GOD'S TEST
WORLD SERIES

Book 2

Corruption
AND
Catastrophe

(GENESIS CHAPTERS 3 - 9)

DAVID G. WOLD

TRILOGY
PROFESSIONAL PUBLISHING MEETS POWERFUL PROMOTION
A wholly owned subsidiary of TBN

Trilogy Christian Publishers

A Wholly Owned Subsidiary of Trinity Broadcasting Network

2442 Michelle Drive

Tustin, CA 92780

Copyright © 2025 by David G. Wold

Scripture quotations marked NASB are taken from the New American Standard Bible® (NASB), Copyright © 1960, 1962, 1963, 1968, 1971, 1972, 1973, 1975, 1977, 1995 by The Lockman Foundation. Used by permission. www.Lockman.org. Scripture quotations marked NIV are taken from the Holy Bible, New International Version®, NIV®. Copyright © 1973, 1978, 1984, 2011 by Biblica, Inc.TM Used by permission of Zondervan. All rights reserved worldwide. www.zondervan.com. The "NIV" and "New International Version" are trademarks registered in the United States Patent and Trademark Office by Biblica, Inc.™ Unless otherwise noted, all Scripture quotations are taken from the New King James Version®. Copyright © 1982 by Thomas Nelson. Used by permission. All rights reserved. Scripture quotations marked KJV are taken from the King James Version of the Bible. Public domain.

All rights reserved, including the right to reproduce this book or portions thereof in any form whatsoever.

For information, address Trilogy Christian Publishing

Rights Department, 2442 Michelle Drive, Tustin, Ca 92780.

Trilogy Christian Publishing/ TBN and colophon are trademarks of Trinity Broadcasting Network.

For information about special discounts for bulk purchases, please contact Trilogy Christian Publishing.

Trilogy Disclaimer: The views and content expressed in this book are those of the author and may not necessarily reflect the views and doctrine of Trilogy Christian Publishing or the Trinity Broadcasting Network.

10 9 8 7 6 5 4 3 2 1

Library of Congress Cataloging-in-Publication Data is available.

ISBN 979-8-89333-438-8 | ISBN 979-8-89333-439-5 (ebook)

Dedication

This book is lovingly dedicated to all believers everywhere, hence, you, the reader. It is our fervent hope that Christians will establish their faith solidly upon the Rock, which is Jesus Christ. Only then can one's spiritual life flourish as God intended. Though it may seem stunning to imagine, God yearns to have a relationship with you. He has thought of you from eternity past. He will continue to think about you for eternity in the future. What an amazing concept that is.

> "The LORD is my strength and my shield; my heart trusted in Him, and I am helped; therefore my heart greatly rejoices, and with my song I will praise Him" (Psalm 28:7).

Table of Contents

Introduction 31

Preface 33

CHAPTER 1. BEGINNINGS AND ENDINGS
  (GENESIS 3:1–8: PART A) 39
Objectives for This Chapter 39
An Important Glance at the Future 40
    A brief excursion into the millennial kingdom 41
    Two kinds of people or one? 42
    Who will enter into the kingdom? 44
    The glorious Marriage Supper of the Lamb 45
    Glorified bodies for whom? 47
    Where are the spirits of the Old Testament saints today? 48
    Jesus' proclamation of His glorious victory 50
    Why should there be a difference between the saints? 52
    The parenting issue 54
    Jewish life in the millennium 56
    Who are these elderly people? 57
    Illness even in the millennial kingdom? 59
    To choose or not to choose 60
    Judgments for the unbelievers are coming! 61
The Start of Untold Miseries 62
    Wisdom from Wiersbe 63

    Sin pervades the entire universe, even heaven itself! 64

    The perpetual puzzlement of sin 66

    God's eternal solution to sin. 67

    What of physical death for Adam and Eve? 68

Lessons Learned in This Chapter 70

CHAPTER 2. THE BEGINNING OF EVIL (GENESIS 3:1–8: PART B) 73
Objectives for This Chapter. 73
The Sad Saga of Sin Described 74

    Satan violates God's perfect creation. 75

    When did Lucifer fall from grace? 77

    Who are the mysterious morning stars and sons of God? 78

    When did sin take over Lucifer? 80

    The Judgment of the Sheep and Goats. 83

    Why did Lucifer fall from grace? 84

    Wise words on Isaiah 14:12–15 86

    Further illumination on Lucifer's fall from grace 87

    Observations on Ezekiel 28:11–15. 88

    The illustration of the heavenly tabernacle and temple 90

    Comments by Paul and the author of Hebrews
        on New Jerusalem 91

    Why no temple in the new heavens and new earth? 92

The Temptation of Adam and Eve. 93

    God-ordained differences between man and woman 93

    God created men and women to complement each other. 94

    God granted Adam the leadership role and Eve
        the support role. 95

Table of Contents

    The biblical story of Boaz and Ruth. 96

    A moment for reflection 98

Lessons Learned in This Chapter 98

CHAPTER 3. SATAN'S DIABOLICAL PLOT AGAINST MANKIND (GENESIS 3:1–8: PART C). 103

Objectives for This Chapter. 103

Satan's Method of Temptation. 105

    Get the people to doubt God's Word 106

    Beware of false teachers. 107

    Twisting the truth 109

    Remember the biblical standard. 110

    A denial of the truth 111

    Visions of grandeur now danced in Eve's head 113

    Lies, lies, and more lies 113

    Satan's ploy tragically worked. 116

    Calamity strikes mankind. 117

    Adam failed his wife and humanity 118

A New Testament Solution to an Old Testament Problem 119

    The solution to pollution 120

    God's grace is all-sufficient 121

    The dire consequence of sin. 123

    Seeing through spiritually blinded eyes 124

    Clothing is now required 125

    Man's vain attempt to conceal iniquity 126

    Run, run as fast as you can! 127

Can anyone hide from God?.................................129

Trouble for two, trouble for all.............................130

Lessons Learned in This Chapter **133**

CHAPTER 4. SIN IS FOUND OUT! (GENESIS 3:9–19) **135**
Objectives for This Chapter..............................**135**
God's Cross-Examination with Adam and Eve (3:9–13).......**137**

God's loving desire for mankind 138

Let the "blame game" begin..............................140

God calls out to Adam 141

Adam's unworthy response 143

Eve's equally predictable response........................145

The Threefold Curse (3:14–19) **146**

God's Curse on the Serpent (Genesis 3:14–15) 147

Eat dirt!..148

The Promised Messiah (Genesis 3:15)....................150

Who is the Seed of the woman?.........................151

Women and the "the childbearing".......................153

Women and the rearing of children 154

Further insightful comments on Genesis 3:15 156

God's curse on the woman (Genesis 3:16)................158

Blessing within the midst of the curse 160

Authority is delegated by God 161

Women must choose Whom they will serve 162

The man must exercise biblical authority.................164

God's Curse on the Man (Genesis 3:17–19) 165

Table of Contents

    Let the punishment fit the crime! 167

    The ground is temporarily cursed. 168

    Resurrection morning is coming! 169

    A fitting summary 171

Lessons Learned in This Chapter **172**

CHAPTER 5. EXILED FROM THE GARDEN! (GENESIS 3:20–24) **175**

Objectives for This Chapter. **175**

Adam and Eve Are Exiled (3:20-24) **176**

    Three immediate results of the fall. 177

    Adam gives Eve her name 177

    Death no longer takes a holiday 180

    Adam and Eve are exiled from the Garden 181

    Two unusual guards 182

The Tree of Life **183**

    What is the tree of life? 183

    God spared Adam and Eve from a grievous fate 184

    A New Testament glimpse at the tree of life 185

    Spiritual realities from Genesis chapter 3 186

    Mankind desperately needs the Shepherd 188

    Who created thinking? 189

    The miracle of modern travel: an accident? 190

    A concluding thought 191

Lessons Learned in This Chapter **192**

CHAPTER 6. A CASE OF MISTAKEN IDENTITY (GENESIS 4:1–2A) **197**

Objectives for This Chapter. **197**

The Birth of the Brothers (4:1–2a) **198**
    The birth of Cain and its accompanying confusion 199
    A case of correct theology but wrong timing 200
    Eve's first mistake 202
    A fuller picture of the promised Messiah 203
    Mary, the mother of Jesus, would suffer grievously 204
    Two advents, one Savior 206

A Backward Glimpse at the Future **208**
    The first phase: Christ raptures the Church 208
    The midpoint of the Tribulation 209
    Elaboration on phase #1 210
    A world without the Church 212
    The beginning of the Tribulation 213
    The Church and Israel are two distinct entities 214
    The evil plots of the nations against Israel 215
    The second phase: Christ returns as Judge 216
    Eve's second mistake 218
    The birth of Abel 220
    Trouble in paradise once removed 222
    God is always in control 223
    The New Testament summation 224

Lessons Learned in This Chapter **226**

CHAPTER 7. THE WORLD'S FIRST MURDER (GENESIS 4:1–17) **231**
Objectives for This Chapter **231**
The Brothers' Sacrifices to God (Genesis 4:1–7) **233**

Table of Contents

A brief examination of the sacrifices 234

A blood sacrifice is necessary for the forgiveness of sins 234

Faith is essential to please God 235

God demands the firstfruits 237

The Mosaic code for dedication and sacrifice 238

On the issue of taking vows 239

A godly life is evidenced by character 240

Abel was a model of righteousness 241

The contrast of two brothers. 242

Cain Murders Abel (4:8–10) 244

The downward progression of sin 245

God communicates with Cain before the murder. 246

God's mandate of forgiveness 247

Cain's horrible choice. 248

Cain Is Judged and Banished from God's Presence (4:11–17) . .251

God confronts Cain 251

The blood of Abel cried out to God 253

A note on suffering. 254

God places a twofold curse on Cain .255

A living death sentence. 256

God grants mercy in the midst of judgment 257

Cain's pathetic response. 258

Cain's fourfold punishment 259

God shows mercy in judgment. 261

Lessons Learned in This Chapter 262

CHAPTER 8. THE LINEAGE OF CAIN AND SETH
(GENESIS 4:16–26) 265
Objectives for This Chapter.................................265
The Consequences of Abel's Murder (4:16–17)...............266
    Sin makes a poor master.................................267
    Cain fathers Enoch......................................269
    Cain builds the city Enoch..............................270
    A summary statement.....................................272
The Ungodly Line of Cain (4:18–24)..........................272
    God prefers forgiveness over condemnation...............272
    Cain's family..274
    Names, names, and more names............................276
    Lamech's polygamy.......................................277
    Further examples of polygamy............................278
    A biblical principle regarding polygamy.................279
    Regulations regarding polygamy..........................281
    Lamech's wives and children.............................282
    Lamech's sinful lifestyle...............................283
The Godly Line of Seth (4:25–26)............................285
    Seth is born..285
    Seth becomes the Seed son...............................287
    Enosh: Public worship becomes more prominent............288
    The end of the first toledoth...........................289
Lessons Learned in This Chapter.............................290

Table of Contents

CHAPTER 9. GODLY GENERATIONS FROM ADAM TO NOAH (GENESIS 5:1–32) 295

Objectives for This Chapter.. 295

    Common items of speculation by the unfaithful 296

    An examination of the patriarchs 297

    Methuselah, Lamech, and Noah............................. 298

The Toledoth (Generations) from Adam to Noah (Genesis 5:1–32) 299

    The beginning of the human race........................... 300

    Early man lived to an immense age 302

    A question of gaps in the genealogical record 304

    No genealogical gaps are necessary........................ 305

    Names have meanings 306

    The miracle of learning a language 306

A Succession of Godly Men 308

    The first man, Adam....................................... 308

    Adam fathers Seth, the Seed son 309

    Are such great ages of the patriarchs possible? 310

    Mankind's ongoing struggle with sin....................... 312

    There is freedom in Christ 314

    Seth 315

    Enosh 316

    Cainan.. 316

    Mahalalel 317

    Jared 317

The Exceptional Man Enoch (Genesis 5:21–24)............... 318

    Enoch walked with God...............................318

    Walking with God was like breathing to Enoch...........319

    A striking contrast of two men.........................321

    Enoch was a great prophet............................322

The Grand Finale of the Patriarchs 323

    Methuselah..323

    Lamech..325

    Noah..327

    Humanity and the animal kingdom is spared on the ark......327

    The earth is cleansed of its wickedness temporarily.........328

    The rainbow is the sign of God's covenant 329

    The Seed son, Messiah, comes through Noah's line 330

Lessons Learned in This Chapter 331

CHAPTER 10. A WORLD GONE BAD (GENESIS 6:1–8: PART A).....337

Objectives for This Chapter.............................337

    The difficult circumstances of Elijah....................338

    Noah's days were unparalleled for wickedness............339

    An important glimpse into the Tribulation................340

    God's sovereign protection and witness
during the Tribulation................................342

Man's Steadily Increasing Depravity 343

    Genesis chapters 6 to 9: God's grace versus man's
wickedness..344

    How quickly mankind slid into the depths of depravity!......345

    Be thankful for the faithful few!........................347

Table of Contents

A Prophetic Pause 348

    Who are the elect? 349

    An Old Testament clarification 350

    God's perfect versus His permissive will 351

    The future context of the Tribulation 352

    The world's most peculiar evangelist 353

    The Jews' long-delayed spiritual awakening 356

    Three types of believers in the Bible 357

    Back to Genesis 358

Lessons Learned in This Chapter 359

    God always preserves a believing remnant 359

    God's witnesses during the Tribulation 361

    The ultimate, angelic witness to the world 363

CHAPTER 11. A WORLD GONE BAD (GENESIS 6:1–8: PART B) 365

Objectives for This Chapter 365

An Introduction to Genesis Chapter 6 367

    God must exercise judgment eventually 367

    God yearns to preserve life, not destroy it 368

    Saving faith requires the right Person 370

Who Were the Sons of God and Daughters of Men?
(Genesis 6:1–4) 370

    Observations about life in Noah's day 371

    The daughters of men were very beautiful 373

    The marriage issue 374

    Who were the "sons of God"? 375

The "sons of God" versus the "sons of men"...............376

The mysterious Nephilim......................377

A worthy word from Ezekiel 379

The garden of God versus the Garden of Eden 380

Additional comments on the "sons of God"................381

The "sons of God" question more thoroughly explained......383

A noteworthy comment from Jude......................384

A repeated emphasis on Noah's day......................386

MacArthur's comment on the apostate angels.............386

The debated question: Were the sons of God
humans or demons? 389

Option #1: The sons of God were demon-possessed men 390

Option #2: The demons fully took on human form 392

Sarfati's comments on apostate angels....................393

Newman's comments on apostate angels..................395

A satanic plot to invalidate Genesis 3:15?.................396

What were the Nephilim like? 397

We serve the God of "second chances" 398

Possibility #1: The age of man is restricted 399

Possibility #2: The Flood would come in 120 years 400

God has warned the world thousands of years in advance.....400

Fruchtenbaum's concluding remarks 402

Lessons Learned in This Chapter 405

CHAPTER 12. A WORLD GONE BAD (GENESIS 6:1–8: PART C) 409

Objectives for This Chapter.................................409

Table of Contents

A Deeper Look at the Nephilim (Genesis 6:4) 412

    What do the ancients say? 413

    A review and amplification by Fruchtenbaum 414

    "Giants" is a misleading translation 416

    The evil Nephilims' business was corruption. 417

    Why do some translations call the Nephilim "giants"? 417

    Were the Nephilim still alive in Moses' day?............... 418

    Lies, lies, and more lies!............................... 420

    The Promised Land is described as simultaneously beautiful but dangerous 420

    Had God suddenly become feeble? 421

    If you like sand... 424

    No more Nephilim 424

God's Holy Response to a Wicked World (Genesis 6:5–8) 426

    A great revival is coming! 427

    Those who live godly lives often suffer on this earth 428

    Moral disaster struck the earth 429

    Evil permeated the earth............................... 430

    The thoughts of man were repugnant continually 431

    The Holy Spirit presently restrains evil 432

    God holds the Antichrist back at the present time 434

    God grieves that He made man 436

    Unrepentant sin must ultimately be punished 438

    God preserves humanity through the ark 439

    Guardians of the faith................................. 440

    The tragic spiritual climate of Noah's day 441

    Savory comments by John Gill 442

Lessons Learned in This Chapter 44

CHAPTER 13. WARNINGS OF A UNIVERSAL FLOOD (GENESIS 6:9–17) 449

Objectives for This Chapter. 449

Righteous Noah versus a Corrupt World (6:9–10) 450

    Noah: The man standing in the gap 451

    God's man of the hour: Noah (Genesis 6:9–10). 454

    Three godly men. 455

    Noah proved a truly exceptional man of God 456

    A biblical description of Noah 457

    Noah habitually walked with God 458

    The worldwide defilement of humanity 459

    A note of God-based encouragement 460

    Noah and Enoch were conquerors in God 460

    The righteous example of Moses 462

    Noah's three sons 464

A World Drowning in Corruption (Genesis 6:11–13) 465

    A world gone mad! 465

    No more tolerance could be tolerated. .466

    Judgment was due! 467

    Noah's congregation was unenviable. .468

Instructions regarding the Ark (6:14–17) 469

    God's command concerning the ark. 470

Table of Contents

    The actual construction of the ark 471

    Did the small critters become tasty tidbits? 472

    What was the size and capacity of the ark? 473

    A lot of animals could have fit on the ark! 473

    Examples of other immense wooden vessels 474

    God's hand of protection is never short 476

    A window, a door, and three decks (Genesis 6:16) 477

    The impending Flood (6:17) 479

    Two terrible consequences for mankind's disobedience 480

    No people or land animals outside the ark survived 481

    Should we not trust Jesus Christ's testimony? 483

Lessons Learned in This Chapter **489**

CHAPTER 14. THE DAY OF JUDGMENT ARRIVES
    (GENESIS 6:18–7:5) **491**

Objectives for This Chapter. **491**

How Many Animals Did You Say? (6:18–22) **494**

    God establishes His covenant with Noah 494

    Warnings of the broad way 495

    The ark and the cross provided spiritual deliverance 495

    The ark: the world biggest visible object lesson 497

    Jesus Christ: the matchless Prophet and Son of God 498

    No excuses allowed! 499

    The miracle of the ark 501

    God provides for a "reasonable" faith .503

    Abraham: An example of living faith 505

Have you considered Job? 506

Objections and Answers...................................**509**

    How could those massive dinosaurs fit on the ark? 509

    A more scientific approach to the dinosaur problem 510

    How could the ark contain millions of animals? 512

    What about the vegetation and all those irritating bugs? 513

    What about the humble bacteria and other germs? 516

    What kept the fish alive in the changing salinity of the seas? ..518

Noah Enters the Ark (Genesis 7:1–5) **520**

    Entrance into the ark is commenced.........................521

    The final warning is uttered 523

    Another judgment day is coming 525

Lessons Learned in This Chapter **526**

CHAPTER 15. GLOBAL FLOOD VERSUS LOCAL FLOOD (GENESIS 7:6–24: PART A) **531**

Objectives for This Chapter.................................**531**

The Biblical Account of the Flood (7:6–16) **534**

    The entry into the ark (Genesis 7:6–10) 535

    An extraordinary witness to the Nephilim 536

    The Day of Judgment arrives: the Flood begins (Genesis 7:11–16) 537

    How could the world become so corrupt? 539

    Why? 540

    God's perfect versus His permissive will....................542

    God knows all in advance 542

Table of Contents

Sin remains a perpetual anchor 544

Free at last! 544

Life wasn't just good, it was perfect! 546

Sin personified at its worst! 547

God's grace has always reached out to man 548

Tragic result of unbridled sin! 550

The Flood strikes! 551

The two sources of water for the universal Flood 551

Rain, rain, rain! 552

Not one square foot of dry land remained 554

A local flood? Absolutely not! 556

The Water Covered the Globe (7:17–24) 557

A willful ignorance 558

Those who deny the Flood are playing a game with no rules ..559

The mysteries of a mythical explosion 560

Spiritual life comes through Christ alone 561

Ignorance decidedly is not bliss! 562

Creationists believe in the Bible and science 563

The extent of the Flood is global (Genesis 7:17–24) 564

Potential problem with the highest mountains? 565

Solution to the highest mountain problem 565

Psalm 104:6–9 566

Water, water everywhere! 567

The candid admission of Alfred Russell Wallace 569

The easiest solution is often the best one 571

    Original creation versus post-Flood 571

    A spiritual truth to remember 574

Lessons Learned in This Chapter 574

CHAPTER 16. GLOBAL FLOOD VERSUS LOCAL FLOOD (GENESIS 7:6–24: PART B) 579

Objectives for This Chapter 579

Traditions regarding a Universal Flood 581

    A biblical warning of scoffers 582

    Flood traditions: Mere coincidence or realistic reporting? 582

    A fascinating Flood tradition from China 584

Fossils Validate the Flood 585

    Bones, bones everywhere! 585

    Fossil formation requires a rapid process 586

    Even soft-tissue jellyfish have been fossilized 587

    Fossils of fish giving birth and eating? 588

    Dinosaurs in Antarctica? 589

    Climate change? Yes! 590

    Will fossils never cease? Apparently not! 590

    Clams climbing mountains? 592

    The earth's crust literally cracked during the Flood 594

    Where did all the bison fossils go? 595

    Fossils smother the planet 596

    Where are all the transition fossils between species? 598

    What does the fossil record actually demonstrate? 599

    Fossils stubborn constant state 601

Table of Contents

    The fossil records disqualify Darwinism 602

    The amazing preservation of the fossils. 603

Lessons Learned in This Chapter **605**

**CHAPTER 17. GLOBAL FLOOD VERSUS LOCAL FLOOD
(GENESIS 7:6–24: PART C)** **611**

Objectives for This Chapter. **611**

What Caused the Coal and Oil Deposits? **614**

    How the Flood made oil and coal. 615

    Fossil fuels require decomposed vegetation and animals 616

    What could possibly cause polystrate trees? 617

    What could create a ninety feet thick coal seam? 619

    How did the large boulders arrive? 619

    Carbon 14: The hidden trade secret of evolutionists 620

    How long does it take to make coal and oil? 622

    God's blessing which arose from judgment. 624

The Rocks Cry Out! **625**

    This little river did that? 625

    Does water erosion still take place today? 626

    An island is born! 629

    A fine layering of soil and sediment. 631

    Fossilized footprints? 632

    Where or where is that alleged geologic column? 634

    Why are theoretically older rocks sunning themselves on younger rocks? 636

    Just how big do those overthrusts get? 637

Corruption and Catastrophe

    Can mountains perambulate hither and yon?...............638

    And what if there really was a Flood?....................640

    Cynicism does not equate to science 641

    Prepare yourself!..642

Lessons Learned in This Chapter 643

CHAPTER 18. SEVEN IMPORTANT QUESTIONS CONCERNING THE FLOOD (GENESIS 7:6–24) 649

Objectives for This Chapter................................649

Seven Central Questions regarding the Flood 651

    Question #1: If the flood is local, what killed everything on earth?......................................652

    Question #2: If the Flood is local, did Noah build the ark on Mount Ararat?..653

    Question #3: If the Flood is local, why build the ark at all? ...654

    Question #4: If the Flood is local, what difference does it make?...655

    Question #5: If the Flood is local, why is there evidence for it all over the world?..................................656

    Question #6: If the Flood is local, is Jesus really the God-man or not?...658

    Question #7: If the flood is local, can we believe in the Bible?.660

    Wiersbe's wise summation...............................661

    Patience is an eternal virtue 662

Lessons Learned in This Chapter 664

CHAPTER 19. THE FLOODWATERS BEGIN TO RECEDE (GENESIS 8:1–19) 669

Objectives for This Chapter................................669

Table of Contents

God Stops the Rain and the Fountains (8:1–5) **671**

    For 150 days the waters steadily increased 672

    The earth was radically transformed 673

    Free at last! 674

    Fiery flying serpents 675

    The spiritual reality behind the physical symbol of the snake . . 676

    Every living thing left the ark 677

    A brief overview of the Ice Age 678

    Confusion over how an Ice Age starts 679

    The floodwaters slowly drain away (Genesis 8:1–5) 681

    God remembered Noah 681

    The floodwaters began to subside in three ways
    (Genesis 8:1b–3) 683

    Mountains, canyons, and rocks 685

    A question of canyon formation 686

    A resting place for the ark 687

Noah Sends Out the Raven and Dove (8:6–12) **689**

    The raven (Genesis 8:6–7) 690

    The dove (Genesis 8:8–12) 691

    The dove's depiction and use in the Bible 692

Disembarkation Time from the Ark (8:13–19) **693**

    Noah removes the roof of the ark (Genesis 8:13–17) 694

    Release at long last (Genesis 8:18–19)! 695

    A new but somewhat unwelcoming world (2 Peter 3:5–6) 696

    Changes in the world as a result of the Flood 697

    Lithification 699

    The expected progression of fossil complexity 699

    This writer's characterization of evolution. 701

    The true record of the rocks 702

Lessons Learned in This Chapter 703

CHAPTER 20. THE ICE AGE (GENESIS 8:1–19) 709

Objectives for This Chapter 709

The Ice Age Explained 712

    Why discuss the Ice Age? 712

    An explanation for the Ice Age 713

    Mount Pinatubo as a recent example 714

    What transpired during the global Flood? 715

    A future comparison to the Flood's effects. 716

    A question of repentance in Noah's day 718

How About All Those Animals? 719

    Did the weather change? Absolutely! 719

    There were a lot of critters up north! 720

    Did life end abruptly in a quick "deep freeze"? 721

    A cogent explanation for life and death in the Ice Age 722

    Not all questions can presently be answered 724

What Difference Does All This Make? 725

    Two promises and three commands 725

    Believers are to anticipate God's glorious blessings 727

    God calls His children to holy living 727

Lessons Learned in This Chapter 728

Table of Contents

CHAPTER 21. GOD'S COVENANT WITH NOAH (GENESIS 8:20–22)....733

Objectives for This Chapter....................733

Noah Worships God through Sacrifices 735

    An exercise of proper priorities 736

    An injunction to follow Noah's godly example 737

    Every good gift is from God...................738

Promise #1: Astounding Agricultural Fertility (8:21–22) 740

    Agricultural blessing 741

    The importance of Petra (Amos 9:12) 742

    Blessing in the midst of judgment 744

Promise #2: God Will Bless Israel (Amos 9:11–15) 745

    Blessings on the land and Israel.................746

    The future for Israel according to Amos 747

    God's unilateral promise of His faithfulness to Israel 748

    A promise for the ages 748

    How certain are God's promises to Israel?..........750

    The Jews' misconception of spiritual heritage 751

    God's promise: No more world floods.............752

    The Judgment of the Sheep and Goats.............752

    The finality of God's judgment 753

    Three categories of believers 754

    Free will involves making decisions 755

    The hardness of the heart is incomprehensible 756

    The final rebellion recorded 758

    Mankind retains its evil nature (Genesis 8:21)........759

The Jews' history of stubborn denial 761

Promise #3: The Seasons Continue Unabated (Genesis 8:22) . . . 762

Lessons Learned in This Chapter 763

CHAPTER 22. GOD'S COVENANT WITH NOAH (GENESIS 9:1–7) 767

Objectives for This Chapter 767

God Blessed Noah and His Sons 768

    A moment of honesty 769

    Be fruitful and fill the earth (Genesis 9:1) 770

    The old man versus the new man 771

    The fear and dread of man falls upon the animals
    (Genesis 9:2) 772

    One-fourth of humanity perishes! 773

    The fear of today will be companionship "tomorrow" 774

    A new diet: meat is now on the menu (Genesis 9:3–4) 776

Several New Developments on Earth 776

    Animals now feared mankind 776

    Meat was now on the menu! 777

    Eating blood was and remains forbidden 778

    Scientific observations about blood 780

    Murder now brings a death penalty (Genesis 9:5–7) 782

    Government is established 783

    The role of government 785

    The death penalty 786

    The tragic act of abortion 787

    The mandate 788

Table of Contents

Lessons Learned in This Chapter 790

CHAPTER 23. GOD'S COVENANT WITH NOAH (GENESIS 9:8–29) 795
Objectives for This Chapter 795

God's three Old Testament covenantal signs 795

God's New Testament covenantal sign 798

God Establishes the Noahic Covenant 799

God establishes His covenant with Noah and the animals
(Genesis 9:8–11) 800

A cogent summary of the Noahic covenant 801

The rainbow: God's covenantal sign (Genesis 9:12–17) 802

Man is perpetually accountable to God 803

The benefit of visible signs 804

Noah's Later Years 806

Noah got drunk (Genesis 9:18–21) 807

A closer examination of Noah's drunkenness 808

When did fermentation come into existence? 808

An issue of character 810

The curse on young Canaan 811

Ham sinned against his father (Genesis 9:22–23) 812

Ham's folly and gross disrespect 813

The righteous Shem and Japheth 815

Noah prophesies about Canaan, Shem, and Japheth
(Genesis 9:24–29) 816

A few salient observations 817

Shem and Japheth are blessed by Noah 818

An historical anecdote regarding immoral Semites 819
A summary of Noah's godly life 820
Noah: A life incredibly well invested for God 822
Lessons Learned in This Chapter 822
BIBLIOGRAPHY 827
APPENDIX 1: SCRIPTURE INDEX............................. 835

Introduction

These three volumes, referring to the first book on Genesis chapters 1 to 2, the second book on Genesis chapters 3 to 9, and the third book on Genesis chapters 10 to 11, are written as a set. As the front cover conveys, it is a trilogy. It is our hope that the prospective reader will obtain all three volumes for the sake of completeness. For this reason, we provide the identical introduction to each of the three volumes in question. One may then reason out whether he desires to purchase all three volumes. In our humble opinion, that would prove wise in order to attain a complete picture.

To write one volume with the wealth of information we seek to provide would have proved cumbersome. It would have loomed into a large book indeed. Hence, we have developed this work into three volumes. We have endeavored to make the chapters reasonably short and subdivided them into smaller, more readable segments.

It is our fervent prayer that the systematic study of Genesis chapters 1 to 11 will immeasurably strengthen the believer's walk with his Savior, Jesus Christ. The world persists in its ungodly endeavor of eroding confidence in the historic accuracy of this incredible account. It is our utmost desire to bolster the faith of the unbeliever as well as provide much-needed education (1 Peter 3:15).

For those who have not yet come to faith in Christ, we pray that these three volumes will prove spiritually persuasive. It is our undying commitment that God created the heavens and the earth and everything within them. Not an atom or a particle exists apart from God's creative hands.

God created man in His own image. Hence, man is the pinnacle of God's earthly creation. We alone are possessed of body, soul, and spirit. Having been created in God's image, we are necessarily accountable to our Creator. Lamentably, man chose to disobey God's command regarding the tree of knowledge of good and evil. But if man were legitimately to exercise free will, he must have the ability to choose. Mankind's errant choice was fully known by God from eternity past.

Within God's eternal plan, however, atonement was provided through His Son, Jesus Christ (John 3:16). However, man must choose to receive this offered forgiveness (John 1:10–12). Redemption from sin comes as a free gift to all who will believe (Ephesians 2:8–9; Titus 3:5). As we examine Genesis chapters 1 to 11, we pray that each reader would be examining his or her own life. If an unbeliever, we fervently yearn that you will embrace the forgiveness and eternal life offered through Jesus Christ (John 5:24).

If a believer already, and most of our readers will be, we trust that you will seek out areas in your spiritual life that require further enhancement and development. May each one who works through these three volumes apply the following biblical passage to his life.

> "For God so loved the world that He gave His only begotten Son, that whoever believes in Him should not perish but have everlasting life" (John 3:16).

Preface

Volume 1
(Genesis Chapters 1 to 2)

The primary purpose of this three-volume set is to explore the beginning of God's creative activities and the extraordinary events recorded in Genesis chapters 1 to 11. The kernel of God's eternal Word is beautifully encapsulated in these first eleven chapters. Nearly every doctrine of the Bible is touched upon in this brief but extraordinary narrative. Thus, it is vital that every believer immerse themselves in a studious, systematic, and devotional examination of these chapters.

In our first volume (Genesis chapters 1 to 2), our intent is to explore God's creation narrative. It is our firm, undying conviction that God created the heavens and the earth and everything within them. Genesis chapters 1 to 2 make it abundantly clear that God required no outside assistance to facilitate His creation.

Evolution is a fraudulent crutch man invented in his state of unbelief. The simple reality is that God simply spoke all things into existence. He required no previously existing material. God Himself is the Originator of all physical material from which He lovingly and elegantly fashioned all that man's eyes can see and cannot see.

Our second purpose is to emphasize the glory of God's creation and incredible handiwork. God did not utilize the mythical, pseudoscientific process of evolution to bring anything into existence. In coordination with our second purpose, we thoroughly shred the entire fallacious structure of evolution. That takes place primarily in the final third of this first volume.

The legendary process of evolution is based on a series of six impossible steps. All of these steps must be accepted in blind faith by the adherents of evolution. There is no empirical proof whatsoever for any of these mythical steps.

Some may legitimately object that creationism must also be accepted by faith. That is undeniably true (Hebrews 11:6). God designed it to be so. However, creationism does not in any way contradict established, observable scientific principles. Evolution, on the other hand, turns legitimate science on its head! The reader must choose for himself. Option #1: Is it more prudent to accept provable science coupled with reasonable faith? Option #2: Is it more prudent to accept unprovable theories based on a foundation of empirical "nothingness"?

Throughout the course of this first volume, we repeatedly emphasize the glorious truth that man and woman are created in God's image. Though we may not understand all the marvelous ramifications of this truth, we may rejoice in it. Only mankind has been endowed with this distinct blessing. We are not animals, plants, or minerals. We are human beings. As such, only mankind is blessed with body, soul, and spirit.

Volume 2

(Genesis Chapters 3 to 9)

Volume 2 deals with a variety of interrelated topics. First, we shall examine the lamentable corruption of the human race (Genesis 3:1–6:8). This is in reference to Adam and Eve's sin in the Garden of Eden. They ate the forbidden fruit and tragically brought sin into the world. We examine the many consequences of their mutual sin.

Preface

We also entertain the question as to whether we would have done any better than Adam and Eve in the same circumstances. Sadly, the answer to that question is self-evident: "No, we would not have fared any better."

We also address the question of why God allowed temptation to enter the world. Though we further elaborate on this within the actual text, the answer is actually quite simple. To sum our response up in most succinct fashion: Without free will, there can be no genuine worship. We shall demonstrate precisely why this must be the case.

Second, volume 2 deals with catastrophe, namely, the worldwide Flood (Genesis 6:9–9:29). God is an extremely patient God. But when He finally judges sin, it is thorough and cataclysmic. We discuss the issue as to why God's judgment seems so harsh. There was a distinct reason why the worldwide Flood was necessary. Mankind reached its lowest moral ebb during Noah's day. Only eight righteous souls were alive at the time of the Flood. That is indeed a frightening thought!

We shall also examine the evidence around the globe that demonstrates the reality of the universal Flood. It is almost comical how evolutionists try to "dance around" the worldwide abundance of evidence for an all-encompassing Flood. Many questions are explored, and answers are provided regarding this cataclysmic event.

The believer may rest absolutely secure in the biblical account. Not only was God the cause and witness of the Flood, but He also provided the only escape for humanity. Sadly, only eight souls availed themselves of His merciful refuge from the storm, namely, the ark.

Volume 3
(Genesis Chapters 10 to 11)

Volume 3 first addresses history's early nation-building (Genesis 10:1–32). We shall examine the genealogical tables and explore how the nations came together over the centuries. Though this segment does not instantly enamor many people, it is nonetheless deceptively invaluable. Regrettably, the preponderance of evidence regarding these nations is scanty at best. But we shall glean some crucial historical notes that are instructive to modern man. As the old axiom pronounces, "If we do not learn from our past, we are bound to repeat it."

The reader will also discover that we shall embark on a rather extended discourse on the nation of Egypt during this particular segment. This pagan nation, more than any other, has played a remarkable role in the development and spiritual aspects of Israel. Prophecies regarding Egypt are quite specific but generally ignored. We do not want to make that mistake. Hence, we shall review the significant interplay between Israel and Egypt.

Second, volume 3 examines the confusion of languages (Genesis 11:1–9). This is truly a unique event in mankind's history. God commanded man to spread across the entire globe and populate all lands. But, in his typical stubbornness, man chose to unite in rebellion against his Creator. Thus, they started building what is called the Tower of Babel.

God interrupted this wicked attempt at idolatry by creating the thousands of languages that now permeate the world. He could have chosen to destroy mankind and simply translate the godly to heaven. Thus, the confusion of languages was actually a show of God's benevolence and mercy.

Preface

Third, volume 3's final section is entitled "Old Families and New Beginnings" (Genesis 11:10–32). This entails a comprehensive review of Shem's line. It is also an introduction to the godly man, Abraham. God established the Abrahamic covenant with this highly favored and devout individual.

The Abrahamic covenant is the basis for all the ensuing biblical covenants. As such, Abraham is one of the most influential and inspirational men in history. One does well to acquaint himself with the life of Abraham and his family, as further described in Genesis chapters 12 through 50.

A final note: Our primary objective is to teach God's Word as it is outlined in Genesis chapters 1 to 11. In doing so, we interpret each verse in its literal, grammatical, historical, and contextual sense. We endeavor to allow Scripture to illuminate Scripture. But we shall also try to make this book as practical as is reasonably possible. From time to time, we shall insert applications for the reader. We trust that these pauses in the commentary may prove edifying and helpful.

Colossians 2:6–8 encourages us to godly living as follows:

> As you therefore have received Christ Jesus the Lord, so walk in Him, rooted and build up in Him and established in the faith, as you have been taught, abounding in it with thanksgiving. Beware lest anyone cheat you through philosophy and empty deceit, according to the tradition of men, according to the basic principles of the world, and not according to Christ.

P.S. At the conclusion of each chapter in each volume, there will be a Bible riddle, fondly dubbed a cognitive conundrum. These riddles are written by the author. They are designed to stimulate concentration on God's Word in a unique and hopefully gratifying manner. The answer will be listed on the bottom of the same page.

Chapter 1

Beginnings and Endings

(Genesis 3:1-8: Part A)

In This Chapter

Objectives for This Chapter
An Important Glance at the Future
The Start of Untold Miseries
Lessons Learned in This Chapter

Objectives for This Chapter

Our objectives for this chapter are twofold. First, we shall briefly discuss the woeful fact that Adam and Eve stumbled into sin. This moral failure on their part impacted every human being who will ever live. Preceding mankind's spiritual downfall, Lucifer and one-third of the angels in heaven chose to rebel against God (Revelation 12:4).

The tragic consequence of sin is that it has impacted the entire universe (Romans 8:19–22). Every element and particle in creation groans under its evil domain. All of humanity falls under its dark penalty (Romans 3:23). Sin is a veritable scourge. Only through the shed blood of Christ is restoration possible (Romans 5:8–10).

Second, we shall take a glance into the future millennial kingdom of Christ. That might strike the reader as a bit odd in a series of books discussing Genesis chapters 1 to 11. But, as we trust will soon become evident, certain eschatological issues brought to the forefront can prove helpful. Our goal is to attain a clearer, panoramic picture of earth's theological experience. Thus, in this introductory chapter, we shall be looking backwards and forwards into earth's history.

As one would expect, in ensuing chapters, we shall explore in more detail man's plunge into sin. Naturally accompanying that discussion will be the divine spiritual resuscitation of mankind. God was not taken by surprise when Adam and Eve succumbed to the wiles of the serpent. Tragedy struck, but better days are coming for both man and this planet. We shall also discover that this rejuvenation of man will not be entirely complete, even in the millennial kingdom. That glorious time of total renewal awaits eternity when God dwells among man (Revelation chapters 21 and 22). Then and only then will perfection be found on this earth.

An Important Glance at the Future

Genesis chapter 3 records the historic downfall of man due to sin. It is not only mankind that suffers because of Adam and Eve's reckless sin. The entire creation pays the penalty for their transgression to this day. Wherever one walks or looks, the contamination of sin is present. One cannot physically see sin, but its dire consequences are all too evident. They surround and horrify us on a daily basis. Sin pervades the entire universe and impacts every living creature.

Even nature itself is frequently convulsed because of sin's disruptive presence. In the Garden of Eden, there were no active volcanoes, earthquakes, tornadoes, floods, or destructive tsunamis. All was peace and purity. Fellowship with God was the norm. Adam and Eve took leisurely strolls and conversed with their Creator in the cool of the day. But, as Genesis chapter 3 relates, sin changed everything in the most dramatic of fashion. Only when Christ returns to establish His millennial kingdom will our present scenario witness a powerful, albeit not all-inclusive, change.

A Brief Excursion into the Millennial Kingdom

Let us now take a biblical glance into the future before discussing the past. Contrary to the expectations of many, even in the blissful millennial kingdom of Christ, there will be sinful activity. Though the millennial kingdom begins only with believers, the first generation born to survivors of the Tribulation will slowly start to change that idyllic situation. The believing survivors of the Tribulation will not lose their sinful nature. They will be like present-day believers with both a perfect and an evil nature. When they bear children, they will pass on the evil nature to their progeny. By contrast, those returning from heaven will have only a perfect nature. However, it appears that they will not parent any children.

As generations increase, so will the number of people rebelling against the authority and righteous reign of Christ. Habakkuk 2:14 informs us: "For the earth will be filled with the knowledge of the glory of the LORD, as the waters cover the sea." Yet, in spite of that glorious reality, the impenitent, of which there will be many, will not rest until they vainly attempt to distort God's ways in every facet of life. Their attempts will not only prove futile but also self-condemning.

The consequences of rebellious individuals acting on their own self-centered initiative inevitably lead to chaos and destruction. Sadly, they are incapable of understanding the predictable aftereffects of their illicit actions and attitudes. This will hold true in the millennial kingdom of Christ just as it does in today's world. These unredeemed souls will foster a huge but pointless rebellion at the end of the millennial kingdom (Revelation 20:7–10).

The insubordinate and wretched lifestyles manifested by the ungodly will be forcibly limited by the Messiah. He will rule with a rod of iron. In the context of the millennial kingdom, Psalm 2:9 states: "You shall break them with a rod of iron; You shall dash them to pieces like a potter's vessel" (cf. Psalm 89:23). Of necessity, there will be discipline and even premature death throughout the millennial kingdom (Isaiah 65:20). We shall see more specific examples of this later in this volume.

Two Kinds of People or One?

The question naturally arises: Why is discipline necessary even in the millennial kingdom? The reason for this, as already alluded to, is that during the millennial kingdom, there will be two types of people. Those who return from heaven will possess only a pure, sinless nature. Jude 14 describes their return: "Now Enoch, the seventh from Adam, prophesied about these men also, saying, 'Behold, the Lord comes with ten thousands of His saints'" (cf. Zechariah 14:5).

Question: Who are these saints (holy ones)? The answer is not entirely clear. Some believe it refers only to men and women, some only to angels, and some to both. Support can readily be found for all three of these positions.

John MacArthur offers the following explanatory statement:

> Second, the Lord will not come alone. While He alone is the final judge, He will be accompanied by many thousands of His holy ones. Holy ones ("saints") could refer to believers (cf. 1 Cor. 1:2; 1 Thess. 3:13, who will return with Christ when He comes in judgment (Rev. 19:14; cf. Zech. 14:5).

However, the emphasis on judgment here seems to favor viewing the holy ones as angels, since angels appear in other judgment contexts in the New Testament (Matt. 24:31; 25:31; Mark 8:38; 2 Thess. 1:7). The saints will have a judgment role during the millennial kingdom (Rev. 2:26-27; 3:21; cf. Dan. 7:22; 1 Cor. 6:2), but angels will serve as God's executioners when Christ returns (Matt. 13:39-41, 49-50; 24:29-31; 25:31; 2 Thess. 1:7-10).[1]

It is our personal assessment that the saints and angels will be returning together. Whatever the case may be, blessed are those accompanying Christ. They ride after the King of kings and Lord of lords (Revelation 19:16). Revelation 19:14 describes the accompanying saints: "And the armies in heaven, clothed in fine linen, white and clean, followed Him on white horses."

Not one among them, whether humans or angels, will be vulnerable to temptation. God will have granted the people of the church age a glorified body and completely new soul and spirit. They will be sinless. God will have removed their carnal nature upon their entering into heaven. To be rejoicing in one's new nature found in Christ for all eternity defies the most vivid of Christian's imaginations. Such fellowship is presently impossible for even the most godly of believers to enjoy in our present state.

It is essential to note that the Old Testament saints apparently do not have the same completely transformed body as the Church saints. That is because the Old Testament believers are not physically resurrected until after the Tribulation is completely finished. Their spirits, however, will have already been joyfully received in

---
1 John MacArthur. The MacArthur New Testament Commentary: 2 Peter & Jude (Chicago, IL: Moody Publishers, 2005), p. 189.

heaven. The Old Testament saints are presently experiencing fellowship with their Creator in all of its fantastic fullness. It is more than a curiosity to ponder that the spirits of the Old Testament saints will be sinless. Yet, their physical bodies may be subject to aging, but probably not disease. We shall discuss this shortly.

Who Will Enter into the Kingdom?

Matthew 8:10–12 states:

> When Jesus heard it, He marveled, and said to those who followed, "Assuredly I say to you, I have not found such great faith, not even in Israel! And I say to you that many will come from east and west, and sit down with Abraham, Isaac, and Jacob in the kingdom of heaven. But the sons of the kingdom will be cast out into outer darkness. There will be weeping and gnashing of teeth."

Several features should be noted regarding this passage and its immediate context:

Feature #1: This is given in the context of Jesus ministering to a Roman centurion. Some may question whether the centurion was actually a Roman. Jesus resolves this question in verse 10. He does not include the man as an Israelite. Clearly, this man of faith was a Gentile. He was a Roman either by natural birth, adopted citizenship by a financial acquisition, or possibly by valor of some type.

Feature #2: Those who come from the "east and west" is figurative for the Gentiles. They are outsiders to Israel. Nonetheless, they will be sitting at a banquet with the patriarchs Abraham, Isaac, and Jacob. Such a statement was not well-received by the unbelieving, cynical, and self-righteous Jews. To think that even among the Gentile "dogs," many would be granted entrance into God's kingdom was anathema to them.

God does indeed have a chosen people, namely, the nation of Israel (Genesis 12:1–3; Exodus 19:5–6). Simultaneously, however, God is no respecter of persons (Acts 10:34–35). He honors anyone with faith. To make matters worse, the "sons of the kingdom," representing the Jews themselves, would be cast out into outer darkness, symbolizing the Lake of Fire.

Statements like this coming from the mouth of Jesus infuriated the nationalistic and pious Jews. That is why many sought His death early on in His ministry. Most Jews assumed they would be ushered into Paradise based on their ethnic identity alone. They conveniently forgot the necessity of faith. But God's holy and eternal plans cannot be thwarted (Acts 2:22–24). Nor can He be deceived.

The Glorious Marriage Supper of the Lamb

Feature #3: The kingdom of heaven and the kingdom of God are viewed as synonymous in Hebrew thought. In the context, Jesus is speaking of a banquet for believers. The question of the timing of this passage is somewhat debated among biblical scholars. Some feel this banquet should be viewed as occurring in heaven in our present time. Others believe that it occurs after the second coming of Christ on earth during the Marriage Supper of the Lamb.

It is not absolutely clear which position is correct. Possibly, it can equally be applied to both scenarios and perhaps is presently ongoing in a way that we do not presently understand. Only the second coming of Christ will reveal what is truly intended. In our personal viewpoint, it takes place only after Christ returns to earth with the Church. Whichever the case may be, it will bring immense blessing to all participants. Anyone invited to this banquet will be rejoicing with Christ for all eternity. Those who miss this banquet will be languishing in unimaginable spiritual darkness. They will be permanently isolated from Jesus Christ and the glorious fellowship of the saints.

R. T. France offers the following explanation for this important passage and its context:

> The imagery of reclining at table with the Hebrew patriarchs would inevitably speak to Jewish readers of the messianic banquet which was a popular way of thinking of the ultimate blessedness of the true people of God. In popular Jewish thought it would be taken for granted that, while not every Jew might prove worthy of a place at the banquet, it would be a Jewish gathering, while non-Jews would find themselves outside in the darkness; to be the people of God meant, for all practical purposes, to be Jewish.
>
> Jesus' saying dramatically changes this instinctive assumption, both by including "many" others from foreign parts ("east and west") on the guest list, and also daring to exclude those who were assumed to have a right to be there, the "sons of the kingdom." To add insult to injury, the fate of these "sons of the kingdom" is described in the terms traditionally used in Jewish descriptions of the fate of the ungodly (and therefore, predominantly, the Gentiles), "darkness outside," "weeping and gnashing of teeth."

The reason they are rejected is not explicit within this saying, but in the context in which Matthew has placed it, it must be linked with the fact that Jesus has not found in Israel faith like that of the centurion. Thus belonging to the kingdom of heaven is found to depend not on ancestry but on faith.[2]

Glorified Bodies for Whom?

First John 3:2–3 is a beautiful passage that ultimately describes believers from the past, present, and future: "Beloved, now we are children of God; and it has not yet been revealed what we shall be, but we know that when He is revealed, we shall be like Him, for we shall see Him as He is. And everyone who has this hope in Him purifies himself, just as He is pure."

Question: To whom does this passage specifically apply? Is this passage restricted to only some believers and not others? Answer: Some feel that for our present age, this promise will apply to the saints of the church age. Why is that? We shall note several factors in this intriguing and somewhat befuddling discussion.

Although some have formed rather concrete opinions on this particular matter, dogmatic exuberance is cautioned against. Not everything is crystal clear in the Scripture, as not enough information is always granted. But we shall entertain a few thoughts nonetheless.

First, it is crucial to note that this comparison is not necessarily restricted to a physical likeness to Christ. It undoubtedly holds reference to a spiritual likeness as well. If that is the ultimate intent of the verse, it then must eventually refer to all children of God from every age of the earth. Which saint would not eventually be like

---
[2] R. T. France, The New International Commentary on the New Testament: The Gospel of Matthew (Grand Rapids, MI: William B. Eerdmans Publishing Company, 2007), p. 316.

Christ? Even if there is a distinction between saints in the millennial kingdom, there cannot be in eternity.

Second, many similar promises are scattered throughout the New Testament. The Church is raptured out, both the dead and the living, before the Tribulation commences (John 14:1–3; 1 Corinthians 15:51–53; 1 Thessalonians 4:13–18). In heaven, the Church saints receive their glorified bodies, souls, and pure spirits.

By contrast, the Old Testament saints also have been transferred from their earthly graves up to heaven, but only in spirit. They are not physically resurrected until Christ's second coming (Revelation 20:4–6). This makes them quite distinct from the Church.

Daniel 12:1–2 states:

> At that time Michael shall stand up, the great prince who stands watch over the sons of your people; and there shall be a time of trouble, such as never was since there was a nation, even to that time. And at that time your people shall be delivered, every one who is found written in the book. And many of those who sleep in the dust of the earth shall awake, some to everlasting life, some to shame and everlasting contempt (cf. John 5:28–29).

Where Are the Spirits of the Old Testament Saints Today?

As Daniel 12:1–2 indicates, the bodies of the Old Testament individuals, whether believers or unbelievers, still reside in the dust of the earth. Only after the final days of the Tribulation are they physically resurrected. However, the spirits of the Old Testament saints were taken to heaven when Paradise was emptied. The spirits of the

Old Testament unbelievers to this day still reside in the torments of hell. Only after the millennial kingdom will they be transferred from this place of torment to an even worse fate, the eternal Lake of Fire.

(Writer's note: The terms "hell" and "Hades" denote the same location in Scripture. They are used as synonyms with many translations.)

Revelation 20:11–15 certainly qualifies as one of the most sobering passages in all of Scripture:

> Then I saw a great white throne and Him who sat on it, from whose face the earth and the heaven fled away. And there was found no place for them. And I saw the dead, small and great, standing before God, and books were opened. And another book was opened, which is the Book of Life. And the dead were judged according to their works, by the things which were written in the books.
>
> The sea gave up the dead who were in it, and Death and Hades delivered up the dead who were in them. And they were judged, each one according to his works. Then Death and Hades were cast into the lake of fire. This is the second death. And anyone not found written in the Book of Life was cast into the lake of fire.

Few, if any, passages in Scripture stand as a greater warning than Revelation 20:11–15. To be cast into the Lake of Fire for all eternity manifests any reasonable person's greatest fear. What is even more terrible is that this destiny is entirely avoidable. No one but the unrepentant will be cast into its treacherous flames. Contrary to what many false religions teach, there is no escaping or release from this permanent prison. One will never be privileged to sense the calm and blessed presence of God again (2 Thessalonians 1:6–10).

Charles C. Ryrie comments on Revelation 20:11–15 as follows:

> Here is pictured the judgment of the unbelieving dead. It occurs at the close of the millennium; it is based on works, in order to show that the punishment is deserved (v. 12, though of course these unsaved people are first of all in this judgment because they rejected Christ as Savior during their lifetimes); and it results in everyone in this judgment being cast into the lake of fire. This is the resurrection of judgment (John 5:29).[3]

Jesus' Proclamation of His Glorious Victory

Jesus made a poignant statement to the repentant thief on the cross. Luke 23:42–43 records this precious scene: "Then he said to Jesus, 'Lord, remember me when you come into Your kingdom.' And Jesus said to him, 'Assuredly, I say to you, today you will be with me in Paradise.'" What a phenomenal, bitter-sweet occurrence! Can there be any greater privilege than to have been crucified alongside your Creator and Lord? This writer can think of nothing. Tragically, the other thief, as far as we know, remained unrepentant.

Christ did indeed go to Paradise that day and declare His triumph over sin and the devil. The thief on the cross was present with Him to witness that triumph. For the duration of eternity, the war had finally been won. Of course, this victory was announced as early as Genesis 3:15. But all events must take place in God's perfect timing. This is not to deny that countless spiritual battles still await

---
3 Charles Caldwell Ryrie, The Ryrie Study Bible (Chicago, Moody Press, 1976, 1978), p. 1920.

and will besiege the believer, but the ultimate victory is already in hand. Christ won that victory of victories on the bloodstained cross. Colossians 2:13–15 relates this marvelous truth:

> And you, being dead in your trespasses and the uncircumcision of your flesh, He has made alive together with Him, having forgiven you all trespasses, having wiped out the handwriting of requirements that was against us, which was contrary to us. And He has taken it out of the way, having nailed it to the cross. Having disarmed principalities and powers, He made a public spectacle of them, triumphing over them in it.

When Christ later ascended to heaven, He took the thief and all other believing inhabitants in Paradise with Him (Ephesians 4:8–10). That is now presently true of all believers when they pass from this earth (2 Corinthians 5:8; Philippians 1:22–24). But the Old Testament saints still await the physical reunification of their bodies until after the Tribulation. Hence, they do not presently have glorified bodies in quite the same fashion as do the Church saints.

If the reader recalls, Jesus presented a demonstration of His new, glorified body to the apostles (Luke 24:36–45). Jesus could just suddenly appear in their midst, yet the disciples could see His scars. Jesus also ate food in front of them. This is not to say that the believers' glorified bodies will retain precisely the same similarities as Jesus demonstrated. But it should be understood that the appearance of our new bodies will probably not be too huge a contrast (1 John 3:2).

Why Should There Be a Difference between the Saints?

The natural question that arises in the reader's mind is: Why is there a difference between saints? The ramification of this scenario seems to indicate that the Old Testament saints will be able to procreate in the millennial kingdom. The New Testament saints apparently will not. This view also receives support from the amazing promises granted to Abraham and other Jewish believers.

Genesis 15:5 states: "Then He brought him outside and said, 'Look now toward heaven, and count the stars if you are able to number them.' And He said to him, 'So shall your descendants be'" (cf. Genesis 22:17, 32:12). Certainly, this prophecy, even if intended as a simile, awaits the future. A similar promise was extended to David and the Levites in Jeremiah 33:22: "As the host of heaven cannot be numbered, nor the sand of the sea measured, so will I multiply the descendants of David My servant and the Levites who minister to Me."

Clearly, this promise has not seen fruition in our present age or in the past. Hence, it must remain for the future. Though some accurately stress that this is stated in the form of a simile, one must take caution never to underestimate God's power. Admittedly, using human reckoning, it is almost impossible for us to imagine this prophecy taking place literally as written.

Let us bear in mind, however, that the finite can never comprehend the infinite. At the very least, the nation of Israel and the Levites will grow to immense proportions compared to today. This will take place during the millennial kingdom of Christ. Jewish believers will all believe and hence not be subject to death (Jeremiah 31:34; cf. Isaiah 65:20).

At first glance, it appears that none of the blessed former inhabitants of heaven will be able to have children. (We say "former" because they do return with Christ for the millennial kingdom.) Why should this be? If they could procreate, they would have no old nature to pass on to their children. Those children, then, would seemingly be denied free choice as they would have a will essentially preprogrammed to serve God. But is that actually the case? Scripture offers little elaboration.

It is quite clear that no one returning from heaven will be encumbered with a sinful nature. This includes the Old Testament saints as well as the church age. However, it must always be borne in mind that the Old Testament saints are not yet physically resurrected. That does not happen until the first resurrection of Revelation 20:4–6. Their spirits go to heaven, but their bodies remain in the grave. By contrast, the saints of the church age will have been both spiritually and physically resurrected. Hence, there does appear to be a physical distinction between those of the church age and those of the Old Testament.

But it must be remembered that the Old Testament saints returning from heaven will not be possessed of an evil nature either. Thus, even when they are physically resurrected at the end of the Tribulation, they will be absent of a sinful nature. So, how can they pass on the evil nature to their children? Certainly, those returning from heaven will not be vulnerable to double jeopardy. Scripture does not thoroughly explain how this will work. It hardly seems possible that Jewish children born after this first generation will be born sinless. That would be contrary to written Scripture (Romans 3:23). However, this does not entirely dismiss the possibility that they could acquire a sinful nature, as did Adam and Eve.

Only Jesus Christ will ever be born sinless. Every mortal born will stand besmirched by the plague of sin. Can one resolve this parenting mystery? Not entirely. Scripture is rather silent on this mystery. Where Scripture is silent, it behooves us to be silent as well. Still, a little sanctified theological contemplation can prove spiritually instructive. But one must always bear in mind that many things are understood only in the mind of our omniscient God. We must rest content with that.

The Parenting Issue

Any biblical scholar will agree that our picture regarding this special time frame is far from absolute. God may orchestrate events in ways we cannot anticipate. Some might argue that Adam and Eve did not originally have a sinful nature. Yet, they were nonetheless vulnerable to temptation. Free will automatically entails such possibilities. Could that also be true in the millennial kingdom, it has been asked?

As the reader is well aware, Adam and Eve brought upon themselves a sinful nature through their disobedience. Thus, they passed on to Cain that which they sadly earned, an evil nature. But it also must be remembered that this was a unique situation in earth's history. One must take care not to establish a theological pattern from this most singular of events. The saints returning from heaven will be sinless and always remain sinless. They will have already made their decision for Christ and been sealed by the Holy Spirit (Ephesians 1:13–14). Hence, it would seem inconceivable that they could pass on an evil nature since they will not possess one.

In the minds of some, all returning humans from heaven could parent children. After all, they reason it is a well-established biblical fact that children are a blessing from the Lord (Psalm 127:3–5). While that is certainly true, it is hardly the grounds for establishing doctrine. Sentiment does not overrule Scripture.

It is a well-established biblical fact that those who dwell in heaven are like the angels. They neither marry nor are they given in marriage (Matthew 22:30). This may, however, be describing the believer's status in heaven. It does not necessarily carry over to their condition on the earth upon their return, some will argue. Such a possibility cannot be entirely discounted, though we find it rather dubious.

The believers returning from heaven would not themselves be placed in spiritual double jeopardy. But it is at least conceivable that each child born, even if absent of a sinful nature initially, would inevitably obtain one. That holds particularly true since there will be no child mortality (Isaiah 65:20). Indeed, from a human perspective, it seems nearly inescapable that an otherwise innocent child would eventually fall into sin. What they are not born with, namely, a sinful nature, could easily be acquired. That would make a choice for or against Christ an absolute must for each child.

One final note, however, does seem to argue against the returning Church saints from parenting children in the millennial kingdom. First John 3:2 states: "Beloved, now we are children of God, and it has not yet been revealed what we shall be, but we know that when He is revealed, we shall be like Him, for we shall see Him as He is."

The members of the Church compose the bride of Christ. We are, in a sense, "married" to Christ (Revelation 19:7). The reader can sense that since the Bible does not make a definitive statement on this matter, we should not either. All such things are conclusively known only to our triune God. Still, our sense is that the heavenly saints of the church age will not procreate. Those who survive the Tribulation and possibly the Old Testament saints apparently will.

Jewish Life in the Millennium

It is intriguing to note that all Jewish people during the millennial kingdom will be followers of Christ. Jeremiah 31:34 states the following: "No more shall every man teach his neighbor, and every man his brother, saying, 'Know the LORD,' for they all shall know Me, from the least of them to the greatest of them, says the LORD. For I will forgive their iniquity, and their sin I will remember no more" (cf. Isaiah 54:13; John 6:45).

Does this mean that the Jewish children born during the millennial kingdom will be sinless? We think not! That would contradict other well-known passages of Scripture (Ecclesiastes 7:20; Isaiah 53:6; Romans 3:23, 6:23). However, at the very least, it must mean that every Jewish child will come to faith before he reaches the age of one hundred (Isaiah 65:20).

Fruchtenbaum comments as follows:

> It is also clear from the New Covenant of Jeremiah 31:31-34 that there will be no Jewish unbelievers in the kingdom; all Jews born during that time will accept the Messiah by their hundredth year. Unbelief will be among the Gentiles only, and therefore, death will exist only among them.[4]

Unfortunately, this unanimous belief in Christ cannot be said of all Gentile children. It is the Gentiles who will foment the final rebellion against Christ. Satan is released from his 1,000-year prison and is allowed once again to tempt the world. Why should he be released?

Satan, like the Antichrist, is the catalyst that will force people to come to a spiritual turning point in their lives. Will they worship

---

[4] Arnold G. Fruchtenbaum, The Footsteps of the Messiah: A Study of the Sequence of Prophetic Events (San Antonio, TX: Ariel Ministries, 2021), p. 377.

Jesus Christ or the devil? Incredibly, many will come to the wrong decision. Scripture describes the rebellious as the sand of the sea in multitude. Once again, unbelieving mankind will foolishly follow the pernicious lies of the devil (Revelation 20:7–9). How inescapably stubborn is the heart of man (Jeremiah 17:9).

It must be understood that the millennial kingdom is a glorious precursor to eternity with God. But it is not heaven in the oft-understood, classical sense. During the millennial kingdom, sin is not entirely eradicated. Sin shall only be permanently removed in the eternal state (Isaiah 65:17; 2 Peter 3:10–14; Revelation chapters 21 and 22).

By great contrast to those returning from heaven, the believing remnant who actually live through the Tribulation on earth will still be fettered with a sinful nature. As believing survivors of the Tribulation, their salvation is obviously secure. Only believers are allowed to enter Christ's kingdom. Those precious individuals will have made their commitment to Jesus Christ. Indeed, a great multitude of people from all around the world profess Christ as their Savior during this time (Revelation 6:9–11, 7:13–17). There will be a phenomenal spiritual awakening throughout the Tribulation. Sadly, though untold multitudes do come to faith in Christ, the majority of humanity will follow the Antichrist (13:8).

Who Are These Elderly People?

One additional factor in this puzzlement between two types of people during the millennium concerns physical aging. In 1 John 3:2, we recognize that the saints will receive glorified bodies. However, will some bodies be more glorified than others? It would almost appear so.

Zechariah 8:3–5 indicates that at least some within the millennial kingdom will become old and at least somewhat infirm:

"Thus says the LORD:

'I will return to Zion,

And dwell in the midst of Jerusalem.

Jerusalem shall be called the City of Truth,

The Mountain of the LORD of hosts,

The Holy Mountain.'

Thus says the LORD of hosts:

'Old men and old women shall again sit

In the streets of Jerusalem,

Each one with his staff in his hand

Because of great age.

The streets of the city

Shall be full of boys and girls

Playing in its streets.'"

It seems quite implausible to entertain the thought that those with fully glorified bodies should age as described in Zechariah. However, Scripture does not specifically deny that possibility. Still, it appears more likely that these aging saints speak in reference to the believers who survived the Tribulation. They seem to retain both their sinful nature and physical nature. This does not mean that these saints will die. But they will be able to age.

Illness Even in the Millennial Kingdom?

In addition to Tribulation survivors regarding Zechariah 8:3–5, one should add the Old Testament saints. They will be physically resurrected at the time of Christ's second coming (Daniel 12:1–2). They may also have the potential to age. It must be understood, however, that this first generation of aging saints will not be vulnerable to death. Will this aging generation be beset with all the debilitating diseases, aches, and pains that now afflict the aged (and even the younger)? If so, it will certainly not be to the degree of today's world.

It is much more conceivable that the children born to this first generation may experience such illnesses. That could be true of both Jew and Gentile. God may very well use illness to bring young Jewish and Gentile individuals to their knees in repentance. It is amazing how physical infirmity often sharpens the spiritual senses.

In the context of the millennial kingdom, Ezekiel 47:12 states:

> Along the bank of the river, on this side and that, will grow all kinds of trees used for food; their leaves will not wither, and their fruit will not fail. They will bear fruit every month, because their water flows from the sanctuary. Their fruit will be for food, and their leaves for medicine.

Clearly, there will be illness during the millennial kingdom. It is quite probable that those most frequently beset with such physical infirmities will be the unrepentant.

There is no doubt that every believer's body will be at least partially transformed. Only the sinner will die during the millennial kingdom (Isaiah 65:20). This aging process does seem to support the view that there will indeed be two types of believers in a physical sense within the kingdom. There will also be those unfettered with a sinful nature and those who retain it.

In addition, some will be able to age while others probably will stay the same physically. Regrettably, there will be a growing multitude of unbelievers. Each generation will see an increase. The unrepentant alone, however, will be subject to physical death. They will die at the age of one hundred (Isaiah 65:20).

To Choose or Not to Choose

God demands that every individual must make a personal choice for or against Christ. This includes all the children born during the millennial kingdom. Regarding the future millennial kingdom, this eventuality may seem a rather confusing scenario to us today. But this has been God's pattern ever since He created man. A relationship with God without a decision to follow Christ is not possible. We cannot answer every question or potential objection that may arise in an individual's mind. Where the Scripture remains silent, we must as well.

What is clear, however, is this: Every person born must be granted the option of following or rejecting Christ. Tragically, a multitude, even in the midst of great material abundance, joy, and biblical knowledge during the millennium, will nonetheless choose against Him (Revelation 20:7–9).

All surviving unbelievers of the Tribulation are judged and cast into hell immediately after being put to death (Matthew 25:31–46). Their sentence is pronounced at the Judgment of the Sheep and Goats. The basis of that particular judgment stems from how they treated Christ's Jewish brethren during the Tribulation. Their appropriate treatment of Christ's brethren did not earn their salvation

(Ephesians 2:8–9). Rather, it indicated that they were either saved people or unbelievers. Their works will demonstrate their relationship with God (John 15:1–6).

This future judgment stands as a grim reminder to the insufferable hardness of man's unrepentant heart (Revelation 6:12–17, 9:20–21, 16:11). The unbelievers' final insurrection takes place at the end of the millennial kingdom. After this final rebellion against Christ, the unrepentant sinners of all history will face God's wrath at the Great White Throne Judgment.

Every individual at this last climactic judgment will be condemned and cast into the Lake of Fire (Revelation 20:11–15). Such a passage should frighten every human being into repentance, but it does not phase many in the least. They reject the truth of the Scripture and so ignore its many warnings. How eternally tragic for them!

Jude 22 and 23 admonish believers to tell unbelievers the complete truth about the coming judgment: "And on some have compassion, making a distinction, but others save with fear, pulling them out of the fire, hating even the garment defiled by the flesh." People need to know that they are sinners and that God will punish them if they remain in their unrepentant state. Romans 6:23 pointedly reminds mankind: "For the wages of sin is death, but the gift of God is eternal life in Christ Jesus our Lord."

Judgments for the Unbelievers Are Coming!

The Judgment of the Sheep and Goats and the Great White Throne Judgment bear solemn witness to God's decisive judgment on those who reject His holy Son. Second Thessalonians 2:11–12 states: "And for this reason God will send them strong delusion, that they should believe the lie, that they all may be condemned who did not believe the truth but had pleasure in unrighteousness."

God has made His witness clear through both His special (the Bible) and general revelation (nature). As Romans 1:20 so poignantly reminds us, man has no excuse whatsoever: "For since the creation of the world His invisible attributes are clearly seen, being understood by the things that are made, even His eternal power and Godhead, so that they are without excuse."

It will not be until after the Great White Throne Judgment of Revelation 20:11–15 that all unmitigated rebellion against God will cease. The condemned will eternally be ushered into the Lake of Fire. The redeemed will be welcomed into eternity for perpetual bliss and freedom from sin and its curse (Revelation 21:1–4). But until that glorious day of eternity, mankind must struggle within its own self-inflicted, sinful quagmire (Ecclesiastes 7:20). Free will is a marvelous servant but a terrible master.

A note to our readers: Regarding some of the above-mentioned future situations, it is unwise to be overly dogmatic. This writer deems it unwise to take a firm position on some of the cited potential scenarios. Why? This is because the information available is scanty. Wisdom dictates that, at times, it is preferable to simply present the primary possibilities. It is always prudent to give credence to other well-informed saints who may differ slightly in their own personal interpretations.

The Start of Untold Miseries

Romans 8:20–22 states:

> For the creation was subjected to futility, not willingly, but because of Him who subjected it in hope; because the creation itself also will be delivered from the bondage of corruption into the glorious liberty of the

children of God. For we know that the whole creation groans and labors with birth pangs together until now.

Wisdom from Wiersbe

Warren Wiersbe adroitly comments as follows on this noteworthy passage:

> When God finished His Creation, it was a good Creation (Gen. 1:31); but today it is a groaning Creation. There is suffering and death; there is pain, all of which is, of course, the result of Adam's sin. It is not the fault of creation. Note the words that Paul used to describe the plight of creation: suffering (Rom. 8:18), vanity (Rom. 8:20), bondage (Rom. 8:21), decay (Rom. 8:21), and pain (Rom. 8:22).
>
> However, this groaning is not a useless thing: Paul compared it to a woman in travail. There is pain, but the pain will end when the child is delivered. One day creation will be delivered, and the groaning creation will become a glorious creation! The believer does not focus on today's sufferings; he looks forward to tomorrow's glory (Rom. 8:18; 2 Cor. 4:15-18). Today's groaning bondage will be exchanged for tomorrow's glorious liberty![5]

It should be noted that the term "fall" into sin is somewhat misleading. Both Eve and Adam sinned quite deliberately. The only redeeming aspect to Eve's transgression is that she was deceived at

---
[5] Warren W. Wiersbe, The Bible Exposition Commentary: Volume 1: Matthew-Galatians (Wheaton, IL: Victor Books, 1989), p. 540.

the time. But both stand guilty for bringing phenomenal misery into the world. However, lest we in our modern world vent unjustified hostilities at the first couple, we should ask ourselves the following rather simple question: "Would I or anyone else have fared any better than Adam and Eve did?"

The answer is an unequivocal "no!" Our triune God knew from eternity when He created man that he would morally fail. Nothing is hidden from the omniscient eyes of our Creator. Thus, God provided the covering atonement for man's sin before he was even created.

John 1:29 states: "The next day John saw Jesus coming toward him, and said, 'Behold! The Lamb of God who takes away the sin of the world!'" (cf. Revelation 13:8) Christ's holy sacrifice was planned before creation ever took place. God never plans in half measures. All things are complete and finalized in eternity past. As mere mortals, we must wait for the proper timing of God's preordained events.

The first promise of this redemption through the woman's Seed is recorded in Genesis 3:15: "And I will put enmity between you and the woman, and between your seed and her Seed; He shall bruise your head, and you shall bruise His heel.'" This crucial prophetic passage will receive a more detailed examination later. For now, however, it is important to note that God's glorious plan of redemption has always existed.

Sin Pervades the Entire Universe, Even Heaven Itself!

Everything in the universe is, for now, tainted by sin. Even the heavenly realm, where God reigns, suffers defilement. How is that possible? Lucifer, who is also called Satan and a host of other descriptive names, is the most evil created being in the universe. Satan was not created evil; he became evil. No one understands how that

Beginnings and Endings

happened, but happen it did. This is one of the many mysteries of Scripture. Man, being a finite creature, is not privy to understand all mysteries that occur throughout eternity.

Lucifer is still allowed access into God's presence (Job chapters 1 and 2). At this very moment, Lucifer is actively accusing the brethren of their sins to God. How ironic that is! Satan, who led man into sin, now stands as the chief accuser of their sin. Satan is evil through and through. His hypocrisy knows no bounds! One can imagine his wicked smile as he reports the repeated failings of God's precious saints. Sadly, mankind gives Satan ample ammunition for accusation.

But the believer may take great comfort in the thought that God knows all things in advance (Isaiah 46:10). He is willing to forgive because of the incalculable gift of His holy Son, Jesus Christ (2 Corinthians 9:15). His sacrificial and bloody payment on the cruel cross was sufficient to forgive any sin. The only three exceptions to that rule are blasphemy against the Holy Spirit (Matthew 12:31), the sin of perpetual unbelief (2 Thessalonians 2:10), and receiving the mark of the beast in the Tribulation (Revelation 14:9–11).

God's grace overflows in abundance. No one can add to or subtract from it! Neither can any mortal comprehend its fullness and satisfaction to the Father above who rules in the heavens. The perfect sacrifice of Jesus Christ provided perfect redemption for the penitent.

Referring back again to Lucifer, Revelation 12:10 states: "Then I heard a loud voice saying in heaven, 'Now salvation, and strength, and the kingdom of our God, and the power of His Christ have come, for the accuser of our brethren, who accused them before our God day and night, has been cast down" (cf. Job 1:6–12, 2:1–7). Satan, who is also called the dragon (Revelation 12:3, 13), will be cast out of heaven halfway through the Tribulation.

When he suffers this humiliating and permanent exile, he knows that the time for his own personal judgment is imminent. He has three and a half years remaining in the Tribulation to carry out his wicked vendetta against God and His adopted children. He enlists every wicked demonic slave in his vile camp and energizes them into battle. Their primary targets will be against the Jews and the saints during the latter half of the Tribulation (Revelation 12:17).

The Perpetual Puzzlement of Sin

Question: Why did God allow sin to enter the world? God had created everything perfect. There was no sin in the original creation. That included Adam and Eve, who were also sinless. But one necessary circumstance permitted sin to happen. Answer: God granted man a free will. Along with that free will came "desire." Desire in itself certainly is not wrong. However, it can easily be corrupted, and, as we know, it was.

God did not create man to be a mindless and unresponsive robot. It's not possible to have a meaningful relationship with a pre-programmed robot. Thus, it was that God presented Adam with one recorded prohibition. Such a prohibition for that time period was necessary. Free worship without free choice is not genuine worship. It is just blind, volitionless obedience.

One should observe that, as far as we know, God did not directly give the same command to Eve as He did to Adam. It seems more likely that Adam repeated it to her. But, one way or the other, she obviously did know about the "forbidden" fruit.

Genesis 2:16–17 states: "And the Lord God commanded the man saying, 'Of every tree of the garden you may freely eat; but of the tree of the knowledge of good and evil you shall not eat, for in the day that you eat of it you shall surely die.'" The Hebrew is best translated as "dying, you shall surely die." That is precisely what happened.

Although man did not die physically on the day of the transgression, he decidedly died spiritually. Consequently, something had to be done. As already stated, that "something" was in God's eternal plan. God never has to change His mind, and He is never surprised by anything. That is truly hard for a finite creature to fathom.

God's Eternal Solution to Sin

In Genesis chapter 3, when Adam and Eve ate the fruit, an instantaneous death sentence was passed upon mankind. But as noted, that instantaneous death was a spiritual death. This spiritual death caused a separation from God. Only God could rebuild that relationship. He did so through His Son. But man must also participate in the reconciliation through faith. It is not merely a one-sided affair. God desires a living relationship with mankind, not one of dead orthodoxy established by human tradition and practices.

Though the provision for salvation is all of God, the reception thereof is, in a mysterious sense, of both God and man. John 6:44 states: "No one can come to Me unless the Father who sent Me draws him; and I will raise him up at the last day."

In reference to God's wondrous gift of salvation, Second Corinthians 9:15 states: "Thanks be to God for His indescribable gift!" While it is patently true that man cannot add to the salvation offered through Christ, he still must accept it by faith. If that were not the case, then salvation would truly be offered only to the elect. And who then, but God, could determine who the elect might be? It could then be erroneously argued (and it has) that Christ died only for the select few. Scripture entirely discounts that possibility (John

3:16, 36; 5:24). Christ died for all.

John 1:12 states: "But as many as received Him, to them He gave the right to become children of God, to those who believe in His name." Christ offers salvation to all. Sadly, few embrace it (Matthew 7:13–14). It is our fervent prayer that anyone reading this book will fully trust in Christ as their Savior. Apart from Christ, only spiritual condemnation exists! Within Christ, spiritual life is reborn within the sinner. What greater gift can anyone receive than that?

What of Physical Death for Adam and Eve?

The physical aspect of death was more slow in coming to the first couple. In fact, Adam lived for a total of 930 years (Genesis 5:5). That is a marvelous example of God's considerable forbearance! But death did arrive earlier at Adam and Eve's doorstep in a most tragic and unexpected development in Genesis chapter 4, as we shall later see.

Fruchtenbaum offers the following comments on Genesis 2:17b:

> The seventh provision, in verse 17b, has to do with the penalty for disobedience, and spiritual death: *for in the day that you eat thereof you shall surely die.* According to this statement, death was to come on the very same day as the violation. Therefore, this cannot refer to physical death since Adam did not die physically on the day he partook of the fruit; but he did die spiritually on the day that he ate.
>
> Spiritual death means "separation from God." The Hebrew form is a special construction, *mot tamut*, using

the same Hebrew root together twice to make it emphatic, which is why it is translated, you shall surely die.

In this form it appears fourteen times in the Hebrew Bible: Genesis 2:17, 3:4, and 20:7; 1 Samuel 14:44 and 22:16; 1 Kings 2:37 and 2:42; II Kings 1:4, 1:6, and 1:16; Jeremiah 26:8; and Ezekiel 3:18, 33:8, and 33:14. It implies an announcement of a death sentence either by a divine decree or by a royal decree.

This is what is meant by Original Sin: The day that man partakes of the fruit, on that day he will die spiritually; and the spiritual death will be transmitted to his progeny. Therefore, those who are born to Adam and Eve are born spiritually dead.[6]

Fruchtenbaum correctly emphasizes that the primary result of the transgression was spiritual death, thus fulfilling God's precise words. But, as humanity soon learned, physical death also proved a most negative consequence. It must have proved quite a shock to Adam and Eve when they first witnessed the death of a creature. This would have been particularly personalized to them when they recognized that this same creature had to be killed to provide clothing for them.

Life irrevocably changed, including Adam and Eve's attitudes toward one another. The defiled sin nature crept into their lives, never again to leave in our present age. Only in heaven can it be removed. Adam and Eve never again experienced the same tender-

---

6 Arnold G. Fruchtenbaum, Ariel's Bible Commentary: The Book of Genesis: Exposition from a Messianic Jewish Perspective (San Antonio, TX: Ariel Ministries, 2009), p. 81.

ness and innocence toward each other they originally had. Regrettably, the battle of the sexes had begun!

Lessons Learned in This Chapter

In this introductory chapter, we discussed several aspects of Genesis chapter 3. We first examined the fact that sin has besmirched God's entire universe. The ramifications of sin surround humanity, even heaven itself, on a daily, ongoing basis. Only through the sacrifice of Jesus Christ can forgiveness and reconciliation with God be accomplished. The amazing fact is that this costs mankind nothing. Salvation is free to man but incredibly costly to God (Titus 3:5). Not only did God create man, but He also provided redemption for him (Genesis 3:15).

Second, we delved into a variety of questions surrounding the future of mankind. This particularly held true regarding the millennial kingdom of Christ. We pondered the question of the differences between the Old and New Testament saints. We reviewed the fact that sin and sinner also will be present during the millennial kingdom. The unrepentant culprits will foster rebellion during the millennial kingdom, hard as that may seem to grasp in our present age.

We also explored the possibility of procreation within the godly host during the millennial kingdom. Clearly, there will be children born (Genesis 15:5). Who will be the parents? The Scripture does not entirely answer that question. It remains for the future to fully understand this issue. Our assessment, however, is that the saints of the church age will not parent children. This will be the privilege of the Old Testament saints and the survivors of the Tribulation.

Scripture also portrays the fact that there will be aged people inhabiting the millennial kingdom (Zechariah 8:3–5). Who are these elderly people? If one has a glorified body, how can it age (1 John

3:2)? Again, this presently remains something of mystery. We believe that those who age are the survivors of the Tribulation and the Old Testament saints who receive their resurrected bodies at the first resurrection (Revelation 20:4–6). That viewpoint, however, is not fully demonstrated in the Scripture.

Our personal assessment on the types of people in the millennium is admittedly a bit tenuous. However, it leans to the concept that there is a decided difference between the glorified bodies of Christians from the church age and those of Old Testament vintage. One of the reasons for this is that only the New Testament saints are both spiritually and physically resurrected at the time of the Rapture. Hence, they receive their glorified bodies and spirits simultaneously.

The Old Testament saints will be physically resurrected only after Christ's second coming. However, their spirits were ushered into the kingdom of heaven when Christ ascended (Ephesians 4:8–10). Paradise was emptied out 2,000 years ago. Abraham is no longer conversing with the rich man in hell (Luke 16:19–31). He is fellowshipping with his marvelous Savior in heaven, as is Lazarus, the beggar.

In our next chapter, we delve more deeply into the actual temptation of Adam and Eve. It is a tragic story but one that needs discussion. We also examine Lucifer's unique situation. How, why, and when did he fall into sin? Though scholars are divided on these issues, we shall offer our perspective on these difficult interpretive matters.

Cognitive Conundrum #1

A mighty man of valor I was reputed to be; in battle, I was not to be trifled with, you see. But my impressive instincts did not always prevail; one time, God's interference led me to fail. A competitor I vainly struggled to soundly defeat, but gross deception led to blood at my feet. The future of a kingdom I deemed in my hand, but God's sovereign choice governed the land.

Who am I?

Answer: Abner

Chapter 2

The Beginning of Evil

(Genesis 3:1-8: Part B)

In This Chapter

Objectives for This Chapter
The Sad Saga of Sin Described
The Temptation of Adam and Eve
Lessons Learned in This Chapter

Objectives for This Chapter

In this chapter, we shall first discuss Lucifer's (Satan's) fall from grace. He was the pinnacle of God's creative handiwork (Isaiah 14:12–15; Ezekiel 28:11–15). His was the most highly exalted position for a created being. But, in a dark mystery understood only by our omniscient God, iniquity reared its ugly head within him. People may ponder how that was possible. But in our present era, it will remain a mystery.

The important issue is this: Mankind must deal with the consequences of both Lucifer's and Adam's transgression. Isaiah 53:6 poignantly points out: "All we like sheep have gone astray; we have turned, every one, to his own way; and the LORD has laid on Him the iniquity of us all." Their moral collapse affected all of humanity, indeed, the entire universe.

Second, we shall delve into a discussion of the spiritual prefiguring of the physical in the Scripture. Generally speaking, the reverse is often the case. The physical quite frequently prefigures Jesus Christ in a beautiful fashion. For example, the sacred offerings and festivals in Israel represented Jesus Christ in splendid ways. Though the Jews could not comprehend the spiritual and eternal meaning of everything commanded of them, God understood their purpose. Indeed, He devised the spiritual intent of all things from eternity.

Third, we shall discuss certain ramifications of Adam and Eve's fall into sin. The world, and they themselves, paid a big price for their iniquity. However, no other human being would have fared any better. All would have fallen prey to the allurements cast about by Satan. Free will creates desire. Desire often leads to sin and sin to death (James 1:13–15).

Incredibly, God willingly laid the full iniquity of mankind on His own precious Son. The Son painfully paid the price for a largely unrepentant and ungrateful mankind. Romans 5:8 states: "But God demonstrates His own love toward us, in that while we were still sinners, Christ died for us." Such a gift bestowed on humanity by the triune God exceeds mankind's limited and sin-stained imagination. We can only humbly say, "Thank You, Lord!"

The Sad Saga of Sin Described

The melancholy story of Adam and Eve's transgression begins in Genesis 3:1–8:

> Now the serpent was more cunning than any beast of the field which the LORD God had made. And he said to the woman, "Has God indeed said, You shall not eat of every tree of the garden'?" And the woman said to the serpent, "We may eat the fruit of the trees of the

garden; but of the fruit of the tree which is in the midst of the garden, God has said, 'You shall not eat it, nor shall you touch it, lest you die.'"

Then the serpent said to the woman, "You will not surely die, for God knows that in the day you eat of it your eyes will be opened, and you will be like God, knowing good and evil." So when the woman saw that the tree was good for food, that it was pleasant to the eyes, and a tree desirable to make one wise, she took of its fruit and ate. She also gave to her husband with her, and he ate.

Then the eyes of both of them were opened, and they knew that they were naked; and they sewed fig leaves together and made themselves coverings. And they heard the sound of the LORD God walking in the garden in the cool of the day, and Adam and his wife hid themselves from the presence of the LORD God among the trees of the garden.

Satan Violates God's Perfect Creation

The fall of mankind began when Eve was first tempted by Lucifer. He came to her in disguise by spiritually possessing a serpent. The serpent spoke to Eve, but remarkably, she was not frightened. Before sin defiled the creation, things were obviously much different. Perhaps all the animals could speak, but that is admittedly speculation. A question quite naturally arises in the minds of many believers when they read the account of Genesis chapter 3. We presented this same question earlier, but we shall now provide a fuller response.

Question: Why did God allow Satan to tempt Adam and Eve? H. C. Leupold astutely answers this perplexing question as follows:

> Yet a word on the question often raised at this point: "Why must there be a temptation?" or "Why does God permit His chief creature on earth to be tempted? Does He not desire man's supreme happiness? Why, then, does He permit a temptation which leads to death and all our woe?
>
> The answer must always be that God will have only that count as moral behavior worthy of a being made in God's image, which is freely given and maintained even where the possibility of doing otherwise offers itself. To do what God desires merely because one cannot do otherwise, has no moral worth.
>
> It would be a morality like unto that of beams which uphold the house because they have been put in place and cannot but bear their load. To do the right where there has never been an opportunity of doing wrong is not moral behavior. The opportunity to do otherwise must present itself. This is temptation.
>
> A being who could not even suffer to be tempted would be a poor specimen of God's handiwork. But the true

wisdom of God appears in this, that, though His creature falls, God is still able to achieve His original purpose through the redemption which is in Christ Jesus, a redemption for which provisions are already beginning to be made in this chapter.[7]

Leupold sagaciously demonstrates the necessity of free choice. Without free choice, man would be nothing more than an elaborate computer program. True, free choice brings its own set of heartaches, but what would life be like without it? Of course, no one will ever experience the-like scenario of Adam and Eve in our present era. Their experience was a once-in-human history situation.

Nonetheless, it does not require an elongated period of contemplation to recognize that an absence of free will would be far less than gratifying. Any slightly introspective individual can immediately see problems without the liberty of personal decision-making. Worship is not genuine worship without free choice! It would simply be a mandate impossible to resist. Where would be the gratification in that? God, in His infinite wisdom, always knows what is best for His creation.

When Did Lucifer Fall from Grace?

A second question frequently arises after the first. Question: When did Satan fall from grace into sin? The Bible does not give a clear answer to that question. However, there are some judicious thoughts about which one may cogitate.

Lucifer's fall is generally held by many to have happened after the creation week was finished. Why? God declared all things to be very good on the sixth day, did He not? A rebellion by Satan could

---

[7] H. C. Leupold, Exposition of Genesis (Grand Rapids, MI: Baker Book House, 1942), pp. 145–146.

hardly be described as "very good." It should be noted that when Satan fell, a third of the angels, who are now demons, fell with him (Revelation 12:4). That certainly cannot qualify as "very good." It was a tragedy of epic proportions. However, there are other thoughts concerning this question that are worthy of deliberation.

Consideration #1: The timing of Lucifer's fall is oft assumed to have been after the creation of man. That, however, is not an essential conclusion if the spiritual, angelic host was created before the physical universe. It is quite conceivable that God was speaking only in reference to the physical universe of the creation week in Genesis chapters 1 and 2. If that be so, the angels, being in the spiritual domain, may well have not been included in His statements about everything being "very good."

Lucifer and his gang may have sinned much earlier. Scripture is inconclusive as to precisely when the angels were actually created. But, based on Job 38:7, the good angels rejoiced when the foundations of the earth were laid. They had to be in existence to be rejoicing over God's creative abilities and goodness. The evil angels, quite naturally, would have mocked and scorned God's creation. They had become evil to the core of their being. No redemption was provided for the evil angels. Hence, there was no motivation for them to improve their lot. Their eternal destiny was already well known to them.

Who Are the Mysterious Morning Stars and Sons of God?

There is no expressed biblical reason to discount an earlier creation of the angelic beings. Since they are spiritual beings and not physical, perhaps the angelic beings are unimaginably old. It must be remembered that Genesis chapters 1 and 2 describe the physical creation. Angels are not mentioned, and possibly for good reason. Job 38:4–7 seems to hint at that possibility quite strongly:

> Where were you when I laid the foundations of the earth? Tell Me, if you have understanding. Who determined its measurements? Surely you know! Or who stretched the line upon it? To what were its foundations fastened? Or who laid the cornerstone when the morning stars sang together, and all the sons of God shouted for joy?

Question: Who are the morning stars and sons of God in Job 38:7? Answer: The most reasonable assessment is that these represent the angels. Elsewhere in the Old Testament, the term "sons of God" represents angelic beings (Genesis 6:2, 4). The "morning stars" and "sons of God" are used in synonymous parallelism to each other. This means they both symbolize the same creatures, the angelic beings.

This is a strong indication that the angels were created before God's creation of the physical universe. Hence, it is a likely, albeit not definitive, conclusion that Genesis chapters 1 and 2 do not describe the creation of the angels but exclusively the physical heavens and earth.

John E. Hartley comments as follows:

> On the occasion of laying the earth's cornerstone, the morning stars were assembled as an angelic chorus to sing praises to God for the glory of his world. At the moment the stone was set in place the sons of God, i.e., the angels, broke out in joyous singing, praising God, the Creator. Since no human being was present at this

occasion, the inner structure of the universe remains a secret hidden from mankind. ...

In Gen. 1 the stars were created on the fourth day, but here they existed at the initial stages of creation. This apparent discrepancy indicates that "the morning stars" in this context is primarily a term that forms a synonymous parallelism with "the sons of God," who, it is assumed, existed prior to the creation of the earth. It is, therefore, used metaphorically to refer to these heavenly creatures independent of the existence of the physical stars.[8]

Consideration #2: Adam and Eve were told to multiply and fill the earth. One can reasonably assume that they began their husband-and-wife conjugal intimacies immediately. Since both of them had perfect bodies, pregnancy would probably take place relatively quickly.

When Cain was born, he proved to be clearly wicked, so the fall had to have already occurred before his conception. Cain was definitely born with a sinful nature, as is true of all humanity save Jesus Christ. If he had been conceived prior to his parents' transgression, he would have been born sinless.

When Did Sin Take Over Lucifer?

Consideration #3: Adam and Eve were in the habit of walking in the Garden with God and enjoying fellowship. It should, therefore, be assumed that they enjoyed at least some interim period of spiritual intimacy with God. However, this period possibly did not

---

[8] John E. Hartley, The New International Commentary on the Old Testament: The Book of Job (Grand Rapids, MI: William B. Eerdmans Publishing Company, 1988), p. 495.

exceed a few months. It is perhaps limited even to a few precious days. Scripture is silent on the time frame.

Keil and Delitzsch offer the following comments:

> There was a fall, therefore, in the higher spiritual world before the fall of man, and this is not only plainly taught in 2 Peter 2:4 and Jude 1:6, but assumed in everything that the Scriptures say of Satan. But this event in the world of spirits neither compels us to place the fall of Satan before the six days' work of creation, nor to assume that the days represent long periods.
>
> For as man did not continue long in communion with God, so the angel-prince may have rebelled against God shortly after his creation, and not only have involved a host of angels in his apostasy and fall, but have proceeded immediately to tempt the men, who were created in the image of God, to abuse their liberty by transgressing the divine command. ...
>
> The temptation of Christ is the counterpart of that of Adam. Christ was tempted by the devil, not only like Adam, but because Adam had been tempted and overcome, in order that by overcoming the tempter He might wrest from the devil that dominion over the whole race which he had secured by his victory over the first human pair. The tempter approached the Savior openly, to the first man he came in disguise.[9]

---
9 C. F. Keil and F. Delitzsch, Commentary on the Old Testament: The Pentateuch (Grand Rapids, MI: William B. Eerdmans Publishing Company, 1986), pp. 92–93.

Scenario #1: Since God described His creation as "very good," most assume that the downfall of Lucifer and the angels occurred shortly after the creation of the heavens and the earth. That is a distinct possibility. Perhaps jealousy of God's relationship with Adam and Eve entered into Lucifer's heart. They clearly had a relationship with God that Lucifer could not have. God created only mankind in His image, not the angelic beings. Though the angels were created superior in strength and undoubtedly intellect, they lacked the all-important image of God.

Scenario #2: As we have already discussed, Satan's downfall possibly occurred long before the creation of the physical heavens and earth. It must be remembered that the angels are spiritual beings, not physical. The fact that the morning stars and sons of God in Job 38:7 rejoiced over the foundations of the earth lends solid support to this view. If they were already there, it seems reasonable to suspect that they existed prior to Genesis chapters 1 and 2.

There really is no way of biblically determining this puzzlement. Neither is it necessary. Either of the scenarios could be true. Mankind must simply deal with the spiritual realities as they confront us today. The painful reality is that Lucifer, one-third of the heavenly host, and mankind all suffer under the heavy weight of sin. Thankfully for man, there is at least the possibility of forgiveness and spiritual reconciliation (John 14:6; Titus 3:5). Mankind simply has to believe, acknowledge their sin, and ask for Christ's forgiveness (John 1:12).

No such hope is offered to the wicked angels. Matthew 25:41 states: "Then He will also say to those on the left hand, 'Depart from Me, you cursed, into the everlasting fire prepared for the devil and his angels'" (cf. Matthew 7:23). This passage is part of the discussion on the Judgment of the Sheep and Goats in Matthew 25:31–46.

It should be noted that this judgment takes place immediately after the Tribulation. All remaining unbelievers will be found guilty, put to death, and sentenced to hell. It will be a truly tragic day for the unrepentant.

The Judgment of the Sheep and Goats

Walvoord and Dyer offer the following appropriate comments on Matthew 25:31–46:

> The King will then address the goats and dismiss them into everlasting fire, declaring that they have not done these deeds of kindness. This judgment is in keeping with Christ's previous predictions in the parable of the wheat and tares and the parable of the dragnet (Matt. 13:24-30, 31-43, 47-50), and is also clearly taught in Revelation 14:11 and 19:15. No unconverted adults will be allowed to enter the millennial kingdom.
>
> The judgment here is not the same as the final great white throne judgment (Rev. 20:11-15), but is preparatory to establishing the kingdom of righteousness and peace, of which many Scriptures speak. Carson writes: "Hell was prepared for the Devil (see on 4:1) and his angels (demons, see on 8:31; cf. Jude 6; Rev. 12:7) but also serves as the doom of those guilty of the sins of omission of which Jesus here speaks: they have refused to show compassion to King Messiah through helping the least of his brothers.

This judgment fits naturally and easily into the prophetic program as usually outlined by premillenarians. The throne is an earthly throne, fulfilling the prediction of Jeremiah 23:5. Those who are judged are Gentiles (Gr. ethne), which, although sometimes used for Jews (Luke 7:5; 23:2; John 11:48, 51, 52; 18:35; Acts 10:22) is more characteristically used of Gentiles as distinguished from Jews. See, for instance, Romans 3:29; 9:24; 11:13; 15:27; 16:4; and Galatians 2:12, where the term is used consistently in this way.[10]

Why Did Lucifer Fall From Grace?

This is a most natural follow-up question to the timing of Satan's fall. Why did he fall? Although we shall never understand all the reasons in this present age, Scripture does provide sufficient answer for inquiring mankind. Clearly, there are parallels between Lucifer's fall and mankind's. It is generally a question of personal will, ambition, and jealousy.

Lucifer wanted not only to be like God (as did Eve and Adam), but he also wanted to be greater than God. Lucifer coveted the highest position in all of creation. It did not seem to occur to him that the created can never become greater than the Creator. The pot can never become greater than the Potter (Jeremiah 18:6).

Sin entirely corrupted Lucifer's ability to extrapolate the difference between truth and fiction. He became the father of lies. That is his new, nonretractable nature. It is his native language, so to speak. Not only does Lucifer lie to others, but he lies to himself. He apparently believes his own lies of grandeur and power. How utterly

---
10 John F. Walvoord and Charles H. Dyer, The John Walvoord Prophecy Commentaries: Matthew (Chicago, IL: Moody Publishers, 1974, 2013), p. 346.

The Beginning of Evil

pathetic that is!

Concerning Lucifer, Isaiah 14:12–15 states:

"How you are fallen from heaven, O Lucifer, son of the morning! How you are cut down to the ground, you who weakened the nations! For you have said in your heart: 'I will ascend into heaven, I will exalt my throne above the stars of God; I will also sit on the mount of the congregation on the farthest sides of the north: I will ascend above the heights of the clouds, I will be like the Most High.' Yet you shall be brought down to Sheol, to the lowest depths of the Pit" (cf. Ezekiel 28:11–15).

Pride is the one-word summary of Lucifer's downfall. He not only wanted to be like God, but he also wanted to replace Him on His throne. Lucifer thought he could become God! How such foolishness entered into his vain heart is inexplicable. Lucifer, the most exalted of God's creation, thought he could become greater than his Creator. This is the worst example of self-aggrandizement and self-deception the universe has ever witnessed.

But there really never was any contest. The created and finite, no matter how powerful or magnificent, cannot do battle with the omnipotent Creator. Sadly, his downfall impacted one-third of the angelic host (Revelation 12:4). Satan then successfully tempted Adam and Eve to disobey God. Tragically, they complied. Our present sinful status is the tragic result.

Proverbs 16:18 astutely reminds us: "Pride goes before destruction, and a haughty spirit before a fall." That is wise counsel that all of mankind would do well to remember. Satan refused to heed those words of wisdom. Pride has led to the downfall of many.

Wise Words on Isaiah 14:12–15

F. C. Jennings offers the following comments on Isaiah 14:12–15:

> Let us trace the ambitious path of this "Lucifer" further. He who reads all hearts has read this in his: "I will exalt my throne above the stars of God," that is, above the other angelic powers, for the term "stars of God," as that other, "the host of heaven ," covers both the material and spiritual, both the visible and invisible. This Bright Star of the Morning aims to place his throne above all other stars. "I will also sit upon the mount of the assembly, in the extremity of the north."
>
> The term "Mount of the Assembly" is strikingly suggestive of that other mount, Har-Mageddon, for that also means when translated from the Hebrew tongue, "mount of assembly, or gathering;" but the last part of the word (maggedon) has in it the idea of a military gathering of troops, in undisguised warfare, and speaks of the final gathering of all the children of pride in open conflict with "Him that sits on the horse" (Rev. 19:19), in whom we recognize our Lord Himself.
>
> But this idea of a military gathering is quite lacking in the word "congregation" (ver. 13). That is the peaceful word used for those appointed feasts in Israel's

day, when Jehovah gathered His people around Himself; and we can see how perfectly consistent is this peaceful word with the time in which the proud king is speaking in his heart.

No rebellion had as yet broken the calm waters of that sinless past, and introduced the storm that is to this day raging. All angelic "assemblies" then were in willing submission to the Throne of God. It is with this assembly in mind, that this Bright Morning Star aims to place his throne, in the "extremity of the north," the highest possible elevation.[11]

Sadly, chaos and misery would soon erupt over the heavens and eventually the earth because of Lucifer. Pride led to his inglorious downfall. The same held true for Eve and Adam. They, too, wanted to be like God in the sense of knowing good and evil. At least the human pair were not so foolish as to think they could become greater than God. Again, however, we must exercise caution in hypocritically condemning Adam and Eve. No other human being would have fared any better. All would have equally succumbed to Satan's beguiling temptation. One must remember that the first couple did not know what sin was or any of its ugly ramifications. They were pure and innocent.

Further Illumination on Lucifer's Fall from Grace

In order to attain the fullest picture possible regarding Lucifer, it is incumbent upon us to examine another text, namely, Ezekiel 28:11–15. We might mention that this text has caused ongoing

---

[11] F. C. Jennings, Studies in Isaiah (Neptune, NJ: Loizeaux Brothers, 1935), pp. 184–185.

Creation

confusion over the centuries. That is also true of Isaiah 14:12–15. Scholars debate back and forth on the meaning of both passages. We shall endeavor to present the proper interpretation of this text as we see it. In fairness to our readers, we extend the warning that undue dogmatism on this text is inadvisable.

Ezekiel 28:11–15 states the following:

> Moreover the word of the Lord came to me saying, "Son of man, take up a lamentation for the king of Tyre, and say to him, 'Thus says the Lord God: "You were the seal of perfection, full of wisdom and perfect in beauty, you were in Eden, the garden of God; every precious stone was your covering: the sardius, topaz, and diamond, beryl, onyx, and jasper, sapphire, turquoise, and emerald with gold.
>
> The workmanship of your timbrels and pipes was prepared for you on the day you were created. "You were the anointed cherub who covers; I established you; you were on the holy mountain of God; you walked back and forth in the midst of fiery stones. You were perfect in your ways from the day you were created, till iniquity was found in you.""'"

Observations on Ezekiel 28:11–15

Several observations are in order at this point:

Observation #1: The king of Tyre clearly symbolizes someone else. No human being can be characterized by the splendid claims made of this individual. Based on Isaiah 14:12–15, our comparative passage, we believe that the king of Tyre represents Lucifer. Who else could possibly qualify?

Why did God select the king of Tyre as this symbol? Perhaps it was based on his enormous power and pride. We are not informed of any precise reason. The men of Tyre were renowned for grotesque wickedness in the midst of their considerable military achievements. The city of Carthage, for instance, was founded by the people of Tyre. They were also highly renowned for enormous wealth based on their extensive trade and mastery of the seas.

Observation #2: This being was described as the "seal of perfection." The attributes accorded to this reputed king of Tyre could only represent an absolutely perfect being. Certainly, that disqualifies any king of Tyre. It is likely that few men who sat on the throne of Tyre arrived there by peaceful means. Most of them were probably excessively cruel and vindictive masters. Certainly, none could be described as perfect, even if legitimate.

Observation #3: The garden of God is apparently a spiritual garden. It prefigures the literal, physical Garden of Eden, where Adam and Eve traversed. Is there any reason to believe that Ezekiel 28:11–15 is speaking only of a spiritual state? Yes, we believe so. The context seems to mandate that interpretation.

Certainly, the garden of God does not equate to the Garden of Eden in its limited description. The garden of God contained precious jewels and even fire. Lucifer walked there adorned with precious stones and in unequaled glory in comparison to all other created beings. Since the angels live in a different dimension than mankind, it would seem reasonable to believe that these gems were of a spiritual nature. Thus, they probably prefigured the physical gems of the physical universe.

The Garden of Eden is described as a lush paradise replete with living animals and sumptuous fruits. We must remember that Lucifer was a spirit being. It seems counterintuitive that God would place him in a physical garden. True, with our limited imaginations and experience, we cannot truthfully imagine such a scenario as we are attempting to describe. But that is true in many avenues of life. A lack of understanding does not necessitate a lack of our belief and acceptance.

There are other examples of the spiritual prefiguring of the physical, which we shall mention momentarily. More frequently, however, it is the reverse. The physical generally prefigures the spiritual. As Paul writes in Colossians 2:16–17: "So let no one judge you in food or in drink, or regarding a festival or a new moon or sabbaths, which are a shadow of things to come, but the substance is of Christ." Christ is the ultimate spiritual fulfillment of many different physical practices and festivals in the Old Testament.

The Illustration of the Heavenly Tabernacle and Temple

Observation #4: Lucifer walked in the midst of this spiritual garden. Again, why do we believe that the garden of God was spiritual? One must call to mind that there is a heavenly temple and tabernacle. They prefigured the physical temple and tabernacle on earth.

Regarding the tabernacle, Exodus 25:40 informs us: "And see to it that you make them according to the pattern which was shown you on the mountain." Moses was to follow the pattern of the tabernacle God had previously shown him in heaven. Moses was thus able to precisely follow the instructions God imposed for the tabernacle.

Regarding the temple in heaven, Revelation 11:19 proves quite instructive: "Then the temple of God was opened in heaven, and the ark of His covenant was seen in His temple. And there were lightnings, noises, thunderings, an earthquake, and great hail." Clearly, there is both a temple and an ark of the covenant in heaven. These are the spiritual originals that were then physically duplicated on earth.

To this passage, we might add Revelation 3:12:

> He who overcomes, I will make him a pillar in the temple of My God, and he shall go out no more, I will write on him the name of My God and the name of the city of My God, the New Jerusalem which comes down out of heaven from My God. And I will write on him My new name (cf. 7:15).

Comments by Paul and the Author of Hebrews on New Jerusalem

One must note that a spiritual New Jerusalem also exists, which predates the physical Jerusalem. Its importance is emphasized in numerous places in Scripture. Paul refers to the New Jerusalem and the Old Jerusalem in Galatians 4:22–26:

> For it is written that Abraham had two sons: the one by a bondwoman, the other by a freewoman. But he who was of the bondwoman was born according to the flesh, and he of the freewoman through promise, which things are symbolic.

> For these are the two covenants: the one from Mount Sinai which gives birth to bondage, which is Hagar—for this Hagar is Mount Sinai in Arabia, and corresponds to Jerusalem which now is, and is in bondage with her children—but the Jerusalem above is free,

which is the mother of us all.

To this, Hebrews 11:8–10 further testifies:

> By faith Abraham obeyed when he was called to go out to the place which he would receive as an inheritance. And he went out, not knowing where he was going. By faith he dwelt in the land of promise as in a foreign country, dwelling in tents with Isaac and Jacob, the heirs with him of the same promise; for he waited for the city which has foundations, whose builder and maker is God.

We would be remiss if we did not add Hebrews 12:22–24:

> But you have come to Mount Zion, and to the city of the living God, the heavenly Jerusalem, to an innumerable company of angels, to the general assembly and church of the firstborn who are registered in heaven, to God the Judge of all, to the saints of just men made perfect, to Jesus the Mediator of the new covenant, and to the blood of sprinkling that speaks better things than that of Abel.

Why No Temple in the New Heavens and New Earth?

One other note of interest regarding the temple is recorded in Revelation 21:22–23: "But I saw no temple in it, for the Lord God Almighty and the Lamb are its temple. The city had no need of the sun or the moon to shine in it, for the glory of God illuminated it. The Lamb is its light." In the eternal state, the temple is not physically present on the earth. Why should that be? The secret to this conundrum is not particularly complex.

One must ask themselves this question: What does the temple represent? It represents the need for atonement and forgiveness. This is literally defined by the blood and grain sacrifices and also the necessity of faith. There certainly is a glorious temple in the millennial kingdom. What is the difference? In the millennial kingdom, sin will still be present. Not so in the eternal state.

The advent of the eternal state removes all necessity for forgiveness. All present will be redeemed believers. Sin will be a curse no longer. For the first time since the fall of man, sin will no longer be a blemish on humanity and the universe. Hence, God and the Lamb are the temple. Atonement is finished! The need for the temple and its accompanying sacrifices is permanently satisfied through the unquenchable power of Christ's blood.

The Temptation of Adam and Eve

God-Ordained Differences between Man and Woman

One should make an initial observation regarding Eve's temptation since she was tempted first: Eve was deceived into sinning. First Timothy 2:14 states: "And Adam was not deceived, but the woman being deceived, fell into transgression." Eve was fully aware of God's prohibition, but it may have been communicated to her by Adam and not God Himself. Scripture does not clarify this. Whatever the case may be, Satan twisted God's words, and Eve was enticed into disobedience.

Women are by nature more trusting and thus more vulnerable toward such a clever ploy as Satan's. God granted woman a tender and loving heart, generally more so than a man's. Satan then used this marvelous and endearing quality against her. He twisted her wonderful strength into a weakness. He continues to use the same tactic with people to this day.

Satan understands the human fallen nature since he shares in that fallen nature himself. The difference is that Satan and his demonic hordes cannot be redeemed (Matthew 25:41). They are condemned for eternity! This makes them all the more dangerous and wicked. They have nothing to lose. The demonic horde called Legion fearfully confessed this truth in the case of a demonically possessed man (Mark 5:1–13). They did not want Jesus to send them to their preordained torment prematurely.

God Created Men and Women to Complement Each Other

Some might object to the above statements regarding women as sexist and justifiably posit the following natural question. Question: How do you know what life was like before the fall? The answer to this inquiry must be surmised as it is not explicitly addressed in Scripture. But, we offer the following reasoning:

(a) God created Adam and Eve with distinct personalities. If they were mere copies of each other, where would the joy be in that? How could they have been of any actual benefit or even interest to each other? Furthermore, it is reasonable to say that most men and women would prefer to be thought of respectively as men and women, not vice versa.

One of the reasons that men and women are attracted to each other is because they are so different from one another. That is part of the spice of life. God engineered the two sexes to be quite distinct in many ways. To pretend otherwise is to hurl into oblivion God's heartfelt and wise design. It also creates ongoing frustration and hurt.

Part of the secret of a happy marriage is to celebrate the differences. In certain circumstances, men and women almost entirely reflect the opposite in attitude. While this may cause conflict and irritation at times, it can also help develop a growing maturity in both the man and the woman. This is particularly true in the relationship of husband and wife.

God Granted Adam the Leadership Role and Eve the Support Role

(b) Adam was created first. He was immediately granted the authority to name all the animals. He also named his wife. In Old Testament times, the ability to name someone or something demonstrated personal authority over it. Adam, not Eve, exercised that authority. Even in the New Testament, the people did not accept the naming of John the Baptist by Elizabeth, the mother, until Zacharias, the father, affirmed him as John (Luke 1:63).

This order is also emphasized within the teaching role of the Church. First Timothy 2:11–14 brings God's ordained roles back to creation itself: "Let a woman learn in silence with all submission. And I do not permit a woman to teach or to have authority over a man, but to be in silence. For Adam was formed first, then Eve. And Adam was not deceived, but the woman being deceived, fell into transgression." This is not a cultural mandate, as so many suppose. It is a permanent order of responsibility instituted by God Himself from the first week of creation.

(c) Eve was created as Adam's helpmate. She was his assistant. This is not to say she was lesser in the intellectual realm or not his equal in the image of God (Galatians 3:28). But she did have a specific role to play, as did Adam. He was to serve as the head of the family. Having two heads over one family does not work. Many couples have tried it and continue to do so, but it only creates friction. Every well-functioning organization has a designated leader.

(d) Throughout the remainder of Scriptures, the headship of man is taught and officially demonstrated. This is particularly true in the spiritual realm. The priests were all men, as were the apostles. Although there were several female prophets in the Old and New Testaments, none of them wrote any books of the Bible.

Masculine leadership is the prominent theme throughout the entire Bible. This is not at all to say that women did not have important roles in biblical leadership. Indeed, they certainly did. But both men and women need to stay within their God-directed parameters.

First Corinthians 11:3 explicitly states: "But I want you to know that the head of every man is Christ, the head of woman is man, and the head of Christ is God." The woman was never intended to exercise authority over the man. When men and women perform their God-ordained responsibilities, functions, and instinctive skill sets, things go relatively well, certainly much better than when they do not.

The Biblical Story of Boaz and Ruth

Anyone would profit by considering the marvelous story of Boaz and Ruth and how they approached each other in such a biblical fashion. Ruth is a story for the ages! The primary teaching of the book of Ruth is about the kinsman-redeemer concept, thus demonstrating Christ's relationship to humanity. Christ paid the price for humanity's sins. Hence, He became their Redeemer. We become His kinsmen as His adopted sons or daughters (Romans 8:14–17).

Two things need to be noted about the kinsman-redeemer concept. First, the nearest kinsman must be willing to redeem his relative. Refusal to do so simply for reasons of stubbornness was not acceptable in Jewish culture. Second, the kinsman had to be able to redeem his relative. In the case of Boaz and Ruth, the closest kinsman was not financially equipped to perform his obligation. Boaz, the next closest relative, was both willing and able. Thus, he redeemed Ruth and Naomi. From their marital relationship, Jesus Christ would eventually become a descendant.

The book of Ruth also does include a touching story on human interpersonal relationships. However, the story is not so much a romance as it is a model illustration of a man and woman acting in obedience to biblical standards. Both lovingly assumed their respective roles in God's spiritual system. Modern marriages have much to learn from their touching example of biblical love and obedience to God's will.

John Phillips offers the following comments:

> His (Satan) plan of attack in the Garden of Eden was based on subtlety. It was God's intention that headship should be invested in Adam. Eve was created second, not first. She was not made for headship; her inmost center of rule was not her head but her heart. Adam, on the other hand, was made to rule, his inmost center of rule was his intellect.
>
> Satan twisted God's order. He began the temptation with Eve, putting her in the place of headship, engaging her in an intellectual discussion concerning right and wrong. He thoroughly deceived her and plunged the race into ruin (1 Tim. 2:11-14; 1 Cor. 11:3). So then, the temptation began with an appeal to Eve's intellect.[12]

---

12 John Phillips, The John Phillip's Commentary Series: Exploring Genesis (Grand Rapids, MI: Kregel Publications, 1980), p. 57.

A Moment for Reflection

Both men and women would profit greatly by examining their respective roles in life by the penetrating light of God's Word. As Phillips has correctly stated, man was designed for headship. Women were designed as nurturers and supporters. A wife can greatly encourage her husband with kind words and gentle support. Many a husband has excelled far beyond his own expectations because of the consistent encouragement and gracious prodding of his wife.

By the same token, husbands must love their wives unreservedly. Women are emotional in God's design and thrive on positive reinforcement, particularly when the man articulates his love for her (1 Peter 3:7–9). God knew precisely what He was doing when He orchestrated relationships between men and women. Learning from God's Word and applying its principles leads to relational success on all fronts.

Lessons Learned in This Chapter

In this chapter, we first reviewed some of the background of Lucifer's fall from grace. Though largely a mystery, the consequences of his rebellion were severe. He dragged one-third of the angels down with him in his sinful and futile plot against God (Revelation 12:4). We examined the Scripture pertaining to both when and why Lucifer disgraced himself. Pride was the primary cause for his downfall (Isaiah 14:12–15; Ezekiel 28:11–15). Regarding that particular temptation, mankind all too frequently falls victim.

We also examined the fact that the spiritual sometimes prefigures the literal. That is true in a number of cases we discussed. For instance, there is a heavenly temple and tabernacle. The temple and tabernacle on earth were replicas of the heavenly. Satan, at one time, walked around the garden of God and was clothed with precious stones. This seems to prefigure the literal, physical Garden of Eden, where Adam and Eve lived.

A heavenly New Jerusalem shall someday come down to the earth. Presently, a physical Jerusalem represents that which is coming in glorious splendor. Abraham looked for such a spiritual Jerusalem (Hebrews 11:8–10). The present earthly city of Jerusalem pales into insignificance when compared to the heavenly (Revelation chapters 21 and 22).

We also noted that the more typical pattern is that the physical prefigures the spiritual. Oftentimes, that spiritual reality is fulfilled in Jesus Christ. This happens repeatedly throughout the Old Testament. That is why one must take the entire Word of God literally unless a passage is clearly intended to be figurative. Colossians 2:16–17 states: "So let no one judge you in food or in drink, or regarding a festival or a new moon or sabbaths, which are a shadow of things to come, but the substance is of Christ."

Second, we discussed additional aspects of the temptation of Adam and Eve. In line with that, we reviewed some of the pre-fall roles of Adam and Eve. From Scripture, it is clear that God designed the headship of Adam over Eve from the beginning. These roles were determined based on the sixth day of the creation week. This was not designed in any way to undermine Eve's importance. Both man and woman are equally created in the image of God.

God created the first couple to complement each other. Both the man and the woman have particular realms in which they operate best. When man and woman function within their God-appointed spheres, life can prove most fulfilling. When men and women ignore their roles as God has so appointed, dissatisfaction and misery are generally the result.

In our next chapter, we shall delve even deeper into Satan's successful attempt to corrupt the human race. We shall discover that his strategies have not changed over the millennia. Why should they? Human nature has not changed appreciably. What worked historically for Satan works today and will also work in the future. That is the sad plight of mankind. In spite of that, however, mankind has the offer of salvation and forgiveness through Christ. We pray that each person reading this manual will fully embrace Christ's love and free gift of salvation.

Cognitive Conundrum #2

A most singular ministry is mine to claim; its fulfillment was sure to bring me fame. Prophecy is mostly what I am known for. Godly rejuvenation, I claimed, is in store. A distinctive man proved I in ministry; I almost finished my task with vigor and glee. But brief moral lapses caused consternation; I never made it back to my home nation.

Who am I?

Answer: the unnamed prophet of 1 Kings chapter 13

Chapter 3

Satan's Diabolical Plot Against Mankind

(Genesis 3:1-8: Part C)

In This Chapter

Objectives for This Chapter
Satan's Method of Temptation
A New Testament Solution to an Old Testament Problem
Lessons Learned in This Chapter

Objectives for This Chapter

In this chapter, we shall first review the various steps taken by Satan in his sinister temptation of Adam and Eve. His primary tools were deception and desire. He promised that those who partook of the forbidden fruit would become like God. Adam and Eve naturally found such a scenario extremely inviting. Who would not want to become like God? The first couple had no concept of deception, sin, or any of its horrid consequences.

Eve was designed by God to have a more trusting and gracious nature. Hence, Satan took advantage of her God-given and endearing qualities to entice her. Adam, as the federal head of humanity (though there were but two humans at the time), was responsible for protecting his wife. Of course, neither Adam nor Eve had ever faced any threats or beguilement of any kind.

So, from what or whom was Adam to protect her? They were entirely alone and sinless. No one had ever lied to them or threatened them in any way. Hence, they were both easily blindsided. Innocence is frequently abused by the less scrupulous. The suspicious nature instinctive to mankind today had not been developed in the least within their pure natures. They had never known pain, deprivation, or emotional disturbance of any kind.

Still, they did have the unwavering command of God. They willfully chose to disobey that command. Both failed for reasons that are not entirely communicated to us today. Pure innocence is not something to which any living mortal can relate. Whatever the reasons may all have been, we must deal with life as it is today. But through all the ugly ramifications of sin, God promised deliverance through His Son, Jesus Christ (Genesis 3:15). We shall explore that potential forgiveness and reconciliation in much more depth as the book proceeds (Acts 4:12).

The strategy incorporated by Satan to deceive the innocent first couple was quite successful. His sinister methods are still effectively used both by the demonic hordes and wicked individuals to this day. The quintessential deceiver in the future will be the evil Antichrist. He and his wicked cohort, the false prophet, will entice the majority of the world to worship both Satan and the Antichrist. We shall examine in more detail the lamentable events of Genesis 3:1–8. It is advisable to always bear in mind that no human being would have fared any better than Adam and Eve.

Second, we shall discuss God's New Testament solution to the Old Testament problem of sin. In reality, the same solution was offered in the Old Testament as in the New. What was that solution? The coming Messiah would conquer Satan and sin. Through His death and resurrection, there could come forgiveness. That forgiveness is garnered through simple faith in and submission to the efficacy of Christ's sacrifice (Habakkuk 2:4; John 1:12).

The Old Testament saints looked forward to the coming Messiah. New Testament saints look back upon the crucifixion, death, and resurrection of the Lord Jesus Christ. God's plans of creation and redemption were all established in eternity. It is impossible for mortal man to envision or understand this blessed truth completely. But one does well to steadfastly meditate on that timeless principle conveyed in Luke 1:37: "For with God nothing will be impossible."

Satan's Method of Temptation

As Scripture states, Satan appeared in the guise of a serpent. Remarkably, this did not startle either Adam or Eve. The abnormality of said situation helps us recognize how different things once were from the beginning of creation until our present era. Today, a talking serpent, or any other animal, would terrify anyone. But we must remember Adam and Eve had no sense of fear. They had never experienced anything adverse in their lives. Furthermore, it is entirely possible that other, and perhaps all, animals could speak. Scripture does not comment on this.

Needless to say, Satan took advantage of the status quo to carry out his nefarious plot. He employed a definite strategy to entice Eve to eat of the fruit. Deception is a most common and effective tool. He continues to use the same stratagem to this day. It works beautifully on men and women alike.

Adam's situation is more troublesome to define. He, too, was deceived, but God had instilled within him a spirit and mentality different from Eve's. He should automatically have been more wary. But again, we must remember nothing untoward had ever occurred in his life. In his state of naïve innocence, Adam still deliberately disobeyed God's clear command. As federal head of humanity, he justifiably receives the harshest criticism for his moral failing (Romans 5:18–19). It is for this reason that the sinful nature passes on through the man, not the woman (5:12).

Get the People to Doubt God's Word

It is incumbent upon us to more closely examine the progression of sin's entry into the world and our first parents. Step #1: Satan got Eve to doubt God's Word. Eve possibly was not told directly about the prohibition of eating the fruit by God Himself. As previously mentioned, Scripture does not specifically address that question. But Adam certainly had told her because she definitely knew of the prohibition.

Genesis 3:1 records Satan's words: "Now the serpent was more cunning than any beast of the field which the LORD God had made. And he said to the woman, 'Has God indeed said, You shall not eat of every tree of the garden?'" A question that naturally occurs in the reader's mind regards the fact that the serpent was "cunning." Precisely what this means is not entirely clear.

We do see, however, a certain level of cleverness and coordination among some predators in the wild even today. Lions will single out a solitary zebra and run it down. Wild dogs hunt extremely well in packs. Dolphins in the ocean will intimidate smaller fish into a frenzied ball of activity. They are all packed in together like the proverbial "sardines." They then become lunch for the hungry larger fish. Even birds will engage in this activity in coordination with this fishing frenzy.

Who taught beavers how to construct dams or birds to make nests? How does a cow know to feed her calf? One also hears of how clever the fox is in avoiding the hounds. Indeed, the illustrations of instinct within nature, even downright cleverness, abound in the mind of any naturalist. Clearly, there were unknown qualities about the serpent that earned this appreciable accolade. We must bear in mind that the animal world also came under a curse. Undoubtedly, they lost some of the greater instincts they once possessed. Someday, according to Scripture, we will see these original qualities restored (Isaiah 11:6–9) during the millennial kingdom.

How did Satan get Eve to doubt God's Word? He twisted the original message. Satan continuously utilizes the same diabolical method to this day. One of the lies Satan constantly promotes to the unsuspecting is that the Bible is full of contradictions and errors.

To the uninitiated, this sounds reasonable. After all, the Bible is a large ancient book. People can easily assume that it must contain many mistakes. Only a small percentage of Christians will ever read it through annually. Many will never read the full Bible, even once in their lifetime. That lie has thus effectively deceived multitudes over the centuries. Without proper guidance and biblical education, many are led down this diabolical path. The truth is available, but one must avail himself of that truth.

Beware of False Teachers

The popular policy of many ungodly governments and individuals is to cast doubt on the authority of God's Word. Tragically, many misguided pastors have intentionally followed suit. They shall answer to God for being false shepherds. Such men and women have been the plague of the earth since history began.

Paul issued the following warning to the elders of Ephesus in Acts 20:27–31:

> For I have not shunned to declare to you the whole

counsel of God. Therefore take heed to yourselves and to all the flock, among which the Holy Spirit has made you overseers, to shepherd the church of God which He purchased with His own blood.

For I know this, that after my departure savage wolves will come in among you, not sparing the flock. Also from among yourselves men will rise up, speaking perverse things, to draw away the disciples after themselves. Therefore watch, and remember that for three years I did not cease to warn everyone night and day with tears.

Worthless and immoral shepherds lead people away from a genuine and saving faith in God. Such unsavory individuals will perpetually multiply themselves until the Lord returns. There is no escaping the fact that these misguided individuals will beset the Church with their false doctrines. Because of this, it is the responsibility of every believer to prepare themselves biblically and in the arena of apologetics to more capably defend the truth (1 Peter 3:15).

Ezekiel 34:1–5 issues the following warning concerning false shepherds:

> And the word of the Lord came to me, saying, "Son of man, prophecy against the shepherds of Israel, prophesy and say to them, 'Thus says the Lord God to the shepherds: "Woe to the shepherds of Israel who feed themselves! Should not the shepherds feed the flocks? You eat the fat and clothe yourselves with the wool; you slaughter the fatlings, but you do not feed the flock.

"The weak you have not strengthened, nor have you healed those who were sick, nor bound up the broken, nor brought back what was driven away, nor sought what was lost; but with force and cruelty you have ruled them. So they were scattered because there was no shepherd; and they became food for all the beasts of the field when they were scattered.""

Twisting the Truth

Regarding this intentional misrepresentation of God's words, which Satan conveyed to Eve, Keil and Delitzsch offer these comments:

['aph ki] is an interrogative expressing surprise (as in 1 Sam. 23:3, 2 Sam. 4:11): "Is it really the fact that God has prohibited you from eating of all the trees of the garden?" The Hebrew may, indeed, bear the meaning, "hath God said, you shall not eat of every tree?" but from the context, and especially the conjunction, it is obvious that the meaning is, "you shall not eat of any tree."

The serpent calls God by the name of Elohim alone, and the woman does the same. In this more general and indefinite name the personality of the living God is obscured. To attain his end, the tempter felt it necessary to change the living, personal God into a merely general numen divinum, and to exaggerate the prohibition, in the hope of exciting in the woman's mind partly distrust of God Himself and partly a doubt as to the truth of His word. And his words were listened to.[13]

Eve incorrectly added to God's word by saying, "Nor shall you touch it." This added prohibition under normal circumstances would make the possibility of disobedience even more tempting. What mankind is forbidden to do is what it then craves to do. However, we must remember that Eve did not, as of yet, have a sinful nature. But God does warn us that under no circumstance are we to revise His holy Word. If we do so, we can easily change its meaning, even though it may be inadvertently. The latter portion of this book deals with that very situation at some length.

Remember the Biblical Standard

Deuteronomy 4:2 states: "You shall not add to the word which I command you, nor take from it, that you may keep the commandments of the LORD your God which I command you." God's Word is absolutely sacred and eternal. We are strictly forbidden to modify or ignore it in any way. It is impossible for us to fully understand how this additional clause of "nor shall you touch it" may have impacted Eve. She was still sinless. Because of that, she cannot be equated with how modern man would have been impacted.

But one thing remains clear: In the evil nature of modern, sin-stained man, it definitely would enhance the incitement to disobey. We do not like being told what to do or not to do! That is an inevitable result of our fallen nature. To be forbidden to eat something or, even more, not to even touch it clearly arouses one's interest in that object.

---

13 Keil, C. F. and Delitzsch, F., Commentary on the Old Testament: The Pentateuch, p. 94.

Two of the first questions that pop into a person's head today are: "Why can't we eat that fruit? Who does God think He is anyway?" Immediately, the curiosity grows, often to the demise or at least unwanted trouble to the tempted individual. We are insatiably curious and rebellious creatures because of the original sin that resides within our natures. We cannot escape our evil tendencies, though we can, by God's grace, combat them (1 Corinthians 10:13).

Paul writes of Eve's deception in 2 Corinthians 11:3: "But I fear, lest somehow, as the serpent deceived Eve by his craftiness, so your minds may be corrupted from the simplicity that is in Christ." How exactly does that happen? One of the most natural temptations of man is to believe that he must work for his salvation. We must generally work for everything else in life.

Athletes must strive for mastery in their sport. Farmers must put in long days to plant and harvest their crops. Soldiers must serve their commanding officers with excellence and strenuous activity. Each of these types of men and women must be disciplined if they are to excel in their particular vocations.

Paul uses these three types of individuals as examples for sincere Christians. However, this mentality can easily be twisted as demonstrating a need to work for salvation. That, of course, was not Paul's intent. He makes clear elsewhere that salvation is a gift (Romans 4:20–21; Ephesians 2:8–9; Titus 3:5). Not everyone seems to understand that simple truth. Just as modern-day theologians can distort God's clear teaching, so Satan did to Eve in the Garden of Eden.

A Denial of the Truth

Step #2: Satan denied the authenticity of God's word. Genesis 3:4 states: "Then the serpent said to the woman, 'You will not surely die.'" This is a complete denial of God's sovereignty. When Satan fell into sin, his entire character was permanently ruined. Though he knows he can never overcome his Creator, he will do anything he can to harm God's creation. The seed of temptation for Eve has now advanced from mere doubt and confusion to a level of denial. But, at this point, Eve had not yet sinned. To be lied to or be slightly confused is not a sin.

Warren Wiersbe astutely comments:

> By questioning what God said, Satan raised doubts in Eve's mind concerning the truthfulness of God's Word and the goodness of God's heart. ... Eve's reply showed that she was following Satan's example and altering the very Word of God. Compare 3:2-3 with 2:16-17 and you'll see that she omitted the word 'freely,' added the phrase "nor shall you touch it" (NKJV), and failed to say that God "commanded" them to obey.
>
> Note too that Eve copied the devil further when she spoke of "God" (Elohim) and not the Lord [Jehovah] God," the God of the covenant. Finally she said "lest you die"--a possibility—instead of "You shall surely die"—an actuality. So, she took from God's Word, and changed God's Word, which are serious offenses indeed (Deut. 4:2; 12:32; Prov. 30:6; Rev. 22:19). She was starting to doubt God's goodness and truthfulness.[14]

---

[14] Wiersbe, Warren. The Bible Exposition Commentary: Old Testament: Pentateuch (Wheaton, IL: Victor Books, 2001), p. 30.

Visions of Grandeur Now Danced in Eve's Head

Step #3: Third, Satan offered an enticing delusion to Eve: she would become like God. Who would not want to be like God? Genesis 3:5 states: "For God knows that in the day you eat of it your eyes will be opened, and you will be like God, knowing good and evil."

It should be immediately noted that Satan lied to Eve three times in this verse alone. He was correct in his statement that their eyes would be opened in the sense that they would soon regrettably understand evil. But his three lies are quite subtle. One of the most effective tools of the devil is to incorporate some truth with his evil deceptions. This worked quite effectively with Eve, and it continues to work with humanity today. Mankind must always be on the watch for Satan's "shiny toys," which turn out to be treacherous bear traps, figuratively speaking.

Lies, Lies, and More Lies

Lie #1: "Their eyes would be opened" is only a partial truth. What is closer to reality is that they would soon be spiritually blinded because of their sin. That is what sin always does to a person. So, the reality of Satan's promise was just the reverse. Only through the forgiveness of a loving God can that spiritual blindness be partially removed.

But even as Christians, our sinful nature continues to operate. Hence, until we reach heaven, we can only see the glories of God in a limited fashion. That, however, is to be expected when one is surrounded by the presence of evil in this sin-darkened world.

Lie #2: They would become like God. Ironically, they already were like God as they were created in His image and were flawless in character. They were sinless. Indeed, at that exact moment, they were immortal. They could not die! Falling into sin did not make them more like God; it made them like the devil. So, this promise is again a reversal of reality. Mankind grovels in the same foolish philosophy today. But today, it is even more dire. Instead of wanting to be like God, they want to knock God off His throne and make all their own decisions.

Lie #3: God does not experientially know evil; He is completely holy. He knows and decrees what is evil and what is not, but He cannot personally indulge in it. He is incapable of sin (Leviticus 11:44; 1 Samuel 2:2; Isaiah 5:16, 6:3; Titus 1:2; James 1:13; 1 Peter 1:15; 1 John 1:5).

Sin is outside of His eternal and holy character. In other words, everything the devil said was untrue. Of course, Eve did not understand that in her pure state. But that purity was about to be abruptly terminated, and that termination would be permanent. She would slip from moral spotlessness to moral filthiness. Adam would quickly follow suit.

Fruchtenbaum adds these comments regarding Eve's sin:

> When Satan said, You shall be as God, he wanted to create in Eve the desire to be like God. In fact, this was the very desire that brought about the fall of Satan. Isaiah 14:12-14, which records the fall of Satan, relates that Satan fell when he made a declaration of five "I will's."
>
> His fifth I will was: I will make myself like the Most High. Rashi interpreted this declaration to be the desire to be like God in being able to create the world. It was

Satan's desire to become like the Most High—to become like God—that brought about Satan's fall. Now the same desire to be like God will cause the fall of man.

According to Satan, the knowledge of good and evil is what makes one God. In verse 5, Satan presented a denial of God's goodness, because Satan accused God of selfishness and jealousness. Therefore, the good God who gave them good is now charged with withholding the greater good.

Satan's implication is twofold: First, man was capable of knowing good and evil as perfectly and as completely as God did, and so man could be like God; and second, God was jealous of His knowledge of good and evil, in the sense of not willing to share it.

Satan's methodology was threefold: First, he raised doubts as to the wisdom, justice, and love of God; second, he made a direct contradiction of the Word of God; and third, he claimed that disobedience to God will result in the highest good. However, in reality Adam and Eve will know good and evil only from the standpoint of sinners. Romans 7:19 teaches that Paul knew the good but was unable to do it. He also knew the evil, but was unable to resist it. Adam and Eve will know the evil, but will be unable to resist it.[15]

---
15 Arnold G. Fruchtenbaum, Ariel's Bible Commentary: The Book of Genesis: Exposition from a Messianic Jewish Perspective (San Antonio, TX: Ariel Ministries, 2009), pp. 94–95.

Satan's Ploy Tragically Worked

Step #4: Satan succeeded in getting Eve to disobey God's word. Genesis 3:6 states: "So when the woman saw that the tree was good for food, that it was pleasant to the eyes, and a tree desirable to make one wise, she took of its fruit and ate. She also gave to her husband with her, and he ate." Tragically, not only did Eve fall into Satan's snare, she led her husband down the same thorny path. Sin always wants company.

Eve unwittingly fulfilled 1 John 2:16 long before it was written: "For all that is in the world—the lust of the flesh, the lust of the eyes, and the pride of life—is not of the Father but is of the world." Regarding this passage, Phillips comments: "We all have legitimate drives and desires placed in our hearts by an all-wise Creator, and the world knows how to whet our appetites and inflame them into lusts. Satan fans them into flames and they become roaring infernos, destructive to ourselves and those around us."[16]

Eve rebelled against the command of the Lord. She was now a sinner! In the next moment, she became a seducer. She immediately enticed her husband to sin as well. One cannot say for certain if Eve already felt guilty before she coaxed Adam into sinning with her. It is a lamentable tendency that those who are guilty of sin enjoy taking the righteous down the same evil path. Evil, like misery, loves company. Verse 7, however, seems to indicate that she had not yet realized the magnitude of her disobedience. No hint of embarrassment is conveyed in the text.

The critical point is this: they both fell into sin. The difference is that Adam sinned deliberately, with eyes more wide open, so to speak. Eve was deceived. Hence, Adam, as the head of the human

---

16 John Phillips, The John Phillips Commentary Series, Exploring the Epistles of John: An Expository Commentary (Grand Rapids, MI: Kregel Publications, 2003), p. 62.

race, bears the ultimate responsibility. He abdicated his role of federal headship, and the woeful consequences plague mankind today.

Calamity Strikes Mankind

Step #5: Satan rejoiced to see the disaster he brought upon the human race. The text does not specifically state that sentiment, but it obviously was Satan's evil intent. He accomplished it, but not as thoroughly as he thought.

Satan is a created being and is not privy to the eternal mind of God. He could not have known that the plan of salvation had always been in the foreknowledge and plan of the triune God. He was not aware of the future substitutionary atonement of Christ at that juncture. He can only be fully aware of what is revealed in the Scripture, as can we. And no Scripture had yet been written. Of course, before he sinned, Lucifer enjoyed perfect companionship with and adoration of his Creator. He was privileged to hear God's communications. Sin changed all that irrevocably.

Without question, Satan now recognizes the entirety of God's complete revelation. He knew it extremely well just as soon as the book of Revelation was penned by the apostle John. That blessed prophetic book by itself shows that Satan is on the losing side. Why should anyone want to follow the loser? Sadly, multitudes do precisely that.

Satan also understands that resistance to God's ultimate will cannot be successful. But his unlimited evil nature and burning hatred against all that is holy propel him forward nonetheless. He will resist and revile God and His spiritually adopted children until he is finally stopped.

Satan is on a crusade of unquenchable hatred. Man cannot fathom how deep and inextinguishable his hatred of God and humanity truly is. Man lives within the potential scope of eternal redemption. There is no forgiveness or redemption for Satan and his evil minions. Their destiny is the Lake of Fire. Tragically, they shall take many victims with them.

Adam Failed His Wife and Humanity

Step #6: A further tragedy: Adam sinned deliberately. Thus, his transgression was worse. He should have assisted Eve and helped her resist this potential and then eventual sin. But he neglected his responsibility for her and instead intentionally sinned with her. Satan and sin always seem attractive and, hence, beguiling. Second Corinthians 11:14–15 warns: "And no wonder! For Satan himself transforms himself into an angel of light. Therefore it is no great thing if his ministers also transform themselves into ministers of righteousness, whose end will be according to their works."

It appears that Adam was standing right alongside Eve when this entire ugly scenario unfolded. Verse 6 states that Adam was with her. Some speculate that Satan approached Eve in a moment when she was alone, and Adam came at the end of the temptation. The text indicates the opposite. Adam failed his wife and all of humanity dismally. He ended up bearing the primary blame for their tragic disobedience.

As the head of this small family, Adam should have intervened and protected his more vulnerable wife. That is every man's God-given responsibility! Indeed, it is the natural instinct of every decent man. Eve was his helper; he was her leader! As such, he stands responsible both for his actions as well as for hers, at least to a degree.

Eve is not to be excused of any responsibility for her transgression. But, for reasons the Scripture does not reveal, Adam tragically neglected his God-appointed task. Because of their mutual transgression, but particularly Adam's, mankind needs a Savior. Jesus Christ is the second Adam. Only through Him can forgiveness be granted.

A New Testament Solution to an Old Testament Problem

In Romans 5:12–19, Paul presents a doctrinal summary of Adam and Eve's sin:

> Therefore, just as through one man sin entered the world, and death through sin, and thus death spread to all men, because all sinned—(For until the law sin was in the world, but sin is not imputed when there is no law. Nevertheless death reigned from Adam to Moses, even over those who had not sinned according to the likeness of the transgression of Adam, who is a type of Him who was to come. But the free gift is not like the offense.

> For if by the one man's offense many died, much more the grace of God and the gift by the grace of the one Man, Jesus Christ, abounded to many. And the gift is not like that which came through the one who sinned. For the judgment which came from one offense resulted in condemnation, but the free gift which came from many offenses resulted in justification.

> For if by the one man's offense death reigned through the one, much more those who receive abundance of

grace and of the gift of righteousness will reign in life through the One, Jesus Christ.)

Therefore, as through one man's offense judgment came to all men, resulting in condemnation, even so through one Man's righteous act the free gift came to all men, resulting in justification of life. For as by one man's disobedience many were made sinners, so also by one Man's obedience many will be made righteous.

The Solution to Pollution

Paul offers numerous salient points about this fatal temptation that one should note.

Point #1: The primary responsibility for sin entering this world falls upon Adam (Romans 5:12a). This could hardly be considered justifiable unless Adam was already the designated head of the family. It was Eve, after all, who sinned first. But it is Adam, quite justly due to his position, who received the primary blame.

Point #2: Sin came upon all men because all have sinned (Romans 5:12b). Some have pondered, "Why should all the world be pronounced guilty for one man's transgression?" The answer is simple enough. (a) Adam was the representative head of all humanity. We all descend from him. (b) Every man, woman, and child would have failed the same or a similar test. No reasonable person, save Jesus Christ Himself, can testify that they are flawless and would have passed this test (John 8:46).

(c) Because sin came through one fallible man, forgiveness likewise can come through one perfect man, namely, Jesus Christ. Just as the temptation did not need to be repeated endlessly of every man, so Christ's substitutionary atonement only needed to occur once to bring forgiveness to all who believe. One act of transgression was rectified by one holy act of atonement!

Referring to Christ's one-time sacrifice, Hebrews 9:12 states: "Not with the blood of goats and calves, but with His own blood He entered the Most Holy Place once for all, having obtained eternal redemption." The fact that Christ's redemptive sacrifice is eternal speaks for itself. Nothing or no one can possibly add to it. It is supreme in its blessedness and efficacy before a holy God.

God's Grace Is All-Sufficient

Point #3: God's grace to mankind became immediately evident through His provision of the Savior, Jesus Christ (Romans 5:17–18). Adam's fall into sin came as no surprise to Him, who knows and declares the end from the beginning (Isaiah 46:10). As we shall later see, Genesis 3:15 establishes promise and redemption in the midst of judgment.

In God's eternal mind and plan, Christ was crucified before the foundation of the world was laid (Revelation 13:8). As stated previously, a proper and meaningful relationship is only possible through an exercise of the free will. Hence, God had to allow the possibility of the fall. But He also, at profound personal cost, provided atonement through His Son.

Warren Wiersbe offers the following explanatory comments regarding Romans 5:12–21. This entire passage demonstrates the incredible contrast between Adam and Christ, the first and second Adams. It should be noted, because of the specific words he cites in his comments, that Wiersbe is using the King James Version of the Bible.

Wiersbe writes:

To understand these verses a few general truths about this section need to be understood. First, note the repetition of the little word one. It is used eleven times. The key idea here is our identification with Adam and with Christ. Second, note the repetition of the word reign which is used five times. Paul saw two men—Adam and Christ—each of them reigning over a kingdom. Finally, note that the phrase much more is repeated five times.

This means that in Jesus Christ we have gained much more than we ever lost in Adam! In short, this section is a contrast of Adam and Christ. Adam was given dominion over the old creation, he sinned, and he lost his kingdom. Because of Adam's sin, all mankind is under condemnation and death. Christ came as the King over a new creation (2 Cor. 5:17).

By His obedience on the cross, He brought in righteousness and justification. Christ not only undid all the damage that Adam's sin effected, but He accomplished "much more" by making us the very sons of God. Some of this "much more' Paul has already explained in Romans 5:1-11.[17]

The grace of God manifests itself abundantly through the ultimate sacrifice of Jesus Christ. He is the only One who can bring about reconciliation to God. His blood so cruelly shed on the cross pays the redemption price so that all who believe may be forgiven

---
[17] Wiersbe, Warren, The Bible Exposition Commentary: Volume 1: Matthew-Galatians, p. 528.

(John 1:12, 5:24).

The Dire Consequence of Sin

Genesis 3:7–8 records the terrible reality that shattered the serenity of the earth:

> Then the eyes of both of them were opened, and they knew that they were naked; and they sewed fig leaves together and made themselves coverings. And they heard the sound of the Lord God walking in the garden in the cool of the day, and Adam and his wife hid themselves from the presence of the Lord God among the trees of the garden.

These two verses usher in a horrendous scenario that has endlessly reaped a whirlwind of catastrophe. One moment, the world was a Paradise with nothing but peace and bliss. Everything was provided for Adam and Eve, and their fellowship with God was assured. Yet, in the twinkling of an eye, darkness, humiliation, shame, pain, deprivation, and sorrow became the norm for humanity. It has remained so ever since for all people. Sin comes with a huge price tag!

Numerous grievous ramifications developed from the first couple's sin. Mankind has groaned under these unenviable consequences ever since. These tragic results have spread throughout the entire world. No country or culture has been spared the travesties of immorality and decadence. Only when Jesus Christ returns to establish His millennial kingdom will the sinful activities of mankind be drastically curtailed. However, they will not be entirely eliminated until eternity.

Seeing Through Spiritually Blinded Eyes

Consequence #1: Their eyes were opened. However, this did not bring about the idyllic situation that they were led to believe by Satan. Their eyes were now opened to their own newborn, sinful natures. This was not quite in line with what that habitual liar Satan had promised. They did not become like God! They became less like Him, much, much less.

Instead of attaining to the spiritual and intellectual stars, so to speak, the exact opposite stunned them into a new and poisonous reality. They, and all humanity since that fateful moment, have become spiritually blinded with their eyes wide open. Mankind's eyes have been staring wide-eyed and largely "unseeing" toward wickedness ever since.

Tragically, those now exposed eyes frequently approve of their own evil ways. Mankind has suffered through endless wars and vile atrocities since Adam and Eve's eyes became spiritually guilty. Not only were their eyes shut toward genuine spirituality, but their hearts irrevocably changed for the worse (Jeremiah 17:9). Until Christ returns, nothing will dissuade mankind from its immorality.

A heart surgeon understands surgical procedure and almost everything there is humanly to know about the heart. But it does not necessarily mean that he suffers heart difficulties himself. His patients certainly hope he doesn't! In that limited sense, you can have knowledge without actual experience.

Not so with sin! Before sin, Adam and Eve had no clue as to what a "spiritual heart problem" meant. Now, they experienced it firsthand. Their darkened hearts became the hereditary condition within all their descendants. No human being escapes the plight of spiritual heart contamination. All are equally impacted. Even those who experience redemption through Christ must wrestle all their lives with the old, evil nature. Only through death or the Rapture will we be removed from our sinful inclinations.

Happily, God offers mankind the solution. This promise came from the very beginning, right in the midst of their judgment. A Messiah and Deliverer would come. Although God patiently waited until the optimal moment in His timing 4,000 years later, He kept His promise. Only the blood of Jesus Christ can cleanse the heart (John 14:6; Acts 4:12).

First John 1:7 offers the singular solution for spiritual heart disease: "But if we walk in the light as He is in the light, we have fellowship with one another, and the blood of Jesus Christ His Son cleanses us from all sin." Sin cost man a huge price; forgiveness for that sin cost God infinitely more! Man can receive; God gave. The remarkable aspect of this entire scenario is that God chose to create man in the first place. He knew from eternity the incredible and painful cost.

Clothing Is Now Required

Consequence #2: Adam and Eve realized they were naked. The Jewish rabbis have traditionally taught that Adam and Eve were clothed, in a limited fashion, in the Shekinah glory. Radiance covered them. That is likely true, although it cannot be conclusively demonstrated from Scripture. However, considering the fact that Moses' face literally shone from his much more limited interaction with God, this potential radiance seems quite plausible (Exodus 34:29–35). This is especially true when one considers that Adam and Eve were living in a sinless state.

The primary point is that there were no moral complications with nakedness before sin entered the picture. God created the human body, after all, and He clearly is not ashamed of that fact. He designed it perfectly for His glory and man's gratification. But sin permanently tarnished that which had previously been holy and fully satisfying. It had now turned into a source of embarrassment and lust. Instead of being clothed in God's glory, Adam and Eve were now clothed in shame.

Henry Morris cogently writes:

> As they remembered that the divine injunction had been to "multiply and fill the earth," they realized that the very fountainhead of human life had now become corrupted by their disobedience and they became acutely aware of their nakedness. Their children would all be contaminated with the seed of rebellion, so that their feeling of guilt centered especially on their own procreative organs. The result was that they suddenly desired to hide these from each other, and from God.[18]

Man's Vain Attempt to Conceal Iniquity

Consequence #3: They sewed fig leaves to cover themselves. Genesis 3:7 states: "Then the eyes of both of them were opened, and they knew that they were naked; and they sewed fig leaves together and made themselves coverings."

It is intriguing to note how quickly shame and embarrassment invaded the human race. The stunning change was instantaneous once both had eaten of the forbidden fruit. Observation: Their new and evil human nature did not automatically motivate them to seek out God for forgiveness. In fact, the reverse proved true. They tried

---

18 Henry Morris, The Genesis Record: A Scientific and Devotional Commentary on the Book of Beginnings (Grand Rapids, MI: Baker Book House, 1976), p. 115.

to cover up their sins and hide.

Of course, Adam and Eve really had no comprehension of forgiveness. They had never before encountered sin. The sinful nature steadfastly resists reconciliation with the Creator. This was one of the many "somethings" they could not have possibly anticipated. Instead, the two guilty culprits endeavored to hide their disobedience. That does not work with an all-seeing God (Hebrews 4:13). Countless people have, nonetheless, adopted the same foolish scheme throughout the long and dusty annals of history.

Man still either tries to deny or to atone for his own sins in foolish ways. But no one can atone for or add to the forgiveness of their sins. This can only be done through divine intervention (Ephesians 2:8–9; Titus 3:5). The scribes were correct when they stated that only God can forgive sins (Mark 2:7).

Of course, what these ancient legal scholars steadfastly rejected was that Jesus Christ was God in the flesh. John 1:14 declares: "And the Word became flesh and dwelt among us, and we beheld His glory, the glory as of the only begotten of the Father, full of grace and truth." Jesus' pronouncement of forgiveness for the paralytic's sins was a tacit admission of His genuine identity. The scribes certainly understood that. But, as history makes clear, they violently spurned Jesus' claim for Himself. Instead, they sought His death for blasphemy.

Run, Run as Fast as You Can!

Consequence #4: Adam and Eve tried to hide from God. Genesis 3:8 states: "And they heard the sound of the LORD God walking in the garden in the cool of the day, and Adam and his wife hid themselves from the presence of the LORD God among the trees of the garden."

Quite naturally, one cannot hide from the omnipresent, all-seeing God. But it instantly became man's instinct to hide from God because they now knew that their singular deed was evil (John 3:19–21). Their consciences had been awakened in a way they could never have anticipated. For the first time in human history, man experienced guilt. It was not a pleasant sensation.

Although in a different context, the prophet Amos aptly describes the impossibility of escaping God's judgment in Amos 5:18–20:

> Woe to you who desire the day of the LORD! For what good is the day of the LORD to you? It will be darkness, and not light. It will be as though a man fled from a lion, and a bear met him! Or as though he went into the house, leaned his hand on the wall, and a serpent bit him! Is not the day of the LORD darkness, and not light? It is not very dark, with no brightness in it?

In this particular context, it should be observed that God's reaction to Adam and Eve was just the opposite of theirs. They tried to hide; God lovingly sought them out. Genesis 3:9 states: "Then the LORD God called to Adam and said to him, 'Where are you?'" God had always known that sin would besmirch mankind. But His love for His creation stands infinite in measure. He still extends His hands to all with an open invitation to call upon Him. Jeremiah 33:3 states: "Call to Me, and I will answer you, and show you great and mighty things, which you do not know" (cf. John 3:16, 14:6).

God demonstrates His eternal love for mankind both by what He does and by what He does not do. He did not destroy Adam and Eve instantly. It was certainly His right to immediately extinguish their lives. He could have terminated mankind and His entire creation instantaneously. Who, after all, had the power to object? No one did or does.

Knowing mankind's incredible capacity for evil, one ponders why He did not take that course of action. But God chose not to do so. By sparing humanity, He provided an eternal example for mankind that we should emulate His holy behavior. Unfortunately, we repeatedly fall short!

God reveals His grace to mankind in many ways. First, He has steadily revealed His will through the progressive writing of the Scriptures. This is called special revelation. Second, each morning, the sun rises. The rain falls throughout the earth. The seasons come and go. This is called general revelation. Third, He offered His holy Son on the cross as the perfect substitutionary sacrifice. He grants eternal life in heaven with all its glories to the repentant. Yet, in spite of these and countless other notable demonstrations of God's unending mercy and love, man generally persists in going his own stubborn way (Matthew 7:13–14).

Can Anyone Hide from God?

Victor Hamilton offers the following salient comments:

> Toward sundown the man and the woman heard Yahweh walking in the garden. The verb used here to describe the divine movement—mithallek—is a type of Hithpael that suggests iterative and habitual aspects. Such walks would take place in the early evening (the cooler time of day) rather than "in the heat of the day" (cf. 18:1).
>
> Far from anticipating another time of fellowship with

deity, the couple—who have just previously "hid" their nakedness from each other by clothing themselves—now attempt to hide even from God. Concealment is the order of the day. The narrator refrains from commenting on exactly how one can camouflage himself and thus escape detection by God. Can trees or shrubbery really come between deity and humanity?[19]

Trouble for Two, Trouble for All

Consequence #5: Adam and Eve's sinful nature passed on to all their descendants. Ecclesiastes 7:20 states: "For there is not a just man on earth who does good and does not sin" (cf. Isaiah 53:6, 64:6; Romans 3:23, 7:14–25). The tragic reality is that all people are now born with a sinful nature. Everyone suffers under the curse of sin (Romans 6:23). Only God-granted forgiveness through the perfect Son of God can bring forgiveness and reconciliation (John 1:29, 14:6).

John MacArthur offers the following enlightening comments on the curse of sinful nature and the oftentimes sorrowful death it causes:

> No truth is more self-evident than the inevitability of death. The earth is pock-marked with graves, and the most incontestable testimony of history is that all men, whatever their wealth, status, or accomplishments, are subject to death. Since creation, every person but two, Enoch and Elijah, have died. And were it not for Christ's Rapture of His church, all men would continue

---

[19] Victor Hamilton, The New International Commentary on the Old Testament: The Book of Genesis Chapters 1–17 (Grand Rapids, MI: Eerdmans Publishing, 1990), p. 192.

to die.

The painful reality of death touches mankind without interruption and without exception. According to an Oriental proverb, "The black camel death kneeleth once at each door and each mortal must mount to return nevermore." The very term mortal means "subject to death."

The seventeenth-century poet James Shirley wrote the following in The Contention of Ajax and Ulysses,

> The glories of our birth and state
>
> Are shadows, not substantial things;
>
> There is no armour against fate;
>
> Death lays his icy hands on kings:
>
> Sceptre and crown
>
> Must tumble down,
>
> And in the dust be equal made
>
> With the poor crooked scythe and spade.[20]

Mankind shall suffer unrelentingly until the Lord Jesus Christ returns to exact judgment upon the earth. From many believers' perspective, this divine retribution is long overdue. Fortunately for humanity, God does not act swiftly upon the unholy actions of an

---

20 John MacArthur, The MacArthur New Testament Commentary: Romans 1-8 (Chicago: IL, Moody Bible Institute, 1991), pp. 290-291.

ever-ungrateful, sinful, and misunderstanding mankind. His benevolence and patience are phenomenal, but it is not infinite. Sin and unrepentant sinner alike will eventually receive their just reward from the hands of an almighty God.

Sarfati relates Augustine's brief threefold statement regarding sin:

- Adam and Eve were created with the ability not to sin.

- After the Fall, humans had no ability to completely avoid sin.

- In the Eternal State, redeemed humans will have no ability to sin.[21]

It is to this eternal state that all believers yearn to someday sojourn. One must first pass through the valley of the shadow of death. The exceptions would be the aforementioned Enoch and Elijah, those who ascend to heaven in the Rapture, or those who are still alive at Christ's second coming. But all believers shall ultimately enter into God's eternal kingdom. There, each believer shall be met by our loving Savior. There will be no more troubles, no more struggling with sin, no more separation from loved ones.

The passage through death is fleeting, indeed, essentially instantaneous. We are suffering on earth one moment and rejoicing in heaven the next. Furthermore, God accompanies us through the dark valley of death. Absent from the body for the believer means to be present with the Lord.

Paul pens these comforting words in 2 Corinthians 5:6–8: "So

---

21 Jonathan D. Sarfati, The Genesis Account: A theological, historical, and scientific commentary on Genesis 1–11 (Powder Springs, GA: Creation Book Publishers, 2015), p. 357.

we are always confident, knowing that while we are at home in the body we are absent from the Lord. For we walk by faith, not by sight. We are confident, yes, well pleased rather to be absent from the body and to be present with the Lord" (cf. Philippians 1:23–25). May every believer rejoice in that promise. Believers never need to fear death.

Lessons Learned in This Chapter

In this chapter, we first examined some of the steps by which Satan enticed Adam and Eve to partake of the forbidden fruit. A similar pattern of temptation surrounds all of humanity today as well. But it must always be remembered: For there to be genuine worship, free will must also be present. Many have contemplated the wisdom of God, providing an avenue of temptation. But God knew from the beginning the entire scope of eternity. Though skeptical man sometimes falters at God's infinite wisdom, he can nonetheless rest assured that His plans are perfect.

Second, we focused on numerous unenviable consequences that Adam and Eve's transgression foisted on the earth. Our entire planet suffers with incivility and spiritual darkness. Only through the light of Jesus Christ can mankind truly be enlightened. John 8:12 declares: "Then Jesus spoke to them again, saying, 'I am the light of the world, he who follows Me shall not walk in darkness, but have the light of life.'"

Our next chapter continues with the temptation of Adam and Eve. Even in the midst of this chaos, we shall see that God's plans cannot be forfeited. As Jesus prayed to the Father: "Your will be done" (Matthew 6:10). God's grace always prevails!

Cognitive Conundrum #3

Well-versed was I in God's holy command; upon His statement, I was to take a stand. My family life proved quiet and serene; my most beautiful wife was truly a dream. A leader of men was I in so many ways. This would never change throughout all my days. But times would change; this was for sure: my unsavory actions have only one cure.

Who am I?

Answer: Adam

Chapter 4

Sin Is Found Out!

(Genesis 3:9–19)

In This Chapter

Objectives for This Chapter
God's Cross-Examination with Adam and Eve (3:9–13)
The Threefold Curse (3:14–19)
Lessons Learned in This Chapter

Objectives for This Chapter

In this chapter, we shall first examine God's examination with His created couple. It is important to note that God sought out mankind. Adam and Eve tried to hide from their Creator. That has been the pattern throughout human history. Though all of their previous interaction with God had been wondrous beyond description, sin initially, albeit not permanently, ruined it all.

In God's great benevolence and mercy, He sought out reconciliation with Adam and Eve. As we shall see, God sought them out in the Garden. As John 3:19–21 reveals, mankind's natural instinct is to hide from God. Why? It is because man's deeds are evil. Wicked deeds fall under sore conviction when placed alongside the radiance of God's holiness. Yet, we must recognize that nothing surprises God in all eternity, mind-boggling as that is to comprehend. Hence, God was fully prepared for this eventuality.

God inquired of Adam and Eve regarding the course of events

that led to their downfall. Not surprisingly, blame was passed from one to another. Adam was the most guilty and also the most accusatory. He not only blamed God for giving him his wife, but he also blamed Eve. Such a ridiculous accusation would be almost laughable if it were not so pathetic. Adam set the pattern of trying to shift the blame onto someone else for all of mankind. Intriguingly enough, there is no corresponding record of Eve blaming Adam for not supporting her in a moment of weakness.

Second, we shall review the threefold curse God placed respectively upon the serpent, Eve, and Adam. How culpable was the serpent itself in this temptation? That is impossible to say. Whatever the situation was, God effectively cursed the cunning creature for all time.

However, in the millennial kingdom of Christ, the curse on the serpent will be largely lifted. During that future time, even small children will be able to play with the most poisonous of snakes alive in our present age. The snakes will, by then, have been rendered harmless. However, dust shall still be the serpent's food. In other words, they will still be relegated to crawling around in the dirt as a reminder of their role in the temptation of Adam and Eve.

Isaiah 65:25 states: "'The wolf and the lamb shall feed together, the lion shall eat straw like the ox, and dust shall be the serpent's food. They shall not hurt nor destroy in all My holy mountain,' says the LORD."

Third, we shall discuss the separate curses placed on the woman and the man. Those curses remain valid to this day. The curse on woman is related to her strongest instincts, that of the relational. By contrast, the predominant curse on man is vocational. However, along with the curses, God granted accompanying blessings. This is consistent with the gracious manner of God. In the midst of judgment, God often offers mercy.

Through this entire biblical scenario, God's grace is manifestly evident. Genesis 3:15 gives promise of the coming Messiah. Through Him, all things can be made right once again. Christ is the great hope of reconciliation with man's Creator. Through Him, all things were made, and through Him, all things can be restored. Hence, from the onset of sin, God has reached out to mankind through His glorious and eternal Son.

First Corinthians 8:6 beautifully summarizes this truth: "Yet for us there is one God, the Father, of whom are all things, and we for Him; and one Lord Jesus Christ, through whom are all things, and through whom we live." It is our fervent prayer that every individual reading this book will embrace that eternal truth.

God's Cross-Examination with Adam and Eve (3:9–13)

In our present passage, we see the new "tendencies" of human nature regrettably emerging. Prior to the sin of eating the forbidden fruit, life was balanced, bountiful, and beautiful in every aspect. After sin entered the picture, life became tumultuous and discomfiting relationally.

Adam and Eve were in for some rather unpleasant awakenings due to their fresh "knowledge" of sin. Naturally, they had no clue as to the severe ramifications of their disobedience. We must exercise caution not to become complacent or critical in our present mentality towards them. Rest assured, no human being would have bettered their faulty performance.

Cultivation of fellowship with the Creator should be the chief objective of every human being. Adam and Eve were the only two human beings to enjoy such fellowship to perfection. But then sin changed everything. Lamentably, the reverse objective for humanity is now generally the case (John 3:19–21; Romans 3:10–18). Instead of fleeing to the Creator and Redeemer of this universe, man instinctively gravitates toward the opposite pole of spiritual indiscretion.

God's Loving Desire for Mankind

The tragic reality is that Satan became our spiritual father (John 8:44). The Jews were understandably incensed when Jesus stated that provocative but true allegation. Thankfully, we can and must be adopted into God's spiritual family. By God's eternal grace, such an adoption is full and permanent. Believers are sealed by the Holy Spirit. To break the Roman government's seal without permission carried the death sentence. How much more secure, then, is the Holy Spirit's seal? It cannot be broken by any power in heaven or on earth.

Romans 8:14–15 presents the following wondrous assurance to God's children: "For as many as are led by the Spirit of God, these are the sons of God. For you did not receive the spirit of bondage again to fear, but you received the Spirit of adoption by whom we cry out, 'Abba, Father.'" "Abba" is an Aramaic term of tender endearment, similar to "papa" or "daddy." Paul did not pen this as a conditional statement; it is a guarantee to God's spiritually adopted family.

Ephesians 1:13–14 marvelously declares:

> In Him you also trusted, after you heard the word of truth, the gospel of your salvation; in whom also, having believed, you were sealed with the Holy Spirit of promise, who is the guarantee of our inheritance until the redemption of the purchased possession, to the praise of His glory.

Who, after all, can break the seal of the almighty God of this universe? No one can! Who can undermine the praise of God's glory? Again, no one can.

Regarding Ephesians 1:13–14, Harold Hoehner writes:

> The last part of verse 13 is literally, "They were sealed in Him [Christ] with the Holy Spirit of promise." The word "seal" indicates security (Matt. 27:66; Eph. 4:30), authentication and approval (John 6:27), certification of genuineness (John 6:33), and identification of ownership (2 Cor. 1:22; Rev. 7:2; 9:4). God is the One who seals, Christ is the sphere in which the seal is done, and the Holy Spirit is the instrument of the seal. "The promised Holy Spirit" refers to Christ's promise to His disciples that He would send the Spirit (Luke 24:49; John 14:16; 15:26; 16:13; Acts 1:5).[22]

Only through the gracious intervention of our triune God can our relationship with God be resuscitated (John 6:44). That is because mankind is now cursed with a sin-darkened soul in the midst of a sin-sickened world. But there is hope! God has poetically and respectfully been called the "Hound of Heaven." That is so true. God, in His great mercy, continuously extends His benevolent hands toward unrepentant mankind.

In the context of Israel, Isaiah 65:1–2 further speaks of God's graciousness:

> "I was sought by those who did not ask for Me, I was found by those who did not seek Me. I said, 'Here I am, here I am,' to a nation that was not called by My name. I have stretched out My hands all day long to a

---
22 Harold W. Hoehner, The Bible Knowledge Commentary: Ephesians (Wheaton, IL: Victor Books, 1983), p. 619.

rebellious people, who walk in a way that is not good, according to their own thoughts" (cf. Romans 10:21).

Simultaneously, however, God will exercise judgment when judgment becomes necessary (Jeremiah 32:17–19). Nonetheless, He utters with clarion voice His desire that man repent and be restored to fellowship with Him (Ezekiel 18:31–32). This has been God's declared and fervent intent since Adam and Eve fell into sin (Genesis 3:15).

Let the "Blame Game" Begin

Genesis 3:9–13 states:

> Then the LORD God called to Adam and said to him, "Where are you?" So he said, "I heard Your voice in the garden, and I was afraid because I was naked; and I hid myself." And He said, "Who told you that you were naked? Have you eaten from the tree of which I commanded you that you should not eat?"

> Then the man said, "The woman whom You gave to be with me, she gave me of the tree, and I ate. And the LORD God said to the woman, "What is this you have done?" The woman said, "The serpent deceived me, and I ate."

In this passage, we mournfully witness the beginning of the "blame game." Sadly, it has become a permanent fixture in human relations ever since. Adam, in a sense, blamed God for giving him the woman in the first place. That was certainly an exercise in futility or, as one might be more tempted to say, unbelievable stupidity. What's more, Adam simultaneously blamed Eve, his wife. Was God really to believe that Eve overpowered Adam and forced him to eat of the forbidden fruit? Depraved instinct within Adam's new "old nature" overruled sagacity.

Eve, in her turn, predictably blamed the serpent. After all, the pattern was established by her husband. She simply followed suit. The serpent didn't get to blame anyone, although Satan certainly deserved the blame for this transgression. Serpents have been getting blamed for many things ever since. It is now time to further examine God's response to the serpent, Eve, and then Adam.

God Calls Out to Adam

How did God respond? God called out to Adam to identify his location. Obviously, God knew exactly where Adam and Eve were hiding in the garden. He then asked Adam what had transpired, thereby granting him an opportunity to respond. The fact that God called for Adam and not Eve once again shows Adam's headship over his wife. Accompanying that headship was a moral and governing responsibility. Adam had not only shirked his responsibility, but he also failed it completely.

Throughout the Scriptures, God constantly poses questions to mankind. The questions are designed for man's sake, not God's. Jesus often ministered to people by asking questions. The most prolific question-and-answer Old Testament prophet was Malachi.

Asking questions is one of the best teaching tools available to any teacher or parent. The reader will note that we use that same methodology quite extensively.

God called out to Adam: "Where are you?" Adam answered: "I heard Your voice in the garden, and I was afraid because I was naked; and I hid myself" (3:9–10). Question: Why was Adam afraid? All of his previous experiences with God had been splendid. They had enjoyed nothing but sweet communion together. He never had any cause to fear God prior to eating the fruit.

Answer: Sin changed everything! The first recorded symptom of that sin was awareness of their disobedience, which was quickly followed by fear. They suddenly realized they were naked. Instead of fleeing to God for forgiveness and reconciliation, Adam and Eve tried to hide from Him and, in a sense, from each other. They covered themselves with leaves.

That tendency of intimidation and fear has not changed appreciably over the millennia. Guilt and shame immediately overwhelmed them because of their unclothed bodies. They had been naked since their creation with no sense of embarrassment. But no more was that the case. Sin ruined perfection.

Eugene H. Merrill writes:

> First, when Adam and Eve sinned, they were keenly aware of what they had done. Their eyes were opened, as the serpent had said they would be (Gen. 3:5), and they took note that they were naked (v. 7). The nakedness here is more than physical nudity—they surely had observed this before—but a sense of shame and responsibility before God.

The physical nakedness betokened a loss of innocence, a stripping away of the glory that partly accounted for their being made in the image of God. They had known the good, and now they knew the bad, and beyond that they knew evil.

Desperate to cover their bodies and the act of rebellion that had enlightened them as to their nakedness, Adam and Eve made themselves loincloths of fig leaves (v. 7). This futile resort to a human remedy for sin is the first evidence in the Old Testament of a man-made religion based on works and not on grace.[23]

Adam's Unworthy Response

Mankind has been trying to cover up their sins ever since. God next asked two rhetorical questions: "Who told you that you were naked? Have you eaten from the tree of which I commanded you that you should not eat?" (Genesis 3:11)

Obviously, God knew the answers to His questions. It is striking that from the first sin of humanity, Adam tried to avoid answering the question of guilt regarding himself. He tried to shift the blame on Eve. Many people do not want to take personal responsibility for their actions. That resolves nothing! Neither does that ploy work with God. But man continues to play this foolish and pointless game of "passing the buck."

Sin immediately distorts the mind and twists the emotions. An inevitable consequence of sin is the tendency toward self-gratification, self-deception, and self-righteousness. Adam conveyed all

---
[23] Eugene H. Merrill, Everlasting Dominion: A Theology of the Old Testament (Nashville, TN: B & H Publishing Group, 2006), pp. 216–217.

three repulsive emotions toward his wife. His attempts at self-exoneration failed dismally. Eve undoubtedly stared back at him in crushed disbelief.

Genesis 2:23 records a previously different sentiment voiced by Adam. He stated this marvelous response when God first brought Eve to him: "This is now bone of my bones and flesh of my flesh: she shall be called Woman, because she was taken out of Man." Adam was originally ecstatic when a mate was brought to him. He had just named all the animals and knew of a certainty that their male/female pattern was an example for him as well. He, too, needed and desired a mate. God had appropriately whetted his appetite! God then lovingly fashioned Eve to be his perfect counterpart.

James McKeown cogently writes:

> Adam's acceptance of his new partner and his delight in her are conveyed in three ways in the text. First, Adam's reaction when he meets Eve is presented as a poetic couplet, the first formal poetry in Genesis. Second, the words he speaks convey his relief that finally his ideal partner has been produced. Third, Adam declares that his partner shall be known as "Woman." This name acknowledges that she is part of himself and they need each other to be complete.
>
> This is more than just a beautiful story, since it provides a powerful polemic against polygamy. Although polygamy is practiced throughout the OT and many prominent characters have several wives, the ideal of one man and one woman is presented unequivocally in this passage.[24]

---

24 James McKeown, Genesis, Two Horizons Old Testament Commentary series (Grand Rapids, MI: Eerdmans, 2008), p. 34.

Sin Is Found Out!

How quickly sin changes perspectives and attitudes. Adam did not look upon his wife with the same adoring eyes as when he first saw her. Genesis 3:12 states: "Then the man said, 'The woman whom You gave to be with me, she gave me of the tree, and I ate.'" While that was certainly true, the only person fooled by such an answer was Adam himself. He knew exactly what the forbidden fruit was, and yet he deliberately ate it. Was God actually supposed to believe that Eve forced Adam to eat it? God did not bother answering his impertinent statement.

Eve's Equally Predictable Response

The questioning continued when God turned to Eve in verse 13: "And the LORD God said to the woman, 'What is this you have done?' The woman said, 'The serpent deceived me, and I ate.'" Eve learned very quickly from Adam on how to shift the blame. Of course, this strategy did not work any better for Eve than it did for Adam. In fact, since Eve initiated the problem, it proved even less effective. In God's judicial system, each individual must answer for himself or herself.

John Phillips offers the following salient comments on the illicit habit of blaming others:

> It is always somebody else's fault. The classic demonstration of that was at the Nuremberg Trials where the Nazi war criminals were indicted for their crimes against humanity. Josef Seuss, an administrative assistant, whimpered, "A solder can only carry out his orders." Walter Langlesit, a battalion commander, declared, "I was just a little man. Those things were done on orders from the big shots."

Colonel Hoess, commandant of the notorious Auschwitz Concentration Camp, who personally supervised the extermination of two and a half million Jews, explained; "In Germany it was understood that if something went wrong the man who gave the orders was responsible. So I didn't think I would ever have to answer for it myself."

Hermann Goering, the former Reichmarschall and second-ranking man in Germany blustered, "We had a Fuherstaat. We had to obey orders." Hitler copped out by committing suicide, but no doubt he would have blamed the Treaty of Versailles.[25]

How foolish and vain are the efforts of man to avoid personal responsibility. God has granted each person a free will. We are born with it. Each person must decide how to utilize that free will. If he chooses badly, he will be opposing the general and special revelation of God. If he chooses wisely, it will be in accordance and harmony with God's complete revelation found in the Bible. But no man can claim complete ignorance and hence avoid the penalty due to his guilt. That is not an alternative God left open to us!

The Threefold Curse (3:14–24)

Numbers 32:23 states the following axiomatic truth: "But if you do not do so, then take note, you have sinned against the LORD; and be sure your sin will find you out." As was true in Genesis chapter 3 for Adam and Eve, so life has proven consistent throughout all of humanity's existence. Our actions do merit consequences. Thankfully, in God's graciousness and benevolence, we are often spared

---
[25] Phillips, John, The John Phillips Commentary Series: Exploring Genesis, p. 60.

from many of those consequences.

God's Curse on the Serpent (Genesis 3:14–15)

Genesis 3:14–15 states:

> So the LORD God said to the serpent: "Because you have done this, you are cursed more than all cattle, and more than every beast of the field; on your belly you shall go, and you shall eat dust all the days of your life. And I will put enmity between you and the woman, and between your seed and her Seed; He shall bruise your head, and you shall bruise His heel."

There was no good news for the serpent. God cursed him in a variety of ways. Curse #1: The serpent was now the most cursed creature on the earth. That is a distinction no human or any animal would covet. That curse on the serpent apparently will never be entirely lifted.

Genesis 3:1 states that the serpent was more cunning than any other animal. That sounds very foreign to the modern ear. We cannot particularly grasp how an animal could have such a quality as cunningness. Yet, in our modern age, we do have such expressions as "sly as a fox." However, that is based on the fox's instinct, not on his inherent sagacity.

We may never have a full understanding of how the serpent was known to be so cunning. It is not known for its cunningness anymore, though the serpent certainly is stealthy and patient. We should also note that all the animal kingdom suffered from the penalty of sin in that they became vicious and carnivorous. However, no animal has suffered as much as the serpent. It is under a permanent curse, although in the millennial kingdom, the serpent will finally become harmless. At that time, a child will safely play with the formerly poisonous viper (Isaiah 11:8).

Eat Dirt!

Curse #2: The serpent must now crawl on its belly and eat dust all its life. Apparently, the serpent used to walk upright. Scripture does not reveal how many changes came over the animal kingdom. Probably at this point, many animals became carnivorous.

Victor Hamilton offers the following comments on the serpent's new mode of locomotion. He also alludes to an interesting observation of a Hebrew wordplay regarding the serpent:

> But one element distinguishes God's decree to the serpent from his decree to the human couple. It—but not they—is banned. This ban involves a unique form of locomotion for the snake—he is to crawl on his belly. This posture will make him eat dust. Such a penalty matches the serpent's sin. He who tempted Eve to eat now himself will eat dust. He who is 'arum, "subtle," is now 'arur, banned. The most subtle of all the animals now becomes the loneliest and oddest of the animals.[26]

The snake was thoroughly humbled by having to crawl on its belly. Previously, it must have walked upright and even had the gift of speech. Even today, a parrot can mimic human speech. Perhaps other animals spoke as well. As previously mentioned, it was not just the snake that was cursed and changed. The snake simply received the greatest curse. But every creature in the animal kingdom was transformed to some degree.

---

26 Hamilton, V. P., The Book of Genesis: Chapters 1–17, p. 196.

The diets of at least certain creatures were modified. Some animals remained vegetarian. Others went from being purely vegetarian to carnivorous. Yet others will eat both vegetation and meat. There is no way to know the extent of these changes as details are not provided. Sadly, however, the idyllic life of the animal kingdom was no more! It had not lasted very long.

In ways that are not comprehensible to us today, Satan used the serpent's limited "personality" to approach the woman. As we have mentioned, the serpent was cunning. Something about the serpent allowed for that description. If that were not the case, and if the serpent was an entirely innocent and helpless victim and was itself abused and possessed by Satan, why the curse?

However, Scripture does not reveal why the serpent was characterized as crafty, and so there is little point in speculating about it. God's ways are sometimes inexplicable. Job found this out the hard way. Hence, we may simply assume that, somehow, the serpent was, in some mysterious fashion, cooperative in the temptation of Adam and Eve.

As far as their diets go, modern-day snakes generally live on other small creatures, such as rodents. The size of its victims depends on the size of the snake. The snake actually does have an organ that "eats" dust. The flickering tongue picks up tiny bits of dust or dirt and carries it to what is called the vomeronasal organ.

This organ can detect chemical traces in the soil, which helps expedite its hunting for its lunch. Ironically, God, as He so often graciously does, enables the serpent to utilize its curse for a blessing. Furthermore, snakes are useful in keeping unwanted pests in better control.

The Promised Messiah (Genesis 3:15)

Curse #3: There would be enmity between the woman and her Seed and the serpent and its seed. The relationship between women and snakes is generally one of spite and fear on the part of the woman. However, a tiny minority of women actually like snakes! How can this be? Should not all women automatically hate snakes? Not necessarily! The reason for these "exceptions" is quite simple.

The primary intent of verse 15 is not about women and snakes. It is about two other entirely different individuals, namely, Satan and Jesus Christ. The primary focus is on the Seed of the woman and the seed of the serpent. So, who is this Seed of the woman and seed of the serpent? This verse seems quite enigmatic at first read. Scholars have studied it thoroughly over the centuries and written copiously about it.

Question: Who could possibly fulfill this verse? Who has such power? Who are the potential candidates? The serpent, which represents Satan and his singular seed (the Antichrist), is represented here. They would be defeated by the woman's singular Seed.

Answer: Who can defeat Satan but God alone? The Seed of the woman can be none other than Jesus Christ. He will bruise Satan's head. This means that Christ will defeat him. That ultimate defeat does not come about until the end of Christ's millennial kingdom. Regrettably, Satan is clearly alive and well on planet Earth today (1 Peter 5:8). He persists in his warlike and evil opposition to his Creator and His spiritually adopted children.

We shall further engage on this rather disturbing conversation about Satan and his seed in Genesis chapter 6. The Nephilim were fathered by demonic spirits. Suffice it for now to say that the Antichrist will be the final Nephilim. His father will literally be Satan himself. The phenomenal power of Satan will someday be encapsulated in one human being. Though John warns of many antichrists, there will be only one final Antichrist.

First John 2:18 states: "Little children, it is the last hour; and as you have heard that the Antichrist is coming, even now many antichrists have come, by which we know that it is the last hour." This prophecy was recorded approximately 3,500 years in advance by Moses. Its ultimate fulfillment does not take place until the end of the millennial kingdom of Christ, thus spanning at least 7,000 years or longer. That will be the minimum duration of this present earth.

The final rebellion takes place at the conclusion of the millennial kingdom. That is when Satan will be thrown into the Lake of Fire along with the Antichrist, the false prophet, and all those who reject God (Revelation 20:7–15). God knows the end from the beginning (Isaiah 46:10). Nothing remains a secret to Him. God has certainly granted mankind sufficient advance warning of coming terrors and ultimate deliverance.

Who Is the Seed of the Woman?

Sarfati quotes Martin Luther as follows:

3:15 – Seed of the woman. The promise and the threat [in this text] are both clear and obscure. It left the serpent in the dark about which woman should give birth to the Seed of the Woman, so that he had to think of every woman as [possibly] becoming the mother of the blessed Seed [Christ].

On the other hand, it gave our first parents great faith that from that very hour they expected the Savior.

When Eve brought forth her first son, she surely believed that she had given birth to Him. [Luther rightly translates Genesis 4:1: thus, I have the man, the Lord." This properly is the meaning of the Hebrew original.]

Isaiah added clarity to the promise by saying, "Behold, a virgin shall conceive." This prophecy made it clear that the Savior was not to be the offspring of the union of a man and wife. In the NT this [fact] was revealed still more clearly by the angel (Luke 1:26-28).

Since, then, there was promised man, through the Seed of the Woman, deliverance from the Law, sin and death, and there was given to him a clear and sure hope of the resurrection and renewal in the future life, it is clear that he could not by his own power remove sin and its punishment.

Nor could he [by his own power] escape death and make amends for his disobedience. Therefore the Son of God had to sacrifice himself and secure all this for mankind. He had to remove sin, overcome death, and restore what Adam had lost by his disobedience.[27]

What woman can give birth with her own seed? What does that mean? Women do not have seeds; they have eggs. The only possible exception to this occurred just once in human history. The Holy Spirit miraculously implanted the Virgin Mary with the Seed and

---

27 Sarfati, Jonathan. The Genesis Account: A theological, historical, and scientific account of Genesis 1–11, p. 408.

combined it with her egg. Jesus Christ, the unique God-man, was the result. He and He alone can defeat the power of the diabolical Satan. Hence, this passage is the first messianic promise.

The futuristic promise of Romans 16:20 alludes back to Genesis 3:15: "And the God of peace will crush Satan under your feet shortly. The grace of our Lord Jesus Christ be with you. Amen." Though Satan is still allowed to wander the earth as a roaring lion seeking whom he may devour (1 Peter 5:8), he will someday be permanently incarcerated in the Lake of Fire. Tragically, he will succeed in bringing one-third of the now-fallen angels with him, as well as an untold multitude of human souls.

Women and the "the Childbearing"

Paul offers an interesting comment on the birth of the Christ-child. First Timothy 2:14–15, although sometimes debated, is best understood as referring back to the messianic promise of Genesis 3:15: "And Adam was not deceived, but the woman being deceived, fell into transgression. Nevertheless she will be saved in childbearing if they continue in faith, love, and holiness, with self-control."

Unfortunately, the translators have generally left out a very important word in the translation of verse 15, namely, "the." A more proper translation, therefore, is "the childbearing." When you include the article and examine the context, it becomes quite obvious that this passage refers to the birth of Christ, not childbearing in general.

If the above interpretation is correct, God then grants a great honor to the woman. Women are often, although certainly not legitimately, viewed as second-class citizens. But the Virgin Mary was privileged to give birth to the Christ child. Eve's punishment for first bringing sin into the world was accompanied with the gracious blessing of bringing the ultimate Peacemaker, the Messiah, into the world.

God often manifests His everlasting mercy in the midst of harsh judgment. All faithful Jewish women yearned for the privilege of being the Messiah-bearer. Only one, of course, could enjoy such a singular blessing. The Virgin Mary was predestined to play that magnificent role. She is indeed the most blessed of all women.

Regarding 1 Timothy 2:14–15, Sarfati sagaciously comments:

> Superficially, some might gain the impression that women can earn salvation by having children. Clearly this is wrong, because it would be salvation by works, contradicting Ephesians 2:8-9. The best solution involves analyzing the original Greek. The word for 'childbearing' is teknogonia.
>
> But it has a definite article in the Greek, which is usually not translated, although Young's Literal Translation indeed does have, "She shall be saved through the childbearing." So this seems to be referring to a specific childbearing that saves them—the Christ-child. And here is the valuable role of women that Satan hates; one of them would bear the One who would doom him.[28]

Women and the Rearing of Children

A secondary meaning to 1 Timothy 2:14–15 is that women are also privileged to play a prominent role in raising godly children. It is the mother, after all, who gets pregnant and carries the child in her womb for nine months. It is the loving mother who nurses

---
28 Ibid., pp. 365–366.

her children and spends more time traditionally with them than the father does. It is the mother who nurtures and comforts her children on a daily basis. The mother weaves the greatest tapestry of early childhood experience and tenderness toward her child.

Women are indeed blessed and splendidly equipped by God for this most blessed of earthly responsibilities. If a woman is not blessed to have children of her own, she can ably assist other busy mothers. God has thus graciously granted women the blessing to eradicate some of their earlier shame of being deceived by Satan and sinning first.

Joseph, Mary's betrothed husband, was not sexually involved in this phenomenal privilege of bringing the Messiah into the world. Part of the reason for this is that the sinful nature is passed on through the man, odd as that may sound (Romans 5:12, 18–19). This is not because women are less sinful but because man is the designated head of the human race. He, therefore, bears the primary responsibility for sin entering the world even though he sinned after Eve.

Eve was more easily deceived due to her trusting nature. Adam sinned deliberately. He was not deceived! This is not to say that Adam understood the ramifications of his disobedience. We must remember that neither Eve nor Adam was possessed of a sinful nature. Hence, both of them sinned in "ignorance" of the gruesome consequences. It should not be construed that they ate of the fruit with an arrogant or actively defiant intent.

Christ's birth had to be from a virgin (cf. Isaiah 7:14, 9:6–7) to prevent the sinful nature from passing on to Christ. Needless to say, that could not be allowed to happen. The Messiah must be totally pure to be acceptable to God. The condition for a woman's personal blessing is faith, evidenced by her love and holiness. A believing woman's instinctive nature is to encourage and help mold children into godliness.

Further Insightful Comments on Genesis 3:15

Sarfati offers the following comments on the first messianic prophecy (3:15):

> This seed who will finally defeat Satan is no ordinary man. It is not hard to show that the biblical norm is to trace genealogies through the fathers (e.g. Genesis 5, 11, 1 Chronicles 1—9; Matthew 1:1-17; Luke 3:23-38). But this particular seed is of the woman. God later reveals in the Bible that the coming unique seed, the Messiah, would be born of a virgin, i.e. without a human father. So Genesis 3:15 is the first mention of the Virginal Conception of Christ.
>
> A major but partial fulfilment was the Crucifixion and Resurrection of the Messiah. The Messiah's heels were wounded by the nails on the Cross, and Satan was "bruised" in the sense of his power drastically weakened. But the final crushing of the head is still future (Romans 16:20), and will be accomplished when Satan is thrown into the Lake of Fire for eternity (Revelation 20:10).[29]

Morris adds the following similar comments:

> The "seed of the woman" can only be an allusion to a future descendant of Eve who would have no human father. Biologically, a woman produces no seed, and except in this case biblical usage always speaks only

---

[29] Jonathan Sarfati, The Genesis Account: A theological, historical, and scientific commentary on Genesis 1-11, p. 363.

of the seed of men. This promised Seed would, therefore, have to be miraculously implanted in the womb. In this way, He would not inherit the sin nature which would disqualify every son of Adam from becoming a Savior from sin. This prophecy thus clearly anticipates the future virgin birth of Christ.[30]

Even in the midst of judgment, God provided good news. Adam and Eve had just defiled themselves and brought calamity into the entire universe. In spite of that, God reached out to them with a promise of hope. From that point on, it became the dream of every godly woman that she might bear the Child of Hope, the Messiah. Eve undoubtedly thought that she would have that privilege. It did not occur to her or Adam that the promised Messiah would not arrive until 4,000 years later! But all comes to proper order in God's timing, not man's.

God's love and intervention for humanity is shown in the fact that He does not delight in the death of the wicked. Ezekiel 18:23, 32 states:

> "Do I have any pleasure at all that the wicked should die?" says the Lord GOD, "and not that he should turn from his ways and live?"

> "For I have no pleasure in the death of one who dies," says the Lord GOD. "Therefore turn and live!"

Scripture makes it quite clear that God desires all to be saved and to come to a knowledge of the truth (cf. 1 Timothy 2:4; 2 Peter 3:9). One must simply be willing to come and surrender to the

---
[30] Henry Morris, The New Defender's Study Bible (Nashville, TN: World Publishing, Inc., 1995, 2006), p. 21.

eternal love offered by the Savior. How can anyone possibly lose by accepting God's salvation? How can a person possibly win if he neglects this loving offer? He condemns himself to hell. That would be the worst possible choice and destination imaginable.

God's Curse on the Woman (Genesis 3:16)

Genesis 3:16 states: "To the woman He said: 'I will greatly multiply your sorrow and your conception; in pain you shall bring forth children; your desire shall be for your husband, and he shall rule over you.'" Like the serpent, Eve was afflicted with a multi-level curse. Still, in the midst of the curses, God offers profound blessings, as we shall see.

Four specific items are mentioned: Item #1: God would multiply her sorrow and conception (3:16a). It is relatively easy to understand how a woman's sorrow greatly increased. Sin causes nothing but destruction. Hence, her feminine sensibilities would now frequently be offended. This would stem largely from the frequent misunderstandings between husband and wife.

Women are largely motivated through heart issues. Men are inclined more toward vocational and intellectual concerns. Both, quite naturally, are important. But the lack of sensitivity toward each other lends itself to increased stress. This is generally felt more keenly by the women because they are more emotional by God's design. That is not a fault on the woman's part; God's planned it this way. It is precisely because of a woman's keener emotional nature that she is qualified to be a loving and nurturing mother. Her thoughts unceasingly flow toward those around her, particularly her children. Being a godly mother will always be, by God's design, her greatest earthly passion and fulfillment.

The "conception" clearly conveys the idea of difficulties that now accompany pregnancy. Before sin entered the world, pregnancy was perfectly safe. After sin, pregnancy became susceptible to danger. Indeed, it is an exceedingly rare woman (if it has actually ever happened) who has experienced an entirely painless pregnancy and delivery. Some women feel quite comfortable throughout their pregnancies. Not all are so fortunate, however. Many women feel morning sickness quite often. In addition to that, other physical discomforts can also occur.

Item #2: Women would give birth in great pain (3:16a). Previously, the Lord had planned to allow childbirth to be free of pain. God now changed the situation. Eve herself never experienced a pain-free childbirth. She and Adam had sinned before Cain was even conceived. If that were not the case, they would not have passed on the sinful nature to Cain. Indeed, only with Jesus Christ was there no sin nature conveyed.

The curse on the woman was giving birth in pain. Yet, in spite of the pain, God granted within women such a strong maternal instinct that the pain is well worth the little "bundle of joy" created in pregnancy. Jesus stated in John 16:21: "A woman when she is in labor, has sorrow because her hour has come, but as soon as she has given birth to the child, she no longer remembers the anguish, for joy that a human being has been born into the world."

Quite naturally, a man cannot comprehend how much pain a woman endures in giving birth. But even more amazing to a husband is that his wife is willing to go through the same agony repeatedly. Her love for her children cannot be paralleled save God's love for His children. That is a fantastic blessing for father, mother, and child alike.

Blessing within the Midst of the Curse

Item #3: "Your desire shall be for your husband" (3:16b). With rare exceptions, very young girls start thinking about getting married and taking care of children. This, of course, varies with young girls depending on the happiness of their own upbringing. It also explains why girls take an earlier interest in boys than boys do in girls. God grants this marvelous instinct of homemaking to them. Oftentimes, this is manifested in nurturing dolls and playing "house." In this sense, the desire for a husband, when brought to fruition, is a profound blessing.

Leupold pens the following interesting comments:

> The second part of the penalty is: "Unto thy husband thou shalt be attracted." Teshuqah might be rendered "desire" or even better "yearning." This yearning is morbid. It is not merely sexual yearning. It includes the attraction that woman experiences for man which she cannot root from her nature.
>
> Independent feminists may seek to banish it, but it persists in cropping out. ... It is a just penalty. She who sought to strive apart from man and to act independently of him in the temptation finds a continual attraction for him to be her unavoidable lot.[31]

It should be noted that when Leupold states, "this yearning is morbid," he does not mean it is strange or unnatural. Indeed, it is ordained by God. His meaning is that this desire is unalterable to the point of being a fixation. Women cannot escape from it. Even wom-

---
31 H. C. Leupold, Exposition of Genesis: Volume 1: Chapters 1–19 (Grand Rapids, MI: Baker Book House, 1942), p. 172.

en who have suffered bad marriages still focus on relationships. But as already stated, this curse also functions as an incredible and incurable blessing. Men do not always manifest the most desirable of personality traits. Indeed, some of them are outright cads!

Yet, strangely enough, some women generally will find themselves attracted to even the least admirable of men. It is almost a befuddlement! King Solomon wrote of this in Proverbs 30:18–19: "There are three things which are too wonderful for me, yes, four which I do not understand: the way of an eagle in the air; the way of a serpent on a rock, the way of a ship in the midst of the sea, and the way of a man with a virgin."

How does this curse render itself into a blessing? One word: marriage! Young women have pondered the mysteries of marriage since their youngest days. Finally, the men come around as well. Proverbs 18:22 states: "He who finds a wife finds a good thing, and obtains favor from the LORD."

God clearly stated in Genesis 2:18: "And the LORD God said, 'It is not good that man should be alone; I will make him a helper suitable to him.'" Marriage was God's holy plan for humanity from the beginning. We see once again that God transforms a curse into a blessing. He exercises grace in the midst of judgment.

Authority Is Delegated by God

Item #4: Your husband "shall rule over you" (3:16b). Women were not designed for leadership within the family. She is to be a loving support and help to her husband (Genesis 2:18). She can strengthen, encourage, and motivate her husband far beyond the vocational or spiritual levels that he might have normally attained. An excellent wife performs this task splendidly. If, on the other hand, the wife takes a competitive or, worse yet, a domineering role over her husband, both shall lose. How much better is a loving embrace between husband and wife than an impertinent: "I won!"

This is not at all to say that women are less capable than men. However, the God-given role within the family is that the husband is the head of the household. Indeed, even within the text of Scripture, some women were elevated to lofty positions. One must remember that our present passage is talking about the context of marriage, not politics, business, engineering, or being an astronaut. Women have excelled in all of these and many other categories of life. However, within the institution of marriage, she is to play a submissive role to her husband.

The woman of Proverbs chapter 31 was a truly industrious wife and mother who was highly skilled and motivated. She was praised by everyone who knew her, particularly by her husband and children. Proverbs 31:28 states: "Her children rise up and call her blessed; her husband also, and he praises her." Clearly, there is nothing unspiritual about godly success.

Women Must Choose Whom They Will Serve

Proverbs 14:1 offers a striking contrast of two types of women: "The wise woman builds her house, but the foolish pulls it down with her hands." Women, just like men, must make a choice as to which type of person they will be. Moral responsibilities and some type of response to God are common among all people: men, women, and children alike. Women need to make their decisions wisely, just as do men and children.

Leupold comments as follows:

> The third part of the penalty is: "he shall rule over thee." She sought to control him by taking control into

her own hands (II Tim. 2:14) and even by leading him on in the temptation. As a result her penalty is that she shall be the one that is controlled. Man's position in reference to woman now is fixed; he bears the rule. When all is done in the spirit of Christ, such rule is not harsh or unnatural; nor is it cancelled. There it expresses itself in such a way that it is not to be felt as a burden.

But where sin prevails, such rule may be degraded into a miserable domination, such as the East has particularly experienced. God did not ordain this harshness, but man transcended his rights, and sin poisoned a necessary restriction. This word, then, does not reflect the narrowness of the East, but is a wholesome restraint and reminder for womankind.[32]

To the already mentioned comments, Fruchtenbaum adds the following:

Therefore the woman is placed into a subordinate role, and the point of 3:16 is that the woman will desire to rule over her husband who is to master her. She will seek to gain authority over the husband just as sin desired to rule over Cain. However, Adam should master her. Teshukah is a word that emphasizes a desire to possess.

The woman chose to act independently of the man, and

---
[32] Ibid., 172.

now she will have a desire to rule and possess him. She shall desire to control the man, and to dispute the headship of the husband. Man was already in authority over the woman before the Fall, but now she will have a tendency to rebel and try to rule him.[33]

The Man Must Exercise Biblical Authority

The New Testament also emphasizes the headship of the man within the context of marriage. Ephesians 5:22–24 presents the summary statement: "Wives, submit yourselves to your own husbands, as to the Lord. For the husband is head of the wife, as also Christ is head of the church; and He is the Savior of the body. Therefore, just as the church is subject to Christ, so let the wives be to their own husbands in everything." God's ordained role for leadership within marriage was established in the days of Adam and Eve, and it has not changed.

However, it must be again emphasized that this is leadership based on two principles. We shall not take them in order within the text but in the order of their instinctive roles.

Principle #1: A man must love his wife as he loves himself. Ephesians 5:28 states: "So husbands ought to love their own wives as their own bodies; he who loves his wife loves himself." Though this normally does work, some men do not foster a great love or respect for themselves. In those peculiar instances, this unproductive, even hostile attitude will almost inevitably be conveyed to his wife. Such an illicit mentality will inevitably lend itself to marital friction.

Therefore, Paul gave us an earlier and much superior principle. Principle #2: Husbands are to love their wives as Christ loved the

---

[33] Arnold Fruchtenbaum, Ariel's Bible Commentary; The Book of Genesis, p. 106.

Church and gave Himself for it. Ephesians 5:25 states: "Husbands, love your wives, just as Christ also loved the church and gave Himself for her." That is the ultimate sacrificial love. No higher example can be set. Within many cultures and marital relationships, such a command is breathtaking! It even sounds nonsensical and counterproductive to some distorted minds. It shatters the typical abrasive relationship often fostered between husband and wife.

How sadly ironic that many modern-day feminists completely ignore this biblical standard. It is largely because they have not been personal recipients of this godly love. Hence, they would rather fight than submit. They choose to ignore and even outright reject the pattern set by Christ to the Father. When a woman refuses to biblically submit to her husband's authority, his job of loving her becomes all the more difficult. In such a scenario, everyone loses.

Jesus Christ, our Creator and Redeemer, offered the greatest example of love possible. Obeying the eternal, God-ordained principles of biblical Christianity is the only faith that makes truly blessed relationships possible. It is true that no husband can actually fulfill this principle of love at the same level as Christ. Nonetheless, Paul presented this standard to the husband under the inspiration of the Holy Spirit. Both husband and wife must do their utmost in carrying out this engaging and blessed relationship called marriage. Additional principles are addressed in Ephesians 5:22–33. When these responsibilities are followed, a wonderful marital relationship is possible.

God's Curse on the Man (Genesis 3:17–19)

Just like the serpent and the woman, the man was also cursed. Genesis 3:17–19 states:

Then to Adam He said, "Because you have heeded the voice of your wife, and have eaten from the tree of which I commanded you, saying, 'You shall not eat of it, cursed is the ground for your sake; in toil you shall eat of it all the days of your life. Both thorns and thistles it shall bring forth for you, and you shall eat the herb of the field. In the sweat of your face you shall eat bread till you return to the ground, for out of it you were taken; for dust you are, and to dust you shall return.'"

Adam was also adversely affected by his sinful behavior. As previously stated, he actually stood more responsible before God since he was the federal head of humanity. Problem #1: He was accountable to God for not intervening on the behalf of his wife. He was standing right beside her and apparently did not assist her in the least. Problem #2: God accused him of listening to his wife's persuasive words. As the federal head, he was to lead, not to follow. In a military situation, the captain does not consult the private. The captain is to lead his soldiers into battle.

Problem #3: Adam ate the fruit with her. He should have been instructing and preventing her from indulging in her disobedience. On the contrary, he sinned alongside her. Instead of capably leading his wife, he was being led by her into spiritual captivity.

The further irony is that she was presented to him as his helpmate, but he, in turn, did not help her! This, of course, does not discount Eve's guilt, but Adam's overall culpability is much worse. He failed in his God-given responsibility. President Harry Truman placed a sign on his desk that he read every day, "The buck stops here!" The sign reminded him that he was ultimately responsible for all of the decisions made under his direct jurisdiction. That was doubly true for Adam.

Let the Punishment Fit the Crime!

We could summarize the entire situation as follows: The serpent was possessed. Eve was deceived. Adam disobeyed. Lucifer rejoiced!

Let us now reflect on the various curses directed toward Adam. It is important to remember that with the curses, we often find an accompanying blessing. God continuously shows His mercy and grace toward man in that way. Punishment #1: Adam would now have to work much harder to make a living (3:17). It should be noted that work itself is not a curse. But the earthly situation would now change and would not be for the better.

Adam, from the beginning, had been commanded to tend the garden (2:15). It probably was a relatively easy job, however, since no nasty "encumbrances" were constantly sprouting out of the soil. Furthermore, the fertility would have been fantastic. That amazing fertility would quickly change with the curse. Though the earth may have still given plentifully, there was a marked decline in productivity.

The "grace" part of this curse is that God originally had made man vocational in perspective. Adam undoubtedly was designed by God as vocational since he was responsible for caring for his family. Now, he must become even more so. But most men enjoy working as it gives them a sense of real purpose. Thus, God brought a blessing into the curse. Ironically, when men retire from work due to age or infirmity, they often suffer for it. A man's identity is frequently wrapped up in his work. Although many women also work outside the home, they are and will always remain much more relational than men. That is to the woman's great emotional advantage.

The Ground Is Temporarily Cursed

Punishment #2: The ground was cursed because of Adam's sin (3:17). This cursing of the ground is directed at Adam because he was created directly from the ground. Eve, by contrast, was taken from one of Adam's ribs. Men typically have a stronger affinity toward the soil in the normal vocational situations throughout history. But because of sin, the ground would no longer yield its full potential. It is impossible to know for certain how productive the ground was before sin.

Times, however, will change. God will not curse the earth forever. Amos 9:13 gives us a strong indication of what life will be like in the millennial kingdom of Christ:

"Behold, the days are coming," says the LORD,
"When the plowman shall overtake the reaper,
And the treader of grapes him who sows seed;
The mountains shall drip with sweet wine,
And all the hills shall flow with it."

In other words, the productivity of the land will be so immense that the reapers will still be harvesting their bonanza crop when the season for tilling the soil comes upon them. The mountains will be literally dripping with the excess grape juices from the overabundant grapevines. Such a beautiful agrarian picture inspires broad smiles from every farmer and gardener! Perhaps the millennial kingdom will once again equal the productivity level Adam and Eve were experiencing in the original creation.

Punishment #3: Weeds and thistles would spring up everywhere

(3:18). This decree tends to hamper those broad agrarian smiles. Every farmer and gardener experiences the never-ending battle with weeds. It is almost astonishing how hardy the weeds are in comparison to the normal crop or vegetables. Gardens and crops must be carefully tended; weeds take care of themselves quite brilliantly!

Ironically, even if there is no rain whatsoever, some kind of weed will almost always sprout and grow! (The writer grew up on the farm.) Weeds can be found in the driest of deserts and growing out of the rocks in the mountains with almost no soil whatsoever. Their roots, like the tenacious roots of sin, tunnel deeply into the soil.

Admittedly, one must be somewhat imaginative to see any possible blessing that might accompany this curse! Weeds are the scourge of mankind. Bread would now have to be earned by the sweat of the brow. Much of the previous joy of work was now replaced by drudgery and intensive labor. If weeds were even moderately thinking entities like animals (which they are not), they certainly could see the blessing in this curse. God made them next to impossible to kill! One blessing is that mankind can look forward to the restoration of God's beauty when Christ establishes His kingdom. The curse of weeds and thorns will not last forever!

Resurrection Morning Is Coming!

Punishment #4: Finally, from the ground, God created man, and to the ground, he would return in death (3:19). This once again emphasizes the curse of both spiritual and physical death. Although the physical death was definitely delayed for Adam, who lived 930 years, the spiritual death was immediate. He and his wife were separated from God and desperately needed reconciliation. Little could they have anticipated that unwelcome scenario.

That separation is true for all humanity. Only Christ can accomplish our reconciliation (Romans 5:8–11; 2 Corinthians 5:18–21). The blessing is, however, for the believer; there will be resurrection unto both spiritual and physical life. Tragically, for the unbeliever, there will be a resurrection unto a "double death," both spiritual and physical (Daniel 12:2; John 5:28–29). That can be avoided entirely simply by embracing the wonderful gift of eternal life. It is freely offered to anyone who will believe (John 5:24). But God will not compel a man to believe.

Death in the animal kingdom was physically more instant, however, as the following verses will reveal. The eating of the fruit proved a fateful day for humanity and the entire universe.

Regarding Adam's shame and guilt, C. H. Mackintosh writes:

> It was through the sustaining energy of faith that Adam was enabled to endure the terrible results of what he had done. It was God's wondrous mercy to allow him to hear what He said to the serpent, before he was called to listen to what He had to say to himself. Had it not been so, he must have been plunged in despair. It is despair to be called upon to look at myself without being able to look at God as revealed in the cross for my salvation.
>
> There is no child of fallen Adam who could bear to have his eyes opened to the reality of what he is and what he has done, without being plunged in despair, unless he could take refuge in the cross.[34]

---

[34] C. H. Mackintosh, Notes on the Pentateuch: Genesis to Deuteronomy (Neptune, NJ: Loizeaux Brothers, 1972), p. 35.

Sin Is Found Out!

How absolutely true Mackintosh's statement is. Thankfully, all believers can and have taken refuge in the Savior of the cross. God seems always ready to extend grace to His creatures. The promise of the Messiah came in the midst of their judgment. Adam and Eve were given immediate consolation in Genesis 3:15 that victory over Satan was coming. They undoubtedly expected the Messiah sooner than He actually arrived, but He eventually did come.

A Fitting Summary

Regarding this terrible story of the fall of man, Phillips offers this summary statement on the threefold curses:

> There was to be sorrow—sorrow centering in the area of a woman's greatest fulfillment, in the bringing forth and the bringing up of children. There was to be subservience. Sin would bring anguish in its train. The headship of the man, ordained of God in creation, would often be replaced by tyranny. More than ever a woman would need the protective covering provided by the headship of husband and home. …
>
> Death is a horrifying thing. Men mock it. They seek to rob it of its gruesomeness by embalming the dead and surrounding their coffins with garlands of flowers. But death is still death—the king of terrors, the last enemy, the final catastrophe this side of eternity—the ultimate wages of sin.[35]

---

35 John Phillips, Exploring Genesis, p. 62.

Corruption and Catastrophe

Lessons Learned in This Chapter

We first began this chapter with a look at God's questioning of the serpent, Eve, and Adam. God spoke to the serpent in language just as He did to the humans. Each one received a pronouncement of God's punishment on them. But with Eve and Adam, God also incorporated blessings within the curses. The primary blessing came on Eve, who had been deceived. As such, she was less culpable than her husband, Adam. God extended to Eve a wonderful promise.

Genesis 3:15 is the first and certainly one of the most famous prophecies in Scripture: "And I will put enmity between you and the woman, and between your seed and her Seed; He shall crush your head, and you shall bruise His heel." It must be noted that these two seeds are each in the singular. Satan's seed is the future Antichrist, who will be the most diabolical and evil man who will ever live. The second Seed is none other than Jesus Christ. He is born of the Virgin Mary, the most blessed of all women. He is the God-man.

Sadly, most translations of the following passage are not complete. We shall include the Greek article into the New King James Version, which is indeed in the original Greek. First Timothy 2:14–15 more precisely states the following: "And Adam was not deceived, but the woman being deceived, fell into transgression. Nevertheless she will be saved in [the] childbearing if they continue in faith, love, and holiness, with self-control."[36] What childbearing could this possibly refer to other than that of Jesus Christ? When you include the article "the," the passage makes perfect sense.

Galatians 4:16 provides further revelation of the Seed of the woman: "Now to Abraham and his Seed were the promises made. He does not say, 'And to seeds,' as of many, but as of one, 'And to your Seed,' who is Christ." The wicked seed of Satan shall meet

---
36 Hereinafter, brackets added for clarity.

his ultimate demise at the end of the Tribulation. He and his evil companion, the false prophet, will be defeated and cast alive into the Lake of Fire (Revelation 19:20).

Second, we examined the respective curses leveled against the participants in the world's first temptation. God will lift the respective curses on the serpent, Eve, and Adam in the millennial kingdom of Christ. Though the serpent will still crawl in the dust, it will no longer be harmful. In fact, the entire animal kingdom will become vegetarians and no longer consume one another. Peace, joy, and the knowledge of the Lord will characterize this 1,000-year period. Until that glorious time, man is destined to grovel in sin and despair.

In our next chapter, we shall witness the tragic exile of Adam and Eve from the Garden of Eden. They were forever banned from God's paradise on earth, which was specifically designed for them. However, through the atoning blood of Jesus Christ, mankind can be reconciled with His Creator. Jesus Christ died on the cross to provide salvation for all who would believe.

Though Adam and Eve did not understand everything about this coming Messiah, they clearly understood enough to put their faith in Him. That is the privilege of every man, woman, and child today as well. Salvation is offered to all who will receive it.

Cognitive Conundrum #4

A man of intemperance proved I in early years, acts of hypocrisy my conscience did sear. Pangs of remorse danced through my head; I buried loved ones who, by God's hand, were dead. Repentance entered my heart as time passed by. Prophecy would leave me spiritually high. My descendant left me thankful—that is certain; timely demise of said echoed by the curtain.

Who am I?

Answer: Judah

Chapter 5

Exiled from the Garden!

(Genesis 3:20-24)

In This Chapter

Objectives for This Chapter
Adam and Eve Are Exiled (3:20–24)
The Tree of Life
Lessons Learned in This Chapter

Objectives for This Chapter

In this chapter, we shall first examine three immediate consequences of the fall. Adam and Eve clearly had no comprehension of the impact of their disobedience. One of the first changes they observed was that they were naked. They had been naked since the sixth day of creation but suffered no embarrassment. That is inconceivable to mankind today. But no living mortal has ever experienced pure innocence. Only Adam and Eve enjoyed that privilege. When they lost their sinless perfection, they simultaneously gained guilt and shame.

God had mercy upon them and clothed them with animals he killed for that purpose. From that point on in human history, creatures have been used in a subservient role for the benefit of man. Prior to sin, every creature lived in complete independence. How? Every living creature's needs were met by a sovereign and gracious God. Sin erased that provision to a significant degree and brought dependence into the world. It also brought carnivorous appetites into the animal kingdom.

Adam and Eve were driven out of the Garden. The reason for this was twofold. First, this unquestionably was a disciplinary action taken by God. Since they had abused their incredible privileges and exchanged them for transgression, they needed to be punished. This principle of punishment and retribution became the norm in human relations from that point forward.

Second, and more important, they could no longer eat of the tree of life. It is possible that they had never eaten of this unique tree. Scripture does not comment on that. But after sin upset everything, they were entirely forbidden to consume its fruit. If they had, they would have lived forever in their sin-defiled bodies. God spared them from that fate.

In our second item of discussion, we shall examine the tree of life to our limited ability. Little is known of this tree save that it offered eternal physical life. Once God removed Adam and Eve from the Garden, He also transplanted the tree of life up into heaven. It will be available for all believers who enter into eternity with God (Revelation chapters 21 and 22). Clearly, this tree's amazing power is granted by divine providence. It could have no supernatural power on its own. God chose to place it in the Garden, possibly to reinforce the blessings He had bestowed upon humanity. Sin tragically forfeited that blessing.

Adam and Eve Exiled (3:20–24)

The penalties for sin could not possibly be anticipated by the world's first young couple. Adam and Eve opened up Pandora's box in a way that defied the imagination. Mankind has been corporately suffering pain and anguish ever since. Mankind's sin opened a gulf between God and man, which seems unbridgeable. Indeed, it is uncrossable save for the atoning sacrifice of our Lord and Savior, Jesus Christ. He is the way, the truth, and the life. When an individual avails himself of His grace, all transgressions can be forgiven and reconciliation made complete.

Three Immediate Results of the Fall

Genesis 3:20–24 relates the story of Adam naming Eve and their unfortunate expulsion from the Garden of Eden:

> And Adam called his wife's name Eve, because she was the mother of all living.
>
> Also for Adam and his wife the Lord God made tunics of skin, and clothed them.
>
> Then the Lord God said, "Behold, the man has become like one of Us, to know good and evil. And now, lest he put out his hand and take also of the tree of life, and eat, and live forever"—therefore the Lord God sent him out of the garden of Eden to till the ground from which he was taken. So He drove out the man; and He placed cherubim at the east of the garden of Eden, and a flaming sword which turned every way, to guard the way to the tree of life.

Adam Gives Eve Her Name

Result #1: Adam named his wife Eve. Why is this important? First, it demonstrated his headship over her. The husband is to lead the wife and children in family relations. That is his assigned task by God. Adam had not exercised that headship, which included an umbrella of protection, with any distinction during the temptation. In a word, he failed his wife badly. One must at least acknowledge that there is no biblical record of his intervention in that scenario. Absent of a sinful nature, it is difficult to imagine Eve resisting her husband's loving directions. But Adam at least now availed himself of his divinely appointed prerogatives.

Lest one be overly judgmental against Adam; however, it must be acknowledged that he had no idea of what sin truly was or of its consequences. He also was deceived by its allurement, though he would not have understood why. Having received God's command from God Himself, he stands as the more culpable. In our modern age, we approach this moral dilemma from experience and historical knowledge. Neither Adam nor Eve had these benefits.

Second, Adam's naming of his wife was a demonstration of his faith in the messianic promise of Genesis 3:15. They understood that a Messiah was to come. That Messiah would be the promised Seed. As demonstrated in Genesis 4:1, they anticipated that a child who would be the Messiah would be born almost immediately. In fact, they thought that Cain, the first son born, was indeed that Messiah.

They were not mistaken in their theology, but they certainly were mistaken in their timing and in the manner in which this child would be born. It would be a virgin birth. However, Adam and Eve did not have the benefit of the Old and New Testaments to study these matters, as do we today. Though he and Eve could not comprehend all of the ramifications of Genesis 3:15 at this time, Adam showed his stalwart faith in God's promise. It becomes clear that Eve equally shared his belief.

Of course, no one truly understood the outworking of God's

plan of salvation for mankind until Christ came and revealed Himself. Even then, it was not until after Christ's resurrection from the dead that His sacrificial atonement became clear. Indeed, Christ's twelve apostles did not understand the full truth until after Christ rose from the dead. Their understanding of these matters was hidden from them until the time of God's choosing.

Fruchtenbaum offers the following explanation over the significance of Eve's name:

> Verses 20-24 describe three results of the Fall. The first result is in verse 20, the naming of Eve: The man called his wife's name Eve, in Hebrew, Chavah. Before the Fall, she was merely called "Woman," isha (2:23), but now she is to be called Chavah, which means "life."
>
> Chavah, which comes from the Hebrew word chayah, means "to live." The Hebrew word for living here is chai, from the same root chayah, "to live." The man gave her the name, and this was his first exercise of lordship over Eve after the Fall, since he had the authority to name her.
>
> The fact that he called her "life" shows Adam's faith in the promise of the Seed in verse 15. The reason he called her Chavah or Eve was because she was the mother of all living. ... The word was is in the perfect tense, although Eve had not as yet produced. This is the common prophetic perfect, a common element in the Hebrew language. This shows that the command to populate the earth had not been withdrawn.[37]

---
37 Arnold G. Fruchtenbaum, The Book of Genesis: Exposition from a Messianic Jewish Perspective, pp. 109–110.

Death No Longer Takes a Holiday

Result #2: God killed some animal or animals to provide physical coverings for Adam and Eve. This was the first time they experienced physical death in their now sin-defiled world. It is not certain whether Adam and Eve watched the killing of the creatures, but they knew what had happened. Something had to die because of their sins. God then graciously covered them with the skins He fashioned for them. Little did they know how bloodshed and death would become the normal pattern of human history.

Mankind would do far more than kill animals for coverings. They soon became specialists at killing each other. The first murder happened between their first two sons. What never-ending tragedies sin has ushered into the world of man! The encroachment of sin reared its ugly head in mankind with the fall. Life then changed for the worse from that point. Only when Christ reigns in His millennial kingdom will there be improvement. Even then, however, sin will still be present. Rebellion will be tightly controlled, but it will be present.

Only when God comes to live with man in permanent fashion will life be completely transformed (Revelation chapters 21 and 22). Then, all believers will be freed entirely from the presence of sin. All believers yearn for that glorious day that is coming. Finally and fully, believers from all ages will rejoice without interference in their God.

Fruchtenbaum offers the following comments:

> The lessons to be drawn from this verse are as follows. First, to approach God, one must have a proper covering. Second, the man-made covering was not acceptable. Third, God Himself must provide the covering.

Fourth, the proper covering required the shedding of blood. Fifth, God's grace provided for them, for the covering was given before the actual expulsion from the Garden.[38]

Adam and Eve Are Exiled from the Garden

Result #3: Adam and Eve were driven from the Garden of Eden. The reason given for this is found in verse 22: "Then the LORD God said, 'Behold, the man has become like one of Us, to know good and evil. And now, lest he put out his hand and take also of the tree of life, and eat, and live forever.'" Yes, Adam and Eve now experientially knew good and evil. They got their wish, but not in the way they had imagined.

Furthermore, their wish decidedly did not coincide with or parallel God's knowledge. God does not know evil experientially, nor shall He ever know it in this sense. He is beyond evil and any form of temptation. He decrees what is evil. Adam and Eve found out, to their great chagrin, that they now understood good and evil, but they could not master their newfound acquisition of this evil. It mastered them! Indeed, it has been mastering mankind ever since.

God drove them out of the garden to till the ground from which he, Adam, had been taken. The difference was that the ground was now cursed. Adam would find this out the hard way through intensive labor. Their expulsion certainly proved a dramatic and frightening experience. Two fascinating "guards" were appointed to watch the entrance to the garden.

Two Unusual Guards

---
[38] Ibid., p. 110.

The first guard was a cherub, which appeared and ushered them out of the garden. Just seeing the cherubim was undoubtedly terrifying. Next to Lucifer, the cherubim were among the highest order of created beings. They are frequently associated with the divine glory (Isaiah 37:16; Ezekiel 10:1).

The three highest categories of angels would seem to be in this order: (1) Michael, the archangel and protector of Israel (Daniel 12:1; Jude 9); (2) the cherubim who served as the protectors of God's glory (Exodus 25:22; Ezekiel 10:2–22); (3) the seraphim who proclaimed God's glory (Isaiah 6:1–3, 6). This would seem to be the first time Adam and Eve had ever experienced such an angelic visitation. Angels can appear incredible in appearance, particularly cherubim.

The second guard was a flaming sword that turned every way. It does not appear that the sword was being held by the cherubim. Adam and Eve were driven out to keep them from the tree of life. If they had eaten of it after the fall, they would have physically lived forever in their sinful state. As it stands today, only through death or the Rapture or the second coming of Christ can individuals be delivered from this present life and directly into heavenly glory.

Another possible instance of instantaneous transformation may be the 144,000 witnesses of Revelation. That scenario is debated among scholars. Thus, the only two exceptions to the rule of death so far have been Enoch and Elijah. The general rule is summed up in Hebrews 9:27: "And as it is appointed for me to die once, but after this the judgment."

The Tree of Life

Question: When did God remove the tree of life from the garden? Scripture does not say. Some speculate that it remained until the Flood. That does not seem at all likely. However, there is no way of knowing for certain. Scholars debate the identity and function of the tree of life. We see the tree of life resurface in the eternal state. Revelation 22:2 states: "In the middle of its street, and on either side of the river, was the tree of life, which bore twelve fruits, each tree yielding its fruit every month. The leaves of the tree were for the healing of the nations."

What Is the Tree of Life?

This issue has produced a considerable amount of discussion over the years. In essence, the tree of life remains something of a mystery. As seen above, it once again becomes prominent in the eternal state. Until then, man can only ponder its complete significance. In this present discussion, we shall employ the comments of two highly capable scholars. Their comments, though far from complete, do offer insights for the benefit of all.

H. C. Leupold writes as follows:

> At the same time, there is one very necessary step that must be taken before this episode of the Fall is completely adjusted, and that is, man must be completely shut off from access to "the tree of life." About the purpose of this tree we learn only from its name and from the remark here made in reference to it. It had the power to impart imperishable physical life – for the plain statement of the case is that had man eaten, he would have "lived forever."

But since, to the best of our knowledge, no tree of itself can possess such virtue, it seems best again with Luther to assume that this remarkable power was characteristic of the power of the Word of God, who was pleased to ordain that such should be the effect of partaking of the fruit of this tree. For man in his fallen and sadly altered state the acquisition of the quality of imperishability for this sin-torn and sin-defaced body would have been a grievous calamity.

He would never have been able to "shuffle off this mortal coil." Christ's work of restoration would have been precluded, where He "changes this body of humiliation that it may be fashioned like unto His glorious body, according to the working whereby He is able even to subdue all things unto Himself" (Phil. 3:21).[39]

God Spared Adam and Eve from a Grievous Fate

Indeed, being shackled permanently to a sin-stricken body would decidedly have been a fate worse than death. To the believer, death, although not generally welcomed, is nonetheless the ultimate liberty from the presence of sin. Though even believers often fear the unknown, it is the known beyond the unknown that fosters great hope. The unknown is physical death. The known is eternal life. In our present existence, of course, eternal life is a belief. We cannot demonstrate it empirically. But we can nonetheless take comfort in its anticipation.

This great optimism is illuminated in Romans 8:24–25: "For we

---

39 H. C. Leupold, Exposition of Genesis: Volume 1: Chapters 1–19, pp. 181–182.

were saved in this hope, but hope that is seen is not hope; for why does one still hope for what he sees? But if we hope for what we do not see, we eagerly wait for it with perseverance."

In spite of their sin, God did not stop loving Adam and Eve. He immediately provided for them clothing, forgiveness, and a promised Savior. In fact, He allowed for this Savior, the Seed of the woman, to be brought into the world by the female. She had first brought sin into the world. God, in His great mercy and compassion, would eventually allow the woman to bring the Savior into the world as well.

An important aspect of God's love was to spare Adam and Eve from living forever in their present, sin-defiled bodies. He thus forbade them to eat of the tree of life. It must be remembered that this tree was not forbidden before the fall into sin. It is entirely possible that they had been eating of its fruit already. Scripture does not address this.

But once sin entered into the picture, new and frightening developments emerged. The power of granting physical life was not excised from the tree of life. It still apparently retains this capacity in its eternal state. Due to the God-endowed nature of this tree, its physical presence must be removed. This was accomplished initially by exiling Adam and Eve from the Garden. Man was not designed to live in a carnal, fleshly state for all time. How long it remained in the Garden after their expulsion is not revealed.

A New Testament Glimpse at the Tree of Life

John Walvoord adds the following comments:

> The tree of life seems to have reference to a similar tree in the Garden of Eden (Gen. 3:22, 24). Its character is

revealed in Genesis 3:22 as being such that if Adam and Eve had eaten of the tree of life, physical death would have been an impossibility.

The tree in the new Jerusalem seems to have a similar quality and a similar intent, and though it is difficult to determine where the literal and the symbolic should be distinguished, the tree is represented as bearing fruit every month which apparently can be eaten, though the text does not say so and also to provide leaves described as "for the healing of the nations."

... The word for 'healing" is therapeian, from which the English word therapeutic is derived, almost directly transliterated from the Greek. Rather than specifically meaning "healing," it should be understood as "health-giving," as the word in its root meaning has the idea of serving or ministering. In other words, the leaves of the tree promote the enjoyment of life in the new Jerusalem, and are not for correcting ills which do not exist. This, of course, is confirmed by the fact that there is no more curse as indicated in verse 3.[40]

Spiritual Realities from Genesis Chapter 3

Genesis chapter 3 is arguably the saddest passage in all of Scripture. It introduces the moral fallibility of a fallen mankind. By stunning contrast, Genesis chapters 1 and 2 convey the extraordinary story of God's creation. He formed everything to be perfectly suited

---
40 John Walvoord, The Revelation of Jesus Christ (Chicago, IL: Moody Press, 1966), p. 330.

for life for man and animal alike. The phenomenal original creation was perfection itself. Yet, in spite of that, sin crept into the near ruin of God's gracious provision.

But as alluded to before, God's grace can triumph over all of hell's fury. Along with the punishment for sin came the wherewithal for forgiveness. This atoning endowment was not free; it cost God His eternal Son's death on the cross. But it was followed by His all-victorious resurrection.

Leupold offers the following comments on Genesis chapter 3:

> We leave this chapter with a sigh over the glory that was lost and with deep regret over the loss of man's original innocence. There is no chapter in the Scriptures that more effectively reveals the source of all evil that is in the world; and so it becomes a very helpful chapter for the man that is ready to accept its truth.[41]

Indeed, without accepting and bowing to its truth, salvation is not possible. A cohesive understanding of life's genuine meaning is impossible without this biblical knowledge.

One must acknowledge his sin, or it will not be forgiven. Some are so spiritually blinded that they refuse to even recognize that they are sinners. But 1 John 1:8–10 clearly states: "If we say that we have no sin, we deceive ourselves, and the truth is not in us. If we confess our sins, He is faithful and just to forgive us our sins and to cleanse us from all unrighteousness. If we say that we have not sinned, we make Him a liar, and His word is not in us."

---

41 H. C. Leupold, Exposition of Genesis: Volume 1: Chapters 1–19, p. 185.

Mankind Desperately Needs the Shepherd

Isaiah 53:6 also summarizes the sinful plight of every man, woman, and child: "All we like sheep have gone astray; we have turned, every one, to his own way; and the LORD has laid on Him the iniquity of us all." Sheep are defenseless and not particularly intelligent animals. If they do not have a shepherd or protector, such as a sheepdog or a human, they are highly vulnerable to predators. Christ offers spiritual protection for every man, woman, and child.

Christ is the great Shepherd. Ezekiel 34:12 states: "As a shepherd seeks out his flock on the day he is among his scattered sheep, so will I seek out My sheep and deliver them from all the places where they were scattered on a cloudy and dark day." That earnestly seeking heart of the earthly shepherd characterizes that of the heavenly Shepherd as well. God never tires in His ongoing search for reconciliation to mankind, His most special creation.

Christ is not only our willing Shepherd. He came to pay for the sins of man. He offers spiritual life (John 10:10). Sadly, man often stubbornly refuses this astounding gift of forgiveness. Christ took upon Himself the sins of an entire world (John 1:29). Only the God-man could fulfill the exacting standards of a holy God. Yet, many people simply yawn and turn away. Though salvation is free to man, it is often just left lying on the table, so to speak.

Mankind all too frequently praises itself for its great accomplishments. Self is elevated; God is ignored! Wayward mankind is frequently fixated on the created, not on the Creator. Science has become king over the One who created the laws of science. It is certainly true that technological advances have benefited man in countless ways. God has endowed man with phenomenal intelligence. But man all too often forgets that his abilities come from his Creator.

Who Created Thinking?

God-granted intelligence in itself should demonstrate the foolishness of mindless evolution. How can brainless evolution give birth to brainy people? The two are antithetical to each other. The greatest scientists, indeed, not even the mediocre ones, do not follow the directionless and haphazard methodology of evolution in their own private research. They employ proven scientific methods and laws. This includes all atheistic, evolutionary scientists.

Why should they behave so? If they desire to receive government grants for demonstrable progress in their area of research, they have no alternative. Is this not a tacit acknowledgment of the systematic organization of information? Does this not point to a divine Designer who orchestrated the universe, especially life? While they gleefully deny the Creator's existence, they enthusiastically employ His divinely created laws. Without those laws, research would be impossible. Do they not see the inconsistency in their methods? Apparently not!

If evolution is true, why bother with research at all? Should not everything be just left up to time and chance? One small example may suffice: Would any government employ military-industrial giants to build the next generation of fighter jets that used evolutionary principles? We certainly hope not. It is our assessment that such a corporation would soon go out of business. To complicate matters even more, such a government and its hapless citizens would immediately become vulnerable to enemy encroachment or outright attack.

Evolution is an empty shell, a blank slate, a godless philosophy entirely void of all common sense or empirical reality. To believe in evolution is to cast one's fate to the wind and to despise all provable empirical realities. It is anything but science!

The Miracle of Modern Travel: An Accident?

One demonstration of man's intelligence, which was benevolently granted to him by God, is modern transportation. Travel around the world has become a relatively simple matter today. To fly halfway around the globe in a modern airplane has become a commonplace. Ancient man could not even begin to imagine the remarkable scientific breakthroughs man has accomplished. Now, a person can circle the entire planet in ninety minutes if traveling in a spaceship.

Though admittedly a debated interpretation, Daniel 12:4 possibly hints of these advances: "But you, Daniel, shut up the words, and seal the book until the time of the end; many shall run to and fro, and knowledge shall increase." Times have indeed changed. Mankind has even left the solar system with some of its spaceships. Remarkable advances in space exploration shall probably increase exponentially for the foreseeable future. The glory and creative acts of God discovered have proven stunning indeed through this impressive research and exploration.

Tragically, in a moral sense, mankind, in general, has not improved one bit. We remain in the same morally degraded state. Wars continue to erupt across the globe, crime continues to escalate, abortion snuffs out the lives of millions, and sexual sins destroy the lives of countless victims. Mankind lost its way in the Garden of Eden and has ever since largely remained so. God's counsel and His warnings often go unheeded. Though He stretches out His hand in compassion every day, mankind generally refuses to take it.

In the context of appealing to Israel, Isaiah 65:1–2 speaks of God's compassion:

"I was sought by those who did not ask for Me; I was

found by those who did not seek Me. I said, 'Here I am, here I am,' to a nation that was not called by My name. I have stretched out My hands all day long to a rebellious people, who walk in a way that is not good, according to their own thoughts" (cf. Romans 10:20–21).

God sought out man from the beginning. That is evidenced by His calling out for Adam and Eve while walking in the garden (Genesis 3:9). He continues to seek mankind out today through His eternal Son and Holy Spirit. His love for His creation never falters. But it must be remembered that though God loves the sinner, He hates the sin. He must punish unrepentant sinners to fulfill His perfect justice. People tend to forget that God is just and perfect in all His attributes. Hence, He must punish willful, unrepentant sinners.

A Concluding Thought

Warren Wiersbe summarizes chapter 3 with these sobering thoughts:

> Daily life would now become a struggle for the man and woman outside the garden as they toiled for their bread and raised their family. They could still have fellowship with God, but they would daily suffer the consequences of their sin, and so would their descendants after them. The law of sin and death would now operate in the human family until the end of time, but the death and resurrection of the Savior would introduce a new law; "For the law of the Spirit of life in Christ Jesus has made me free from the law of sin and death" (Rom. 8:2, NKJV).[42]

---
42 Warren Wiersbe, The Bible Exposition Commentary; Old Testament: Genesis-Deuteronomy (Wheaton, IL: Victor Books, 2001), p. 34.

It is in this new law of the Spirit of life in Christ Jesus that believing men and women rejoice. We need not fear the valley of the shadow of death. It is a momentary passage that is over instantaneously. As was once stated in a famous movie: "Death is only the beginning." The movie certainly did not have the context correct spiritually, but the statement was true.

Death is not the end. Indeed, it ushers in eternity for us who have previously been time-bound. For the believer, this represents a glorious eternity in Paradise with God. For the unbeliever, it sadly represents an eternity in condemnation (John 5:28–29). Our prayer is that every individual reading this treatise will bend their knees in fervent worship of our Creator God.

Lessons Learned in This Chapter

In this chapter, we first reviewed the forlorn fact that sin has entered into the world through the disobedience of Adam and Eve. It brought about immediate changes. Earlier in this book, we emphasized that the battle of the sexes was one of the more unfortunate revisions in life that took place. A sometimes uneasy truce has frequently replaced a pure love and fellowship between husband and wife. Still, God's grace does make a marvelous relationship possible even today, though it requires more diligence and patience.

A demonstration of Adam's headship was mentioned in the sense that he named his wife Eve. The one who names another thus demonstrates their authority over the other individual. But it also reminds the reader that Adam failed in his earlier responsibilities of protecting his wife from the serpent. Still, neither Adam nor Eve possessed a suspicious nature. Hence, they were easily persuaded by Satan's mistruths. When Adam named Eve the mother of all living, it represented his belief in the coming Messiah. Eve shared with him in that sincere belief and hope.

The consequence of their disobedience revealed their sin in a sudden and embarrassing manner. They realized that they were both naked. Though this had been true all along, sin, in a true sense, uncovered not just their conscience but their eyes as well. Clothing became necessary. At least one creature had to die for their transgression to provide this clothing. This was their first taste with the ugliness and finality of death. Sadly, it was just the beginning.

Second, we discussed the fact that Adam and Eve were driven out of the Garden of Eden. This was necessary so they would understand that sin brought unpleasant consequences. Even more importantly, however, it was so they could not eat of the tree of life. Originally, only the tree of the knowledge of good and evil had been forbidden to them. It is entirely possible that they had been eating from the tree of life all along. But now that sin had entered into the picture, it was instantly prohibited.

God had granted the tree of life the supernatural quality of granting eternal physical human life to anyone who ate of it. Before sin disrupted everything that posed no problem whatsoever. But to eat of this tree after sin would have caused Adam and Eve to live forever in their sin-besmirched bodies. That would have proven a terrible fate.

Scripture reveals precious little information about the tree of life. We examined the comments of two highly respected scholars on the subject. Beyond what they said, little more can be put forth. Genesis chapter 3 is indeed a sad chapter for humanity. Sin entered into the world. Sin requires payment. Not just any payment will suffice. Only Christ, the Son of God, can provide perfect and necessary atonement.

Third, we closed with an examination of the need for a spiritual Shepherd. That Shepherd is none other than Jesus Christ. Only through His shed blood on the cross can that payment be made. John 10:11 reiterates this truth: "I am the good shepherd. The good shepherd gives His life for the sheep."

Jesus made the following truism possible: "Genuine worship is not possible without free will." If Adam and Eve had no such possibility as disobedience, neither could they have ever experienced the choice of free and living worship. They would have been highly preprogrammed robots. Though we may grieve over the consequences elucidated in Genesis chapter 3, we may rejoice in the promise of Genesis 3:15. Provision for forgiveness was immediately brought to the forefront by our loving God.

In our next chapter, we shall see the tragic murder of Abel by Cain. Adam and Eve undoubtedly mourned many times over their eating of the fruit. This mourning, however, was just the beginning. How much more reprehensible Cain's actions must have proven to them. From the age of innocence, man descends ever deeper into the age of alienation from God. Thankfully, God continues to reach out and rescue many from the fire.

We close this chapter with these wise words of counsel from Jude 20–23:

> But you, beloved, building yourselves up on your most holy faith, praying in the Holy Spirit, keep yourselves in the love of God, looking for the mercy of our Lord Jesus Christ unto eternal life. And on some have compassion, making a distinction; but others save with fear, pulling them out of the fire, hating even the garment defiled by the flesh.

Cognitive Conundrum #5

Enthusiastic was I for the royal reign; my ministry and rule I did proudly proclaim. Detractors connived and against me did plot, but to their opinions gave I little thought. Jezebel proved a model of temperance for me; I followed her designs with additional glee. A relative and a priest sought my undoing; my treachery was ended by sword with rejoicing.

Who am I?

Answer: the imposter Queen Athaliah (2 Kings chapter 11)

Chapter 6

A Case of Mistaken Identity

(Genesis 4:1–2a)

In This Chapter

Objectives for This Chapter
The Birth of the Brothers (4:1–2a)
A Backward Glimpse at the Future
Lessons Learned in This Chapter

Objectives for This Chapter

In this chapter, we shall first review the birth of Cain and Abel. Based on Genesis 3:15, Adam and Eve were clearly expecting the Messiah to be their firstborn child. Hence, Eve mistakenly believed that she had given birth to the Lord (Genesis 4:1). Her theology of giving birth to the Messiah was correct, but her timing was wrong. Nor was she the woman chosen for this unparalleled privilege.

Neither Adam nor Eve understood that for a sinless Messiah to be born, the Seed must be implanted by the Holy Spirit. If that were not the case, Adam would have passed on his sinful nature to the Messiah. That obviously could not be allowed. One cannot produce the divine from the carnal. It must be emphasized that the sinful nature is passed on through the man, not through the woman. Adam and Eve were not blessed to possess the full picture that God's complete revelation grants to believers today. That explains their historical confusion.

The wicked Cain turned out to be anything but the Lord. Indeed, he permanently shall be remembered as a notorious figure for murdering his righteous brother Abel. Fratricide is one of the most reprehensible sins imaginable. Cain brought untold grief to his parents. We shall discuss in more detail this horrendous sin of jealousy and homicide in our ensuing chapter.

Second, we shall take a glimpse of both future and past simultaneously. The past lays the groundwork for the future. The future helps believers to more fully comprehend the past. Even the apostles understood relatively little about Christ's purpose on life until after His resurrection. It was only then that their eyes were opened to a greater clarity of eternal and redemptive truth.

The culminating book for the New Testament is Revelation. It was penned approximately sixty years after Christ's ascension to heaven. Believers sometimes ponder why God took so long to issue His entire Word to mankind. To that natural inquiry, we do not venture to respond. We are not privy to all of God's reasoning. We simply rest assured that God's ways are always the best. The primary issue is how one presently utilizes the complete Word of God in his possession, not how long it took to be written. May that be the concerted focus of all believers everywhere.

The Birth of the Brothers

Genesis chapter 4, although not as negative as chapter 3, still presents material that weighs heavily on the heart. Cain, the first child born into humanity, committed the first murder. Cain was quite an inauspicious beginning for the human race. To make the crime even more heinous, Cain murdered his own blood brother, Abel. Complicating matters further, Cain manifested no degree of penitence. We shall examine this ugly scenario in more detail in our following chapter.

Like his parents, Cain futilely tried to conceal his transgression from the Lord. That tendency has manifested itself with every human being since Adam and Eve. Why? Men love evil actions but do not want fair retribution. Jesus makes that abundantly clear in John 3:19–21. Men attempt to hide from God, fruitless, though that may be because their deeds are evil. But God sees and knows all (Hebrews 4:13).

The Birth of Cain and Its Accompanying Confusion

Genesis 4:1–2a introduces the births of the first two brothers: "Now Adam knew Eve his wife, and she conceived and bore Cain, and said, 'I have acquired a man from the LORD.' Then she bore again, this time his brother Abel." To "know" is a euphemism for sexual intercourse. This euphemism is used in other passages as well.

As one can see from the New King James Version, in verse 1b, the translation is: "I have acquired a man from the LORD." We feel it incumbent to notify the reader that verse 1 is not generally translated literally by English translators. That is unfortunate because it changes the meaning of the text quite markedly!

The Hebrew literally reads, "I have gotten a man; YHWH." The English translation likewise should read, "I have gotten a man; the Lord." There is no "from" in the Hebrew. Reformer Martin Luther translates it in literal fashion: "I have received a man, namely, Jehovah." This is not difficult to translate from Hebrew. It is quite straightforward to even beginning students of Hebrew.

The reason for the mistranslation is that Eve was mistaken in her claim. But Eve's mistake certainly does not give license to modify the straightforward Hebrew translation. The Scripture frequently records the mistakes of individuals in the Bible just as they were stated or as believed by them. This just happens to be one of the first biblical examples of a mistaken statement or viewpoint. Man is fallible, and thus, frequently are his beliefs.

If our readers recall, Eve was also mistaken in what God said about the tree of the knowledge of good and evil. Her conversation with the serpent bears that out. In Genesis 4:1, the less-than-literal translation hides an important biblical truth. Indeed, it is almost entirely lost upon the general reader. That is most unfortunate.

The reality is that Eve thought she had given birth to the God-man, the Messiah. Was this an unrealistic expectation on her part? No, it was not. As it most dreadfully turned out in the course of life, Cain decidedly was not who she thought he would be. However, her mistake nonetheless reflects an accurate belief.

A Case of Correct Theology but Wrong Timing

Eve was not wrong in her understanding that a promised Messiah was coming. This was clearly forecast in Genesis 3:15. Indeed, Eve was absolutely correct. As mentioned before, Adam's naming his wife as he did testified to his belief that she would become the mother of all living. Within that act of naming Eve was the recognition of the promised Seed (Genesis 3:15). But neither Adam nor Eve could have understood all the unrevealed details.

Revelation is progressive. None of the Scripture had been written and would not be for another 2,550 years. People often envision some of the Old Testament saints meditating on God's Word. It is easy to envision Enoch holding a Bible in one hand and prophesying of future events. Would not Noah have read Scripture condemning the sins of those errant unbelievers surrounding him?

And what of Abraham? Did he not pass many an evening studying God's Word? The answer is "no" on all accounts. No Scripture was penned until the days of Moses, counterintuitive though that may seem to the modern reader. Although the Pentateuch cannot be precisely dated, it must have been completed by Moses' death in 1450 BC.

In the days of Moses, God spoke face-to-face with His servant. Only Moses experienced such an intimate relationship with God (Numbers 12:6–8). What a privilege was his. However, in eternity, all believers will be so blessed, astonishing as that may be to contemplate (Revelation chapters 21 to 22). In a way far exceeding our imaginations, God will dwell with man.

We are not aware of all the ways in which God communicated to man in the days before Moses. Obviously, He used visions, dreams, and even personal appearances with Adam and Eve. Only the first couple were ever privileged to experience such blissful and sin-free fellowship with their Creator. God walked and talked with them in the Garden of Eden.

Tragically, all of this changed after they fell into sin. If God did, on occasion, walk in the Garden with them after sin, it is not mentioned in Scripture. It is impossible to imagine the sense of profound loss Adam and Eve felt over this disruption of pure fellowship. The young couple did understand, however, that a Redeemer was coming. God had lovingly promised them this in the midst of His pronouncement of judgment.

In doing so, God set a profound example on how humans should likewise interact with each other. Encouragement, followed by punishment, followed by encouragement, demonstrates love and a desire for reconciliation. One does well to practice such a loving pattern in his or her walk of life. The encouragement they received is recorded in Genesis 3:15: a Redeemer was coming. Adam and

Eve assumed that they would be the parents of that Redeemer, the coming Messiah. In that optimistic viewpoint, however, they were mistaken.

Eve erred on at least two counts:

Eve's First Mistake

Mistake #1: Eve's timing was premature. The Messiah would not appear until 4,000 years later. But who could possibly have anticipated that? Isaiah confirmed her correct belief in the coming Messiah approximately 3,250 years later. Clearly, a great deal of time elapsed before this fuller revelation became available. But even then, precious few people, if any at all, considered that the Messiah might come in two advents. The church age was a mystery unrevealed in the Old Testament. God used Paul to clarify His purposes regarding the Church.

Isaiah 9:6–7 proclaims the wonderful news of Christ's birth and reign. The reader should observe that Isaiah deals with both the first and second advents of Christ in this most singular passage. Zechariah 9:9–10 and Luke 1:31–33 present other examples of both the first and second advents being shown back to back. Isaiah 61:1–2a also contrasts Christ's first coming with His second in the remainder of the chapter.

This admittedly sometimes makes interpreting prophecy difficult. One does not naturally separate such close verses into two distinct events. But that is precisely what God did in the Scriptures. The student of Scripture must observe closely what is being said. He must also cross-reference quite extensively to garner a more complete understanding of such passages. The God-man was indeed coming, but only in God's perfect timing. God is eternal and is not to be rushed! He, unlike man, is not bound by time.

Christ's first coming was to serve and provide salvation for mankind. Luke 19:10 states: "For the Son of Man has come to seek and to save that which was lost" (cf. Mark 10:45). Christ's second coming will be to reign as King of kings and Lord of lords. Zechariah 14:9 proclaims: "And the Lord shall be King over all the earth, in that day it shall be—'The Lord is one, and His name one'" (cf. Titus 2:13; Revelation 11:15).

Application: What does this mean for the average believer? God will reveal His will in His own perfect timing. His chosen children are responsible for complying with the revelation granted to them. In the Old Testament, this revelation was far from complete. Nonetheless, it was sufficient. God never leaves His children floundering in frustration. This does not mean, however, that He is required to cater to our every whim and curiosity. It is the privilege of God's spiritually adopted sons and daughters to live and thrive by faith (Romans 4:20–21; Hebrews 11:6). May we do so with enthusiasm and rejoicing.

A Fuller Picture of the Promised Messiah

Isaiah 9:6–7 declares:

> For unto us a Child is born, unto us a Son is given; and the government will be upon His shoulder. And His name will be called Wonderful, Counselor, Mighty God, Everlasting Father, Prince of Peace. Of the increase of His government and peace, there will be no end, upon the throne of David and over His kingdom, from that time forward, even forever. The zeal of the Lord of hosts will perform this (cf. Zechariah 9:9–10).

As already mentioned, the first part of these two verses refers clearly to Christ being born as a baby. It was the highest hope and dream of every godly Jewish woman to give birth to the anticipated Messiah. Mary was blessed to be chosen from eternity and among all womanhood for this unique privilege. This same noble wish was also shared by Eve. But Eve, like the later Jewish women, did not know the timing of this grand event.

Mary, the Mother of Jesus, Would Suffer Grievously

What young Jewish women probably did not anticipate was what Simeon prophesied to Mary, mother of Jesus, in Luke 2:35: "Yes, a sword will pierce through your own soul also, that the thoughts of many hearts may be revealed." We say "probably" because Isaiah chapter 53, though generally misunderstood by the Jewish people, spoke quite specifically of the Messiah.

If the Jews had interpreted this passage properly, it would have been widely known that the Messiah would suffer grievously. The Jews, however, were fixated on a military Messiah, not a suffering One. They wanted someone to overthrow the hated Roman government. Most Jewish citizens could not and did not get beyond that obsession of hatred.

A moment for introspection: Hatred is an evil characteristic. It is the sign of an unbeliever. First John 3:13–15 offers sound counsel on this matter:

> Do not marvel, my brethren, if the world hates you. We know that we have passed from death to life, because we love the brethren. He who does not love his brother abides in death. Whoever hates his brother is a murderer, and you know that no murderer has eternal life abiding in him.

A Case of Mistaken Identity

Clearly, this signified the spiritual status of most Israelites during the days of Jesus. Their hatred blinded them to the Messiah who stood right in their midst.

Returning to Mary: Mary truly is the most blessed of all women, but she also endured great emotional distress in her life. This mother's love for her glorious Son, Jesus, moved her in a heart-riveting fashion. Indeed, Mary experienced every extreme of emotions, from deep distress to overwhelming joy. Her Son was the long-awaited Messiah, but only a few anticipated His immediate destiny. He was reviled, condemned, crucified, and then rose again.

It is likely that only a precious few actually envisioned the Messiah's initial destiny in His first advent. Those who may have understood partially, such as Simeon (Luke 2:34–35), would not have understood the entire picture. This was a mystery understood only by the triune God.

Years later, Mary stood at the foot of the cross, watching the nerve-shattering death throes of her beloved Son. Her heart ached with overwhelming sorrow, and the tears flooded unchecked down her cheeks. Her body shook with uncontrollable agony over her Son's horrible yet inevitable and preordained fate. Every fiber of her being shuddered with pain over her holy Son, Jesus. Short of the eternal love of God, no mortal's love can exceed that of a godly mother's.

She undoubtedly felt like she was dying with Him and would have gladly died in His place over and over again. But Mary was not able to pay for mankind's sins. Only the God-man could do that. Payment for mankind's sins required the highest price possible. God Himself had to make that payment. That momentous decision was made back in the unsearchable eons of eternity. Mankind's unrelenting sins demanded an eternal and "priceless" payment of blood. All believers should weep with Mary.

The meaning of Isaiah chapter 53, which speaks of Christ's suffering, seemed so implausible that the Jewish rabbis assumed it referred to someone other than the Messiah. As noted, only a select few contemporaries of Jesus, such as Simeon, John the Baptist, and possibly Anna, understood that the Messiah must suffer.

The Holy Spirit revealed this knowledge to them. Otherwise, it made no sense whatsoever in the minds of Jewish believers. Their eyes were veiled to Scripture's full meaning. But Christ did indeed come to suffer and die for the sins of humanity. This was the plan from eternity past. God's price for creating humanity was enormous beyond comprehension.

Two Advents, One Savior

Christ is coming to earth in two distinct advents. The Jews certainly did not anticipate that. But it was because of their lack of belief that this was necessary. Advent #1: Christ came as a baby 2,000 years ago. Scripture records this miraculous event in a beautiful fashion. A star in the east led the way to His birthplace.

This star, incidentally, is best thought to be a special and unique reflection of God's Shekinah glory. It clearly was not a literal star. It stood directly over the house where the young Christ child lay wrapped in swaddling clothes (Matthew 2:9). If a literal star did that, not only would the young family have been incinerated, but the entire planet would have been burned into ashes.

Advent #2: Christ will return as the indisputable King of kings and Lord of lords (Isaiah 63:1–6; Zechariah 14:3–9; Revelation 1:7, 19:16). It is at His second advent that He sets up His millennial kingdom. For this 1,000-year reign of Christ, joy, peace, and the knowledge of the Lord will be evident throughout the entire globe

(Habakkuk 2:14). Indeed, all nations shall flock to Jerusalem to hear the word of the Lord from Jesus Christ Himself (Isaiah 2:2–4; Zechariah 8:2–3, 20–23, 14:16–21).

Zechariah 9:9–10 elegantly clarifies the two separate advents:

> "Rejoice greatly, O daughter of Zion! Shout, O daughter of Jerusalem! Behold, your King is coming to you: He is just and having salvation, lowly and riding on a donkey, a colt, the foal of a donkey. I will cut off the chariot from Ephraim and the horse from Jerusalem; the battle bow shall be cut off. He shall speak peace to the nations; His dominion shall be 'from sea to sea, and from the River to the ends of the earth'" (cf. Luke 1:31–33).

Verse 9 clearly speaks of the day Christ entered into Jerusalem and was proclaimed King. This is commonly known as Palm Sunday. Tragically, He was rejected by the populace. This was, of course, all within God's sovereign plan (Acts 2:22–24). Verse 10 refers to Christ's eventual reign in His millennial kingdom. He returns to the earth victorious and establishes Himself as King of kings and Lord of lords (Revelation 19:11–21). All believers from every age yearn for this wondrous time.

It should be noted that Israel will no longer have to defend herself or make war (Isaiah 2:4). Joel 3:20–21 presents this fabulous promise to Judah: "But Judah shall abide forever; and Jerusalem from generation to generation. For I will acquit them of the guilt of bloodshed, who I had not acquitted; for the LORD dwells in Zion." The reader should note that Israel and Judah will be reestablished as one nation at this time (cf. Ezekiel 37:15–28). Christ will establish His sovereign peace. The millennial kingdom, although not perfect, will be a time of unparalleled peace and of God's knowledge.

A Backward Glimpse at the Future

In order to have a clear picture of the past, it is sometimes advisable to peer into the future. Scripture presents a broad panorama of earth's entire history. It begins at the creation of the universe and its first couple, expands on to their immediate family and all human descendants, and extends all the way into eternity. The complete picture is necessary for clarity's sake. Hence, we shall delve for a moment into future events to assist in our explanation of the past.

We have already recognized that Christ comes to earth in two distinct advents. The first advent is past; the second is yet coming. We shall invest some time in exploring the two aspects of Christ's second coming. It consists of two phases: (1) the Rapture of the Church and (2) His glorious return to establish His kingdom at the end of the Tribulation.

Simultaneously, we shall take a backward glance at Adam and Eve regarding the coming Messiah. Everything makes perfect sense when one has the entire biblical revelation in front of him. Adam and Eve did not have that enlightening advantage. The modern-day believer does have the complete revelation of God available to him. But to garner a thorough understanding, the believer must apply himself to a systematic study of the Bible.

The First Phase: Christ Raptures the Church

As we have already noted, Christ's second advent will take place in two phases. His first phase will be as the believers' holy Deliverer from an unjust, sin-sickened world. This particular view to be presented represents what is called the Pre-tribulation, premillennial perspective. It is generally referred to as the Rapture. This means, in short, that we believe the Church will be removed from the earth before the Tribulation begins (1 Thessalonians 4:13–18; Revelation 3:10).

Some have accused adherents of this viewpoint of shameful escapism. Nothing could be further from the truth. We hold to this position because, in our view, it best represents the teaching of Scripture. When one considers the many distinctions between the Rapture and the second coming of Christ, the evidence speaks for itself.

We shall mention just one. In Matthew 24:36, Jesus states the following: "But of that day and hour no one knows, not even the angels of heaven, but My Father only." Jesus is speaking in reference to the Rapture. The timing of the Rapture is a secret known only to the triune God. Those who seek to identify a specific date should not be heeded.

The Midpoint of the Tribulation

Let us now couple Matthew 24:36 with Christ's second coming to establish His millennial kingdom. Satan and his minions are cast out of heaven for the last time at the midpoint of the seven-year Tribulation. Revelation 12:12–14 summarizes this momentous occasion, although one needs to read the entire context of Revelation chapter 12 for the full picture.

Revelation 12:12–14 states:

> Therefore rejoice, O heavens, and you who dwell in them! Woe to the inhabitants of the earth and the sea! For the devil has come down to you, having great wrath, because he knows that he has a short time. Now

when the dragon saw that he had been cast to the earth, he persecuted the woman who had gave birth to the male Child. But the woman was given two wings of a great eagle, that she might fly into the wilderness to her place, where she is nourished for a time and times and half a time, from the presence of the serpent.

This means there are 1,260 days or three-and-a-half years or forty-two months or a time, times, and half a time remaining for the second half of the Tribulation. The Bible uses all four descriptions to describe the second half of the Tribulation.

There are 1,260 days remaining for the tortures of the Tribulation to unfold. On the final day of this horrible time, Christ will return to deliver the believing individuals remaining in the world (Hosea 5:15–6:3; Zechariah 12:10–13:1, 8–9; Revelation 1:7). These particular believers will never have to pass through the dark valley of the shadow of death (Psalm 23:4). Remarkably, these surviving children of God will be able to pinpoint exactly when their Messiah will arrive. They only need to count down the days. That is quite a marked contrast to Matthew 24:36. When He returns, Christ will rescue these surviving saints from the evil hands of the Antichrist and the false prophet.

Elaboration on Phase #1

Phase #1: Christ will return in the air at the Rapture to rescue His Church from the impending Tribulation. His feet do not even touch the ground in this first return (1 Thessalonians 4:13–18). All believers of the church age, both dead and living, will, at that point, be translated directly into heaven. Those who are alive at the Rapture will never have to pass through the portals of death. They will be spared that journey of trepidation, brief though it may be.

A lesser-known fact to many believers is that the Rapture does not directly initiate the Tribulation. This is not to deny that the two events could coincide, but it seems rather unlikely. It is true that the Tribulation must follow within a reasonably short time of perhaps a few years or even less (Daniel 9:24–27). We shall discuss the beginning of the Tribulation momentarily. Let it be said, however, that the Rapture will cause an astounding upheaval around the world. "Where did all those people go?" will be the question of the day.

Many who formerly knew the gospel but did not respond will instantly recognize the folly of their delay. Undoubtedly, a huge number of such people will trust in Christ immediately. Many will be martyred for their faith (Revelation 13:7). The Holy Spirit will stop restraining wickedness to the degree He presently does. That in itself will create chaos.

But this does not mean that He will not stop convicting men of sin (2 Thessalonians 2:6–7). If the Holy Spirit did not continue to convict mankind, no one could come to faith in Christ (John 16:8–11). Unregenerate man has no capacity to seek after God on his own. God must first seek him (Genesis 3:9; Romans 3:10–12).

After the Rapture, unimaginable immorality will explode all over the globe. In the context of the Tribulation, Jesus lamented in Matthew 24:12: "And because lawlessness will abound, the love of many will grow cold." Families will be fractured, communities divided, and nations will crumble into anarchy. These horrendous circumstances will definitely set the stage for the Antichrist's rise to power. Somehow, the Antichrist will explain the absence of so many people. He shall successfully persuade most. Spiritual discernment by the masses will have largely evaporated.

A further motivation to follow the Antichrist: People will crave an iron hand that can bring peace. Fear of brutality by others will push people to accept any ruler who can bring back law and order. The Antichrist will be brilliantly successful at convincing the masses that he is just the man to do that. His motto almost certainly will parallel Neville Chamberlain's haunting and historically inaccurate cry: "Peace in our time!" His godless ally, the false prophet, will play the same supportive role that Joseph Goebbels did for Adolf Hitler. Coupled with a godless and ever-supportive media, most people will believe their repugnant lies.

A World without the Church

The influence of the Church will be missing for the first time in 2,000 years. Still, through the ongoing witness of the Holy Spirit in people's lives, an immense and diverse multitude will come to faith in Christ during this time. Countless individuals will become believers (Revelation 6:9–11, 7:9–17). The world will witness an unequaled revival. The gospel will be spread as never before throughout the entire globe (11:1–13, 14:6–7). God will provide many witnesses to His eternal glory and gracious offer of salvation.

Many of these new believers will lose their lives as martyrs for Christ. But what better way to die is there than to die for Christ? He, after all, first died for us (1 Peter 2:23–24). Though the world will be at its darkest since the days of Noah, Christ's light will shine brightest in those perilous times (2 Timothy 3:1–5).

Romans 8:32–34 brings great comfort to every believer:

> He who did not spare His own Son, but delivered Him up for us all, how shall He not with Him also freely give us all things? Who shall bring a charge against God's elect? It is God who justifies. Who is he who condemns? It is Christ who died, and furthermore is

also risen, who is even at the right hand of God, who also makes intercession for us.

The Beginning of the Tribulation

The signing of a treaty between the as-of-yet-unknown Antichrist and the nation of Israel will begin the Tribulation (Daniel 9:24–27). Israel certainly would not knowingly sign an agreement with the worst man in history if they were aware of his true identity. This infamous treaty signals the beginning of the seven-year Tribulation period.

For the first three and a half years, the Antichrist will be Israel's primary protector. It is partly because of his guardianship that Israel can dwell securely. Though they are capable of significant military strength, which in itself cannot make them secure, they are and will still be surrounded by fierce enemies. Though the Israelis are a formidable and extremely capable people blessed by God, they have a major vulnerability.

What is that vulnerability? It is a lack of faith in their Messiah, Jesus Christ. As a nation, only a tiny minority of Jews worship the Lord Jesus Christ. Before Christ returns as their divine Messiah, however, they shall all worship Him.

Since the rebirth of the nation in May 1948, Israel's very existence has stood in constant peril, humanly speaking. The nation's rebirth foreshadows amazing prophecies to come. The hundreds of prophecies regarding Israel cannot be fulfilled if they are not an actual nation. Hence, 1948 is truly a banner year regarding the fulfillment of many future biblical prophecies. To simply allegorize these hundreds of prophecies regarding Israel is an inexcusable abuse of written Scripture.

The Church and Israel Are Two Distinct Entities

A biblical axiom to remember: The Church has not replaced Israel. The Church actually receives its spiritual blessings as a "junior partner" of Israel, so to speak. The Abrahamic covenant of Genesis 12:1–3, though given primarily to Abraham, included all of his spiritual descendants. Those spiritual descendants came through David and then Jesus Christ.

All Jewish and Gentile believers are Abraham's spiritual descendants (Galatians 3:14, 28–29). They are also all adopted members of the Church. All Jews are Abraham's physical descendants, but that does not make them spiritual descendants (Romans 9:6–8, 30–33). The unbelieving Jews of Jesus' day rejected His statements regarding that precise issue (John 8:39–44). Jesus identified their father as not Abraham but the devil. He could not have insulted them in greater fashion than this.

Spiritual application:

All believers would profit greatly by immersing themselves in the study of biblical prophecy (2 Timothy 2:15). It is one of the most educational and encouraging arenas of personal spiritual development possible. It is also exceedingly useful for evangelism. God has provided a blueprint for the future literally thousands of years in advance. How much of an excuse do believers have for not familiarizing themselves with God's blueprint for the future? None! If prophecy were not so important, why would God have included it in Holy Writ? A full 28 percent of the Bible was prophetic when written.

Romans 15:4 reminds believers of the benefit for systematic study of God's Word: "For whatever things were written before were written for our learning, that we through the patience and comfort of the Scriptures might have hope." It is our fervent desire that all believers will focus much more intently on the wonderful promises God grants to His people through prophecy. That includes both Jewish and Gentile believers.

The Future Evil Plots of the Nations against Israel

Ezekiel 38:10–12 describes the thoughts and evil plans concocted by Israel's future enemies:

> Thus says the LORD GOD: "On that day it shall come to pass that thoughts will arise in your mind, and you will make an evil plan: You will say, 'I will go up against a land of unwalled villages; I will go to a peaceful people, who dwell safely, all of them dwelling without walls, and having neither bars nor gates'—to take plunder and to take booty, to stretch out your hand against the waste places that are again inhabited, and against a people gathered from the nations, who have acquired livestock and goods, who dwell in the midst of the land."

By great contrast to the first half of the Tribulation, for the final three and a half years, the Antichrist becomes Israel's primary persecutor. Revelation 12:17 summarizes the Antichrist's zeal to destroy both Israel and God's spiritually adopted children: "And the dragon was enraged with the woman, and he went to make war with the rest of her offspring, who keep the commandments of God and have the testimony of Jesus Christ" (cf. Revelation 12:1–3).

The woman represents the nation of Israel. The offspring represents both Jewish and Gentile believers in Christ. The Antichrist and his evil cohorts shall find out, to their eternal dismay, that one cannot fight God and win. Every single individual in his wicked army shall perish at the hands of God and the Jewish people. By God's providential care, Israel shall be triumphant!

No one will know the Antichrist's true identity for certain until the midpoint of the Tribulation. Undoubtedly, many will suspect who he is. But it is only when the Antichrist invades the Tribulation temple, proclaims himself as God, and demands worship that he can truly be identified. Satan will also be worshiped along with the Antichrist. The false prophet, who is the Antichrist's right-hand man, promotes the worship of both.

The Second Phase: Christ Returns as Judge

Phase #2: Christ returns as the all-conquering Judge. When Christ returns to reign, He defeats the Antichrist and his evil forces, settles upon the earth, judges the wicked (Matthew 25:31–46), and establishes His millennial kingdom (Revelation 19:11–21). All believers look forward to that day. It reflects Christ's comment that the believer's redemption draws nigh. All believers shall return from heaven with Christ (Jude 14–15).

Titus 2:13 states: "Looking for the blessed hope and glorious appearing of our great God and Savior Jesus Christ." There has been some controversy over the centuries regarding the identity of the Person(s) in this passage. Are there two being referred to or just one? We believe there is just one Person, that of Jesus Christ. That means that Christ is definitively identified as God, hence part of the triune God.

John MacArthur offers the following comments:

A Case of Mistaken Identity

Our great God and Savior is one of the many plain declarations in Scripture of the deity of Jesus Christ (see, e.g., John 1:1-18; Rom. 9:5; Heb. 1:1-3). Some interpreters hold that in this passage God and Savior refer to different beings, the first (great God) to the divine Father and the second (Savior) to the human Son, Christ Jesus.

But that explanation has several insurmountable problems. Besides the other clear affirmations of the divinity of Christ in Scripture are several grammatical reasons found in this passage itself.

First, there is but one definite article (the, tou), which indicates the singularity and identity of God and Savior. Second, both of the singular pronouns in the following verse ("who," hos; and "Himself," heauton) refer back to a single person. And, although the Old Testament makes countless references to God the Father as great, in the New Testament that description is used only of God the Son (see, e.g., Matt. 5:35; Luke 1:32; 7:16; Heb. 10:21; 13:20). Perhaps most importantly, the New Testament nowhere speaks of the appearing or Second Coming of God the Father but only of the Son.[43]

---

43 John MacArthur, The MacArthur New Testament Commentary: Titus (Chicago; Moody Press, 1996), pp. 120–121.

Eve's Second Mistake

Mistake #2: Eve did not realize that the Holy Spirit must provide the Seed to the mother of the Messiah. No earthly father, namely Adam or Joseph, could be involved in the sexual process of fathering the holy Messiah. If either man had been involved, he would have passed on his sinful nature to the Messiah. As the federal head of humanity, the evil nature passes on through the man, not the woman. To keep the Messiah pure, He must not have an earthly father, though He can and did have an earthly mother.

Sarfati alludes to Martin Luther's interpretation of this rather surprising statement by Eve:

> Gen. 4:1—The words of Eve, "I have the Man, the Lord" [In his commentary, Luther translates, "I have gotten a Man of the Lord," that is the Redeemer. In his Bible Luther translates more correctly, "I have the Man, the Lord."—Mueller] supply another reason why she did not call Cain a son. In her great joy and reverence she did not want to call her offspring a son, for she believed that he was to be much more, the Man who was to bruise the serpent's head. Therefore she called him "the Man, the Lord."
>
> She thought that he [Cain] was the one whom the Lord had meant when He said, "Thy Seed shall bruise the serpent's head." Though Eve was mistaken in her hope, her words show that she was a pious woman who believed the promise of the coming salvation by the blessed Saviour. Therefore she did not call him a son,

but the Man, the Lord, whom God promised and gave [to her]. Her faith in the promised seed was laudable.

By faith in this promised Saviour all saints [in the OT] were justified and saved. But her faith that Cain was the one who would end the misery of sin was misplaced, for this she believed without a definite sign and Word [from God] by her own conviction.

Just because she was so sure of the promise that she regarded her first son as the one who would carry out what the Lord had promised. Her mistake was that she did not know that from [sinful] flesh nothing could be born but (sinful) flesh, and that sin and death could not be overcome by flesh [corrupt nature].[44]

Genesis 4:1 must be translated properly to understand the theology behind it. Eve was correct in her understanding that a Messiah figure, a God-man, was coming. She simply misidentified who He would be. Knowing that she and her husband had sinned against the Lord, she naturally desired forgiveness and reconciliation to the fullest extent possible.

She assumed, erroneously, that her firstborn child would be that God-man. Thus, the young couple awaited the birth of Cain with great enthusiasm. What a shattering disappointment that proved to be for her and Adam. Instead of being their anticipated Messiah figure, Cain eventually became his own brother's murderer!

It probably did not take long for Adam and Eve to understand their premature expectation had not been fulfilled. One can safely

---
[44] Jonathan Sarfati, The Genesis Account: A theological, historical, and scientific commentary on Genesis 1–11, pp. 408–409.

assume that Cain's later unbridled behavior manifested itself in his younger years. One does not generally become a cold-blooded murderer overnight. Such unbridled mischief in the heart takes time to develop. It must fester and molder over the years.

The proper translation of Genesis 4:1 accentuates the necessity of honoring Christ's statement in Matthew 5:17–18: "Do not think that I came to destroy the Law or the Prophets, I did not come to destroy but to fulfill. For assuredly, I say to you till heaven and earth pass away, one jot or one tittle will by no means pass from the law till all is fulfilled." Certainly, Genesis 3:15 is included in that promise.

Louis A. Barbieri offers the following explanation of Jesus' statement:

> Jesus' fulfillment would extend to the smallest Hebrew letter, the "jot" (lit., yod), and even to the smallest stroke of a Hebrew letter, the "tittle." In English a jot would correspond to the dot above the letter "I" (and look like an apostrophe), and a tittle would be seen in the difference between a "P" and an "R". The small angled line that completes the "R" is like a tittle. These things are important because letters make up words and even a slight change in a letter might change the meaning of a word.[45]

The Birth of Abel

It is not possible to discern how long Eve lived under her mistaken impression regarding Cain. Cain was obviously born with a

---
45 Louis A. Barbieri, The Bible Knowledge Commentary: Matthew, John F. Walvoord and Roy B. Zuck, Roy B., eds. (Wheaton, IL: Victor Books, 1983), p. 30.

sinful nature fully intact. Adam and Eve had sinned before Eve became pregnant. If they had not sinned, they could not have passed the sinful nature on to Cain. Adam and Eve's sinless state probably lasted a lamentably short time in the Garden.

Lucifer, having rebelled against God, would quite instinctively have proceeded to the earth to tempt Adam and Eve. His evil nature craved the opportunity to lead them also into sin. Strange as it may sound, he had to have God's permission to do his diabolical deed. But such a temptation regarding the forbidden fruit was necessary for genuine worship. As discussed previously, there is no way of knowing when Lucifer fell into sin. From the description of Isaiah 14:12–15, it appears to have been long before the creation of the physical universe.

Lucifer was jealous of God. He wanted to replace God, ridiculous though that may be. But that is how twisted his mind became because of sin. It is also likely that he was envious of Adam and Eve's special relationship with God. He knew and envied the fact that he was not created in the image of God, powerful though he was.

Eve named her second son "Abel," which has the primary meaning of "breath." But it also means "vanity." This name is a rather peculiar one, at least from a westerner's perspective. It is exactly the same word used in the none-too-cheerful passage of Ecclesiastes 1:2: "'Vanity of vanities,' says the Preacher; 'Vanity of vanities, all is vanity.'"

If one interprets Abel by its primary meaning, "breath," as opposed to its secondary meaning, "vanity," it may be understood that life is fleeting like a breath. It is conjecture to affirm that this name was prophetic of Abel's life being cut short, thus like the proverbial "vapor" in James 4:14. However, that is precisely how Abel's life would turn out. If God did indeed give Eve prophetic insight, Scripture does not mention it. But this unusual name, being a mere coincidence, does seem rather doubtful.

Trouble in Paradise Once Removed

The first family on earth did not fare too well. Though created directly by God, Adam and Eve fell into sin in tragically short order. They unwittingly brought the entire future human race down with them. Years later, their eldest son would murder his younger brother, thereby enhancing the wickedness of the inhabitants of earth immeasurably.

Jeremiah 17:9 reiterates the theme of the ongoing evil tendencies of man's heart: "The heart is deceitful above all things, and desperately wicked; who can know it?" For the first sin, Eve was deceived by an outside source, the serpent. Adam sinned with much greater knowledge. But now, man needs no outside source of temptation. His own heart deceives and beguiles him into sin. With glorious exceptions in the millennial kingdom, that pattern shall relentlessly continue until eternity for mankind commences (Revelation chapters 21 to 22).

It has often been observed that the Bible is a book that could not have been written by man without the superintendence of the Holy Spirit. How true that is! The Bible demonstrates a divine hand. Its mysteries and prophesies are impossible utterances if left to man's own knowledge or "educated guesses." The fact that no prophecy has ever "fallen to the ground" is evidence by itself of the Bible's divine origin. No book on earth has ever been penned like it, nor shall there ever be one. Only God's words are eternal (Matthew 24:35). Believers can take great comfort in the omniscience and sovereignty of our everlasting God.

A Case of Mistaken Identity

One can also safely say that the Bible would not have been written by men because it reveals too much of his wicked nature. It hides or conceals nothing from the prying eyes and morbid interests of others. Clearly, it is the work of the Holy Spirit operating through men. Otherwise, what committee of men and women would have included Cain's murder of his brother Abel? Surely, this tragic affair would have been "swept under the rug" by prideful humanity. But God always declares the truth in all its completeness.

God Is Always in Control

Warren Wiersbe comments as follows:

Genesis is a "family book" and has a good deal to say about brothers. Being the firstborn son, Cain was special, but because of his sin, he lost everything and Seth took his place (Gen. 4:25). Ishmael was Abraham's firstborn, but God bypassed him and chose Isaac. Esau was Isaac's firstborn son, but he was rejected for Jacob; and Jacob's firstborn son Reuben was replaced by Joseph's two sons (Gen. 49:3-4; 1 Chron. 5:1-2).

In fact, God even rearranged the birth order of Joseph's sons (Gen. 48:8-22). Throughout Old Testament history, God's sovereignty is displayed in His choices of those who receive His blessing, for all that we receive is because of God's grace.

Sibling rivalry among brothers is another theme in Genesis. Ishmael persecuted Isaac; Jacob left home so

Esau couldn't kill him; and Joseph's brothers intended to kill him but decided to sell him as a slave. When sin entered the human race, it gave us dysfunctional and fractured families, and only the Lord can put families together again.[46]

Following up on that thought, we recognize that Judah, the fourth son, ultimately became the Seed son in Jacob's family. Genesis 49:10 states: "The scepter shall not depart from Judah, nor a lawgiver from between his feet, until Shiloh comes; and to Him shall be the obedience of the people." Shiloh refers to the coming Messiah. Oddly enough, down the entire line of the patriarchs, not even one firstborn son became the prominent or Seed son through whom the Messiah would eventually come. This shows that God is always in control, not man.

The New Testament Summation

Going back to the days of Abraham, Paul writes the following summation in Romans 9:6–13:

> But it is not that the word of God has taken no effect. For they are not all Israel who are of Israel, nor are they all children because they are the seed of Abraham; but, "In Isaac your seed shall be called." That is, those who are the children of the flesh, these are not the children of God; but the children of the promise are counted as the seed. For this is the word of promise: "At this time I will come and Sarah shall have a son."

---

46 Wiersbe, Warren. The Bible Exposition Commentary: Old Testament: Genesis-Deuteronomy, p. 36.

And not only this, but when Rebecca also had conceived by one man, even by our father Isaac (for the children not yet being born, nor having done any good or evil, that the purpose of God according to election might stand, not of works but of him who calls), it was said to her, "The older shall serve the younger." As it is written, "Jacob I have loved, but Esau I have hated."

Tim LaHaye and Ed Hindson offer the following excellent comments on this passage:

> When God gave the prophecies about His program to the patriarch Abraham (Genesis 12:1-3), He later showed that the promises would not be for all of his descendants. The promises were for the line of Isaac (Romans 9:7, 9) and not Ishmael (Genesis 17:15-19), through Jacob (Romans 9:10-12; Genesis 25:23) and not Esau, Jacob's older twin (Romans 9:23; Genesis 25:33-34).
>
> God drew the boundaries of His covenant line and passed it along to whom He pleased. Not all Jews who are "the children of the flesh" are "children of God," but only those whom the Lord called in order to work out His plan.
>
> Paul revealed God's choices concerning Esau and Jacob when he wrote, "Though the twins were not yet born and had not done anything good or bad, so that God's purpose according to His choice would stand,

[God elected Jacob over Esau] not because of works, but because of Him who calls" (Romans 9:11).

God has a right to reject sinners from His plans. Esau, the first of the twins out of Rebekah's womb, as a grown man, "despised his birthright" and gave it to his brother Jacob (Genesis 25:34). This is why the Lord later said, "Jacob I loved, but, Esau I hated" (Malachi 2:1; Romans 9:12). No one can fully explain this. Though people are held responsible for the choices they make, still, God's mysterious plans and purposes in various people's lives defy human understanding.[47]

Lessons Learned in This Chapter

In this chapter, we noted the birth of the first two sons. We saw that Genesis 4:1 should be translated more literally than most English translations do. Based on the Hebrew, this passage conveys that Eve thought she had given birth to the promised Messiah. She was mistaken both on the timing of the Messiah's birth and the fatherhood thereof. Christ can have an earthly mother but not an earthly father. The father passes on the sinful nature to the children. The mother is spared of that ignominy even though she is sinful herself.

Cain turned out to be a truly wicked individual. As we shall see in our following chapter, he murdered his more righteous brother, Abel. The murder was premeditated and senseless. Cain simply needed to rectify his behavior in line with God's previous revelation regarding sacrifices. He adamantly refused to do so and instead spilled his brother's innocent blood on the ground.

---

47 Tim LaHaye and Ed Hindson, The Popular Bible Prophecy Commentary (Eugene, OR: Harvest House Publishers, 2006), p. 396.

Second, we discussed more details regarding the coming Messiah. Though Adam and Eve were not historically privy to God's complete revelation, we are blessed with its fullness today. Their eager expectation of the coming Messiah was in accordance with the limited revelation they possessed. We ventured into some detail regarding future events predicted in Scripture. As becomes quite evident, the past is key to the future, and the future unlocks the past. The entirety of Scripture unveils what was previously hidden to man's prying eyes and searching hearts.

We also discussed the fact that Christ's coming was in two separate advents. He first arrived on earth 2,000 years ago as a baby. His first advent was to provide salvation for a spiritually desperate world. Sadly, most spurn His painful crucifixion and glorious resurrection. His return will be as the King of kings and Lord of lords (Revelation 19:16). The second coming will be divided into two phases. First, Christ returns for His Church at the Rapture (1 Thessalonians 4:13–18). Second, He returns to establish His millennial kingdom.

At the time of His second advent, all the earth will acknowledge Him as the true God of eternity. Those who have rejected Him, however, will be put to death and thrown into hell (Matthew 25:31–46). Following that judgment, Christ establishes His millennial kingdom. Unbelievably, in spite of all the evidence of Christ's deity and His glorious rule, many will rebel even during the millennial kingdom.

Third, we included a fascinating quote by Warren Wiersbe concerning how the promised Seed descended through the patriarchal family. Not even in one instance was the first child born to any patriarchal family granted the honor of being the promised Seed son. This shows how God is in control of all human events. The ultimate Seed, the Messiah, would come from the tribe of Judah. They will always be the most blessed of the twelve tribes. A quotation from LaHaye and Hindson amplified the biblical reality of Wiersbe's previous comments.

In our next chapter, we shall examine in more detail the repugnant story of Cain's murderous assault on Abel. It qualifies as one of the most sordid events in all of human history. Scripture never hides or covers up the truth. That in itself is strong evidence of its divine authorship.

A Case of Mistaken Identity

Cognitive Conundrum #6

Of royal heritage, I proved quite unworthy; my reign was short and admirable as scurvy. If rings were in my future, I would have no luck; I tried to no avail to pass the sinful buck. But God knows all truth to my great distress; my reign of evil would end in harsh duress. My future in David's line ended so abruptly, yet my final days were not too bad as I did see.

Who am I?

Answer: Jeconiah (2 Kings 25:27–30; Jeremiah 22:24–30)

Chapter 7

The World's First Murder

(Genesis 4:1–17)

In This Chapter

Objectives for This Chapter
The Brothers' Sacrifices to God (Genesis 4:1–7)
Cain Murders Abel (4:8–10)
Cain Is Judged and Banished from God's Presence (4:11–17)
Lessons Learned in This Chapter

Objectives for This Chapter

In this chapter, we shall first examine the sacrifices that Cain and Abel offered to God. Though the details of the biblical account are relatively few, several distinctions between their sacrifices can be enumerated.

Three of the primary qualifications in this instance were as follows: (1) If this was a sacrifice for sin, it required the shedding of blood. (2) The sacrifice must be of the firstfruits: in other words, the very first and best. (3) It must be offered in faith. A sacrifice without all three of these qualifications fell short of God's expectation. Abel faithfully followed the requirements, but Cain decidedly did not.

Second, we shall review the disheartening account of Cain rising up against Abel and murdering him. This appears to be an act of premeditation, which makes it all the more repugnant. God questioned Cain about what he had done. Not only did Cain foolishly deny the murder, but he did so with an impudent spirit. Did Cain really believe he could deceive the Creator?

Even if Cain did know better, and it seems highly likely that he did, the elders of Israel 3,500 years later did not. Ezekiel 8:12 reports this remorseful situation:

> Then He said to me, "Son of man, have you seen what the elders of the house of Israel do in the dark, every man in the room of his idols? For they say, 'The LORD does not see us, the LORD has forsaken the land.'"

Perpetual, unrepentant sin blinds man to the most obvious of spiritual realities. How could God be omniscient and not know what His chosen nation was doing?

Third, we shall discuss God's sentence upon Cain for his horrible homicide. It becomes evident that even in the midst of Cain's judgment, mercy is exercised by God. Cain is physically marked by God so others might not attack him. Cain did not want the same treatment measured against him that he had viciously taken against his righteous brother Abel. Cain was also driven away from the ground's productivity. This curse seemed to be directed toward Cain alone.

Cain left the land and dwelt in Nod. He placed himself into self-exile from God. Though he claimed that his punishment was more than could be borne, that was far from the truth. If Cain had repented, he could have been forgiven. But Cain did not manifest the slightest remorse over his heinous actions. He truly was a despicable person. Although Cain deserved the death sentence, God instead imposed what was, in essence, a "living death sentence" upon him. For the remainder of his life, Cain apparently lived largely in isolation from most, but not all, of his family.

The Brothers' Sacrifices to God (Genesis 4:1–5)

Genesis 4:1–5 records the sacrifices brothers Cain and Abel man brought to the Lord:

> Now Adam knew his wife and she conceived and bore Cain, and said, "I have acquired a man from the LORD." Then she bore again, this time his brother Abel. Now Abel was a keeper of sheep, but Cain was a tiller of the ground; and in the process of time it came to pass that Cain brought an offering of the fruit of the ground to the LORD. Abel also brought of the firstborn of his flock and of their fat. And the LORD respected Abel and his offering, but He did not respect Cain and his offering. And Cain was very angry, and his countenance fell.

In our previous chapter, we discussed the fact that Eve thought she had given birth to the predicted Messiah. Hence, a more literal translation of verse 1 is that she said, "I have acquired a man, the LORD." She and Adam were soon enough convinced that Cain was anything but the Lord. His genuine character undoubtedly manifested itself relatively soon in his early childhood years. Adam and Eve's theology was correct: the Messiah was to be born into the world. A Redeemer was needed to purchase the price of sins. Their timing, however, was premature.

Our text mentions nothing of the early childhoods of either Cain or Abel. We begin with an incident of their offering sacrifices to the Lord as fully grown adults. Was this the first time they had ever offered a sacrifice? Scripture does not address that question. Undue speculation as to their knowledge of sacrifices is thus unprofitable.

However, it should be relatively safe to assume that God, or

Adam, had granted them sufficient instructions so they knew which types of sacrifices were acceptable and which were not. If that had not been the case, how could Cain have been faulted or Abel praised?

A Brief Examination of the Sacrifices

Question: Why did God not accept Cain's offering? Certainly, being a tiller of the soil was not a dishonorable profession. Indeed, God had commanded his father, Adam, to till the soil. That was mankind's first vocation. So, nothing was wrong with Cain's agricultural background. Indeed, after the earth was cursed, it became mandatory to grow food.

Furthermore, God did accept grain offerings in the days of the nation Israel and the wilderness wanderings. So grain offerings in themselves were not wrong, at least not in Moses' time and certainly not afterwards. Again, however, one must exercise caution in taking principles from Moses' time 2,500 years later and attempting to shoehorn them into Cain and Abel's time.

The immediate context in Genesis chapter 4 itself does not provide many clues as to why Cain and his sacrifice were rejected. The New Testament, however, offers a strong hint as to the major problem with Cain's sacrifice. The book of Hebrews, for instance, provides us with some glimpses into this otherwise rather piecemeal account. That is why cross-referencing is so important. Scripture sheds light on Scripture.

A Blood Sacrifice Is Necessary for the Forgiveness of Sins

Insight #1: The shedding of blood was necessary for the forgiveness of sins. Hebrews 9:22 records: "And according to the law almost all things are purified with blood, and without shedding of blood there is no remission." God requires a blood sacrifice for sins to be forgiven. That is why He sacrificed His own Son on the cross (John 3:16).

If, by chance, and the Bible does not explicitly state this, this sacrifice was for sin, then Cain's sacrifice would not be acceptable. A thanksgiving offering of fruits and vegetables may have been appropriate at other times, but not for forgiveness of sin. One must exercise caution in stating this as the primary cause for its rejection since that information is not provided.

Faith Is Essential to Please God

Insight #2: Abel offered his sacrifice by faith. Hebrews 11:4 states the following regarding this scenario with Cain and Abel: "By faith Abel offered to God a more excellent sacrifice than Cain, through which he obtained witness that he was righteous, God testifying of his gifts; and through it he being dead still speaks."

This passage offers a keen observation regarding Abel in this verse. Abel is credited with exercising faith in God. The obvious inference, then, is that Cain did not exercise faith. Perhaps for Cain, the sacrifice was more of a begrudging obligation. By his soon-to-follow actions, Cain clearly was not a follower of God in any pure sense of the word. One does not just casually murder his own brother.

Cain understood who God was, but he apparently refused to bend his knees and heart in complete submission and worship. He exercised a strong spirit of independence. Malachi condemned the Israelites for their insincerity in offering sacrifices 3,500 years later. They were treating God contemptuously, as if He were blind, deaf, and dumb.

Malachi 1:7–8 states:

"You offer defiled food on My altar, but say, 'In what way have we defiled You?' By saying, 'The table of the LORD is contemptible.' And when you offer the blind as a sacrifice, is it not evil? And when you offer the lame and sick, is it not evil? Offer it then to your governor! Would he be pleased with you? Would he accept you favorably?" says the LORD of hosts.

Craig Blaising astutely comments on Malachi 1:7–8 as follows:

> The charge that the priests were calling the Lord's table contemptible was substantiated by their actions (Mal. 1:8). They were treating it with contempt by disregarding God's requirements concerning the kinds of sacrifices that should be placed on it. This made them guilty, deserving of death (Lev. 22:9). Also their contempt was deepened as they ate some of those unacceptable sacrifices (the priests received their food from the offerings, Lev. 24:5-9).[48]

Israel, as a nation in Malachi's time, operated not just insincerely but condescendingly. They insulted God with their unacceptable sacrifices. God always honors faith. Without faith, you cannot please God. Interestingly, this principle is stated in Hebrews 11:6, which is just two verses after Abel is commended for his faith. The even more remarkable shame regarding Israel's sacrifices is this: the memories of her Babylonian captivity were fresh in their history but apparently not in the citizens' all-too-porous minds.

The following context of Genesis chapter 4 clearly demonstrates that Cain was lacking in faith. Even more revolting is that this was

---

[48] Craig A. Blaising, The Bible Knowledge Commentary: Malachi (Wheaton, IL: Victor Books), p. 1578.

not a case of a lack of faith due to an absence of knowledge. His lack of faith was based on a stubborn refusal to submit to his Creator God. Cain preferred to do things his own way, not God's way. He had an excessively independent streak that proved quite counterproductive. Man's intended independence from God always yields a harvest of disaster. Not only is such a belligerent attitude nonsensical, but it is also counterproductive. Indeed, in Cain's sordid case, it led him to commit murder!

God Demands the Firstfruits

Insight #3: Abel's sacrifice was of the firstborn of his flock and of their fat. He brought the best that he could offer. Furthermore, it was a blood sacrifice. It is reasonable to assume the brothers knew of this principle for forgiveness. True, the text does not specify that. Yet one might reasonably conclude that they knew this either from the Lord Himself or from their father, Adam. Proverbs 3:9–10 states: "Honor the Lord with your possessions, and with the firstfruits of all your increase. So your barns will be filled with plenty, and your vats will overflow with new wine."

Cain apparently decided not to bring the best of his agricultural produce. Why should Genesis 4:4 otherwise mention that Abel brought the firstborn of his flock and of their fat? That was considered the best. "Firstborn" is plural, further implying that Abel sacrificed all of the firstborn, which was indeed a later requirement of the Mosaic Law. When one faithfully adhered to the stipulations of the law, God would, in turn, provide fruitful wombs for the life of the creature. The sheep, for instance, would bear young every year.

Since God's special revelation to man was progressive over the centuries (it took approximately 1,500 years for the Bible to be completely written), we do not know for certain what Cain and Abel knew about sacrifices. However, it seems reasonable that they knew it was necessary for blood to be shed for the forgiveness of sins.

They also should have recognized that one honors God by bringing to Him the best from either one's produce or from the flock. After all, it is only because of God's provision that one could bring any sacrifice at all. Aside from God's providence, we would have nothing at all. Finally, it is reasonable to conclude that a sacrifice absent of faith cannot, in reality, even be considered a sacrifice. It is a mockery, an exercise in baseless futility. One cannot mock God and win. What is the point of offering a sacrifice absent of faith?

The Mosaic Code for Dedication and Sacrifice

This principle is further amplified in Exodus 13:11–16:

> "And it shall be, when the LORD brings you into the land of the Canaanites, as He swore to you and your fathers, and gives it to you, that you shall set apart to the LORD all that open the womb, that is, every firstborn that comes from an animal which you have; the males shall be the LORD's. But every firstborn of a donkey you shall redeem with a lamb; and if you will not redeem it, then you shall break its neck.
>
> And all the firstborn of man among your sons you shall redeem. So it shall be, when your son asks you in time to come, saying, 'What is this?' that you shall say to him, 'By strength of hand the LORD brought us out of Egypt, out of the house of bondage. And it came to pass, when Pharaoh was stubborn about letting us

go, that the Lord killed all the firstborn in the land of Egypt, both the firstborn of man and the firstborn of beast.

'Therefore I sacrifice to the Lord all males that open the womb, but all the firstborn of my sons I redeem.' It shall be as a sign on your hand and as frontlets between your eyes, for by strength of hand the Lord brought us out of Egypt" (cf. Exodus 22:29–30).

The firstborn male from a Jewish family was redeemed for five shekels of silver according to the sanctuary shekel, which is approximately two ounces (Numbers 18:16). For a female, the cost was three shekels. The firstborn always belonged to the Lord, and a redemption price was thus paid. If the family was poor, as was Jesus' family, they could offer two turtledoves or two pigeons as a replacement sacrifice (Luke 2:22–24). The price was set by a priest (Leviticus 27:8).

On the Issue of Taking Vows

Leviticus 27:1–8 gives a breakdown for the redemption price depending on the age of the individual. It must be noted that the redemption price noted here was in the context of a vow that was taken for a variety of reasons. Vows were permitted for numerous causes but were not encouraged. When one made a vow, he must perform it with great sincerity and diligence. Ecclesiastes 5:4–5 states: "When you make a vow to God, do not delay to pay it; for He has no pleasure in fools. Pay what you have vowed—better not to vow than to vow and not pay."

Men aged from twenty to sixty had the highest redemption price for a vow. This was not based on their intrinsic value as a human being. Men and women are created equally in the image of God. Rather, it was based on their ability to labor intensely in an agrarian society. Men are stronger than women and can perform more physically demanding labor, such as plowing the fields behind oxen. In addition, it was men who fought as soldiers, not the women. The men generally earned the money for the family.

The valuation cost for a man was higher also because their vows were entirely their own responsibility. If a wife made an unwise vow, her husband could annul it on the day he heard about it. Likewise, if an unmarried daughter made a vow, her father could cancel it if he deemed it imprudent. He had to do this on the day he heard of it (Numbers 30:1–15). Delay on annulling a vow was not permitted without heavy cost.

If that did prove the case, the husband or father, whichever the case may have been, would bear the moral and financial responsibility for the vow (30:15). No one could annul the adult male's vow (30:2). He alone was responsible to either fulfill it or to pay the price for its invalidation as recorded in Leviticus chapter 27. In this way, the sometimes present inclination to make insincere vows was highly discouraged.

A Godly Life Is Evidenced by Character

Insight #4: Abel's actions testified to his righteousness. One may safely assume that Abel followed the unwritten directives of God more closely than did his brother. Their difference in character becomes all too obvious quite soon afterwards. As already stated, the brothers must have had sufficient understanding of the type of sacrifice God desired. If not, how could God fault Cain for something he did not know? That would seem quite unreasonable. God cannot be accused of being unreasonable or capricious in any way.

Furthermore, one cannot be characterized as righteous by accident. Abel was righteous by his faith and obedience. He lived a life that reflected an ongoing relationship with his Creator. We have sufficient information to recognize that both Cain's sacrifice and his character were definitely lacking in many commendable or righteous aspects. As evidenced later, Cain certainly was a man given over to raging jealousy. He did not master sin; sin mastered him.

Abel Was a Model of Righteousness

Insight #5: Abel's obedience provides an example to believers of all generations. He followed the directives of God even though we are not necessarily privy to what all of them were in our present age. Believers of all generations need to emulate Abel's godly example. Though we no longer need to offer sacrifices from our flocks or herds, we are commanded to live Christ-honoring lives (Romans 12:1–2).

Christ provided the perfect sacrifice of Himself (Hebrews 9:14). The principle of bringing to God the best of our spiritual gifts, talents, time, and financial resources still applies to all God's children. We should offer to God the best of everything of which we have been entrusted as stewards.

King David prayed this insightful prayer in 1 Chronicles 29:13–14: "Now therefore, our God, we thank You and praise Your glorious name. But who am I, and who are my people, that we should be able to offer so willingly as this? For all things come from You, and of Your own we have given you." How true that is. Everything that exists already belongs to God. That includes our very being: body, soul, and spirit.

What do we possess that is exclusively our own? Nothing!

Should we not then return the "firstborn," so to speak, of our time, possessions, and talents to the Lord? In a godly and Christ-centered mentality, that "firstborn" includes our own individual lives. Even the forgiveness of our sins is a gift from God; it cannot be earned (Ephesians 2:8–9).

That forgiveness, ultimately through Jesus Christ, is the greatest gift anyone can receive (2 Corinthians 9:15). It is worth far more than our every possession. As Mark candidly asks, what can we give in exchange for our souls (Mark 8:34–38)? Our lives on earth are temporal, but our souls are eternal. How, then, can we logically withhold anything from our Creator and Redeemer God?

The Contrast of Two Brothers

Insight #6: Abel's character and integrity were superior to Cain's. God approved of both Abel and his sacrifice. He disapproved of both Cain and his sacrifice. God knows every intent of the heart. If it was entirely a matter of the wrong type of sacrifice, a repentant Cain would have willingly and even eagerly rectified his errant behavior.

He could have easily brought a lamb for a new sacrifice if that was what God required. He did just the opposite. Instead of seeking reconciliation with God, he actually heartlessly and premeditatively murdered his brother instead! This was such an extreme reaction that it almost defies the imagination. He gained nothing by his vicious action and lost everything.

It is no small wonder that both Cain and his sacrifice were rejected. Even if the sacrifice was appropriate (which it was not), Cain's behavior betrayed an already darkened and unrepentant heart. His character was deplorable! We are not told why hatred had already so consumed him as to commit such a heinous sin. The Bible repeatedly warns of the dangers of an unrepentant and sin-blackened heart.

In essence, Cain's sin cost both of the brothers their lives. Fruchtenbaum summarizes this passage as follows:

> Then came the offering of Abel: And Abel, he also brought of the firstlings of his flock. Abel's offering was different from Cain's in two ways: It was a firstling, a firstborn; and it was a blood sacrifice. The text adds that Abel brought of the fat thereof, which was created as the best part (Lev. 3:16). For Abel, this sacrifice was an act of faith, to perform his spiritual duty. The mention of the fat shows that the issue was the sacrifice of blood.

Popular relational theology tries to claim that the whole thing was an issue of attitude, that Cain had the wrong attitude but Abel had the right attitude. However, there is simply no indication of this in the text, and the thrust of Scripture is that the problem was a lack of blood, as shown in Hebrews: By faith Abel offered unto God a more excellent sacrifice than Cain (Heb. 11:4); Messiah's blood that speaks better than that of Abel (Heb. 12:24).

The clear emphasis here is on blood, not merely attitude. Both Cain and Abel were sinners; both were born after the Fall and outside the Garden of Eden; both had the same parents, the same upbringing, the same environment and the same knowledge. However, Cain's offering was not of faith, while Abel's offering was an act of faith in response to revelation and knowledge.[49]

As is so commonly the case, the entire scenario boils down to faith and obedience. Cain did not exercise faith. Therefore, he simultaneously did not exercise obedience either. Abel was both faithful and obedient. We can safely assume, as Fruchtenbaum stated, that both men shared common experiences and knowledge. However, contrary to Fruchtenbaum's opinion, we feel that attitude did indeed play a role. No one's character could have changed so rapidly and diabolically over a rejected sacrifice. Cain clearly was already in the wrong in numerous ways.

It was not a matter of God revealing Himself differently to the two men. All men have access to general revelation (nature) and most to special revelation (the Bible). However, not everyone respects what they can see and experience firsthand. So it was with Cain and Abel. Abel's testimony shines for all time; Cain's shame darkens his name permanently.

Cain Murders Abel (Genesis 4:5b–10)

The heartbreaking travesty of the world's first murder is recorded in Genesis 4:5b–10:

> And Cain was very angry and his countenance fell. So the LORD said to Cain, "Why are you angry? And why has your countenance fallen? If you do well, will you not be accepted? And if you do not do well, sin lies at the door, but you should rule over it." Now Cain talked with Abel his brother; and it came to pass, when they were in the field, that Cain rose up against Abel his brother and killed him.

---
49 Fruchtenbaum, Arnold. Ariel's Bible Commentary: The Book of Genesis, p. 118.

Then the LORD said to Cain, "Where is Abel your brother?" He said, "I do not know. Am I my brother's keeper?" And He said, "What have you done? The voice of your brother's blood cries out to Me from the ground."

This story is devastating partly because it is so pathetically unnecessary. Murder, of course, never is necessary, but this murder strikes one as particularly deplorable. Cain nursed bitterness over a gracious correction by God regarding his sacrifice. This senseless bitterness mushroomed into a mountain of unquenchable hatred. That Cain would commit premeditated murder seems almost impossible to fathom under such rectifiable circumstances. Nonetheless, that is precisely what happened.

We shall examine several steps leading to the finale of this entirely repugnant scene. An uncountable multitude of similar and even more depraved scenarios have been repeated endlessly ever since. Humanity's history is replete with atrocities of unimaginable wickedness.

The Downward Progression of Sin

Step #1: Cain refused to acknowledge and repent of his sin. That is the stubborn and unnecessary plight of so many sinners. The motivations for resistance to God are sundry among unrepentant sinners, but the result is always the same … unmitigated disaster. In Cain's situation, the primary motivation was probably injured pride based on infantile jealousy. That misshaped seed of rebellion quickly blossomed into catastrophe.

Simply put, Cain didn't get his way! He and Abel both paid an enormous price for this. Even more ironically, neither ended up getting their way. Cain did not want to be exiled, and Abel did not want to be murdered. Abel wanted to serve the Lord with gratitude and appropriate worship. Indeed, he is honored precisely for that commendable spirit in the book of Hebrews. As such, he is an ongoing testimony to all believers of steadfast faithfulness and righteousness.

Numbers 32:23 warns: "But if you do not do so, then take note, you have sinned against the Lord, and be sure your sin will find you out." That principle haunted Cain for the rest of his life. How ironic it is that Cain claimed to be honoring God with his sacrifice. He was self-righteously offering his sacrifice in his own preferred and egotistical method. He did not act in accordance to God's divinely ordained regulations. You do not honor God by disobeying Him! That was true in Cain's day, and it remains equally true today in the church age.

God Communicates with Cain before the Murder

Step #2: God counsels Cain to godly living and victory over sin. It is interesting to note that God was still reaching out to Cain and Abel verbally. Scripture does not indicate that the Lord was walking alongside Cain as He did previously with His parents. Nonetheless, communication was quite open and free. God spoke to Cain verbally. He offered Cain ample opportunity for reconciliation with Himself. This all occurred before Cain lifted up his hand against Abel with a murder weapon.

God probed deeper by asking Cain why his countenance had fallen. Did Cain have a right to be angry? The obvious answer was no. Centuries later, God asked Jonah the same question, not once but twice. In Jonah 4:4, 9, the Bible states: "Then the Lord said, 'Is it right for you to be angry?'" Jonah twice defiantly responded, "Yes!" But in both cases, the correct answer was a definite "no."

Jonah, at least for that moment, did not recognize his own arrogance and unforgiving spirit.

Jonah's response to God was truly stunning. Had he already forgotten his own astounding rescue from the great fish just days before the spiritual awakening in Nineveh? One could not easily forget such an incredible adventure. Jonah willingly, one would assume enthusiastically, accepted God's mercy upon him.

Being in the dark, hot, and wet belly of the great fish for three days decidedly would not have been a pleasant experience. It certainly would have been memorable. But after being delivered from this unique prayer room, Jonah turned right around and rejected God's same mercy toward the Ninevites. Extraordinary! Ironically, in the book of Jonah, the only person who did not repent was Jonah.

God's Mandate of Forgiveness

Jonah, the wayward prophet of God, was so consumed with hatred toward the Ninevites that his hatred, in turn, nearly consumed him. Unforgiveness is one sin that hurts the offended more than the offender! Christ warned believers that if we are not willing to forgive, neither will we be forgiven. Matthew 6:14–15, which immediately follows the Lord's Prayer, states the following: "For if you forgive men their trespasses, your heavenly Father will also forgive you. But if you do not forgive men their trespasses, neither will your Father forgive your trespasses." Let every man, woman, and child take that passage to heart. Bitterness consistently destroys the bitter.

As previously mentioned, the only person who is not recorded as repenting in the book of Jonah is the prophet Jonah himself. Amazing! Both Cain and Jonah refused to listen to God's patient counsel. Although the Bible does not express this, archaeological history seems to indicate that Jonah did finally repent of his ungodly attitude. A tomb was set up in his honor in the region near Nineveh. Apparently, Jonah relinquished his anger and allowed the grace of God to once more rule in his soul. His tomb was honored among the Muslims until recent years. Sadly, it was destroyed on July 24, 2014, by the radical group ISIS.

As difficult as it may seem at times, sin can be held in check. Victory is available for the believer, although admittedly, that sometimes seems impossible. First Corinthians 10:12–13 conveys this simultaneous warning and promise to all believers:

> Therefore let him who thinks he stands take heed lest he fall. No temptation has overtaken you except such as is common to man: but God is faithful, who will not allow you to be tempted beyond what you are able, but with the temptation will also make the way of escape, that you may be able to bear it.

Cain's Horrible Choice

Step #3: Cain allowed sin to stimulate its ugly fruit to a full and morbid ripeness. The consequence? He murdered his brother. Cain enticed Abel to go out to the field with him. Very likely, it was customary for them to go on walks together and enjoy the freshness of God's creation. But this day, it involved a diabolical intent on Cain's part. This almost certainly proved a premeditated murder, not merely an abrupt crime of passion. Cain desired to get Abel away from any possible witnesses. But where can one flee from God's all-seeing eyes (Psalm 139:7–12)?

Contrary to popular belief, there were already other people in the world, although not many. It was not just Adam and Eve and their two sons. We know this because Cain was married, and he started a city after leaving behind the rest of his family. The tragic reality is that others, who were his close relatives, clearly followed Cain in spite of his wicked ways. One cannot start a city all by himself. Evil was steadily creeping into humanity. Cain willfully fomented its incipient growth. He led the way in depravity.

After walking and talking for a short time with Abel, Cain committed his dastardly deed of fratricide. Jesus testified to the historicity of this attack in Matthew 23:35: "That on you may come all the righteous blood shed on the earth, from the blood of righteous Abel to the blood of Zechariah, son of Berechiah; whom you murdered between the temple and the altar."

How it must grieve God's heart to see the innocent slaughtered by the guilty. It is ironic that God's righteous children are oftentimes the victims of these wretched crimes. But this is the sum total of earth's history. Someday, God will set everything right again. Believers must remember the injunction of Romans 12:19: "Beloved, do not avenge yourselves, but rather give place to wrath; for it is written, 'Vengeance is Mine, I will repay,' says the Lord." Patience is required by the redeemed, especially in the Tribulation period (Revelation 13:10).

James G. Murphy comments:

> Cain did not act on the divine counsel. He did not amend his offering to God, either in point of internal feeling or external form. Though one speak to him from heaven he will not hear. He conversed with Abel his brother. The topic is not stated. The Septuagint supplies the words, "Let us go into the field." If in walking side by side with his brother he touched upon the

divine communication, the conference did not lead to any better results.

If the divine expostulation failed, much more the human. Perhaps it only increased his irritation. When they were in the field, and therefore out of view, he rose up against his brother and slew him. The deed is done that cannot be recalled. The motives to it were various. Selfishness, wounded pride, jealousy, and a guilty conscience were all at work (1 John 3:12). Here, then, is sin following upon sin, proving the truth of the warning given in the merciful forbearance of God.[50]

Thus ends the tragic consequence of unrepented sin and lack of reconciliation. When one dismisses the warning of God, he is asking for tragic consequences. Abel stands in the presence of God; Cain suffers in eternal punishment. Jesus asks this eternal question in Mark 8:36–37: "For what will it profit a man if he gains the whole world, and loses his own soul? Or what will a man give in exchange for his soul?" The answer is clear: "Nothing!"

We pray that each reader will attend to the eternal salvation of his soul. What could possibly matter more? Even now, God reaches out to those needing forgiveness. We do not want to meet God in the Court of Justice. By then, the opportunity for repentance will have long passed. Rather, meet Him in the Court of Redemption. His Son, Jesus Christ, lovingly awaits you.

---

50 James G. Murphy, *Barnes's Notes: A Commentary on the Book of Genesis* (Grand Rapids, MI: Baker Books, 1847 by Blackie & Son, London, reprinted 2005), p. 153.

Cain Is Judged and Banished from God's Presence

(Genesis 4:11–17)

Just as his parents were expelled from the Garden of Eden, so the first son born into the world also experienced banishment. Sin inevitably produces terrible consequences. Shed blood cannot be unshed; it is a permanent blight upon the murderer. The innocent victim can never be resuscitated save in the resurrection or in the Rapture. Fortunately, all believers will one day be privileged to meet the righteous Abel in the glories of eternity. What a reunion that will be!

God Confronts Cain

In Genesis 4:9–12, Cain experiences a confrontation with the all-seeing God. If Cain, for one impious moment, thought he had gotten away with the perfect murder, he was sadly mistaken. He should have known that God, in His omnipresence, watched the entire grievous affair. Yet Cain's hatred was so intense that nothing short of direct divine intervention would dissuade him from taking his wicked path.

It appears that Cain was already so hardened in his heart that he could not even be reached by almighty God. He shamelessly and deliberately shunned God and His righteous ways. He willfully chose the dark side! He never returned to God's grace, as far as we know. Though even Cain's calamitous sin could have been forgiven by God, no repentance is ever recorded.

Genesis 4:9–12 states:

> Then the LORD said to Cain, "Where is Abel your brother?" He said, "I do not know. Am I my brother's

keeper?" And He said, "What have you done? The voice of your brother's blood cries out to Me from the ground. So now you are cursed from the earth, which has opened its mouth to receive your brother's blood from your hand. When you till the ground, it shall no longer yield its strength to you. A fugitive and a vagabond you shall be on the earth."

God clearly knew the answers to His questions to Cain. They are all rhetorical. It would seem obvious enough that Cain also knew this. But in spite of Cain's profound and personal knowledge of God, he still remained obstinate in his sin. We must recognize that Adam and Eve undoubtedly taught their boys all they knew about their Creator. They were privy to information presently withheld from mortal man.

Adam and Eve had literally walked and talked with God! What manner of conversations they must have experienced! What better school of knowledge and inspiration has any mortal ever attended? How foolish it was for Cain, as well as his parents, to try to conceal anything from God. They all knew God as the omnipotent, omnipresent, and omniscient Creator.

Leupold offers the following comments:

> As always, God does not ask in order to secure information. The question is pedagogic, in order to remind Cain that God knows where Abel is. To ascribe those words to Adam as a spokesman for God is farfetched. Here is the second cross-examination found in the Scriptures. The contrast with the first is apparent. The first found Adam and Eve humble, though given to

evasion and excuses. The second finds Cain impudent and hardened, at least at the beginning of the interview.

Yet the first question had effectually presented to Cain the startling reminder of the slain man lying inert in his own blood out in the field. The heartless lie and bold rejoinder on Cain's part is: "I do not know; am I my brother's keeper?"

The question gains a slightly different force in the Hebrew, where the predicate stands first for emphasis: "Am keeper of my brother I?" like "Am I supposed to watch him all the while?" He feels too guilty to draw attention to himself by way of contrast and to say: "Am I my brother's keeper?" The interrogative ha anticipates a negative answer.[51]

The Blood of Abel Cried Out to God

As the Scripture would later reveal, the life is in the blood (Leviticus 17:11). Those who shed man's blood unjustly deserve to have their blood shed in righteous retribution (Genesis 9:6). Instruction regarding capital punishment was not instituted, however, until after the Flood. The fact that Abel's blood was crying out to God indicates proof of the hereafter. As Jesus would later attest, God is not the God of the dead but of the living.

Luke 20:37–38 states: "But even Moses showed in the burning bush passage that the dead are raised, when he called the Lord the God of Abraham, the God of Isaac, and the God of Jacob. For He is

---

51 Leupold, H. C., Exposition of Genesis: Volume 1: Chapters 1–19, pp. 204–205.

not the God of the dead but of the living, for all live to Him." Moses thus recognized that man does not live to himself. He is accountable to the God of the living (Romans 14:11–12).

Abel was the first resident in Sheol. In the era of the Old Testament, Sheol was divided into two sections. The first section was sometimes called the place of "Abraham's bosom." It was also called Paradise. While languishing on the cross, Jesus stated the following in Luke 23:43 to the believing and contrite thief on the cross: "And Jesus said to him, 'Assuredly, I say to you, today you will be with Me in Paradise.'"

A Note on Suffering

Although Abraham himself would not descend to Sheol for many centuries, this was a place of comfortable rest for the believer. Abraham offered great comfort to the beggar Lazarus, who, although impoverished and diseased, faithfully believed in God. Suffering on this earth by God's children, contrary to the opinion of many, is not automatically a sign of God's disapproval. God has His own purposes in the blessings and occasional lack thereof for His children. It is almost axiomatic that suffering can greatly enhance faith. Luxury rarely does so.

In John 9:1–3, Jesus clarifies this truth to His disciples:

> Now as Jesus passed by, He saw a man who was blind from birth. And His disciples asked Him, saying, "Rabbi, who sinned, this man or his parents, that he was born blind?" Jesus answered, "Neither this man nor his parents sinned, but that the works of God should be revealed in him."

Jesus then healed the blind man who, in turn, brought Him great glory. This message was particularly pertinent to the apostles as all of them would suffer grievously for their faith in Christ not many years hence (cf. Hebrews 11:35b–40). Indeed, all but John died as martyrs for their faith.

The other half of Sheol was designated for unrepentant sinners. It was a region of torment and alienation from God and is frequently called hell or hades (Luke 16:19–31). The rich man suffered there but, amazingly, was allowed to hold a conversation with Abraham. However, his desire for water brought over by Lazarus to quench his thirst was not granted. Neither was his wish honored to send Lazarus back from the dead to warn his brothers of their impending judgment.

One of the greatest truths of Scripture uttered by Abraham is then recorded in Luke 16:31: "But he said to him, 'If they do not hear Moses and the prophets, neither will they be persuaded though one rise from the dead.'" The same holds true throughout all of earth's history. If one refuses to acknowledge God's special and general revelation, he willfully destines himself to eternal retribution. No excuses will be tolerated in God's court of justice. Cain did precisely that, even with God's personal intervention. How much greater persuasion can one expect than God Himself? Cain, probably more than any man in history, was absolutely without excuse.

God Places a Twofold Curse on Cain

The first curse on Cain was similar to that which was afflicted on Adam. By the sweat of his brow, Adam would earn his bread. Curse #1: Cain would be cursed from the earth (4:11). This obviously does not mean that Cain was exiled from the planet. He moved east to the land of Nod. It appears that the ground would no longer bountifully yield for Cain. That is the explanation offered in verse 12.

This curse was leveled directly against Cain himself. He had shed Abel's blood, and the earth had "opened its mouth" to receive that blood (cf. Numbers 16:30–35; Deuteronomy 11:6). It is not clear whether this agricultural dilemma affected anyone else allied to Cain to a similar extent. But certainly, Cain himself would truly struggle to make his living from farming. The earth he had previously loved to work on now rejected him. The ground he had defiled with Abel's blood was now defiled for him.

A Living Death Sentence

Curse #2: Cain would become a fugitive and a vagabond on the earth (4:12). Why was Cain not simply executed? As previously noted, the sentence of execution for murder was not enacted until after the Flood (Genesis 9:6). Furthermore, the only people who could have executed him were his own immediate family. His punishment served as a living death sentence.

Everyone alive in Cain's day remembered him as the evil murderer of his own brother. In fact, even biblically illiterate people of today have generally heard about the wretched murderer Cain. Cain was fully aware of how people would feel about him. There would be a universal sense of revulsion towards him. His wife, however, remained faithful to him and bore him children.

Warren Wiersbe comments as follows:

> A vagabond has no home; a fugitive is running from home; a stranger is away from home; but a pilgrim is heading home. "I have set before you life and death, blessing and cursing, therefore, choose life" (Deut. 30:19). Cain made the wrong choice, and instead of

being a pilgrim in life, he became a stranger and a fugitive, wandering the land.[52]

It is impossible to envision the drastic change that came upon Cain's life. One ponders how many times he relived those fateful moments in his mind. He had murdered his own more righteous and younger brother. He certainly had proved not to be his brother's keeper! He was anything but that. His defiant answer to God undoubtedly haunted him for all his remaining days. Cain cut himself off from the most important relationship possible, namely, that with God.

God Grants Mercy in the Midst of Judgment

God's justice is thorough and perfect. But even more admirable than that is His ever-consistent and patient mercy. Some may feel that God is not justified in His patience. He should be quicker to exact punishment, many assert. Perhaps that individual should voluntarily offer himself up to the throne of God's holy wrath immediately instead of reveling in His loving benevolence.

Few would feel personally inclined to voluntarily endure the possibility of deserved divine retribution. All too many, however, would be agreeable to wish the wrath of God upon someone else. How do such people reflect God's love and patience? Thankfully, believers do not have to suffer the "kindly graces" of others for all eternity. There is forgiveness for the penitent. But there remains condemnation for the unredeemed. They have, in a real sense, thrown themselves into the flames of hell through their individual complacency or outright disbelief.

Genesis 4:13–17 recounts God's punishment on Cain. It, as is

---

52 Warren Wiersbe, The Bible Exposition Commentary: Genesis–Deuteronomy (Wheaton, IL: Victor Books, 2001), p. 38.

almost always the case, was sprinkled with His ever-present mercies:

> And Cain said to the LORD, "My punishment is greater than I can bear! Surely You have driven me out this day from the face of the ground; I shall be hidden from Your face; I shall be a fugitive and a vagabond on the earth, and it will happen that anyone who finds me will kill me." And the LORD said to him, "Therefore, whoever kills Cain, vengeance shall be taken on him sevenfold." And the LORD set a mark on Cain, lest anyone finding him should kill him.
>
> Then Cain went out from the presence of the LORD and dwelt in the land of Nod on the east of Eden. And Cain knew his wife, and she conceived and bore Enoch. And he built a city; and called the name of the city after the name of his son—Enoch.

Cain's Pathetic Response

One cannot but notice the "crybaby" response of Cain to the Lord. He cannot bear his punishment. Woe to poor Cain! He apparently gave little or no thought to his murdered brother. Abel did not deserve to be slaughtered like a sheep. Instead of complaining, Cain should have been lying flat on the ground with his face in the dirt, repenting and thanking the Lord for sparing his wretched life. He had just finished murdering his own brother! His pathetic response was truly one for the ages. Self-pity is a common characteristic for the unrepentant.

It is interesting that the Hebrew in verse 13 should be more literally translated: "My sin is greater than can be borne." That perspective is from Cain's viewpoint. But his sin could be borne, and indeed it was, by Christ on the cross (John 3:16). Only the sin against the Holy Spirit, perpetual unbelief, and the receiving of the mark of the beast can never be forgiven. Even Cain's murder of his brother could have been forgiven if he had genuinely repented.

How many times in human history have other brothers committed the same or similar heinous crimes? The number is far too many to count! Sadly, there does not seem to be any actual repentance from Cain over his actions. He certainly expressed remorse over his coming punishment. Remorse is personal and self-centered. Repentance is sincere regret directed toward others, particularly toward God.

But unlike his parents, Cain did not utter any sincere confession to the Lord. Second Corinthians 7:10 reminds us: "For godly sorrow produces repentance leading to salvation, not to be regretted; but the sorrow of the world produces death."

Cain's Fourfold Punishment

What was Cain's punishment? It is fourfold. First, as previously stated, the ground was cursed for him. He could no longer make a good living through agriculture. If he did plant crops, the yield would be poor. This would force him to become more reliant on others. But he would also have available fruits and vegetables that grew of themselves.

Second, he would be hidden from God's face. This means, in Cain's opinion, that his fellowship with God was now permanently broken. That would truly have been an incomprehensible curse! If it literally meant he no longer had access to the throne of grace in prayer, it would be the worst possible curse. But it should be observed that God Himself did not state this; Cain alone did.

Verse 16 states that Cain went out from the presence of the Lord. This is an action taken by Cain; it was not mandated by God. That type of banishment is the description of hell in the New Testament. Lest anyone think that Cain's punishment was too mild, they need to reflect on what this part of the curse on him really meant. It would be a curse far worse than death! Cain would experience a "living death."

Second Thessalonians 1:8–9 is arguably the most terrifying passage in all of Scripture: "In flaming fire taking vengeance on those who do not know God, and on those who do not obey the gospel of our Lord Jesus Christ. These shall be punished with everlasting destruction from the presence of the Lord and from the glory of His power."

However, it must be observed that this second curse was Cain's pronouncement upon himself. God did not declare this as part of the curse in Genesis 4:11–12. Hence, if this literally describes Cain's future activity, it was his personal choice! It was not part of God's holy punishment. The same holds true for the multitudes around the world today. God calls out to everyone to repent. He does not want any to perish apart from the Savior. Tragically, only a tiny percentage respond to Christ's extended hands (Matthew 7:13–14; 2 Peter 3:9).

Third, Cain would be a fugitive and vagabond on the earth. This does not mean that he would never again have a home. Verse 17 records that he built the city of Enoch, which he named after his son. But he would live with a perpetual sense of isolation. He probably remained largely friendless for the remainder of his life.

Fourth, he feared that anyone who met him would kill him. He did not want to be treated by others as he had treated Abel. Ironically, Cain feared the wrath of man more than the wrath of God. Had he genuinely feared God, he would never have murdered his brother in the first place.

God Shows Mercy in Judgment

God intervened for Cain in two noteworthy ways: Intervention #1: God decreed that anyone who killed Cain would be punished sevenfold himself. That certainly would motivate most people to stay far away from Cain. One quite naturally asks why God made such a powerful statement and defense of the scoundrel Cain. Why should Cain be so openly defended?

Certainly, it was not because Cain deserved divine protection in light of his transgression. It was because God was establishing for all just how heinous murder and revenge truly were. Hence, He would not allow anyone else to commit the same action against Cain that he had committed against Abel. Furthermore, it would have to be another close family member who would take action against Cain.

Intervention #2: God put a clear mark on Cain to protect him. Scripture does not identify what that mark was, but people indisputably understood it. "Do not touch this man!" was its obvious message. This actually would have contributed to Cain's sense of loneliness. He was, in a real sense, branded. A steer does not desire the searing heat of the branding iron. Though God did not utilize such a primitive tool, the effect was the same. Cain was a marked man!

What was the end result for Cain? Cain went out from the presence of the Lord and dwelt in the land of Nod on the east of Eden. This should not simply be interpreted as Cain leaving a certain geographical region. God dwells everywhere. It means that his fellowship with God truly was over. But again, it must be remembered that this was Cain's own wicked choice. He hardened his own heart. He could have been forgiven had he genuinely repented of his sins. No man is beyond redemption save those who refuse to believe.

Cain's obstinate heart truly staggers the imagination. He was privileged to speak to God verbally. He was part of the original family God created. He was the first son ever born to humanity. He could have learned from the example of his more spiritually sensitive younger brother. Instead, he viciously murdered him! Cain spurned every conceivable advantage and chose the path of unremitting darkness. It is a spiritual tragedy almost without equal.

Lessons Learned in This Chapter

In this chapter, we first reviewed the truly lamentable story of the world's first murder. What makes matters even worse is that this murder took place between brothers. It is hard to imagine that in the world's very first family, such a despicable action could have occurred.

Even more painful is the fact that this calloused murder took place over a sacrifice to God. Abel, the younger brother, offered his sacrifice to God in an appropriate fashion. Cain, the older brother, did not act in accordance to God's unwritten instructions. Clearly, both knew the proper procedures. If that were not the case, Abel could not have done so well, and Cain could not have behaved so impiously.

Second, we discussed the details regarding this atrocious act of fratricide. A brother murdering another physical brother happens but rarely. Families generally will defend each other, not take one another's life. So insanely jealous did Cain become of his righteous brother Abel that he viciously attacked and killed him. He did this out in the field to avoid witnesses. Hence, the murder should be viewed as premeditated, not as a momentary act of illicit passion.

Third, we observed how, even in the midst of God's judgment, He was willing to show mercy and forgiveness. However, Cain foolishly disclaimed any responsibility for the shameful incident. He asked God, "Am I my brother's keeper?" Such impudence is breathtaking. Instead of repenting in sackcloth and ashes, so to speak, Cain actually got worse in his insolence. By today's standards, Cain should have been put to death for his grievous crime. But God had not yet instituted the death penalty. That was not enacted until Genesis 9:6, which was after the worldwide Flood.

We also noted that much of Cain's punishment was self-imposed. He purposely left the presence of God. Though he geographically moved to the land of Nod, he spiritually broke off his prior relations with his Creator. It appears that he no longer interacted with his immediate family but instead started his own line. However, some members of his family must have followed him. Certainly, his wife did. More details of this separation shall become evident as we proceed through Genesis chapters 1 to 11.

Next to the fall of Adam and Eve into sin, this chapter is perhaps the most tragic in Scripture. It establishes the despicably low standard to which mankind progressively sinks. The benevolence of God is commonly ignored. Indeed, acts of insurrection against His holy commands quickly became the norm for the majority of humanity. Such attitudes eventually ended in worldwide tragedy through the all-destructive Flood.

In our next chapter, we shall examine certain aspects of the ungodly line of Cain. He stands in stark contrast to both Abel and his yet-to-be-born brother Seth. Unfortunately, much of the world has ungraciously and unwisely patterned itself after the godless Cain, not after the righteous Abel (Luke 13:24). May Abel's memory remain a positive influence on believers worldwide.

Cognitive Conundrum #7

A person of solitary means was I in my life; simplicity eliminates a great deal of strife. Health enthusiasts would have frowned at my diet, and my character tended to start a riot. The Old Testament spoke of me in mysterious way, but my position in marriage is here to stay. Against sin, I strove until good and dead; because of godliness, I soon lost my head.

Who am I?

Answer: John the Baptist

Chapter 8

The Lineage of Cain and Seth

(Genesis 4:16–26)

In This Chapter

Objectives for This Chapter
The Consequences of Abel's Murder (4:16–17)
The Ungodly Line of Cain (4:18–24)
The Godly Line of Seth (4:25–26)
Lessons Learned in This Chapter

Objectives for This Chapter

Rebellion against an almighty God only ends up as "gravel in one's mouth." No good can ever come of it. Fortunately, in God's profound mercy and yearning for reconciliation, forgiveness is available. However, this forgiveness must be accepted with a sincere and humble spirit. Psalm 51:17 states: "The sacrifices of God are a broken spirit, a broken and a contrite heart—these, O God, You will not despise."

Sadly, Cain did not seek forgiveness. His heart had become so darkened with sin that he murdered his brother, Abel. The cause for this heinous act strikes one today as completely senseless. His brother's blood would follow him all his remaining days. Even cynical criminals generally act with at least some sense of profit in mind. Cain's actions were pointless and permanent. His sacrifice to God was unacceptable for reasons not entirely disclosed. However, rectification of his error was easily within his grasp. We discussed several of those reasons previously.

A simple modification of his behavior would have resolved all troubles. He could have offered the appropriate type of sacrifice. But Cain chose another path. It was more than just the proper type of sacrifice. His was a heart issue. That proved the kernel of the matter. In this chapter, we shall first examine the regrettable consequences of Cain's murderous behavior. He established the immoral path which most of his direct descendants would tragically follow.

Second, we shall review the largely ungodly line of Cain. His descendants were skilled individuals. Many people tend to view ancient man as primitive in their understanding. Though inventions and technology have steadily progressed through the millennia, early man was by no means lacking in intelligence or vocational finesse.

They advanced themselves almost immediately in many aspects, such as metallurgy and musical talents. Other avenues of exploration and development obviously took place that are not mentioned. Agrarian advances also certainly came about quickly.

Third, we shall see the initial progression of Abel's line. Seth became the third son mentioned in Scripture, though there may have been others. But the Seed son would be derived from Seth. His son Enosh perhaps assisted in orchestrating public worship. With each ensuing generation, God presented Himself more rarely on an individual level than He had with Adam, Eve, Cain, and Abel. However, He continued to interact with man in ways that were not revealed.

The Consequences of Abel's Murder (4:16–17)

Genesis 4:16–17 records the immediate consequences of Cain's encounter with God: "Then Cain went out from the presence of the

LORD and dwelt in the land of Nod on the east of Eden. And Cain knew his wife, and she conceived and bore Enoch. And he built a city, and called the name of the city after the name of his son—Enoch."

Sin Makes a Poor Master

Result #1: Cain abandoned God. Perhaps one of the most traumatic statements in Scripture is that "Cain went out from the presence of the LORD." That obviously does not mean that Cain could travel to an area where God was not present or forbidden entry. God is everywhere! God can, however, remove the sense of His presence so that mankind can no longer reach out to Him.

Such an eventuality will be the fate of those in the Lake of Fire. Nothing imaginable can be worse than the deprivation of sensing the warmth and love of God's presence. No mortal has entirely experienced that on this side of the grave. Not even Cain could accomplish that, though he tried. Second Thessalonians 1:9 presents a summary of this eventual terrible scenario to those who reject the Savior: "These shall be punished with everlasting destruction from the presence of the Lord and from the glory of His power."

In eloquent and yet the simplest of fashion, Psalm 139:7–12 makes the truth of God's omnipresence crystal clear:

> Where can I go from Your Spirit? Or where can I flee from Your presence? If I ascend into heaven, You are there; if I make my bed in hell, behold, You are there. If I take the wings of the morning, and dwell in the uttermost parts of the sea, even there Your hand shall lead me, and Your right hand shall hold me. If I say, "Surely the darkness shall fall on me," even the night shall

be light about me; indeed, the darkness shall not hide from You, but the night shines as the day; the darkness and the light are both alike to You.

One obviously cannot escape from God physically, but one can abandon Him spiritually and emotionally. That is precisely what the sin-hardened Cain did. He and most of his descendants paid the consequences by following suit. It was largely for this reason that the world progressively worsened.

The world and its people became so wicked by the time of Noah's day that, save eight souls, the destruction of all mankind became necessary. In our present age, we cannot imagine the depths of depravity to which the world has sunk. Cain fiendishly and intentionally contributed to this depravity.

R. S. Candlish summarizes this sorrowful scenario of Cain's character as follows:

> His anxiety at first, when his sentence was pronounced, arose chiefly from his selfish fear of death at the hands of justly indignant brethren (ver. 13-15). When that fear is removed, he thinks little of his exclusion from the sanctuary of his God and the society of the faithful. He can still turn to account his natural talents and powers. He goes forth (ver. 16-17), to live without God in the world, -- building cities and begetting children, -- himself and his seed prospering and prevailing – until the flood comes – to purge the world of them all.[53]

---

53 R. S. Candlish, An Exposition of Genesis (Wilmington, DE: Sovereign Grace Publishers, 1972), p. 71.

The Lineage of Cain and Seth

Cain Fathers Enoch

Result #2: Cain was intimate with his wife, and she bore a son whom they named Enoch. Bible skeptics are frequently consumed with the question of where Cain got his wife. They claim that it was immoral to marry a sister or niece. That is a mistake on the skeptics' part. Marrying a close relative was not forbidden until the days of Moses, approximately 2,500 years later. Even Abraham married Sarah, his half-sister.

In the beginning of humanity, mutations did not affect the human body to the degree they have today. There was no danger or prohibition in marrying a close relative. Indeed, what choice did they have? None! You had to marry either a sister or a niece. As Jesus stated to the Sadducees in Matthew 22:29: "You are mistaken, not knowing the Scriptures nor the power of God." That still remains the case with Bible skeptics of our modern era.

As Jesus Himself noted, the vast majority of mistaken theology stems from an inadequate and unsystematic knowledge of Scripture. Far too many believers read only select portions of Scripture that they favor and that are relatively easy to understand. They avoid the difficult books such as the Major and Minor Prophets. But prophecy entails 28 percent of the Bible. One cannot just ignore such a vast percentage of God's Word. He included these books for a purpose, not merely to take up space. Furthermore, Scripture sheds light on Scripture. It is its own greatest interpreter.

Without an adequate comprehension of all the books of the Bible, one is prey to any whimsical doctrine that false teachers are all too eager to propagate. In Ephesians 4:14, Paul warns of this danger: "That we should no longer be children, tossed to and fro and carried about with every wind of doctrine, by the trickery of men, in the cunning craftiness of deceitful plotting."

One such modern fallacy is that God wants all His children to be healthy and wealthy. Where is that recorded in the Scripture? Quite simply, it isn't. But it is one of the most popular teachings of preachers today within the Church. It is also patently false. Prosperity may sound wonderful to the unschooled ear. And, within the kingdom of God, there are affluent believers who utilize their funds to advance the Gospel in fantastic ways. The overall reality of the matter, however, is that suffering and deprivation develop faith much more than comfort and luxury do.

Cain Builds the City Enoch

Result #3: Cain and his wife built a city and named it Enoch, after their son. At this point in history, there may have already been hundreds of people on earth. Cain did not kill Abel when they were mere children. Scripture does not reveal their ages. Birth defects and miscarriages were probably unknown. Women and men both were likely quite vigorous, and pregnancy was the order of the day. The population undoubtedly exploded rapidly.

It should be noted that this Enoch was not the prophet alluded to in Jude 14. The godly Enoch of Jude was the seventh from Adam and will be mentioned in Genesis chapter 5. He is truly a remarkable character and never died. He was translated directly into heaven. Only Elijah has since experienced such a divine deliverance from the valley of the shadow of death.

Aside from Enoch being a noteworthy prophet, relatively little is known of him. However, God certainly knew and honored his godliness. He was a man who walked with God, reminiscent of Adam and Eve, though not in the same personalized way. Only three men in Scripture receive this high praise of walking with God:

The Lineage of Cain and Seth

Enoch, Noah, and Levi (Genesis 5:22, 6:9; Malachi 2:6). Obviously, other men and women also developed a keen relationship with God, particularly Moses.

Cain built a city in which to dwell. It is the natural tendency of mankind to congregate together. But God's original mandate was for people to spread out and fill the earth (Genesis 1:28). Cities offer many benefits and mutual protection. Ironically, the protection was needed because of Cain's own immoral descendants, not his righteous brother Abel's. Large cities lend themselves to immoral behavior, as will be seen in Genesis chapter 11. This action indicates Cain's ongoing rebellion against the Lord. There is no indication that he ever repented of his gross immorality.

Warren Wiersbe offers the following comments:

> Why would God allow a diabolical murderer like Cain to go free? In His mercy, God doesn't give us what we deserve, and in His grace, He gives us what we don't deserve. That's the nature of God. God spared Cain's life, but that wasn't the end of the story. Eventually Cain died and "after this the judgment" (Heb. 9:27). The entire civilization that he built was destroyed in the Flood, and the record of his life is left in Holy Scripture as a warning to anybody who pretends to worship, plays with sin, and doesn't take temptation seriously. "The way of Cain" (Jude 11) is not the narrow way that leads to life (Matt. 7:13-14).[54]

---

54 Wiersbe, Warren, The Bible Exposition Commentary: Genesis–Deuteronomy, p. 38.

A Summary Statement

A similar summary of God's characteristic working has often been expressed as follows:

Justice: We get what we deserve.

Mercy: We don't get what we deserve.

Grace: We get what we don't deserve.

The story of Cain and Abel should prove instructive to every human being who is privileged to hear it. The moral repercussions and principles are quite obvious. Sin produces misery and judgment; obedience produces blessing. That is a truism that is not always presently witnessed in our sin-sickened generation, but it certainly bears fruit in eternity. God sees all and knows all. He shall bring every evil deed to judgment if not repented of on this side of eternity. May each of us live our lives in the marvelous example of godly Abel. He is a testimony for the ages!

The Ungodly Line of Cain (Genesis 4:18–24)

As already stated, Cain voluntarily left the presence of the Lord. God did not decree that drastic spiritual alienation upon him. That was Cain's choice. What God did decree is that Cain would be a "fugitive and a vagabond" upon the earth (4:12b). That does not qualify as a permanent judgment and pronouncement of eternal condemnation. God wants all to repent.

God Prefers Forgiveness over Condemnation

In the context of God's chosen nation, Israel, Ezekiel 18:30–32 reminds us of God's intent for all mankind, even for a murderer like Cain:

"Therefore I will judge you, O house of Israel, every one according to his ways," says the Lord God. "Repent, and turn from all your transgressions, so that iniquity will not be your ruin. Cast away from you all the transgressions which you have committed, and get yourselves a new heart and a new spirit. For why should you die, O house of Israel? For I have no pleasure in the death of one who dies," says the Lord God. "Therefore turn and live!"

God patiently approached Cain with the allegations of his murder. He interacted with him about the dastardly deed, but Cain refused to repent of his actions. He even went so far as to initially deny the murder. The foolishness of doing so to an omniscient God nearly defies the imagination. Sin had thoroughly twisted Cain's conscience and reasoning (Jeremiah 17:9). It can do the same to anyone in any age.

God ensured with the physical mark He placed upon his body that Cain would not be killed. We have previously examined the reasons for this clemency toward Cain. Scripture does not say what this identifying mark was. It did serve its purpose in sparing his life. By contrast, during the future Tribulation, the believers who do not receive the mark of the beast may pay with their lives immediately upon being caught. They become martyrs for their Lord Jesus Christ (Revelation 13:7).

Ironically, those who receive the mark of the Antichrist will ultimately suffer both physical and eternal death (Revelation 14:9–11). They will be temporarily spared by the Antichrist, but their soon-to-follow destiny is tragic and unending. They will be put to death at Christ's return and immediately be sent to hell (Matthew 25:46).

Ultimately, one thousand years later, after facing the Great White Throne Judgment, unbelievers will be exiled forever to the lake of fire (Matthew 25:31–46; Revelation 20:11–15). A one-thousand-year period, the millennial kingdom of Christ, must first transpire before this final judgment.

Cain's banishment from his family was geographical, emotional, and, most importantly, spiritual. But as already noted, the spiritual aspect was of his own choosing. He thus decreed the bulk of his judgment upon himself through his intransigence and lack of repentance.

This did not prevent Cain from starting a family line of his own. He was already married and perhaps had fathered numerous children. There is no way of knowing. The first child born is not always the most prominent child. David is a sterling example of this. He is actually called the firstborn in spite of the fact that his seven brothers were born before him. Psalm 89:27 declares: "Also I will make him My firstborn, the highest of the kings of the earth" (cf. 1 Samuel 16:10).

We do not know how old Cain and Abel were when this diabolical murder took place. They certainly were not children. By then, they possibly had many relatives. If that is the case, it lends even further insight into Cain's wicked character. He would have had a good number of years to learn, understand, and apply God's principles regarding the proper sacrificial system. It appears, however, that he largely chose to ignore such guidelines.

Cain's Family

Genesis 4:18–24 records his descendants and their respective abilities:

To Enoch was born Irad; and Irad begot Mehujael, and Mehujael begot Methushael, and Methushael begot Lamech. Then Lamech took for himself two wives: the name of one was Adah, and the name of the second was Zillah. And Adah bore Jabal. He was the father of those who dwell in tents and have livestock. Hs brother's name was Jubal. He was the father of all those who play the harp and flute.

And as for Zillah, she also bore Tubal-Cain, an instructor of every craftsman in bronze and iron. And the sister of Tubal-Cain was Naamah. Then Lamech said to his wives:

"Adah and Zillah, hear my voice; wives of Lamech, listen to my speech! For I have killed a man for wounding me, even a young man for hurting me. If Cain shall be avenged sevenfold, then Lamech seventy-sevenfold."

As already noted, Enoch was Cain's prominent son, through whom the family line continued. It is also possible that he was his firstborn son. Cain named the city that he built after Enoch. Five generations are mentioned in verse 18. The only one of these five of which we know much about is Lamech. His sons and sundry details about their occupations are listed. They were clearly men of considerable intelligence and skill.

Commentary is made about Lamech's unorthodox and sinful lifestyle. Illicit behavior was sadly becoming more acceptable. He followed in the immoral footsteps of his ancestor, Cain. It should be mentioned that there is a similarity of these names to those of the godly line of Seth in Genesis chapter 5. In fact, Enoch and Lamech are found in both genealogies.

Names, Names, and More Names

Kiel and Delitzsch offer the following comments:

> Some of these names resemble those of the Sethite genealogy, viz., Irad and Jared, Mehujael and Mahalaleel, Methusael and Methuselah, also Cain and Cainan; and the names Enoch and Lamech occur in both families. But neither the recurrence of similar names, nor even of the same names, warrants the conclusion that the two genealogical tables are simply different forms of one primary legend.
>
> For the names, though similar in sound, are very different in meaning. Irad probably signifies the townsman, Jared, descent, or that which has descended; Mehujael, smitten of God, and Mahalaleel, praise of God; Methusael, man of prayer, and Methuselah, man of the sword or of increase.
>
> The repetition of the two names Enoch and Lamech even loses all significance, when we consider the different places which they occupy in the respective lines, and observe also that in the case of these very names, the more precise descriptions which are given so thoroughly establish the difference of character in the two individuals, as to preclude the possibility of their being the same, not to mention the fact, that in the later histo-

ry the same names frequently occur in totally different families.[55]

One encouraging name found in the Cainite line is Methushael, which means "man of El(ohim)" or "man of prayer." If names genuinely reflected the attitudes and beliefs of individuals, this may indicate that within the line of Cain, there were some believers. This certainly was true for Rahab, the harlot who lived in the godless city of Jericho. The wicked people of Canaan knew of the miraculous intervention by God on behalf of His children, Israel.

Amazingly, only a few such individuals, such as Rahab, a woman of ill repute, and her family, were willing to acknowledge the God of Israel. Even in wicked Jericho, God had a small remnant of those who were open to belief. They obediently recognized the true God of Israel and repented accordingly. If God could save immoral Rahab and her extended family, He can save anyone else who will respond to His grace.

Lamech's Polygamy

Genesis 4:19 states: "Then Lamech took for himself two wives: the name of one was Adah, and the name of the second was Zillah." Genesis 2:23–24 clearly demonstrates the superiority of monogamy. A man cannot be genuinely intimate with two women at the same time. They cannot become one flesh in its broader and fuller meaning. Becoming one flesh entails much more than mere sexual contact. It refers to being one in spirit as well.

Sexual activity is obviously possible with more than one partner. However, a private and endearing love, as God intended, can only be possible one-on-one. This is as equally true for a woman as it is for a man. Lamech is the first recorded polygamist in Scripture,

---
55 Keil and Delitzsch, Commentary on the Old Testament: Pentateuch, p. 117.

but he certainly is not the last. Was Lamech wrong to have two wives? This brings us to a rather divisive issue among scholars. This would seem an appropriate time to address the subject of polygamy.

Question: Is polygamy strictly forbidden in Scripture? Answer: Strictly speaking, no, but it is rarely encouraged. It must be recognized that even godly men occasionally took more than one wife. Abraham married Sarah. But he also had sexual intimacy with Hagar in order to raise up a child. Hagar was a concubine, not an actual wife.

The reason for this arrangement is that Abraham and Sarah faltered in their faith. Sarah herself enticed Abraham to produce a child by Hagar. Sarah would then claim the child for her own. That was an accepted cultural practice in their time, though it was quite alien to those of a Christian background. Other religions, such as Islam and Mormonism, not only allow polygamy but openly encourage it. The reasoning partly has to do with the concept that each woman should marry even if she has to share her husband with other wives.

Further Examples of Polygamy

If Abraham and Sarah had waited, however, Ishmael would not have been born. Much of the world's conflict could thus have been avoided. Ishmael grew up to be a violent man who fought against almost everyone. Genesis 16:12 states: "He shall be a wild man, his hand shall be against every man, and every man's hand against him, and he shall dwell in the presence of all his brethren." His descendants particularly fought against the Jews in later times.

The Patriarch Jacob had only wanted to marry Rachel but was tricked into marrying Leah and then two servant girls. This caused a miserable marriage and endless controversy between the women. Still, it cannot be denied that God formed the twelve tribes of Israel from Jacob's union with these four women. So God still blessed the arrangement. But marital happiness undoubtedly eluded all four women and Jacob.

Hannah was the barren wife of Elkanah. She suffered under the harsh mockery of Penninah, his other wife. Nonetheless, God blessed Hannah, and she gave birth to the prophet, priest, and judge Samuel. First Samuel 2:21 states: "And the LORD visited Hannah, so that she conceived and bore three sons and two daughters. Meanwhile the child Samuel grew before the LORD."

David also fell into the trap of marrying more than one wife, although he normally followed God's pattern for living. His many wives caused much consternation within his family due to competition between the sons. Solomon was led far astray from the Lord by his 700 wives and 300 concubines.

Polygamy is rarely put in a positive light in Scripture, although it is not strictly forbidden. The primary and only expressed purpose for polygamy would be to raise up children for a brother who died and had fathered no children. We shall examine that situation below.

A Biblical Principle regarding Polygamy

Deuteronomy 25:5–6 states:

> If brothers dwell together, and one of them dies and has no son, the widow of the dead man shall not be married to a stranger outside the family; her husband's brother shall go in to her, take her as his wife, and perform the duty of a husband's brother to her. And it shall be that the firstborn son which she bears will succeed to the name of his dead brother, that his name may not be blotted out of Israel.

To obey this command required the living brother to marry his sister-in-law. The first son they parented would be considered the deceased brother's son. The purpose was so that his name would be carried on and not be blotted out of Israel. To the modern, non-Jewish ear, this sounds strange indeed. But God always has a purpose for every ordinance.

Jack Deere, in The Bible Knowledge Commentary, explains this exceptional case for polygamy as follows:

> In only one kind of circumstance was marriage to a close relative permitted. Marriage to a divorced or widowed sister-in-law was forbidden (Lev. 18:16) unless the following conditions were met. The brothers must have been living together (i.e., they inherited their father's property jointly), and the deceased brother must have died without a male heir.
>
> If both of these conditions were met, the levirate (from the Latin levir, "brother-in-law" or husband's brother), marriage was to take place. Levirate marriage thus would provide a male heir who in turn could care for the parents in their old age and prevent the alienation of family property.
>
> Furthermore, the first son born from the levirate marriage was given the deceased brother's name ... so that his name would not be blotted out from Israel. In this way, even though a man died before the Lord fulfilled the covenant promises made to Abraham and his de-

scendants (Gen. 15:5, 18-21; 17:19; 22:17-18; 28:13-14; 35:12) he could participate in a sense, in the glorious future of Israel through his descendants.[56]

The context does not actually say if the brother who marries his sister-in-law is already married. The silence on that issue would seem to indicate that permission is granted for marriage in either case, whether he is already married or not. If a man does take a second wife, however, his first wife is not to be deprived of any of her natural marital rights.

Regulations Regarding Polygamy

In a slightly different context, Exodus 21:10 states: "If he takes another wife, he shall not diminish her food, her clothing, and her marriage rights." This seems to be dealing primarily with slaves. Nonetheless, this second woman is called a wife, not a concubine. Concubines, a strange concept to believers today, were often treated differently. This was the situation with Abraham and Hagar. She was not officially his wife. She was a concubine. Concubines were on a lower status than a wife. However, they were not mere slaves.

Modern man does not have concubines, and so this seems rather confusing today. But it was a situation occasionally dealt with in Israel and possibly elsewhere. The point is that if a man took a second wife, the first wife was to be treated equally. There was to be no discrimination in any fashion. This was the rather lamentable situation Jacob found himself in with Rachel and Leah. The two servant girls further added to the marital imbalance.

Polygamy might also be considered more socially acceptable under other mitigating circumstances. As history has long borne

---

[56] Jack Deere, The Bible Knowledge Commentary: Volume 1, Deuteronomy, John F. Walvoord and Roy B. Zuck, general editors (Wheaton, IL: Victor Books, 1985), p. 306.

out, hundreds of thousands of men die in warfare. Then you have a situation of many more women available for marriage than men. In those cases, rather than a woman being forever deprived of marriage and raising children, polygamy becomes more acceptable from a pragmatic viewpoint. Warfare can be so catastrophic that a rapid repopulation becomes essential. This can happen more readily if polygamy is sanctioned.

As an apt illustration of an absence of men, Isaiah 4:1 is written in the context of severe judgment on Israel. Many of the men would have been killed in battle by their enemies. Isaiah pictures the situation in 4:1 as follows: "And in that day seven women shall take hold of one man, saying, 'We will eat our own food, and wear our own apparel; only let us be called by your name, to take away our reproach.'"

To remain single in ancient cultures such as Israel was socially unacceptable. Indeed, it was considered a humiliation. Even in our modern, free-thinking society, most men and women desire a marital relationship at some point in their lives.

God's primary plan unquestionably is one man and one woman together. Polygamy is never a more acceptable situation than monogamy. Polygamy greatly diminishes intimacy! It should only be resorted to in unusual extenuating circumstances. Solomon took polygamy to extraordinary lengths. His foreign wives subsequently led him astray spiritually. But, as we have seen, polygamy was not entirely prohibited.

Lamech's Wives and Children

Genesis 4:19–22 states:

Then Lamech took for himself two wives: the name of

one was Adah, and the name of the second was Zillah. And Adah bore Jabal. He was the father of those who dwell in tents and have livestock. Hs brother's name was Jubal. He was the father of all those who play the harp and flute. And as for Zillah, she also bore Tubal-Cain, an instructor of every craftsman in bronze and iron. And the sister of Tubal-Cain was Naamah.

No matter what one may think of Lamech, he seems to have raised up competent children. His wife, Adah, is mentioned first. Their son Jabal was a nomadic herdsman who dwelled in tents. In that sense, they were the precursors of the modern-day Bedouins, a vanishing lifestyle. Since no one ate meat, they apparently just used the wool for clothing and the milk to produce butter and cheese. Their second son was Jubal. His name means "jubilee." He was a musician and played the harp and flute.

The second wife mentioned is Zillah. Their first child was Tubal-Cain. He invented metallurgy. He also taught others the art. This certainly was quite an advancement in technology. It enabled Cain's descendants to be well-equipped for future battles. Knowing the propensity of mankind toward evil, it probably did not take long before the bronze and iron were put to military use. Contrary to what anthropologists would have us believe, early man was not primitive. They were highly competent and industrious. Tubal-Cain's sister, Naamah, is also mentioned, but nothing further is told about her.

Lamech's Sinful Lifestyle

Genesis 4:23–24 states: "Then Lamech said to his wives: 'Adah and Zillah, hear my voice; wives of Lamech, listen to my speech! For I have killed a man for wounding me, even a young man for

283

hurting me. If Cain shall be avenged sevenfold, then Lamech seventy-sevenfold.'" Lamech murdered a man for injuring him. We are not informed what the injury actually was or how serious it was, but the context seems to indicate that Lamech's retribution was completely disproportional. Even beyond that, however, he seems to be mocking the graciousness of God.

If God was willing to show mercy to Cain and even to protect him sevenfold, Lamech esteemed himself as being worthy of seventy-sevenfold, eleven times the amount. This smacks of arrogance to the extreme. It also flatly contradicts the teaching of the Savior regarding forgiveness (Matthew 18:22).

John Phillips writes:

> Lamech's song was the first song in Scripture. It has been called "the song of the sword" because it glorified human independence, power, and vengefulness. The father of Tubal-Cain, exulting in the power placed in his hands by his son's weaponry, arrogantly threatened with death anyone who might try to injure him.
>
> With boastful impiety he promised vengeance to anyone who might attack him, vengeance greater than that promised by God to Cain. Such a song was in keeping with Lamech's character and with the spirit of the age. An age of military defiance had come, when men flung down the gauntlet, as it were, in the very face of God Himself.[57]

Lamech seems to be a precursor to the terrible wickedness that would soon encompass the earth. Actions and attitudes like his led

---

[57] John Phillips, The John Phillips Commentary Series; Exploring Genesis, pp. 74–75.

to the great judgment of the Flood. Cain at least had the understanding that God would defend him, unworthy though he was. Lamech manifests an independent and vicious quality that degenerates the very soul. Mankind continued to descend morally downward toward total lawlessness. When man deliberately suppresses the knowledge of God long enough, only judgment remains. Pity the generation that makes "itself" their own god. That will be the generation of the Antichrist's rule.

The Godly Line of Seth (Genesis 4:25–26)

The final two verses in chapter 4 introduce Seth. During his day, men began to call on the Lord. Genesis 4:25–26 states:

> And Adam knew his wife again, and she bore a son and named him Seth, "For God has appointed another seed for me instead of Abel, whom Cain killed." And as for Seth, to him also a son was born; and he named him Enosh. Then men began to call on the name of the LORD.

Seth Is Born

W. H. Griffith Thomas offers the following summary of the line of Seth:

> By contrast with the line of Cain we are now introduced to the new line of Seth, his brother. The points of contrast are many and significant. The first is the birth of Seth. The death of Abel had left an indelible mark on the soul of Eve, and now with the birth of her

third son her hopes of the fulfillment of the primeval promise again spring up, and she calls him Seth, and recognizes in his birth a Divine appointment and providence.

It is noteworthy that when Cain was born she associated his birth with the Covenant God of Grace (Jehovah). With Seth's birth she associates the God of Creation and Power (Elohim). This distinctness of usage of the Divine names should be carefully noted at each stage of the narrative, for it is full of spiritual significance and cannot be satisfactorily accounted for in any other way.

Another point of emphasis is associated with the son of Seth. It is interesting that in the same chapter we have the record of the birth of Cain's son and also the son of Seth. Still more interesting is the fact that with the birth of Seth's son there came what may very fairly be called a revival of true religion, for "then began men to call on the Name of Jehovah."

This may mean, as is our A.V., a revival of prayer; or it may mean still more than this, and indicate consecration to Jehovah, "calling themselves by His Name," and thereby separating themselves from all those who were not prepared to take the same action. They realized that they were in covenant with the God of their father, Who had promised victory over sin.[58]

Seth Becomes the Seed Son

Seth was not necessarily the first child born after Cain and Abel. The first couple must have had daughters and possibly other sons in the interim. Adam was already 130 years old when Seth was born (Genesis 5:3). They certainly had additional sons and daughters following Seth. If there were other sons born before Seth, they are not named. Seth became the most prominent of their sons. He was the Seed son. The replacement of the firstborn son by another later son was a familiar refrain in the book of Genesis. This shows God's sovereign control over the affairs of men.

One must bear in mind that the population of the earth was undoubtedly growing very rapidly. Death and disease were probably quite rare. People lived for hundreds of years. The childbearing years also seemed to parallel the great ages. Cain was married and started a city.

One does not generally establish a city with just one family. Seth's name is related to the Hebrew term that means "appointed." As such, he was the one appointed to replace the righteous Abel. Seth gave his son Enosh a rather intriguing name. Enosh means "frail man" or to "be weak, sick." Why would any father give his son such a name as that?

Keil and Delitzsch comment:

> In this name, therefore, the feeling and knowledge of human weakness and frailty were expressed (the opposite of the pride and arrogance displayed by the Canaanitish [sic—Cainite?] family); and this feeling led to

---
[58] Griffith W. H. Thomas, *Genesis: A Devotional Commentary* (Grand Rapids, MI: William B. Eerdmans Publishing Co., 1946), pp. 63–64.

God, to that invocation of the name of Jehovah which commenced under Enos.[59]

Enosh: Public Worship Becomes More Prominent

During the days of Enosh, men began to call on the name of the Lord. This seems to point to public worship. Certainly, every man had and continues to have the right to converse with the Lord privately. Adam, Eve, Cain, and Abel experienced such a personal interaction with God. Now, it appears that corporate worship has become a regular part of life among the godly.

Although God would still have verbal interaction with chosen people throughout the Old Testament, this was becoming more of a rarity. The prophets, for example, received direct communication with God in one way or another. Moses was extraordinarily blessed to see God in His glory, even if in a subdued sense. He spoke to God "face-to-face." The life of Enosh stands in stark contrast to the line of Cain and the boastful arrogance of Lamech.

Henry Morris adds the following comments:

> To "call upon the name of the Lord" normally implies a definite act of prayer and worship. It was evidently at this time that godly men and women first initiated public services of sacrifice, worship and prayer, replacing the earlier practice of meeting personally with God, as Cain and Abel had done. The practice of individual prayer is also intimated, implying that God's personal presence was no longer regularly available. In any case, an act of faith is implied.

---

[59] Keil and Delitzsch, Commentary on the Old Testament: Pentateuch, p. 119.

In later times, "calling upon the name of the LORD" was accompanied by the building of an altar and the offering of a sacrifice (12:8; 26:25). Since Christ's sacrifice on Calvary, however, men need only call in faith on the name of the Lord Jesus Christ. "For whosoever shall call upon the name of the Lord shall be saved" (Ro. 10:13).[60]

God has always preserved a small remnant of believers. As time got closer to the days of the Flood, that remnant became remarkably small. Noah eventually was the only man who merited God's praise and commendation as a godly man (Genesis 6:8). Together with his family, only eight survived the peril of the worldwide Flood.

The End of the First Toledoth

Sarfati offers the following concluding remarks concerning chapters 1 to 4. It is the end of the first toledoth:

> The toledot of the heavens and earth (Genesis 2:4-4:26) starts with the high point of the creation of man and woman, and the ordination of marriage. But not too long after that, the First Couple, Adam and Eve, sinned, and brought death into the world. Their firstborn Cain compounded the sin by taking a human life made in God's image. His lineage produced the vengeful Lamech who threatened fearful vengeance in his own power, and showed the results of living apart from God.

---
60 Henry Morris, The New Defender's Study Bible (Nashville, TN: World Publishing, Inc., 1995, 2007), pp. 28–29.

However, the toledot ends on a high note. Adam and Eve have another son, whose line would produce the Redeemer whom God promised in 3:15. This is Seth. He and his son Enosh are righteous men who institute public worship of the true God YHWH. But what results from them must await the second toledot.[61]

Lessons Learned in This Chapter

In this chapter, we first briefly reviewed the horrific account of Cain murdering his brother, Abel. The penalties imposed on Cain by God were, in reality, quite merciful. God sought forgiveness and reconciliation. Cain, however, was not interested in reestablishing his relationship with God.

Genesis 4:16a utters one of the most disconcerting statements in Scripture: "Then Cain went out from the presence of the LORD." His leaving indicated a spiritual abandonment. To the best of our knowledge, Cain never returned. For all practical purposes, he lived the life of an atheist in spite of personally encountering God.

The second part of this chapter examined the family life of Cain and his descendants. When Cain left, he brought his wife with him. It is entirely possible that he had already been married for some years and had fathered many children. However, the first child mentioned is Enoch. It was through Enoch that his descendants would be traced. Cain built a city and named it after his son Enoch. We continued to trace Enoch's children. They clearly were highly intelligent and talented.

The descendant of whom we have the most information is Lamech. In the first recorded instance of polygamy, Lamech mar-

---
61 Jonathan Sarfati, The Genesis Account: A theological, historical, and scientific commentary on Genesis 1–11, p. 444.

ried Adah and Zillah. Adah's son Jabal is credited with establishing a nomadic lifestyle herding livestock. However, they probably did not have to travel too far as the earth was undoubtedly much more fertile than it is today. Nonetheless, he would have been the precursor of modern-day Bedouins. His brother Jubal invented the harp and flute. He initiated music that is soothing to the soul.

Zillah's son Tubal-Cain invented metallurgy. He worked with bronze and iron. It is quite likely that Lamech quickly utilized these metals for militaristic purposes. He bragged about killing a young man who had wounded him in some fashion. In a mocking manner, he stated that if God would avenge Cain sevenfold, he should be avenged seventy-sevenfold. This should be understood as a direct affront to God and His mercy. Mankind was turning increasingly wicked.

Third, we discussed Seth's son, Enosh. During his lifetime, men began to call on the name of the Lord. This implies public worship. Clearly, men and women had been calling on the name of the Lord privately ever since creation. As time passed, however, God's appearance to individuals began to lessen. By no means did it cease, however, as is evidenced by Moses and the prophets. Prior to then, God also appeared to the patriarchs Abraham, Isaac, and Jacob.

However, God first appeared to Adam and Eve in the Garden of Eden. No other mortal has ever enjoyed the sweet fellowship they experienced. They were sinless and thrived in a perfect environment. Such an idyllic situation will not be replicated until eternity (Revelation chapters 21 to 22). But in spite of those unimaginable advantages, sin stealthily invaded the world nonetheless. Thankfully, God knows all and provides redemption to all who will receive it (Genesis 3:15; Isaiah 46:10; John 1:12).

We conclude this chapter with the following worthy quotation from Leupold:

> Men do not first in the age of Abraham or Moses begin to comprehend God's faithfulness, unchangeableness, and mercy. Since this calling out by the use of the name definitely implies public worship, we have here the first record of regular public worship. Private worship is presupposed as preceding.
>
> The great importance of public worship, both as a matter of personal necessity as well as a matter of public confession, is beautifully set forth by this brief record. This act bears eloquent testimony to the courage of this group, who wanted to be known as such whose hope was placed only in Yahweh. It is not enough to say that "Yahweh's religion begins with Enoch." It began with Adam and developed into regular public worship in three generations.[62]

In our next chapter, we shall examine the toledoth of Adam and Eve down to the time of Moses. This is the second toledoth mentioned in the book of Genesis. It covers a period of 1,656 years. During this tumultuous period, the world grows steadily more wicked. Finally, when the ark was prepared to take Noah and his family into safety, only eight human beings were spared.

Mankind had been reduced to just one godly family remaining. Ironically, only Noah actually receives the accolade of godliness. Genesis 6:8 states: "But Noah found grace in the eyes of the LORD." We trust, however, that his influence was sufficient and that his family willingly followed his example. Such a spiritual condition of the

---
[62] H. C. Leupold, Exposition of Genesis, p. 228.

earth down to eight people truly boggles the imagination.

We shall also examine the great ages to which man lived. Nothing like that time frame of longevity has been witnessed since the age of early man. However, the millennial kingdom of Christ will once again witness great lifespans of men and women. People will once again live to 1,000 years of age. As such, they will exceed even the vast ages recorded in Genesis chapter 5.

Cognitive Conundrum #8

Fidelity to loved ones marked my entire life; though faithful, my life with pain was rife. That two sought my consolation held true, I, in turn, would see another in pain through. My heritage proved unworthy, I must confide, but God, in great mercy, did turn the tide. A man sought me as his bride in devotion; our descendant would prove our redemption.

Who am I?

Answer: Ruth

Chapter 9

Godly Generations from Adam to Noah

(Genesis 5:1–32)

In This Chapter

Objectives for This Chapter
The "Toledoth" (Generations) from Adam to Noah (Genesis 5:1–32)
A Succession of Godly Men
The Exceptional Man Enoch (Genesis 5:21–24)
The Grand Finale of the Patriarchs
Lessons Learned in This Chapter

Objectives for This Chapter

Genesis chapter 5 is a most exceptional chapter. It covers a period of 1,656 years. That would be the time from creation until the Flood. During this time, two lines of men were developing. The ungodly line of Cain ultimately took over nearly the entire character of humanity. As we shall see in Genesis chapter 6, mankind became almost completely corrupt. Judgment was needed and was thoroughly exercised by the Creator. It is called the universal Flood.

In this chapter, we shall review the succession of godly men. Though details are quite sketchy about most of these men, other passages of Scripture often help shed additional light on the lives of some of them, such as Adam, Enoch, and Noah. Enoch lived such a godly life as a prophet that God directly translated him alive up to heaven. This has occurred only twice in history, the other being

Elijah. It is thought by many, although it cannot be proven, that Enoch and Elijah will be the two magnificent witnesses spoken of in Revelation chapter 11.

Common Items of Speculation by the Unfaithful

Our first topic of discussion revolves around a few frequently debated items. Many stumble at the great age of the patriarchs. They reason that living for hundreds of years is not possible simply because we do not live hundreds of years in our present age. Such speculation ignores the plain teachings of Scripture. If one is to caustically cast off the teachings of Scripture based on personal experience, what then remains? There is no foundation for truth left, save the arrogant pontifications of man.

These same individuals frequently believe that the Flood in Noah's day was only local. Such a viewpoint is not only unbiblical, it is ridiculous. Why would the animals and the people simply not wander a short distance away to dry ground? Furthermore, why is the evidence for a worldwide Flood just that, worldwide? Again, when one abandons the clear teaching and literal sense of Scripture, little remains but nonsense. We reject that venue of thinking wholeheartedly. Though we may not fully understand all the teachings of Scripture, we accept them nonetheless.

The biblical account must be acknowledged precisely for what it says. Matthew 24:35 declares: "Heaven and earth will pass away, but My words will by no means pass away." Jesus Christ is the living Word of God (John 1:1–5). Whatever He teaches is eternally true. And Jesus unquestionably taught that the Flood was universal.

In Matthew 24:37–39, Jesus unequivocally states:

> But as the days of Noah were, so also will the coming

of the Son of Man be, for as in the days that were before the flood, they were eating and drinking, marrying and giving in marriage, until the day that Noah entered the ark, and did not know until the flood came and took them all away, so also will the coming of the Son of Man be.

How can one question the words of the Messiah and simultaneously claim that he worships Him as the God-man? Such a lack of biblical logic is nothing less than stupefying!

An Examination of the Patriarchs

Our second topic of discussion will be a review of each of the patriarchs. Although with some of them we are granted but a minuscule glimpse, we shall examine what is available in the biblical text. Admittedly, with several of them, little more is recorded than who their Seed son was and how long they lived.

We must await the millennial kingdom of Christ to discover more about their lives. What an incredible privilege reliving their lives historically via personal interview will be! Believers shall have not just the millennial kingdom to make acquaintance with these saints of old but all eternity besides. It is ironic that a common misconception of eternity is that it will be boring. Eternity holds adventures for believers beyond our most fervent imaginations.

Third, we shall indulge ourselves in a more detailed review of the godly prophet Enoch. He certainly qualifies as one of the most mysterious and yet honored men in all of biblical history. Sadly, we are privileged at this time to know very little about his powerful and godly life. Jude 14–15 presents a summary of his extraordinary prophetic message. Enoch was truly a man for the ages. His faithfulness and exemplary lifestyle are presently known only to God.

Ironically, another man of the same name lived in the same time period as Enoch. Cain named the first city he founded after his son, Enoch (Genesis 4:17). Scripture notes one of Enoch's descendants a few generations thereafter. His name is Lamech. He stemmed from the ungodly line of Cain, both physically and spiritually. These two men, Enoch from Adam and Lamech from Cain, are remarkable contrasts in character. Enoch was incredibly godly; Lamech was a pathetic illustration of wickedness. We have already reflected on Lamech's sordid lifestyle in our examination of Genesis 4:19–24.

The reader must exercise caution not to confuse the wicked Lamech from Cain's ungodly line from the righteous Lamech stemming from Seth's godly line. Though their names are the same, their characters are completely antithetical. They are the reverse one from the other.

Methuselah, Lamech, and Noah

Fourth, we shall invest some time focusing on the final three generations listed: Methuselah, Lamech, and Noah. Methuselah had the distinction of becoming the oldest man in biblical history. He lived to the ripe old age of 969!

It is understood by the rabbis (but this is not biblically substantiated) that Methuselah died one week before the Flood. It is often thought that after God shut the door of the ark, there was a week-long delay of mourning for Methuselah's passing. Only then did the rains come down and the Flood begin. Methuselah outlived his son, Lamech, by five years.

Lamech is distinguished because he accurately prophesied of his son, Noah. Some of his prophecy remains a bit unclear to us today. However, Lamech clearly understood through the Holy Spirit that Noah was to be a man of exceptional character. God clearly granted him this insight, just as he does with all prophets.

Peter affirms this in 2 Peter 1:20–21: "Knowing this first, that no prophecy of Scripture is of any private interpretation, for prophecy never came by the will of man, but holy men of God spoke as they were moved by the Holy Spirit."

Finally, we close with an examination of Noah's life. God worked through this solitary man in powerful, unparalleled ways. Short of Jesus Christ and John the Baptist, Noah would be the third most important man ever born. God saved humanity through his faithful efforts. Noah and his immediate family, totaling eight people, appear to have been the only righteous people left on earth after the death of Methuselah. Noah's tragic time was incomparable for perverseness and wickedness of every sort imaginable.

The Toledoth (Generations) from Adam to Noah (Genesis 5:1–32)

Many students of Scripture rather unwisely skim over Genesis chapter 5. The repeated sequence of "so and so begot so and so" seems redundant and unimportant to our modern-day lives. While such a sentiment is understandable, it is not appropriate. The genealogies, though perhaps not thrilling to simply read through, are vital for biblical accuracy.

The historical veracity of Scripture rests upon its reliability. In our modern age, there exists a growing interest in people tracing their family tree. Many people consult corporations that search out a person's genealogical heritage. In these cases, no name is considered unimportant. How much more so with Scripture?

It is not within the scope of this book to delve into every detail of Genesis chapter 5. Much has been written of great value. We shall endeavor to examine details that are more relevant and practical for the modern reader, though we stress that no detail is unimportant. God included all of this material because it is relevant for a variety of reasons, some obvious, others perhaps not so clear. But every jot and tittle is important, nonetheless.

The Beginning of the Human Race

Genesis 5:1–8 states:

> This is the book of the genealogy of Adam. In the day that God created man, He made him in the likeness of God. He created them male and female, and blessed them and called them Mankind in the day they were created. And Adam lived one hundred and thirty years, and begot a son in his own likeness, after his image, and named him Seth.
>
> After he begot Seth, the days of Adam were eight hundred years; and he had sons and daughters. So all the days that Adam lived were nine hundred and thirty years; and he died. Seth lived one hundred and five years, and begot Enosh. After he begot Enosh, Seth lived eight hundred and seven years, and had sons and daughters. So all the days of Seth were nine hundred and twelve years, and he died.

(Note to the reader: Toledot and toledoth are both spellings of the same word. Scholars differ in how they choose to spell the term. Both spellings are equally acceptable.)

In Genesis 5:1–2, it is intriguing to note that, unlike the other toledoth, the "generations of Adam," this one refers to a book or a scroll. A book in relation to toledoth is not mentioned again until Mathew 1:1: "The book of the genealogy of Jesus Christ, the son of David, the son of Abraham." Why should a book be mentioned in these two particular toledoth?

Sarfati offers the following explanation:

> Genesis 5 provides the generations which proceeded from "the first man, Adam"; Matthew 1 provides the 'generations' which preceded Christ, "the last Adam" (1 Cor. 15:45). These two verses recapitulate Genesis 1:26-27, when God created Adam and Eve in His image on Day 6. The previous toledot (2:4-4:26) had expanded greatly on this brief mention in the Prologue (1:1—2:3).
>
> That toledot dismissed the line of the murderer Cain, and returned to the Seed son, Seth. We are told of only one more generation, Enosh, but the toledot left on the high note of the beginning of public worship to YHWH. The toledot of Adam recapitulates the first two generations from him, then continues much further.[63]

As Sarfati points out, the previous, or first toledot (2:4–4:26), concluded with Adam, Seth, and Enosh. The second toledot, Genesis 5:1, picks up where the first one left off, reiterating and adding additional information regarding the same three men. Numerous observations regarding this fascinating chapter are in order.

Romans 15:4 reminds us of the benefits of learning from even the genealogies: "For whatever things were written before were written for our learning, that we through the patience and comfort

---

[63] Ibid., p. 446.

of the Scriptures might have hope." All Scripture is for the benefit of man.

Early Man Lived to an Immense Age

Observation #1: Men lived extraordinarily long lives. For 1,656 after the creation of man, the individual men listed in Genesis chapter 5 lived incredibly extended lives. The most remarkable aspect to contemplate is that many of these men were contemporaries of Adam himself. Either that, or they were personally acquainted with someone else who had been.

Excluding Enoch, who was directly translated to heaven at the age of 365, the other ten patriarchs who preceded the Great Flood lived to a remarkable average of 912 years! Lamech, the youngster of the group, died at the tender age of 777. Methuselah, the granddaddy of them all, lived to 969 years of age! His grandfather, Jared, who fathered Enoch, lived the second longest life at 962 years. Ironically, Methuselah's son, Lamech, had the shortest lifespan save that of Enoch, who never died.

Scripture does not explicitly reveal why people lived so long before the Flood. Some believe that an atmospheric "canopy" somehow shielded humanity from harmful effects from the sun. Such a canopy may have produced additional benefits of which modern science is not aware. However, Noah still lived until he was 950 (Genesis 9:29). He was thus the third longest-living man in history. If the canopy effect was genuine, it would have been removed during the course of the Flood. But God could easily have supernaturally lengthened Noah's days.

Noah turned 600 at the time of the Flood, which means he outlived it by 350 years. As already stated, it can be argued that God gave Noah an unnaturally long life, although not particularly different than his forebears. This longevity may have been granted because of his faithfulness in building the ark. Others, however, also lived after the Flood for durations of hundreds of years. It should be noted, however, that Shem, Noah's Seed son, lived to only 600 years of age. That is a 350-year difference between father and son in one generation!

Some feel that mankind's lifespan progressively got shorter because of genetic mutations. There has been considerable speculation over the lifespan issue over the years. One thing is certain: Genesis chapter 11 does make it abundantly clear that lifespans diminished over time. No immediate biblical explanation for that drastic reduction is offered.

It has been asserted that this proclamation of a shorter lifespan is announced in Genesis 6:3: "And the LORD said, 'My Spirit shall not strive with man forever, for he is indeed flesh; yet his days shall be one hundred and twenty years.'" One cannot conclusively deny that this was a prophetic statement regarding the longevity of man. Contextually, however, it seems better to understand this as a divine warning that the universal judgment of the Flood would take place in 120 years. If that be the case, Noah was 480 years old at this time.

Perhaps the most definitive statement on the longevity of man is recorded by Moses in Psalm 90:10: "The days of our lives are seventy years; and if by reason of strength they are eighty years, yet their boast is only labor and sorrow; for it is soon cut off, and we fly away." Ironically, Moses himself lived 120 years. However, that was exceptionally long, even in his day. The average lifespan of people in the world today is precisely what is recorded in Psalm 90:10. Only a select few live to one hundred and beyond. Most die between the ages of seventy and eighty.

A Question of Gaps in the Genealogical Record

Question: Were there gaps within the genealogical record? James Barr (1924–2006), then regius professor of Hebrew at Oxford University, commented as follows in 1984:

> ... probably, so far as I know, there is no professor of Hebrew or Old Testament at any world-class university who does not believe that the writer(s) of Genesis 1-11 intended to convey to their readers the ideas that:
> ... the figures contained in the Genesis genealogies provide by simple addition a chronology from the beginning of the world up to later stages in the biblical story.[64]

It is fascinating to note that Barr himself did not accept the Genesis record at face value. However, he did believe that a strict, uninterrupted genealogy was what Genesis clearly taught. Many scholars have unwisely rejected the clear counsel and teaching of Scripture because it doesn't mesh with the pseudoscience of the day called evolution. They thus place the folly of fallible man above the eternal truisms of an eternal and omnipotent God.

Evolution has so ingrained itself into modern man's thinking that it seems nearly impossible to wrest it from many "educated" individual's obstinate minds. The true tragedy is how compromised people have become just for the sake of popular thinking. Yet that popular thinking is entirely devoid of scientific substance.

Many people have forgotten how to think for themselves. In blunt reality, they never learned how to think. They blindly allow so-called authorities to do their thinking for them. They then just "parrot" out the answers provided by others without any contempla-

---
64 James Barr, Letter to David C. C. Watson, 1984.

tive effort whatsoever. That is a woeful and dangerous "lack-of-cogitation" scenario in which to voluntarily place oneself. God provided brains to every man and woman. He expects us to utilize them to His glory, not to our own mindless acceptance of pseudoscientific and philosophical drivel.

No Genealogical Gaps Are Necessary

Regarding gaps in the genealogical records, Sarfati offers the following sagacious observations:

- Seth; definitely a direct son of Adam and Eve, named by both of them, and seen as a replacement for Abel, killed by Cain (4:25).
- Enosh: must be a son of Seth, because Seth named him (4:25).
- Jude 14 says Enoch was seventh from Adam, which indicates straight-forward father-son relationships from Adam to Enoch.
- Methuselah: Enoch, a pre-Flood prophet (Jude 14), gave his son a name meaning 'when he dies it shall be sent', and the Masoretic chronology without any gaps would place his death in the year of the Flood.
- Noah: Lamech named him, so Lamech must be his father, not just an ancestor (5:29).
- Shem, Ham, and Japheth were definitely ordinary sons of Noah, since they accompanied him on the Ark.
- Arphaxad was plainly a son of Shem, because he was born two years after the Flood (11:10).
- Abram, Haran, and Nahor were Terah's ordinary sons, since they journeyed together from Ur of the Chaldees (11:31).[65]

---

65 Jonathan Sarfati, The Genesis Account: A theological, historical, and scientific commentary on Genesis 1–11, p. 467.

To the objective mind, what Sarfati writes above should provide abundant proof of the complete reliability of the genealogical record. It does not skip generations. Rather, it should be understood just as it is read: a simple chronological record. People are perfectly willing to accept today's genealogical records, which are based on far less accurate data. But some of those same people, for no plausible reason whatsoever, will then reject the biblical record.

Names Have Meanings

Observation #2: The names of the patriarchs have definite meanings. It is amazing to note how a person's name frequently matches his character. A brief review of the names, although at times it is somewhat debated as to those meanings, proves helpful in understanding the text. It is fascinating to note that the names of the ten patriarchs are all of Hebrew origin. This seems to suggest that Hebrew was the original language up until the Tower of Babel. Only after the Tower of Babel does one find non-Hebrew names.

The first non-Hebrew names recorded occur in Genesis chapter 14. In that particular scenario, the chapter chronicles the foreign names of four invading kings. Thus, foreign names would be expected. However, based on the names preceding this chapter, it seems quite probable that the language of the early patriarchs, that of the millennial kingdom, and perhaps even eternity will be Hebrew. The Hebrews are God's chosen people. Why should Hebrew not be the eternal language?

The Miracle of Learning a Language

Some have questioned how Hebrew ever became a language. That is, truthfully, a nonstarter of a question. How did any language become a language? The simple and accurate answer is that God created every language. He then placed the ability to become fluent thereof within the human mind (Genesis chapter 11). It matters not what the language may be or the level of its complexity. God enables the smallest of children, babies really, to begin understanding any language. Could evolution provide such a miracle in action? We think not.

Chinese babies learn Chinese, Arabic children learn Arabic, Hebrews learn Hebrew, and English babies learn English. This is a marvelous miracle to behold in all small children. They begin learning as babies without effort, study, or impatience. Many children around the world master several different languages simultaneously.

How could evolution ever create a language, much less engender the capacity to learn several at a time? Evolution is, according to the evolutionists themselves, completely brainless and random. One ponders, then, why the evolutionist does not claim for himself those same unflattering qualities. Is that not a rather discriminatory denial of his own alleged ancient history? Would that not be the consistent and logical conclusion? Evolutionists tend to bridle against such "reasonable reasoning" with firmly gritted teeth and a noticeably sparse sense of humor.

So how could this witless, unsystematic, and invisible process of evolution create systematic and highly complex methods of communication called languages? Furthermore, why would it create so many thousands of them? Is there not a tad bit of incongruity in this picture? Perhaps the evolutionists could "talk it out" regarding how the non-talking process of evolution allows them to "talk it out." Evolution wittingly, even pompously, embraces a system "devoid of intelligence." That is an unenviable mental straitjacket. Alas! In accordance to their own unrelenting principles, we must allow them to devise their own brainless and unsystematic response. Remember: Evolution cannot give what it does not have.

A Succession of Godly Men

The First Man, Adam

Adam (Genesis 5:1–5): His name means "man" or "mankind." He is noted for being God's first and only created man. God formed Adam out of the dust of the earth. Adam is the federal head of humanity and tragically, along with his wife Eve, brought sin into the world through his disobedience. Adam's sin is doubly tragic because it was deliberate. Eve was deceived by the serpent and was thus less culpable, though both are unquestionably guilty.

Genesis 5:1–5 states:

> This is the book of the genealogy of Adam. In the day that God created man, He made him in the likeness of God. He created them male and female, and blessed them and called them Mankind in the day they were created.

> And Adam lived one hundred and thirty years, and begot a son in his own likeness, after his image, and named him Seth. After he begot Seth, the days of Adam were eight hundred years; and he had sons and daughters. So all the days that Adam lived were nine hundred and thirty years; and he died.

On the positive side of the coin, Adam could testify of God's goodness and mercy in providing a Seed of the woman who would redeem the world. He knew little of this coming Messiah. It is certain that Eve, and probably Adam as well, thought Cain was that promised Seed, the Messiah. They were badly mistaken in their timing but absolutely correct in their theology.

Scripture records people's mistakes as well as their accurate thinking. Still, it must be recognized that history's first couple firmly believed God's promise. Genesis 4:1 emphasizes that they thought the man born to them was indeed God in the flesh. Considering that God had walked with them in the Garden of Eden in some visible form, this unique God-man concept was not difficult for them to envision. Thus, they readily believed in a God-man to be their Messiah.

Imagine their grave disappointment when they realized Cain was not the fervently hoped-for Messiah. Indeed, he proved to be anything but the promised Seed. Their case of mistaken identity did not in any way contravene the reality of the messianic promises (Genesis 3:15). Man's temporal errors do not circumvent God's eternal decrees. The Messiah did indeed arrive on the scene 4,000 years later to accomplish His mission of redemption for mankind.

Adam Fathers Seth, the Seed Son

Adam fathered Seth at the age of 130. Seth was to become the Seed son through whom the Messiah would eventually come. Adam's specific age testifies to the fact that there could not have been millions of years during the creation week or before the fall. If one chooses to interpret Scripture in such a haphazard fashion, as do the day-age theorists with their billions of years, how can one possibly determine actual truth vs. fiction? Bible interpretation becomes impossible.

What point would there be in even reading Sacred Writ? Adam

lived until he was 930. That is a plain, straightforward fact. It requires no deep, internal contemplation or undue discussion. God means what God says! Either the Scripture is true in all, or it is not true at all.

If one is inclined to pick and choose what he believes or does not believe in the Scripture, he may as well read Shakespeare instead. It is well-written and spins a good yarn. If Scripture is not the truth and nothing but the truth, where then is truth recorded? It is only in the mind of the reader. At our present time, that means there are approximately eight billion varying definitions of truth. That is not a comforting thought. Some individuals' definition of peace and goodwill toward man is somewhat less than serene and contemplative.

Are Such Great Ages of the Patriarchs Possible?

Regarding the incredibly long lifespans of these pre-Flood patriarchs, Leupold offers the following astute observations:

> At once we are struck by the longevity of these patriarchs; all except three lived in excess of nine hundred years. It is useless to attempt to evade this fact. The attempt to let the personal names represent tribes shatters in the clear statement of how old each father was when he begot a son. A complete generation is not thus brought forth within a tribe.
>
> Equally abortive is the attempt to claim that numerous links in the chain may have been omitted. Again the precise measuring of each forward step in reference to successive individuals peremptorily rules out such a

claim. The most common suggestion by way of escape from the difficulty is to make "year" mean a shorter period, either one month or two, etc.

Unfortunately, the term "year" knows of no such usage, and the suggestion must be treated as a mere surmise. He, however, who is duly impressed by the excellence of man's original estate, will have no difficulty in accepting the common explanation that even under the curse of sin man's constitution displayed such vitality that it did not at first submit to the ravages of time until after many centuries had passed.

Besides—a fact established by fossil finds—there are ample indications of a more salubrious climate in the antediluvian days. Nor should we forget that here is the race of godly men who lived temperately and sanely.[66]

Moses wrote that Adam and Eve "begot a son in his own likeness, after his image, and named him Seth." Clearly, this does not mean that Seth wasn't made in God's image as that would contradict earlier and later Scripture (Genesis 1:26–28, 9:6; 1 Corinthians 11:7; James 3:9). Nor, even though women are not specifically mentioned in Genesis chapter 5, does it deny their being made in the image of God. Nothing could be further from the truth. Adam and Eve shared equally in God's image from the beginning of creation.

James McKeown offers the following explanation:

> The NIV Study Bible jumps to the logical conclusion that "As God created man in His own perfect image,

---
[66] H. C. Leupold, Exposition of Genesis, pp. 233–234.

so now sinful Adam has a son in his own imperfect image." However, given that the main message of this passage is that the line of Adam's firstborn son Cain has been rejected in favor of his younger brother Seth, the most likely interpretation is that Adam, who is made in the image of God, passes this image on to Seth. This argument is supported by the later affirmation that, even after the flood, human beings are superior to animals because they are made in the image of God (9:6).[67]

Mankind's Ongoing Struggle with Sin Foreshadows Deliverance

It must be noted that man inherits his fallen nature from Adam. That nature is corrupt. But, as previously stated, mankind blessedly still retains the image of God even though it has been marred by sin. That image is no longer pure, like it was from the initial creation of Adam and Eve. Indeed, it is impossible for modern man to comprehend a perfect nature. As some have compellingly expressed it, our image of God has been effaced but not erased.

The apostle Paul emphasizes that while we are believers on this present earth, we retain Adam's fallen nature. But even in this present life, we are privileged to inherit Christ's perfect nature, though not in its full manifestation. In a mysterious sense, we are granted a fuller restoration of God's image. Second Corinthians 5:21 represents one of the most stunning proclamations of that truth recorded in Scripture: "For He made Him who knew no sin to be sin for us, that we might become the righteousness of God in Him."

When God looks at a redeemed individual, He sees them through the perfect blood of Christ. This makes the believer positionally per-

---
[67] James McKeown, Genesis, p. 45.

fect in Christ. Sadly, believers remain morally flawed from a practical standpoint. Only when believers ascend to glory will they be perfectly restored to what Adam and Eve were originally.

Eventually, but not in this present life, believers shall entirely leave the fallen nature behind. Believers' new and sinless nature is constantly battling with our ever-present old nature (Romans 7:5–7, 14–25). So it is that believers have both a new and old nature (Romans 6:5–8, 15–18; 2 Corinthians 5:17; Colossians 3:1–12).

The old nature, which we retain from Adam, cannot help but sin (1 John 1:8–10). It is condemned to evil while on this earth. Believers will continuously struggle to follow God's holy decrees. Thankfully, as our passage below informs us, we shall eventually be liberated from the very presence of sin. We shall become completely transformed creatures. Until that glorious moment of spiritual deliverance, our old nature will be in perpetual struggle against our new nature.

First Corinthians 15:45–49 states:

> And so it is written, "The first man Adam became a living being." The last Adam became a life-giving spirit. However, the spiritual is not first, but the natural, and afterward the spiritual. The first man was of the earth, made of dust; the second Man is the Lord from heaven. As was the man of dust, so also are those who are made of dust; and as is the heavenly Man, so also are those who are heavenly. And as we have borne the image of the man of dust, we shall also bear the image of the heavenly Man.

There Is Freedom in Christ

John MacArthur comments as follows:

> Adam and Eve originally were in a probationary period. Had they proved faithful rather than disobedient, their bodies would have been glorified and immortalized by eating the fruit of the tree of life, which they then could have eaten (see Gen. 2:9). Because they sinned, however, they were put out of the garden lest they eat of the tree of life and live forever in a state of sin (3:22).
>
> The last Adam, however, became a life-giving spirit. The last Adam is Jesus Christ (Rom. 5:19, 21; cf. vv. 12, 15). Through Adam we have inherited our natural bodies; through Christ we will inherit spiritual bodies in the resurrection. …
>
> Adam, the first man, from whom came the natural race, originated on the earth, in fact was created directly from the earth (Gen. 2:7). In every way he was earthy. But Christ, called the second man because He has produced a spiritual race, existed eternally before He became a man. He lived on earth in a natural body, but He came from heaven. Adam was tied to earth; Christ was tied to heaven.

Because of our natural descent from Adam we are a part of those who are earthy. But because of our inheritance in Jesus Christ, we also have become a part of those who are heavenly. In Adam we are earthy; in Christ we have become heavenly.

One day our natural bodies from Adam will be changed into our heavenly bodies from Christ. And just as we have borne the image of the earthy, we shall also bear the image of the heavenly. Just as we will exchange Adam's natural body for Christ's spiritual body, we will also exchange Adam's image for Christ's.[68]

Seth

Seth (Genesis 5:6–8): The name Seth means to "set something in place" or "appointed." It would appear that the idea behind his name was that he replaced Abel, who had been murdered by Cain. Seth was 105 years old when he begot Enosh. After that, he lived another 807 years, making a total of 912.

Genesis 5:6–8 states: "Seth lived one hundred and five years, and begot Enosh. After he begot Enosh, Seth lived eight hundred and seven years, and had sons and daughters. So all the days of Seth were nine hundred and twelve years, and he died."

It was during the days of Seth and his son Enosh that men began to call on the name of the Lord (Genesis 4:26), which seems to indicate public worship services. The ungodly line of Cain had not entirely ruled out the faithful to the Lord. However, over the following centuries, that faithful remnant to the Lord perpetually

---
[68] John MacArthur, The MacArthur's New Testament Commentary: 1 Corinthians (Chicago, IL: Moody Press, 1984), pp. 438–439.

declined among their descendants. Finally, only Noah was left to be described as a man who pleased the Lord (6:8–9).

Enosh

Enosh (Genesis 5:9–11): His name means "frail man." This seems a rather odd name for a father to give to his son. Seth is possibly reacting to the line of Cain, which had rapidly become repugnant to God. He chose a name demonstrating humility and dependence on the Lord as a contrast to the rebellious spirit of Cain and his descendants. The ungodly line of Cain tended to boastfulness and arrogance, as demonstrated by Lamech.

Enosh begot Kenan when he was ninety, lived an additional 815 years, and died at the age of 905. It should be noted that the Seed son, or primary son, is always the one listed. It does not necessitate that Enosh or the following did not father other children, whether sons or daughters, before the one that is actually listed. God selected certain young men within these rather large extended families through whom He chose to extend His future messianic blessing. As one can see below, the information provided for these individuals is quite limited.

Genesis 5:9–11 states: "Enosh lived ninety years, and begot Cainan. After he begot Cainan, Enosh eight hundred and fifteen years, and had sons and daughters. So all the days of Enosh were nine hundred and five years; and he died."

Cainan

Kenan or Cainan (Genesis 5:12–14): His name means "smith." His name is similar to but not identical to Cain. Cainan begot Mahalalel when he was seventy and then lived 840 more years, dying at the age of 910. Genesis 5:12–14 states: "Cainan lived seventy years, and begot Mahalalel. After he begot Mahalalel, Cainan lived eight hundred and forty years, and he had sons and daughters. So all the days of Cainan were nine hundred and ten years; and he died."

Mahalalel

Mahalalel (Genesis 5:15–17): His name means "praise of Elohim." His father apparently wanted to bring praise to the Lord in the naming of his son. This demonstrates an ongoing celebration and worship of the Creator. However, as each succeeding generation passed, the faithful steadily declined in number. Mahalalel fathered Jared at the age of sixty-five. He then lived an additional 830 years and died at the age of 895. He was the first patriarch to die a natural death under the age of 900.

Genesis 5:15–17 states: "Mahalalel lived sixty-five years, and begot Jared. After he begot Jared, Mahalalel lived eight hundred and thirty years, and had sons and daughters. So all the days of Mahalalel were eight hundred and ninety-five years; and he died."

Jared

Jared (Genesis 5:18–20): His name means "descent." Jared had the honor of living the second-longest lifespan in biblical history. His grandson alone would surpass him. He fathered Enoch at 162, lived 800 more years, and died at 962. Jared apparently proved an exceptional father. It is admittedly true that, at times, sons far surpassed their fathers in spirituality. This was particularly true for the kings of Judah many centuries later.

We favor the belief, however, that Jared raised up his unique son, Enoch, in a highly commendable fashion. As revealed in our set of verses, Enoch never died but was translated straight to heaven. His was an exceptionally godly lifestyle. The name that Jared bestowed upon his son also supports the view of his heartfelt dedication of his son to God.

Genesis 5:18–20 states: "Jared lived one hundred and sixty-two years, and begot Enoch. After he begot Enoch, Jared lived eight hundred years, and had sons and daughters. So all the days of Jared were nine hundred and sixty-two years; and he died." Although the Scripture does not specify how Jared raised his son, Enoch, we assume that it was in exemplary style. It would strike us as quite unusual that Enoch would turn out to be such a uniquely godly man without strong biblical guidance.

The Exceptional Man Enoch (Genesis 5:21–24)

Enoch (Genesis 5:21–24): Enoch's name means "dedication." Ironically, this is the same name as Cain's son (Genesis 4:17). Cain was dedicating the city he founded after the name of his son. Jared was apparently dedicating his son to God. Enoch lived sixty-five years and fathered Methuselah. He then lived an additional 300 years, and God took him. So, Enoch lived on the earth for 365 years but never died! He was translated straight into heaven! The only other man in world history to experience such a translation is Elijah.

Enoch Walked with God

Genesis 5:21–24 states:

> Enoch lived sixty-five years, and begot Methuselah. After he begot Methuselah, Enoch walked with God three hundred years, and had sons and daughters. So all the days of Enoch were three hundred and sixty-five

years. And Enoch walked with God; and he was not, for God took him.

Verse 24 states: "And Enoch walked with God; and he was not, for God took him." The verb "walked" in Hebrew is in the Hithpael stem, which is intensive and reflexive. It reflects a habitual, never-ending habit. This shows that Enoch lived his entire life in the closest communion humanly possible with God. He was an extraordinary man who pleased God.

The same Hithpael verbal pattern was used only of Noah regarding his walk with God (Genesis 6:9). These two men exemplify godly living to all believers today and throughout history. Although very little is personally known of Enoch, one can remember and emulate his extremely commendable lifestyle.

Walking with God Was Like Breathing to Enoch

Leupold comments:

Now the significant thing reported concerning him is that he "walked with God" (hithhallekh 'eth ha'elohim). The Hithpael stem signifies "to walk about" = "to live." The particular preposition used, 'eth, denotes "intimacy, fellowship" (BDB). ...

We are thus driven to take the expression "to walk with God," figuratively, in the sense of inner communion, as living one's life in such a way that in faith one remains uninterruptedly conscious of the nearness of the almighty God and so walks as the thought of that presence determines. Life was lived to please God, so far as this was humanly possible.

... One side of such walking with God is very fortunately stressed by Luther on good scriptural grounds over against the purely mystical and contemplative aspect of it that we might be inclined to overstress. Developing the thought expressed in Jude 14, 15, Luther rightly contends that Enoch's communion with God was coupled with aggressive testimony to the unbelievers of his generation, and, therefore, he is to be regarded as a man who manifested "great boldness in testifying for the Lord and His church against Satan's church and that of the Cainites."[69]

Historically, only Enoch and Elijah (2 Kings 2:11) were directly translated into heaven without first dying. This scenario will take place again at the Rapture for the living believers. Thus, these living believers will never face the remorseful pangs of death. Those of the Church age who had previously died will be resurrected first and then immediately followed by the living saints (1 Corinthians 15:51–54; 1 Thessalonians 4:13–18). It is wise for the believer to contemplate such illustrious lives as Enoch, Elijah, Noah, and other assorted heroes of the faith.

In a world replete with unbelievers, much encouragement can be garnered from these men of incredible faith. We have much to be gained from the study and emulation of their godly lives. In this ever-increasingly dark world, such inspirational examples are a tremendous blessing. Their godly lifestyles need to be passed on to one's children and grandchildren.

---

[69] H. C. Leupold, Exposition of Genesis, pp. 241–243.

A Striking Contrast of Two Men

Sarfati offers the following salient comments:

> Jude 14-15 affirms that Enoch was "the seventh from Adam", which is further support for a strict, gapless chronogenealogy. It's notable that while this Enoch comes via Seth, the seventh from Adam via Cain was Lamech. As shown in chapter 14, this Lamech was a violent and vengeful man who cared nothing for God. This could have been the beginning of a marked morally downward slide to the general depravity and violence revealed in Genesis 6:5-12.
>
> Because the Sethite Enoch and the Cainite Lamech were in the same generation, they could have been rough contemporaries, and a marked contrast: Lamech wicked and Enoch righteous. So while Genesis says that Enoch walked with God, the NT reveals one way this was expressed. Enoch was a prophet who preached righteousness and denounced the wickedness developing in mankind, who by contrast "walked in the way of Cain" (Jude 11).[70]

Enoch clearly grew up to be an extremely righteous man. He was a prophet of whom we know very little, but what we do know is extremely impressive.

---

[70] Jonathan Sarfati, The Genesis Account: A theological, historical, and scientific commentary on Genesis 1–11, p. 453.

Enoch Was a Great Prophet

Jude 14–15 states:

> Now Enoch, the seventh from Adam, prophesied about these men also, saying, "Behold, the Lord comes with ten thousands of His saints, to execute judgment on all, to convict all who are ungodly among them of all their ungodly deeds which they have committed in an ungodly way, and of all the harsh things which ungodly sinners have spoken against them."

John Macarthur adroitly systematizes these verses as follows:

> First, the final aspect of God's divine wrath relates to a specific future event—namely, the second coming of Jesus Christ. At the end of the age, the Lord will return to earth to execute judgment: "He has fixed a day in which He will judge the world in righteousness through a Man whom He has appointed, having furnished proof to all men by raising Him from the dead" (Acts 17:31; cf. Matt. 24:29-30; Rom. 2:5-8, 16; 2 Peter 2:9b; Jude 6b; Rev. 6:16-17). ...
>
> Second, this judgment will be general and public. For instance, at the sheep and goat judgment (which immediately precedes the millennial kingdom), Christ will call to account all the nations of the earth. ... Third, God's judgment will be just and impartial (Rom. 2:11; Gal. 2:6; cf. Gen. 18:25). ... Fourth, the promise of divine judgment is intended as a warning. ...

Fifth, God's judgment is based on His law (Deut. 27:26; Rom. 2:12; 3:19; Gal. 3:10; James 2:10). ... Sixth, God's judgement will occur in specific phases. It will begin during the seven-year tribulation period (which immediately follows the rapture—1 Thess. 4:13-17; cf. Rev. 3:10). ... Finally, God's retribution ultimately results in eternal damnation in hell (Matt. 13:40-42; cf. 24:50-51; John 5:29).[71]

Enoch's prophecy concerns the return of Christ to establish His millennial kingdom. He will simultaneously judge the wicked and punish them with death. But for the living saints who survive the tumultuous Tribulation, much joy and reward awaits them. Hebrews 11:5 offers further testimony of Enoch's spiritual character: "By faith Enoch was taken away so that he did not see death, 'and was not found because God had taken him'; for before he was taken he had this testimony, that he pleased God." What greater compliment can any man receive than that which is recorded in this verse?

The Grand Finale of the Patriarchs

Methuselah

Methuselah (Genesis 5:25–27): Methuselah holds the distinction of being the oldest man in biblical history. At the age of 187, he fathered Lamech. He then lived an additional 782 years and fathered many other children. He died at the tender age of 969, a memorable attainment, to say the least. That represents a lot of birthday celebrations!

---

[71] John MacArthur, The MacArthur New Testament Commentary: 2 Peter & Jude (Chicago, IL: Moody Publishers, 2005), pp. 184–186.

Genesis 5:25–27 states:

> Methuselah lived one hundred eighty-seven years, and begot Lamech. After he begot Lamech, Methuselah lived seven hundred and eighty-two years, and had sons and daughters. So all the days of Methuselah were nine hundred and sixty-nine years; and he died.

Methuselah's name has a twofold meaning. It could mean "man of the spear," but it can also mean "when he dies, it shall be sent." The latter meaning seems to make more contextual sense. It must be remembered that his father was the exemplary prophet, Enoch. It would seem characteristic that Enoch would name Methuselah with a prophetic message intended.

What was this "potential" prophecy? It appears that Methuselah died in the same year as the Flood. Rabbinic tradition holds that Methuselah died one week before the Flood. When Noah and his family entered into the ark, there was a one-week period of mourning for Methuselah. It was only after that the rain started pouring down from the heavens.

Again, one cannot positively affirm that this was Enoch's veiled prophetic message since the name Methuselah is debated as to its precise meaning. But if it does refer to the year of the Flood, that would have been a truly sensational prophecy. God always gives ample warning to the wicked before He enacts judgment. The Flood occurred 1,656 years after creation. According to a strict biblical genealogy, that is indeed the precise year Methuselah died. So, it is quite conceivable that the duration of Methuselah's life was a literal countdown to judgment.

Lamech

Lamech (Genesis 5:28–31): Lamech's name means "warrior" or "conqueror." He holds the prestigious title of fathering and, arguably, the most important man in humanity, save the Lord Jesus Christ and John the Baptist. That individual is Noah, the man who built the ark.

Lamech was 182 years old when Noah was born. He then lived an additional 595 years, making a total of 777 years. This was the youngest lifespan of the original patriarchs. Ironically, Methuselah, his father, actually outlived Lamech, his son, by five years. Lamech also fathered many other children, but Noah was the Seed son. Sadly, it appears that Noah's brothers and sisters did not walk by the same biblical creed and lifestyle he did. None of them entered into the ark of God's refuge. This reality must have broken Noah's faithful and loving heart.

Genesis 5:28–31 states:

> Lamech lived one hundred eighty-two years, and had a son. And he called his name Noah, saying, "This one will comfort us concerning our work and the toil of our hands, because of the ground which the LORD has cursed." After he begot Noah, Lamech lived five hundred and ninety-five years, and had sons and daughters. So all the days of Lamech were seven hundred and seventy-seven years; and he died.

Unlike the Lamech of Genesis 4:23–24, who was the descendant of the wicked Cain, this descendant from the line of Seth was a very godly man. In Genesis 5:29, he utters these prophetic words: "And he called his name Noah, saying, 'This one will comfort us concerning our work and the toil of our hands, because of the ground which the LORD has cursed.'"

Sarfati comments on Noah as follows:

> This name was "Noah." In Hebrew this is Noach ... Lamech explained that this Noach "shall bring us relief from our work and from the painful toil of our hands" caused by "ground that the LORD has cursed." This is yet another word-play that works only in Hebrew—the verb "comfort" is nacham, which is only one Hebrew letter different from Noach. There is another similar proper name, Nehum (Nechum) in Nehemiah 7:7, which also means "comfort." There is another word similarity: Noach and nuach meaning "rest."[72]

Lamech's blessing and prediction about his son Noah strikes one as a bit confusing. It is not entirely clear how Noah comforted mankind in relationship to the ground that God had cursed. That lack of our present understanding, however, in no way means that Lamech was mistaken in his prophecy. It is true that Eve was mistaken about the coming Messiah being fulfilled in Cain. However, that allegation of similar error should not be superimposed on Lamech.

Lamech himself possibly did not understand everything about how his prophecy concerning Noah would be fulfilled. Still, that was not uncommon among prophetic statements by other prophets, as Peter mentions (cf. 1 Peter 1:10–11). Still, as we shall see, Noah turned out to be a comfort in many different ways. We shall examine a number of ways in which Noah did prove to be a comfort to humanity.

---
[72] Jonathan Sarfati, The Genesis Account: A theological, historical, and scientific commentary on Genesis 1–11, p. 456.

Noah

Noah (Genesis 5:32): When Noah was 500 years old, he fathered three sons. Although a superficial reading of the text seems to indicate that the three sons were triplets, that is not correct. Genesis 11:10 states that Shem fathered Arphaxad at the age of one hundred, two years after the Flood. So Shem was only ninety-eight when the Flood began. In Genesis 9:24, Ham is called the youngest son. Consequently, Japheth must be the oldest. Noah fathered him at the age of 500.

Genesis 5:32 states: "And Noah was five hundred years old, and Noah begot Shem, Ham, and Japheth." As already noted, Lamech made a compelling prophecy about Noah. How did his prophecy come to pass? His son Noah brought comfort and rest to the earth in at least seven ways that we can presently ascertain:

Humanity and the Animal Kingdom Is Spared on the Ark

Comfort #1: The primary comfort is that humanity itself was spared because of Noah's obedience to God. That should be "comfort" enough for anyone! If there had been no Noah, the Bible itself would not have been written. Of whom would one write? And who would be there to read it? Humanity would have been completely obliterated in the Flood's watery depths.

Comfort #2: Noah provided a powerful and permanent example of obeying the Lord in the face of extremely adverse circumstances. No one had ever seen or imagined the Flood that was destined to destroy the world and every air-breathing creature on it. Thus, Noah acted in complete faith and unrelenting obedience to God's holy commands.

The ensuing evidence for the Flood is literally worldwide. To the unbiased observer, it is absolutely compelling in its phenomenal abundance. It is literally everywhere one turns his unbiased eye to observe. Yet scientists and laypeople alike in our modern era stubbornly reject the historical fact that there ever was a Flood of such magnitude. The avalanche of pertinent data supporting the Flood is either ignored or blatantly misinterpreted. How much evidence does man need?

How ironic it is that even after this cataclysmic event occurred, its worldwide destruction is still vehemently denied. In his day, people scoffed at Noah before succumbing to their watery fate. It is unlikely that they continued laughing, however, while the water encroached upon their outstretched necks and flaring nostrils. But by then, it was too late. Today, people continue to mock Noah and the Bible's account (2 Peter 3:5–7). It is true that they shall escape a worldwide water event (Genesis 9:11). But they shall not be able to flee from the Great White Throne Judgment (Revelation 20:11–15). There will be no laughing then.

Ironically, these same individuals will accept local, catastrophic floods as an explanation for the fossil record and other assorted geological phenomena. This is true in spite of the fact that local floods cannot possibly explain the evidence which literally covers the globe. Furthermore, this clearly contradicts the plain teaching of Scripture that there was a universal Flood.

The Earth Is Cleansed of Its Wickedness Temporarily

Comfort #3: Noah brought comfort and rest to the earth by ridding it, at least temporarily, of its perpetual wickedness. The Flood allowed everything to start anew. As Genesis 6:5 states, "Then the LORD saw that the wickedness of man was great in the earth, and that every intent of the thoughts of his heart was only evil continually."

The earth and all of humanity groaned under this staggering burden of wickedness (cf. Romans 8:19–23; 2 Peter 2:4; Jude 1:7). As Romans 1:18 reveals, when men suppress the truth long enough, no opportunity remains for repentance. One cannot spurn the gentle call of the Holy Spirit forever without consequence. Second Corinthians 6:2 emphasizes: "For He says: 'In an acceptable time I have heard you, and in the day of salvation I have helped you.' Behold, now is the accepted time; behold, now is the day of salvation."

Comfort #4: Noah obediently sacrificed the clean animals to God on the altar. He thus exemplified a pattern for honoring God to the instruction of mankind ever afterwards. This was a significant act of worship. A lesser man may have panicked, thinking that they needed every animal preserved alive for the purpose of procreation. By Noah's faith and obedience, he brought comfort and rest through the threefold promise of God: (a) not to curse the ground anymore; (b) not to again destroy every living creature; (c) to permanently establish the seasons.

Genesis 8:21–22 states:

> And the LORD smelled a soothing aroma. Then the LORD said in His heart, "I will never again curse the ground for man's sake, although the imagination of man's heart is evil from his youth; nor will I again destroy every living thing as I have done. While the earth remains, seedtime and harvest, cold and heat, winter and summer, and day and night shall not cease."

The Rainbow Is the Sign of God's Covenant

Comfort #5: God blessed the earth through the Noahic covenant, accompanied by the symbol of the rainbow. We shall later examine this Noahic covenant in greater detail. The rainbow remains a glorious sign to the entire globe of God's faithfulness. Unfortunately, most people don't realize or contemplate the significance of the rainbow. Biblical ignorance is not bliss! Every believer who sees the beautiful rainbow brilliantly displayed across the sky should lift their hearts in praise and thanksgiving for God's mercy and love.

It is hard to imagine the light that shone in Noah's eyes the first time he saw a rainbow. If the perspective is correct that it had not rained before the Flood, then there had never been a rainbow either. God consistently shows grace even in the midst of His most severe judgments.

Comfort #6: Noah brought comfort and rest to the earth by passing along God's message of hope and reconciliation to humanity. He started with his own small family. No one knew this message of God's love and offer of salvation better than Noah. Their training program of enduring the Flood in the ark and seeing God's preservation firsthand was unquestionably superior to any seminary classroom. God's methods of spiritual instruction and discipline are immeasurably better than any of man's tools or skills.

The Seed Son, Messiah, Comes Through Noah's Line

Comfort #7: Through Noah and his son Shem, the promised Seed of Genesis 3:15 was preserved. It steadfastly endured until the actual birth of the Messiah Jesus Christ (Matthew 1:1, 20–23). The genealogy of Christ can be traced all the way back to Adam and Eve, but it narrowed down to Noah and his family during the Flood. God's promises cannot in any way ever be thwarted. Yet, man continues to rebel against Him. God laughs at man's impunity and futile arrogance.

Regarding the Messiah, Psalm 2:4–9 states:

> He who sits in the heavens shall laugh; the Lord shall hold them in derision. Then He shall speak to them in His wrath, and distress them in His deep displeasure:

> "Yet I have set My King on My holy hill of Zion."

> "I will declare the decree: The LORD has said to Me, 'You are My Son, today I have begotten You. Ask of Me, and I will give You the nations for Your inheritance, and the ends of the earth for your possession. You shall break them with a rod of iron; You shall dash them to pieces like a potter's vessel.'"

The Messiah shall one day reign on the earth and set up His millennial kingdom. This is the great hope of all believers. Titus 2:13–14 states: "Looking for the blessed hope and glorious appearing of our great God and Savior Jesus Christ, who gave Himself for us, that He might redeem us from every lawless deed and purify for Himself His own special people, zealous for good works."

Life will be perpetually blessed when the Savior of humanity takes His rightful place on the throne. Noah was instrumental in God's plan for all of these things to transpire. What a tremendous privilege it is for any human being to play a role in God's vineyard and kingdom! Noah played an intrinsic role, as few people ever will.

Lessons Learned in This Chapter

In this chapter, we first discussed several issues regarding the narrative of Genesis chapter 5. Many people have struggled with the immense ages people lived to back in the earlier days of the earth. It does not seem to occur to them that God had created a perfect world. Adam and Eve did not even require clothing before their fall into sin. The world had a uniform climate, as evidenced by the coal and oil deposits all over the globe. When God finished His act of creation, He described it as "very good" (Genesis 1:31). That statement by itself testifies to its perfection.

Sin was the downfall of the earth. When sin became so pervasive around the globe, God acted. He severely judged the world and mankind with the universal Flood. The Flood changed everything to a much harsher environment. This change included the climate itself.

Many large species of animals, such as the dinosaurs, could not adapt to the new and varying climates around the globe. Even though the dinosaurs were on the ark as juveniles, they did not survive many generations. However, the behemoth and the leviathan were still alive and flourishing as late as the days of Job.

Although we cannot accurately date the book of Job, he possibly was an approximate contemporary of Abraham (Job chapters 40 and 41). The Hebrew of Job predates the writing of the Mosaic Pentateuch. God also decreed that the lifespans of man and animals would diminish over time. They did so quite rapidly a few generations after the Flood.

Second, we explored the succession of godly men listed in the patriarchal line of Seth. It must be remembered that Adam founded the line of Cain as well as the line of Seth, who was the third son recorded. Seth was seen as a replacement for the murdered Abel. These two lines of men were morally quite distinct from each other. There may have been godly men within the line of Cain, but they would likely have been far and few in between. The ungodly line of men eventually overwhelmed the world with their horrid wickedness.

Third, we touched upon the exceptional life of the godly prophet Enoch. He was such a righteous man that God directly translated him into heaven at the intriguing age of 365. He lived one year for every day of the year. The only other man thus far in history so honored was the prophet Elijah. He was translated into heaven in a whirlwind and accompanied by a chariot of fire (2 Kings 2:11). Enoch prophesied about the coming of the Lord with an innumerable multitude of his saints, which included both angels and redeemed mankind.

We do well to repeat Jude 14–15 at this point:

> "Now Enoch, the seventh from Adam, prophesied about these men also, saying, 'Behold, the Lord comes with ten thousands of His saints, to execute judgment on all, to convict all who are ungodly among them of all their ungodly deeds which they have committed in an ungodly way, and of all the harsh things which ungodly sinners have spoken against them.'"

Fourth, we focused in some detail on the lives of the final three patriarchs, Methuselah, Lamech, and Noah. Methuselah lived to be the oldest man on earth, a whopping 969 years. He actually outlived his son, Lamech, by five years. Lamech, quite ironically, proved the youngest of the patriarchs; he died a natural death at the age of 777. His father, Methuselah, lived 192 years longer than he did. Lamech prophesied of Noah's prominence. Though we may not understand the entirety of his prophecy, much can be discerned.

Finally, we closed with some introductory statements regarding Noah and his family. Clearly, Noah was the third most important man in human history. Only the God-man Jesus Christ (Genesis 3:15) and John the Baptist were more important (Matthew 11:11). Indeed, it was through Noah's lineage that the Seed son was passed down to Jesus Christ.

God used Noah in powerful ways. It was through Noah that the entire world was spared. Immense, incalculable destruction occurred in God's judgment of the Flood. Nonetheless, as God always does, He exercised mercy in the midst of judgment. He did not wipe out mankind or the animal kingdom entirely. The ark parallels the cross. Both are the avenues of deliverance. One was physical, the other spiritual. Each individual is obligated to bend his knees at the cross for forgiveness and salvation.

Our next chapter turns to the lamentable specter of a world gone horribly wrong. As we shall see, demonic influence pervaded the entire human race. The attempt was made by Satan's minions to entirely corrupt humanity. They came perilously close to doing so. The following is not a comfortable chapter to read or study. Further enlightenment is shared in the New Testament by Peter and Jude. We shall examine their teachings as a necessary supplement to what is recorded in Genesis chapter 6.

Cognitive Conundrum #9

Solitude embraced me with a cold, malevolent grip; the pains of stark loneliness did I sadly sip. Miracles performed by me brought glory to God, yet multitudes rejected me as uniquely odd. The Christ celebrated I in a special fashion; my friend and I jointly witnessed transfiguration. With fire did I testify to God our Father above, of God's holy prophets I am second most loved.

Who am I?

Answer: Elijah

Chapter 10

A World Gone Bad

(Genesis 6:1-8: Part A)

In This Chapter

Objectives for This Chapter
Man's Steadily Increasing Depravity
A Prophetic Pause
Lessons Learned in This Chapter

Objectives for This Chapter

We now embark on one of the most tragic periods of earth's history. From the time of Adam and Eve's fall into sin until the Flood, morality continues to decline. There were certainly some notable exceptions to this general rule, such as Enoch and Noah. Other patriarchs from the line of Seth may also have lived truly exemplary lives, but we are presented with few details.

It is a sad reality that mankind generally gravitates toward that which is morally repugnant. To embrace the darkness seems instinctive within man's sin-besmirched heart. Relatively few individuals in the population eagerly yearn to develop a relationship with God. As a historical reality, that stands self-evident. It shall become painfully obvious as we explore Genesis chapter 6.

In this chapter, we shall first review the tendency of man to revert to ungodliness. John 3:19–21 declares that this has always been man's natural bent. He loves darkness because his deeds are evil. Scripture abounds with examples and statements concerning the inherent evil which lies resident within man's unrepentant heart (Ecclesiastes 7:20; Jeremiah 17:9). This evil is unrelenting and will persist to one degree or another until the eternal state (Revelation chapters 21 to 22).

Second, we shall more happily note that some godly men and women have always traversed the earth. The patriarch Abraham represents a powerful example of a man whose testimony of godliness shone brilliantly in the midst of a largely godless society. Sometimes, this righteous minority has shrunk to extremely low numbers. We refer to the example of Elijah immediately below.

The Difficult Circumstances of Elijah

It is instructive to recall the great prophet Elijah's depressed sentiment regarding the abysmal moral estate of Israel. Elijah had just experienced the fantastic spiritual victory of God sending down fire on Mount Carmel (1 Kings chapter 18). Immediately thereafter, however, he is threatened by the wicked Queen Jezebel and plummeted to the depths of despair. Elijah was dumbfounded that the nation of Israel did not rise up in concerted and permanent worship of God. How was that possible?

This was an understandable yet somewhat indefensible reaction on his part. Elijah undoubtedly reasoned within his heart: "What more did God need to do to persuade the people?" He would have done well to contemplate how Moses must have felt after the ten plagues of Egypt had devastated the country. Did the Egyptians or even the Israelites repent? No, they did not. We are by no means criticizing Elijah. The question each reader (and the author) should ask himself is this: "Would I have reacted any differently than Elijah? Would I have done better?" The honest answer may prove somewhat disquieting. Reality check: We would not have fared any better.

In 1 Kings 19:10, Elijah poured out his plaintive plea to God: "So he said, 'I have been very zealous for the LORD God of hosts; for the children of Israel have forsaken Your covenant, torn down Your altars, and killed Your prophets with the sword. I alone am left; and they seek to take my life'" (cf. v. 14). Yet, in spite of Elijah's forlorn but understandable outlook, God had all things in control. Note His response to Elijah in 1 Kings 19:18: "Yet I have reserved seven thousand in Israel, all whose knees have not bowed to Baal, and every mouth that has not kissed him."

Many a pastor, teacher, evangelist, and layperson have groveled in self-pity and discouragement over similar, albeit less dramatic, circumstances than Elijah. That is quite natural. However, when one allows his eyes to focus only on his immediate surroundings, his vision becomes skewed. The world is a large place, and God is working throughout the globe in sundry manners. But ... He is always working!

What is unnatural even for believers is to reflect consistently upon the fact that God is sovereign. He reigns from His throne. No one shall ever remove Him from power. He knows the end from the beginning (Isaiah 46:10). Hence, the believer has no real foundation or cause for discouragement. One must simply embrace the truths and promises of God with unremitting faith. Admittedly, this is not always easy. Eternity is known by our omniscient God alone.

Noah's Days Were Unparalleled for Wickedness

Never was the besetting plight of evil more evident than in Noah's day. When he and his family entered the ark, there were only eight righteous people left alive on the planet. All others were destined to perish! There was and will never again be a parallel to the wickedness experienced in Noah's day. All the world save eight had become corrupt.

Such a cesspool of sin is thankfully well beyond our imagination. God will never allow sin to pervade society on this level again. We shall examine the cause of this excessive wickedness more thoroughly in our following chapter. It does not make for pleasant writing or reading. Nonetheless, Scripture relates these wicked days as a warning to mankind. It is the believer's responsibility to take instruction from God's eternal words.

An Important Glimpse into the Tribulation

Third, we shall take a brief prophetic excursus into future events. This is important because the past is predictive and illustrative of what will take place in the seven-year Tribulation. The time frame of the Tribulation is compared to the days of Noah. The Tribulation will be a time of terror and sinful activity. But it will not be as spiritually devoid of believers as were the days in which the ark was being prepared.

The destruction of the Tribulation, although truly unimaginable, will not be as thorough as the Flood. No human or oxygen-breathing animal outside the safety of the ark survived. Many will survive the Tribulation, both believers and unbelievers. However, as Scripture reveals, the unbelievers will be immediately judged, put to death, and thrown into hell (Matthew 25:31–46). No theological reprobates will be spared from God's holy wrath.

The godly, by contrast, will be ushered into the millennial kingdom without passing through the dark valley of death. No unbelievers will be allowed to enter into the millennial kingdom. In that spiritual sense, the end result is the same as Noah's Flood. But the entire world will not be totally destroyed, although it shall come perilously close when one examines the seal, trumpet, and bowl judgments. The climactic bowl judgments are almost beyond imagination.

There is, however, a bright side to the future. In contrast to the days of the ark, there will be significant spiritual victories to be won during the Tribulation period. Indeed, the Scripture indicates that multitudes of individuals from every tribe and nation will come to a personal, saving faith in Christ (Revelation 6:9–11, 7:9–17). Oftentimes, God uses miseries and sufferings to bring people to their theological senses in a most efficient manner. Pain frequently produces penance!

The world's most wicked man, the Antichrist, and his cohort, the false prophet, will actually drive many to faith in Christ. That, of course, will not be their ungodly intent. However, one must worship the Antichrist and the devil or worship Jesus Christ (Revelation 13:12). They unintentionally, in concert with God's other witnesses, will motivate many people to worship Christ. It will be decision time for the peoples of the world!

A minority will initially choose not to worship anyone or anything at all. If that were not the case, Israel as a nation could not experience a great spiritual awakening at the end of the Tribulation. Clearly, they would not have been worshiping the Antichrist. If they had been, there would be no repentance available to them (Revelation 14:9–11). But until the final three days of the Tribulation, most of them would not have been worshiping Jesus Christ either. One may safely assume that others will refuse to worship the Antichrist. This does not necessarily mean, however, that they will worship Jesus Christ.

The Holy Spirit will finally bring Israel to her knees in spiritual submission in the final three days of the Tribulation (Hosea

5:15–6:3). There will be an unparalleled spiritual awakening among the Jews (Zechariah 13:8–9). Everyone, save a tiny minority, will embrace Christ. As a nation, the people will mourn and recognize that for 2,000 years, they had rejected their Messiah. Now, on the brink of annihilation, they come to their spiritual senses (Zechariah 12:10–13:1).

God's Sovereign Protection and Witness During the Tribulation

A minority of Jews will already be believers and flee to Petra or Bozrah (modern-day Jordan) for protection from the Antichrist (cf. Isaiah 34:6, 63:1–6; Daniel 11:41; Micah 2:12; Revelation 12:14). Others outside of Israel, though at the risk of death, will probably also resist worshiping the Antichrist. Their numbers shall be relatively few (13:8).

Those who retain some biblical literacy will recognize the deception of the Antichrist and false prophet for what it is. Though it will probably cost them their lives, those blessed individuals wisely choose to follow Christ. They will lose their bodies physically but gain their souls eternally. What wiser choice can there be than that (Mark 8:34–38)?

Thankfully, those who make the Holy Spirit-inspired decision to follow Christ will not be just a few. There will be an immense number of new believers (Revelation 6:9–11). We refer to them as Tribulation saints because the Church has been removed in the Rapture. When they are martyred for Christ, they ascend to heaven to a specific place and are comforted by Christ. Never again shall they experience suffering or persecution.

The one somewhat curious advantage of the Antichrist is that he allows essentially no one on earth to remain undecided. In that limited sense, he will compel people not to hesitate regarding their declared faith. The undecided will no longer be tolerated. To not worship the Antichrist is an automatic death sentence. Thus, being either a Christian or religiously undecided equally merits the Antichrist's implacable wrath.

Of course, the Antichrist must first catch such individuals in order to put them to death. That will not be an overnight process. As we have already noted, many Jews clearly resist worshiping the Antichrist or Jesus Christ until the final three days of the Tribulation. At that officious time, they finally embrace Christ as Savior and Lord.

We shall also discuss the various evangelists that will be ministering during the Tribulation. There will be more than just a few. Their ministries will prove powerfully effective. The greatest "minister," so to speak, will be the Holy Spirit Himself. In truly miraculous fashion, He shall reach down to unrepentant Israel. A spirit of acknowledgment and open confession of Christ envelops the entire country. Israel as a nation shall corporately and finally trust in their promised Seed Son, the Messiah Jesus Christ.

Mankind's Steadily Increasing Depravity

As we have already stated, the Bible is not the kind of book that man could have written, nor would he have written it. Honesty is the never-ending quality of God's Word throughout its every page, paragraph, verse, letter, and portion of a letter. That particularly holds true concerning the accounts in Genesis.

Man's obstreperous spirit manifests itself in ever-increasing ghoulish fashion. Within the very first family, the unthinkable abomination of fratricide occurs. An older brother viciously and callously kills his younger brother. The assumed protector became the predator.

Simultaneously, while the repugnant deeds of man are recorded, the magnificent charity and grace of God are likewise noted. Adam and Eve, though somewhat fearfully at first, received and acknowledged God's forgiveness, benevolence, and provision. Cain, their eldest son, stubbornly and completely spurned it. He, at first, even foolishly denied his culpability for Abel's death. To lie to a sovereign, all-seeing God is pointless at best.

When God confronted him with the evidence, Cain still did not repent or relent. Rather, he willingly left the presence of God. In his spiritual rebellion, he carried along with him the majority of his descendants. One trusts, however, that there were some shining exceptions to his unrelenting godlessness.

Genesis Chapters 6 to 9: God's Grace versus Man's Wickedness

One cannot conscientiously read Genesis chapters 6 to 9 without uncomfortably experiencing a roller coaster of emotions. Emotion #1: The reader inevitably experiences a disturbing fascination regarding the mysterious Nephilim. Questions swarm the mind. Who were they? Do such people still exist in some fashion? Were they completely wicked, or were some of them good? We shall endeavor to examine these and other questions in fuller detail later.

Emotion #2: One grieves immeasurably over not just the propensity of man toward unremitting evil but the wholesale embracement of it. What is recorded almost seems to be some manner of nightmarish hyperbole. The Bible informs us that the thoughts of man were wicked continually. Could things really have taken that nasty of a turn? Was the Bible perhaps "stretching things" just a bit? Sadly, we shall see that God was not exaggerating the situation in the least. The morality of mankind plummeted to near zero.

A World Gone Bad

How Quickly Mankind Slid into the Depths of Depravity!

The line of descendants from Adam to and including Noah consists of only ten generations! Excluding Adam, Seth, and Enoch, who were translated, Noah himself could have met six out of the first ten patriarchs—such was their longevity. It is quite evident that these men passed down the oral traditions of their forebears. That is precisely how many cultures operated for centuries until writing became predominant. If there was writing before the Flood took place, all evidence of it was destroyed.

One should not understand that all of these men from the line of Seth had become spiritually corrupt. Indeed, that particular line of men apparently retained their godliness. The Seed son passed through them. Regrettably, we know very little about some of them. But it is evident that the spiritual torch was being passed from generation to generation. Sadly, it was being passed by fewer and fewer individuals as time went on. The godly line was dwindling drastically.

Lamentably, the godly line is almost always in the minority. That has characteristically been the case throughout man's history. The vast majority of humanity morally stems from the line of Cain, who inherited his sinful nature from his parents. Even if that originally were not the case, which it definitely is, most of humanity would have unthinkingly followed in Cain's godless footsteps anyway. His sins became generational. Sinfulness is the easy path to blindly wander down. Just follow the crowd! Godliness requires discipline and resistance.

Lamech serves as an early example of the contagion of godlessness (Genesis 4:23–24). What one generation does inappropriately, the next generation frequently takes to wild excess. Two such modern-day heinous examples are abortion and homosexuality. Though both were considered reprehensible only a scant generation ago, now they are considered natural human rights. Even beyond that, now the deplorable sin of exercising transgender operations is skyrocketing among the young.

It matters not to such individuals what God teaches in His Word. When one casts off the eternal Word of God, he revolts against God Himself. You cannot separate the one from the other. When one dismisses God, he foolishly discards all sensitivity to his own lack of morality. The convicting power of the Holy Spirit is spurned. Indeed, as in the days of Noah, such individuals become blind to their own sin. The heart becomes thoroughly hardened. The nation of Israel all too frequently exemplifies this wicked pattern. Such a diabolical propensity certainly did not end with Israel.

This evil trend has continuously operated within all generations of mankind up to our present day. From time to time, it rears its ugly head in bewildering and horrific fashion. How many individuals and entire nations have enslaved and butchered their fellow man? The annals of history are saturated in bloody conflict. Sin captivates and increasingly enslaves the unrepentant and immoral heart.

Thankfully, and only by God's grace, society will occasionally repent en masse, and a great spiritual awakening will take place. This is generally the outcome of concerted prayer by believers (2 Chronicles 7:14). Severe judgment also frequently precedes the humbling and contrition of man's heart. It is the responsibility of every believer to share his faith and to testify of God's grace and forgiveness through Jesus Christ alone. Unfortunately, many will be unreceptive to this message of grace and salvation. That, however, does not release the Christian from his obligation to pass on the message of eternal salvation (1 Thessalonians 1:2–5, 5:17).

Be Thankful for the Faithful Few!

Emotion #3: One rejoices over God's redemptive love coupled with His righteous judgment. The benevolent Father is patient, almost beyond belief. Indeed, in Abraham's day, He made this memorable statement regarding the wicked Amorites in Genesis 15:13, 16:

> Then He said to Abram: "Know certainly that your descendants will be strangers in a land that is not theirs, and will serve them, and they will afflict them four hundred years. ... But in the fourth generation they shall return here, for the iniquity of the Amorites is not yet complete."

A four-hundred-year time frame qualifies as patient in nearly everyone's perspective. Perhaps the only people who might have disagreed with that sentiment were the Amorites themselves. They wanted to continue groveling in their indescribable depravities. At times, the only cure for such immorality is divine intervention. With the Amorites, they meant judgment by death (cf. Genesis chapter 19).

God is holy and must eventually punish sin (Isaiah 53:6). If He did not do so, mankind would exist in a permanent dog-eat-dog mentality. Indeed, man would have accomplished self-annihilation long ago. The advent of nuclear weapons, biological and chemical warfare, and more conventional weaponry would have ensured that. Many people who lack biblical faith lie awake at night, dreading what the next day will bring. Some wonder if there will be a next day. The believer can always rest easy. He knows that God alone controls the future. All will happen in accordance to His eternal plan.

Jesus is not going to allow humanity's self-destruction to happen. In reference to the end times, Matthew 24:22 declares: "And unless those days were shortened, no flesh would be saved; but for the elect's sake those days will be shortened." In one way or another, God intervenes to prevent mankind's self-annihilation.

Pessimistic thinkers have long proclaimed that the end is near. They have set the earth's imagined history clock at 11:55 p.m. "Only five minutes remain for earth," they zealously and with clarion voices announce. Their gloomy assessment is understandable but in error. God has a different plan and solution in mind. It is all recorded in His holy book for anyone who takes time to read it. Mankind does not control their own fate. They never have, and they never will.

In retrospect, however, if such pessimists had lived in the days of Noah and company, their warnings of impending cataclysm would have proven entirely accurate. Sadly, few individuals lived righteous enough lives to discern the repugnance of their moral standing. Even fewer of the depraved inhabitants of the earth cared. Their hearts were obsessed with evil thoughts. Their hands and feet ran straight into those wicked thoughts and actions. The dwellers on earth in Noah's day personified Proverbs 1:16: "For their feet run to evil, and they make haste to shed blood."

A Prophetic Pause

Let us, for a moment, recess for an interlude in our Genesis discussion. The following abbreviated analysis regards the future. We shall take a sneak preview of what is coming prophetically. Why should we do so? It is because the past of Noah's day reflects quite markedly on what is coming to the earth in the future.

This encroaching horrendous and unprecedented seven-year

span is called the Tribulation. As we have already noted in our introduction, many will encounter Christ as Savior during this time of horrendous conflict. These individuals are numbered among what Scripture calls the "elect." It must always be remembered that God will consistently preserve for Himself a people. Elijah needed to be reminded that God still had 7,000 men who had not bowed their knees to Baal.

Who Are the Elect?

Matthew 24:22 states the following: "And unless those days were shortened, no flesh would be saved; but for the elect's sake those days will be shortened." In discussing future events of the end times, Jesus mentioned the elect. Question: Who are the elect? Answer: During the future seven-year Tribulation, countless multitudes will embrace Jesus Christ as their Savior. Those new believers are the elect.

But the elect also include all believers: past, present, and future. Acts 13:48 describes all such individuals: "Now when the Gentiles heard this, they were glad and glorified the word of the Lord. And as many as had been appointed to eternal life believed." Certainly, in God's infinite and omniscient mind, He knew who would trust in His Son Jesus Christ. Indeed, such blessed individuals are described as "appointed" or, as the King James Version states, "ordained."

First Peter 1:2 further amplifies this issue of predestination and election. In describing the saints, Peter writes the following: "Elect according to the foreknowledge of God the Father, in sanctification of the Spirit, for obedience and sprinkling of the blood of Jesus Christ." The reader should take careful note of the clear description of the Trinity in this passage. This is one of the most fundamental verses in the Bible regarding our triune God. Every believer would do well to mark it in his Bible, memorize it, or write it in a notebook for further reference.

Furthermore, the reader should take note that the term "elect" is utilized. The elect are known by God from eternity. How could it be otherwise? If that were not the case, God would not be omniscient. Such a lack of omniscience would also mean the lack of God's absolute sovereignty, a monstrous doctrine indeed! God would not be in control; His plans would have to be adjusted according to man's decisions. Placing God as subservient to man's personal initiative and decisions is not how He is portrayed in Holy Writ.

An Old Testament Clarification

Isaiah 46:9–10 helps to clarify this issue: "Remember the former things of old, for I am God, and there is no other; I am God and there is none like Me. Declaring the end from the beginning, and from ancient times things that are not yet done, saying, 'My counsel shall stand, and I will do all My pleasure.'"

In the minds of some, this raises the question of what is called "double predestination." Did God intentionally create some men and women solely for the purpose of eternal punishment? Did they have no choice but to reject the Savior? The Bible decidedly does not teach that. God wants all to be saved and to come to the knowledge of the truth (Deuteronomy 30:19–20; Joshua 24:15; Psalm 116:15; Ezekiel 18:23, 32; John 3:16; 1 Timothy 2:4; 2 Peter 3:9).

Another sometimes overlooked passage regarding God's sovereign will for mankind is written in Matthew 25:41: "Then He will also say to those on the left hand, 'Depart from Me, you cursed, into the everlasting fire prepared for the devil and his angels.'" The fire of punishment was originally designed for the devil and his evil minions. These are the fallen angels, the demons. Sadly, much of humanity willingly chooses to join the devil based on their immoral decision against Christ.

God's Perfect versus His Permissive Will

God's perfect will was that all mankind would develop a stimulating and eternal relationship with Him. However, for that to be an actual living reality, God had to allow mankind free will. Without free will, there can be no free worship. Hence, His permissive will had to allow for potential unpleasantries. Without God's permissive will, man would be preprogrammed robot.

One such inevitable unpleasantry is the fact that much of humanity would choose to walk away from Him in unbelief. Mankind often spurned the option of worshiping their Creator. This is not the same thing as a predetermined, unalterable double predestination. On the contrary, it is a simple reality of choice. God knows what all the individual choices of mankind will be from eternity past. Indeed, He knows mankind's every thought. Hence, in that limited sense, man's choices are admittedly predetermined. But this is not arbitrated by force; rather, it is by free choice.

From the beginning, man has had the option of choosing for or against God. Why do some choose to follow God and others spurn Him? That remains a mystery in this present age. A simple recognition of its reality must remain sufficient for us. We can go no further than the expressed statements of Scripture. Indeed, why should feeble mankind even attempt to explain what God has not?

The error of theologians is spawned when they endeavor to answer questions that God Himself has not fully addressed. We must allow biblical mysteries to remain mysteries (Deuteronomy 29:29). Where man is not asked to tread, he must remain silent. God does not require our counsel. Romans 11:34 declares: "For who has known the mind of the Lord? Or who has become His counselor?"

The Future Context of the Tribulation

The context of Matthew 24:22 regards the Tribulation period. Before the Tribulation begins, the Church will have been raptured out from the earth (John 14:1–3; 1 Thessalonians 4:13–18; Revelation 3:10). That removes every living Christian in one moment from the entire planet. Not a single Christian remains! All Christians from the entire Church age are resurrected from the dead or translated alive up to heaven. The Rapture is an indescribably glorious event. Every Christian should yearn for that day. But what happens next?

Though the Church has been raptured out, the Bible and other Christian literature and videos will remain behind. In addition, many unsaved and yet biblically knowledgeable individuals remain. They know the Word of God but have failed to embrace it. The study of prophecy will be resuscitated to an amazing level. People will be watching prophecy take place right before their eyes. The Holy Spirit no longer restrains evil as He has done historically, but He continues to work in His convicting and enlightening ministry nonetheless (John 16:8–11).

God will provide many witnesses to His eternal gospel during the Tribulation. These include the following: (1) the Bible, Christian tapes and videos. This would include the prophetic fulfillments of the seal, trumpet, and bowl judgments; (2) the millions of Christian martyrs; (3) the 144,000 Jewish evangelists of Revelation chapters 7 and 14; (4) the two witnesses of Revelation chapter 11; (5) the ministry of Elijah (possibly he will be one of the two witnesses); (6) the angel proclaiming the gospel to the entire world (Revelation 14:6–7); (7) and the Holy Spirit being poured out on Israel (Zechariah 12:10–13:1).

Millions will be influenced to follow Christ by these testimonies (Revelation 6:9–11, 7:9–17). Sadly, many of these new believers will be martyred. But upon their death, they shall be immediately ushered into heaven to receive comfort from and fellowship with their God. Incredibly, during the world's second darkest period, the gospel will shine brightest.

The World's Most Peculiar Evangelist

In a rather ironic and unintentional sense, the Antichrist himself will prove to be a great evangelist. Quite naturally, as his name indicates, he is diametrically opposed to Jesus Christ. But his actions will shock untold millions of people into choosing either for him and his evil kingdom or for Jesus Christ. The wicked Antichrist will demand worship and proclaim himself God! Incredibly, the majority of the world will blindly follow him (Revelation 13:8).

Speaking of the Antichrist, Paul writes the following in 2 Thessalonians 2:3–4:

> Let no man deceive you by any means; for that Day will not come unless the falling away comes first, and the man of sin is revealed, the son of perdition, who opposes and exalts himself above all that is called God or that is worshiped, so that he sits as God in the temple of God, showing himself that he is God.

Enough biblical knowledge will remain on earth that multitudes will be profoundly shocked and moved by this diabolical pronouncement of the Antichrist's alleged deity. The false prophet will demand that people worship Antichrist. He will construct an image of him that seems to be alive. People will be commanded to worship this image or be killed (Revelation 13:14–15).

Once an individual takes the unforgivable step to worship this vile image, there will no longer be any repentance granted to them by the Holy Spirit (14:9–11). They will be required to receive the mark of the beast on their right hand or on their forehead (13:16). The number of the mark will be 666. Once a person has received this mark, his eternal condemnation is assured. This will be the culminating point in history for spiritual decision-making. Nothing before or after this time will ever force such a dramatic spiritual determination.

Revelation 14:9–11 summarizes this twofold step into the Lake of Fire:

> Then a third angel followed them, saying with a loud voice, "If anyone worships the beast and his image, and receives his mark on his forehead or on his hand, he himself shall also drink of the wine of the wrath of God, which is poured out full strength into the cup of His indignation.
>
> He shall be tormented with fire and brimstone in the presence of the holy angels and in the presence of the Lamb. And the smoke of their torment ascends forever and ever; and they have no rest day or night, who worship the beast and his image, and whoever receives the mark of his name."

It is because of this decisive future moment that we believe all the major witnesses to Christ will be ministering in the first half of the Tribulation. In this perspective, no one will be able to say they received the mark of the beast in complete ignorance. However, we do stress that the Bible itself does not present the actual time frame. Some scholars believe that the two witnesses, for instance, will be ministering in the second half of the Tribulation. We readily acknowledge that is a possibility, but it is not our preferred view.

Thankfully, there will be multitudes who will be granted spiritual insight by the Holy Spirit at that time. They will recognize this grandstanding and evil deceiver for who he really is. The Antichrist will try to force a decision on the part of everyone on earth. There are to be no fence-sitters. In spite of his worst efforts, however, there will be those who remain undecided. They do so at their own peril, humanly speaking. Such individuals, which will include all Tribulation saints, will not be allowed to buy or sell. But the believers' choice means eternal life. The unbelievers' choice means eternal condemnation.

Those who choose to follow Christ will flee to His loving and forgiving arms. Tragically, the overwhelming majority will opt to follow this repulsive human usurper to the Lord, namely, the Antichrist. Their eternal fate will be befitting them. God will have provided overwhelming evidence of salvation through His Son, Jesus Christ.

Revelation 13:8 portrays this great dichotomy amongst mankind: "All who dwell on the earth will worship him, whose names have not been written in the Book of Life of the Lamb slain from the foundation of the world." So it shall be that the majority of mankind will stampede into the hands of wickedness and gross idolatry by worshiping the Antichrist and Satan himself (13:4). But God always preserves a faithful remnant. They shall embrace the eternal Savior and receive justification for their sins. Their eternal home will be with the triune God (John 14:1–6; Revelation chapters 21 to 22).

The Jews' Long-Delayed Spiritual Awakening

The final and greatest witness will be directed toward the Jews. The Holy Spirit will be poured out on the previously unbelieving nation just as the Antichrist and his evil hordes are poised to obliterate the Jewish people (Hosea 5:15–6:3; Zechariah 12:10–13:1). Amazingly, this takes place in the final three days of the Tribulation. A great spiritual awakening takes place, and Israel finally turns to Christ.

The Jews will finally recognize that their forefathers for the past 2,000-plus years have rejected the promised Seed Son, namely, Jesus Christ (Genesis 3:15). Their spiritual agony of repentance will be unparalleled. Their intense remorse and recognition are eloquently described by Zechariah.

After millennia of unbelief, Israel will finally accept their Messiah, the promised Seed Son. With utter compliance and heartfelt worship, the nation will turn to Him. Accompanying this change of heart will come unprecedented grief for their almost perpetual disobedience and idolatrous ways.

We refer now to Zechariah 12:10 and 13:1:

> "And I will pour on the house of David and on the inhabitants of Jerusalem the Spirit of grace and supplication; then they will look on Me whom they pierced. Yes, they will mourn for Him as one mourns for his only son, and grieve for Him as one grieves for a firstborn. ... In that day a fountain shall be opened for the house of David and for the inhabitants of Jerusalem, for sin and for uncleanness" (cf. Zechariah 13:8–9; Matthew 23:37–39).

It is at this point of spiritual renewal that Jesus Christ comes in His glorious second advent. He annihilates the forces of the Antichrist, returns to His newly redeemed people, and establishes His millennial kingdom (Zechariah chapter 14). The Jews will be physically rescued and spiritually rejuvenated in their otherwise last hour.

God's grace always shines brightest during His harshest judgments. This has been His consistent mode of operation from the beginning of humanity. Many millions around the world will become what we call "Tribulation saints." They will have the same belief system as Christians today. Those who are martyred for their faith during the Tribulation will go straight to heaven. There, they shall receive comfort and blessing from their beloved Savior.

Three Types of Believers in the Bible

The reader should note that there are three types of believers in earth's history. While the belief systems of all three are inexorably based on the Scripture, the time frames are decidedly distinct. The understanding of these divisions facilitates what otherwise may prove bewildering portions of Scripture.

These three distinct divisions of believers are as follows: #1. Old Testament believers. They were saved by faith and looked forward to the coming of the Messiah (Habakkuk 2:4). #2. New Testament believers (the Church). They look back at the first advent of the Savior. The members of the Church are likewise saved by faith (Ephesians 2:8–9; Titus 3:5; Hebrews 11:6).

#3. Tribulation saints. Their belief system is identical to their brethren in the Church. They also are saved by faith in the returning Messiah. In all three time frames or dispensations, many believers have lived and died for their faith. But during the intense and horrific time of the Tribulation, relatively few believers will be spared

Corruption and Catastrophe

from martyrdom. It will be a difficult time for the Tribulation saints (Revelation 13:7).

The Tribulation will be the most wicked time in earth's history since the Flood. Noah's day was actually much worse. During that time, the wicked Nephilim essentially ruled the earth. We shall discuss them in more depth in our ensuing chapter. At the actual time of the Flood, the righteous were reduced to eight souls. Satan and his evil hordes had nearly conquered the world in a counterfeit religious sense.

By contrast, in the Tribulation, there will be multitudes who follow Christ. At the end of the Tribulation, the surviving saints will be blessed to enter into the millennial kingdom alive (Revelation 1:7). Mere survival of the Tribulation is nearly incomprehensible. Imagine the unsurpassed joy when the remaining believers witness Christ in all His glory descending on a white horse in battle array. Also, imagine the terror of unrepentant humanity. It will be one of the most pivotal points in human history. The believers surviving the Tribulation will never have to pass through the portals of physical death.

Back to Genesis

Having now glanced at some of the future aspects of prophecy, we must now turn back to the most spiritually corrupt time in earth's history. Genesis chapters 6 to 9 reveal an appalling chapter for our planet. Chapter 6, in particular, leaves the reader with an uncomfortable knot in his stomach. The thought that should enter every believer's mind is this: There but for the grace of God go I. In our following chapter, we will elaborate on this distressing time.

Lessons Learned in This Chapter

In this chapter, we first reviewed the fact that mankind steadily lowered itself into the darkest pits of sin. This shall become even more tangible in our following chapter. The discussion of demonically influenced mankind stands as one of the most frightening periods recorded in the Bible. Our statements in this particular chapter were more of an introduction to the lamentable discussion we shall have on the Nephilim (fallen ones).

God Always Preserves a Believing Remnant

Second, we discussed the fact that no matter how degraded mankind may choose to plummet itself morally, God always preserves a remnant of believers. That remnant reached its lowest ebb during the days of Noah. Though staggering to imagine, godly mankind dropped down to a scant eight souls. But through this one solitary family, God preserved humanity. When the Flood actually arrived, mankind frantically sought refuge on higher ground. Finally, there was no higher ground remaining. Only water covered the surface of the earth.

The door of the ark was shut by God Himself (Genesis 7:16), which qualifies as one of the most terrifying thoughts in Scripture. When God shuts the door, all hope is truly lost. Throughout the history of man God faithfully beckons to his largely unresponsive creation (Isaiah 62:11–12; Ezekiel 34:11, 16; Matthew 18:12; Luke 19:10). Man may sputter and complain, but in God's eyes, he is entirely devoid of excuse (Romans 1:18–20). God has provided overwhelming evidence to demonstrate His existence.

The nation of Israel, in particular, had no excuse for rebelling against God. As the reader is aware, Israel plays a major role throughout Scripture. This nation is God's chosen people (Genesis 12:1–3; Exodus 19:5–6; Psalm 135:4). God certainly did not choose them, however, because of their worshipful or submissive attitude. Generally speaking, they proved to be stiff-necked and disobedient people. This came as no surprise to an omniscient, all-seeing God.

Malachi 1:1–3 states:

> The burden of the word of the LORD to Israel by Malachi. "I have loved you," says the LORD. "Yet you say, 'In what way have you loved us?' Was not Esau Jacob's brother?" says the LORD. "Yet Jacob I have loved; but Esau I have hated, and laid waste his mountains and his heritage for the jackals of the wilderness."

In spite of God's provision and care for Israel, they still largely ignored Him. They even actively turned away to worship false gods. Isaiah strongly ridicules both Israel and Judah for their idolatrous ways (Isaiah chapter 44).

Third, because the Old Testament is the foundation stone for the New Testament, we briefly indulged in a prophetic excursus, so to speak. We examined numerous prophetic passages. As the days of Noah were, so shall be the future days of the Tribulation (Matthew 24:37–39).

However, we noted that there would be much greater spiritual vitality during the Tribulation than there existed in Noah's time. Satan and his minions had almost entirely captivated the hearts and minds of humanity in Noah's day. Only eight souls remained who had pledged their faithfulness to God; all were within Noah's family.

God's Witnesses during the Tribulation

We also delved into numerous aspects of the seven-year Tribulation. God will faithfully provide many different witnesses during these dark days. Included in these witnesses are the following: (1) the Bible, Christian books and videos; (2) the many millions of martyrs for Christ; (3) the 144,000 Jewish evangelists; (4) the two unidentified witness; (5) Elijah, who possibly is one of the two witnesses; (6) the angel who proclaims the everlasting gospel to all the world; (7) the Holy Spirit who pours out conviction on the nation of Israel.

Witness #8 is not generally counted or even considered. Why? It is because this witness is the Antichrist. How does the Antichrist qualify as a witness for Christ? He doesn't. He is categorically against Christ, hence his name. But what he does do is bring all dwellers on earth to a point of decision. He does not allow people to vacillate between himself and Jesus Christ.

Still, there will be many who do not worship either the Antichrist or Jesus Christ. If that were not the case, no one in Israel would be left to repent during the final three days of the Tribulation. Yet, as Scripture indicates, the nation of Israel will experience a phenomenal spiritual awakening (Hosea 5:15–6:3; Zechariah 12:1–13:1, 8–9).

The Antichrist's future decree will be as follows: You must worship the Antichrist in his godless system or pay the price of physical death. What the wretched Antichrist does not tell the people is that if they worship him, they will then suffer an eternal spiritual death. Only through Christ is their spiritual life (John 1:29, 3:16, 14:6; Acts 4:12).

Many millions will choose Christ. Enough biblical literacy remains that people will not be entirely ignorant of what is happening spiritually. In addition, God will spread the gospel all over the world through His stellar group of witnesses. For example, the entire unredeemed world will recognize and hate the two unidentified witnesses. They are granted great power by God to perform many miracles. No one can harm them. If they try, they are killed by fire coming out of the mouths of the two witnesses.

Finally, the Antichrist is granted permission by God to kill the two witnesses (Revelation 11:1–13). They are left unburied in the streets of Jerusalem for three and a half days. The world rejoices that these two troublemakers have finally been killed. But then comes the shock of shocks! By divine call, they are raised again from the dead. They go straight into heaven when God summons them. The entire world witnesses their resurrection and ascension. Modern technology has made that possible.

Indeed, during the Tribulation, the gospel, for the first time, will saturate the entire world simultaneously. Everyone will hear the gospel from the angel who proclaims it in every tongue to each person on earth (Revelation 14:6–7). We believe that this occurs before the decision forced upon humanity by the Antichrist takes place. At the midpoint of the Tribulation, the Antichrist demands worship and the wearing of the mark of the beast.

Before that eventful day occurs, it seems reasonable to believe that God will first offer salvation and forgiveness to every individual on the planet. That way, no one can claim that he received the mark of the beast in ignorance. All will have heard in their own tongue the everlasting story of the gospel. It is nearly impossible to imagine still refusing to heed its glorious message. Tragically, most will turn a blind eye and harden their hearts even further to the redemption story.

The Ultimate, Angelic Witness to the World

Revelation 14:6–7, which speaks of this angel, stands as one of the most fascinating and encouraging passages in all of Scripture:

> Then I saw another angel flying in the midst of heaven, having the everlasting gospel to preach to those who dwell on the earth—to every nation, tribe, tongue, and people—saying with a loud voice, "Fear God and give glory to Him, for the hour of his judgment has come; and worship Him who made heaven and earth, the sea and springs of water."

In our next chapter, we shall examine more closely the sordid details of how sin crept into and took hold of humanity in Noah's day. Although we are not informed as to how God spread His word in the days before the Flood, we may rest assured that He did. Certainly, He used the godly line of Seth. There were also undoubtedly other methods in which His truth was communicated, of which we are uninformed. God never leaves humanity without a witness.

Cognitive Conundrum #10

My family was partly good and partly bad; my own testimony at times was really sad. All in all, however, I lived a good life; sadly, I endured a big struggle with my wife. An active warrior I could not claim to be, but my relative rescued me from trouble, you see. A father of countries that was my destiny, but their untoward creation brought me no glee.

Who am I?

Answer: Lot

Chapter 11

A World Gone Bad

(Genesis 6:1-8: Part B)

In This Chapter

Objectives for This Chapter
An Introduction to Genesis Chapter 6
Who Were the Sons of God and Daughters of Men (Genesis 6:1–4)?
Lessons Learned in This Chapter

Objectives for This Chapter

In this chapter, we shall first examine the graciousness of God. He desires that all men be saved. Yet, in light of His permissive will, that blessed hope will not see complete fulfillment. Genuine worship is not possible without free will. Due to man's self-centered volition and sinful preferences, the majority will steadfastly refuse to pursue a relationship with God. They unthinkingly prefer the momentary "pleasures" of sin to the riches of eternal life and fellowship with God. How tragic that is. They trade eternal life in heaven for a living death in hell.

Micah 6:8 summarizes God's perfect will for man in a brilliant and concise fashion: "He has shown you, O man, what is good; and what does the LORD require of you but to do justly, to love mercy, and to walk humbly with your God?" (cf. Deuteronomy 10:12) What a marvelous condition earth would find itself in if all men heeded this simple counsel.

Second, we shall venture into the disquieting discussion of the Nephilim. Debate over this somewhat thorny issue has vacillated back and forth between theologians and laymen alike for millennia. The Nephilim are the offspring of those called the sons of God and the daughters of men. Generally speaking, most understand that the daughters of men represent all females. No actual distinction is made in the pertinent Scripture under review regarding the daughters of Seth versus the daughters of Cain.

The fervent debate centers on the sons of God. Who were they? Our preferred understanding is that they were actually demons who took on human flesh. Though this sounds quite repugnant, and it is, this seems to be the most logical and biblical conclusion. These demonic spirits, who took on human flesh, married the daughters of men and had children by them.

Their hybrid offspring were called the Nephilim, which means "fallen ones." Unfortunately, the Septuagint and many English translations have translated Nephilim into "giants." That is not the original meaning of the Hebrew. Although it is possible that these progeny were physically imposing, that is not the primary understanding. It refers to those who are morally and spiritually degenerate. If one has a literal demon for his father, he is not only a mixed hybrid, but he will also be a morally corrupt one. What else could he be?

Does this mean that the Nephilim were beyond redemption? Were they born automatically sentenced to hell? Though that may sound logical, it is biblically indefensible. God's declared intention is that all come to Him in faith (1 Timothy 2:4). However, it is quite probable that precious few, if any, of such demented individuals embraced the Lord's loving offer of forgiveness.

The biblical data regarding the Nephilim is scanty at best. We may be extremely grateful that God has put a stop to such horrendous sinful activity. The natural question on everyone's lips is this: Why did God allow these unholy cohabitations in the first place? That, admittedly, is impossible for this writer to answer. One must take caution, however, not to bring accusation against the Almighty. As in other cases, some mysteries must remain mysteries in our present age.

An Introduction to Genesis Chapter 6

It is human nature to excuse one's own unworthy behavior and many transgressions. When man sins, he persistently looks for the "back door" to escape from his personal responsibilities and liabilities. However, this fleeting fancy of immoral man does not alleviate his guilt. Man is inherently sinful. If he will only acknowledge his sins and ask forgiveness, forgiveness is available from our gracious God. But he must first ask! God is not blind; He is just.

God Must Exercise Judgment Eventually

In light of God's righteous judgment, some postulate that everyone should be given a second chance. The reality is that God has granted each human countless "second chances." Some crimes, however, are so heinous, such as murder and kidnapping, that the punishment must be severe and prompt. Though the sin may be forgiven by God, the consequences of the sin must be carried out.

Ecclesiastes 8:11 proclaims the following truth: "Because the sentence against an evil work is not executed speedily; therefore the heart of the sons of men is fully set in them to do evil." When the court systems delay justice and oftentimes completely disregard it, society pays a high price. Evil must be punished, or it flourishes.

If someone in Israel entered into a village and tempted others to grovel in idolatry, he was to be severely punished. Such a person generally was stoned by the entire community. Why? Deuteronomy 13:11 gives the answer: "So all Israel shall hear and fear, and not again do such wickedness as this among you." When punishment is fair, complete, and processed expeditiously, the intent of the wicked man's heart is given healthy pause for reflection.

For example, if kidnapping is always and immediately punishable by death, the desire to gain ransom from the wealthy is considerably lessened. If the criminal is caught, he will never be able to spend his ill-gotten gain. Instead, he will be dead, and that right quickly. Thus, the potential kidnapper will arguably be inclined to contemplate a different and more commendable avenue of enterprise. Many innocent lives will thus be spared, and much misery averted when justice is swift and fair. The Bible knows whereof it speaks. God knows man's heart.

God Yearns to Preserve Life, Not Destroy It

Yet, in spite of God's perfect and holy sense of justice, He foremost desires repentance and forgiveness. He did not create man merely to destroy him. God is a relational God who loves to minister to His spiritually adopted children. For those who do not yet know Him, He provides opportunity after opportunity to begin worshiping Him.

Daily, our loving Lord provides an untold and unimagined amount of benefits to all mankind. He extends grace in a seemingly infinite number of ways to humanity. So it is only natural, not to mention biblical, to recognize that God desires a relationship with the pinnacle of his phenomenal creation, namely, man. Though man may be the "high point" of creation, all of nature cries out in testimony to a Creator God. Where can one turn his head and not see the blueprint of creation from God's hands? The answer is simple: Nowhere!

Ezekiel 18:23, 32 conveys God's sense of mercy and compassion:

> "Do I have any pleasure at all that the wicked should die?" says the Lord God, "and not that he should turn from his ways and live? ... For I have no pleasure in the death of one who dies," says the Lord GOD. "Therefore turn and live!" (cf. Psalm 103:8–11; Lamentations 3:22–23, 33)

God consistently seeks opportunity to show mercy. But that mercy is dependent on the individual sinner. God exercises justice when mercy no longer stimulates spiritual change!

It is for this reason that God gave His promise of the Seed in Genesis 3:15. Though Eve mistakenly thought that their first child, Cain, would serve as that Seed (Genesis 4:1), she was not misguided in her faith concerning God's promise. Her theology was accurate, but her timing was incorrect. Furthermore, contrary to what she had hoped, she was not destined to be the mother of the Messiah.

While Eve and the Old Testament saints anticipated the Godman's (Messiah's) coming, modern-day believers lovingly look back at Christ's first advent. Both Old and New Testament believers are justified by faith. Habakkuk 2:4 states: "Behold the proud, His soul is not upright in him; but the just shall live by his faith." But is faith alone sufficient?

Saving Faith Requires the Right Person

It is not faith alone that saves. That faith must be placed in the right Person, and that Person is Jesus Christ. The object of one's faith is vital. One cannot just believe in anything or anybody. Christ's first advent was designed for His substitutionary atonement on the cruel cross of Calvary (John 3:16). What a spiritual and eternal harvest it yielded. Eternal forgiveness was provided for all who believe (5:24). Believers now eagerly await His second coming.

It is at the time of His return that Christ shall judge sin and establish righteousness on the earth. Revelation 1:7 states: "Behold, He is coming with clouds, and every eye will see Him, even they who pierced Him. And all the tribes of the earth will mourn because of Him. Even so. Amen" (cf. Acts 1:9–11). This will be one of the most momentous events in eternity.

Christ will return as the ruling Messiah and build His 1,000-year kingdom on earth. It will be the most glorious time on earth since Adam and Eve's sinless state in the Garden of Eden. Every premillennial believer prayerfully awaits the earthly reign of Christ. In other words, they take the 1,000-year reign of Christ on earth literally, not allegorically. With this brief introduction, we shall now address some of the thornier questions raised in the biblical text.

Who Were the Sons of God and Daughters of Men?

(Genesis 6:1–4)

Much speculation has been aired, and considerable ink has been spilled over this perplexing question. Although we shall postulate the most reasonable explanation we can, this passage will probably always foment some debate among biblical scholars. The discussion certainly provides a fountainhead for many perplexing questions.

Genesis 6:1–4 states:

> Now it came to pass, when men began to multiply on the face of the earth, and daughters were born to them, that the sons of God saw the daughters of men, that they were beautiful; and they took wives for themselves of all whom they chose. And the LORD said, "My Spirit shall not strive with man forever, for he is indeed flesh; yet his days shall be one hundred and twenty years." There were giants on the earth in those days, and also afterward, when the sons of God came in to the daughters of men and they bore children to them. Those were the mighty men who were of old, men of renown.

We shall make numerous observations on this passage while seeking to extrapolate its meaning.

Observations about Life in Noah's Day

Observation #1: The population of the earth was rapidly increasing. People tend to assume that the wickedness God referred to was excessive physical violence. Indeed, it undoubtedly did entail much violence, as in the tragic case of Lamech (Genesis 4:23–24). But wickedness has many faces. Sexual immorality is certainly one of the more prominent. It appears that men and women have become consumed with deviant sexual practices. The context certainly supports that view.

But another factor also appears quite certain. Despite the probability of violence during Noah's day, the population was probably steadily increasing. It must be remembered that people lived to a great age. That undoubtedly included unbelievers as well as believers. If all unbelievers died at an early age due to God's direct intervention (and Scripture does not imply this), that punishment would be a physical warning to impede the unrighteous lifestyles of the wicked.

Most people would prefer to remain alive than to pass through the frightening valley of the shadow of death. But since God ordains free will and allows man to go his own way, it is best to assume that everyone, believers and unbelievers alike, were living to an advanced age.

However, a comparatively early death will quite literally occur in the millennial kingdom of Christ for the impenitent. Isaiah 65:20 states: "No more shall an infant from there live but a few days, nor an old man who has not fulfilled his days; for the child shall die one hundred years old, but the sinner being one hundred years old shall be accursed."

Tim LaHaye and Ed Hindson comment as follows on Isaiah 65:20:

> Verse 20 is especially significant, for it raises key points about life and death in the kingdom. First, there will no longer be any infant mortality in the millennium; everyone who is born in the kingdom will reach at least a certain age. Second, the reference to one dying at 100 as being a child emphasizes the blessing of longevity in the millennium. And third, those who die at the age of 100 evidently are sinners (unbelievers), for only they would be considered "accursed."[73]

---

[73] Tim LaHaye and Ed Hindson, The Popular Bible Prophecy Commentary (Eugene, OR: Harvest House Publishers, 2006), p. 148.

The Daughters of Men Were Very Beautiful

Observation #2: The women were considered very beautiful. This statement seems to be referring to an exceptional period of time. This is by no means intended to say that women today are not all beautiful in their own way. But there may have been something particularly exemplary about the women or "daughters of men" back in Noah's day. It is not possible, however, to know more than what is succinctly stated. At any rate, the sons of God were greatly attracted to them.

There is no compelling reason to see these women as anything but normal, albeit beautiful women. Genesis 6:1 was simply a continuation of the normal procreation of men and women. Men and women would marry and beget children. That had been occurring since Adam and Eve.

Indeed, in verse 4, in the phrase "the daughters of men," a more literal and proper interpretation should be "the daughters of the man." In other words, it refers to a man, singular. This man could only represent Adam. This implies that the "daughters" were the natural byproduct of Adam, in other words, his biological descendants. Hence, they were normal human females. This agrees with verse 1. But we shall soon see that something rather significant changes.

Fruchtenbaum comments as follows:

> Genesis 6:1 continues, Daughters were born unto them, referring back to Genesis 5, which repeats for each son and grandson of Adam in Seth's and Cain's lines that they bear sons and daughters. The Hebrew word for daughters means "females," and the emphasis here is on the female portion of humanity. The first phrase, when men began to multiply on the face of the ground,

is a reference to humanity in general, which includes both male and female; the second phrase focuses on the female portion of humanity.

Once again, the term cannot be limited to the female descendants of Cain. The basic translation of the first verse is: Mankind, adam, (singular) multiplied; and daughters, (plural) were born unto males and females. By this time there were many more than just two lines, since Adam and Eve had other sons than those named.

There is something more unique in this context, as seen from what is missing in the text as well as what is mentioned. The text states sons of God and daughters of men, not "sons of man and daughters of God," which would be the case if this were purely a human endeavor.[74]

The Marriage Issue

Observation #3: The "sons of God" married the "daughters of men." Verse 2b states that these sons of God "took wives for themselves of all whom they chose." This would seem to imply polygamy, as was exemplified by Lamech (Genesis 4:23–24). If so, this would have hastened even more rapidly the degenerative erosion of mankind's morality, or absence thereof.

It may be quite likely that no woman was left single. Why? The primary intent was to ruin the prospect of Genesis 3:15 being ful-

---

[74] Arnold Fruchtenbaum, Ariel's Bible Commentary: The Book of Genesis: Exposition from a Messianic Jewish Perspective, pp. 144–145.

filled. Hence, the sons of God, if in reality fallen demons, would choose to corrupt the entire human race. They came perilously close!

There seems to be little disagreement about the daughters of men. No distinction is ever specifically made regarding the daughters of men as to whether they were from the line of Seth or Cain. However, it may be argued that the moral daughters of the Sethites (though no such distinction is actually made) would have scrupulously avoided marriages with immoral men and certainly with demonic ones. However, that argument cannot be established from Genesis chapter 6.

In 1 Corinthians 6:14–15, Paul reiterates a timeless commandment that God did not want evil and good to be united in matrimony: "Do not be unequally yoked together with unbelievers. For what fellowship has righteousness with lawlessness? And what communion has light with darkness? And what accord has Christ with Belial? Or what part has a believer with an unbeliever?" Sadly, many young men and women have strayed from God's holy commandment regarding marriage and paid a terrible price. That is quite likely the scenario of Genesis 6.

Who Were the "Sons of God?"

In Genesis 6:1–4, as we have already alluded to, these "sons of God" may have been literal demons who took on human flesh. That is a frightening possibility. It is one that a pious individual cringes at even contemplating. The specter of demonic beings masquerading as men with their full physical abilities is truly horrible to imagine.

But it must be remembered that God also enables good angels to take on human flesh (cf. Genesis chapter 18; Matthew 28:1–7; Mark 16:5; Luke 24:4; John 20:12). That possibility remains to this day within the "good angels" capabilities. Hebrews 13:2 states: "Do not forget to entertain strangers, for by so doing some have unwittingly entertained angels." Clearly, good angels can take on human flesh to this day. The fallen angels of Noah's day are no longer permitted to do so. Indeed, those particular demons are languishing in eternal punishment.

Another less reprehensible option is that these sons of God were demonically possessed individuals. That is alarming enough in its own right, but that spiritual tragedy is also thoroughly demonstrated in the New Testament. Jesus cast out many demons in His ministry (Matthew 4:24; Luke 4:41). Yet, there is clearly a distinction between demonic possession and demons taking on human flesh with all of its identical properties.

The primary issue revolves around the identity of the "sons of God" versus the daughters of men. Who were the sons of God? If the sons of God were merely human beings, why were they not simply identified as the sons of Adam? It should be remembered that Genesis 5:3 states: "And Adam lived one hundred and thirty years, and begot a son in his own likeness, after his image, and named him Seth."

The "Sons of God" versus the "Sons of Men"

The "sons of God" is almost certainly an expression of distinction to separate them from the "sons of men." It is the somewhat begrudging contention of this author that this distinction concerns itself with the spirit world versus the world of flesh and blood. There are several supporting reasons for this admittedly rather unpalatable viewpoint. We shall examine these reasons as closely as we can.

We do point out that competent scholars have argued rather vociferously in opposition to the position we shall adopt. They clearly have their reasons for doing so. However, we find that their objections do not adequately explain the comments that arise later in Scripture. That stands particularly true in the New Testament with Peter and Jude. But as we explore this matter more deeply, the reader must decide for himself which position he will adopt. No savory conclusion is possible in this disconcerting biblical scenario.

Our conclusion is succinctly stated as follows: The sons of God are fallen angels (demons) who married normal, physical women (daughters of men). Their offspring are called the Nephilim (the fallen ones). The Nephilim are the mighty men of old, the men of renown. Tragically, they are also half-demon and half-men. We shall now endeavor to provide reasons for our assessment.

The Mysterious Nephilim

Reason #1: The immediate context indicates that an unusual offspring, namely, the Nephilim, was the result of these marriages (6:4). The Hebrew term Nephilim means "the fallen ones." This offspring shall receive more attention momentarily in our ensuing discussion. At this point, it suffices to say that these offspring certainly seemed to be more than just ordinary human beings. There was something quite exceptional about them.

Reason #2: Other Old Testament passages of Scripture indicate that the sons of God are angelic beings (Job 1:6, 2:1, 38:7). The three passages of Job are almost unquestionably angelic beings. It should be noted, by contrast, that in the New Testament, the phrase "sons of God" refers to human believers (John 1:12; Romans 8:14, 19; Philippians 2:15; 1 John 3:1–2). That, admittedly, lends itself to some understandable confusion. One must consciously be aware of the broad panorama of Scripture while simultaneously paying copious attention to the biblical context.

It may be contended by some that the sons of God in Job 1:6

and 2:1 refer to godly humans. That perspective is unlikely, however, when one considers the rather decisive case of Job 38:6–7. This latter passage speaks of the time of creation. Job 38:6–7 states: "To what were its foundations fastened? Or who laid its cornerstone? When the morning stars sang together, and all the sons of God shouted for joy." Certainly, in this passage, the sons of God could not have been human beings. They had not yet been created.

Furthermore, the context of Job 1 and 2 does not support the idea of godly humans in the context. It seems to indicate angelic beings since the locality of the story is in heaven. It should be noted that it is not necessarily possible to distinguish whether the "sons of God" in Job were fallen or good angels. In that particular context, both were undoubtedly included.

Many cogently postulate that the angels were created in creation week. That is a reasonable assessment. However, we caution that this is not an essential conclusion. The creation of angelic beings is not precisely revealed in Scripture. Genesis 1 refers to a physical creation, except for the soul and spirit of animals and man (animals have souls, not spirits). Hence, it is entirely conceivable that the angels, which are spiritual beings, were possibly created long eons before the creation week. Job 38:6–7 lends support to that perspective.

Thus, it may be the case that angels (spiritual beings) existed long before God created the physical universe. However, in the opinion of many, Lucifer's fall from a sinless state to an entirely wicked one would not seem possible until after the conclusion of the creation week. That is because everything is described by God as "very good" on the sixth day of creation. Sin cannot be included in that description. This holds particularly true considering the deplorable level of total wickedness to which Lucifer and his fellow demons fell.

However, assuming that the spirit beings were created prior to the physical creation, Lucifer's fall into sin could have happened in eons past. Some will reasonably argue that Lucifer became jealous of God's relationship with Adam and Eve. They were created in God's image. Lucifer was not. However, the reality is that Scripture never indicates such jealousy of Adam and Eve. Lucifer was jealous, however, of God Himself. He wanted to become greater than God!

A Worthy Word from Ezekiel

Ezekiel 28:11–15 lends support to the view that Lucifer's downfall took place prior to the creation week of Genesis chapters 1 to 2:

> Moreover the word of the Lord came to me, saying, "Son of man, take up a lamentation for the king of Tyre, and say to him, 'Thus says the Lord God: "You were the seal of perfection, full of wisdom and perfect in beauty. You were in Eden, the garden of God; every precious stone was your covering: the sardius, topaz, and diamond, beryl, onyx, and jasper, sapphire, turquoise, and emerald with gold. The workmanship of your timbrels and pipes was prepared for you on the day you were created.
>
> "You were the anointed cherub who covers; I established you; you were on the holy mountain of God; you walked back and forth in the midst of fiery stones. You were perfect in your ways from the day you were created, till iniquity was found in you."'"

The Garden of God versus the Garden of Eden

One should exercise due caution in establishing dogma on this somewhat controversial passage. Nonetheless, it seems to indicate that Lucifer (symbolized by the king of Tyre) walked in the garden of God. While doing so initially, he was perfect in all his ways. The Garden of Eden was part of God's original creation in Genesis chapters 1 to 2. But was the garden of God the same as the Garden of Eden? That does not seem to be the case. Their descriptions are quite different from one another. We shall examine two differing viewpoints on this rather enigmatic discussion.

Viewpoint #1 on Lucifer's fall: At some inexplicable point, possibly quite early after the creation of Adam and Eve, sin invaded Lucifer's spirit. Why? Was it jealousy of God's relationship with Adam and Eve? Clearly, their relationship was different and, one might surmise, closer than God's relationship with Lucifer. The humans had the God-ordained capacity to develop a loving relationship with their Creator.

This special relationship is something that perhaps was not possible at the same intimate level for the angels. We advise the reader that those who hold to this viewpoint are speculating. It cannot be proven. Scripture does not offer any such explanation. In this viewpoint, the garden of God and the Garden of Eden are generally thought to be one and the same.

Viewpoint #2 on Lucifer's fall: The garden of God and the Garden of Eden are two entirely different places representing two different times. The first is spiritual, and the second is physical. The time frame for Lucifer and all the angelic hosts' creation was prior to the physical creation of the universe. At some point, Lucifer became intensely jealous of God. He foolishly thought he could become greater than his Creator. Such is the twisting and degrading power of sin. Lucifer's fall into sin cannot be calculated in terms of time. But when God created the universe and mankind 6,000 years ago, Lucifer immediately desired to corrupt it.

When Lucifer surrendered to temptation, whenever that was, he enticed one-third of the angels to follow him down the same wretched path (Revelation 12:4). There was no return back to God made available to them (Matthew 25:41). Christ did not die for the angels. They had the capacity to remain in their sinless state. Two-thirds of them did precisely that. Since that inglorious time of Lucifer's fall, they have been indefatigably attempting to counter every one of God's benevolent wishes for mankind.

In this second viewpoint, God is speaking only in reference to the creation week in Genesis chapters 1 to 2. It was then that He created the physical universe. The spiritual universe had already been created long ago in the past. If that understanding is correct, Lucifer's fall into sin may have been eons prior to earth's creation.

A word to the wise: Dogmatism coupled with speculation creates an unhealthy theological bond. Thus, one must exercise caution in forcing unwarranted conclusions. Our preference is admittedly viewpoint #2. We fully recognize, however, that viewpoint #1 is most definitely a viable option. Caution is the order of the day.

Additional Comments on the "Sons of God"

Fruchtenbaum offers the following comments regarding the "sons of God":

> Genesis 6:2 records the actual intermarriage that occurred. The first statement, that the sons of God saw the daughters of men that they were fair, presents the crisis. The sons of God in Hebrew is bnei ha-Elohim.

This term, in the Hebrew Bible, is always a reference to angels, both good and bad ones. Examples occur in Job 1:6 and 2:1, where Satan was among the sons of God and in Job 38:7 where the sons of God were present at creation.

The Septuagint uses the same term in Deuteronomy 32:8, where it refers to angels. A variation of this term is bnei eilim, which is usually translated as "the sons of the Mighty," a term also used of angels. Examples include: Psalm 29:1, the sons of the mighty or the sons of God; Psalm 89:6, the son of the mighty or the sons of God; and Psalm 82:6 uses a different variation, the sons of the Most High. Another form is the Aramaic bar Elohim, which means a son of God.

So everywhere else this word is used, it is always in reference to angels, a point on which all expositors concur. Nevertheless, some wish to make Genesis 6 the one exception. However, it is not wise to make exceptions unless there are very good exegetical reasons to do so, and there is no good reason to make this one passage the exception to the rule.

As in all other passages, the term sons of God should be understood as being angels. They are sons in the sense of being directly created by God, and this includes angels, both fallen and unfallen. In the New Testament, the Greek term sons of God is applied to other entities besides angels, but the common element is that of being directly created by God.

Adam, in Luke 1:38, is called the son of God, since he was directly created by God. Believers are called the children of God in John 1:12 because believers are viewed as a new creation, created by God. The term sons of God has the meaning to be created by God. The exception is the uniqueness of the only begotten Son of God; the word "only" emphasizes His uniqueness in that He was always in existence and not created.[75]

The "Sons of God" Question More Thoroughly Explained

Reason #3: Two New Testament passages allude to fallen angels (demons) condemned for illicit practices in Noah's day. The first passage pertains to Noah's time frame.

Second Peter 2:4–8 states:

> For if God did not spare the angels who sinned, but cast them down to hell and delivered them into chains of darkness, to be reserved for judgment; and did not spare the ancient world, but saved Noah, one of eight people, a preacher of righteousness, bringing in the flood on the world of the ungodly; and turning the cities of Sodom and Gomorrah into ashes, condemned them to destruction, making them an example to those who afterward would live ungodly; and delivered righteous Lot, who was oppressed by the filthy conduct of

---
[75] Arnold Fruchtenbaum, Ariel's Bible Commentary: The Book of Genesis: Exposition from a Messianic Jewish Perspective, pp. 145–146.

the wicked (for that righteous man, dwelling among them, tormented his righteous soul from day to day by seeing and hearing their lawless deeds)—

Quite clearly, the context in 2 Peter 2:4–8 involves the time of Noah. The angels who sinned (the "sons of God") were confined in the lowest pits of hell. As one can readily see, Peter absolutely identifies the immoral predators on human female flesh as fallen angelic beings. These angels have never been released from hell, nor shall they ever be. They did the bidding of their master, Lucifer, at great personal cost. Since their knowledge was incomplete, they perhaps assumed they could get away with their abominable sins.

A Noteworthy Comment from Jude

In addition, Jude 1:6–7 states:

And the angels who did not keep their proper domain, but left their own abode, He has reserved in everlasting chains under darkness for the judgment of the great day; as Sodom and Gomorrah, and the cities around them in a similar manner to these, having given themselves over to sexual immorality and gone after strange flesh, are set forth as an example, suffering the vengeance of eternal fire (cf. 2 Peter 2:4–8).

Second Peter 2:4–8 is very similar to Jude in its message. Both indicate that certain angels are isolated from others for a particularly heinous sin. The place to which these wicked angels were assigned is called Tartarus, *tartarosas*.

Gene L. Green comments on the historical ramifications regarding this awful place as follows:

This verb, found only here in the NT, refers to being sent to Tartarus, the "deepest region of the underworld, lower even than Hades" (OCD 1476). As Zeus says in Homer's Iliad (8:13-14), "I shall take and hurl him into murky Tartarus, far, far away, where is the deepest gulf beneath the earth ..., as far beneath Hades as heaven is above earth."

Hesiod (Theogony 617-25; 715-25) told the story of the Titans who were consigned to this place of "misty gloom, in a dark place where are the ends of the huge earth" (729-31). Here, according to Hesiod, they were "bound ... in bitter chains" 718-19; see also Apollodorus, Library and Epitome 1.1.2). ...

Jewish thinking modified reflection on the theme, however, as God now becomes the one who consigns the evil to "Tartarus itself and profound darkness" (Philo, Rewards 26 152). ... A small step was made from seeing this as the place of punishment of the Titans to speaking of it as the place where sinful angels were consigned (Glasson 1961:62-67).[76]

One gets the idea from historical writings that Tartarus definitely was not a desirable destination. It was, in actuality, the ultimate punishment possible before the eventual Lake of Fire (Revelation 20:11–15). God handed over these particular demons to unrelenting punishment in Tartarus. There is no hope of forgiveness or rescue

---

76 Gene L. Green, Baker Exegetical Commentary on the New Testament: Jude & 2 Peter (Grand Rapids, MI: Baker Academic, 2008), pp. 250–251.

for these wicked demons.

A repeated emphasis on Noah's day

First Peter 3:18–20 also refers to the wickedness of these demonic spirits in their sinful lifestyle:

> For Christ also once suffered for sins, the just for the unjust, that He might bring us to God, being put to death in the flesh but made alive by the Spirit, by whom also He went and preached to the spirits in prison, who formerly were disobedient, when once the Divine longsuffering waited in the days of Noah, while the ark was being prepared, in which a few, that is eight souls, were saved through water (cf. Colossians 2:15).

This passage refers to the "victory" parade in the depths of hell, where Christ proclaimed His triumph over sin and the devil. This took place after His crucifixion and before His resurrection. In the context of the above-cited passages, sexual immorality of a severely repugnant type plays a major theme.

MacArthur's Comment on the Apostate Angels

John MacArthur offers the following comments:

> The second example that Jude gave was that of apostate angels. The fact that these angels are not specifically identified indicates that Jude assumed his audience was already familiar with the details of their extraordinary defection.

Commentators have offered three main views as to the identity of these angels. Some argue that Jude's reference is to an episode his readers knew nothing about. But that does not fit the larger context in which, as noted above, Jude reminded his readers of things they already knew (cf. v. 5). Thus one has to assume that Jude wrote of an Old Testament account familiar to his audience.

Others assert that Jude referred to the original fall of Satan (Isa. 14:12-15; Ezek. 28:12-17; cf. Luke 10:18; Rev. 12:7-10). That is a possible interpretation, but it fails to explain Jude's mention of eternal bonds, which does not apply to the current status of Satan and demons. The apostle Peter correctly wrote that the devil "prowls around like a roaring lion, seeking someone to devour" (1 Peter 5:8; cf. Job 1:6-7). Therefore it is unlikely that Jude is referring to Satan's fall.

The third and most plausible viewpoint is that Jude referred to an extraordinarily heinous infraction by some of the fallen angels. That sin, recorded in the Old Testament (Gen. 6:1-4), was so severe that God placed the offending demons in chains to prevent them from committing such perversity ever again. Peter said they sinned, whereas Jude described two closely related aspects of the fallen angels' sin.

First, they did not keep their own domain. Instead of staying in their own realm of authority given by God, they went outside it. Second, they abandoned their proper abode. With Lucifer they rebelled against their created role and place in heaven (cf. Isa. 14:12, NKJV).

When God expelled them from heaven for that rebellion (cf. Rev. 12:4, 9), some continued their downward fall to the point of taking masculine human form and cohabitating with human women to seduce a generation of demon-influenced, thoroughly corrupt children (cf. Gen. 6:11-13). God sent those particularly apostate angels (demons) to a place under darkness for the judgment of the great day. Peter wrote that God "committed them to pits of darkness, reserved for judgment" (2 Peter 2:4).[77]

MacArthur summarizes the above two passages in most noteworthy fashion. However, in our perspective, he overstates one thing: children are not born "thoroughly corrupt." This seems to imply that they were beyond redemption. It is true that everyone is born with a sinful nature. That cannot be disputed. Certainly, the children born in Noah's day who are called Nephilim, "fallen ones," were exceptional in their ungodly heritage. This fallen state refers to their spiritual and moral nature.

But to say that they were "thoroughly corrupt" implies that they were completely beyond any hope of forgiveness. They were spiritually lost forever, even before they were born. That would be double-predestination. That means some are born to be saved and

---
[77] John MacArthur, The MacArthur New Testament Commentary: 2 Peter and Jude (Chicago, IL: Moody Publishers, 2005), pp. 164–165.

others to be lost. That may seem like a logical conclusion based on the depravity of man. But it is biblically inconsistent (cf. John 3:16; 2 Peter 3:9).

We do not look upon the concept of double predestination with favor. It proves inconsistent with God's all-pervading grace and ongoing outreach to mankind. Hence, we cannot concur with that particular aspect of MacArthur's otherwise well-stated explanation. In a word, we hope that he is mistaken in that limited sense.

However, it must be emphasized that MacArthur certainly stands correct in emphasizing the wholesale depravity of the world. Evil permeated all of society. The time of moral distress and rebellion has never since seen its equal. In fact, at the very end, only Noah's family seemed to have been preserved from the total corruption that enslaved the earth.

The Debated Question: Were the Sons of God Human or Demons?

Though our position accepts the view that these sons of God were demons, a general consensus on this divisive issue does not exist among biblical scholars. That is understandable, as this is not merely a spiritual matter. It is also one shrouded in high-strung emotion. It is an uncomfortable discussion. That is why there is disagreement among biblical scholars. So, we will examine the two primary options in slightly more detail.

Demonic possession was a terrible problem in Jesus' day. He encountered demon-possessed people both in Israel and the surrounding territories. It is impossible to genuinely estimate how the present world compares to the world in Jesus' day. But if our understanding is correct, the days of Noah were truly incomparable to any age. What an ongoing horrible experience it must have been for the sons of Seth. They were forced to watch the world around them slide into a horrendous slime pit of sin.

Option #1: The Sons of God Were Demon-Possessed Men

Option #1: The sons of men are demonically-possessed men who cohabited with the daughters of men. This option has the quality of being somewhat more familiar to the believer's mind. It does not bring any particular level of comfort, however. Furthermore, it does not address every issue. At least two unresolved problems concerning this first option must be addressed.

Problem #1: Demon-possessed men and women exist in society today. This clearly was also the case in Jesus' day. Many such men have fathered children. This has been occurring throughout human history. However, modern demon-possessed men are not accomplishing what happened in Genesis 6:4. They are not producing ungodly offspring that possess the same characteristics as those elucidated in Noah's day, in other words, the Nephilim.

The offspring in Genesis 6:4 were men of great renown. They were exceptional individuals. It is not revealed what all of those exceptional qualities were. But their primary exceptional quality was undoubtedly their gross immorality. Nephilim means "fallen ones" and refers to their evil nature. In that respect, they were like the fallen angels.

The difference is that the Nephilim apparently could still be forgiven; fallen angels cannot. If they could not have been forgiven, why did God send Noah out to preach to them? It would have been a spiritual mockery to extend grace where no grace was actually available. Considering Noah's preaching ministry was a minimum of 120 years, that would entail a considerable amount of communication. He may well have been preaching most of his life.

Problem #2: It does not address the question as to why these demons, which allegedly possessed men, are not automatically bound today with chains in Tartarus. This definitely was the case of the demons in Noah's day. The harsh penalty, in other words, does not seem to fit the crime if it is merely a matter of demonic possession, awful though that is.

Jesus and the apostles cast demons out of many individuals, men and women alike, but they did not cast those possessing demons into Tartarus. In Luke 8:26–39, Jesus cast out so many demons from just one man that they, in turn, possessed about 2,000 swine (cf. Mark 5:13). The swine ran into the Sea of Galilee and drowned.

One must observe the request of the demons who possessed the unfortunate man in Luke 8:31: "And they begged Him that He would not command them to go out into the abyss." According to Greek scholar Gerhard Kittel, the primary definition of "abyss" is as follows: "A description of the underworld as a. 'the place of imprisonment for disobedient spirits' (Lk. 8:31, Rev. 9:1, 2, 11; 11:7; 17:8; 20:1, 3) and b. the 'realm of the dead' (Rom. 10:7)."[78] A secondary definition includes the great Flood or other floods of water.

Based on this secondary definition, John Martin offers the following comment:

> In answer to Jesus, the demon said that his name was Legion, a Latin term denoting a group of about 6,000 Roman soldiers. The point of the name was that a large number of demons were inhabiting the man. The demons asked that Jesus not torment them (Matt. 8:29 adds "before the appointed time") by asking that they not be sent into the abyss, which was thought of as a place of the dead.

---

78 Gerhard Kittel, Editor of Theological Dictionary of the New Testament: Volume 1, Translator and Editor Geoffrey W. Bromiley, (Grand Rapids, MI: Eerdmans Publishing Company, 1964), p. 9.

The abyss was also thought of as a "watery place," which made the outcome of this encounter all the more ironic and climactic. At the request of the demons Jesus let them enter into a large herd of pigs nearby which immediately rushed over a cliff into the lake and were drowned. Thus the request not to be sent into the abyss was granted by Jesus, but they were sent to a watery place anyhow.[79]

Although scholars debate the difference between the abyss and Tartarus, it appears that Tartarus was the worst possible place of confinement. It was reserved only for the angels who sinned in Noah's day. The abyss is also a place of torment, but Tartarus was at the bottom level, so to speak, and was the most isolated area within the abyss.

Option #2: The Demons Fully Took On Human Form

Option #2: The sons of God were literally demons who were allowed by God to take on human flesh. These demons quite literally took on human flesh, married women, and produced children. Angels are always identified in the masculine order. However, this does not mean they have sexuality in their angelic form. This option admittedly bridles against the believer's spirit. It is a repugnant thought, to say the least.

Matthew 22:30 states: "For in the resurrection they neither marry nor are given in marriage, but are like angels of God in heaven." However, one must remember that Jesus is making reference to good angels in heaven, not to fallen demons on earth. When the demons took on human flesh, they also took on the ability of reproduction. One must assume that they fully possessed all human features.

---
[79] John Martin, The Bible Knowledge Commentary. Editors John F. Walvoord and Roy B. Zuck (Wheaton, IL: Victor Books, 1983), p. 227.

When Christ appeared with two angels in their visit with Abraham in Genesis 18:7–8, they all ate food together. Later on, those same two angels traveled to Sodom and also ate food with Lot (19:3). God allowed those good angels to eat with a fully functioning digestive system for at least a short period. It can be argued that these angels were allowed to take on all the systems of a normal human being. The male homosexuals of Sodom and Gomorrah were convinced that these two angels were normal, sexually-equipped men. Indeed, it had to be the case if the sons of God fathered children.

Sarfati's Comments on Apostate Angels

Sarfati comments as follows:

> Also, 2 Peter indicates that this gross angelic sin occurred not long before the Flood. Then he makes a connection with the sin of Sodom and Gomorrah which he said was 'sensual'. While 2 Peter provides the timing of this event, and what befell these angels, Jude explains more about what this sin entailed.
>
> The angels didn't stay where they belonged, "within their own position of authority", that is, within the demonic realm. Instead, they left this "proper dwelling", which is consistent with entering the realm of humanity by intermarriage. For these crimes, Jude 6 corroborates Peter: that they are chained in darkness until Judgment Day.

Jude 7 explains the nature of the unforgiveable and particularly grievous angelic sin: they are compared with the Sodomites and Gomorrhites. That is, 'just as' these evil people did, the angels did 'likewise.' And what these people did was commit sexual immorality (Greek ekporneuo, from the same root whence we derive 'pornography'). Further, this sexual sin includes pursuing 'unnatural desire", literally "other (strange) flesh". ...

This makes sense, because 'sodomite' is an eponym for male homosexual, "men likewise gave up natural relations with women and were consumed with passion for one another, men committing shameless acts with men and receiving in themselves the due penalty for their error" (Romans 1:27). And these angels sought what was an unnatural flesh for them: human females.

We know that the NT writers expected their readers to understand an OT context for what they wrote, and we should interpret Scripture by Scripture. If Genesis 6 is not referring to sinning angels, 2 Peter and Jude are left dangling without any prior biblical referent.[80]

It seems most reasonable, although we do so begrudgingly, to conclude that the sons of God, as is consistent with other Old Testament Scripture, refer to angelic beings. In the case of Genesis chapter 6, however, they were demons who rebelled against God,

---

80 Jonathan Sarfati, The Genesis Account: A theological, historical, and scientific commentary on Genesis 1–11, pp. 478–479.

clothed themselves with human flesh, and cohabited with women.

Although this transgression seems unimaginable today, so does God creating the universe in six days seem beyond comprehension. Nonetheless, we accept it as true. God is all-powerful. He did not need any time at all for His creative purposes. We must always remember that the supernatural world is not confined by the same restrictions as the natural world is.

Newman's Comments on Apostate Angels

R. C. Newman writes:

> The earliest extant view is the supernatural one, that the 'sons of God' were angels and that the 'Nephilim' were their gigantic offspring. The sin in this case was the unnatural union between angels and humans. Going beyond the text of Genesis, this view pictures the offending angels as being bound and cast into dark pits until the day of judgment. This interpretation seems to have been popular at the time of Christ. The nonsupernatural interpretations are not extant until later ...
>
> After investigating possible NT references in this passage, it appears highly likely that the NT does refer to this incident, almost certainly in Jude 6 and 2 Peter 2:4 [which] clearly favor the supernatural position ...
>
> May it not be possible that we enlightened, 20th century Christians can learn something positive from the ancient exegetes? Perhaps they were right in seeing an

angelic incursion in Gen. 6:1-4 and we are wrong in denying it. Perhaps with a great interest in the supernatural and angels, some ancient interpreters scoured the Scriptures to locate any hints it might contain on this subject. In such a case, they might well have reached some valid insights which God preserved by inscripturation in the NT.[81]

A Satanic Plot to Invalidate Genesis 3:15?

Question: Why did these demons choose to marry earthly women? Answer: Satan perhaps vainly aspired to disrupt the possibility of the promised Seed Son ever being born (Genesis 3:15). He likely surmised that if he could physically and spiritually corrupt all women, the messianic Seed could not be born.

In Satan's demented mentality, he and all his demonic hordes would thus destroy the Messiah's holy mission. From a believer's biblically based understanding of God's omnipotence, such a mindset is ridiculous to the extreme. But believers must remember that Satan's mind has become thoroughly deranged by his wickedness. If that is true of Satan, how much more true it would be for his lesser minions?

One must remember that Satan cannot see the end from the beginning like God. The almighty and omniscient God knows and controls all things. How foolish that Satan could entertain thwarting His holy will. Not only does Satan deceive others, but he also deceives himself. He actually thought he could replace almighty God! He wanted the throne and fashioned himself as the master of God. Such is the folly of sin.

---

[81] R. C. Newman, The Ancient Exegesis of Genesis 6:2, 4, Grace Theological Journal 5(1):13-36, 1984.

One cannot even imagine a more demented thought pattern than that! The created thought he could overthrow the Creator. How nonsensical! But does not modern man attempt to do the same thing? When one stubbornly refuses to submit to the Creator, he is, in essence, trying to overthrow God, even if subconsciously. His sin parallels that of Satan.

Quite naturally, God could not allow this demonic infiltration to spread to all women. Their seed would become so corrupted that redemption for them and their offspring would have proven nearly impossible. We do not hold to the view that these women or their children would have no hope of redemption. God's grace is far more powerful than Satan's corrupting influence. But the contamination of their spirits would have been enormous. The fact that only eight righteous people remained on the earth is a powerful statement of sin's illicit influence.

What Were the Nephilim Like?

It is imprudent to make comparisons of what the Nephilim were like physically. The translation of "giants" is an unfortunate one. The Nephilim could have been of large stature, but that is not necessarily the case. Regrettably, the Septuagint, a Greek translation of the original Hebrew manuscripts, popularized the translation of "giants." These individuals were exceptional, that much we do know. We also know that Nephilim literally means "fallen ones."

We can safely assume that this speaks in reference to their spiritual status. It was due to this corruption that God chose to completely wipe out humanity. He chose to rid the world of these half-human, half-demonic beings. Beyond the meaning of the term "Nephilim," no physical description of these individuals is granted. The fact that they were mighty men of renown does, however, contribute to the mindset that they were large in stature. We certainly do not contest that distinct possibility. But it is not specifically stated.

To some biblical skeptics, the entire concept of the Nephilim smacks of sensationalism. That is understandable but unfortunate. The Bible does not spin fairy tales. Whatever the Nephilim were, they definitely existed. Furthermore, they had a very negative impact on the world. If they were really demon-men, as repulsive as that sounds, how could their moral status and influence be otherwise?

How long did God allow this cohabitation to continue? How many women actually became sexually intimate with demons? How many children were born to these unholy unions? The biggest question of all is: Why did God allow it to happen? Much to our regret, Scripture does not answer these questions. Perhaps the reason that the Bible is largely silent on the discussion is that this topic can so easily become an unhealthy fixation. People, including believers, tend to gravitate toward the sensational. One should focus on God and His holiness, not on the devil and his wickedness.

We Serve the God of "Second Chances"

Drastic action became necessary. This was all in keeping with God's foreknowledge and permissive will. We must always bear in mind that genuine worship is not possible without free will. With God's warning of impending judgment, grace was consistently offered for the duration of 120 years. Noah was a preacher of righteousness, not just a builder of an ark (2 Peter 2:5).

Genesis 6:3 states: "And the LORD said, 'My Spirit shall not strive with man forever, for he is indeed flesh; yet his days shall be one hundred twenty years.'" Question: Does this verse mean that the lifespan of man progressively decreased to 120 years? Eventually, that became true. But that is not the complete answer.

One thing is certain: men and women no longer live for hundreds of years. No one in the modern era is ever going to match the 969 years of Methuselah. Psalm 90:10 states: "The days of our lives are seventy years; and if by reason of strength they are eighty years, yet their boast is only labor and sorrow; for it is soon cut off, and we fly away." Ironically, Moses wrote this. He himself lived to 120 years of age. We shall review two possibilities for this question of the 120 years.

Possibility #1: The Age of Man Is Restricted

Answer: In brief, the answer to our question is more than likely twofold. Possibility #1: We must first note that the 120 years in question, if relating to age spans, certainly did not come to fruition immediately. Noah himself lived until he was 950 years old. That was the third longest lifespan recorded in Scripture. He lived for 350 years after the Flood, nearly three times the length of the 120 years cited.

Noah's sons also lived for hundreds of years. The oldest living human in recent times was the Frenchwoman Jeanne Louise Calment, who lived until the ripe old age of 122 years and 164 days. She is the most notable exception of which we are presently aware. It is quite rare that anyone lives past 110.

Even Abraham, who was many generations later, lived until he was 175. Amazingly, Noah would have died just two years before Abraham was born. So, contrary to popular myth, they never met each other. Noah easily lived long enough to see the dispersion at the Tower of Babel! Indeed, he would have lived approximately 250 years beyond the Tower of Babel. Thus, Noah saw two great judgments by God take place on the earth.

Possibility #2: The Flood Would Come in 120 Years

If we are to take Scripture at face value, another option of meaning must be explored. Possibility #2: The simplest and contextually most plausible solution is that God would bring the Flood upon the world 120 years from His statement of doom. God gave His warning when Noah was 480 years old.

Why would God give a 120-year advance warning? First, God is merciful and patient. He doesn't want anyone to perish spiritually (2 Peter 3:9). Second, with the primitive tools Noah had available to him and the immense size of the ark, it would take him 120 years to build it. Third, Noah invested some of his time in preaching. For 120 long years, he preached righteousness and repentance to an ever-increasingly godless world.

Yet, the only people who entered the ark with him were his wife, three sons, and three daughters-in-law. However, he may have had some converts who died before the Flood. But if he did, they were probably relatively few in number. Scripture does not mention any at all. How Noah's heart must have broken over the intransigence of the people! Many of them were undoubtedly his friends and relatives. Noah lived a long time and would have known hundreds of people.

God Has Warned the World Thousands of Years in Advance

God has given mankind warning of a future impending judgment thousands of years in advance. The warnings about the coming seven-year Tribulation are interlaced heavily throughout the prophets. Only the prophet Jonah does not speak of the future. Ironically, just as in the days of Noah, men of today still pay little or no attention.

Many excellent Bible teachers presently proclaim God's truth, and hundreds of worthy books are available. Sadly, the general public still largely ignores their message. Even if some knew their lives would end the next day, many of them would still neglect the salvation of their souls (Matthew 24:37–39; Hebrews 2:3). How tragic is the hard-heartedness of man!

To sum up this section, it seems "almost" unavoidable not to conclude that the sons of God were angels who sinned and became demonic beings. While this is certainly an unsavory conclusion, we are left with little biblical or logical recourse. Some of these demons then took on human flesh and married women. They bore children and thoroughly corrupted the human race.

This admittedly is a most unsettling doctrine. It stifles the Christian spirit to even contemplate such a state of wretchedness in the world. But the demonic forces of hell take no prisoners! Sin only seeks to destroy the soul and spirit and sentence it to the everlasting Lake of Fire. As previously stated, one of Satan's motivations during Noah's day was to prevent the prophecy of Genesis 3:15 from being fulfilled. If he could morally corrupt all of humanity, in his faulty reasoning, the Messiah could not be born. His wicked plans were thwarted by our almighty God.

Beyond that motivation, he and his wicked hordes perhaps yearned to destroy God's beautiful creation. If that was a genuine motivation, they were partially successful. The Flood changed significant aspects of our originally perfect earth. However, God shall eventually restore the world to its pre-Flood majesty and splendor.

Satan's objective to fight against God and His spiritually adopted children has not diminished over the millennia. It will only increase in intensity during the seven-year Tribulation. But, thankfully, Satan's horrid, immoral objectives will always be defeated by our almighty God.

Thankfully, the Church will have been raptured before that future and unprecedented time of misery and woe. Those who become believers during the Tribulation will suffer greatly at the hands of Satan, the Antichrist, the false prophet, and their wicked followers. Millions will face torture and martyrdom. Let all readers be warned who have not fully embraced Jesus Christ as their Savior and Lord. Repent today while you still have time and opportunity! God awaits you with loving and open arms.

Fruchtenbaum's Concluding Remarks

We turn once again to the capable remarks of Hebraist Arnold Fruchtenbaum. In concise and yet meticulous form, he offers the following explanation regarding Genesis 6:1–4:

> Then Genesis 6:4 goes on to say: and also after that to explain how the Nephilim came into existence. Following the opening statement: The Nephilim were in the earth in those days, it explains how they came into being, and the explanation is introduced by the phrase also after that.
>
> The phrase does not mean that the Nephilim existed after the Flood. Also after that introduces the phrase: when the sons of God came unto the daughters of men, which repeats the facts of 6:2, and then adds: They bore children unto them. These children were the Nephilim.

So the Nephilim were the children of human woman and fallen angels. They were human on one side but superhuman on the other: the same were the mighty men that were of old, the men of renown. The term the mighty men is the Hebrew word giborim. Because of their unique origin, they proved to be exceptional. The rabbis interpret this to mean that they were the mighty in their rebellion against God. This is a valid conclusion since the same terminology will be used of Nimrod in chapter 10.

It also states that they were the men of renown. The rabbis interpret this to mean that they were men who brought desolation upon the world because of the correlation in Hebrew between the word renown and the word desolation. At any rate, this intermarriage produced a grotesque race that was superhuman both mentally and physically in strength, but not necessarily in size. Genesis 6 is the account of what really happened. This actual historical event became the source of Greek and Roman mythology, where the gods and goddesses intermarry with humans, producing great men such as Achilles.

The difference between Genesis and Greek mythology is that Genesis states what really happened while mythology is a corrupted account. In Genesis the intermarriage is expressed negatively in all its sinfulness; in the mythology it is glorified. This shows why the

Flood was necessary—to destroy the product of fallen angels and human women.

Interpreting Genesis 6:1-2 as being an intermarriage of human women with fallen angels provides the only adequate explanation for the statements found in II Peter and Jude. In these passages, three points are made. First, this phenomenon of intermarriage was a peculiar, unique sin; second, the sin was timed in conjunction with the Flood; and third, it is different from the original fall of angels; otherwise, all angels would end up being in permanent confinement.[82]

The lessons of this short section of Scripture may prove highly disturbing to believers. To think that such corruption was once not just present on the earth but overwhelming is a sickening feeling. We regrettably concur with Fruchtenbaum's assessment as written immediately above this paragraph. Though unsettling to contemplate, it does reflect the horrid ugliness of the Nephilim and godlessness of Noah's day in graphic description.

We may corporately thank God that such a vile sin is not surging throughout humanity in our present age. All the human perpetrators were destroyed by the Flood. The unholy demons who committed these abominable sins have been locked up in Tartarus. God will allow one more period of intense godlessness to encompass the world, namely, the Tribulation. But even during this infamous seven-year period, God's grace will bring millions into proper fellowship with Him.

---

[82] Arnold G. Fruchtenbaum, Ariel's Bible Commentary: The Book of Genesis: Exposition from a Messianic Jewish Perspective, pp. 150–151.

Lessons Learned in This Chapter

This rather disturbing passage of Scripture produces an unsavory taste in one's mouth and an upsetting feeling in one's stomach. It accurately reflects the revolting level of sin to which both Lucifer and his ungodly minions coupled with mankind can plunge. The degradations of sin can completely obliterate any semblance of godly conscience or moral aptitude.

We first discussed an overview of God's continual outreach to mankind. He does this through both His special and general revelation. God's mercy and His "second chances" seem to be infinite in number. However, as gracious as God truly is, He is also just. He must eventually punish the unrepentant sinner. Ecclesiastes 8:11 testifies to the unfortunate propensity of man: "Because the sentence against an evil work is not executed speedily, therefore the heart of the sons of men is fully set in them to do evil."

Second, we engaged in the disturbing question concerning the identity of the sons of God, the daughters of men, and the Nephilim. After considerable review, we concluded that the sons of God in Genesis chapter 6 can refer to none other than the fallen angels. These fallen angels, or demons, had the capacity to take on human flesh. They then married earthly women, the daughters of men, and bore children. The children were called the Nephilim.

These Nephilim were extraordinary half-demon, half-human hybrids. They were described as the mighty men who were of old, men of renown (Genesis 6:4b). We can safely assume that they were morally bankrupt. Details of their lives are not offered. Thankfully, the Flood swept all the wicked human perpetrators away into a watery tomb. No more Nephilim are wandering the earth. However, one final Nephilim is coming. He will be the son of Lucifer himself.

His future identity is well known. He will be none other than the Antichrist.

This assessment is based on a proper interpretation of Genesis 3:15. There are two Seed (singular) mentioned in Genesis 3:15. The first and holy Seed will be the Messiah. He has already come to this earth and will return a second time (Acts 1:9–11; Revelation 1:7).

The second and degenerate seed will be the Antichrist, the most wicked man to ever live. It is possible that the Antichrist may be alive even today, but that cannot be established until the midpoint of the Tribulation. He will be responsible for bringing almost unparalleled misery and destruction on this earth. There will only be one Antichrist who will be fathered by Satan.

The offending demons who cohabited with women in Noah's day have been permanently incarcerated in Tartarus, which is the lowest pit of hell. Peter and Jude's statements about these angels only make sense if interpreted in this manner. Though a frightening doctrine indeed, it seems by far the most reasonable conclusion.

In making reference to Peter and Jude's statements, we once again repeat Fruchtenbaum's enlightening assessment: "First, this phenomenon of intermarriage was a peculiar, unique sin; second, the sin was timed in conjunction with the Flood; and third, it is different from the original fall of angels; otherwise, all angels would end up being in permanent confinement."[83]

In our following chapter, we shall continue in our discussion of Genesis 6:1–8. Though not a pleasant discussion, Scripture presents life in a most realistic sense. This includes the glorious descriptions of God's power and majesty. But it also relates to the ugliness and

---
[83] Ibid., p. 151.

warts of ungodly mankind.

Thankfully, because of Christ's eternal love and sacrifice, even the most unworthy of humanity can come to saving faith. But, so we may keep a balanced perspective, we encourage our every reader to pose this question to themselves: Who is worthy of God's grace? The answer is that no one is. Thus, every believer should daily lift up his redeemed and godly arms, covered by Christ's justifying blood and grace, and utter a heartfelt: "Thank you!"

Cognitive Conundrum #11

From an industrious family, I may claim to be; a vendetta was mine, I shouted with glee. My offspring proved talented to the supreme, but their godliness was in doubt, it would seem. My wives supported my endeavors, so it appears of my Creator God I showed very few fears. My past heritage came directly from God; my reaction thereof proved pathetically odd.

Who am I?

Answer: Lamech (Genesis 4:19–24)

Chapter 12

A World Gone Bad

(Genesis 6:1–8: Part C)

In This Chapter

Objectives for This Chapter
A Deeper Look at the Nephilim (Genesis 6:4)
God's Holy Response to a Wicked World (Genesis 6:5–8)
Lessons Learned in This Chapter

Objectives for This Chapter

In this chapter, the reader will note a slight amount of reiteration regarding the Nephilim. This is a complex theological issue and merits a thorough review. The discussion regarding the Nephilim's identity has proven fairly intense over the centuries. Undue disgruntlement betwixt scholars certainly is not warranted, however.

All Bible-believing students seek out the truth, nothing more, nothing less, nothing else. In this particular situation, the truth strikes one as quite unpalatable, even deplorable. The student must be prepared to accept the seemingly unacceptable. God's truth shines in glorious majesty; evil grovels in its perpetually besmirched ugliness.

We shall first examine some of the ancient historical perspectives on the identity of the Nephilim. Those who lived closer to the events of Noah's day and understood the culture better should be given an ear. Modern man sometimes tends to think that his knowledge is superior. This decidedly is not always the case, particularly regarding historical attestations.

Second, we shall review the wickedness and physical qualities frequently attributed to the Nephilim. They were not necessarily giants, as many translations assert. Nephilim means "fallen ones" and refers to their immoral status as half-demonic and half-human. It is possible that they may have been physically imposing and large in size. That cannot be categorically denied. But even if that were the case, that was not the emphasis of the Hebrew term Nephilim. They were men of renown for largely unknown reasons.

Third, we shall discuss the issue of when the Nephilim were destroyed. In Numbers 13:33, ten of the spies reported seeing the Nephilim living in the Promised Land. Their report was characterized by at least four lies, which we shall cite. Scripture unerringly reports men's temporal lies and misunderstandings just as it does the eternal truth. The student of Scripture must examine the whole context of God's holy Word to evaluate these recorded lies. When the broad panorama of Holy Writ is thoroughly studied, such mistruths become patently evident to the diligent believer.

Reality check: There were no more Nephilim alive in Moses' day. They had all perished in the Flood. That was one of the primary purposes for the universal water judgment. God eradicated the vile Nephilim for all time… with one notable exception. The Antichrist will be that solitary exception in the future Tribulation period. Satan will father, through a normal woman, the Antichrist. This monstrous figure will truly be the last Nephilim of all time.

First John 2:22 conveys the thoughts of many antichrists and also defines them: "Who is a liar but he who denies that Jesus is the Christ? He is antichrist who denies the Father and the Son." One can readily observe that the term "antichrist" can be conveyed in a general sense. In addition, 2 John 7 adds the following explanation: "For many deceivers have gone out into the world who do not confess Jesus Christ as coming in the flesh. This is a deceiver and an antichrist" (cf. 1 John 2:18, 4:3). But there is clearly one final Antichrist who will rule over the world. In Revelation chapter 13, this ultimate Antichrist is called the beast (cf. 2 Thessalonians 2:1–12).

The ten lying spies who explored the Promised Land were put to death by the Lord for their false report. But their influence was such that the entire older generation of Israel also perished in the wilderness through forty years of wandering. They rebelled against God the Creator, Moses, and Aaron. They paid for their rebellion with their lives. Ultimately, it was their children, for whom they claimed to fear, that actually invaded the land and conquered it.

Numbers 14:30–32 presents God's judgment on the older generation of Israel:

> Except for Caleb the son of Jephunneh and Joshua the son of Nun, you shall by no means enter the land which I swore I would make you dwell in. But your little ones, whom you said would be victims, I will bring in, and they shall know the land which you have despised. But as for you, your carcasses shall fall in the wilderness.

Fourth, we shall delve into the spiritual climate of Noah's day. It was truly the worst period in earth's history, morally speaking. The Nephilim essentially corrupted nearly all of humanity. Though Noah was blessed with impressive spiritual mentoring and examples during his life, they became fewer and fewer. Corruption invaded the world, and mankind became spiritually degenerated by godlessness. Though Noah faithfully preached for 120 years, his converts were precious few, if any at all.

As we shall see, however, God always faithfully preserves a remnant. That remnant was delivered through the ark. God brought the animals to the ark and thus preserved humanity and the animal kingdom. Such a spellbinding parade that must have been to behold! Eyeballs must have nearly been popping out of the Nephilim's heads. Incredibly, the sagging jaws were not accompanied by repentance. This simultaneously tragic and glorious story shall be the topic of our next chapter and those following. It is truly a story for the ages.

A Deeper Look at the Nephilim (Genesis 6:4)

To the inquisitive student, Genesis 6:4 opens a veritable pandora's box of questions: "There were giants on the earth in those days, and also afterward, when the sons of God came in to the daughters of men and they bore children to them. Those were the mighty men who were of old, men of renown." This question instantly leaps to the foreground: Who were these mysterious "giants," or as it is more properly translated, "Nephilim"? The Hebrew word, although frequently translated as "giants" (as in our NKJV), is actually "Nephilim," which means "fallen ones." As we shall see, "giants" is not a precise translation.

Much insight can often be gained from ancient Jewish writers. They were closer to the historical context and retained insights into the cultural settings that we no longer possess today. In agreement with what we have already concluded, the Jewish mentality is that the sons of God were fallen angels, in other words, demons. They intermarried with women and produced the offspring called the Nephilim.

What Do the Ancients Say?

Sarfati quotes Jewish historian Josephus as follows: "For many angels of God accompanied with women, and begat sons that proved unjust, and despisers of all that was good, on account of the confidence they had in their own strength; for the tradition is, that these men did what resembled the acts of those whom the Grecians call giants."[84]

In addition, Sarfati quotes from the pseudepigraphic book of Enoch:

> And it came to pass when the children of men had multiplied that in those days were born unto them beautiful and comely daughters. And the angels, the children of the heaven, saw and lusted after them, and said to one another: "Come, let us choose us wives from among the children of men and beget us children." And Semjaza, who was their leader, said unto them: "I fear ye will not indeed agree to do this deed, and I alone shall have to pay the penalty of a great sin" (Enoch 6:1-3).[85]

Hebraist scholar Arnold Fruchtenbaum delves into a lengthy discussion on the phrase "sons of God." He also asserts that this phrase in the Old Testament refers to angelic beings, whether good or bad. Some resist his conclusions because the doctrine of half-demon, half-men (the Nephilim) is such a repugnant one. As unsavory as this doctrine may be, the fallen angels' half-demonic, half-human offspring, namely, the Nephilim, seems to be well-established in Scripture. Fruchtenbaum's conclusions are well-supported and coherent.

---
84 Jonathan Sarfati, The Genesis Account: A theological, historical, and scientific account of Genesis 1–11, p. 477.
85 Ibid., p. 477.

A Review and Amplification by Fruchtenbaum

For the sake of a more complete context, we shall repeat some of what we quoted earlier by Fruchtenbaum:

> Genesis 6:2 records the actual intermarriage that occurred. The first statement, that the sons of God saw the daughters of men that they were fair, presents the crisis. The sons of God in Hebrew is bnei ha-Elohim. This term, in the Hebrew Bible, is always a reference to angels, both good and bad ones. ...
>
> So everywhere else this word is used, it is always in reference to angels, a point on which all expositors concur. Nevertheless, some wish to make Genesis 6 the one exception. However, it is not wise to make exceptions unless there are very good exegetical reasons to do so, and there is no good reason to make this one passage the exception to the rule.
>
> As in all other passages, the term sons of God should be understood as being angels. They are sons in the sense of being directly created by God, and this includes angels, both fallen and unfallen. In the New Testament, the Greek term sons of God is applied to other entities besides angels, but the common element is that of being directly created by God. For example, Adam, in Luke 3:38 is called the son of God, since he was directly created by God.

Believers are called the children of God in John 1:12 because believers are viewed as a new creation, created by God. The terms sons of God has the meaning to be created by God. The exception is the uniqueness of the only begotten Son of God, the word "only" emphasizes His uniqueness in that He was always in existence and not created.

The ancients viewed this term to mean "angels", and the oldest Jewish view of this verse, and those living closest to the time when these things were written, took sons of God to be angels, not humans. For example, the Septuagint, dated from about 250 B.C., translates this verse as angels of God. Josephus understood this as angels, and so do the Book of Enoch and the Dead Sea Scrolls documents of Qumran. Furthermore, in the Targum Pseudo-Jonathan, 6:1, 6:2, and 6:4 also make these angels.

Also seven books in the Pseudopigrapha interpret this as a reference to angels (1 Enoch 6:1-2; Jubilees 4:15, 5:6, II Enoch 18; II Baruch 56; and The Testament of the Twelve Patriarchs [Reuben 5:5-6 and Naphtali 3:3-5]). Philo and the Midrashim also adhere to this view. Finally, this was also the meaning in other Semitic languages. For example, the Canaanite bn il signifies deities in general. In the Ugaritic Texts, the god El married the daughter of men by whom he had two sons, Shcht and Shim, who both became gods.

To summarize the point, the term man (Genesis 6:1) refers to humanity; and the term sons of God in 6:2 refers to "angelanity," to coin a word. Therefore, the contrast is not Sethites versus Cainites, but the contrast is humanity and angelanity.[86]

"Giants" Is a Misleading Translation

The reader may have recognized that we choose not to use the term "giants," as does the KJV and NKJV. The literal word is not "giants" but "Nephilim." This Hebrew term means "fallen ones." The term is used in a moral sense, not a physical one. Obviously, it is not talking about people who fell on their faces or were slain in battle. Quite the contrary, these were very imposing individuals. Probably, they were both intellectually and physically superior to other normal human beings, but they were not necessarily giants. We shall address this issue momentarily.

Ancient rabbinic interpretation clearly supports the view that the primary meaning of the term Nephilim refers to their morally fallen natures. They were reprobates to the extreme! Because their fathers were literal demons clothed in human flesh, the Nephilim were born with an unusually corrupt nature. These children, though potentially redeemable as far as their human spirits, undoubtedly manifested an unusually rebellious and cantankerous nature. When you are possessed by an unclean demonic spirit from conception, a particularly wicked nature is inevitable.

Disciplining such children must have proven nearly impossible. But, then again, their mothers and fathers were also so corrupt that they undoubtedly encouraged evil within them. Such is not a pleas-

---

[86] Arnold Fruchtenbaum, Ariel's Bible Commentary: The Book of Genesis, pp. 145–146.

ant thought, but parents of today are capable of doing exactly the same thing. Some parents literally coach their children on how to cheat, steal, and engage in other despicable acts.

The Evil Nephilim's Business Was Corruption

The Nephilim endeavored quite successfully to corrupt the rest of humanity with evil. Their presence essentially transformed the world into a completely wicked environment. Satan's ultimate plot was to thwart the fulfillment of the messianic promise of Genesis 3:15. We may be thankful that the Bible does not offer commentary on what those wicked practices were. The fallen human nature of mankind today would instantly desire to emulate the atrocious habits of those bygone and immoral demon-men.

Genesis 6:11 states: "The earth also was corrupt before God, and the earth was filled with violence." God was grieved that He had even created man (6:6). Hence, He chose to destroy mankind down to just eight people. Tragically, the Nephilim had already accomplished their heinous task of corrupting humanity. One must always contemplate the fact that God created man with free will. At times, this free will turns potential blessing into treacherous and repulsive behavior. Still, humanity would not be humanity without a free will.

Why Do Some Translations Call the Nephilim "Giants"?

There is a logical explanation for this question. The Septuagint (LXX) was the first translation of the Hebrew Bible into Greek. When the translators of the Hebrew Bible were trying to convey the concept of these "fallen ones," the Nephilim, they pondered how to best communicate it.

As already noted, the Nephilim, according to the ancient Jewish interpreters, were believed to be half-demonic and half-human. Other false ancient religions taught the same belief. These false religions characterized their own gods and goddesses as powerful beings. Hercules is a well-known mythical example of a half-god, half-man. He was a very imposing warrior, almost invincible to death.

In order to better convey the idea of these extraordinary individuals who were half-demon and half-men to their Greek audience, the LXX translated the word "Nephilim" as the Greek word "*gigentes.*" Our English word giant stems from that root. Hence, the tradition began that the Nephilim were physically large people. It is quite possible that some were physically imposing, but that is not the primary meaning of the term.

The concept of large stature also receives support in Numbers 13:33, which states: "There we saw the giants (the descendants of Anak came from the giants); and we were like grasshoppers in our own sight, and so we were in their sight." There are numerous lies involved in the spies' report. Ten of the twelve spies proved fraudulent, and they accomplished their foolhardy purposes. They got the people to rebel against God. It cost that entire dust-covered generation their lives. They ended up meandering through the barren wilderness until all succumbed to the stifling hot grip of icy cold death.

Were the Nephilim Still Alive in Moses' Day?

Question: If the Nephilim were destroyed by the Flood, why are they then mentioned in Numbers 13:33? Were demons still cohabiting with women? Answer: No, they decidedly were not! Those offending demons had already been cast into Tartarus. No women were wittingly or unwittingly cavorting about sexually with demons. Thus, there were no Nephilim left on the earth. The ten spies had given a false report. Were there giants on the earth? Yes, unquestionably, there were. One need only consider Goliath, who lived centuries later.

Punishment for the spies' false report immediately ensued. God put the ten lying spies to death (Numbers 14:36–38). One might be disposed to think that this immediate consequence would have swayed the rest of the Israelites to repentance. Alas! God's direct punishment had little effect but to produce more whining and lamentations.

However, one salient point must be remembered. God's decree of death for that unworthy generation in the wilderness occurred before He put the ten spies to death. Some might argue, then, that God was being premature in His unremitting punishment. Really? Such an argument is pathetic. Had God not overwhelmingly shown His power and grace in the ten plagues of Egypt? Had He not delivered His people through the Red Sea? Had He not drowned the Egyptian army? Was He not providing the Israelites with food and water even in that moment? How much more evidence did Israel need? Was God incapable, then, of defeating the nearby wicked nations in battle?

Ultimately, the entire generation of fighting men and women twenty years old and above that left Egypt perished in the deserts. Only Joshua and Caleb and those under the age of twenty would be permitted to enter the Promised Land (14:29–31). The older generation would liberally sprinkle the hostile wilderness with their decaying bones. Such is the price of blatant disobedience! Let the modern-day believer learn wisdom and obedience from this lamentable history lesson.

As already noted, the reader must remember that Scripture records the mistruths of people just as it does true statements. Certainly, that was true of the lies of the serpent in Genesis chapter 3. That practice holds true throughout the Scriptures. Let us note, for a moment, the falsehoods perpetrated upon the masses of Israelites who were nervously assembled before Moses and Aaron.

Lies, Lies, and More Lies!

Lie #1: The ten witnesses had seen the Nephilim. The reality is that there were no Nephilim alive on planet earth to see. All of those wicked half-demon, half-men (the Nephilim), had been destroyed in the Flood. That was one of the primary purposes of the Flood. Everyone on earth, save the eight in the ark, perished. All the offending demons had long since been cast into Tartarus, where they presently languish in torment, awaiting God's final judgment.

Lie #2: The sons of Anak, who truly were giants, did not descend from the Nephilim. No one alive in Noah's day had descended from the Nephilim. They were completely wiped off the face of the earth. It is true, however, that there were many giants in those ancient days. One need only consider Goliath, who lived centuries later during the days of David. That was approximately 400 years after the death of Moses. The Bible records other groups of men who also were of great height and size.

In our present age, we still find giants on the earth, although they are not generally as big as Goliath. But even as late as 1940, Robert Pershing Wadlow grew to the extraordinary height of eight feet and eleven inches. Goliath was only half a foot taller. During Moses' time, this phenomenon of huge people was much more prevalent.

Again, let the reader note that the actual term, which is used twice in Numbers 13:33, is Nephilim, not giants. However, in support of this translation "giants," it is known that the sons of Anak were physical giants (cf. Deuteronomy 9:2; Joshua 14:15, 15:13–14, 21:11; Judges 1:20). Thus, the context of these verses admittedly lends itself quite naturally to translating Nephilim as "giants." It should be observed that other ethnic groups, such as that of Og, king of Bashan, are also translated as giants by the NKJV instead of utilizing the actual ethnicity as recorded in the Hebrew manuscript.

The more literal translation of Deuteronomy 3:11a should be: "For only Og king of Bashan remained of the remnant of the Rephaim" ("giants," NKJV). King Og was the last Rephaite. He was called a giant because his bed was so large. It was approximately thirteen feet long and six feet wide. If Og really needed a bed that big, then he truly was immense. But the more literal translation in this passage is to be preferred. Og was the last of the Rephaites.

It is much better to translate the Hebrew term "Nephilim" as "fallen ones." This more accurately conveys the moral quality, or decided lack thereof, as intended in Genesis 6:4. Furthermore, we simply are not informed of all the qualities of the Nephilim. Limiting it to physical stature, as many translations tend to do, is not wise.

The Promised Land Is Described as Simultaneously Beautiful but Dangerous

Lie #3: The ten spies reported that the land devoured its inhabitants. That was truly a ridiculous statement. How could the land devour its inhabitants while simultaneously supporting such an immense and healthy population? How could the people have grown so large and been such fierce warriors in such an inhospitable place? How could they have built such large and fortified cities? Their statement was not just nonsensical; it was laughable.

Furthermore, the spies had already described the land as flowing with milk and honey. Numbers 13:27 states: "Then they told him, and said: 'We went to the land where you sent us. It truly flows with milk and honey, and this is its fruit.'" But they also claimed that the land devoured its inhabitants. Somehow, the gullible people did not see through this lie.

The spies showed the Israelites the incredible bounty of grapes that they had carried back between two poles (13:23). They also brought and displayed sumptuous pomegranates and figs. The land was incredibly fertile! How could that possibly be interpreted as "devouring" its inhabitants? But sadly enough, humanity tends to believe what they choose. That holds particularly true in times of potential danger. Panic easily sways the crowds. Facts are frequently deemed less important than feelings. That is the sad state in which our world still grovels. It will continue to so vacillate until the eternal state.

Had God Suddenly Become Feeble?

Lie #4: The cities are built up and fortified to the heavens. Although this is clearly an exaggeration, even such pathetic statements can influence a terrified and faithless crowd of people. Those who are perilously dangling on the precipice of panic are prone to believe almost anything, no matter how ridiculous. How many times has history witnessed such irrational behavior?

The Israelites had completely forgotten that it was the same God who had so effectively destroyed Egypt who was leading them. If He could rain down such judgments as the ten plagues of Egypt, could He not also destroy large cities and physically imposing men? Can a human warrior defeat the Creator God? For Israel to panic so soon after being delivered from Egypt in such stupendous fashion is truly stupefying. Man's heart is all too easily hardened and swayed by circumstances.

The book of Deuteronomy is a review of the previous four books. It covers the entire wilderness wanderings. So, after the forty years of wandering in the wilderness are nearly over, Moses speaks to the surviving children of that disobedient generation. He relates the historical response of their disobedient fathers in Deuteronomy 1:28: "Where can we go up? Our brethren have discouraged our hearts, saying, 'The people are greater and taller than we; the cities are great and fortified up to heaven; moreover we have seen the sons of the Anakim there.'"

Numbers 13:32 states that ten of the twelve spies sent out gave a bad report. This does not mean their report was of poor quality grammatically or communicated in a sloppy fashion. It means that they lied through their quail-encrusted teeth (cf. Numbers chapter 12). They even stated that the land devours its own inhabitants. What a pathetic falsehood that was!

Such allegations were a direct contradiction to it being the Promised Land. They were calling God a liar! In actuality, it was a land flowing with milk and honey, an incredibly fruitful land. The spies themselves admitted and even demonstrated that truth with the fruits they brought back. The Promised Land was exceedingly prosperous and fruitful. Its inhabitants were clearly very healthy and large.

Yet ten of the spies notoriously planted a thoroughly depressing view of God's faithfulness and promises in the minds of the people. They reported that the land itself was dangerous and depressing. That was a boldfaced lie. Nothing could have been further from the truth. If the land was so dangerous, why were so many people thriving in it? Farmers instinctively seek out fertile land in which to grow their crops. The Promised Land was an agrarian society. It supported a prosperous population, thus demonstrating its fruitfulness.

If You Like Sand...

Considering the Israelites' consistent lack of faith, the spies' infamous report sadly does not prove overly surprising. The people's predictable response was that they should have just died in the wilderness or gone back to Egypt. How ironic! They would soon get their demented wish! Many wanted to return back to their bondage in Egypt. Even if they did not desire freedom for themselves, should they not have aspired to freedom for their children? Apparently not! How short were their memories. Did they really want to return to a land where the Pharaoh had sworn to slaughter the newborn baby boys?

Some parts of the spies' report were accurate, but other parts were wildly exaggerated or even shameful lies. They deliberately lied about the Nephilim being in the land. As important leaders of their tribes, they surely should have known better. The ten evil spies were trying to frighten the Israelites about these half-demonic, half-human men. They succeeded! After all, who could defeat the Nephilim in battle? Truthfully, probably no one could. That is why they were men of renown.

But it must be remembered that one of the purposes of the Flood was to destroy such hybrid, demonically-bred individuals. If they actually did exist, would they not once again corrupt humanity to destroy the future messianic Seed? They would not hesitate to do so. But God would preserve the messianic Seed through Noah, Shem, and their many descendants. His holy will cannot be stymied.

No More Nephilim

Fruchtenbaum capably argues that the Nephilim did not exist on the earth anymore. He comments as follows:

When the Jewish translators were trying to find a Greek word that would express to the Greek reader what the Nephilim were, the best word in Greek was gigentes. In English, however, the word giant gives the wrong connotation altogether. So it is best to transliterate the word Nephilim or "fallen ones."

These are the products of the union of the sons of God and the daughters of men, as is explained in the remainder of the verse. According to rabbinic interpretation, these beings were so named, meaning Nephilim, because they fell and caused the world to fall.

Moreover, this is more in keeping with the meaning of the term. The phrase were in the earth in those days means the days of the intermarriage, but not after the Flood. Some use Numbers 13:33 to teach that they existed after the Flood because, when the spies came back, ten of the spies said that the Nephilim were in the Land. Some assume that these ten spies were telling the truth; but they were not. The reported existence of the Nephilim after the Flood was a lie of the ten spies, as they tried to discourage the people.

This was one of several lies they told. When Joshua conquers the land, he never runs into any Nephilim. Therefore it seems apparent that these Nephilim were the product of the intermarriage of the fallen angels and human women, and they only existed before the

Flood in keeping with the phrase "in those days"; they did not remain after the Flood.[87]

Needless to say, the topic of the Nephilim creates considerable discussion among scholars and laypeople alike. Genesis 6:1–4 ranks as one of the most discussed passages in all of Scripture. There will never be total satisfaction among scholars on any one interpretation. But that is a rather familiar refrain in theological circles.

McKeown offers these wise words regarding this rather perplexing text: "While a fully satisfactory explanation of this obscure passage is elusive, its purpose in the overall context is clear: the created order once declared 'good' is now on a collision course with the Creator and sinister anti-God forces are on the increase."[88] Indeed, this was a terrible saga in earth's history. The moral record of humanity hit its lowest ebb of all time during the days of Noah with the Nephilim. Even the Tribulation period of the end times prophecy will not exceed the wretchedness of this fateful period.

God, in His grace and mercy, has eliminated at least this one particular scenario by which mankind can defile itself. Humanity has an almost unimaginable capacity for creating and participating in the depths of evil. Believers can praise God that one exemplary man, Noah, stood the test and is celebrated by all as a genuine hero of the faith. Believers of every generation would do well to study and emulate his stellar life.

God's Holy Response to a Wicked World (Genesis 6:5–8)

We now turn our attention to one of the saddest, if not the saddest, passages in all of Scripture, Genesis 6:5–8. God gives His commentary on a world gone mad. The solution will be the utter

---
87 Arnold Fruchtenbaum, The Book of Genesis, p. 150.
88 James McKeown, Genesis, p. 50.

destruction of the earth and mankind, save the tiny remnant preserved in the ark. The faithlessness and wickedness of man reached its lowest ebb in human history during Noah's day.

Even during the darkest days of the future seven-year Tribulation, there will be many who turn to Christ. Indeed, the Tribulation period may see an almost unprecedented period of spiritual revival among humanity. God faithfully provides many opportunities for unbelievers to understand the truth of Scripture, repent of their sins, and turn by faith to Christ. God's grace always shines brightest when sin reaches its most treacherous levels.

A Great Revival Is Coming!

Revelation 6:9–11 presents an awesome testimony of living and sacrificial faith during the coming horrible days of the seven-year Tribulation:

> When He opened the fifth seal, I saw under the altar the souls of those who had been slain for the word of God and for the testimony which they held. And they cried with a loud voice, saying, "How long, O Lord, holy and true, until You judge and avenge our blood on those who dwell on the earth?" Then a white robe was given to each of them; and it was said to them that they should rest a little while longer, until both the number of their fellow servants and their brethren, who would be killed as they were, was completed (cf. Revelation 7:9–17).

The ultimate human tools of Satan, who are the Antichrist and the false prophet, will reign absolutely supreme during the second half of the Tribulation. Their influence will permeate the globe during the first half of the Tribulation, but the second half fully reveals their true nature (Revelation chapter 13). Mankind will be faced with a choice: worship the Antichrist or die. Many will become believers during this time period and die as martyrs for Jesus Christ. Some believers will be spared and enter into the millennial kingdom of Christ alive.

But none of the unbelievers of the world will be spared. They will all die! The unbelievers will die at the hands of the Antichrist, the plagues raining down on the world, or from Jesus Christ's judgment at His return (Matthew 25:31–46). Every single unbeliever will suffer the fate of physical death. There is absolutely no hope outside of Christ. There never has been.

One can take great courage from passages such as Revelation, chapters 6 and 7. Yes, there will be unparalleled misery and persecution of the Tribulation saints, but the glorious final destination for the saints far surpasses anything endured on their arduous journey. Eternity with God goes on for a very long time; indeed, it is endless!

Those Who Live Godly Lives Often Suffer on This Earth

Second Timothy 3:12 solemnly declares: "Yes, and all who desire to live godly in Christ Jesus will suffer persecution." That is the unfortunate lot of many Christians. But Paul also writes this in Romans 8:18: "For I consider that the sufferings of this present time are not worthy to be compared with the glory which shall be revealed in us" (cf. 8:28). The Christian may always look up to heaven because his redemption draws nigh (Luke 21:38).

Our present passage, however, paints no such pleasant picture of future redemption. Genesis 6:5–8 presents bad news, save for one redeeming point of light: Noah found grace in God's eyes:

Then the LORD saw that the wickedness of man was great in the earth, and that every intent of the thoughts of his heart was only evil continually. And the LORD was sorry that He had made man on the earth, and He was grieved in His heart. So the LORD said, "I will destroy man whom I have created from the face of the earth, both man and beast, creeping things and birds of the air, for I am sorry that I have made them." But Noah found grace in the eyes of the LORD.

Moral Disaster Struck the Earth

This passage lists two major moral disasters. It is hard to imagine a worse commentary anywhere. The entire planet was characterized by evil. Everywhere one would turn his head, his eyes would be shocked. Every conversation was laced with ribald, lustful comments. Even the scent of sin would prove pervasive. Wherever your feet would tread, it would take your body and spirit into a sinful display of sensuous pleasure.

Isaiah 32:6 describes the wicked: "For the foolish person will speak foolishness, and his heart will work iniquity: to practice ungodliness, to utter error against the LORD, to keep the hungry unsatisfied, and he will cause the drink of the thirsty to fall." Tragically, history has witnessed such a bounty of wretched men and women that it makes one weep. To this, we add Jeremiah's somber refrain in 17:9: "The heart is deceitful above all things, and desperately wicked; who can know it?" Indeed, the wickedness of the heart frequently defies the imagination.

Regarding Jeremiah 17:9, Theodore Laetsch comments as follows:

The "heart" in Hebrew thought is the center and fountainhead of life in its every form and phase (Prov. 4:23). This heart is "deceitful," literally, following the heel, dogging one's footsteps for the purpose of betraying him. Compare "Jacob" Gen. 25:26, 27:35-36, the name derived from the same root word. In point of deceitfulness, treachery, the human heart exceeds all things.

And the greatest deception it has conceived is the lie of the natural goodness of man's heart. On this fallacy all efforts of man at self-reform and national reform are based. This treacherous lie is the greatest obstacle to a humble return to God.[89]

Evil Permeated the Earth

Moral disaster #1: The evil acts of man smothered the earth in a blanket of wickedness. One must remember the diabolical circumstances that transformed the world into this state of immoral catastrophe. The Nephilim were largely responsible for these enormous acts of wickedness, which, thankfully, are not listed in the text. People would want to imitate them today if they could.

John Phillips writes:

> Those doubly fallen angels defied the law of their being, not merely by deceiving and consorting with members of the human race, but by the actual marriage act itself. Jude and Peter both put the sin of those fallen

---

[89] Theodore Laetsch, Concordia Classic Commentary Series: Jeremiah (St. Louis, MO: Concordia Publishing House, 1952), p. 163.

ones alongside the sin of Sodom and Gomorrah, the sin of going after "strange flesh."

So then, Genesis 6 sets before us the great apostasy of the antediluvians, an apostasy that gave rise to a perversion of the human race. Sodom-like sins became common, sins of even greater enormity indeed because they involved the lawless intercourse of alien races with human beings. The result was the Flood.[90]

The Thoughts of Man Were Repugnant Continually

Moral disaster #2: The thoughts of man were evil continuously. Genesis 6:5 states: "Then the LORD saw that the wickedness of man was great in the earth, and that every intent of the thoughts of his heart was only evil continually." The Hebrew literally says, "All the day." From morning until night, men and women alike were focused on vile thoughts. It is hard to imagine what such a society was like or how it could even function. One must not imagine that the situation of Noah's day compares to present day immorality in the world. Noah's day was unspeakably worse.

The amazing thing is that someone like Noah could have even existed in the midst of such moral chaos and depravity. Truly, he was an extraordinary individual. Equally true is that God preserved his life and the life of his family during this tumultuous time. His family's corporate resistance to evil proved incredible. However, one should not assume that they literally fought off evil men. God protected them from the Nephilim and all who would be in opposition, which would be nearly everyone.

---

[90] John Phillips, Exploring Genesis, p. 80.

Henry Morris writes of the world situation in Noah's day as follows:

> Though it is true of the natural man in general that "they are all under sin" (Romans 3:39), this description of antediluvian man in verse 5 (also in verses 11-13) can hardly be correctly applied to all men everywhere. Outward wickedness is certainly not "great" in the case of every self-righteous unbeliever, nor do any but the most depraved imagine "only evil continually."
>
> There are certainly degrees of sin, and therefore degrees of punishment, in the case of unbelievers is something grotesque and abnormal, and thus reflects a grotesque and abnormal cause. It therefore required a cataclysmic remedy, nothing less than the unique cleansing of a worldwide baptism in the waters of the great Flood. Before demonic wickedness could gain control of every man, woman, and child throughout the entire world, thus destroying God's redemptive promises, God must intervene in catastrophic judgment.[91]

The Holy Spirit Presently Restrains Evil

In our modern era, the faith of the believer and the presence of the Church constantly restrain the evil tendencies of society. Most important of all, however, is the restraining influence of the Holy Spirit. What happens when the Church is raptured and the Restrainer (the Holy Spirit) stops restraining evil people from their wicked

---
91 Henry Morris, The Genesis Record, p. 176.

impulses?

Second Thessalonians 2:6–8 warns:

> And now you know what is restraining, that he may be revealed in his own time. For the mystery of lawlessness is already at work; only He who now restrains will do so until He is taken out of the way. And then the lawless one will be revealed, whom the Lord will consume with the breath of His mouth and destroy with the brightness of His coming.

The reader may note that the Restrainer is not specifically identified. Some feel that it is actually government or some other powerful entity. However, the only individual who adequately qualifies for such a monumental task is the Holy Spirit Himself. This is not to declare that He will stop convicting man of their sins (John 16:8–11). If He did that, no one could come to faith in Christ during the Tribulation. But in ways that are unclear to us today, He will cease restraining sinful activity. Remarkably, even the future darkest days of the Tribulation will shine brighter spiritually than the historic days of Noah.

Unrestrained bedlam and evil will reign with little or no positive influence to modify mankind's monstrous behavior. Mankind does not and cannot understand in our present age the activity of the Holy Spirit in restraining evil. It is far more appreciable than we can imagine. But the Restrainer (the Holy Spirit) will cease restraining the sinful proclivities of man at some point in the future. That shall undoubtedly take place immediately after the Rapture of the Church.

Eventually, however, the Antichrist will seize the situation and bring some temporary semblance of order to the world. But he will do so at a phenomenally high cost to mankind. All freedoms will be stripped away at the midpoint of the Tribulation. A person must comply to the dictates of the Antichrist and his false prophet or face execution. The Antichrist will make all former dictators look like raw and goodhearted amateurs. His reign of terror will know no equals in the history of the earth. Simultaneously, God will be judging the earth with the seal, trumpet, and bowl judgments. It will not be a pleasant season to be an earth dweller.

God Holds the Antichrist Back at the Present Time

LaHaye and Hindson offer the following comments:

God will not allow the Antichrist to appear until the time of the Tribulation. The Antichrist is being restrained until "in his time he will be revealed" (2 Thessalonians 2:6). The word "restrain" (Greek, katecho, "to hold down") in both verses 6 and 7 is a present active participle, but in verse 6 it appears in the neuter gender ("what restrains") while in verse 7 it is in the masculine ("he who restrains, holds down"). Such usage also occurs in reference to the Spirit of God.

The Greek word for "spirit," pneuma, is a neuter-gender word, but the masculine pronoun is used when referring to the Person of the Holy Spirit. The one doing the restraining, then, in all likelihood, is the Spirit of God. In church history some believed the restrainer was the Roman Empire or the witness of the church. But neither of these suggestions seems feasible.

Constable says, "The Holy Spirit of God is the only Person with sufficient [supernatural] power to do this restraining ... The removal of the Restrainer at the time of the Rapture must obviously precede the day of the Lord" ("2 Thessalonians," Bible Knowledge Commentary, p. 219).[92]

Tragically, signs of the future are already saturating the world. There is no end for cries to enhance abortion rights. Some are demanding the right to murder babies even after they are born if they do not measure up to the parents' or to society's expectations. Divorce is as common inside the Church as it is outside. How far is society from advocating the "mercy killing" of the elderly or hopelessly informed? The Nazis of Germany not only indulged in this heinous action, but they also included the mentally or physically handicapped. Indeed, they slaughtered millions of perfectly healthy men and women without hesitation.

Pornography has degraded men, women, and children alike. Many crave sexual "freedom" without restraints, no matter all the evidence to the contrary, which shows its harmful effects. Sin-sickened adults want to force small children to perform sexual acts. Perhaps the most insane of all is the recent craze to change one's sexual orientation. This will ultimately lead to the devastation of many a young person's life. It is incredible that any medical "doctor" would go along with this mental deviation and perform so-called corrective surgery. Our preferred word for such individuals is "genetic butcherer."

All of these and many other vices are becoming more common and readily accepted by the world in general. Violence around the world is steadily increasing. Accompanying that violence, indeed

---

[92] Tim LaHaye and Ed Hindson, The Popular Bible Prophecy Commentary, p. 455.

encouraging it, is a judicial system that would rather focus on legal technicalities than punishing the criminals. Even the most violent criminals are, at times, released after their arrests. These same criminals leave the jails and commit exactly the same crimes. They are later once again released by an immoral legal system.

How long will God's patience endure? Jesus warned believers what the end times would be like. Matthew 24:12 states: "And because lawlessness will abound, the love of many will grow cold." When the Holy Spirit withdraws His restraining ministry, evil will escalate exponentially. Our present systems of government control, to at least some minimal degree, criminal activity. During the horrendous days of the Tribulation, even much of government control will be corrupted. The Antichrist will initially restore some semblance of order but at a tremendous cost. Those who do not please him will simply and quickly be put to death.

God Grieves that He Made Man

We return now to our passage at hand, Genesis 6:5–8. Three crucial truths are revealed about God's attitudes and actions.

Truth #1 (God's perspective): He was grieved that He had created man. Genesis 6:6 records: "And the LORD was sorry that He had made man on the earth, and He was grieved in His heart." That is truly a remarkable statement! What can it possibly mean? God knows all things in advance; He was not surprised how events turned out (Isaiah 46:10). So how can He be grieved? We must always bear in mind that Scripture is the best interpreter of Scripture.

Numbers 23:19 states: "God is not a man, that He should lie, nor a son of man, that He should repent. Has He said, and will He not do? Or has He spoken, and will He not make it good?" First Samuel 15:11 says that God regretted that He had made Saul king. But in the same context, 1 Samuel 15:29 states that God does not lie or relent. Is this a contradiction?

We must remember that the Bible speaks in human language. These communications can and frequently are uttered in the unusual manner of God possessing physical qualities like arms or even feathers and wings (Deuteronomy 33:27; Psalm 91:4). Yet the Bible makes it very clear that God is a Spirit (John 4:24). He does not have arms, feathers, or wings. The technical terms for these types of statements are anthropomorphisms and zoomorphisms, respectively.

The Bible can also refer to God's emotions in comparison to man's, such as God's love (John 3:16). Only God can love with a perfect love. These emotional descriptions, inherent within the Godhead, are called an anthropopathism. In our present context, the emotion we are referring to concerns God's grief. Admittedly, this concept of God's grief seems a bit difficult to understand.

Fruchtenbaum offers the following explanation:

> Here is the resolution. Because the Bible teaches that God does not repent (1 Sam. 15:29), it is only from our own perspective that He seems to repent, meaning He seems to change His mind because man has changed his attitude toward Him (1 Sam. 15:11). Therefore, God may seem to repent when man changes his mind, for God's attitude toward man is conditioned by man's attitude. So God responds to man in one way when man obeys; He responds another way when man disobeys.

Initially, Saul was obedient; and he was made king. He then became disobedient, so God removed the kingship from him. It appears from the human perspective that God repented; He changed his mind. Actually no change has taken place. God simply responds one way to obedience, and He responds a different way to disobedience.[93]

Unrepentant Sin Must Ultimately Be Punished

Truth #2 (God's judgment): He declared that He would destroy the world and all its inhabitants. Genesis 6:7 declares: "So the LORD said, 'I will destroy man whom I have created from the face of the earth, both man and beast, creeping thing and birds of the air, for I am sorry that I have made them.'"

This declaration of destruction signified the utter depravity of man. Even the animals were to fall under the curse. Of necessity, God's patience had run out. He could not allow humanity to continue relentlessly down his path of moral destruction. The Nephilim ensured that man's depravity would grow worse and worse. They were on the brink of defiling all mankind. God could tolerate the wickedness of man no more.

Yet, God would not completely blot out His creation. As always, He had a remnant, though a small remnant indeed. In fact, that remnant may have been down to one man and his family. Is it truly possible that all of humanity save one family had been infiltrated by the wickedness of the Nephilim corruption? That may have actually been the case. The fact that no one alive in Noah's day is reported to have responded to his preaching the truth for 120 years is a sobering reality. Few evangelists in history have ever experienced such minimal success. That is not a commentary on Noah's abilities. Rather,

---

[93] Arnold Fruchtenbaum, Ariel's Bible Commentary: The Book of Genesis, pp. 153–154.

it is a stark testimony to the immoral realities of his day.

However, this tragic scenario does not necessitate that only eight faithful people were alive in Noah's time frame of preaching. Methuselah, for instance, died in the year of the Flood. Other godly men and women would also have been present during those 120 years. They may have been encouraging and even assisting Noah to build the Ark. However, when those 120 years of God's forbearance ended, it was down to just Noah and his own family. Incredible!

God Preserves Humanity Through the Ark

Truth #3 (God's thread of redemption): He spared humanity through Noah and the ark. Genesis 6:8 offers a glimpse into God's forbearance and mercy: "But Noah found grace in the eyes of the LORD" (cf. Exodus 33:12–13; Psalm 84:11). What a remarkable statement that is. In all the earth, one exceptional man found grace in God's sight.

This should not be interpreted as necessarily meaning that Noah was the only man on earth who found grace in God's sight. But he certainly was God's man for his own generation. Noah stood out above all others, as did Enoch, Job, Moses, Elijah, Daniel, and John the Baptist in their respective generations. The vast majority of the earth followed their own morally polluted paths. One ponders how the world could have been so sorely afflicted and stained by sin. Was it any wonder why God had to take such drastic action?

What does this say regarding the rest of Noah's family? His three named sons had not yet been born when God told Noah that only 120 years remained before judgment (Genesis 6:3). If he fathered children before his sons Shem, Ham, and Japheth, they apparently did not follow in their father's footsteps. They are never mentioned. Noah did have brothers and sisters (Genesis 5:30), but they apparently were not committed believers. It is either that or they mercifully died before the Flood.

God spoke to Noah regarding the impending Flood when he turned 480 years of age. His three believing sons were not born until he was 500. One must assume that they took their father's message to heart since they entered the ark with him. If Noah began work on the ark immediately, and we should take it for granted that he did, he must have hired helpers to assist him. His sons would not have been much help for at least thirty years after God first spoke to him. They would have been too young to assist him.

Guardians of the Faith

As already alluded to, Noah did have godly influences around him. He was eighty years old when Enoch was translated up to heaven. That gave him abundant opportunity to hear the word of the Lord from this godly saint. Clearly, Noah listened attentively and took to heart the spiritual lessons he learned from this astonishing and learned prophet of God.

When Enoch was translated to heaven, Noah undoubtedly did not know whether to rejoice or weep. He would truly miss his godly instructor and inspiration. It is amazing to think that an additional 400 years passed before God's warning came to him regarding the fact that man's days would be ended after 120 years.

It is also quite probable that Methuselah encouraged Noah in his building of the ark. God graciously allowed Noah's grandfather, Methuselah, to remain alive until the year of the Flood. The rabbis teach that Methuselah died on the same day that Noah and his family entered into the ark. The week-long delay for the rain was spent in mourning over Methuselah's memory.

Considering that he was the son of godly Enoch and the fact that he was the Seed son, Methuselah followed in his father's righteous footsteps. If that truly be the case, he would have provided much encouragement and inspiration for his grandson, Noah. Considering that Noah's father, Lamech, prophesied that Noah would bring the earth comfort, he almost certainly was a believer.

Ironically, Methuselah outlived his own son, Lamech, by five years. One must also bear in mind that the men mentioned descending from Seth were the Seed sons. It is quite reasonable to assume that they were all devout believers. That is particularly evident since each of these ten patriarchs probably fathered many, many children. If those mentioned had not been godly, another son would have been selected. God has always been in control of these matters. This is clearly evidenced in the line of Abraham, Isaac, and Jacob. None of them were the firstborn, but all fathered the eventual Seed sons. The same held true of David centuries later. David was the eighth son born.

It is amazing that God always preserves a remnant who believes on Him. Never before or after in earth's history did the remnant become so small. We cannot be certain how dedicated Noah's three sons were in their walk with God. Scripture does give indication that Ham was not a very respectable son toward his father. His son Canaan was even cursed by Noah. The chosen Seed son in Noah's family was Shem. He was undoubtedly the most spiritually-minded of the three brothers.

The Tragic Spiritual Climate of Noah's Day

As already noted, the Jewish rabbis teach that Methuselah died just one week before the Flood began, but that cannot be categorically supported from Scripture. Genesis 6:8 should be understood as meaning the following: At the actual commencement of the Flood, outside of his own family, Noah was the only righteous man still alive on the earth. That is a truly remarkable and disconcerting thought! All other righteous men and women had passed from the scene. This is not to say, however, that his sons did not follow in his footsteps.

The world had passed into a stage of almost total spiritual corruption. If there were other righteous people, why did they not join Noah in the ark? One must assume that there were none beyond his own family. Abraham interceded with the Lord on behalf of the righteous within Sodom and Gomorrah centuries later. He asked this rather pointed question of the Lord in Genesis 18:23: "And Abraham came near and said, 'Would you also destroy the righteous with the wicked?'"

God agreed to spare the city if there were even ten righteous people in those two cities. There were not! Hence, Sodom and Gomorrah were destroyed. But consider this: In Noah's day, there were only eight righteous individuals left, not just in the local cities but on planet Earth. The Nephilim had entirely corrupted the world.

Unlike the days immediately before the Flood, even in the future dark days of the Tribulation, many will turn to faith in Christ. In the midst of the spiritual darkness, Christ's light will shine brilliantly even in that time. All believers around the world can take great confidence in the promise of Romans 8:31: "What then shall we say to these things? If God is for us, who can be against us?" That has always been the reassurance for the believer.

Savory Comments by John Gill

John Gill, in his characteristically lengthy but highly insightful sentences, capably summarizes Genesis 6:8 and the surrounding context as follows:

This man and his family were the only exception to the general apostasy; God always reserves some, in the worst of times, for himself; there is a remnant, according to the election of grace; it was but a small one, and now appeared, and this owing to the grace of God, and His choice upon that, and not by the merits of the creature.

This grace, which Noah found and shared in, was the favor and good will of God; Noah was grateful and acceptable to him; he was well-pleased with him in Christ; his person, services, and sacrifices, were acceptable to him through the Beloved;

through he might not be acceptable in the eyes of men, who derided him for his piety and devotion, and especially for his prediction of the flood, and making an ark to save him and his family from it; yet he was very acceptable in the eyes of the Lord, and grateful in his sight, and was favored with grace from Him, who is the God of all grace, and with all the supplies of it: the Jerusalem Targum is, he "found grace and mercy" the grace he found was not on account of his own merit, but on account of the mercy of God,

and this shows that he was not without sin, or he would have stood in need of no mercy and grace of God to save him, and as he found grace and favor in things spiritual, so in things temporal he found favor with

God, and therefore he and his family were spared, when the whole world of the ungodly were destroyed; he found favor with God and therefore was directed by him to build an ark, for the saving of himself and his, and therefore he had the honor of being the preserver of mankind, and the father of a new world.[94]

All believers can rejoice in being the unworthy recipients of God's grace (Ephesians 2:8–9; Titus 3:5). Not one believer has ever merited such forgiveness, love, and mercy. We are simply blessed to receive it. Noah was a man who received God's grace in the midst of the world's most horrendous moral meltdown. As such, he provides an inspirational example to all believers for all time. Every believer would do well to examine his life and learn. Noah certainly qualifies as one of the greatest and most faithful believers of all time. Genesis 6:8 reminds us: "But Noah found grace in the eyes of the LORD." May that be the heartfelt yearning of our every reader.

Lessons Learned in This Chapter

In this chapter, we first reviewed the perspective of ancient commentators regarding the Nephilim. It is wise to listen to what the ancients have to say as they were so much closer to the actual events than modern man is. It was their general assessment that the demonic world thoroughly corrupted the inhabitants of the earth in Noah's day.

Second, we examined more deeply who the Nephilim really were. Though the information is far from complete, we do know that they were morally fallen creatures. If your father is literally a demon, who married and produced offspring with your human

---

[94] John Gill, *Exposition of the Old & New Testaments: Volume 1 of 9* (Paris, AR: The Baptist Standard Bearer, Inc. Reprinted in 2016), p. 48.

mother, what kind of morality could you possess?

Although we do not teach that the Nephilim were beyond redemption, it would probably be rare that any ever followed God. Though some of the Nephilim may have been physically imposing, the term should not be translated as "giants." That is misleading. Nephilim means "fallen ones" and refers to their moral status, not their physical size.

Third, we addressed the question as to whether any Nephilim survived the Flood. In a word, they did not. The Flood destroyed the entire society of Noah's day save his own immediate family. The offending demons who impregnated women were confined permanently to Tartarus. They are waiting there in torment for their final judgment. Not all demons participated in this vile sin, as is evidenced in the gospels. Jesus cast out many demons from possessed people. Clearly, they were not imprisoned in Tartarus. They are free to roam about as of yet.

The spies' report recorded in Numbers chapter 13 contains at least four lies, which we elucidated. Sadly, the common people listened to these lies and rebelled against God and His appointed spiritual leaders, Moses and Aaron. The consequence was that the older generation whom God had so gloriously rescued from Egypt perished in the wilderness. They had forty years to contemplate their incredible foolishness. It was their children, for whom they expressed such fear, that eventually conquered the Promised Land.

Fourth, we touched upon the moral qualities of Noah's day. Never again will the world become so corrupt. Though the Tribulation will see terrifying days and immense immorality, it will not parallel Noah's time. It is almost impossible to imagine how Noah and his family kept themselves morally pure in a time of such unimaginable sinful activity.

In our present day, the Holy Spirit restrains the sinful penchants of mankind. But when the Rapture of the Church takes place, He will cease His restraining activity (2 Thessalonians 2:6–8). The degradation of mankind will then plummet to new depths. Still, it will not be as horrendous as in Noah's day. Indeed, in the coming Tribulation, untold multitudes will embrace the truth of Jesus Christ. This indicates that the Holy Spirit will still be involved in convicting man of sin and drawing them to Christ. Most of those new believers will be martyred for their faith (Revelation 6:9–11).

In our next chapter and following, we shall observe the instructions God gave to Noah regarding the ark. The study of the Flood is both fascinating and distressing simultaneously. We may rejoice to see how God preserved a tiny remnant for Himself. But the harsh reality is that the vast majority of humanity, along with the animal kingdom, succumbed to the violent waters. One cannot hope to fight against a sovereign God and win! The Nephilim were history's most poignant and frightening example of that truth.

Cognitive Conundrum #12

Ill-treatment received I from those closest to me, but by God's help, He destined me to be. A matriarch beloved by a warrior people, yet we together resist God's blessed Church steeple. As a mother, I cried out to the Lord who sees; He answered the prayers I made from my knees. My son to me was the direct blessing of God, yet he grew to fight against all, the even and odd.

Who am I?

Answer: Hagar

Chapter 13

Warnings of a Universal Flood

(Genesis 6:9–17)

In This Chapter

Objectives for This Chapter
Righteous Noah versus a Corrupt World (6:9–10)
A World Drowning in Corruption (Genesis 6:11–13)
Instructions Regarding the Ark (6:14–17)
Lessons Learned in This Chapter

Objectives for This Chapter

Noah was a man outstanding in his generations (plural). He was one of the most exemplary men among the ten listed in the first line of patriarchs. However, one must not forget the godly man Enoch, Noah's great-grandfather, who was directly translated into heaven. In this chapter, we shall first examine the lives of these two godly men. Our overview of them must, of necessity, be painfully brief. Much blessedness awaits the diligent student of Scripture who faithfully reviews their incredible lives. God used them both in most singular fashion.

Second, we shall review the world in which Noah lived and preached. He was given the awesome responsibility of constructing an ark. Through this immense wooden vessel, God would spare humanity and the land-dwelling creatures. Noah's audience proved the most incorrigible in the history of mankind. The Nephilim had nearly taken over the entire world. Still, God reached out to these corrupt half-demon, half-men, through the preaching of Noah.

Though Scripture does not mention any converts in Noah's ministry, it is possible that there were some. If some deed heed his message, they died before the Flood took place. The godly people, such as Methuselah, had completely disappeared by the time the first raindrops of judgment wetted the earth. Noah and his family alone were righteous on God's unique biosphere for humanity.

Third, we shall delve into the instructions God gave to Noah concerning the ark. It was to be of immense size. Its dimensions were approximately 450 feet long, 75 feet wide, and 45 feet high. We also present data regarding the window, door, and three decks of the ark. Because of this gargantuan size for a wooden vessel, skeptics throughout the millennia have scoffed at this story. However, history reveals that comparable boats have actually been built by other nations. They approached but more than likely did not exceed the dimensions of the ark.

The skeptics must not only vainly attempt to refute the biblical account; they must also call Jesus either misguided or a liar. Jesus testified to the reality of the ark. He was there, after all, when it was being constructed. No critics can make the same claim. Their pomposity in calling the Lord a liar invites severe discipline by the Lord. God does not make jokes or tell false stories. Nor does He tolerate mockers and scorners forever.

Righteous Noah versus a Corrupt World (Genesis 6:9–10)

The singular most catastrophic event in earth's history thus far has been the universal Flood. Indeed, nothing shall ever equal it, including the future Tribulation. It wiped out every air-breathing creature on the earth, man and animal alike. Aside from Noah and his family, which consisted of his wife, three sons, and daughters-in-law, no human lives were spared.

God judged the entire world because man had become incomprehensibly wicked. The Nephilim had corrupted earth's human society to an unparalleled level. Such grotesque sinfulness will thankfully never characterize the earth again. God's patience had come to an end (cf. 2 Kings 17:20–23). His judgment was exceptionally thorough and well-deserved.

Though distressing to contemplate and write about, man and animals alike deservedly suffered the ultimate punishment of their watery tomb. The entire globe itself was convulsed in ways that defy the imagination. As we shall see in later chapters, physical and literary evidence of the universal Flood smothers the globe. Never again will the earth be convulsed in such fashion short of its recreation (2 Peter 3:10–13).

Noah: The Man Standing in the Gap

Many centuries later, in a much less encompassing yet similar context, God states the following in Ezekiel 22:30–31:

> "So I sought for a man among them who would make a wall, and stand in the gap before Me on behalf of the land, that I should not destroy it; but I found none. Therefore I have poured out My indignation on them; I have consumed them with the fire of My wrath; and I have recompensed their deeds on their own heads," says the Lord God.

God punished both Israel and Judah severely. Other nations also suffered alongside them under the harsh and grinding heels of the Egyptians, Assyrians, Babylonians, Medo-Persians, Greek, and Roman Empires. Sin must eventually be punished. When God's forbearance finally runs out, let treacherous mankind beware. Hebrews 10:31 summarizes such folly well: "It is a fearful thing to fall into the hands of the living God."

Hearkening back to our present context, in the midst of this immediate pre-Flood moral chaos, there was one man who pleased God. Noah was that godly and exceptional man. He "walked with God" (Genesis 6:9). He enjoyed a rare fellowship with his Maker, which few humans have ever equaled. Only three men, namely Noah, Enoch, and, much later, Levi (Malachi 2:6), received this marvelous accolade from God regarding their spiritual walk and vitality.

Enoch was translated directly into heaven by God and thus never died (Genesis 5:24). Elijah, Israel's quintessential prophet, was also translated directly into heaven via whirlwind and fiery horse and chariot (2 Kings 2:11). Levi died a natural death. Little is known of his spiritual walk. But, in accordance with God's holy will, it was the descendants of Levi who oversaw the worship in Israel.

Clearly, Levi's personal spiritual awakening came later in his life. It must be remembered that he and his brother Simeon shamefully murdered all the men of Shechem. They did this in abhorrent revenge of their sister Dinah's rape (Genesis chapter 34). The other ten brothers then participated in ransacking the city and kidnapping all the women and children. Did all the men of Shechem deserve to die for one man's sin? Obviously not!

Indeed, the guilty perpetrator of the rape, namely, Shechem, sought to marry Dinah and thus at least partially atone for his wickedness (34:8–12). He offered a large dowry and desired to take her hand in marriage. The sons of Jacob maliciously lied to them regarding the necessity of their all being circumcised. Their diabolical intent was to take revenge on one and all. This premeditated atrocity was the most shameful act ever perpetrated by Jacob's family.

Yet, in spite of his wicked beginnings, God had a plan for Levi. Though unrecorded in Scripture, Levi obviously experienced a spiritual epiphany of considerable magnitude. God perpetually reaches out to those who are willing to heed His quiet voice (cf. 1 Kings 19:11–14). The tribe of Levi generally turned in faith to God. The Levites in Moses' day righteously attacked their brothers in the tragic situation of the idolatrous golden calf incident (Exodus 32:25–29). Sadly, they would later on have to be sorely punished for a foolish and arrogant rebellion against Moses and Aaron (Numbers chapter 16). That serves as a reminder that godliness is to be cultivated steadily, not arrogantly assumed.

Let us now return to Noah and the judgment of God. Many outstanding books have been written on the Flood by highly capable authors. It is highly recommended that our readers avail themselves of such materials written from a biblical perspective. We shall make numerous observations from selected passages to present an overview of this terrifying judgment. The account of the Flood demonstrates both God's holy wrath and His marvelous grace in one grand picture.

The physical confirmations for the universal Flood, as already noted, cover the entire planet. In this day and age, such evidence demonstrates the reliability of Scripture as few other extra-biblical avenues of substantiation can. To ignore these findings is irresponsible at best. God has provided this essentially unlimited physical data to edify the believer and to evangelize the lost.

It is the responsibility of every believer to learn these ample verifications regarding the Flood as thoroughly as possible. Flood "evangelism" can be a very effective tool to reach the lost. As 1 Peter 3:15 reminds believers, we need to be prepared to defend our faith. The believer has all the advantages. Why is that? Truth is on his side. Falsehood is on the side of the unbelieving skeptic. Believers need not be intimidated by the boastful and preposterous claims of those who teach in opposition to the Word of God. As the Bible clearly teaches in Romans 8:31: "What then shall we say to these things? If God is for us, who can be against us?"

God's Man of the Hour: Noah (Genesis 6:9–10)

Scripture offers a momentary breath of fresh air. We transition from the most wicked of humanity, the Nephilim, to the most righteous. Genesis 6:9–10 states: "This is the genealogy of Noah. Noah was a just man, perfect in his generations. Noah walked with God. And Noah begot three sons: Shem, Ham, and Japheth."

Noah was indeed a godly man. He was noted throughout the Old Testament for his exemplary standing before God. Short of Jesus Christ Himself and John the Baptist, it is hard to fathom a more significant man in all of humanity's existence than Noah.

In Matthew 11:11, Jesus declared: "Assuredly I say to you, among those born of women there has not risen one greater than John the Baptist; but he who is least in the kingdom of heaven is greater than he." No man has ever received a higher compliment than that given to John the Baptist. Outside of Christ, he is the most blessed man to ever live. This is not a commonly understood fact among believers. But this honor bestowed to John the Baptist certainly does not detract from other spectacular believers, of which there have been many.

Humanly speaking, God spared the entire world through one saintly individual, namely Noah. Noah's task, however, was by no means an easy one. It required tremendous faith, the enduring of untold mockery, and a phenomenal amount of physical labor. Most importantly, it necessitated God's blessing. Without God operating behind the scenes, Noah's ark would have been the most stupendous boondoggle of all time. It succeeded because God commanded the mission and provided the grace.

Three Godly Men

The prophet Ezekiel mentions three godly men highly reputed for their intercessory practices. They clearly spent considerable time praying for others, particularly for the repentance of their fellow human beings. As such, these three men set a remarkable example for all believers to follow. God honors prayer in ways that we cannot fathom. It is the responsibility of every believer to pray for his fellow believers as well as for the unsaved.

Ezekiel 14:14, 20 declares:

> "Even if these three men, Noah, Daniel, and Job, were in it, they would deliver only themselves by their righteousness," says the Lord GOD. … "even though Noah, Daniel, and Job were in it, as I live," says the Lord GOD, "they would deliver neither son nor daughter; they would deliver only themselves by their righteousness."

All three of these men enjoyed outstanding reputations for their godly living and character. Every believer would do well to study their lives and emulate their godly disciplines.

Hebrews 11:7 also provides testimony to Noah's godly lifestyle: "By faith Noah, being divinely warned of things not yet seen, moved with godly fear, prepared an ark for the saving of his household, by which he condemned the world and became heir of the righteousness which is according to faith." It is interesting to note that Hebrews chapter 11 would have ended rather abruptly with Noah had he not been obedient and built the ark. Indeed, Hebrews chapter 11 would have never been written at all. There would have been nobody to write had Noah and his family not lived!

Noah Proved a Truly Exceptional Man of God

Noah was just and perfect in his generations. This does not mean he was sinless. All men have sinned (Ecclesiastes 7:20; Isaiah 53:6). But some men, such as Noah, Daniel, and Job, were noted for their godly lifestyles. To this select group, we can add Enoch and Elijah, who were directly translated into heaven.

A host of other godly saints could also be mentioned. For a moment, let us consider the incredible man, Job. He has a distinct honor accorded to him. Job 1:8 states: "Then the LORD said to Satan, 'Have you considered my servant Job, that there is none like him on the earth, a blameless and upright man, one who fears God and shuns evil?'" Job was the most righteous man on the earth. No other man has ever received that particular accolade. Job was truly unique. How ironic that he had to suffer such grievous affliction. God selected His best and allowed Satan to sling his worst at him.

Morris offers the following comments about Job:

> If not a contemporary of Abraham, Job lived shortly before or shortly after him. Even though God chose Abraham to carry on the line of promise, he regarded

Job as such a paragon of true faith and righteousness that he said: "there is none like him in the earth." Three times, in fact, we are told that Job was "perfect and upright, and one that feared God, and eschewed evil" (Job 1:1, 8; 2:3).[95]

Such godly men deserve our focused attention and heartfelt emulation. They are exceptional! Scripture blesses us with accounts of numerous such men. The student of Scripture has no shortage of great men on which to meditate. It must be remembered, however, that no man or woman is great save by the grace of God. God's grace is available to all, but all do not avail themselves of that grace.

A Biblical Description of Noah

Genesis 6:9 states: "This is the genealogy of Noah. Noah was a just man, perfect in his generations. Noah walked with God."

Fruchtenbaum explains the two terms, "righteous" and "perfect," describing Noah as follows:

> Genesis 6:9b describes the spirituality of Noah in two ways. First: Noah was a righteous man, he was a tzaddik, meaning righteous. This emphasizes justification; it is inward, and it shows salvation. Second: Noah was perfect in his generations. The Hebrew word for "perfect" here is tamim. It means "without blemish," as is used of the sacrifices (Lev. 1:3, 1:10; 3:1, 3:6). It means "free from defect," and this emphasizes Noah outwardly. Therefore, he was inwardly and outwardly right before God.

---
[95] Henry M. Morris, The Remarkable Record of Job (Green Forest, AR: Master Books, 1988, 2000), p. 57.

The next phrase is: in his generations, meaning unlike others of his generation, he was not contaminated by the intermarriage. According to rabbinic tradition, the term generations is used in the plural, because he was the most righteous of the ten generations. So he is described as being both tzaddik and tamim; both righteous and perfect.[96]

Noah Habitually Walked with God

The verb "walked" is in the Hithpael stem in Hebrew. In grammatical terms, this indicates an iterative and intensive value for the term. In other words, it shows a self-imposed and heartfelt habit or pattern. Another grammatical factor is that the term for "walk" is "reflexive" or "applying to oneself." One could accurately translate the phrase as "Noah himself habitually walked with God." He never ceased his communion with God. This was his life's custom. When people saw Noah, they could not help but think about his ongoing and special relationship with God.

As Fruchtenbaum noted, Noah was perfect in his "generations" in that he had not been in any way personally affected by the Nephilim. Considering God's drastic action with the global Flood and also taking the Hebrew language literally, it appears that at the time of the Flood only Noah and his family were not affected by the demonic Nephilim. Again, this should be understood as referring to the time of the actual commencement of the Flood. Clearly, other godly men and women lived during Noah's lifetime before the Flood was initiated by God.

The total lack of repentance by all others living at the time of

---

[96] Arnold Fruchtenbaum, Ariel's Bible Commentary: The Book of Genesis, p. 159.

the Flood indicates the complete corruption of humanity. That is incredible! In a fascinating tradition, the rabbis teach that Methuselah died on the very day that Noah, his family, and the animals entered the ark. With his passing, all was finally in readiness. The week-long delay before the rains descended was spent in mourning for his passing. That, however, though a marvelous tradition, cannot be substantiated from the biblical record.

The Worldwide Defilement of Humanity

Such a possibility of worldwide godlessness sobers the mind. How could the world have turned so completely evil? Through the influence of the Nephilim, it had. God had no choice but to enact severe judgment and start over with Noah and his family. If something drastic had not been done, Satan could have defiled the messianic Seed before Christ was born (Genesis 3:15). He came amazingly close to doing so.

Sinful men and women throughout earth's long and sordid history have been riveted in morbid fascination with evil. Due to this aberrant engrossment, tragedy upon tragedy has unfolded upon saint and sinner alike. The fruits of wickedness taste pleasureful but for a scant few seconds, comparatively speaking. Then, the undying indigestion of sin's contamination pollutes the hearts and minds of humanity.

Sorrow and untold misery have unnecessarily blighted the world and its inhabitants. All could be avoided if man chose to serve his Creator rather than serving himself. Alas, that is the double-edged sword of free will. God does allow man to amble off in his own perverse and misguided steps. But without free will, there could be no free life or worship.

A Note of God-Based Encouragement

However, no one can defeat the purposes of God. Though the world may seem blackened with the soot of sin and foul with its malodorous scent, though the believer may be depressed with harsh spiritual realities surrounding him, though stinging circumstances besiege the lonely saint isolated on an island of howling sinners, he cannot be defeated either on this day or any day? Why?

It is because believers are the spiritually adopted children of the sovereign, almighty God who shall quench all the fiery darts of the wicked (Ephesians 6:16). In Christ, we are, and we shall ever remain unconquerable and invincible (Romans 8:35–39). This is not by our strength but by our omnipotent God's power. Believers have no need to fear (Matthew 10:28). We are to go forth and conquer in Christ. Amen and amen!

Noah and Enoch Were Conquerors in God

One final comment summarized Noah's righteous life: he walked with God. As previously mentioned, this truly memorable comment is directed toward Enoch and Noah and, later in history, to Levi. Enoch, as we have learned, was translated into heaven and never died. He shall someday return with the saints of which he so elegantly prophesied.

Jude 14–15 contains Enoch's prophecy:

> Now Enoch, the seventh from Adam, prophesied about these men also, saying, "Behold, the Lord comes with ten thousands of His saints, to execute judgment on all, to convict all who are ungodly among them of all their ungodly deeds which they have committed in an un-

godly way, and of all the harsh things which ungodly sinners have spoken against Him."

Question: If Noah was as righteous as Enoch, and perhaps even more so, why was he not also translated directly to heaven?

Answer: God is not obligated to act toward one individual as He does toward another, even though the circumstances may be similar. Each believer has his own divinely orchestrated purpose directed by God's individualized composition written just for him. That is a marvelous truth and one that should be fully embraced by every follower of Christ. One can safely assume that God accomplished His sacred purposes through Enoch and thus took him home. He does the same for all believers throughout history.

It is possible, though by no means certain, that Enoch might be one of the two witnesses in the book of Revelation (Revelation chapter 11). This is often speculated because he and Elijah have yet to die. Hebrews 9:27 states that all men must die and then be judged. However, there are going to be exceptions to this general principle. Those who are living when the Church is raptured will not die (1 Thessalonians 4:13–18). Furthermore, those believers who survive the Tribulation will be ushered directly into Christ's millennial kingdom without experiencing the dark valley of the shadow of death (Revelation 1:7).

God clearly had different purposes for Noah than He did for Enoch. Through Noah, God planned to save the world and all the air-breathing animals. Save Christ's substitutionary death on the cross, what greater human accomplishment than that can even be imagined? As believers on earth, we presently see through a glass darkly (1 Corinthians 13:12, KJV). Not all is presently revealed to us. If it was, where would be the need of faith? If anyone ever exercised faith, it was the beloved Noah.

Hence, each must yield his will to the plans of a sovereign God. We see only a short distance toward the horizon. We cannot see over the horizon with human eyes. God sees all eternity as if it were sitting in an open vessel beside Him on His eternal throne. Nothing is hidden from God. Shall we not then place our full confidence in this omniscient, omnipotent, and omnipresent God? How can the believer lose by exercising faith in his sovereign God?

Noah was a man who walked with God. Can a man be paid a higher compliment than that? Perhaps the only other humans who experienced such a close relationship with God, that is, after the fall of Adam and Eve, were Enoch, Moses, and John the Baptist.

The Righteous Example of Moses

We would do well for a moment to consider another giant of the faith, namely, Moses. In a mysterious way, God spoke to Moses "face-to-face." This statement of such a deep relationship is made of no other human being. At one point in Moses' ministry in the wilderness, Aaron and Miriam, his brother and sister, attacked him verbally in a most outlandish fashion. That was both foolish and completely unrighteous on their part. If it had not been for Moses, no one would have ever heard of either Aaron or Miriam. God thus called all three out to the tabernacle for an encounter. His words of reproof are memorable.

Numbers 12:6–8 states:

> Then He said, "Hear now My words: If there is a prophet among you, I, the LORD, make Myself known to him in a vision, I speak to him in a dream. Not so with My servant Moses; he is faithful in all My house, I speak with him face to face, even plainly, and not in

dark sayings; and he sees the form of the LORD. Why then were you not afraid to speak against My servant Moses?"

No other man experienced such an incredibly blessed experience as this. Moses, in an incomprehensible way to us, spoke face-to-face with God. This does not mean that Moses saw God in all His glory. No man can see God in all His glory and live. Exodus 33:20 declares: "But He said, 'You cannot see My face; for no man shall see Me and live.'" Since this opportunity was granted only to Moses, it is not possible to genuinely define what this experience really was like. There is no other earthly comparison.

R. K. Harrison offers the following comments:

> The reasons for Moses' uniqueness are made clear to the complainants. Whereas God would reveal Himself indirectly in dealing with a prophet, with Moses He spoke face to face. This distinction was maintained, with the possible exception of Isaiah (6:1), throughout the entire history of Hebrew prophetism.
>
> But even Isaiah's experience of "seeing" was essentially visionary, whereas Moses met periodically face to face—i.e., "openly"—with God. Although God had in fact spoken through others, such as the elders who prophesied when part of the gifts of Moses were bestowed upon them, it was the great Israelite leader himself who was commissioned to convey the Lord's will to the covenant community (cf. Heb. 3:2-6).[97]

---

[97] R. K. Harrison, The Wycliffe Exegetical Commentary: Numbers (Chicago, IL:: Moody Press, 1990), p. 196.

Noah's Three Sons

Let us return now to Noah: Noah fathered three sons that are noted in Scripture: Shem, Ham, and Japheth (Genesis 6:10). It seems reasonable that he had more sons before he turned 500, but only these are mentioned. It is possible that only these three sons followed in their father's godly example if, indeed, there were other children. Of these three sons, Shem, the progenitor of the promised Seed, is by far the most prominent. From Shem ultimately descended the well-known Abraham, the first of the Hebrews.

From the Hebrew nation comes the Christ child, the promised Messiah. Genesis 49:10 narrows the Seed line down from Abraham to his great-grandson Judah: "The scepter shall not depart from Judah, nor a lawgiver from between his feet, until Shiloh comes; and to Him shall be the obedience of the people" (cf. Isaiah 9:6–7). Judah eventually came to represent the southern kingdom when the twelve tribes split apart. Judah was coupled with the tribe of Benjamin but overshadowed Benjamin and all the other tribes in importance. The ten northern tribes were known corporately as Israel or, sometimes, as Ephraim. When Christ returns, the twelve tribes will be reunited (Ezekiel 37:15–28).

It is intriguing to note that the Bible's first glimpse of Judah was far from complimentary (Genesis chapter 38). However, God clearly worked in Judah's life, and he became one of the most exemplary of the twelve sons, the godly Joseph excepted. From Judah's line, David was born. From David descended Jesus Christ. God retained control of the entire process.

The other two sons, Japheth and Ham, have their own distinct contribution, but they are not as important as Shem. From these three sons and their wives, the entire world was repopulated. The genealogy of the Messiah is methodically traced throughout the book of Genesis. Hence, the study of the genealogies is indeed important. Nothing in Scripture was inserted merely to take up room (Romans 15:4).

A World Drowning in Corruption (Genesis 6:11–13)

Genesis 6:11–13 conveys this sad reality:

> The earth also was corrupt before God, and the earth was filled with violence. So God looked upon the earth, and indeed it was corrupt; for all flesh had corrupted their way on the earth. And God said to Noah, "The end of all flesh has come before Me, for the earth is filled with violence through them; and behold, I will destroy them with the earth."

A World Gone Mad!

We shall make two observations regarding this passage. Observation #1: The world had abandoned God and wholeheartedly embraced wickedness. These three verses stand in stark contrast to the previous discussion on Noah. The text goes from the sacred to the sinful in just a few words. The dissimilarity is both breathtaking and heartbreaking.

The perpetuators of the Nephilim eagerly gave themselves over to corruption. Thankfully, the Nephilim no longer exist. However, personal decisions still must be made by modern man. One either decides for or against God. In Mark 9:39–40, Jesus declares: "But Jesus said, 'Do not forbid him, for no one who works a miracle in My name can soon afterward speak evil of Me. For he who is not against us is on our side.'" Every individual must make a choice as to whom he will serve. His eternal destiny depends upon it. God and Satan are the only two choices available.

Noah was surrounded by immoral reprobates and a world that scorned the holy. Only he and his small family remained pure. At least they, as individuals, had not been corrupted by the Nephilim. How trying the world's immorality must have been to Noah's soul and spirit. Undoubtedly, he often yearned to be translated straight up to heaven as his great-grandfather Enoch had been.

No More Tolerance Could Be Tolerated

Leupold comments on man's depravity as follows:

> There come times in the events of this world when God's gracious dealings with men are definitely terminated. Such times come only when grace has been offered in richest measure. But when the end is resolved upon, there is no recall. Such a case is marked by the "end" that God here determines. His reason for His steps show this course to be entirely just: "the earth is filled with violence through them." ...
>
> Man has no one to blame but himself. But this end is not coming on like a blind fate. God indicates His initiative in the work of destruction, in fact, vividly points to His participation by a "behold." Works of retribution are as much holy as good works and worthy of God as any other. ... Thus, when man is wiped away and his habitation with him, men realize more fully how serious the nature of their misdeeds is.[98]

---
98 H. C. Leupold, Leupold on the Old Testament: Genesis, pp. 268–269.

This corruption should not be thought to include the animal kingdom in a moral sense. Sadly, the animal kingdom was also negatively impacted by man's sinfulness. Though animals do have a soul, nephesh, they do not possess a moral spirit as does man. However, once the fall occurred, the animal kingdom turned upon itself. Its all-encompassing philosophy became and has ever since remained "eat or be eaten." That was not God's original intent, but sin ruined His originally peaceful and vegetarian animal kingdom. Thankfully, this curse will be lifted from the animal kingdom in the millennial kingdom of Christ.

The carnivorous habits of the animal kingdom must have been a most distressing scenario to observe for the early line of humans. However, that early line of individuals likewise fell into two camps all too quickly: the godly and the ungodly. Gross immorality invaded the first family on earth. It immediately split into two lines, morally speaking. Cain, the wicked firstborn of Adam and Eve, murdered righteous Abel, the second son born on earth. It was a tragic development. Like humanity, even the animals have changed and remain so to this day.

Judgment Was Due!

Observation #2: God pronounced judgment on the entire world (verse 13). The carnality, lasciviousness, wickedness, and total depravity of man were complete. No room remained for repentance. Man had stifled the message of God heralded for 120 years so faithfully and persistently by Noah. When an individual casts off the conviction of the Holy Spirit long enough, He stops calling on that person to repent. Then, all hope is truly forfeited and lost forever.

Considering the longevity of man in Noah's day and the length of his preaching, there is no doubt that everyone who desired to hear him had the opportunity to listen. This may have happened personally or through someone else conveying Noah's message. God always faithfully reaches out to mankind through the communication of His Word (Isaiah 42:6–7, 49:5–8; 2 Corinthians 6:2). Sadly, the majority of mankind refuses to listen (Matthew 7:13–14; Revelation 9:20–21).

It must be remembered that God had commanded mankind to populate the earth. Based on Genesis 11:1–9, it becomes clear that they had resisted this commandment. They clumped together in cities where immorality inevitably was conceived, bore its ungodly fruit, and infected all of humanity. Sin inevitably breeds more sin (James 1:13–15).

Noah's Congregation Was Unenviable

Noah's earnest preaching proved to no avail except for the salvation of his own family. In that ironic sense, Noah was arguably the least successful preacher of all time. However, there may have been converts of which we are not informed. One must also consider his Nephilim-plagued audience. How terrible are the works of Satan, and how influential are his evil deceptions. Second Corinthians 11:14 states: "And no wonder! For Satan himself transforms into an angel of light."

Sarfati offers the following remarks:

> In particular, God tells Noah that He will 'destroy' the evil people on the earth. The word 'destroy' is shachat, the same word translated 'corrupted' in the previous section. So God is connecting the two: as man ruined the earth, God will ruin man. But nowhere does the account tell us of any response by Noah; we are re-

peatedly told that he just obeyed. In fact, although we know that Noah was "a herald of righteousness" (2 Peter 2:5), his only recorded words in the Bible are the curse on Ham's son Canaan after the Flood (9:25-27).[99]

God's testimony regarding the evil of man is frightening. We cannot envision how desperate the situation on the earth had become, morally speaking. Only eight righteous souls were left on the earth. If there were more (and we pray that this was the case), they died before the day of the Flood.

And, we must confess, the righteousness of even Noah's sons and daughters-in-law is not overly certain. However, they were not defiled by the corruption of the Nephilim. After the Flood, Ham did not show much respect for his father when Noah inadvertently became drunk in his tent. As the Seed son, Shem certainly followed faithfully in his father's footsteps. We can state without hesitation, however, that Noah was a righteous man… a righteous man for the ages!

Instructions Regarding the Ark (Genesis 6:14–16)

God provided a means of escape for the precious few righteous among mankind, namely, the ark. He also gave instructions to Noah on how to build this massive ship (6:14–22). Nothing like this had ever been done in the history of the earth. The ark was designed to preserve and feed representatives of all the land animals and birds. Once again, we see God's mercy extended in the midst of judgment.

That is how God graciously operates throughout all of human history. The ark was an immense ship. Most people assume that such a huge ship could not possibly be constructed until relatively

---
[99] Jonathan Sarfati, The Genesis Account: A theological, historical, and scientific commentary on Genesis 1–11, pp. 494–495.

modern times. That strikes one as a reasonable perspective. However, it is not a correct one. It certainly is not a biblical one. We shall soon examine that question in more depth.

God's Command Concerning the Ark

Considering the importance of this vessel, God's instructions to Noah are amazingly succinct. Indeed, compared to the detailed instructions regarding the millennial temple, they are incredibly brief (cf. Ezekiel chapters 40 to 48).

Genesis 6:14–17 describes the ark and states its dimensions as follows:

> Make yourself an ark of gopher wood; make rooms in the ark, and cover it inside and outside with pitch. And this is how you shall make it: The length of the ark shall be three hundred cubits, its width fifty cubits, and its height thirty cubits. You shall make a window for the ark, and you shall finish it to a cubit from above; and set the door of the ark in its side. You shall make it with lower, second, and third decks. And behold, I Myself am bringing floodwaters on the earth, to destroy from under heaven all flesh in which is the breath of life; everything that is on the earth shall die.

The Hebrew term for ark is "teivah." This is the same term used for the ark in which Moses was placed by his mother for safekeeping (Exodus 2:3–5). Both arks preserved life from drowning. In both situations, the individuals within the arks brought deliverance. In both cases, the future deliverer was largely innocent of immorality. Indeed, in both cases, the men were characterized as possessing a highly intimate relationship with God.

Although not entirely perfect, Noah was the most upright man on the earth in his generations. Moses was just a baby and so not a volitional sinner as of yet. Noah delivered humanity from certain destruction; Moses delivered the fledgling nation of Israel. Both men were used mightily by God. Never underestimate the power of an individual whose life is dedicated to serving God!

The Actual Construction of the Ark

Noah built the ark out of gopher wood. The term "gopher" is a hapax legomenon; in other words, it is used only once in the Old Testament. No one knows what type of wood this really was. It very likely was a tree that God allowed to go extinct after the Flood. Others have suggested cypress wood or perhaps teak. Teak resists rot and mildew and is a very low-maintenance wood. In fact, some ships constructed out of teak have gone for thirty-five years of continual use with minimal maintenance.

John Woodmorappe, who has done extensive study on the ark and the Flood, writes as follows:

> But what kind of wood was the Ark made of? Indian teak has been found in ancient Babylon ... so it had been known to the peoples immediately after the Flood, and—by implication—also to the antediluvians. Because of its strength and durability, teak is probably the best wood of all for the construction of ships.
>
> Teak structures have resisted deterioration for thousands of years ... and the possible survival of the Ark in Ararat to this day may be due to this fact. Moreover,

the Chinese practice a method of burying teak underground in order to make it even harder ... and Noah may also have employed this technique.[100]

Did the Small Critters Become Tasty Tidbits?

The answer to our above question is "no." Noah was told to build rooms or, more literally, "nests" within the ark. The various animals were to have their own compartments and could thus be kept separate. It must be remembered that the animal kingdom had become carnivorous after the fall. A hungry Tyrannosaurus might be tempted to look at an ostrich as a tasty little "chicken" snack!

Having all of those wild animals in one small area like the ark could have proven a bit unnerving, particularly to the chickens. God faithfully preserved all the animals that entered the ark. Why would He otherwise have had them enter? God does nothing pointlessly! God clearly allowed the normal carnivores to survive as vegetarians for the duration of the Flood. If that were not the case, their keen sense of smell would have caused considerable consternation and indigestion for the smaller, helpless animals. Without God's direct intervention, the ark would have become a slaughterhouse!

With furrowed brows and sweaty palms (figuratively speaking), the smaller animals would all have been perpetually anxious. They would have wondered when they themselves would become the key feature on the menu. The normal craving for meat would have been insatiable to the carnivores. That is especially true since they were all in such close proximity.

The entire process of life and feeding within the ark was an ongoing miracle that few people take time to consider. God possibly

---
[100] John Woodmorappe, Noah's Ark: A Feasibility Study (El Cajon, CA: Institute for Creation Research, 1996), p. 51.

induced an unnatural hibernation within some of the larger meat-eating animals. They may have slept through a significant portion of the Flood. Even today, a variety of animals spend a considerable amount of time in hibernation and sleep.

What Was the Size and Capacity of the Ark?

Noah was to cover the inside and outside of the ark with pitch. The term used for "pitch" is not the typical term used for a petroleum product. Moses penned the word "kaphar," which means "a covering." Fruchtenbaum comments: "It is the same Hebrew root for 'atonement.' There is a correlation, because the covering of the outward with pitch saved them physically from water seepage, keeping the ark from sinking. As a parallel, the covering of blood saved spiritually."[101]

The cubit was the length of the arm from the elbow to the tip of the middle finger. By definition, this is not a precise measurement. The average length most scholars use is eighteen inches. If using that approximate figure, the ark would have been 450 feet long, 75 feet wide, and 45 feet high. It was not a small boat! No civilization has ever constructed a wooden framed boat that was larger than this, though some have come close to or possibly equaled it. The Romans, Greeks, and Chinese were known to have constructed some very large wooden vessels.

A Lot of Animals Could Have Fit on the Ark!

Morris comments:

With the dimensions as calculated, the total volumetric capacity of the Ark was approximately 1,400,000 cubic feet, which is equal to the volumetric capacity

---
101 Arnold Fruchtenbaum, Ariel's Bible Commentary: The Book of Genesis, p. 163.

of 522 standard livestock cars such as used on modern American railroads. Since it is known that about 240 sheep can be transported in one stock car, a total of 125,000 sheep could have been carried in the Ark.[102]

That is a lot of livestock.

Some estimate that the actual number of animals was probably somewhere between 35,000 and 70,000. Others have calculated that as few as 16,000 animals and birds would have represented all the different types. Whatever the actual number was in the ark is obviously debatable. But one may safely assert that there would have been plenty of room for Noah and his family, all the animals, and an ample food and water supply for one year. Skeptics abound, however, who question the plausibility of Noah constructing such a huge ship.

Examples of Other Immense Wooden Vessels

Woodmorappe comments as follows:

There is evidence that ships approaching Ark length have in fact existed in ancient times. The ancient Greeks had a ship named Syracusia (or Alexandris) whose cargo is described by a writer named Moschion (Casson, 1971, p. 185) as carrying around 4,000 tons of cargo.

Most of the details of the ship described by Moschion have been corroborated, and Casson (1971, p. 185) acknowledges that Moschion's account cannot any

---
[102] Henry Morris, The Genesis Record: A Scientific and Devotional Commentary on the Book of Beginnings, p. 181.

longer be dismissed as mythology. However, Casson, 1971, p. 186) cannot bring himself to acknowledge the validity of the ship's cargo capacity because of his admitted preconception that ships of that size did not exist prior to the 19th century.

The pre-modern Chinese also built giant wooden ships. The 15th century sea-going junks of the ambassador Cheng Ho approached the size of the Ark (Mills 1960, p. 147; McWhirter 1985, pp. 284-5), and some 8th century (AD) vessels, intended for use in lakes, were even larger (Mills, 1960, p. 147).

Again, these figures have been disputed because of preconceptions against their validity, but there is independent corroboration from archaeological evidence (a huge rudder) that Cheng Ho's junks were in the size range claimed (Needham 1971, pp. 481-2). Other scholars (Levathes 1994, p. 80) are prepared to accept somewhat smaller figures for the size of these ships which nevertheless keep them within the general size range of the Ark.[103]

It has often been contended that the ark would not have been a stable craft. The Flood undoubtedly produced immense waves and tsunamis that devastated the continents. How could the ark possibly have stayed afloat? It must be remembered that tsunamis cause no real damage in the ocean. They only impact the land when they come up on shore. But rogue waves can become quite huge even in

---
[103] Woodmorappe, John. Noah's Ark: A Feasibility Study, p. 50.

modern times. What protected the ark from such monster waves? Actually, two items need to be mentioned.

God's Hand of Protection Is Never Short

First, God supernaturally protected the ark. Surely, God would not have allowed the ark or its precious inhabitants to perish. Noah had faithfully built and preached for 120 years. If Noah proved that faithful, would God be less faithful to him? Of course not! What would have been the point of the ark in the first place if it were simply to capsize and all the inhabitants and creatures died? How would that have preserved the messianic Seed?

Did not the same God open the Red Sea for Moses and the Israelites and then close it on Pharaoh and his army? Did not the same God go before the Israelites when they conquered the Promised Land and destroy the much superior military forces before them? Did not the same God preserve tiny Judah from the powerful Assyrian forces? One night, the Angel of the Lord wiped out 185,000 Assyrian soldiers (Isaiah 37:36). Protecting the ark from capsizing was not a concern in the least. God's "hand" steadied the ark through the roughest waters.

Second, the dimensions of the ark actually created extreme stability. With the particular dimensions God gave to Noah, it would have been nearly impossible to roll the ark over, no matter what the sea conditions proved to be. Naval architects have done considerable research into the dimensions of the ark. They have concluded that it was optimally stable. The ark was probably somewhat similar to a floating barge.

Ironically, in the Gilgamesh Epic, which is an ancient and mythical Babylonian account of the Flood, the ark was a floating cube. A more ridiculous shape could scarcely be imagined. It would have been completely unseaworthy. The Gilgamesh Epic is merely a poorly devised imitation of the genuine ark story. However, the benefit of the Gilgamesh Epic is that it helps authenticate the real biblical story. We shall see much more on that in ensuing chapters.

A Window, a Door, and Three Decks (Genesis 6:16)

Genesis 6:16 states: "You shall make a window for the ark, and you shall finish it to a cubit from above; and set the door of the ark in its side. You shall make it with lower, second, and third decks." Obviously, this verse does not delve deeply into details. Consequently, there have been many fascinating artists' depictions of the ark and its various elements. Some portray the ark as a rectangular block, not much different than the shape of a box. Others picture it with curved lines, which are aesthetically pleasing and navigationally more up-to-date. The truth of the matter is that we do not have much to go on save the dimensions recorded in the Bible.

The window: It is not possible, based on the limited description, to envision precisely what this window looked like. It certainly was not like a standard, small window in a modern house. One of the complicating factors is that the term for "window," tzohar, is yet another hapax legomenon; in other words, a word used only once in the Old Testament.

The term literally means an "opening for daylight." This window would have served a triple purpose: light, ventilation, and heat dissipation. Clearly, it could not provide much light unless it extended a considerable distance, perhaps the entire length of the ark. That is almost certainly what it did.

The window, however it was designed, obviously met the requirements for the ark. If man could not devise an appropriate window for the purpose, it seems reasonable that the God who created the universe could have done so quite nicely! However, it is well-known that man can indeed devise just such a window. Modern factories often have a covered or at least sheltered window running the entire length of the building. This allows for sunlight to filter in, ventilation to occur, and heat to be dissipated. The technology required is not difficult. Noah, who built the ark, could have also done this.

The door: The door served the function of allowing Noah and his family, the animals, and all of the supplies to be brought into the ark. There was only one physical door for the temporal deliverance and safety of those who entered. In like manner, there exists only one spiritual door for eternal deliverance and safety—Jesus Christ.

Using the symbolism of sheep and a sheepfold, Jesus proclaimed in John 10:9: "I am the door. If anyone enters by Me, he will be saved, and will go in and out and find pasture." Those who teach that there are many ways to heaven clearly do not recognize Christ's statement that He alone is that way (John 14:6). Such individuals remain in their state of spiritual confusion and folly. This, sadly, is largely their own choice.

To reject the Messiah is to tragically forfeit eternal life and willingly embrace eternal condemnation (John 5:24). Let every man, woman, and child be warned! Indeed, they have already been warned. That is why the Bible was written. But it must be heeded. The Bible (special revelation) and nature (general revelation) contain all the spiritual answers mankind will ever need answered while on this earth.

The three decks: The Bible does not communicate the purpose of these three respective decks. Perhaps one deck was for food, but that is mere speculation. Probably, these decks categorized the animals and had food and water supplies on each floor. If each deck was ten cubits high (approximately fifteen feet), this would have helped stabilize the ark. Some have commented that there is no rudder mentioned and no way or need to steer the craft. A rudder also helps to stabilize the ship.

However, it has been reasonably asked: To what destination would Noah have sailed since the entire globe was covered with water? God Himself ensured that the ark docked at an appropriate place and at the correct time. That destination was Mount Ararat. In addition, just because a rudder is not mentioned does not mean that there wasn't one. The Bible does not provide all the myriad details of which people might reasonably inquire. If it did, the Bible's contents would swell to a book of unimaginable size.

The Impending Flood (6:17)

"And behold, I Myself am bringing floodwaters on the earth, to destroy from under heaven all flesh in which is the breath of life; everything that is on the earth shall die." One should observe how God personalizes His warning of judgment. He states that "'I Myself' am bringing the floodwaters on the earth." When man is attacked by man, there is some hope of resistance and self-defense. But when God attacks, no defense is possible. All hope is lost!

God's wrath cannot be averted, not even by Satan himself. What greater motivation can there be to make oneself right with God? But in the final days of the Nephilim, no fear of God existed, save with Noah and his family. The darkness of volitional sin no longer enabled the light of God to pierce through to their implacable hearts. It is not, however, that God's saving light cannot permeate the hardest of situations. But He does not force Himself on a closed and completely resistant mankind. If He did, then free will would be necessarily annulled.

Joshua 24:14–15 reminds us of this important principle:

"Now therefore, fear the LORD, serve Him in sincerity and in truth, and put away the gods which your fathers served on the other side of the River and in Egypt. Serve the LORD! And if it seems evil to you to serve the LORD, choose for yourselves this day whom you will serve, whether the gods which your fathers served that were on the other side of the River, or the gods of the Amorites, in whose land you dwell. But as for me and my house, we will serve the LORD."

Two Terrible Consequences for Mankind's Disobedience

God warned of two dire consequences because of mankind's sins. In spite of that, they refused to listen. Tragically, that has proven the propensity of mankind since Adam and Eve's fall into sin. The old nature has proven powerful and all too convincing to unredeemed mankind.

Consequence #1: God Himself would bring the floodwaters upon the earth. Scholars debate whether it rained on the earth after Creation week or if a mist continued to water the earth (Genesis 2:5–6). It is impossible to know for certain. One thing is clear, however. The Flood was not an act of "Mother Nature" gone berserk! There is no such thing as "Mother Nature." There is only Father God.

Unquestionably, the Flood was an act of God. No comparable flood had ever been witnessed by early man. Nor shall modern man ever again witness such a watery inundation. If there had been no rain, that would be one contributing factor as to why ancient man did not take God's warnings through Noah seriously. No one had ever experienced rain, much less an impending worldwide Flood.

Hebrews 11:7 seems to indicate that there had not yet been any rain but that the mist continued to water the earth. This mist would have been made possible if the earth retained a biosphere as originally created. Though modern science may not understand it, the water canopy could have maintained such conditions. We must not err in stating that the present is a key to the past. It decidedly is not, save in limited fashion. Let us not repeat the mistake of the evolutionist.

Hebrews 11:7 states: "By faith Noah being warned of things not yet seen, moved with godly fear, prepared an ark for the saving of his household, by which he condemned the world and became heir of the righteousness which is according to faith."

Creationists will continue this debate regarding the water canopy versus the concept that early mankind was familiar with rain. Neither side can prove their point unequivocally. Personally, we favor the water canopy view. The real point, however, is that God unleashed a Flood to end all floods. It matters not how He did it. The important thing is that He did it. He punished the world's inhabitants for their outrageous iniquities in a most conclusive manner. He also permanently ended the reign of the blasphemous Nephilim.

No People or Land Animals Outside the Ark Survived

Consequence #2: All life on earth would perish. If one chooses to take the Bible seriously, "all" means everything! No air-breathing life would be spared. This also refutes the preposterous view that the Flood was local. Indeed, if it was only a local Flood, an even greater miracle was necessary than the universal Flood.

All air-breathing animals and every man, woman, and child had to willingly journey to the region of the local flood, wander into its limited depths, and intentionally drown themselves. Self-drowning parties are not historically popular or well-known among humans or animals. And, if that was indeed the case, why does the Bible not teach it? Are we really to believe that God got confused? We think not!

This viewpoint of the local flood strikes one as being more than a bit foolish. A further question involves the presence of worldwide fossils. If the Flood did not create the trillions of fossils found everywhere on the planet, including mountaintops, what did? Did clams, for instance, decide en masse to climb to the highest peaks without the benefit of legs? They are generally not noted for their climbing skills nor for any bizarre yearnings to climb mountains... not even small hills. So how did they get there without the universal Flood?

The terminology describing the Flood is quite specific. There are several words in Hebrew that describe floods. But for the universal Flood, special words are involved. Nonlinguists will not notice that distinction in their English Bibles. However, for those scholars who have studied Hebrew, it becomes readily apparent.

Sarfati comments:

> This is no ordinary flood, but a globe-covering flood that would exterminate all land vertebrates outside the Ark. The Bible uses special words for Noah's Flood: Hebrew mabbul, which in the LXX is kataklysmos. Compare the words used to describe ordinary localized floods, e.g. Hebrew sheteph (Nahum 1:8), zaram (Psalm 90:5); Greek plemmyra (Luke 16:48). Also in the Hebrew, the word has an article, so hammabbul.

Thus a more precise translation would be the "the flood," as the NASB puts it. The words mabbul and kataklysmos don't by themselves specify water. So the word is qualified as a watery cataclysm: "the flood of waters" (mayim).[104]

Should We Not Trust Jesus Christ's Testimony?

Jesus also testified to the historicity of the Flood account in Luke 17:26–27: "And as it was in the days of Noah, so it will be also in the days of the Son of Man: They ate, they drank, they married wives, they were given in marriage, until the day that Noah entered the ark, and the flood came and destroyed them all."

How could a local flood destroy "them all"? If one cannot trust the words of Jesus Christ, the God-man, then who does one trust? Man then becomes his own petty and pathetic little god. Such a perspective, if carried far enough, involves eternal ramifications. If you cannot even trust the Bible and the God who wrote it, can you be a genuine believer? Does not one's own fleeting words and frothy imaginations then supersede God's eternal Word? Doubts are one thing; denials are quite another. Man cannot force God off His throne and witlessly take His place.

Peter also alludes to the Flood in 2 Peter 3:6: "By which the world that then existed perished, being flooded with water." For the earnest student of Scripture, there is no debate. The Flood occurred in the days of Noah; it was universal, and all air-breathing creatures, save what was in the ark, died. End of story!

Gene Green comments:

---

[104] Jonathan Sarfati, The Genesis Account: A theological, historical, and scientific commentary on Genesis 1–11, pp. 511–512.

Over against the opinion of the false teachers, Peter has shown that God is not only the creator but also actively sustains the world. The present verse advances his argument one step further as he reminds his readers that God has already judged the world in the past by means of the cataclysmic flood.

By recalling the flood, our author cuts the heart out of the heretic's claim that "all things remain as they were from the beginning of creation" (3:4b) and at the same time lays the foundation for his assertion in the following verse that God will indeed judge the world in the future, just as he has done in the past.[105]

What God writes, God means. He does not mislead His children. Though some passages of Scripture may prove a bit difficult to understand, they are not beyond the scope of normal, systematic study and intelligence (2 Timothy 2:15). The narrative of Genesis chapters 6 to 9 is simple enough that a child can understand the primary issues. God punishes the sinner but spares the faithful. The choice is quite simple: Believe the biblical truth or reject it. But one must live with the consequences of his choice. Choose wisely!

Lessons Learned in This Chapter

Our present chapter involves two spiritually significant figures: Enoch and Noah. The prophet Enoch is the lesser-known of the two. However, as Noah's great-grandfather, he undoubtedly profoundly impacted his life. His ministry should not be underrated. He is

---

[105] Gene L. Green, Baker Exegetical Commentary on the New Testament: Jude & 2 Peter (Grand Rapids, MI: Baker Academic, 2008), p. 320.

quoted in the book of Jude. Only Enoch and Elijah were directly translated into heaven (Hebrews 11:5; 2 Kings 2:11), which places them in a unique category.

We first briefly examined these two patriarchs of the faith. The Bible makes clear that Jesus Christ, who is the God-man, and John the Baptist were the two most important men ever born. Would it not be reasonable to place Noah in the third position? How many other men have been used by God to save humanity? Noah was truly a man for the ages!

The Old Testament, as well as the New, bears eloquent testimony to Noah's godliness. Two other intercessors were also noted alongside Noah. Those two are Job and Daniel. Ezekiel 14:14, 20 declares:

> "Even if these three men, Noah, Daniel, and Job, were in it, they would deliver only themselves by their righteousness," says the Lord GOD. ... "even though Noah, Daniel, and Job were in it, as I live," says the Lord GOD, "they would deliver neither son nor daughter; they would deliver only themselves by their righteousness" (cf. Hebrews 11:7).

It is one thing to be listed among the top three of David's mighty men (2 Samuel 23:8–12). It is quite another to be mentioned in God's heroic trio. What greater honor can there possibly be than that? No modern-day prayer warrior will be placed on equal footing with Noah, Daniel, and Job. Nonetheless, they provide an example for all believers to emulate. As Paul exhorted the believers in 1 Thessalonians 5:17: "Pray without ceasing."

We also took a moment to review the life of the faithful Moses. He and Noah shared the common adventure of being rescued in an ark. Noah's ark was immense; Moses' ark was tiny enough to hold one baby boy. Moses experienced a prayer relationship with God not equaled among humanity. He spoke face to face with almighty God. Though we cannot envision what that relationship was like, it truly was unique and remarkable. Moses was the man through whom God gave the Law. Noah delivered the world; Moses delivered the nation of Israel. Both accomplishments were done through the almighty power of God.

Second, we reviewed the world of corruption in which Noah labored and preached. For 120 long years, God used Noah as a part-time construction worker and a part-time evangelist. He faithfully poured out his pure soul in heartfelt, passionate messages to save the lost. Perhaps he did witness a precious few who came to faith in the Lord throughout his ministry. Evidence does not seem to indicate there would have been many, if any at all. When the time of the Flood inundated the earth, only Noah and his immediate family were safely tucked away in the dry interiors of the ark.

There has never been nor will there ever be a more inhospitable time to proclaim God's holy Word than in Noah's day. The Nephilim had essentially corrupted the entire earth. Believers of today may find the average person resistant and occasionally hostile to the gospel. But no time frame can compare to the continually wicked thoughts of man's heart in Noah's day. How discouraging that must have been.

Third, we touched upon the dimensions of the ark. It was approximately 450 feet long, 75 feet wide, and 45 feet high. The Bible presents only the barest of information about its construction. It contained a window, a door, and three decks. Within the ark were individual pens for the animals. The Hebrew term describes them as "nests." That terminology paints a cozy picture for the animal's individual protection and solitude. The ark was overladen with pitch on the inside and the outside (6:14). This was to prevent water from seeping into the ark. The term for pitch is not the typical word used for a petroleum product.

Fruchtenbaum offered the following comments regarding the pitch: "It is the same Hebrew root for 'atonement.' There is a correlation, because the covering of the outward with pitch saved them physically from water seepage, keeping the ark from sinking. As a parallel, the covering of blood saved spiritually."[106]

The story of the ark is paralleled by the infinitely greater reality of Jesus Christ and His atoning crucifixion and resurrection (John 3:16). Christ testified to the historical reality of Noah and the ark. If this story is good enough for Christ, who was there, should it not be good enough for mankind today?

It is one thing to be an unbeliever and reject the Bible out of hand. That is to be expected. But it is inexcusable for the believer to heap scorn on the narrative of the Flood. That will reap strong and negative consequences in his own spiritual life. God does not honor those who refuse to honor Him and His Word. If a believer cannot trust God's eternal Word, does he not also cast doubts upon the Author of that Word? Yes, he does! That is an inescapable conclusion. Nor can any such believer offer any defense in the eternal court of God for his lack of trust (1 Corinthians 3:11–15; Romans 14:11–12).

It is our firm assessment that God truly did send the Flood to destroy all of humanity and land-dwelling creatures on this earth. The world had become irreversibly corrupted through the wicked influence of the Nephilim. Judgment was due! The many evidences supporting the universal Flood, of which we shall examine more thoroughly later, testifies to this worldwide inundation.

---
106 Arnold Fruchtenbaum, Ariel's Bible Commentary: The Book of Genesis, p. 163.

In our next chapter, we shall continue to examine sundry aspects of the universal Flood. We will address numerous common objections and endeavor to provide a reasonable response. One of the more commonly voiced questions concerns how many animals actually entered into the ark. As we shall soon see, this particular objection does not have the merit that so many falsely believe. There is no reason to doubt any aspects of the biblical worldwide Flood.

Cognitive Conundrum #13

Legalities proved my middle name; to me, religion was more than a game. Friends I had in considerable number, my mannerisms could cause some to slumber. Theology marked my area of expertise; unique instruction gave my life a new lease. Rumors of my abrupt death still do abound; my distinctive conversion proved my life sound.

Who am I?

Answer: Paul

Chapter 14

The Day of Judgment Arrives

(Genesis 6:18–7:5)

In This Chapter

Objectives for This Chapter
How Many Animals Did You Say (6:18–22)?
Objections and Answers
Noah Enters the Ark (Genesis 7:1–5)
Lessons Learned in This Chapter

Objectives for This Chapter

God commanded His loyal servant Noah to build an ark. Through that huge wooden vessel, humanity and the animal kingdom were to be preserved. Flood waters encompassing the entire globe enveloped all other land-dwellings and air-breathing creatures. Nothing survived! With the floodwaters, the Nephilim and all the rest of sin-plagued humanity were swept away. The time of Noah's flood witnessed the absolute bottom for morality on the earth. Thankfully, spiritual conditions will never again become so horrendous and abysmal in scope.

In this chapter, we shall first examine the divine purpose of the ark. The ark and the cross of Christ both provided deliverance to all who would embrace their message. The cross of Christ still rings out its clarion call for repentance and eternal life. Though not such a poor response as in the days of Noah, relatively few, even today, heed the warning and invitation of the cross. Lamentably, those who embraced God's grace and forgiveness in Noah's time were limited exclusively to Noah and his family. That was just eight souls! But from those eight souls, the world has been repopulated.

The ark was a visible, tangible warning of coming judgment. As we shall see, all the human senses could be physically impacted by the presence and the construction of the ark. It took 120 years to build. The ark was the world's biggest object lesson. During its construction, the faithful Noah kept on proclaiming God's call for forgiveness and reconciliation. He was largely ignored. Although there may have been some converts who died before the Flood, we have no record of such.

No excuses were acceptable in Noah's day for continued rebellion against God. They were not tolerated in the days of Christ either. Indeed, to this day, God deems no excuses satisfactory. He has steadfastly provided ample witness of His sovereignty. Special and general revelation saturate the entire globe. There is no hidden place in the universe where God has not displayed His creative ability. The intricate design of virtually all things in creation shout out their sundry testimonies to God's greatness. Most importantly, the Bible is the pinnacle of God's unparalleled communication to mankind.

It is our privilege to examine biblical information concerning truly godly men in this chapter. Though our primary emphasis will be on Noah, we shall also briefly discuss Enoch, Abraham, Job, Moses, and Daniel. All of them provide incredible testimony to God's faithfulness and their heartfelt response. All believers should be inspired by the example of their undying fidelity to the Creator.

Second, we shall address some of the primary reasons people reject the concept of the worldwide Flood and the ark. These objections are briefly introduced. Other extremely well-written books discuss in greater depth more of the sundry issues that come to the forefront. However, we shall comment on a few of the more common puzzlements that individuals frequently pose. We trust that such questions will be addressed adequately.

Many questions are quite reasonable and certainly are worthy of answers. Believers and unbelievers alike are greatly encouraged to ask questions. What is discouraged is a stubborn inclination to disregard clear facts. Creationists have thoroughly addressed an ample assortment of apparent difficulties to a most satisfactory degree. Some inquiries, however, remain a mystery and perhaps always will. God is not compelled to cater to humanity's every whim and curiosity. The evidences that we can understand testify eloquently to a Creator. All other perplexing mysteries are known and controlled by our sovereign God. In this, believer and unbeliever alike may rest confident.

Third, we shall review the day that Noah entered the ark. All the food and water supplies had been placed in their designated areas. God Himself led the animals to the ark and almost certainly to their designated areas within the ark as well. That was absolutely necessary. Tigers and other such boisterous carnivores rarely smile upon being herded about like cattle.

By God's intervention, the wild animals became docile while under the care and supervision of Noah and his family. For those pagans observing this divinely guided parade of animals, one would think that alone should have proven sufficient warning of dire days soon to come. It wasn't! They were beyond conviction and even common sense. Sadly, the day of grace was over; the day of retribution had arrived. No air-breathing mortal would escape it, save those safely ensconced in the ark.

How Many Animals Did You Say (Genesis 6:18–22)?

Genesis 6:18–22 states:

> But I will establish My covenant with you; and you shall go into the ark—you, your sons, your wife, and your sons' wives with you. And of every living thing of all flesh you shall bring two of every sort into the ark, to keep them alive with you; they shall be male and female.
>
> Of the birds after their kind, of animals after their kind, and of every creeping thing of the earth after its kind, two of every kind will come to you to keep them alive. And you shall take for yourself of all food that is eaten, and you shall gather it to yourself and it shall be food for you and for them. Thus Noah did; according to all that God commanded him, so he did.

God Establishes His Covenant with Noah

In verse 18, God promises a covenant with Noah. The details of this covenant are explained more precisely in Genesis chapter 9. Thus, they shall be dealt with in more detail later. Before the Flood actually began, however, Noah and his family had the promise of a covenant with their Creator. This, incidentally, is the first specific mention of a covenant in Scripture.

It should be noted that many consider Genesis 1:26–28 as a covenant, although the term "covenant" is not actually used in the context. It is better described as a command or mandate to fill and exercise stewardship over the earth. Others include Genesis 3:15 as a covenant. But this is not really a covenant either. It is a promise of future deliverance by the Seed of the woman. It was fulfilled in Jesus Christ. Covenants are specifically identified through precise language.

Only eight human beings were going to be spared in the ark. That is a remarkably small number. The offer was extended to all who would repent and believe, but the takers were only those of Noah's family! The human race began with just two people: Adam and Eve. It exploded in number exponentially. But now, after 1656 years, the entire population would be reduced to just eight souls.

Warnings of the Broad Way

How lamentably true rings Matthew 7:13–14: "Enter by the narrow gate; for wide is the gate and broad is the way that leads to destruction, and there are many who go in by it. Because narrow is the gate and difficult is the way which leads to life, and there are few who find it."

One cannot find much of a narrower gate than the door leading into the ark. Salvation is not found on the broad path or in numerous imaginative avenues. God knows of only one way of salvation. That is through His holy Son, Jesus Christ (John 14:6). Jesus' sacred words hauntingly remind us of the natural and sinful proclivities of mankind. Each man, woman, and child is fettered with an old nature. This nature manifests itself at a very young age. One of the first words a baby learns to say is "no!"

The broad way Jesus spoke of fills the eyeballs with enticing allurements. It appeals to all the senses with carnal and sensual pleasures. It radiates throughout the mind in seemingly unceasing waves. The broad way is lined with temptations that are clothed in radiance and neon signs, but in reality, they are filthy rags. Second Corinthians 11:14 warns believers: "And no wonder! For Satan himself transforms himself into an angel of light."

The broad way leads to a spiritual graveyard lined to the cemetery fence with earthly remorse and eternal regrets. It must and can be daily battled by God's grace (1 Corinthians 10:12–13). God, even in unseen ways, provides the grace for resisting the apparently irresistible. He affords a narrow avenue for escape. That was true in Noah's day; it was true in Jesus' day; it is true in our present day; it shall be true in the future Tribulation.

The Ark and the Cross Provided Spiritual Deliverance

Considering the world largely rejects the truth of Scripture, one should not be surprised by a reaction of skepticism to the Flood. Discussing the Flood story, however, presents a marvelous opportunity to share the eternal principles of God's Word. A primary truth regarding the Flood is that God does eventually punish sin and, of course, the sinners (John 3:16–18; Ephesians 2:1–3). That is an inescapable axiom of life. God must punish sin, or He would no longer be a complete and holy God. His justice must and will prevail.

But God also demonstrates phenomenal patience (Ephesians 2:4–7). At the time of the Flood, the entire world was morally bankrupt except for Noah and his immediate family. God provided potential salvation through Noah and the ark, but it was rejected. Jesus Christ is the more modern "ark" for humanity. He is the one and only way of salvation (1 Corinthians 15:1–4). If Jesus were not the only way, why should He have suffered the agonies of crucifixion in the first place? Was such pain and spiritual agony only for grandstanding purposes? Obviously not!

He died so that all can live through and for Him. One must simply be willing to believe and follow Him (1 Peter 2:24–25). He is the only avenue of escape from God's wrath (1 Peter 3:18). Just as Noah, his family, and the animals entered the physical ark and escaped the floodwaters, even so each individual must proceed down the path of life through the Savior Jesus Christ. He is the fulfillment of Genesis 3:15. He is the one who can and has already defeated the power of Satan.

The Ark: The World's Biggest Visible Object Lesson

God patiently waited for 120 years while Noah preached and built the ark. The ark was a huge and visible object lesson for all of humanity. Notice how God allowed humanity's physical senses to be exercised. The people could see their impending doom being constructed right in front of their eyes. They could also observe that there was only one door of deliverance from the coming Flood. Over two millennia later, there would also be one door of salvation offered by Jesus Christ. But one has to walk through that door of his own volition (Revelation 3:20).

The people could listen with their ears to Noah's message regarding both the mercy and the coming judgment of God. They could also hear the sound of nails being pounded into the wood. They could feel the immense ark with their hands. They could touch the slimy pitch with their fingers. They could talk with Noah himself about the ark and impending judgment. Noah would have enthusiastically conversed with all who inquired of the ways of the Lord.

They could smell the freshly cut gopher wood and the pungent odor of the pitch used to cover the wood. Their strong odors filled the air. They could use their minds to contemplate the harshness of the promised punishment for the unrepentant. Their minds also could focus on potential forgiveness and deliverance. In other words, they could use all their senses! The people of Noah's day had no excuse! Tragically, the Nephilim had so distorted their God-granted spiritual reasoning that they did not believe (cf. Isaiah 6:9–10; John 12:40).

Jesus Christ: The Matchless Prophet and Son of God

In like manner, the members of the Sanhedrin and the common people had no excuse in Jesus' day. Jesus performed endless miracles (John 20:30–31, 21:26); He fulfilled prophecies from His conception (Matthew 1:23); He knew people's thoughts (John 2:24–25); He taught with unparalleled authority. Matthew 7:28–29 records His teaching: "And so it was, when Jesus had ended these sayings, that the people were astonished at his teaching, for He taught them as one having authority, and not as the scribes." He relied on the Scriptures entirely for His teaching (Matthew 4:1–11).

Jesus sent out seventy emissaries, whom He enabled to do miracles while He was still dwelling on the earth (Luke 10:1–17). Later, after Jesus' crucifixion, resurrection, and ascension, the apostles carried on an astonishing ministry of miracles (Acts 5:12–16). It appears that, at one point, if even Peter's shadow passed over a sick person, he was healed (5:15). All the apostles could do miracles in the early stages of their ministry.

This was later equally true of Paul (Acts 14:8–10). Paul raised Eutychus from the dead (Acts 20:9–12). The apostles fervently declared that this was all by the power of Jesus Christ. Yet most people still refused to believe. Incredible! Indeed, the unbelievers eventually murdered eleven of the twelve apostles according to Church tradition. What kind of excuses will they offer before God at the Great White Throne Judgment (Revelation 20:11–15)? None! Their terror and unmitigated remorse will leave them utterly speechless.

How much more evidence could the people possibly expect regarding the Messiah? God was not hiding the truth from either the people of Noah's day or the Messiah's. He made His message so obvious it would seem next to impossible to miss it. But in spite of all the evidence portrayed to them, unrepentant and unthinking man ignored God's clear message. God could have written it in the sky, and it apparently would have made no impact on their darkened souls.

In Noah's day, even if it had never rained on the earth before (which is debated among creationists), they could still at least partially envision what a Flood would be like. The human imagination has always been quite fertile. Of course, no one could envision a worldwide Flood. Even today, in spite of all the available evidence for this past cataclysm, many people still vehemently deny it. They can witness an entire world replete with supporting data and still turn a self-blinded eye to it. Seeing for many is not believing!

No Excuses Allowed!

Noah, God's faithful and persevering servant, fully obeyed the words and instructions of his Maker. He did not hesitate to carry out any of God's commands. The question for each reader is: Will he or she follow God's written instructions handed down throughout the millennia? We are each left with a choice to follow God or to reject Him, to comply or to complain.

Some do not choose to actively reject God; they instead simply ignore Him. They muddle through life, not denying God but acting as if He and His holy ordinances do not matter. But ignorance of the law is no excuse for breaking it. Each person in the Old Testament era was required to learn the law to at least a minimal degree. Much of the law was contained in the Ten Commandments.

Let it be remembered by our readers that Christ fulfilled the

Old Testament law (Matthew 5:17–18). We now live under the law of Christ, which is articulated in the New Testament. Galatians 6:2 states: "Bear one another's burdens, and so fulfill the law of Christ." The law of Christ should be considered the entirety of all New Testament instruction for the Church. It should also be noted, however, that the promises of the Old Testament toward Israel and eternal principles for godly living are still considered valid in the New Testament era. The specific sacrifices and festivals of the Old Testament era have been fulfilled through the obedience, death, and resurrection of Christ.

If one follows Christ's law, he would most likely be abiding within the law of the land. However, if the law of the land contradicts scriptural injunctions, then that law must be disobeyed. In many countries throughout the world today, evangelism and the practice of Christianity are prohibited. This causes the lives of many Christians to be quite tumultuous. Many have died for their faith. Sadly, this has proven true since the inception of the Church.

Acts 4:18–20 presents a beautiful example of godly disobedience:

> So they called them and commanded them not to speak at all nor teach in the name of Jesus. But Peter and John answered and said to them: "Whether it is right in the sight of God to listen to you more than to God, you judge. For we cannot but speak the things which we have seen and heard."

To this passage, we add Acts 5:29: "But Peter and the other apostles answered and said: 'We ought to obey God rather than men.'" God honored them for their faithful disobedience.

In like manner, neglect or outright disobedience of God's general and special revelation will not leave one guiltless at the feet of an almighty God. Hebrews 10:26–27 warns: "For if we sin willfully after we have received the knowledge of the truth, there no longer remains a sacrifice for sins, but a certain fearful expectation of judgment, and fiery indignation which shall devour the adversaries" (cf. Zephaniah 1:18).

As Scripture so amply warns us in Galatians 6:7–8: "Do not be deceived, God is not mocked; for whatever a man sows, that he will also reap. For he who sows to his flesh will of the flesh reap corruption, but he who sows to the Spirit will of the Spirit reap everlasting life." By God's grace, believers sow faith in their lives. They reap everlasting life. The unbeliever sows distrust and disobedience. They will reap corruption and punishment in hell. All throughout Scripture, such warnings are plentiful and plainly given.

The Miracle of the Ark

We shall now examine some of the false objections regarding the ark and the Flood. In a rather succinct fashion, we shall endeavor to answer these alleged grievances. It should be noted that many of these objections are quite reasonable and are to be expected. Asking the question "why" is quite natural and should be respected. Hence, we do not respond with a critical spirit in any way. Rather, we encourage such inquiries by questioning souls. After all, how can one learn if he does not ask pointed questions?

The ark was truly a unique boat and has had no known equals in the history of man. However, creationist organizations have supervised the building of an ark that is equal to the biblical dimensions. Their intention is for illustrative purposes. The job was brilliantly done in at least one instance. Such an ark was personally toured by this writer.

It is true that some very large wooden vessels have been made, but none seem to equal the size of the ark. These vessels were built for the conveyance of trade goods, raw materials, and people. They were impressive in size and built for practical ventures. But none of these prodigious vessels were up to the task of ferrying all living types of air-breathing animals and a year's supply of provisions.

Question: Could Noah really have built something that huge? Answer: Yes, he not only could do so, he did it! But he did it by God's grace. Still, the uninitiated skeptic quite understandably finds that difficult to fathom. Admittedly, it seems like a fairy tale! But it is indeed a reality supported by historical, archeological, and scientific facts. Most importantly of all, the Bible teaches it! What greater witness does one need than the Author of Scripture (2 Peter 1:19–21; Hebrews 12:2)?

It is nearly impossible for the average individual to comprehend how a Flood could cover the highest mountains, such as Mount Everest. There simply is not that much water on earth, the skeptics claim. Indeed, their claim is true, considering our present earth! Thus, they raise an interesting and valid point. But that objection can be resolved through a biblical explanation and geological evidences. We shall examine those resolutions momentarily.

Believers should always be preparing themselves to respond to sincere questions and doubts by unbelievers. First Peter 3:15 reminds us: "But sanctify the Lord God in your hearts, and always be ready to give a defense to everyone who asks you a reason for the hope that is in you, with meekness and fear." As this passage instructs all believers, we need to be preparing for a defense of the Christian faith. The primary method of doing so is by studying God's Word systematically (2 Timothy 2:15). Reading books, listening to sermons, and being involved in evangelism also enhances the believer's life and effectiveness.

Regarding 1 Peter 3:15, Martin Luther comments:

> We must here acknowledge that Peter addressed these words to all Christians—clergy and laity, male and female, young and old—of whatever state or condition they may be. Hence, it follows that every Christian should know the ground and reason of his faith, and he should be able to maintain and defend it where it is necessary.[107]

God Provides for a "Reasonable" Faith

God requires faith to believe in Him (Hebrews 11:6). But He leaves tremendous proof to demonstrate His biblical claims (Deuteronomy 4:2; Psalm 19:1–6; Romans 1:18–22). That is particularly true when both general revelation (nature) and special revelation (the Bible) are considered. In all other false religions around the world, the adherents are expected to accept almost everything by faith. Few verifications of their heretical teachings are ever provided. The reason for this is quite simple: There are no legitimate verifications!

False religions are characterized by belligerent showmanship, arrogant verbosity, and a skeletal framework of "truth." These do not equate to a solid foundation of empirical substance. Absent is a reasonable underpinning for their false faith.

Christianity is the most fervently analyzed and criticized faith of all time. Yet, in spite of relentless attacks and denials, it has easily stood the test of history and perpetual examination. The evidences

---
107 Martin Luther, *Commentary on Peter & Jude* (Grand Rapids, MI: Kregel Publications, 1990), p. 158.

for Christianity have converted some of the most venomous of critics. Indeed, many such individuals have become some of Christianity's most notable witnesses and supporters.

In a few rare circumstances, God may not leave empirical substantiations of His commands to us. One must then rely exclusively on faith. Most people don't like living by faith alone; they crave proof. But then again, anyone can live by proof! Where is the challenge in that? It takes a special man or woman to live solely by faith in God's promises. Faith is a necessary component in any meaningful relationship, whether human or divine.

First Corinthians 2:14–16 states:

> But the natural man does not receive the things of the Spirit of God, for they are foolishness to him, nor can he know them, because they are spiritually discerned. But he who is spiritual judges all things, yet he himself is rightly judged by no one. For "who has known the mind of the LORD that he may instruct Him?" But we have the mind of Christ.

C. K. Barrett comments as follows:

> The natural man is most easily defined negatively; he is a man who has not received the Holy Spirit. His natural resources, for example his intellectual resources, are, or may be, complete; he is not in any ordinary sense a 'bad man', or a foolish man, or an irreligious man. But lacking the Spirit of God, he cannot apprehend spiritual truths, for to him they are foolishness, and he cannot know them, because they are investigated spiritually.[108]

---

108 C. K. Barrett, The First Epistle to the Corinthians (Peabody, MA: Hendrickson Publishers, 1968), p. 77.

How true Barrett's comment is. Without the Holy Spirit residing within the unbeliever, his spiritual perceptions are small indeed. This lack of spiritual discernment creates much friction and even hostility toward the believer. The unbeliever simply cannot understand the actions of Christ's followers. This has been the case throughout human history. Having said that, let us for a moment consider two other historic men of faith. Hence, we shall briefly pause from our discussion of the ark.

Abraham: An Example of Living Faith

Abraham was a man of simple but profound faith. He only had God's promise that he would receive an heir, and he eventually did in Isaac. But consider their circumstances. Abraham and Sarah were already quite elderly. They had been eagerly waiting for God's promise for many years already. They even tried to "help God out" by using a servant woman, Hagar, to bear a child on Sarah's behalf. Thus, Ishmael was born. Because of this crucial, albeit temporary, lapse of faith, the child Ishmael eventually proved to be the source of much misery.

However, one must consider the emotional plight of Abraham and Sarah with at least a semblance of sympathy and understanding. How could they become parents? Humanly speaking, Sarah had lived beyond her childbearing years. It is extremely disappointing for most couples not to have children in almost any age. It was devastating in the days of Abraham. That would be the worst possible scenario that could happen to anyone.

Children were understood as a sign of God's blessing by both believer and unbeliever alike (Psalm 127:3–5). The more the merrier, so to speak! Conversely, if you could not have children, it was interpreted as a sign of God's concerted displeasure. This proved particularly onerous on the woman since it was generally assumed to be her fault in those ancient cultures. This, of course, was neither fair nor medically accurate. Nonetheless, it was the painful stigma women suffered under in Abraham's day.

Yet, regarding Abraham, Romans 4:19–22 states:

> And not being weak in faith, he did not consider his own body, already dead (since he was about a hundred years old), and the deadness of Sarah's womb. He did not waver at the promise of God through unbelief, but was strengthened in faith, giving glory to God, and being fully convinced that what He had promised He was also able to perform. And therefore "it was accounted to him for righteousness."

Abraham chose to trust in God. In light of his faith, the Hebrew nation came into being. Isaac was eventually born. Then followed Jacob and Esau. Jacob, the second born, was hardly a man of great faith in his early days. He was actually known as a deceiver. But he ultimately fathered the twelve tribes of Israel through his rather unhappy marriage to four women.

Have You Considered Job?

Another historical example of faith is Job. He was the most righteous man on the earth. But God allowed His beloved servant to be sorely tested. In one tragic day, Job lost most of his property and, infinitely more importantly, all his children. This happened through the actions of enemies, supernatural events such as fire falling from heaven, and natural events such as a great wind that knocked down the house where his children were gathered.

This obviously was not a dark day accentuated merely by remarkable coincidences. God had allowed all of this to happen. From the short-sighted human perspective, the same God who had so bountifully blessed Job now seemed bent on destroying him. Job knew nothing of the cosmic contest taking place in heaven between God and Satan. All he understood at the moment was his phenomenal pain and anguish. No father and mother have ever experienced such calamitous blows in such a unique fashion in such a short time.

Job's remarkable response is recorded in Job 1:20–22:

> "Then Job arose, tore his robe, and shaved his head; and he fell to the ground and worshiped. And he said, "Naked I came from my mother's womb, and naked shall I return there. The LORD gave, and the LORD has taken away; blessed be the name of the LORD." In all this Job did not sin nor charge God with wrong.

However, Job's misery was just beginning. He was then afflicted with painful boils all over his body. He sat in an ash heap and scraped his wounds with a piece of pottery. The primary person remaining to him was his wife. She also, needless to say, was heartbroken. She reacted as almost any destitute mother would. She just wanted to curse God and die! She, in fact, encouraged her husband to do just that!

Job 2:9 states: "Then his wife said to him, 'Do you still hold fast to your integrity? Curse God and die!'" The implication is that she had already done that. If true, God, in His infinite mercy and patience, had graciously not put her to death.

However, one should not be too quick to judge her overly harshly in her statement, morally repugnant though it was. She had just lost her children whom she had borne, nursed, and raised. Her pain was unimaginable. What woman had ever experienced anything like she did on that horrible day? Few, if any, women ever had. Her faith was clearly not as strong as her husband's, so she reacted the way she did. But whose faith is as strong as Job's? The answer is precious few, if any!

God Himself had testified to Satan in Job 1:8: "Then the LORD said to Satan, 'Have you considered My servant Job, that there is no one like him on the earth, a blameless and upright man, one who fears God and shuns evil?'" Job was the most outstanding man on earth from God's perspective. That statement regarding Job's lifestyle helps us to understand his remarkable reaction to God and his wife in Job 2:10: "But he said to her, 'You speak as one of the foolish women speaks. Shall we indeed accept good from God, and shall we not accept adversity?' In all this Job did not sin with his lips."

What an amazing response! The book of Job has proven to be an inspiration down throughout the millennia to millions of people. And one must remember this: Job did not have the book of Job to read for comfort! He lived it. May we allow his amazing example to remind us of the need for faith, obedience, and worship of our sovereign God.

Noah, Abraham, and Job provide believers with incredible examples of faith. One does well to reflect frequently on their extraordinary lives. Each man, in his own unique set of circumstances, offers a veritable smorgasbord of godly character. The faithful of every generation can profit immensely by studying and emulating their lives. Believers are created to be interdependent, not to dwell in seclusion on an island. Those of faith do well to learn from each other. God desires that the Christian body assist one another for mutual spiritual growth (Hebrews 10:24–25).

With these splendid examples of godly living freshly cited, let us now turn to some common objections regarding the ark and the universal Flood.

Objections and Answers

How Could Those Massive Dinosaurs Fit on the Ark?

Objection #1: Noah could not have fit the largest dinosaurs onto the ark, nor could he have provided sufficient food for them to last a year.

Response #1: Noah didn't bring any of the animals onto the ark; God delivered them to the ark Himself (Genesis 7:7–9). Would the largest dinosaurs have fit on the ark? They are not large when they are just a few months old. All that was required was a male and female that would eventually be able to reproduce, not fully grown adults. Furthermore, very young and immature dinosaurs would not eat much. God could have also caused them and other animals to supernaturally hibernate during the Flood. Many animals do just that in this present time for the winter season.

Dinosaurs fascinate people, particularly children. Evolutionists take great advantage of this natural human tendency to promote their false doctrine. More reliable information is needed to correct some of the misunderstandings regarding dinosaurs. Scholars, such as Woodmorappe, have carefully calculated the size of the average juvenile dinosaurs and their various genera. Based on his calculations, the ark contained plenty of space for the dinosaurs and the other animals and the food and water reserves for human and beast alike.

The largest dinosaur eggs located thus far are no bigger than a football. If they got much bigger, their shells would have to be so thick that oxygen could not filter inside of the shell. The embryo needs oxygen for survival and growth. Thus, all dinosaurs started out small. Noah would not have brought any full-grown dinosaurs onto the ark.

A More Scientific Approach to the Dinosaur Problem

Sarfati offers the following research that fully supports the Genesis account of the ark:

1. As shown in 'Dinosaur kinds', ch. 10, information since NAFS was published shows that the number of dinosaur genera has been seriously over-estimated. For example, many juvenile dinosaurs have been wrongly identified as separate genera from the adults.

2. Dinosaur weights have also been badly over-estimated, according to researchers from the University of Manchester. Using a laser scanner and high-speed computing, the British team first created a 3D image of the skeletons of known animals with known weights. They then calculated the minimum amount of skin necessary to cover the skeletons, and used estimates of the average density of modern-day tissues to work out the minimum weight of just the skin and bones. They tested their methods on modern large land animals of known weight.

They then scanned the reconstructed, almost complete, skeleton of the large dinosaur now classified as Giraffititan brancai (formerly Brachiosaurus brancai) from the brachiosaurid created kind. They estimated that if the same formula applied, it would have weighed about 23 tonnes in life. Previously, it had been believed to weigh up to 80 tonnes.

3. Gregory Erickson, a paleontologist at Florida State University in Tallahassee, and other researchers, studied dinosaur bones for the equivalent of growth rings. They showed that dinosaurs had a type of adolescent growth spurt—the pattern is called sigmoidal, or s-shaped. In fact, the growth pattern is more similar to that of birds and mammals than that of reptiles.

Furthermore, dinosaurs didn't need to be fully grown to mate. Female dinosaurs have been discovered to have medullary tissue in their bones—this lines bone marrow and keeps them from losing calcium from their bones when they use it to make egg shells. Furthermore, this tissue has been found in dinosaurs that were not fully grown. It follows that dinosaurs didn't need to be fully grown before they could produce. ...

This study also analyzed other tyrannosaurids called Daspletosaurus, Gorgosaurus, and Albertosaurus. These all had the same growth patterns, but not nearly as extreme. So it seems that they were the same created kind, so represented by one pair on the Ark, and T. Rex was simply a giant form, just as we have in some humans. And as with many giant humans, the giantism comes at a cost.

Superficially, the T. rex body plan might give the impression it was a fast runner. But this structure simply will not allow fast running for this type of animal over one tonne, which the T. rex reached at age 13. So the Jurassic park scene of a T. rex outrunning a jeep is pure fiction—to do that, it would have needed muscle weighing over twice the entire animal![109]

How Could the Ark Contain Millions of Animals?

Objection #2: You cannot hold millions of species of animals on the ark.

Response #2: Noah did not bring millions of species onto the ark; he brought two of every kind, a male and a female. For example, there are many different species of dogs, but only one kind. That original kind was probably something similar to a wolf. There are many species of cattle, but only one kind. Likewise, many species of cats, horses, and even elephants exist. However, one only needs the basic kind of these animals.

The genetic structure contained within the DNA allows for much speciation in every kind of animal. Hence, some estimate the number of animals to be only 16,000. Others put the number between 35,000 and 70,000. No one really knows for sure.

But one thing is certain: there was ample room! If one is going to give any credence at all to the biblical story of the Flood, it should be easy enough to accept the fact that there was sufficient room in the ark. The giraffes did not have their heads sticking out of the roof as so many artists have mockingly portrayed.

Clearly, the animals did not need to fight in order to find refuge

---

[109] Jonathan Sarfati, The Genesis Account: A theological, historical, and scientific commentary on Genesis 1–11, pp. 518–520.

inside the ark. If they had, there would have been a lot of dead animals lying around the entrance! The lions, tigers, bears, and dinosaurs would have been in their glory, slaughtering everything else in sight. That did not happen! God brought them peacefully into the ark. If He hadn't, why would all of these animals, particularly carnivores and herbivores, have ever come to the ark together in the first place? That could never have happened without God's direct intervention.

Considering that God performed the miracle of bringing the animals into the ark, He would also have designed sufficient room for every occupant. Some objections are really quite silly if one thinks about it. Either the account of the Flood and the ark is true, or it is not. Obviously, an omniscient God would have dealt with every possible contingency imaginable.

Two-by-two, the animals traversed their way into their soon-to-be floating home. God required seven animals of the clean kind and seven birds of each kind (7:2–3). Part of this was for the purpose of sacrifice after they left the ark (8:20). Fish, quite naturally, survived in the water. It is almost an absolute certainty that the oceans were not as salty as they are today. Scientists can quite effectively measure the increase of salinity in the ocean as the years pass. Hence, the fish, which are adaptable, could adjust well enough.

What about the Vegetation and All Those Irritating Bugs?

Objection #3: How did Noah manage to keep all the plants and insects alive? Perhaps a better question is, how can one even kill all those nasty bugs? They seem to creep up everywhere. Regarding the plants, Darwin and other contemporaries found that they could submerge regular garden seeds in salt water for up to forty-two days, and they still sprouted beautifully. Plants do not even need the entire plant to propagate.

A plant simply requires a small segment of itself, such as the stem, root, bulb, or other assorted parts. The survivability of plants, particularly weeds, is known to every farmer. Sometimes, it seems impossible to kill the weeds. If action is not taken every year, the weeds will always faithfully sprout and choke out the good plants. The total number of different species of plants and trees is still unknown. New ones are still being found, including some that were supposedly extinct.

Anyone who has gone camping might wish that Noah hadn't kept all those pesky insects alive! Actually, Noah had nothing to do with their survival. They did just fine on their own in spite of the trauma of the Flood. According to scientists, there are over 900,000 known species of insects. New ones are being found almost every day. In addition, probably a few go extinct every day as well. Science is kept quite busy categorizing the insect population.

The number of individual insects is beyond calculation. The ant population alone is estimated to be one quadrillion. That is one million billion ants! It is no surprise that one finds them almost everywhere on the planet, including, rather frustratingly, in the kitchen. There are over 12,000 known species alone among the ant population. Only bacteria outnumber the ants!

Response #3: Noah did not take all of those plants and insects on the ark. So how did they survive? One must recognize that unimaginably immense log jams and other floating plants would have been caused by the Flood. Bear in mind that every tree on earth was uprooted! Entire forests could be floating in one unbelievably massive, jumbled-up pile of trees and assorted vegetation.

The entire globe was a veritable cornucopia of vegetation. This included all the seemingly uncountable different types of vegetation as well. It must be remembered that the entire globe was of a temperate climate. There were no deserts or even mountainous regions in the original creation. These all developed as a consequence of the Flood (Psalm 104:6–9). That makes for a lot of trees and vast regions of vegetation. On our present earth, the Amazon Forest seems to stretch on forever. The entire earth was at least somewhat similar to that profusion of growth in Noah's day.

Insects and bacteria could survive on such floating forests for a long time, and they obviously did. Some of these immense driftwood rafts undoubtedly had untold millions of insects thriving on them while they floated. Beyond these log and vegetation rafts, there are additional methods of survival of which most people are unaware.

Sarfati comments on one such unusual method:

> An alternative in many cases could be pumice. This is a volcanic rock that forms when very hot and high pressure lava is violently ejected from a volcano. Such lava often contains dissolved gases. The sudden drop of pressure causes these gases to bubble out of solution, and the quick solidification traps these gases in a matrix. So the result is this highly buoyant rock.
>
> Researchers from the Queensland University of Technology have found that floating pumice can support tiny marine plants and animals (e.g. coral, algae, crabs, anemones). They even traveled the thousands of kiliometres from Tonga in the South Pacific Ocean to Australia' Great Barrier Reef.[110]

---

[110] Jonathan Sarfati, The Genesis Account: A theological, historical, and scientific commentary on Genesis 1–11, p. 514.

What about the Humble Bacteria and Other Germs?

Objection #4: How did germs survive? How many different kinds of bacteria, viruses, and other microscopic lifeforms are there in the world? This question is almost laughable in some respects. The issue generally is how to eliminate the ever-present germs, not how to preserve them.

Response #4: Microbiology is a major branch of science. It is almost guaranteed that man can likely explore microbiology for tens of thousands more years and never come close to exploring its fascinating depths. God's creative power in the microscopic world is truly mind-boggling. Those who venture into this admirable science will continuously discover new and oftentimes highly beneficial secrets. They will also be reminded of the destructive capabilities of things so small they can only be seen under powerful microscopes. The microscopic world is absolutely extraordinary!

A better question than how the microscopic world survived is: "How can you even kill the little life forms?" Many of them seem capable of resisting almost anything. Thankfully, by God's immeasurable grace, only a certain percentage of germs are dangerous. God created an innumerable array of helpful bacteria and other microscopic life forms.

Evolutionists seem not to cogitate overly much on this remarkable balance in nature. In their esteemed academic circles, such an unnatural but healthy balance is something of an "inconvenient truth." So, they just ignore it. They shrug their shoulders and witlessly respond, "Time and chance!" In reality, it never was a concern how the microscopic world would survive. These bacteria and viruses, both good and bad, easily survived on the inhabitants of the ark. They also thrived on the floating vegetation, in the fish of the sea, and everywhere else imaginable.

Bacteria seem to be able to survive under the most extreme of conditions. Bacteria can thrive in both boiling and freezing conditions. They can live with or without oxygen. They can harm or help other organisms. The following paragraphs offer some poignant examples of the durability of just a few types of microscopic creatures.

Researcher Alan Gillen comments:

> Scientists discovered that water bears can survive pressure up to six times the deepest ocean trench's pressure. When subjected to the complete vacuum of space and direct radiation from the sun, they lived. Water bears can even survive for almost ten years totally dehydrated. To resurrect them, all you have to do is add water. ...
>
> Certain kinds of bacilli are capable of changing into resistant bodies called spores (or endospores). Each individual bacillus becomes converted into a single spore, except in a few rare species where two spores appear to form in a single cell. The spore can withstand comparatively high temperatures and other unfavorable influences, keeping the organism alive when it would otherwise perish. When suitable conditions are supplied, the spore germinates and returns to the original bacillus form.
>
> This remarkable property is confined to a few species of bacilli only, but has great practical importance. The

aerobic, spore-forming bacteria make up the genus Bacillus, and the anaerobic species are classified in the genus Clostridium.[111]

God has designed the microscopic world with astounding resilience. A small matter like the universal Flood would not have even proven an inconvenience to some of these remarkable little creatures. God also provided "good" bacteria to battle the "bad" bacteria. Before the fall, of course, there were no bad bacteria. When this equilibrium is disrupted, and the delicate balance is upset, people and animals get sick and sometimes die. Scientists continue to explore this tiny world, but short of the infinite knowledge of God, they could likely study for eternity and still not discover all of its amazing secrets and capabilities.

What Kept the Fish Alive in the Changing Salinity of the Seas?

Objection #5: How did saltwater and freshwater fish survive in the rapidly changing seas? Many skeptics believe that this objection is the death knell for the Flood story.

Response #5: Contrary to popular belief, many fish types can survive in both salt and fresh water. It is true that massive amounts of marine animals were killed by the Flood. Many of these, along with buried vegetation, provide our supplies of petroleum and coal. God turned the disaster of the Flood into a source of energy for modern man—a blessing indeed. The issue of how fish survived the changing water salinity has perplexed many over the years. While our answer cannot resolve all issues, it will address many of them regarding this issue.

Sarfati comments as follows:

---
111 Alan Gillen, "The Genesis of Germs," *Answers Magazine*, July 24, 2015.

1. Fish can survive a range of salinities if they have a chance to acclimatize gradually. I saw this for myself in 1998 at Underwater World in Queensland, Australia. They had a freshwater and saltwater fish in the same tank. They achieved this by gradual adjustments to salinity in both fish, until they could cope with the same salinity.

2. Freshwater is less dense than saltwater, so can float on top. There is a well-known phenomenon called a halocline, where a vertical salinity gradient persists in a body of water. The resulting vertical density gradient is called a pycnocline.

3. Many fish kinds have both saltwater and freshwater varieties. This suggests that tolerance for a particular degree of salinity is a specialization within the kind. The specialization is likely due to the loss of ability to tolerate other degrees of salinity. Indeed, the creationist zoologist Dr. Arthur Jones studied cichlid speciation for his Ph.D. thesis, and affirmed that starting from the biblical Creation/Flood/Migration model provided him with important research insights. He states: …

After the post-Flood diversification within the kinds we should still find that, in marine kinds, there are some species that can tolerate much fresher water and, in freshwater kinds, some species that can tolerate much saltier water. With my cichlids I found that this was indeed the case. I was able to keep some species in pure seawater for more than two years with no harmful effects—they lived and reproduced normally. Literature searches again revealed that this was a common pattern throughout the fish classes.[112]

Certainly, we have not reviewed exhaustively all the potential questions regarding the Flood. It was not our intention to do so. We simply wanted to demonstrate that most objections have been scientifically met. When one considers the tremendous evidence for the Flood, it becomes almost impossible to intellectually resist the biblical account. We shall be examining many more of these evidences as we continue.

Verse 22 ends this section with this memorable statement: "Thus Noah did: according to all that God commanded him, so he did." What a powerful testimony to believers of all ages. Noah responded in complete faith and obedience. He did not question God's judgment. He simply obeyed God's commands. Every believer should follow Noah's godly example.

Jesus stated in John 14:21: "He who has My commandments and keeps them, it is he who loves Me. And he who loves Me will be loved by My Father, and I will love him and manifest Myself to him." It is easy to articulate love for another; it is quite another to demonstrate it. We show our genuine love for God by obeying His commandments. All of His commandments are for our benefit. We cannot lose by following Jesus Christ's obedient footsteps.

Noah Enters the Ark (Genesis 7:1–5)

After 120 years of faithful ark construction and preaching, the

---

[112] Jonathan Sarfati, The Genesis Account: A theological, historical, and scientific commentary on Genesis 1–11, p. 515.

fateful day finally arrived. Noah, his family, and all the creatures entered the ark.

Genesis 7:1–5 states:

> Then the LORD said to Noah, "Come into the ark, you and all your household, because I have seen that you are righteous before Me in this generation. You shall take with you seven each of every clean animal, a male and his female; two each of animals that are unclean, a male and his female: also seven each of birds of the air; male and female, to keep the species alive on the face of all the earth.
>
> "For after seven more days I will cause it to rain on the earth forty days and forty nights, and I will destroy from the face of the earth all living things that I have made." And Noah did according to all that the LORD commanded him.

Entrance into the Ark Is Commenced

After 120 long years of preaching and building, Noah and his family entered the ark. All the food and water were stored, and all the animals and birds gathered. Genesis 7:1 states: "Then the LORD said to Noah, 'Come into the ark, you and all your household, because I have seen that you are righteous before Me in this generation.'"

According to biblical chronology, Noah's grandfather, Methuselah, died in the same year of the Flood. Noah's father, Lamech, had died just five years previously. It seems highly likely that both of these godly men powerfully influenced Noah. When Methuselah died, Noah alone remained of the ten original patriarchs. But in a particular sense, God had saved the best for last. Noah was the most perfect in his generations.

John Phillips aptly writes:

> The ark was ready. The last tree had been felled, the last timber secured in its place, the last nail driven home, the last pail of pitch applied. Salvation, full and free, was now ready for all. One step of faith was all it took to put a person in the ark, safe from the wrath of God. We see the full commitment demanded of Noah. ...
>
> God was already in the ark. Salvation was simply the shutting in of all the saved with Him. What it meant for Noah to be "in the ark" in his day is what it means for us to be "in Christ" today. Between the saved and the storm were the judgment-proof timbers of the ark. Between the believer and God's wrath is Christ. He bore the storm for all those who now find their safety in Him.[113]

God ushered in the animals (clean and unclean) and the birds. Genesis 7:2–3 states: "You shall take with you seven each of every clean animal, a male and his female; two each of animals that are unclean, a male and his female: also seven each of birds of the air; male and female, to keep the species alive on the face of all the earth."

Most conservative scholars understand that Moses wrote the entire Pentateuch. Hence, what he considered clean in Leviticus chap-

---
[113] John Phillips, Exploring Genesis, p. 85.

ter 11 and Deuteronomy chapter 14 would almost certainly coincide with what Noah considered clean in his day. That, however, cannot be established definitively. It should be noted that in the levitical system under Moses, there were animals that were clean and could be eaten but were not normally offered as sacrifices. The types of clean animals intended for sacrifice were actually quite small.

Seven pairs of every clean animal were brought into the ark so at least one could be offered up as a sacrifice. This was probably fourteen animals, not seven. However, commentators are divided on the issue. Many claim that it means only a total of seven, one being reserved for sacrifice.

The Hebrew text literally says, "Seven seven," which seems to indicate seven pairs. In addition, seven pairs of every kind of bird, clean or unclean, were included. The recorded reason for these numerous pairs of birds was probably to ensure their survival. Also, as already alluded to, some of them would be sacrificed.

The Final Warning Is Uttered

In Genesis 7:4–5, God commanded Noah and his family and all the animals to board the ark: "For after seven more days I will cause it to rain on the earth forty days and forty nights, and I will destroy from the face of the earth all living things that I have made. And Noah did according to all that the LORD commanded him."

One week from the day they entered the ark the Flood would begin. Noah's family had already loaded the food supplies onto the ark since the animals that walked on first in line had to eat immediately. And that would have been a very large job indeed. Noah and his family had possibly devised many self-feeding mechanisms to assist in this otherwise gargantuan task. Scripture is silent on that issue.

Once again, it must be reiterated that the number of animals may have been as few as 16,000. No one can say for certain how many there were. But clearly, God made sure there was ample room and food for all of them. It could also be that some of them quickly settled into hibernation. Certainly, most of them were younger and smaller animals, not full-grown.

Noah complied with all that God commanded. His faithfulness during this entire time is inspirational. No one had experienced what was coming to the earth (Hebrews 11:7). No one had ever seen a Flood. Quite likely, although it is debated, no one had ever even seen it rain. But it would soon begin to rain for forty days and nights. This would be no gentle spring drizzle. The rain almost certainly came down in unequaled torrents. The terror inflicted on the people would have proven nearly heart-stopping!

The result would be that all air-breathing life on the earth would die. This would be accompanied by the subterranean fountains of water erupting and inundating the earth. Pity the individual standing on the spot where such a geyser erupted! Such a cataclysmic judgment seems incomprehensible, but God does not shirk from His holy acts. Noah acted in complete faith and spared humanity from total destruction through God's providence. But Noah could not repent for the rest of humanity. Each man is responsible for his own spiritual decisions. No one can choose for anyone else. That is the blessing of free will.

Leupold comments as follows:

> There is nothing vague about this last direction which is imparted to Noah. God speaks with authority as one who has absolute and perfect control of all issues involved. Noah will have seven days in which to com-

plete his preparations. Then there will break forth a rain whose exact duration divine providence has fixed and foreknows, a rain of forty days and nights. The number "forty" cannot be merely accidental. According to the scriptural use of numbers forty regularly describes a period of trial terminating in the victory of good and the overthrow of evil; see Num. 14:33; Exod. 24:18; 1 Kings 19:8; Jonah 3:4; Matt. 4:2; Acts 1:3.

Since the rule of evil has in this case become well-nigh universal, God determines to "wipe out all existence" (kol yeyum), that is, everything that stands up (allen Bestand). In the adjective clause "which I have made" lies both a sorrow at the thought that His own creatures should have degenerated thus, as well as the assertion of His right to destroy thus. What He has made, He may destroy.[114]

Another Judgment Day Is Coming

God does indeed reign over the entire created universe. He is the sovereign Judge to whom everyone must someday give account. The catastrophe of the worldwide Flood foreshadows the ultimate courtroom scene for man at the Great White Throne Judgment (Revelation 20:11–15). In that trial scene, there shall be no defense lawyers nor hope of acquittal. None will be needed. All present will be guilty by definition. Many tragically refuse salvation because of stubborn unbelief; others through negligence of God's sacred message.

114 H. C. Leupold, Exposition of Genesis: Volume 1, Chapters 1–19, p. 291.

Hebrews 10:28–29 presents this sobering message:

> Anyone who has rejected Moses' law dies without mercy on the testimony of two or three witnesses. Of how much worse punishment, do you suppose, will he be thought worthy who has trampled the Son of God underfoot, counted the blood of the covenant by which he was sanctified a common thing, and insulted the Spirit of grace?

Whichever the case may be, all that remains for them is an eternity in the Lake of Fire. Unbelievers, beware: Make your life right with God while there is still time. Believers: Share these truths with everyone you meet. God has granted us the privilege of being His ambassadors on this earth (2 Corinthians 5:20).

Lessons Learned in This Chapter

In this chapter, we first examined the comparison of the ark and the cross of Christ. Both were designed for the spiritual liberation of sinful mankind. Sadly, only a minority of mankind embraces the wondrous gift of salvation offered to mankind through Christ.

However, the spiritual deadness and wicked rebellion of Noah's day bear no resemblance to today's much more moderate world. In today's society, the Church has impacted the world in large swaths of society. This was not the case in the days of the Nephilim. Mankind had essentially become entirely corrupted save for Noah and his immediate family. A congregation of only eight people would prove discouraging to the average pastor. But imagine an entire world of only eight believers!

We were privileged to examine quite briefly the lives of several saints of God. A common quality among all of them was perseverance in the midst of trials. Paul declared the following in 2 Timothy 3:12: "Yes, and all who desire to live godly in Christ Jesus will suffer persecution." Although no persecution of Noah is recorded in Scripture, he must have suffered extreme mocking at the hands of the Nephilim. God clearly protected him sufficiently so he could carry on his preaching and construction work. But life would have been difficult for Noah and his family.

We also delved into various details regarding the ark. We asked how many animals would have been required. No one can answer that question today with certainty. But God was in charge of the entire operation. We thus rest secure in knowing that every type of land-dwelling creature was represented.

Second, we assessed a sampling of the numerous common objections to the Flood and the ark. The issues we addressed are reasonable inquiries. God does want people to use their minds and contemplate what He writes. One of the more common questions regards the dinosaurs. How could the ark have contained such immense creatures? The answer provided is really quite simple. God did not bring fully grown dinosaurs to Noah. He brought juveniles. They only had to be healthy and later on be able to procreate.

Third, we discussed the day that Noah entered into the ark. That was a fateful day, indeed. Once God shut the door behind Noah and his family, there was no longer any hope for redemption. The scarlet cord of forgiveness had been cut. A similar day awaits every human being. Life for the unbeliever does come to an end. As Hebrews 9:27 so powerfully reminds us: "And as it is appointed for men to die once, but after this the judgment."

The rains did not start for one week after entering the ark. Scripture does not explain the waiting period. The rabbis conjectured that it was a period of mourning for the death of Methuselah. It is possible that the Nephilim and company were laughing outside of the ark and pounding on the walls. They stopped laughing the moment the first raindrops started to fall. Hilarity ended; hysteria took over! One cannot mock God and win.

Many believe that God's grace and patience are infinite. It is not! Many have an entire lifetime allotted to avail themselves of God's benevolence, grace, and forgiveness. If ignored or reputed, all hope is lost. The unbeliever's destiny will be comparable to the Nephilim savagely pounding on the walls of the ark in desperation. But the door was shut, never to be opened to them again. We refer once again to 2 Corinthians 6:2: "For He says: 'In an acceptable time I have heard you, and in the day of salvation I have helped you.' Behold, now is the accepted time; behold, now is the day of salvation."

In our next chapter, we shall explore the issue of the global Flood versus the erroneous concept of a local flood. We shall see that the concept of a local flood is not only unbiblical, it flies in the face of all the evidence. The global Flood has the support of Scripture and a worldwide panorama of provable evidence. The local flood theory has only the fleeting testimony of the skeptic, absent all empirical evidence. It is indeed a pathetic failure.

The Day of Judgment Arrives

Cognitive Conundrum #14

A man of fantastic visions was I. Yes, indeed, the future I did behold; that was my creed. My words of Messiah stand without peer; my witness of truth brings forth much cheer. Life proved quite difficult for a man like me; my prophecies will come to pass for all to see. The Assyrian Empire gave me little fright, but I warned the Babylonians would take a big bite.

Who am I?

Answer: Isaiah

Chapter 15

Global Flood versus Local Flood (Genesis 7:6–24: Part A)

In This Chapter

Objectives for This Chapter
The Biblical Account of the Flood (7:6–16)
The Water Covered the Globe (7:17–24)
Lessons Learned in This Chapter

Objectives for This Chapter

A mere 1,656 years after God created the world and covered it in love He had to smother it in waves of water. In our modern day and age, a frequent mantra people loudly and enthusiastically shout out is that "God is love!" That is true. God is love (1 John 4:16). But God is also just. And God must eventually punish sin and sinner alike (Hebrews 10:26–30). That attribute is generally left out of the equation by the unbeliever.

In this chapter, we shall first discuss the events surrounding Noah's entrance into the ark. He did not go in alone. Noah was accompanied by seven of his faithful family members. It is almost certain that he had many more relatives than that. Unless they had already died before the Flood, they then died in the Flood. If true, how heartbreaking this must have been for this small nuclear family.

God provided a once-in-a-planet witness to the vile Nephilim of His upcoming judgment. They certainly could not miss it. Sadly, it was too late. The particular witness God provided was a seemingly unending parade of all the different types of land-dwelling, air-breathing animals into the ark. Every male was accompanied by its companion female. The unclean came in two-by-two, the clean seven-by-seven. It would appear that God led each type right into its designated pen area.

One does not otherwise herd lions, tigers, and bears about as if they were domesticated beasts. They tend to resent and resist being pushed about like that. They are known to express their discontentment with vigor! The Nephilim would have witnessed this unnatural parade with eyeballs nearly popping out of their heads. Still, they stubbornly did not repent of their wicked ways… not a single one of them! How caustic and cynical their souls had become through the corroding acid of sin. Another variable to remember is that God no longer allowed them to believe. Judgment day had come.

Second, we shall address that ever-perplexing question of why God allowed such wickedness to invade and defile the earth. We shall discuss several factors surrounding the circumstances. However, as the reader will soon discern, we cannot answer this question to complete satisfaction. One is not permitted to explain certain events that God Himself leaves inexplicable. Speculation must have its limits.

We take comfort, however, in the fact that God's grace is always greater than sin's myriad traps and entanglements. Hence, we adhere to the fact that mankind chose his own diabolical path. He was not innocently led with a nose in his ring to a merciless and unpredictable slaughter!

Third, we shall delve into the actual account of the Flood. We address the two sources of rain for the Flood. One perplexing and highly reasonable question in the minds of many concerns how much water is presently on the earth. Is there enough water to cover today's highest mountain peaks? The answer, with our present geography, is "no." There definitely is not sufficient water to cover Mount Everest.

So, how do we account for this? Psalm 104:6–9 provides the answer. This passage addresses the "sufficiency of water" question quite eloquently. However, this powerful passage is often overlooked due to some translation difficulties. Certain phrases can legitimately be translated in two ways due to the Hebrew grammar. We provide what we consider to be the more accurate of the two translations. When understood correctly, this passage of four verses resolves all potential difficulties regarding the sufficient water issue.

Fourth, we shall inspect several quotations that provide a detailed account of what transpired during the Flood. One of these quotations is by Alfred Russell Wallace. Even though an unrepentant biblical skeptic, he acknowledged that massive geological changes took place at some point in earth's history. If the earth had been less fragmented and more spherical historically, the earth would have been covered in water 1.7 miles deep!

Almost all geologists recognize this because of the fossils that are everywhere on the planet. Indeed, this evidence is impossible to ignore even by the most committed of evolutionists. One finds marine fossils on the tops of mountains. How did they get there? Obviously, absent of legs, they did not walk or climb. Hence, the mountains had to have been elevated at some point by massive, unprecedented earth movements. Oddly enough, most geologists willingly explain the fossils by earthly floods but completely deny a universal Flood.

Finally, throughout this chapter, we allude to the spiritual solution of mankind's sinful dilemma. That solution is none other than

Jesus Christ. He is the way, the truth, and the life. Just as God designed one door into the ark, there is only one door into heaven. Jesus proclaimed in John 10:9: "I am the door. If anyone enters by Me, he will be saved, and will go in and out and find pasture." An eternal question to all who read this book is as follows: Have you entered that spiritual door of Christ?

The Biblical Account of the Flood (Genesis 7:6–16)

The Bible makes it abundantly clear that the Flood inundated the entire globe with water. Even the highest mountains were hidden under its depths. During our review of the Flood, we shall be examining the biblical text and extra-biblical sources. This chapter reveals God's eternal attributes as few passages of the Bible can.

In this study, the attentive student will take great satisfaction in recognizing the veracity of Scripture. There is no reason whatsoever to doubt the biblical account, not only here but anywhere in Scripture. If one is to genuinely worship the God of the Bible as supreme, how can that same person accuse God of error or ignorance? That makes no sense whatsoever. If God is truly eternal and all-knowing, mistakes are not possible for Him (Isaiah 46:10). However, they are quite common and predictable for the mortal and fallible beings that He created.

Genesis 7:6–10 states:

> Noah was six hundred years old when the floodwaters were on the earth. So Noah, with his sons, his wife, and his sons' wives, went into the ark because of the waters of the flood. Of clean animals, of animals that are unclean, of birds, and of everything that creeps on the earth, two by two they went into the ark to Noah,

male and female, as God had commanded Noah. And it came to pass after seven days that the waters of the flood were on the earth.

The Entry into the Ark (Genesis 7:6–10)

Noah, the hero of the plot, lived to be the third oldest man in biblical history. He sojourned on this earth until he was 950 (Genesis 9:29). Hence, he outlived the Flood by 350 years, a remarkable feat indeed. This demonstrates that the 120 years mentioned in Genesis 6:3 primarily refers to the timing of the Flood. From the moment of God's warning to Noah a definite timeline was set. People could literally count down to their planned destruction… or potential redemption.

The 120 years may secondarily also refer to the duration of individual lifespans. However, even after the Flood, many individuals still lived to extraordinary ages. Noah's son Shem, for instance, lived until he was 600 (Genesis 11:10–11). That is 350 years less than Noah, but an appreciable age nonetheless.

Of course, lifespans did slowly decline in longevity as history progressed. Psalm 90:10 states: "The days of our lives are seventy years; and if by reason of strength they are eighty years, yet their boast is only labor and sorrow; for it is soon cut off, and we fly away." Incidentally, Moses, who wrote this passage, lived until he was 120.

The Hebrew text indicates the number of clean creatures by using the rather unusual grammatical construction of "two sevens" side by side in the text. As previously noted, scholars debate if this means seven or fourteen animals. From all appearances, however, it seems that fourteen is the proper number of clean animals that God brought into the ark. The extra numbers enabled Noah to perform sacrifices and also to help ensure rapid repopulation.

No "cattle roundup" has ever flowed more efficiently than God's "creature parade." With God, all things are possible (Luke 1:37). He makes the inconceivable a reality, the mysterious as understandable. All good things will eventually come to His children. But while sojourning on this earth, God's children must exercise patience and trust.

An Extraordinary Witness to the Nephilim

Apparently, the defilement of the Nephilim had totally destroyed any spiritual sensitivities within the general population. The Holy Spirit had been so stifled and repressed that He no longer functioned within the hearts of those foul half-demon and half-men. The women had also given themselves over to the service of Satan. Modern man cannot possibly envision the grotesque wickedness of that day and age.

Jesus the Messiah was the one and only God-man (John 1:14). By horrid contrast, in the antediluvian world, people had become demon-men. That is almost beyond comprehension. What kind of a world were Noah and his family inhabiting? One shudders to contemplate it. Is it any wonder that God had to destroy every person in the world outside of Noah and his family?

Satan's diabolical plot to destroy God's plan of redemption failed. The messianic Seed survived the Flood through Noah and his son Shem (Genesis 3:15). Satan foolishly hoped that he could so corrupt mankind that it would morally sink beyond redemption. He came incredibly close to accomplishing this, but nothing or no one can ever stymie the omniscient and omnipotent God.

What God has decreed will inevitably come to pass. Nothing

can stop it. Isaiah 45:22–23 reminds us of this truth:

> "Look to Me, and be saved, all you ends of the earth! For I am God, and there is no other. I have sworn by Myself; the word has gone out of My mouth in righteousness, and shall not return, that to Me every knee shall bow, every tongue shall take an oath" (cf. Philippians 2:9–11).

God, in His great mercy, postponed His judgment until the last moment, the "final Nephilim-plagued generation," so to speak. The demon-men no longer inhabit the earth, nor shall they ever do so again.

It is intriguing to note that in Hebrew mentality, the number "eight" represents restoration. There were eight souls on the ark. Jews also believe that day eight, figuratively speaking, represents the restoration of the earth. They think of it as the eighth day of creation. On that day, God will create everything new once again (2 Peter 3:10–13). It must be borne in mind that this fascinating viewpoint is traditional Jewish thinking; it is not based directly on Scripture.

The Day of Judgment Arrives: The Flood Begins (Genesis 7:11–16)

Genesis 7:11–16 unveils the day the world died, or at least the vast majority of it. Only the selected representatives of the air-breathing creatures that had walked onto the ark would survive. Countless fish would also die in the turbulent, watery cataclysm that was now to be unleashed on the globe by an almighty and sovereign God. Nonetheless, every species of fish survived by God's providence.

The Flood began seven days after Noah, his family, and the

animals were safely established on the ark (Genesis 7:1–4). As already noted, Jewish tradition believes that part of the reason for this one-week delay was to mourn the death of Methuselah. According to their tradition, he died on the same day they entered the ark. Although this is a truly intriguing tradition, it cannot be biblically proven. The waiting time of one week may also have been a test of Noah and his family's faith. Man tends to get impatient all too quickly!

Noah's family and all the animals entered the ark. When all was in readiness, God shut the door! What greater statement of finality can there be than that? Once God shut the door, no hope remained for those outside the ark. The inevitable, long-awaited judgment had arrived!

Genesis 7:11–16 states:

> In the six hundredth year of Noah's life, in the second month, the seventeenth day of the month, on that day all the fountains of the great deep were broken up, and the windows of heaven were opened. And the rain was on the earth forty days and forty nights.
>
> On the very same day Noah and Noah's sons, Shem, Ham, and Japheth, and Noah's wife and the three wives of his sons with them, entered the ark—they and every beast after its kind, all cattle after their kind, every creeping thing that creeps on the earth after its kind, and every bird after its kind, every bird of every sort. And they went into the ark to Noah, two by two, of all flesh in which is the breath of life. So those that entered, male and female of all flesh, went in as God

had commanded him; and the LORD shut him in.

Verse 13 can create confusion in the minds of some. The Flood did not start on the day that Noah, his family, and the animals entered the ark. This verse is referring back to God's initial statement to Noah in Genesis 7:1–4. As already noted, there was still a week's delay before the rains came. The precise day of the year is stated precisely in verse 11 for the start of the Flood in regards to Noah's life. It is: "In the six hundredth year of Noah's life, in the second month, the seventeenth day of the month." According to biblical chronology, the Flood took place 1,656 years after the creation of the world. In that relatively short period of time, all of humanity had corrupted itself.

How Could the World Become So Corrupt?

Question: How is such wholesale corruption possible in 1,656 years? How could mankind have become so spiritually unresponsive and wicked? One must recall that only ten generations had passed. Answer: The total corruption was due to the demonic influence of the Nephilim. These half-demonic, half-human beings caused a near-total moral collapse.

Does this mean that every person outside of the ark had been corrupted by the Nephilim? The text does not specifically state that in so many words, but it does seem to be a distinct possibility, horrifying as it may seem. It certainly would help explain the complete lack of response to Noah's message of faith and repentance. The few remaining righteous people, if any, such as Methuselah, died before God shut the door. Hence, the Jewish tradition emphasizes the possibility that Methuselah lived until the day Noah and his family entered the ark.

It also explains why the particular demons involved in this deviant sexual activity were imprisoned in Tartarus. They shall never be released but will suffer eternal punishment. Their judgment is amply deserved! These particular demons are twice-fallen. They first rebelled against God; they second rebelled against their own spirit nature. We reiterate that not all demonic forces were guilty of this vile transgression. Many are still left to roam free, including Satan himself (1 Peter 5:8).

Scripture makes it abundantly clear that Jesus cast out many demons. But it is not recorded precisely where the demons went when exorcised. Satan will be bound during the millennial kingdom of Christ for 1,000 years. But he will then be released for a time to tempt the nations again. When the final rebellion has taken place, he will perpetually be imprisoned in the Lake of Fire (Revelation 20:7–10). Thankfully, his days of tempting the saints will at last be over permanently. Those who enter into the eternal kingdom of God will never be tempted again (21:1–4).

Why?

This uncomfortable question quite naturally arises in the minds of many: Why did God allow the Nephilim to ever influence the earth? If our understanding is correct, God allowed the "sons of God," which we interpret as fallen angels, to cohabit with the "daughters of men," the women of earth. That very thought sounds repugnant enough. This cohabitation then created the Nephilim. They were the offspring of these unholy and completely unnatural matrimonies. In order to understand this scenario, several factors must be considered.

Factor #1: God created Adam and Eve with a free will. Without a free will, genuine worship is not possible. Even the angels had a free will. Some, to their eternal regret, chose to follow that free will and use it to rebel against their Creator, just as Satan did. They foolishly rejected their perfect Creator and followed the imperfect, indeed the absolutely evil Lucifer. One ponders how the angels could have been so deceived, but deceived one-third of them were.

A major difference between angels and men is that the angels were granted a one-time decision. They could decide for or against God. That decision was permanent, irrevocable. Scripture offers few details on this spiritual status regarding the angels. Tragically, one-third of them chose to rebel (Revelation 12:3–4). Redemption is not possible for the angels! Either they remained in their holy estate, or they abandoned it forever.

Matthew 25:41 reminds us: "Then He will also say to those on the left hand, 'Depart from Me, you cursed, into the everlasting fire prepared for the devil and his angels.'" Jesus Christ died for human beings, not for angels (John 3:16). There is no hope of redemption for the fallen angels.

Regarding Matthew 25:41, MacArthur comments as follows:

> Jesus is speaking of eternal separation from God and from His goodness, righteousness, truth, joy, peace, and every other good thing. He is speaking of eternal association with the devil and his angels in the place of torment God prepared for them. He is speaking of eternal isolation, where there will be no fellowship, no consolation, and no encouragement. He is speaking of eternal duration and of eternal affliction, from which there will be no relief or respite.[115]

---

[115] John MacArthur, The MacArthur's New Testament Commentary: Matthew 24–28 (Chicago: Moody Press, 1989), p. 125.

God's Perfect versus His Permissive Will

Factor #2: God created Adam and Eve to live forever. Spiritual death was not in God's perfect will, but it was allowed in His permissive will (Ezekiel 18:30–32). The potential of death was necessary if man was to exercise his free will. If man had not been granted a free will, he would have existed merely as a highly programmed robot. God did not seek fellowship or worship from a mindless, emotionless, and volition-less creature. He created a limited edition of Himself.

There are those who quite naturally will protest the present state of human affairs. They will assert that this potential for sin was "just not fair"! After all, they argue, God knew that man would fail. Ironically, the only reason they can issue such protests against God's provision for free will is to exercise their own God-given free will. They could not even think such independent thoughts without the benefit of their free will.

While believers and unbelievers alike mourn the results of sin, they would not have the capacity to mourn at all without free will. Life would be nothing more than a monotonous, mindless, spiritless routine. In other words, man would exist, not actually live. As Job openly expressed to his wife, we must receive the bad with the good (Job 2:10).

God Knows All in Advance

Since God is eternal, all things from beginning to end are known by Him, including the plan of redemption through His Son, Jesus Christ (Isaiah 46:10; Revelation 13:8). As hard as it is for the human mind to grasp, God learns nothing! He knows everything already. All His decrees have been established from eternity.

His foreknowledge does not eliminate free will, contrary to what some teach. Scripture admittedly speaks with "conditionally-oriented" language for the purpose of human communication (cf. Genesis 6:6–7). That is because man can only understand things with a time orientation. We cannot think with eternal understanding or principles with our finite minds. We can believe in eternity, but we cannot truly comprehend it.

Ecclesiastes 3:11 states: "He has made everything beautiful in its time. Also He has put eternity in their hearts, except that no one can find out the work that God does from beginning to end." God continuously reaches out to every human being. Every child born has an instinct of a Supreme Being. This is the eternity placed in man's heart. It must be intentionally wrested away from the unsuspecting child by moral reprobates if it is to be entirely removed.

Children only need to have their minds and hearts directed toward God through the Bible. Tragically, the world's present Western-style education system does precisely the opposite. It attempts to excise the holy and eternal and transform into the godless temporal. This is a wretched travesty for everyone involved. All shall answer to the eternal God for their earthly decisions.

Doubly tragic, many ungodly parents drive their children away from the Creator. They teach their children to either doubt or deny God entirely. Those parents are accountable to God for their actions. Not only do such parents drive their children toward immorality, they help deprive them of a sense of well-being and eternal purpose. Is it any small wonder that so many individuals resort to violence? Most direct the violence toward others. But an increasing number are afflicting their own persons with drugs, alcohol, and often suicide. To such individuals, life is nothing more than futility and hopelessness.

Sin Remains a Perpetual Anchor

Factor #3: God created Adam and Eve with the capacity not to sin. Only Adam and Eve of all humanity born, save Jesus Christ, possessed this capacity. This sinless propensity is completely impossible for believers to relate to in our modern age. As Christians, we continuously struggle with both an old and a new nature.

These dual natures should strike one as an unnatural shackling together. Indeed, that is precisely the case. It is unnatural. When we are removed to heaven, the old nature will, at long last, be dissolved and excised from us permanently. Until then, the spiritual struggle continues.

Sadly, this moral coupling remains the reality all believers must continuously deal with while on this earth. Even the apostle Paul constantly fought against his evil tendencies (Romans 7:14–21). Unfortunately, sinning comes almost as naturally as breathing to believer and unbeliever alike. We cannot entirely escape our evil tendencies because we cannot escape ourselves.

Thankfully, believers will someday experience deliverance from their evil nature. That occurs when we pass from this life into heaven or when the Rapture comes. There, we shall at last be gloriously free from the chains of our sinful nature. Romans 7:24–25 states: "O wretched man that I am! Who will deliver me from this body of death? I thank God—through Jesus Christ our Lord! So then, with the mind I myself serve the law of God, but with the flesh the law of sin."

Free at Last!

Paul writes in Romans 8:35–39:

Who shall separate us from the love of Christ? Shall

tribulation, or distress, or persecution, or famine, or nakedness, or peril, or sword? As it is written: "For Your sake we are killed all day long; we are accounted as sheep for the slaughter." Yet, in all these things we are more than conquerors through Him who loved us.

For I am persuaded that neither death nor life, nor angels nor principalities nor powers, nor things present nor things to come, nor height nor depth, nor any other created thing, shall be able to separate us from the love of God which is in Christ Jesus our Lord.

Is there anything, anything at all, that can separate the believer from his Lord? No, nothing in heaven or on earth can remove us from the Father's hand. When we have the power of almighty God supporting us, how can we possibly fail? In John 10:27–30, Jesus declares,

> "My sheep hear My voice, and I know them, and they follow Me. And I give them eternal life, and they shall never perish; neither shall anyone snatch them out of My hand. My Father, who has given them to Me, is greater than all; and no one is able to snatch them out of My Father's hand. I and My Father are one."

Donald Grey Barnhouse offers the following words of comfort regarding Romans 8:35–39:

> Sheep for slaughter! More than conquerors! What a contrast! And how? "Stand still..." "Sit still..." "Be still..." And as we are still, resting in our God, our

seeming losses are turned into gains; our wounds become badges of honor; our trials become precious; our tribulations lead to patience, and patience brings its perfect work.

Our sufferings are not worthy to be compared with the glory that shall be revealed in us (Rom. 8:18). "Therefore [we] take pleasure in infirmities, in reproaches, in necessities, in persecutions, in distresses for Christ's sake: for when [we are] weak, then [we are] strong" (2 Cor. 12:10).[116]

Life Wasn't Just Good; It Was Perfect!

Factor #4: God blessed Adam and Eve with a perfect environment. Consider this! There was no sin, no death, no disease, no anger, no famine, no pain, no sorrow, no marital conflict, no shortage of anything, no separation from loved ones, no danger, and no warfare; they and the animals were vegetarians and lived in total peace with each other. There were not even any taxes!

Adam and Eve experienced a complete, unique, and marvelous relationship with God. They literally walked and talked with God every day. Not even Moses experienced a living relationship like that with God. No sinful nature inhibited their wonderful fellowship. That blessed situation has never been experienced by any other human being since Adam and Eve! Adam and Eve lived in total peace with God and with each other. In addition, they were blessed with a perfect temperature on the earth as they did not even need clothes. They had perfect nutrition; the entire world was lush and

---

[116] Donald Grey Barnhouse, Romans III: God's Grace, God's Freedom, God's Heirs (Grand Rapids: MI: Wm. B. Eerdmans Publishing Company, 1959), p. 204.

fruitful, and the animals were all friendly.

Perhaps man and animal even smiled at one another as they passed! Imagine two tigers grinning at Adam and Eve and bowing to them as they crossed paths. No, the Bible does not actually teach that, but it is a pleasant thought, is it not? If a tiger smiled at a man today, it would decidedly not produce the same heartwarming reaction. Adam and Eve's every conceivable need was met in abundance. And yet, in spite of it all, they chose the wrong path.

Sin Personified at Its Worst!

Factor #5: When you fall from a state of perfection, sin rears its ugly head with every evil device imaginable. God allowed for this tragic scenario. He had provided every possible benefit to mankind only to have His love rejected. Man fell from perfection to an all-consuming perversity. Adam and Eve chose to eat the fruit in disobedience to God's command. This should not be construed as a defiant attitude. They were sinless; they did not know what it meant to be defiant. But they did have curiosity and desires, which led them astray. They wanted to be like God!

It is true that Eve was deceived by the serpent. But Adam sinned willfully and with a more complete knowledge of what he was doing. This is not to say that Adam had full understanding of what he was doing. He did not yet have a sinful nature. So, in a very strange and foreign sense to us today, he did not sin with a rebellious attitude. But Adam, nonetheless, bears the primary responsibility for sin entering the world.

This particular sin does not sound like a terrible transgression in comparison to the terrors of today. But it was this very sin that gave birth to all other sins. The progression of evil went from bad to horrible in short order. Their firstborn son murdered his own brother. But immeasurably worse, it culminated with the unimaginable tragedy of demons cohabiting with women. The result was the vile Nephilim.

God's Grace Has Always Reached Out to Man

Factor #6: God continued to reach out in grace to mankind. He did not immediately send the Flood. In fact, He waited for 1,656 years before passing judgment on wicked mankind. That is the supreme definition of patience! People could still call on the Lord. Adam and Eve could still share, albeit in a much more limited sense, times of intimacy with their Creator. God did not cut off their opportunity for worship and fellowship. Each generation had the privilege and responsibility of passing on the spiritual baton to the next. Adam and Eve did just that. Sadly, the baton was now tainted with sin.

Genesis 15:16 records a similar example of God's patience: "But in the fourth generation they shall return here, for the iniquity of the Amorites is not yet complete." That patience extended a rather lengthy 430 years. That is the time frame from Abraham's initial sojourn into the Promised Land until the fledgling nation Israel left Egypt (Exodus 12:40–41). Then, because of Israel's disobedience, the Amorites were granted an additional forty years to repent. They utterly refused to do so. Their punishment under the hands of God and Israel was well-deserved.

God did not stop His spiritual message from going forth to humanity. In fact, Noah preached it for 120 years. God's messengers and children continue proclaiming His Word to this day. But in spite of all God's gracious and historic efforts to redeem a fallen mankind, they typically have persisted in their disobedience. The end result in Noah's day was the Flood, which destroyed the entirety of the world. Only Noah and his family were saved in the ark.

It must be tacitly admitted that there is much about the pre-Flood world that we do not understand. The observant student recognizes that we cannot fully answer the question of why God allowed the Nephilim scenario. We shall never understand those historic conditions of the earth in our present era. We are limited to discussing extenuating circumstances.

We cannot relate to such a fall from perfection into the worst, vile sins imaginable. But we do know from the rest of Scripture that God always seeks forgiveness and reconciliation. The factors we presented shed some light on the issue, but for the present era, it is not to be fully understood.

It must be remembered that this ongoing spiritual benevolence is largely one-sided. God is the one offended, and yet God does the forgiving of the offender. It is our loving God who first reaches out to man for potential reconciliation. Man cannot do so because he is born sinful and dead in his sins. He stands incapable of reaching out to God without first being drawn by Him (John 6:44; Ephesians 2:1–2).

To make things even more lopsided, God is the one who provides the provision for forgiveness. Man only responds to this potential forgiveness. We have no ability to pay for our sins (Isaiah 64:6; Ephesians 2:8–9). The greatest evidence of God's compassion is the willing sacrifice of His Son for our sins (John 3:16, 5:24). What greater gift can man receive than this?

How the world became so utterly evil remains something of a mystery. We cannot answer every question or curiosity. It admittedly seems highly incongruous that God allowed the demons to cohabit with earthly women. Nonetheless, that is precisely what happened. However, we are not privy to all of God's former methods of communication to mankind. God's grace has always been greater than Satan's ploys and temptations. We may safely assume that it was man's willing choice, not God's desire, for such a calamity to take place.

Tragic Result of Unbridled Sin!

The Nephilim apparently contaminated all of mankind save Noah and his immediate family circle. Those who remained undefiled died before the Flood. Genesis 6:5 reminds us of the calamitous results of sin: "Then the LORD saw that the wickedness of man was great in the earth, and that every intent of the thoughts of his heart was only evil continually."

Concerning the wickedness of man's heart, John Gill offers the following comments:

> That it spread throughout the earth, wherever it was inhabited by men, both among the posterity of Cain and Seth, and who indeed now were mixed together, and became one people; this respects actual transgressions, the wicked actions of men, and those of the grosser sort, which were multiplied, as the word also signifies; they were both great in quality and great in quantity; they were frequently committed, and that everywhere;
>
> the degeneracy was become universal; there was a flood of impiety that spread and covered the whole earth, before the deluge of waters came, and which was the cause of it; this God saw, not only by His omniscience, by which He sees everything, but He took no-

tice of it in His providence, and was displeased with it, and determined in His mind to shew His resentment of it, and let men see that He observed it, and disapproved of it, and would punish for it.[117]

The Flood Strikes!

Punishment of an unimaginable nature did indeed finally arrive. The Flood destroyed all of God's beautiful creation. Mankind, save those in the ark, perished. All land creatures smothered under the powerful waves. Creatures cowered in fear at the sudden and unrelenting deluge of rain, the flashing lightning, and the crashing thunder. The waters grew steadily more violent and ever deeper. Necks stretched higher and higher, but to no avail.

At last, no refuge of open land from the waves beckoned to either man or beast. What a tragedy to find that all hope for deliverance was gone. God spoke firmly, and mankind, who had steadfastly resisted His holy will, succumbed to it at long last. All finally capitulated to God's universal and holy judgment! Sadly, all richly deserved the watery tomb into which they passed. There were no innocents remaining on the earth.

The Two Sources of Water for the Universal Flood

Two sources of water are mentioned for the Flood. First, the fountains of the "great deep" were broken up. An immense amount of subterranean water existed before the Flood and still does to this day in the form of aquifers. God supernaturally broke up the crust of the earth in order to release this water. That almost certainly caused immense geysers of water to rocket skyward.

---
117 John Gill, Exposition of the Old & New Testaments: Volume 1 of 9, p. 47.

The release of these waters under immense pressure resulted in spectacular fountains. Yellowstone National Park and other regions of the world witness similar but much smaller geysers to this day. We also see a parallel of this type of physiological action on a much larger scale in volcanic eruptions. The difference is that one involves water, possibly superheated, and the other magma.

When the fountains of the "great deep" broke up, they were accompanied by immense earthquakes. The resulting compression in certain areas would have sent the geysers soaring to spectacular heights. These earthquakes quite literally cracked the earth's foundational crust in sundry places around the globe. Immense land masses would have dropped drastically in some regions and been uplifted in others (Psalm 104:6–9). The catastrophic results from these geysers of water with the accompanying volcanic action cannot be completely envisioned today.

Rain, Rain, Rain!

Second, the windows of the heavens were opened. It rained nonstop for forty days and nights. This should not be thought of as a gentle spring rain. It was undoubtedly a deluge never since equaled on the earth. This rainfall was initially caused by what may have been a water vapor canopy surrounding the earth. The water canopy theory is debated among creationists today. There are excellent arguments both for and against the canopy theory. One of the objections is that this reputed canopy could not hold that much liquid water, or it would cause other physical problems on earth.

However, the canopy did not have to contain such a huge amount of water, as some people envision. How so? When the fountains of the deep broke up and were accompanied by volcanic action and earthquakes, an unimaginable amount of steam would have been created. This steam, superheated as it was, naturally rose high into the atmosphere, where it would have condensed into liquid form. Hence, the subterranean sources of water could easily have replenished the atmospheric waters for quite some time, forty days at least.

Henry M. Morris III, the son of the eminent Henry Morris, explains as follows:

> The subterranean reservoirs of water broke open, likely a steam mixed with magma. Ocean floors erupted and gaped open. Land-based sources split and spread in a worldwide cataclysm that occurred on the seventeenth day of the Hebrew month Iyar, when Noah was 600 years old. Water surged up and out. Land surfaces collapsed. Continental shelving was broken and sucked down into the widening maw of the ocean deep, and tsunamis began to heave back and forth across the land surfaces.
>
> Such geological energies would have triggered magma rents, and volcanic pressures would have exploded into enormous fire blooms of such intensity that anything in their paths would have been incinerated. Such explosive energies would have pulverized the land surfaces and blown them into the highest reaches of Earth's atmosphere. The "windows of heaven" would have begun to collapse in a deluge that would make a summer thunderstorm seem like a spring sprinkle.

No one knows for sure how the "waters above" were contained. The Bible merely hints at columns and foundations and beams. Something that God did during the second day of the creation week positioned some enormous volume of water above the planet.

Now, with the fountains of the great deep exploding all over the globe, the upper reserves would begin to coalesce around the tiny land-based particles that were rocketing skyward, resulting in a 40-day inundation so rapid and awful that catching a mouthful of air would have been almost impossible. Billions of creatures died during that year. The fossil record is the result of that terrible Flood. Some could swim, waddle, run, flee, and ride out the horror for a time, but ultimately "all flesh died" (Genesis 7:20).[118]

Not One Square Foot of Dry Land Remained

The combined sources of water inundated the world completely. All air-breathing flesh that was not on the ark died in the Flood. This is a distinct, God-caused event that is unique in the history of the earth. No flood like it shall ever occur again. God grants this promise in Genesis chapter 9. The terrors of those days defy the imagination. Mankind had no comprehension of what was headed his way, though Noah had warned them for 120 years.

Jeremiah 17:9–10 states: "The heart is deceitful above all things, and desperately wicked; who can know it? I, the LORD, search the

---

[118] Henry M. Morris III, Unlocking the Mysteries of Genesis: Explore the Science and Miracles of Creation, pp. 97–98.

heart, I test the mind, even to give every man according to his ways, according to the fruit of his doings." The wickedness of man's heart has never known the equal since the days of the Nephilim.

There are many things we do not understand about the Flood and its various causes. Perhaps, we shall receive further revelation of it in the future. For now, however, it is beneficial to examine it for the sake of understanding God's wondrous working power. One must always remember that God is sovereign above all. We worship God because, by definition, God is to be worshipped! We now refer to the father of Henry M. Morris III. Both men are highly regarded as outstanding scientists.

Regarding the subterranean waters, the elder statesman Henry Morris writes as follows:

> Such subterranean reservoirs were apparently all interconnected with each other, as well as with the surface seas into which the rivers drained, so that the entire complex constituted one "great deep." The energy for repressurizing and recycling the waters must have come from the earth's own subterranean heat implanted there at Creation.

> This entire system must have been a marvelous heat engine, which would have operated with wonderful effectiveness indefinitely, as long as the earth's internal heat endured and as long as the system of reservoirs, valves, governors, and conduits maintained their structure. The details of its design were not revealed, but such a system is quite feasible hydraulically and thermodynamically, and there is no reason to question the Creator's ability to

provide it for the world He had made.

When the time for the destruction of this world arrived, however, all that was required was to bring the two "deeps" together again, as they had been when first created. The waters above the firmament must be condensed and precipitated, and the waters below the crust must burst their bonds and escape again to the surface.[119]

A Local Flood? Absolutely Not!

Some people have endeavored to explain how all of these profound actions took place simultaneously through natural causes. Then why has a comparable flood never happened a second or third time? If not a global flood, certainly there should be repetition of cataclysmic floods that inundate entire low-lying countries. Furthermore, if the Flood was entirely natural, what connection can one make with the fact that God was punishing the world for its sinful behavior? The Flood would then have no moral purpose or punishment for sin whatsoever. It would simply be a natural tragedy.

The resolution is really quite simple. God caused it to happen; it had a supernatural origin! End of story! Scientists can today describe what transpired on the earth based on the biblical story. But one should never assume that the Flood came from purely natural explanations. There was nothing natural about the calamity of the Flood.

Furthermore, if the Flood was purely natural, then how did God know when to gather the animals and tell Noah when to get on the

---

[119] Henry M. Morris, The Genesis Record, p. 195.

ark? How did God know that the rain would begin one week after Noah got on the ark? How did He know that the subterranean waters would erupt? How did He predict the Flood 120 years in advance?

Although God used natural forces, the beginning and duration of the Flood were unquestionably supernatural. God controlled the entire process. He decreed that it would rain forty days and nights. The consequences and the evidences for the Flood can and should be explored. But the actual and final cause is God. On that undeniable truth, we rest our case.

The Water Covered the Globe (Genesis 7:17–24)

Ironically, albeit understandably, modern secular scientists are willing to admit that floods caused many of the geological features of our modern world. They also confess that the best way to produce fossils is through a flood. But most of them still deny Noah's Flood. They cannot bring themselves to admit that a flood covered the entire globe. Are these scientists being entirely arbitrary in their skepticism? No, not entirely, even though they are decidedly wrong. After all, how often do you see a global flood? Never! However, local floods occur almost nonstop around the globe.

Quite understandably, skeptics object that there is not enough water to cover Mount Everest, or most other mountain ranges for that matter. They are correct in that assessment. So, how does one resolve that concern? We shall momentarily be addressing that issue.

In addition, no one, save Noah and his family, has ever witnessed the worldwide Flood and lived to tell about it. Some of those same scientists are possibly ignorant of the wealth of extra-biblical testimony regarding the worldwide Flood. We refer not only to fossils and other geological evidence but to written records and traditions as well. Though historical records are frequently vulnerable to error, they are not to be cast off in a wholesale manner. After all, how can modern man improve on even a sketchy secular history? None of us were there!

A Willful Ignorance

Is such ignorance regarding the Flood by well-educated scientists or others reasonable? No, it is not. The array of evidence supporting the Flood is overwhelming! Unfortunately, many modern scientists have been so academically misled that they reject any concept of the universal Flood. Many of these same scientists reject any concept of a Supreme Being as well. So, they simply ignore the worldwide evidence. Such an attitude does not engender a sound scientific method. It makes one wonder whether they are willing to ignore less attractive evidences of research in their own fields.

It is that very same close-minded attitude that allows the evolutionist to accept six completely unsupported false concepts: (1) the quantum fluctuation; (2) the big bang; (3) spontaneous generation; (4) acceptance of a "no-transition" fossil record; (5) punctuated equilibrium; (6) the existence of nonmaterial information. Each one of these six pronouncements carries a scientific death sentence for evolution.

Hence, evolutionists are six times duped! That is tragic. There is no actual evidence for any of these six scientific heresies. Yet highly trained professional scientists casually accept them. It is not because of any justifiable empirical evidence. The true, entirely subjective reason is that they will not "allow a divine foot in the door." They are solely and entirely sold out to materialism.

How ironic that viewpoint is since the immaterial surrounds them on all sides. That includes their own thought processes. How can something that is entirely material, the brain, actually conjure up nonmaterial thoughts, feelings, and opinions? No scientist has ever explained that profound mystery.

Indeed, many evolutionists glibly assert that our brains are merely haphazard arrangements of material stimulated by random electrical impulses. One ponders what manner of purely random electrical impulses allowed so many of them to arrive at that same conclusion. This writer contemplates the mystery of why his own electrical impulses arrived at an entirely different conclusion. Tis' a conundrum! Why should this writer, who believes God created his mind, entertain any faith in the evolutionist's (by his own admission) disorganized and electrically charged mass of gray matter?

Those Who Deny the Flood Are Playing a Game with No Rules

When you start out with a false premise and then use false evidence, you will inevitably end up with a false conclusion. This is obvious to anyone with an unprejudiced mind. Yet, it happens daily with thousands of scientists regarding the origins of this universe. Every day, they faithfully utilize the scientific laws developed by the Creator and then turn around and deny the Creator of those same scientific laws. That is extraordinary! Do they never question why the universe works with clock-like precision? Why are all these laws so consistent?

For example, where did the laws governing mathematics originate? We use mathematics every single day, but these laws are not material. They are abstract. Two plus two equals four. How does evolution account for the consistency of that truth? As far as we know, those same laws work over the entire universe. Why do they work? Did all these laws just happen by accident?

Some explain that man invented the laws of mathematics, but

that is untrue. Indeed, that is preposterous. If math can be invented by man, then man should also be able to un-invent all mathematical formulas. Some may have even tried. What is the result of their vain attempts? Two plus two still equals four. It doesn't change. Man did not create mathematics; he can only discover math's wonderfully consistent laws. They are ironclad.

The Mysteries of a Mythical Explosion

How did this incredible reliability all come about from a massive explosion? The simple answer is: It didn't! You can extend this reality to virtually all branches of science. Somebody or something must have originated these laws. We will vie for Somebody. His name is God.

Scripture clearly relates a law of biology in Leviticus 17:11: "For the life of the flesh is in the blood, and I have given it to you upon the altar to make atonement for your souls; for it is the blood that makes atonement for the soul." This passage, written thousands of years ago by Moses under the inspiration of the Holy Spirit, makes the function of blood quite clear. Blood is essential for physical life. In addition, the blood provides spiritual life through the foreshadowing blood of the sacrificial animals. Those animals, however, only prefigured the later atoning blood sacrifice of Jesus Christ (1 Peter 1:18–19).

Modern science did not recognize the importance of the blood until recent centuries. Medical doctors were still "bleeding" their patients via leeches or cutting open a vein as recently as President George Washington. If medical scientists had paid closer attention to the Scriptures, they would have realized how dangerous their practice really was for the patient. Yet some of the best medical minds of George Washington's day missed the point of Leviticus

17:11 entirely.

Every time the Scriptures speak scientifically, it has been proven true. That is truly extraordinary for a book which, in certain parts, is 3,500 years old. Indeed, many of the parts which do make scientific statements are the oldest sections of Scripture. How many modern science books can make this claim? None! That is why they are constantly being rewritten and expanded.

Spiritual Life Comes Through Christ Alone

The spiritual life aspect was provided by Christ's shedding His perfect blood on the cross. Prior to Christ's crucifixion, animals were sacrificed as a symbol of the coming perfect Sacrifice. This is arguably why Cain's sacrifice was not acceptable. It was not a blood sacrifice. There were undoubtedly other factors involved in that situation, as his murderous behavior attests.

Hebrews 9:14 states: "How much more shall the blood of Christ, who through the eternal Spirit offered Himself without spot to God, cleanse your conscience from dead works to serve the living God?" The perfect blood of Christ alone can satisfy the demands of a holy God. Sin requires a perfect sacrifice. God desired sacrifices from Noah after he left the ark. Again, these symbolized a covering for sin but not a permanent removal of it. That could only come when Christ came to this earth as God's sacrificial and substitutionary Lamb.

Most schoolchildren have heard about Noah's Flood and the ark with all the animals on it. Unfortunately, they are generally introduced to a fake picture of the ark. There often is a couple of giraffes sticking their heads out of a window and other creatures running around the deck. The animals basically look like they are crammed into a small boat with very little room. That picture is designed to create doubt, not faith. Secularists use such pictures to communicate that the story of the Flood and the ark is untrue. Sadly, many children believe them.

Ignorance Decidedly Is Not Bliss!

Ignorance of the ark and the Flood is not a plausible excuse. As already stated numerous times, the evidence is worldwide. We shall review what the Bible specifically teaches about the Flood. We shall also examine the sundry evidences supporting the biblical record. Tragically, even many Christians deny the universal Flood.

Ken Ham and Bodie Hodge cite one professing Christian teacher who erroneously wrote:

> The flood was indeed a river flood. … The language of Genesis allows for a regional flood. … The parts of modern Iraq which were occupied by the ancient Sumerians are extremely flat. The floodplain, surrounding the Tigris and the Euphrates rivers, covers over 50,000 square miles which slope toward the gulf at less than one foot per mile. … Drainage is extremely poor and flooding is quite common, even without large rainstorms during the summer river-level peak (when Noah's flood happened).[120]

That written assessment is completely ridiculous! A child can read and comprehend the biblical story of the Flood better than that particular teacher! Even if the child refuses to believe what he reads, he will not come up with such a nonsensical conclusion that the Bible is referring to a local flood. The Bible is unambiguous in its

---

120 Ken Ham and Bodie Hodge, A Flood of Evidence: 40 Reasons Why Noah and the Ark Still Matter (Green Forest, AR: Master Books, 2016), p. 91.

message. Besides, what is so unusual about a local flood? They happen every day around the earth.

This also means that God is a liar since He promised that never again would He send such a Flood. He stated that the rainbow in the sky was visible proof of His promise. That can only be true if God is referring to a global Flood. How could a local flood kill all of mankind and all the land-dwelling creatures? Why would the living, both man and beast, simply not walk to higher ground? Are we really to believe that humanity and creatures alike were that impossibly stupid or uncoordinated?

Were all humans and animals living in such a tight area as to be within or immediately around the Tigris and Euphrates rivers? According to the viewpoint of the above-quoted Christian teacher, the Bible is either flatly false or God is a liar. Neither position is acceptable in true Christianity.

No fair-minded individual can possibly come up with a local flood position based on Scripture. One has to intentionally be misled by others or mislead himself to believe such a clearly unbiblical viewpoint. No straightforward reading of Scripture can support the local flood theory. One must read the Bible wearing "evolutionary glasses" to be so misled.

Creationists Believe in the Bible and Science

Why do many Christians so willingly reject what the Scripture teaches? They are trying to match up the Bible with the billions of years science falsely claims for the age of the earth. They commit the tragic error of elevating fallible science on a higher plain than infallible Scripture (Romans 1:22). It never seems to occur to them to examine the actual evidence with an open, inquiring, and unprejudiced mind. That is most unfortunate.

There is no excuse for such irresponsible behavior by Christian leaders! The supporting evidence for the veracity of Scripture is massive and grows by the day. Furthermore, the alleged "science" regarding the age of the earth has been proven fallacious repeatedly.

Christians are responsible for what they believe and teach others. If a self-proclaimed Christian leader stands in front of other believers and teaches contrary to the Scriptures, it is time for him to sit down and seek another vocation. James 3:1 warns all of us: "My brethren, let not many of you become teachers, knowing that we shall receive a stricter judgment." Unfortunately, all too many leaders do not take this verse seriously.

The Extent of the Flood Is Global (Genesis 7:17–24)

Genesis 7:17–24 states:

> Now the flood was on the earth forty days. The waters increased and lifted up the ark, and it rose high above the earth. The waters prevailed and greatly increased on the earth, and the ark moved about on the surface of the waters. And the waters prevailed exceedingly on the earth, and all the high hills under the whole heaven were covered. The waters prevailed fifteen cubits upward, and the mountains were covered.

> And all flesh died that moved on the earth: birds and cattle and beasts and every creeping thing that creeps on the earth, and every man. All in whose nostrils was the breath of the spirit of life, all that was on the dry land, died.

So He destroyed all living things which were on the face of the ground: both man and cattle, creeping things and birds of the air. They were destroyed from the earth. Only Noah and those who were with him in the ark remained alive. And the waters prevailed on the earth one hundred and fifty days (cf. Hebrews 11:7; 2 Peter 3:5).

Potential Problem with the Highest Mountains?

One of the most obvious and understandable objections to the global Flood is that there is not enough water in the world to cover Mount Everest. That is correct! Mount Everest is presently 29,029 feet high. The Bible makes it abundantly clear that the waters covered the entire globe. Indeed, if they did not, why would all of the animals and humans have died? They simply would have fled to higher ground.

But how could there have been so much water as to cover Mount Everest? Simply put, there wasn't that much water then or now to cover Mount Everest at its present height. The earth in Noah's day was markedly different than the earth of today. Even secular scientists will acknowledge this, but not for the same reasons. Their solution will be based entirely on topographical solutions. The creationist's solution utilizes both geology and the Bible.

Solution to the Highest Mountain Problem

Mount Everest and other mountain ranges were not always as high as they are in our present day. We shall be examining Psalm 104:6–9. Some commentators feel this entire chapter focuses on

Corruption and Catastrophe

God's original creation of the heavens and earth. Clearly, part of it does, but definitely not all of it. A careful reading of the passage does not allow for such an interpretation.

For example, verse 21 states: "The young lions roar after their prey, and seek their food from God." This describes life after the fall. Before the fall, all creatures were vegetarians. Verse 35 states: "May sinners be consumed from the earth, and the wicked be no more." There were no sinners before the fall. Hence, Psalm 104 must be read with an objective eye. In actuality, it is divided up into several natural sections. In our personal estimation, the chapter begins with creation, expands to the Flood, and then continues on to describe the post-Flood world.

Psalm 104:6–9

Using the New American Standard Bible (NASB), which, in this writer's opinion, more accurately reflects the Hebrew, Psalm 104:6–9 states:

> You covered it with the deep as with a garment; the waters were standing above the mountains. At Your rebuke they fled, at the sound of Your thunder they hurried away. The mountains rose, the valleys sank down to the place which You established for them. You set a boundary that they may not pass over, so that they will not return to cover the earth.

Intriguingly, there are two different ways in which verse 8 is translated in various versions. Both are permissible, but one is contextually preferable.

Translation #1: "They" (referring to the waters) went up over the mountains and went down into the valleys.

Translation #2: The "mountains" rose, and the "valleys" sank down. English translations are split fairly evenly on these two different translations. However, translations in other major languages are essentially unanimous in selecting the second method of translating verse 8. Those other languages include German, French, Italian, Swedish, Spanish, Latin, and the Septuagint (Greek).

Part of the difficulty regarding verses 6 to 9 is that they could possibly be describing the third day of creation. Admittedly, there are striking parallels. Verses 1 to 5 are definitely talking about creation week. However, in our view, it is preferable to see Psalm 104 as a review of the world's history, not just a statement about the first week of creation.

Thus, we deem it reasonable to divide Psalm 104 into three major divisions: (1) verses 1 to 5—creation week; (2) verses 6 to 9—the Flood; (3) verses 10 to 35—post-Flood. Commentators will almost certainly continue an active discussion on whether this division is legitimate. But this threefold division seems to more accurately reflect the meaning of this marvelous psalm.

One of the most compelling arguments that Psalm 104:6–9 is referring to the Flood is the statement of verse 9: "You set a boundary that they may not pass over, so that they will not return to cover the earth." If this passage is speaking in reference only to the creation week, how is verse 9 fulfilled? If this entire psalm is referring to the creation week, it cannot have been fulfilled accurately. Why is that?

Water, Water Everywhere!

The reader must remember that the waters did indeed cover the entire earth in the Flood! That would then glaringly contradict the creation story. Some argue that this passage can be used to describe both the third day of creation and the Flood. However, as already demonstrated, that is not a viable interpretation. Thus, the evidence demonstrates that the concept of verses 6 to 9 describing the Flood is the better of the two viewpoints. The concept of the rising mountains and falling ocean valleys fully resolves the "sufficient water" issue.

One thing is certain: the earth had a much different topography in Noah's day. The mountains were not nearly as high as they are now. The ocean basins were not as deep. God powerfully transformed the globe while the Flood was occurring and afterwards. If the earth were essentially smooth, as it probably was in Noah's day, you could cover the earth in water approximately 1.7 miles deep. But even in Noah's day, there would have been different levels of topography.

Sarfati comments:

> Even allowing for lower mountains than today, one might think that it would take an enormous amount of water to cover it. But there is actually more than enough water in the oceans today to cover the whole surface—that is, if the earth were totally smoothed. The earth's surface is about 70% covered by water. Also, the average ocean depth is about 3.8 km (2.4 miles), while the average continental height above sea level is only 0.84 km (0.52 miles).
>
> The deepest point in the ocean is the Challenger Deep—10,898-10,916 m (35,355—35,814 ft)—at the southern end of the Mariana Trench in the Pacific Ocean. This is over a mile deeper than Everest is high.

So, not surprisingly, it is well known that "If all the land in the world was flattened out, the earth would be a smooth sphere completely covered by a continuous layer of seawater 2,686 metres [1.669 miles] deep."[121]

The Candid Admission of Alfred Russell Wallace

This understanding that the Flood may have changed the topography of the earth in dramatic fashion is not new. Many others have understood that to be precisely the case. One such individual was Alfred Russell Wallace (1823–1913). He was a trained surveyor and one of Charles Darwin's co-laborers in the field of evolutionary contemplation. Hence, he could hardly be described as an ally in the field of biblical creationism.

Indeed, Wallace opposed the truthfulness of Scripture at every opportunity. Yet, he and many others in his day recognized that there was plenty of water on the earth to cover the highest mountains if the mountains rose after the Flood. Even the secular scientists have recognized that this is indeed the case. With the discovery of marine fossils on the tops of mountains, something obviously happened. Marine animals are not generally known to climb to the tops of frigid, snow-covered mountain peaks.

Wallace's knowledge was admittedly not as accurate as Sarfati's because Wallace lived so much earlier. Technology was not as advanced as it is today. Nonetheless, Wallace understood the historical scenario quite well. The mountains clearly had to have risen in elevation.

Sarfati quotes Wallace as follows:

---

[121] Jonathan Sarfati, The Genesis Account: A theological, historical, and scientific commentary on Genesis 1–11, pp. 559–560.

According to the best recent estimates, the land area of the globe is 0.28 of the whole surface, and the water area 0.72. But the mean height of the land above the sea-level is found to be 2250 feet, while the mean depth of the seas and oceans is 13,860 feet; so that though the water area is two and a half times that of the land, the mean depth of the water is more than six times the mean height of the land.

This is, of course, due to the fact that lowlands occupy most of the land-area, the plateaus and high mountains a comparatively small portion of it, while, though the greatest depths of the oceans about equal the greater heights of the mountains, yet over enormous areas the oceans are deep enough to submerge all the mountains of Europe and temperate north America, except the extreme summits of one or two of them.

Hence it follows that the bulk of the oceans, even omitting all the shallow seas, is more than thirteen times that of the land above sea-level, and if all the land surface and ocean floors were reduced to one level, that is, if the solid mass of the globe were a true oblate spheroid, the whole would be covered with water about two miles deep.[122]

---

122 Ibid., 560.

The Easiest Solution Is Often the Best One

Question: What changed topographically in order to allow the mountains to be covered with water? As previously stated, there clearly is not that much water on the earth today. Certainly, such a gargantuan amount of water did not simply evaporate into outer space. The simplest solution is that the highest mountains of the pre-Flood world were much lower than the earth's present topographical status. Scholars will continue to debate and formulate different theories as to precisely what happened.

However, if our understanding of Psalm 104:6–9 is correct, the solution from the Scripture is forthright and resolves any potential difficulties. We have examined both sources of water for the Flood. We have also offered a reasonable explanation as to how they worked in conjunction to flood the world. We believe that the water vapor canopy contained enough water to inundate the entire globe when used in combination with the subterranean waters.

The potentially thousands of erupting geysers conceivably replenished the water vapor canopy for at least forty days. That also assumes a remarkable change in the earth's topography, as reflected in Psalm 104:6–9.

Original Creation versus Post-Flood

Henry Morris ably summarizes this passage as follows:

> Verses 6 through 9 of Psalm 104 obviously refer to the great deluge. Not until the very end of the psalm, however, is mention made of the effect of sin on the earth. The primary purpose of the psalm is simply to describe the mighty creative and providential acts of

God in relation to the earth. Therefore, the narrative jumps directly from the act which called the earth out of the water to that which again plunged it beneath the waters.

"Thou coverest it with the deep as with a garment." This statement notes the contrast between God covering (literally "arraying") himself with light as with a garment, and his covering (literally "hiding" –a different Hebrew word) the earth as with a garment. One was for display of glory, the other for covering its shame.

"The waters stood above the mountains" (see Genesis 7:19-20), so the whole world was inundated. The mountains so mentioned were the gentle mountains of the antediluvian topography; the next verse describes the uplift of the great and rugged mountains of the present world.

Verse 8 speaks of a gigantic earth movement which terminated the universal flood. The eruption of the "fountains of the great deep" and the pouring of huge torrents of rain on the earth from "the windows of heaven" (Gen. 7:11) had left great empty caverns in the earth's crust and piled tremendous beds of sediments in all the antediluvian seas, leaving the crust in a state of complex stress. Eventually, great faults and earth movements began to develop.

The American Standard Version renders this verse accurately as follows: "The mountains rose, the valleys sank down." Great continental uplifts took place, with corresponding sinking of the basins. A great storm of wind (Gen. 8:1) and lightning and thunder (verse 7), none of which had ever been experienced by the earth before the flood, triggered the mighty orogenies. Verse 9 then refers to God's promise to Noah never again to send the flood to destroy the earth (Gen. 9:11). Job 26:10 also refers to this promise: "He hath compassed the waters with bounds, until the day and night come to an end."

The isostatic equilibrium is now sufficiently established so that the seabed can never rise again sufficiently to plunge waters over the mountains. Also, the waters remaining in the heavens and below the ground are no longer present in such quantities as to make possible a worldwide flood.[123]

The water covered the entire globe, and every air-breathing animal died, save what was in the ark. In that scenario, the earth itself contained sufficient water to accomplish this catastrophic task. Judgment was mandatory to destroy the Nephilim. Mankind had almost completely corrupted itself. Still, God provided His gracious way of escape before exacting His judgment. For humanity back then, it was Noah and the ark. Today, Jesus Christ is that solitary way of escape from the penalty of sin.

---

[123] Henry Morris, Treasures in the Psalms (Green Forest, AR: Master Books, 1999), p. 210.

A Spiritual Truth to Remember

First Peter 2:24–25 reminds us of this spiritual truth: "Who Himself bore our sins in His own body on the tree, that we, having died to sins, might live for righteousness—by whose stripes you were healed. For you were like sheep going astray, but have now returned to the Shepherd and Overseer of your souls." Jesus Christ alone can take away the sins of the world. He alone is the perfect and acceptable Sacrifice. But man must be willing to confess those sins and humbly ask His forgiveness (1 John 1:7–9).

Why should mortal man find that redemptive concept so difficult to understand? He finds it difficult because his heart is darkened with sin (John 3:19–21; Romans 3:23). His unclear conscience must be cleared of its spider's web of deceptions and lies. But the blaze of God's glory and the Holy Spirit's conviction can burst through even the most darkened of hearts. However, it must be with the man or woman's permission. That is how God so lovingly and tenderly operates.

Lessons Learned in This Chapter

In this chapter, we first noted the spectacular circumstances surrounding the Flood. Noah and his family entered the ark one week before the rains began. In a never-to-be-repeated fashion, God Himself led the animal kingdom into the ark. He gathered them and then ushered them to the prearranged pens designated for them. This provided a staggering visual witness to the Nephilim. One can imagine that possibly thousands of the Nephilim assembled to observe this nearly heart-stopping parade of wild animals, both small and great.

Second, we addressed the thorny question of why God allowed such wickedness to overcome the world. This theological and spiritual catastrophe begs an answer. However, we are limited to making observations regarding the whys and wherefores of the circumstances. No man can fully answer the question as to why God permitted this spiritual calamity. We may rest confident, however, that God's ways are always best. In unknown ways, He continued to reach out to wicked mankind, even to the Nephilim themselves.

Isaiah 55:8–9 graciously explains: "For My thoughts are not your thoughts, nor are your ways My ways, says the Lord. For as the heavens are higher than the earth, so are My ways higher than your ways, and My thoughts than your thoughts." The believer may rest confident in eternal truths even though they are left unexplained in Scripture. God's truth steadfastly rings forth throughout the earth. Mankind chose to wander down the thorn-plagued path of sin due to his own volition. God never forces man to sin.

The book of James offers an eternal promise to mankind. This passage equally applies even to the Nephilim. James 1:13–15 proclaims:

> Let no one say when he is tempted, "I am tempted by God"; for God cannot be tempted by evil, nor does He Himself tempt anyone. But each one is tempted when he is drawn away by his own desires and enticed. Then, when desire has conceived, it gives birth to sin; and sin, when it is full-grown, brings forth death.

Third, we discussed the Flood itself. With unwavering fervency, we uphold the biblical truth that the Flood was universal. For a believer to proclaim it as a local flood betrays a stark incapacity to read with clarity and understanding. The Bible unequivocally declares that the thoughts of mankind were wicked continually (Genesis 6:5). The Nephilim were contaminating the bloodline of humanity.

They almost succeeded. The intent was to eliminate any possibility of the messianic Seed being born (Genesis 3:15). The elimination of unrighteous mankind was the only solution possible.

Not only does the Bible unerringly declare that the Flood was universal, but the extra-biblical evidence available also demonstrates the same. The fossils all over the world, especially those on the tops of mountains, bear ample witness to the universal Flood. Only an unreasonable and evidence-denying skeptic can think otherwise.

We also dealt with the sources of water for the Flood. They were twofold: (1) the heavens rained down precipitation on a never-after-equal scale; (2) the subterranean waters burst forth when the crust of the earth cracked. This would have created geysers of both water and magma. It is unlikely that mankind and animals outside the ark suffered long. The immensity of God's judgment defies the imagination.

Fourth, we intermixed the only solution to mankind's sinful nature. That is the spiritual door of Jesus Christ. Just as there was but one physical door into Noah's ark, only one spiritual door exists today. If man walks through that spiritual door, his sins can be forgiven, and his soul can reside with God throughout eternity (John 5:24). There is no greater gift than that!

Isaiah 53:5–6 solemnly proclaims:

> But He was wounded for our transgressions, He was bruised for our iniquities; the chastisement for our peace was upon Him, and by His stripes we are healed. All we like sheep have gone astray; we have turned every one, to his own way; and the Lord has laid on Him the iniquity of us all.

In our next chapter, we shall continue to examine evidence regarding the biblical Flood. It is everywhere on earth and of a nature that people often do not anticipate. The believer may rejoice in the abundance of truth God has distributed among mankind. We are truly without excuse if we reject His eternal message.

Cognitive Conundrum #15

A noteworthy prophet did I clearly prove; though my words were scant, they truly did move. God took special note of my faithful ministry; as such, I live on in earth's future history. A great force of angels and men I proclaimed; my service to God brought me much fame. Two men on earth passed not death's weary gate; communion with God was my happy fate.

Who am I?

Answer: Enoch

Chapter 16

Global Flood versus Local Flood

(Genesis 7:6-24: Part B)

In This Chapter

Objectives for This Chapter
Traditions Regarding a Universal Flood
Fossils Validate the Flood
Lessons Learned in This Chapter

Objectives for This Chapter

Throughout the long ages of man, scoffers of God's holy Word have always existed. From the arrogant military leaders of the Assyrian Empire down to our present age, pagans have despised God's principles and His actions. In this chapter, we shall first briefly see what the Bible has to say about such scoffers. They bring their own condemnation upon their heads. God has abundantly revealed Himself in powerful and irrefutable ways. Yet, such individuals prefer to skeptically deny the obvious truths displayed right in front of their persistently disbelieving eyes.

Second, we shall examine a broad array of traditions concerning the Flood. There are hundreds of these traditions scattered around the entire globe. Indeed, no major culture has ever been discovered that does not have some tradition of a worldwide inundation. While the sundry details differ somewhat from each other, the similarities are beyond mere coincidence. Of particular interest is one tradition we quote that comes from China. Its parallels to the biblical account cannot be easily dismissed.

Third, we shall examine the fossil record. Many excellent volumes have been written by eminent scholars on this undeniable testimony to God's judgment on the earth. The globe is saturated with literally trillions of fossils. Though many of these are extremely small, others are as large as dinosaurs. We give account of vast repositories of fossils in one common grave. These include a mixture of many animals that otherwise studiously avoided each other, such as carnivores and herbivores.

There are even fossils of fish giving birth and also swallowing other fish. Clearly, something catastrophic had to occur to fossilize these quick actions. Such fossils demonstrate that fossilization did not take millions of years. It did not even take weeks. For example, the process of fossilizing a jellyfish would have to take less than twenty-four hours. Otherwise, the jellyfish would quickly dissolve into an amorphous blob upon death.

Alarmists of today spout off about climate change. Though we certainly do support man being a good steward of the earth and its resources, it is God who really brings about climate change. He did this historically in Noah's day. He shall do so again during the Tribulation. Intense, suffocating heat will smite the earth during the bowl judgments (Revelation 16:8–9).

Historically, climate change has been abundantly demonstrated by the fact that coal and oil deposits exist in inhospitable locations, such as the Arctic Circle and Antarctica. How could coal and oil have been formed without any vegetation? Obviously, at one time, the entire world had a uniform climate. The entire planet enjoyed luxuriant vegetation. When God created the heavens and the earth, Adam and Eve did not even require clothing (Genesis 2:25). Something drastically changed as a result of the Flood.

During the Flood, all of mankind and the animal kingdom perished. The only exceptions were those safely ensconced on the ark. God is patient in His judgment. But when He acts, it is with a devastating thoroughness. The fossil record leaves us confirmation of Scripture's reliability. The student of Scripture may rejoice that not only does the Bible eloquently testify of God's eternal attributes, but so does nature itself.

The fallaciousness of Darwinism is absolutely refuted by the evidence of the fossil record and the worldwide written traditions concerning the Flood. There is no possibility whatsoever that these should have ever happened in any other way. God's truth has stood, does stand, and will forever endure the test of time and eternity itself. As Jesus Himself stated in Matthew 24:35: "Heaven and earth will pass away, but My words will by no means pass away."

Traditions Regarding a Universal Flood

Over the centuries, skepticism regarding the biblical account of the Flood has steadily grown. That is rather ironic since the proofs of the worldwide Flood have increased exponentially more. But Scripture predicted that such blind cynicism would occur. Why is that? With the popularization of no-evidence, unscientific, and nonsensical Darwinism, scientists have increasingly abandoned the truthfulness of Scripture and often empirical reality itself. As a replacement for the Bible, they have placed "pseudoscience" on the altar of their worship.

Genuine science is a wonderful tool to explore God's creation. It should be. God created it! We rejoice with those who follow demonstrable and verifiable science absent the motives of scientific charlatans. Many such brilliant scholars do exist and add much to society. But when "science" is abused to reject the concept of an almighty Creator, misery and false information follow.

A Biblical Warning of Scoffers

Second Peter 3:3–7 vividly predicts this scenario:

> Knowing this first: that scoffers will come in the last days, walking according to their own lusts, and saying, "Where is the promise of His coming?" For since the fathers fell asleep, all things continue as they were from the beginning of creation. For this they willfully forget: that by the word of God the heavens were of old, the earth standing out of water and in the water, by which the world that then existed perished, being flooded with water. But the heavens and the earth which are now preserved by the same word, are reserved for fire until the day of judgment and perdition of ungodly men.

Question: Is there any reliable extra-biblical evidence that supports the concept of a worldwide Flood? Answer: There is an abundance of just such evidence. Many fact-filled and fascinating books have been written on this subject. In this section, we shall examine just a sampling of such proofs. We encourage the reader to avail himself of some of the splendid books written from a creationist's perspective.

Flood Traditions: Mere Coincidence or Realistic Reporting?

Flood evidence #1: Historical accounts of the Flood are found all over the world. Dr. Richard Andree, a German scholar, has compiled a collection of eighty-eight different flood traditions. Twenty come from Asia, five from Europe, seven from Africa, ten from Australia and the South Sea Islands, and forty-six from the Indians of North, Central, and South America.

Others have recorded many more traditions than this. In fact, some claim that hundreds of slightly different Flood accounts are scattered all over the globe. A final count is not possible as more Flood traditions continue to be discovered. Although these traditions do have some significant differences, there are three areas in which they almost always agree. Those areas of agreement are as follows: (1) there is a universal destruction of the human race and all other living things by water; (2) an ark, or boat, is provided as the means of escape; (3) a small seed of mankind is preserved to continue the human race.

A fourth area occurs very frequently as well: (4) the wickedness of man is given as the cause of the Flood. It is rather astonishing that such widespread accounts of a universal Flood would have occurred by mere chance. What could possibly account for that? The reality of the Flood accounts for it. Why else would any individual or culture conjure up such a fantastic idea that a worldwide Flood would kill all life forms?

Furthermore, how many distinct localities would simply imagine so many similarities regarding this allegedly imaginary Flood? Indeed, why would any culture just dream up a Flood story in the first place? What are the chances that these "story fabricators" would envision an ark to rescue an assortment of humanity and the animal kingdom? That truly defies the imagination. It is obviously beyond the scope of pure luck and coincidence. Something must have happened! Objective prudence demands accepting the straightforward biblical account.

These traditions, in actuality, provide powerful evidence of the reality of God's judgment through the worldwide inundation. Their close parallels with Scripture, without question, go well beyond strange happenstance. It is intriguing to note that some of these traditions come from desert regions. For such traditions to be merely idle tales stretches the limits of credulity.

A Fascinating Flood Tradition from China

Bodie Hodge writes of a Flood tradition from the Miao people of China:

> So it poured forty days in sheets and in torrents. Then fifty-five days of misting and drizzle. The waters surmounted the mountains and ranges. The deluge ascending leapt valley and hollow. An earth with no earth upon which to take refuge! A world with no foothold where one might subsist! The people were baffled, impotent and ruined, despairing, horror-stricken, diminished and finished. But the Patriarch Nuah was righteous. The Matriarch Gaw Bo-lu-en upright. Built a boat very wide. Made a ship very vast. Their household entire got aboard and were floated, the family complete rode the deluge in safety. The animals with him were female and male.
>
> The birds went along and were mated in pairs. When the time was fulfilled, God commanded the waters. The day had arrived, the flood waters receded. Then Nuah liberated a dove from their refuge, sent a bird to

Global Flood versus Local Flood

go forth and bring again tidings. The flood had gone down into lake and to ocean; the mud was confined to the pools and the hollows.

There was land once again where a man might reside; there was a place in the earth now to rear habitations. Buffalo then were brought, an oblation to God, fatter cattle became sacrifice to the Mighty. The Divine One then gave them His blessing; their God then bestowed His good grace.[124]

The similarities to the biblical Flood story in the Chinese account are truly remarkable. This is just one example among hundreds of differing Flood stories scattered around the globe. Indeed, even in the deepest and most remote regions of the Amazon, every tribe thus far discovered has a global Flood legend. There is no region on earth that does not have some type of Flood legend. How is this possible?

It is possible because the Flood was a reality! These Flood stories have been a marvelous stepping stone to share the Gospel with these tribes. It gives an immediate sphere of common interest and agreement. These Flood legends serve as a powerful testimony to secularists who deny the truth of Scripture.

Fossils Validate the Flood

Bones, Bones Everywhere!

Flood evidence #2: Only a universal Flood could account for the huge deposits of bones and fossils buried throughout the planet.

---

[124] Ken Ham and Bodie Hodge, A Flood of Evidence: 40 Reasons Why Noah and the Ark Still Matter, p. 35.

For example, in Nebraska, there lies a huge bone deposit that occupies a hill covering ten acres. This hill of bones was discovered in 1876. It contains the assorted bones of rhinoceroses, camels, giant wild boars, and myriad other animals. They are buried together in a confused jumble as only water would bury them. It is estimated that about 9,000 animals are buried on this one hill. These animals were all buried in a very short time.

Such deposits of bones are found all over the world. In some situations, the bones are all crammed together in a cave or a large fissure (a crack in the earth). One such hill is 1,030 feet high in France. What would cause all these animals, many of them natural enemies, to cram together like this? For instance, why would a deer want to be in the same room with a wolf? Only a major flood could accomplish this. Nothing else can account for it!

The animals were desperately trying to escape the killer waters. This is not to say they all died in the same spot, but they were at least crowding together in the same vicinity. A common fear of the monster storm and the encroaching waters is the only logical explanation for their close proximity. Then, as the floodwaters receded, small streams and rivers would drain into deep crevasses or hollows, dragging dead animals of all descriptions in their current. In the process, they would deposit the remains of thousands of drowned animals into mass graves.

Fossil Formation Requires a Rapid Process

There are literally billions, even trillions, of fossils buried all over the world. What unnatural event could have precipitated such an occurrence? How were these fossils formed? The only logical conclusion is through a universal Flood. Fossils do not come into being through a slow, rotting process.

For example, if a fish dies, it slowly sinks to the lake or ocean floor and is consumed by other fish or microorganisms. Either that or it is entirely consumed on the surface. The dead fish, or whatever other animal one considers, does not automatically turn into a fossil. Fossils must and do form very quickly under precise circumstances.

In a museum in Tasmania, there is a miner's felt hat that dropped into mineral-laden water. When the miner found it again sometime later, it had actually "fossilized" into a hard hat. It had become thoroughly mineralized! That hardly took millions of years. Indeed, scientists, using the proper procedures, have actually produced fossils in their laboratories. The concept of fossils requiring millions of years to form is a nonsensical myth. For example, few creatures on earth are composed of such soft tissue as jellyfish, hence their name.

Even Soft-Tissue Jellyfish Have Been Fossilized

Gary Parker gives the following insightful example of jellyfish:

> Remember the Precambrian Australian jellyfish? Jellyfish often wash ashore, but in a matter of hours they have turned into nondescript "blobs" (although watch out – the stinging cells continue to work for quite a while!). To preserve the markings and detail of the Ediacara jellyfish, the organisms seem to have landed on a wet sand that acted as a natural cement. The sand turned to sandstone before the jellyfish had time to rot, preserving the jellyfish's markings, somewhat as you can preserve your handprint if you push it into cement during that brief time when it's neither too wet nor too dry.

Indeed, the evolutionist who discovered the Ediacara jellyfish said the fossils must have formed in less than 24 hours. He didn't mean one jellyfish in 24 hours; he meant millions of jellyfish and other forms had fossilized throughout the entire Ediacara formation which stretches about 300 miles or 500 km from South Australia into the Northern Territory, in less than 24 hours! In short, floods form fossils fast![125]

Fossils of Fish Giving Birth and Eating?

There are numerous remarkable fossils on display in various places. One such fossil is a marine reptile called an ichthyosaur that was fossilized while giving birth! Clearly, the ichthyosaur was overcome by an incredible natural disaster. Another fish was in the midst of swallowing another fish for its dinner when it and the victim were killed and fossilized.

Ken Ham and Bodie Hodge write as follows:

> The sample of dozens of closed shells that were buried rapidly and fossilized before they could open, which is what shellfish typically do, are in the Andes Mountains of Peru above Cusco, which is over two miles high. A local guide took us to the site. We left the fossils in the care of a local church in Cusco.
>
> A group of turtles were buried and fossilized so fast that all nine pairs were still stuck in the process of mating. Being critical of the report's slow natural expla-

---
[125] Gary Parker, Creation: Facts of Life (Green Forest, AR: Master Books, 1994), pp. 176–177.

nation of fossil formation, these turtle pairs are better explained by catastrophe and rapid events. This happens often, showing the speed at which burial and fossilization took place.[126]

Dinosaurs in Antarctica?

Fossils of all descriptions are found in every country and continent on earth, including Antarctica. In fact, dinosaur fossils have been discovered in frigid Antarctica. How could they have survived there for even one day without adequate heat and food? In a word, they couldn't! Uniformitarianism insists that the present is the key to the past. Is that really true? No, it clearly is not! The existence of dinosaurs in freezing lands by itself disproves that theory.

Dinosaurs are cold-blooded creatures. Even a moderate change in temperature will affect their circulatory system. They cannot tolerate frigid conditions. They need to live in a place where the temperatures are quite consistent. That is why one does not find reptiles and snakes living up in the tundra of Canada or Siberia. The conditions are far too harsh. Only warm-blooded animals can reside in such extremes.

Obviously, the climate in Antarctica was very different at one time than it is today. The fossils, coal, and oil deposits testify to that reality as few things can. Their existence cannot be denied or dismissed. They are glaring contradictions to uniformitarianism. The evolutionist must cling to theoretical and completely implausible straws to dispute the evidence found in Antarctica alone. While secular scientists cannot adequately explain how things were once different, Scripture can and does explain it.

---

[126] Ken Ham and Bodie Hodge, A Flood of Evidence: 40 Reasons Noah and the Ark Still Matter, p. 143.

Climate Change? Yes!

The Flood transformed the entire globe in drastic ways. The entire world was at one time pleasant and ready to be occupied. Before man sinned, clothing was not even needed. The fall itself did not change the weather, although just about everything else was drastically altered. But the fall eventually led to the Flood, which did change the climate drastically. Scripture explains the entire process eloquently and accurately. Evolutionary science does not and cannot.

Modern man frets and fumes over "climate change." Little do most people realize that God is responsible for the climate. He radically changed the entire globe's climate millennia ago. Even today, countries are vying for drilling rights to the oil located in the Arctic Circle. How did oil get up there if it has always been cold? Did it just percolate northward? We think not!

Many evolutionists secretly recognize that the world was at one time much different. Unless they have intentionally blinded themselves to the fantastic extra-biblical evidence surrounding them, they cannot reckon otherwise. However, they chose not to repeat anything that would grant credence to the Word of God. Why? As atheist Lewontin asserted, they do not want to allow a divine foot in the door. But they conveniently forget: If there really is a divine foot, then it must come attached to a divine Being.

Will Fossils Never Cease? Apparently Not!

Regarding fossils, Alfred Rehwinkel writes:

> Fossils of all kinds of animal and plant life both of existing species and of many forms now extinct have

been found. There are fossils of land and sea animals, of fish and of birds, of reptiles and of beautiful insects, of giant trees and delicate leaves and parts of plants. They are found in mountain areas, such as the Rockies, the Alps, the Himalayas, the mountains of Greece and Italy.

They occur in great numbers on the plains and prairies of Nebraska, Kansas, Oklahoma, Texas, Wyoming, South Dakota, Utah, Idaho, Oregon, and Alberta, but they are also found in the Eastern States and the Eastern Provinces of Canada. They are found on the pampas of South America and on the steppes of Russia, in Siberia and on the Sahara, on the Gobi Desert and in Greenland.

In fact, they are found nearly everywhere. Sometimes they have been discovered in caves or in coal mines, in valleys or on mountaintops, near the surface or deep down in the earth, buried under fifty, sixty, one hundred, even thousands of feet of soil, clay, loess, gravel, sand, and hard stratified rock. In a boring of Oklahoma City a fossil shell was brought up from a depth of six thousand feet.[127]

Question: What should we expect to find if, indeed, there really was a worldwide flood?

Answer: We should expect to find an uncountable number of

---

[127] Alfred M. Rehwinkel, The Flood: In the Light of the Bible, Geology, and Archaeology (Saint Louis, MO; Concordia Publishing House, 1951), pp. 210–211.

fossils. If there really was a global flood, what and where would the evidence be? The evidence would be displayed in untold trillions of dead creatures buried in rock layers all around the world. These rock layers would have been laid down by water washing all over the earth. And that is precisely what we find.

The evidence does not lie. Fossils do not have a theological or scientific "axe to grind." They are dead. The question is not whether they exist or not. The question is, how did these fossils come to exist? What else but a universal Flood could have formed such universal evidence? A catastrophic, world-inundating Flood is the only reasonable explanation. Fossils do not form of their own volition.

Clams Climbing Mountains?

As previously mentioned, geologists find marine fossils on the tops of mountains. How did marine fossils get way up on the tops of mountains? Marine fossils, after all, are the types of creatures that live in the ocean. Most of these water-dwelling creatures, such as clams, are not well-known for their ability to climb mountains. Their ambulatory skills are quite minimal, to say the least. Indeed, they are non-existent. But there they are, stubbornly sitting on the tops of mountains.

How could these marine creatures have possibly finished the grueling journey? Did someone or something carry them? That does not strike one as very likely. And even if they did get carried to the top of a mountain, they would still have to go through the arduous process of fossilization. Or is it just possible that the mountain itself rose from a lower elevation during the universal deluge? We believe that is precisely the case. Lo and behold, that is also what the Bible teaches. Even the secular geologists generally concur. What real choice do they have?

Global Flood versus Local Flood

Dr. Andrew Snelling, a world-renowned geologist, writes as follows:

> Marine fossils are also found high in the Himalayas, the world's tallest mountain range, reaching up to 29,029 feet above sea level. For example, fossil ammonites (coiled marine cephalopods) are found in limestone beds in the Himalayas of Nepal. All geologists agree that ocean waters must have buried these marine fossils in these limestone beds. So how did these marine limestone beds get high up in the Himalayas?
>
> We must remember that the rock layers in the Himalayas and other mountain ranges around the globe were deposited during the Flood, well before these mountains were formed. In fact, many of these mountain ranges were pushed up by earth movements to their present high elevations at the end of the Flood. This is recorded in Psalm 104:8, where the Flood waters are described as eroding and retreating down valleys as the mountains rose at the end of the Flood.
>
> The fossilized sea creatures and plants found in rock layers thousands of feet above sea level are thus silent testimonies to the ocean waters that flooded over the continents, carrying billions of sea creatures, which were then buried in the sediments these ocean waters deposited. This is how billions of dead marine creatures were buried in rock layers all over the earth.

We know that the cataclysmic Genesis Flood was an actual event in history because God tells us so in His record, the Bible. Now we can also see persuasive evidences that support what the Bible has so clearly taught all along.[128]

The Earth's Crust Literally Cracked During the Flood

The Bible provides a clear answer for the skeptic regarding these marine fossils. The world convulsed in unimaginable fashion during the global flood. Things were in a transition of catastrophic change for the duration of the Flood. Volcanic action, tidal waves, earthquakes, and other natural disasters, not to mention the Flood itself, transformed everything about the earth. If such things happened today absent the ark, no living flesh would be spared.

During the Flood, the crust of the earth broke apart in places to release the subterranean waters. This entire process contributed to continental shifting that is unimaginable today. One should not confuse the crust of the earth with its foundation, which cannot be moved. Psalm 104:5 states: "You who laid the foundations of the earth, so that it should not be moved forever."

When the crust of the earth cracked open in places during the Flood, it released gargantuan amounts of water to the surface. Under unimaginable pressure, this created geysers of water shooting skyward. Volcanic action also took place beyond modern comprehension. Our most violent volcanic eruptions of today pale into insignificance with what occurred in Noah's day.

During this same time frame, the mountains rose up, and the valleys of the ocean dropped. Psalm 104:8 (NASB) informs us:

---

[128] Andrew Snelling, High and Dry Sea Creatures. Answers Magazine, December 7, 2007.

"The mountains rose, the valleys sank down to the place which Thou didst establish for them." Noah and his family were protected from these cataclysmic effects by the ark and the supernatural protection of God. When God pours forth judgment, it is generally not of a placid nature.

Where Did All the Bison Fossils Go?

Question: Where did all the worldwide fossils come from if there was no worldwide flood to form them? Just a few generations ago, millions of bison wandered over the plains of America. One would think that people walking on the plains should encounter their fossilized remains almost everywhere they walk. So, where are all those bison fossils? Why didn't they form? It is because they were either eaten by scavengers or simply rotted away.

Making a fossil requires specialized conditions. Some of those conditions include considerable pressure, heat, and a complete lack of oxygen. The potential fossil must be buried quickly under proper conditions. Such conditions are rarely encountered today. The fossil record is one of the best windows into earth's past that is available to scientists. It does not lie, but it does need to be properly interpreted.

Rehwinkel comments as follows:

> Nor is it mere speculation to speak of the first world as a "veritable paradise." For though there are but meager written records concerning this first world, there is another kind of record which God has preserved for us in His wisdom. This record is reliable and true and is written in large and legible letters in the very foundation rocks of our present world. The record I refer to are the fossil remains that have been found in great

abundance in every part of the globe.

These fossils may be called the mummified remains of an extinct world. Fossils do not lie. Just as the pyramids of Egypt and the monuments of Greece and Rome are an evidence of the greatness of the civilization that produced them, so these fossils speak an eloquent language of the glories of a world which has passed away. These fossils have been preserved by God for a purpose.[129]

Around the world, large geological formations have been discovered that contain billions of fossils! The Cretaceous chalk beds of England are about 405 meters thick. They extend well beyond the borders of England. The white cliffs of Dover are their best-known region. These chalk beds contain untold trillions of microscopic foraminifera and coccolithophores (calcareous algae). Their formation hardly seems to have been accidental and produced by natural causes. If that is the case, why do we not see those same "natural causes" actively working today?

Fossils Smother the Planet

Museums are teeming with well over 100 million fossils representing over 250,000 different types of plants and animals. There is no shortage of fossils around the world. If this massive formation of fossils occurred in the past, why is it not happening today as well? Secular geologists assert that the past is the key to the present. Really? Where is the evidence of that pious platitude?

The reason why fossils are not forming todays has been reiterat-

---

[129] Alfred Rehwinkel, The Flood: In the Light of the Bible, Geology, and Archaeology, pp. 6–7.

Global Flood versus Local Flood

ed by us numerous times already: Only something like the universal flood is capable of creating the environment necessary to make such massive formations of fossils. To deny that simple truth is to deny reality. No serious scientist will claim, for instance, that a dead fish floating on the surface of a lake is destined to become a fossil over the next few million years. If the fish carcass remains for even a few days, it will be a surprise. Other fish and bacteria will eat it quite quickly.

Nor does one often see the remains of a dead deer lying in the ditch becoming a fossil either. Common observation available to everyone tells the story. The deer will rather quickly be on the menu for the various carnivores gathering about for lunch. Even small children can understand this quite readily. They see the birds assembling in motley fashion for the purposes of dining.

How is it that highly educated and allegedly erudite scientists can so easily miss the obvious lesson on the formation of fossils? What causes this intellectual disconnect? The answer is quite simple: They refuse to acknowledge a divine Creator. Therefore, they must substitute the next available option for creation and all related observable phenomena. The only available option to them is the pathetic side pursuit of evolution.

The observation has been made that 95 percent of the fossil record consists of small marine organisms. Why is that? This is because they are located in the lower level of the aquatic system. Hence, they would have been the first to die and to be buried under the shifting soils.

Body density also would make a difference. Reptiles and amphibians are less buoyant than mammals and birds, so they would sink relatively quickly. The more buoyant creatures would have been prone to being eaten by fish or simply rotting on the water's surface. Microscopic bacteria multiply by untold numbers at fantastic speed. They are quite proficient at consuming that which is deceased. Human beings would climb to the highest regions and be among the last to die. Their avoidance skills also largely prevented them from being fossilized.

Where Are All the Transition Fossils between Species?

Question: Does the fossil record demonstrate a step-by-step transition from one species to another? Evolution teaches that one species changed into another species. For this to be true, there must be demonstrable evidence.

Answer: The fossil record has produced no provable transition fossils whatsoever. None! That is truly remarkable. This fact alone is a death knell to Darwin's entire fallacious theory. How can it possibly be that not even one provable transition fossil has been found as of yet? Many such fossils have been claimed, but all have been eventually rejected. This reality should discourage even the most fanatical of evolutionary proponents.

Still, die-hard evolutionists vainly hope that a straw of evidence may eventually appear in the ocean of contrary truths. Such a struggle both against science and God is tantamount to choosing quicksand over a four-lane interstate highway. One must admire their marked tenacity if not their logic… or total lack thereof.

Even Darwin himself recognized this calamitous encumbrance against his theory. He wrote:

> Why then is not every geological formation and every stratum full of such intermediate links? Geology assuredly does not reveal any such finely graduated organic chain; and this, perhaps, is the most obvious and seri-

ous objection which can be urged against my theory. The explanation lies, as I believe, in the extreme imperfection of the geological record.[130]

Sadly for the evolutionist, this reputed geological imperfection of the fossil record remains geologically imperfect. It has not improved one iota since Darwin's day. The truth of the matter is that there is nothing wrong with the fossil record. It is what it is! But, rather than being a support beam for the theory of evolution, it is more like a gallows on which to hang the absurd, godless philosophy.

What Does the Fossil Record Actually Demonstrate?

The fossil record is, in reality, a champion for the Flood and the veracity of the Bible. Few scientific studies bring more satisfaction to the creationist than the study of the fossil record. It is indeed God's testimony carved into solid rock!

Regarding the lack of transitional fossils in the fossil record, Brian Young writes:

> What once was thought to be the best evidence for evolution is now being reconsidered, since virtually NO evidence surfaced. If evolution is true, there should be a vast record of fossils showing these various animals evolving into higher, more complex creatures.
>
> There should be worms (invertebrates) turning into fish (vertebrates), fish developing legs as they turn into amphibians, amphibians developing into reptiles, and

---

130 Charles Darwin, On the Origin of Species (New York: The Modern Library, 1856 reprint), p. 307.

the legs of reptiles turning into wings like birds, etc. With so many fossils today, there should be a number of these transitions, but in fact, every creature appears fully formed in the fossil record. A snail is always a snail and a bird is always a bird.

Dr. David M. Raup, curator of geology at the Field Museum of Natural History in Chicago, has stated, "Well, we are now about 120 years after Darwin and the knowledge of the fossil record has been greatly expanded. We now have a quarter of a million fossil species and the situation hasn't changed much. The record of evolution is still surprisingly jerky and ironically, we have even fewer examples of evolutionary transitions than we had in Darwin's time.

"By this I mean that some of the classic cases of Darwinian change in the fossil record, such as the evolution of the horse in North America, have had to be discarded or modified as a result of more detailed information."[131]

To complicate matters even further, many modern fossils have been located. The only problem is that these fossils are still alive! The coelacanth, a supposedly extinct fish, was located in 1939. The coelacanth was discovered happily swimming off the coast of Madagascar, blissfully unaware that it no longer existed! Another example was reported by the Associated Press in 1995. David Noble

---

[131] Brian Young, Doubts About Creation? Not After This (Bend, OR: Maverick Publications, 2003), p. 69.

found some trees vigorously growing in Australia. These trees were reported to have gone extinct in the Jurassic era when dinosaurs roamed the earth. Somebody forgot to tell the trees they no longer were supposed to be alive, much less thriving.

Fossils Stubborn Constant State

Fossils dated 50 million years old look identical today. Why haven't they changed? Ants preserved in amber, supposedly tens of million years old, look the same today as back then. This type of scenario occurs again and again and again. When slight changes are discovered, they can easily be explained as occurring within the original DNA makeup.

For example, dogs are still dogs, but there are many subspecies emanating from the original kind of dog. The same holds true of cattle, horses, cats, etc. Incidentally, we categorically reject the dating methods and do not believe that the bat or ant fossils cited are millions of years old. Almost all fossils were produced in the Flood when the conditions were exactly as needed.

The highly respected Dr. Colin Patterson of the British Museum of Natural History published a book called Evolution in 1978. Incredibly, he did not include a single photograph of a transition fossil in his book, which tried to prove the theory of evolution. Naturally, people asked him about this. In a most candid admission regarding the fossil record, he responded to their inquiries as follows:

> I fully agree with your comments on the lack of direct illustration of evolutionary transitions in my book. If I knew of any, fossil or living, I would certainly have included them. You suggest that an artist should be used to visualize [portray] such transformations, but where

would he get the information from? I could not, honestly, provide it.

[Steven] Gould [of Harvard] and the American Museum people are hard to contradict when they say there are no transitional fossils. As a paleontologist myself, I am much occupied with the philosophical problems of identifying ancestral forms in the fossil record. You say that I should at least "show a photo of the fossil from which each type of organism was derived."

I will lay it on the line—there is not one such fossil for which one could make a watertight argument. The reason is that statements about ancestry and descent are not applicable in the fossil record. It is easy enough to make up stories of how one form gave rise to another, and to find reasons why the stages should be favored by natural selection. But such stories are not part of science, for there is no way of putting them to the test.[132]

The Fossil Records Disqualify Darwinism

Question: Does the fossil record support evolution? Answer: Not in the least! Whatever fossils are found are identical, or nearly so, to their modern-day equivalents. No proven transition fossils have ever been found! We should see billions of them. They should be the normal fossil, not the exceptional one. No one sees evolution occurring today. If classical evolution is true, we should see at least some creatures evolving into another type of creature. The fossil

[132] Vance Ferrell, Science vs. Evolution, pp. 451–452.

record remains the missing link, the missing chain, and the missing science! It will never be anything else.

Some may be bold enough to challenge Dr. Patterson's assessment. They might contend we have not yet examined enough fossils. Either that or there simply are not enough fossils available on the earth to examine. However, such a sentiment is not only grossly uninformed; it also borders on informational and evidential lunacy. These individuals have not done their homework! Sentiment does not magically metamorphosize itself into hard facts.

N. O. Newell comments: "There are innumerable, well-documented records of preservation of tissues of animals and plants in pre-Quaternary rocks."[133] Furthermore, he adds: "Robert Broom, the South African paleontologist, estimated that there are eight hundred thousand million skeletons of vertebrate animals in the Karroo formation."[134] The Karroo formation extends over two-thirds of the nation of South Africa, Lesotho, and spreads partially into other bordering countries. To say the least, it is not a small area! Of course, Robert Broom is only estimating, but it demonstrates the vast quantities of fossils available for inspection.

Another vast repository of fossils is located in the Miocene shales of California. It is estimated that more than a billion fish, averaging six to eight inches in length, died and were buried in just four square miles on the bottom of the bay. That is an extraordinary density of fish to congregate together and corporately die.

The Amazing Preservation of the Fossils

Not only are there many examples scattered around the world of vast fossil beds, but the preservation of some of the fossils is

---

133 N. O. Newell, "Adequacy of the Fossil Record," Journal of Paleontology, vol. 33, May 1959, p. 495.
134 Ibid., p. 492.

incredible.

Whitcomb and Morris write:

> One of the most remarkable examples of preservation of organic tissues in antiseptic swamp waters is a "fossil graveyard in Eocene lignite deposits of the Geiseltal in central Germany . ... More than six thousand remains of the vertebrate animals and a great number of insects, molluscs, and plants were found in these deposits. The compressed remains of soft tissues of many of these animals showed details of cellular structure and some of the specimens had undergone but little chemical modification. ...
>
> Well-preserved bits of hair, feathers, and scales probably are among the oldest known examples of essentially unmodified preservation of these structures. The stomach contents of beetles, amphibia, fishes, birds and mammals provided direct evidence about eating habits. Bacteria of two kinds were found in the excrement of crocodiles and another was found in the trachea of a beetle. Fungi were identified on leaves and the original plant pigments, chlorophyll and coproporphyrin, were found preserved in some of the leaves.[135]

To believe that these worldwide fossil beds, some extraordinarily preserved, came about by uniformitarianism testifies to amazing but completely ill-founded faith. Scientifically, it is inexcusable to believe that these billions of fossils dropped into place one by one,

---
135 John Whitcomb and Henry Morris, The Genesis Flood, p. 160.

or even by the dozen, refused to rot, and then slowly mineralized into fossils. That is not just implausible; it is absolutely impossible.

Is it any small wonder that God states in Romans 1:18: "For the wrath of God is revealed from heaven against all ungodliness and unrighteousness of men, who suppress the truth in unrighteousness." Darkening one's heart and blinding one's eyes against the obvious truths of God's revelation does not refute them.

Lessons Learned in This Chapter

The wicked tendencies of mankind have manifested themselves in unrelenting furor since the fall of Adam and Eve. Historically, this culminated in the propagation of the Nephilim. They, in turn, corrupted the entire world. Nothing was left but for God to exercise overwhelming judgment against the humanity He had created. Noah, however, found favor in His sight. God commissioned him to build the ark through which his family and the animal kingdom were spared. The ark sheltered them from the treacherous waters of the great Flood.

In this chapter, we first examined some of the extra-biblical traditions of the Flood. These traditions are scattered throughout the entire world. We noted the following areas of agreement: (1) there is a universal destruction of the human race and all other living things by water; (2) an ark, or boat, is provided as the means of escape; (3) a small seed of mankind is preserved to continue the human race. A fourth area occurs very frequently as well: (4) the wickedness of man is given as the cause of the Flood.

How remarkable it is if all of these hundreds of traditions just appeared by sheer coincidence. While some may choose to believe that, the unlikeliness of such a scenario taking place is self-evident. Even in extremely remote corners of the globe, these Flood traditions persist. We cited a particularly amazing tradition that originated in China.

Second, we examined the phenomenal fossil record. Fossils can be formed only under quite specific conditions. One example we mentioned is the absence of bison fossils on the plains of North America. Though millions of bison historically roamed the plains, almost no fossils of them remain. Why is that? It is because the carcasses of these majestic animals either rotted or were eaten by predators, insects, and bacteria.

Fossils are located everywhere one turns on the planet. Even the highest Himalayan mountain ranges present a huge array of marine fossils. Clams, for instance, have no legs. How did clams manage to climb up to the top of these impressive mountain ranges? Obviously, at one time, the earth was vastly different than today. Fossils have been found as deep as 6,000 feet below the surface of the earth. What could possibly have caused that save a worldwide change of almost unbelievable proportions? Scripture provides the only reasonable answer: the Flood.

Psalm 104:6–9 offers a most satisfactory explanation of what transpired during the Flood. The mountain ranges rose, and the ocean valleys dropped during this topographical catastrophe. Secular geologists are forced to agree with this fact. They may dispute how the mountain ranges came into existence. Nonetheless, they must acknowledge that, at one time, the earth was markedly different than it is today.

The climate also changed dramatically as a result of the Flood. At one time, the earth was replete with verdant vegetation. This is shown by the fact that oil and coal deposits exist in now inhospitable regions such as the Arctic Circle and Antarctica. If the myth of uniformitarianism were actually true, how did coal and oil develop in these regions? These worldwide deposits are produced by the burial of massive amounts of vegetation and animals. As recently as 1990–1991, scientists discovered dinosaur bones in Antarctica. How could the cold-blooded dinosaur live in such a climate if the present is key to the past?

Third, a most disturbing problem for the evolutionist concerns the stubborn tenacity of the fossils. They refuse to show any evidence of transition. The fossils of long-dead creatures are essentially the same as the identical creatures of today. Much to the chagrin of evolutionists, some theoretically extinct creatures, such as the coelacanth, have been located swimming contentedly in the ocean. Though reputed to have died out millions of years ago, they are still flourishing. Little did the poor fish realize that it no longer existed!

Ironically, the coelacanth has not changed in appearance to any appreciable degree whatsoever. That is more than a bit disconcerting for those who claim such a fish had to descend from a bunch of minerals on a moist rock and go through an uncountable number of transitions. Does that theory sound a bit "fishy"? A bit of variation may exist in modern creatures; that is true. However, the DNA inherent in every type of creature known to man allows for these slight variations.

The travesty known as Darwinism has proven unworkable from literally every angle one can approach it. The fossil record, by Darwin's own admission, argued strongly against his anti-God philosophy. This chapter focused on the written and oral traditions concerning a worldwide Flood. These traditions are found in all major cultures. Furthermore, the fossil record amply verifies a worldwide inundation by water. How else could the fossils have formed in such astounding abundance? Only a specific and rapid process can produce fossils.

Our next chapter provides additional evidence regarding the Flood. We shall also address some of the more common questions asked concerning this incredible event.

Global Flood versus Local Flood

Cognitive Conundrum #16

Scoundrels and their deeds did I disdain; their evil manners they thought brought them gain. Destruction upon them I did fully predict; they earned their demise by denying God's edict. A popular man with a message I proved to be, my warnings of death received with great glee. The city I ranted against fostered evil feeling; washed out and ruined, it never had healing.

Who am I?

Answer: the prophet Nahum

though
Chapter 17

Global Flood versus Local Flood

(Genesis 7:6-24: Part C)

In This Chapter

Objectives for This Chapter
What Caused the Coal and Oil Deposits?
The Rocks Cry Out!
Lessons Learned in This Chapter

Objectives for This Chapter

As the reader will readily observe, these chapters progressively build one upon another. We are endeavoring to communicate credible extra-biblical evidence supporting the biblical view of the Flood. Such evidence is actually overwhelming to the unprejudiced mind. However, if one utterly refuses to acknowledge any truths outside of his own biased perceptions, no amount of data will change his heart. Such doubters must be warned not to stymie the convicting work of the Holy Spirit.

We trust that any reader who has made it this far through this book will not foster such an attitude of skepticism or resistance to God's truth. Thus, it is with considerable enthusiasm that we continue this discussion. We pray that it will be of great encouragement to those who may be experiencing lingering doubts about the veracity of Scripture. Most of these doubts are the byproduct of misinformation.

In this chapter, we shall first examine how coal and oil are formed. What are the requirements for them to come into being? As we shall see, the fossil fuels are composed of an immense amount of vegetation and animals buried under proper conditions. They must be placed under tremendous pressure, accompanied by heat, interact with specific chemicals, and be entirely void of oxygen. Various other lesser-known conditions were also inevitably present and active.

Similar conditions for making oil can rather easily be replicated in modern laboratories. Scientists have formed oil in as little as thirty minutes from algae. Many other natural raw materials can also be utilized to form oil. Even coal can be transformed into oil. The primary limiting problem is access to the necessary raw materials and the prohibitive cost of the procedure.

Coal seams as thick as ninety feet have been located. This would require a mass of vegetation up to 900 feet high. Under what possible circumstances could such a gargantuan repository of vegetation be accumulated and then buried? The only reasonable answer is a worldwide Flood.

Only the pre-Flood world was blessed with a worldwide uniform climate that could grow such immense amounts of vegetation. This is demonstrated by the fact that coal and oil are located all over the planet. That includes such inhospitable regions as the Arctic Circle and Antarctica. It is well-known that desert regions also offer huge reserves of oil.

We shall also discover that some trees have been deposited in more than one coal seam. These are called polystrate trees. If, as the evolutionist claims, these coal seams took millions of years to form, why did these polystrate trees not simply rot over these reputed vast epochs of time? In addition, why are some of them buried askew at awkward angles? Some are even found upside down, roots up. Trees do not normally grow that way.

Second, we shall examine the geological evidence that the rocks and canyons of the world provide. For instance, was the Grand Canyon carved out by the comparatively puny Colorado River? How could one river account for the hundreds of separate canyons with all of their twists and turns? We shall also delve into the mythical geologic column. This column is merely a figment of man's overactive imagination. It exists nowhere on the planet in such a systematic order. However, the question must be posed as to what formed all the different rock layers that compose the alleged geologic column. Only the Flood can account for it.

Third, we shall observe a sampling of the many different evidences that support a worldwide Flood. For example, how can such ephemeral fossils as footprints and even raindrops develop over millions of years? In a word, that is utterly impossible. Only during the Flood can the once-in-a-planet circumstances give rise to these essential chemical and physical activities. Our understanding of the actions of the Flood is admittedly minimal. But all the extra-biblical evidence discovered thus far supports the fact that there was just such a cataclysmic event.

We shall close this chapter with an exhortation to all believers to more thoroughly prepare themselves for intellectual discussion with scoffers. People of this generation generally seek proof. Christians, by definition, live by faith. But it is not a faith that stands without accompaniment. God has provided astounding evidences of His existence. It is the believer's responsibility to avail himself of as much information as is reasonably possible.

That God-given responsibility includes proofs of the Flood. The Flood leaves the reader with the chilling message that God does eventually judge sin. As Hebrews 10:31 warns all mankind: "It is a fearful thing to fall into the hands of the living God." God provides the way out of His judgment through His Son, Jesus Christ. Do you know Him?

What Caused the Coal and Oil Deposits?

Flood evidence #3: The world's immense deposits of coal and oil indicate a universal Flood. How do coal and oil form? Vast amounts of vegetation, animal and fish carcasses, heat and pressure, and a lack of oxygen are required. The vegetation and animal material must be buried rapidly, or it will merely rot. Are oil and coal deposits being formed around the world today? No, not in any significant amounts. In fact, some would say not at all.

Most geologists generally agree that coal is formed primarily from vegetation and oil from ancient marine animals and fish. We have vast reserves of both coal and oil. Problem: Neither product is being formed today in any significant measure. This would seem to contradict the ongoing mantra that the present is the key to the past. So why and how did oil form in the past?

Ben B. Cox writes:

> Petroleum occurs in rocks of all ages from the Cambrian to the Pliocene inclusive, but no evidence has been found to prove that any petroleum has been formed since the Pliocene, although sedimentation patterns and thicknesses in Pleistocene and recent sediments are similar to those in the Pliocene where petroleum has formed.[136]

Why is that? Perhaps it is because the mechanism for making oil

---
[136] Vance Farrell, Science vs. Evolution, p. 603.

and coal was temporary and unrepeated. Scientists can make oil in the lab in thirty minutes or less, given the proper controlled conditions. What event in nature could produce the same necessary conditions to create the world's immense deposits of coal and oil? The only known answer to man is a universal Flood.

How the Flood Made Oil and Coal

How did the Flood manage to form oil? Ken Ham and Bodie Hodge answer this question in easily understandable terms:

Most oil deposits that we have are a result of the Flood. There may be other factors (e.g., oil production from bacteria), but most of it came from the Flood and the conditions thereof. Think about the fossils of marine organisms, plants and trees, algae, land creatures, etc. When they fossilize, their organic material is removed by water and replaced by minerals (e.g., limestone) to turn it into rock. Where does all that organic material go? It seeps down with water into pockets in the earth. Then it separates from the water into pools or deposits. What remains is primarily a mixture of hydrocarbons, gases, and water. We call this "crude oil."[137]

Some claim that coal can slowly form over millions of years. Since no one will be around to watch this happen, that is a hard claim to deny. But it is equally hard to prove! Peat bogs are often cited as a good source of coal. While peat may be a source of small amounts of coal, numerous facts demonstrate that they could not possibly have been responsible for the massive coal seams found

---
[137] Ken Ham and Bodie Hodge, A Flood of Evidence: 40 Reasons Noah and the Ark Still Matter, p. 141.

today, many of which are up to thirty to forty feet thick. To make a coal seam that thick requires a deposit of between 300 to 400 feet of vegetation and animal remains.

Some coal seams up to ninety feet thick have been discovered. That would require about 900 feet of vegetation! How is that possible in a peat bog? Coal is found on all seven continents. How could coal seams possibly have formed in ice-bound Antarctica? The obvious answer is that Antarctica was once lush and full of vegetation, just as the entire planet was. No one has ever seen a peat bog form a coal seam anywhere near that thick. Furthermore, the primary ingredients for coal come from plants and trees that do not grow in swampy areas, which is where one finds peat bogs.

The only reasonable alternative to form coal is from the global Flood. Several factors contribute to the formation of coal. These factors demonstrate evidence supporting the occurrence of an unprecedented Flood.

Fossil Fuels Require Decomposed Vegetation and Animals

Factor #1: Immense amounts of vegetation and marine animals had to be mixed together and quickly buried. Heat and pressure must then be applied to guard against premature rotting. How did marine animals end up mixing with land-based vegetation? Obviously, this blending was due to some extraordinary and massive transport device. What transportation device could possibly be better than a universal Flood?

Around the world today, one can witness some rather incredible and highly destructive floods. The capacity of water to scour the channels through which it flows is amazing. Anything that gets in the turbulent water's path will be swept along relentlessly until the water spreads out more evenly. Huge boulders and massive tree jams are frequently carried along great distances. The power of water is more formidable than most people appreciate. If we could witness this today in local floods, what would the power of a universal Flood have been?

Tsunamis, from time to time, inundate coastal areas with extremely destructive power. Coastline property tragically falls claim to its strength, and unsuspecting people lose their lives. Imagine the energy released by unrelenting tsunamis sweeping repeatedly over the same geographical regions. The tsunamis of Noah's day would have unquestionably towered to unthinkable heights. One must bear in mind that the crust of the earth is fragmented in an untold number of locations.

What Could Possibly Cause Polystrate Trees?

Factor #2: Polystrate trees, often ten to thirty meters in length, are frequently found punctuating two or more coal seams. This means that these trees go from one stratum right into the next. But if these coal seams formed over millions of years, as geologists generally contend, the trees would simply have rotted. They could not possibly be found in more than one coal seam.

Apparently, no highly trained geologists were around to inform the offending trees of their transgression. They are theoretically not permitted to punctuate more than one coal seam simultaneously. But they do anyway. Such is life in the coal beds! Obviously, the coal seams materialized rather quickly. In addition, oftentimes, these trees are upside down or at some other strange angle. They certainly did not grow that way. They obviously were transported from somewhere else. What can transport such huge trees? A universal Flood can do it! Nothing else in nature really seems to qualify.

Henry Morris comments on polystrate fossils as follows:

Stratification (or layered sequence) is a universal characteristic of sedimentary rocks. As noted above, a stratum of sediment is formed by deposition under essentially continuous and uniform hydraulic conditions. When the sedimentation stops for a while before another period of deposition, the new stratum will be visibly distinguishable from the earlier by a stratification line (actually a surface).

Distinct strata also result when there is a change in the velocity of flow or other hydraulic characteristics. Sedimentary beds as now found are typically composed of many "strata," and it is in such beds that most fossils are found. Not infrequently, large fossils of animals and plants—especially tree trunks—extend through several strata, often twenty feet or more in thickness. Dutch geologist N. A. Rupke has suggested that these be called "polystrate fossils" and has documented numerous remarkable examples of this phenomenon. ...

It is beyond question that this type of fossil must have been buried quickly or it would not have been preserved intact while the strata accumulated around it. And since the strata entombing these polystrate fossils are no different in appearance or composition from other strata, it is obvious that neither was there any significant difference in the rapidity of deposition.[138]

---

[138] Henry M. Morris, The Biblical Basis for Modern Science (Grand Rapids, MI: Baker Book House, 1984), p. 324.

What Could Create a Ninety-Foot-Thick Coal Seam?

Factor #3: Coal is collected in layers called cyclothem. In between the layers of coal will be other materials such as shale, clay, limestone, sandstone, etc. These coal layers may be relatively thin, as little as approximately five feet. They can also be quite thick, up to ninety feet. It is generally conceded that it requires ten feet of vegetation to make one foot of coal. That is 900 feet of vegetation! One does not witness such piles of vegetation every day. What is additionally shocking is how broad an area these coal seams can cover.

Vance Ferrell writes:

> Each of these layers may be thin—but it can be amazingly wide in area. Modern stratigraphic research has shown that just one of these coal seams reaches from Oklahoma, Missouri, and Iowa, eastward through Indiana to Ohio to Pennsylvania, and southward through Kentucky. This one coal seam alone comprises 100,000 square miles [258,990 km] in central and eastern United States. There are no modern conditions that could duplicate such coal production, yet evolutionary geologists routinely tell us that "the present is the key to the past", i.e., the way things are happening now is the way they happened in past ages.[139]

How Did the Large Boulders Arrive?

Factor #4: Large boulders are frequently found in coal seams that are not native to the region. The only possible way they could be there is if they were washed in by a huge Flood. Boulders do

---
139 Vance Ferrell, Science vs. Evolution, p. 481.

not walk by themselves. These boulders are, on average, about 12 pounds (5 kg), but one was located that weighed 161 pounds (73 kg).

Otto Stutzer comments: "Numerous theories have been advanced to explain the transportation of these boulders to their positions. Phillips' (1855) explanation that the boulders were floated in, held by the roots of floating trees, has still the greatest support among geologists."[140]

Coal, petroleum, and fossils all share one thing in common. They are found only in sedimentary strata. All three are found all over the globe. In other words, they all experienced a rapid burial because of a Flood. Since sedimentary strata are found literally everywhere on earth, the only reasonable conclusion is that a Flood once covered the entire planet. Thus, fossils are God's handwriting in the soil and rock. Equally so, coal and petroleum testify to the Flood.

Carbon 14: The Hidden Trade Secret of Evolutionists

Factor #5: Carbon 14 (C-14) is found in coal seams. Geologists consistently date coal as being millions of years old. But is that true? If it is true, then how could there still be C-14 in the coal? C-14 "supposedly" has a half-life of 5,730 years. We stress "supposedly" because all the radioactive dating methods are fraught with unprovable assumptions. However, we shall assume that the half-life of C-14 is accurate for the moment. If that were really true, then no measurable amount of C-14 should remain in any material after 100,000 years. But that certainly has not been found to be the case.

Bodie Hodge writes:

An interesting thing about coal is that it is made up of

---

140 Otto Stutzer, Geology of Coal, translated by A. C. Noe (Chicago: University of Chicago Press, 1940), p. 277.

Global Flood versus Local Flood

carbon. If coal layers are supposed to be millions of years old, then there should be no C-14 left in it. C-14 can only give dates of thousands of years, not millions of years, otherwise it should all be decayed away. Now as a caveat, C-14 dates have hosts of problems such as living creatures that date to outrageously old dates. For example, we find incorrect dates for:

- Living mollusks supposedly 23,000 years old

- Living snails were supposedly 27,000 years old

- A freshly killed seal was supposedly 1,300 years old

- Dinosaur bones with C-14

People may offer excuses for these, but the fact is that they came out with inaccurate dates. If we can't trust C-14 dating on dates we know, how can we trust it on dates we don't know? That would be illogical. ... Geophysicist Dr. John Baumgardner has a listing of 90 samples from secular literature of things supposedly older than 100,000 years old in the secular reasoning, and yet they have measurable C-14 in them! This means these things cannot be that old![141]

---

141 Ken Ham and Bodie Hodge, A Flood of Evidence: 40 Reasons Noah and the Ark Still Matter, pp. 118–119.

Carbon 14 has been found in coal, oil, and even diamonds. Yet diamonds are dated as billions of years old! Clearly, something is being falsely reported. As previously stated, no measurable C-14 should be found in anything over 100,000 years old. The other listed examples should suffice to cause anyone to pause regarding the accuracy of all dating methods. They have all proven to be highly inconsistent with one another over much-extended research.

How Long Does It Take to Make Coal and Oil?

Factor #6: Coal and oil can be produced very rapidly in laboratory conditions. Given the proper conditions, coal can be transformed into oil in a matter of days. Andrew Snelling writes:

> Thus, for example, it has been demonstrated in the laboratory that moderate heating of the brown coals of the Gippsland Basin of Victoria, Australia, to stimulate their rapid deeper burial, will generate crude oil and natural gas similar to that found in reservoir rocks in only 2-5 days.[142]

Research on the generation of oil constantly takes place around the globe. Many different products are being tested in laboratories, such as animal fats, feathers, algae, the waste products from cows and other animals, and even sewage sludge. The primary limiting factors for the production of oil seem to be the imagination and economics. If the cost factor is higher than the benefit of the product, simple economics rules it out.

Regarding the production of oil in this manner, geologist Andrew Snelling comments:

---

142 Ibid., 121–122.

Turkey and pig slaughterhouse wastes are daily trucked into the world's first biorefinery, a thermal conversion processing plant in Carthage, Missouri. On peak production days, 500 barrels of high-quality fuel oil better than crude oil are made from 270 tons of turkey guts and 20 tons of pig fat.[143]

Algae, surprisingly, provides for the quickest transformation. Under the correct conditions, it can be turned into oil in just thirty minutes. That certainly does not coincide with the viewpoint that it takes millions of years to make coal or oil.

Researcher Brian Thomas writes:

> Researchers at the Pacific Northwest National Laboratory (PNNL) in Washington State have pioneered a new technology that makes diesel fuel from algae – and their cutting edge machine produces the oil in just minutes. ... Simply heat pea-green algae soup to 662 degrees F (350 C) at 3,000 psi for about 60 minutes. ...
>
> Scientists at the Pacific Northwest National Laboratory are claiming success in perfecting a method that can transform a pea-soupy solution of algae into crude oil by pressure cooking it for about 30 minutes. The process, called hydrothermal liquefaction, also works on other streams of organic matter, such as municipal sewage.[144]

---

143 Ibid., 121.
144 Ibid., 122.

Amazingly enough, as time went on and more research was done, the Pacific Northwest National Laboratory cut the time down by half for producing crude oil. Who knows how much further they will refine the process? The point is that what man can do reasonably well, God can do infinitely better.

God's Blessing that Arose from Judgment

God transformed the pre-Flood vegetation and marine and animal carcasses into crude oil and coal through burial, lack of oxygen, heat, and pressure. Just these two important substances provide the majority of heat and energy for the planet. Furthermore, the supplies will last for centuries. Out of a disaster, God provided a blessing! That, characteristically, is God's marvelous and gracious pattern of provision for mankind.

The world once had a uniform climate and was lush with vegetation and animals. Evidence is found for this everywhere we turn. Even Antarctica has large deposits of coal and petrified wood. How did it get there? Vast oil deposits are found north of the Arctic Circle, where almost no vegetation grows today. What happened to all the vegetation? These coal and petroleum deposits could only have happened in a world that was blessed with ideal environmental conditions.

The world once was covered with vegetation and populated with animals over its entire land surface. What a fantastic life God provided for earth's inhabitants. And what was mankind's unholy response? They turned to wickedness on a scale not even imaginable in today's world. The evidence for a worldwide flood is overwhelming! Contrary to what many claim, the earth is not running out of either coal or oil. True, the supply is not infinite, but it is certainly more than adequate for God's purposes until Christ returns.

The Rocks Cry Out!

This Little River Did That?

Flood evidence #4: The Grand Canyon and other canyons around the world indicate a worldwide Flood. Geologists are fond of stating that the Grand Canyon took millions of years to form. The Colorado River supposedly accomplished this all on its own. "It took a little water and a lot of time," geologists and park rangers placidly claim with a yawn. Yet, any reasonable person who visits the Grand Canyon for the first time can readily see how absurd that claim really is.

The Grand Canyon is huge. It is one mile deep, four to eighteen miles wide, and 216 miles long. A different and much more plausible way of summarizing the formation of the Grand Canyon is that: "It took a lot of water and a short time!" The Grand Canyon is not one canyon. It is a jumbled and highly complex array of canyons carved out by many different sources of water. But where and when did all of this water come from to carve out the canyon? Are there modern-day canyons that have formed on a smaller scale than the Grand Canyon? Yes, there are. How did they form? They formed under the influence of a lot of water and a short time.

The Flood quite naturally left many broad and deep lakes behind it. Some of those lakes are still with us today; others did not last so long. During and after the Flood, the valleys dropped; in other words, the ocean basins were greatly deepened. Mountains also were raised up due to massive geological forces not happening today (Psalm 104:8). When the mountains were in the process of being elevated, this by itself would cause immense, unprecedented runoff. Considering that the earth was still saturated with water and the soil was not yet solidified, huge canyons would have been carved out. That is common sense and understandable even by a child.

The continents themselves shifted and convulsed in many ways beyond our present-day comprehension. No one has ever seen its equal since. No one ever shall. Considering the fact that the continents apparently split from each other and moved, floating on water and a shattered crust of the earth, the topographical changes were astronomical in size. This all had to happen quite rapidly.

This combination of factors would have caused an incalculable runoff from the continents into the oceans. The Grand Canyon was formed during this time when the rock was still quite pliable. In other words, the rocks were still moist. How can we say that? Some of the rock within the Grand Canyon is twisted into unnatural shapes. Solid rocks don't bend; they break.

Hence, the initial rock material of necessity had not yet become firm; it was still forming. Undoubtedly, the Grand Canyon was also carved out with the additional help of natural dams bursting from numerous directions. These dams were holding back massive lakes left by the Flood. Rushing water is capable of phenomenal erosive power.

Does Water Erosion Still Take Place Today?

Question: Do we see water erosion comparable today that would support the Flood theory? Answer: Indeed, the evidence abounds, but it is on a much smaller scale.

Roger Patterson writes as follows:

> As we look at the processes forming and eroding geologic structures today, we must admit they cannot

be responsible for the features that we see across the globe. Textbooks and other evolution-based sources suggest Grand Canyon formed gradually over the last 6-17 million years, slicing through layers that go back nearly 2 billion years. This amazing canyon has been interpreted as the result of a little water acting over a very long period of time. However, from the biblical perspective, the canyon formed from a lot of water acting over a short period of time.

Grand Canyon itself is best explained as a result of the erosion caused by the sudden release of water from large lakes left behind after the Flood. The Flood deposited many of the canyon's layers, through which the canyon was later cut. Hopi and Canyonlands Lakes were remnants of the receding Floodwaters, impounded by the Kaibab Upwarp.

While the sediment layers of the Kaibab Upwarp were still relatively soft, these lakes breached that barrier and their waters flowed west toward the Pacific Ocean, scouring the landscape. Could such a catastrophe actually carve such dramatic features? Evidence from the recent eruptions at Mount Saint Helens lends support to these claims.

After the eruption of Mount St. Helens in 1980, pumice and volcanic ash deposits blocked the Toutle River.

Two years later a mud flow breached the area and eroded what is now known as the "Little Grand Canyon of the Toutle River," cutting canyons up to 140 feet deep. The side canyons and channels resemble the appearance of Grand Canyon and mirror the rapid formation of a canyon in a short period.

Nearby, Loowit Canyon was cut out of solid rock to a depth of 100 feet. These observed examples of rapid canyon formation can be used to help us understand how larger canyons and topographic features may have formed as a result of the Flood.[145]

In more recent memory, Mount St. Helens is best known for its power and catastrophic impact on the surrounding territory. However, other lesser-known floods have also seriously impacted their immediate regions. Burlingame Canyon near Walla Walla, Washington, was carved out over a period of six days in 1926. It is about 1,370 feet long (450 meters), 110 feet deep (35 meters), and 110 feet wide (35 meters).

Another example occurred when the Guadalupe River in Texas had excessive flooding. The Canyon Lake spillway (a reservoir) normally experienced 350 cubic feet per second of water going over itself. During this particular flood, 70,000 cubic feet per second of water spilled over! It carved out a canyon 1 mile long (1.6 km) and 50 feet deep (15 meters). This was accomplished through solid limestone.

Sarfati writes of the following example:

---

[145] Roger Patterson, Evolution Exposed: Earth Science (Hebron, KY: Answers in Genesis, 2008), p. 131.

These are the results of comparatively minor floods. No wonder more geologists are recognizing what megafloods could do. So they are recognizing megaflood causes of other canyons, such as Box Canyon, Idaho. But it took four decades to support the theory of J. Harlan Bretz (1882-1981) that the Channeled Scablands of Eastern Washington were caused by a catastrophic flood in the Ice Age, the Lake Missoula Flood. This was the second biggest flood in history, after Noah's Flood, which was about 10^4 times larger. (As shown in Ch. 20, a single Ice Age was an almost inevitable aftermath of the Flood).

The greatest scabland channel by far is the Grand Coulee, a gorge about 80 km long and up to 300 m deep. This includes the Dry Falls about midway along, a huge feature 120 m high and 6 km wide. The 'Dry Falls' is so named because it was clearly carved by a water flow many times that of the Niagara Falls today, but none is flowing over it now. It shows what the catastrophic water action of a single flood can do in rapidly carving solid granite.[146]

An Island Is Born!

Flood evidence #5: Rapid rock formations are taking place in the present. Although it is true that one does not often see large changes quickly taking place, such events do occur from time to

---
146 Sarfati, Jonathan. The Genesis Account: A theological, historical, and scientific commentary on Genesis 1–11, pp. 548–549.

time, given the right conditions. The cited examples listed above of canyons forming very rapidly is one scenario. These occur because of floods and/or a combination of factors.

Other changes can take place solely due to volcanic action. A prime illustration of volcanic activity occurred in recent years and actually created the new island—Surtsey. It is located 51 miles (32 km) off the southern coast of Iceland and came into being in 1963. The volcano began erupting in water 410 feet (130 m) below sea level. By November 14, the magma had breached the surface. It continued erupting until June 5, 1967. The island was 2.7 square km when finished but has now shrunk back down to 1.4 square km due to water erosion.

A book was written on this volcanic activity by the official geologist for Iceland, Sigurdur Thorarinsson (1912–1983), in 1964. The following is an excerpt from his book:

> An Icelander who has studied geology and geomorphology at foreign universities is later taught by experience in his own homeland that the timescale he had been trained to attach to geological developments is misleading when assessments are made of the forces—constructive and destructive—which have molded and are still molding the face of Iceland.
>
> What elsewhere may take thousands of years may be accomplished here in one century. All the same he is amazed whenever he comes to Surtsey, because the same development may take a few weeks or even days here. On Surtsey, only a few months sufficed for a

landscape to be created which was so varied and mature that it was almost beyond belief.[147]

Within a few years after the lava stopped flowing on Surtsey, it had a thriving variety of plant life consisting of ferns, grasses, and flowers. Insects also had arrived in good order, followed by birds. Scientists were amazed at how quickly these developments of nature occurred. The same held true for Mount St. Helens. Though its eruption in 1980 was vastly more powerful, life also returned there in quick procession.

Within five years, the decimated region was once again rapidly repopulating with plants and small animals. Just a scant twenty years after the eruption, the vegetation and animal life had returned to nearly the level of pre-eruption levels! Scientists could not believe their eyes. Clearly, the long-age, uniformitarianism advocates had "missed the boat" in their estimations of how quickly nature takes to rebound from a disaster.

A Fine Layering of Soil and Sediment

Two other features within this category need to be cited. (1) One of the truly fascinating aspects of the canyon formed at the Mount St. Helens volcanic eruption is the finely graded layers of soil and sediment. Within just one afternoon, the volcano produced approximately twenty-five feet of finely distinct and separated layers. Amazingly, these layers sorted themselves out quite automatically as long as there was a horizontal flow of material. The particles differentiated themselves based on their size.

These levels of sediment tend to be quite flat and parallel to each other. This is commonly witnessed in the Grand Canyon. If there had been long periods of time between these layers, as is commonly

---
147 Ibid., p. 543.

taught, one would not find them to be so precise and uniform. The weather and other factors would have interfered and caused considerable disruption.

Fossilized Footprints?

(2) Fossilized ephemeral footprints have been located. This is arguably the most remarkable remnant of the Flood that has been left behind. Ephemeral means "to last for a very short time." If that is the case, how can a footprint possibly survive? The first rainfall or gust of wind should wipe such footprints out, depending on the soil conditions. If a footprint is made in dusty soil, for example, it may last only a few minutes. If it is exceptionally windy, the footprint will disappear in mere seconds.

One of the best places to make a footprint is on the beach. But common experience tells us that such footprints do not last long. Yet, in the fossil record, some footprints are actually fossilized. What could possibly produce that? The only way they can be preserved is if they are covered with an additional sediment layer that quickly hardens. There must be a cementing process. That is precisely what the Flood did.

Sarfati writes:

> A good example is the Winton Formation, Lark Quarry, Queensland, Australia. This is famous for its 3,300 dinosaur footprints. They were exposed by excavations in 1976 that removed 60 tons of overburdening sandstone. This was soon named the Dinosaur Stampeded National Monument. However, it didn't take long for the footprints to start weathering.

First, a sheltering roof was built over the sight, but this was insufficient. So in 2002, a Conservation Building was constructed to cover the tracks. Now, the humidity and temperature are controlled; and running water, humans, and animals, are kept away from the tracks. So it makes little sense that they were exposed for vast ages without such protection. There is a further turn to this story. Many of the tracks are not full footprints, and are instead likely to have been made by a swimming dinosaur whose feet barely touched the bottom. So this trackway was likely not the result of a stampede at all, but dinosaurs fleeing from a flood.[148]

In addition to dinosaur tracks, which quite expectantly make large impressions, many other types of animal footprints have been found. These include quite a range of creatures. One finds the footprints of trilobites, horseshoe crabs, pterosaurs, amphibians, and others. Footprints of human beings have been located in Laetoli, Tanzania, in rock dated by evolutionists as 3.7 million years old. But humans supposedly were not around back in that time period. According to the Scripture, the universe wasn't around 3.7 million years ago either. Remarkably, even raindrops have left fossilized marks!

Whitcomb and Morris write:

> Related to animal tracks that have been thus preserved are the many instances of preservation of ancient ripple marks or raindrop impressions. But that such ephemeral markings could have been preserved in such great numbers and in such perfection is truly a remarkable

[148] Ibid., p. 546.

phenomenon and one for which there is little if any modern parallel. ...

It seems clear that the only way in which such prints could be preserved as fossils is by means of some chemical action permitting rapid lithification and some aqueous action permitting rapid burial. Some sudden and catastrophic action is again necessary for any reasonable explanation of the phenomena.[149]

Quite naturally, one cannot go back in time to see how many topographical changes have taken place on the earth. However, it is quite evident that these geological revisions were of an incredible nature. The Flood saw a restructuring of the entire planet. The mountains rose, and the ocean basins were formed. The continents separated and drifted apart.

Earthquakes of unimaginable magnitude shattered areas in the crust of the earth. Volcanic action covered the world with ash and other residue. The rain and the tsunamis swept over entire continents. All of this happened only about 4,300 years ago, not millions and billions of years. Indeed, the account of it is all recorded in Sacred Writ.

Where Is That Alleged Geologic Column?

Flood evidence #6: The lack of unity in the rock strata. Uniformitarianism teaches that the different levels of rock strata (the geologic column) took approximately two billion years to form. That, of course, denies the scriptural account of the Flood. But it also denies science. There is absolutely no evidence that the laying

---

[149] John C. Whitcomb and Henry M. Morris, The Genesis Flood: The Biblical Flood and its Scientific Implications (Grand Rapids, MI: Baker Book House, 1961), pp. 167–168.

down of the various strata took long periods of time. In fact, the evidence shows precisely the opposite. Examples from Mount St. Helens have clearly demonstrated that this process can take place very rapidly, sometimes within scant hours.

It should be noted that the so-called geologic column, as frequently presented in textbooks, does not exist anywhere on earth. It is merely a compilation of numerous examples of sedimentary and other types of rock stacked one on top of another. Some scientists claim that the various strata came about from a long and extended series of catastrophes.

They are correct in that it was a catastrophe that caused the different layers. However, it was just one catastrophe, the global Flood. There are no real boundaries between the various levels that would represent any time gap. They are simply laid one upon another in what appears to be rapid succession. This implies that the entire column was put together at about the same time.

Vance Ferrell offers the following observations as to why the Flood established the geologic column in just a short time:

(1) Rapid or no Fossils. Each strata had to be laid down rapidly, or fossils would not have resulted.

(2) Rapid or no Rocks. The physical structure and interconnections of the strata require rapid deposition in order for them to form into rocks.

(3) No Erosion between Strata. Each strata was laid directly over the one below it, since there is no trace of erosion between them. Each strata was formed continuously and rapidly, and then—with no time-lapse ero-

sion in between—the next strata formed continuously and rapidly over that. And on and on it went.

(4) Layers not Worldwide. There are many "unconformities," where one stratum ends horizontally and another begins. But there is no worldwide unconformity; instead one stratum will gradually grade imperceptibly into another, which thereupon succeeds it with more continuous and rapid deposition, without a time break at any point.

(5) Generally no Clear Boundaries. There is rarely a clear physical boundary between strata formations. Generally they tend to merge and mingle with each other in a zone of considerable thickness.[150]

Why Are Theoretically Older Rocks Sunning Themselves on Younger Rocks?

Flood evidence #7: How does evolution explain the major overthrust of older rock formations piled on top of allegedly younger rock formations? That is a scenario that most evolutionary geologists do not enjoy discussing. Quite understandably, the lower rock formations are understood to contain the oldest rock. But this oftentimes is not the case, at least not according to radioactive dating methods and the corresponding study of fossils. How can such a thing be? Should not the younger rocks naturally be on the top? Of course, they should. It would take a major event to reverse this natural order.

---
150 Vance Ferrell, Science vs. Evolution, p. 807.

A "quiet" conundrum: According to geologists, the fossils are generally used to help date the rocks, although, and this is exclusively in their opinion, it works the other way around as well. In other words, the rocks date the fossils, and the fossils date the rocks. How utterly convenient! In geology, apparently, one can have his mineral-encrusted cake and eat it too! That is circular reasoning at its worst. You cannot use both factors to explain each other. Either the rock dates the fossil, or the fossil dates the rock. You cannot have it both ways. You must pick one method or the other.

Aside from this impermissible circular reasoning of geologists, what other major problem does one find? The problem is that you frequently find "older" rock formations on top of the "younger" ones. This is rather casually called an overthrust. How is that possible? Some explain it through earthquakes. Some might even acknowledge floods causing some of the problems. That is reasonable to some extent. However, such scenarios would have to be limited to a rather small geographical area. Not all of these situations can be qualified as "small" geographical areas.

Just How Big Do Those Overthrusts Get?

John Whitcomb and Henry Morris comment as follows:

> It is recognized that phenomena of this sort have taken place on a small scale, in certain localities where there is ample evidence of intense past faulting and folding. However, these visible confirmations of the concept are definitely on a small scale, usually in terms of a few hundreds of feet, whereas many of the great overthrust areas occupy hundreds or even thousands of square miles.

637

It seems almost fantastic to conceive of such huge areas and masses of rocks really behaving in such a fashion, unless we are ready to accept catastrophism of an intensity that makes the Noachian Deluge seem quiescent by comparison! Certainly the principle of uniformity is inadequate to account for them.

Nothing we know of present earth movements—of rock compressive and shearing strengths, of the plastic flow of rock materials, or of other modern physical processes—gives any observational basis for believing that such things are happening now or ever could have happened, except under extremely unusual conditions.[151]

Can Mountains Perambulate Hither and Yon?

There are numerous examples of these so-called overthrusts that are quite impressive. One example is the Matterhorn in Switzerland. This entire mountain is sitting on top of rock that is supposedly much younger. It is hard to imagine how an entire mountain could ambulate horizontally many miles in order to settle in its present position. Mountains are not generally known to have such strong legs; indeed, they are not known to have any legs at all.

A more regional area of rather significant size is the Appalachian mountain range in eastern America. Apparently, this mountain range climbed up out of the sea and settled in a new place. They even beat the Indians in their arrival to America! An inquisitive person might suspect that evolutionary geologists may be having

---

[151] John C. Whitcomb and Henry Morris, The Genesis Flood, pp. 180–181.

some problems with their dating of rocks. One of the largest of these overthrusts is found in Yellowstone National Park. To say that it is immense is a classic understatement.

Whitcomb and Morris comment as follows:

> To illustrate the character of these important areas, we might consider the well-known Heart Mountain Thrust of Wyoming. This supposed thrust occupies roughly a triangular area, 30 miles wide by 60 miles long, with its apex at the northeast corner of Yellowstone Park. It consists of about 50 separate blocks of Paleozoic strata (Ordovician, Devonian, and Mississippian) resting essentially horizontally and conformably on Eocene beds, some 250,000,000 years younger![152]

Such a geological difficulty proves a major inconvenience for uniformitarian scientists. However, it is perfectly understandable to the creationist. Such matters are partly resolved with a recognition of the universal Flood. However, the creationist, unlike the evolutionist, also recognizes that the radiometric dating methods are fallacious. Hence, a creationist puts no faith in the alleged ages of these rock formations in the first place. The dates of the rocks are erroneous from the beginning. They are not millions or billions of years old.

If these rocks actually were dated at least in sequence, even though not in age, what might explain the sequence? Certainly, uniformitarianism has no real answers to explain the legendary column or the types of fossils contained therein. But if the Flood was real, then the many puzzles connected with earth's geological features would be resolved quite readily.

---
152 Ibid., p. 181.

And What if There Really Was a Flood?

Assuming the Flood really happened as the Bible describes, and we certainly believe that it did, what would be some of those results? If the floodwaters laid down all of the sedimentary rock layers along with all of their entombed fossils, what might we expect?

Vance Ferrell answers as follows:

(1) Animals living at the lowest levels would tend to be buried in the lowest strata.

(2) Creatures buried together—would tend to be buried with other animals that lived in the same region or ecological community.

(3) Hydrologic forces (the suck and drag of rapidly moving water) would tend to sort out creatures of similar forms. Because of lower hydraulic drag, those with the simplest shapes would tend to be buried first.

(4) Backboneless sea creatures (marine invertebrates), since they live on the sea bottom, would normally be found in the bottom strata.

(5) Fish would be found in a higher strata since they can swim up close to the surface.

(6) Amphibians and reptiles would be buried higher than the fish, but as a rule, below the land animals.

(7) Few land plants or animals would be in the lower strata.

(8) The first land plants would be found where the amphibians were found.

(9) Mammals and birds would generally be found in higher levels than reptiles and amphibians.

Because many animals tend to travel in herds in time of danger, we would find herd animals buried together. In addition, the larger, stronger animals would tend to sort out into levels apart from the slower ones (tigers would not be found with hippopotamuses). Relatively few birds would be found in the strata, since they could fly to the highest points. Few humans would be found in the strata. They would be at the top, trying to stay afloat until they died; following which they would sink to the surface of the sediments and decompose.[153]

Cynicism Does Not Equate to Science

Amazingly enough, this is exactly what we find. It does not take a rocket scientist to analyze the data that encompasses the globe related to the Flood. It is literally everywhere one walks! Only a skeptic of the first order can turn a blind eye to these clearest of evidences. Given some proper guidance and time to think, even a relatively young child would come up with many of the above-listed characteristics of the Flood that Ferrell has listed. Certainly, the

---
153 Vance Ferrell, Science vs. Evolution, p. 610.

child would recognize that people would be best equipped to avoid the rising waters. People climb trees and mountains, for instance, better than your average cow or clam does.

Many more evidences demonstrating the worldwide Flood could be examined. It is advisable that the student of Scripture avail himself to some of these excellent materials found in books and DVDs. We have merely dabbled in some of these evidences. It must be remembered and believed that Scripture unquestionably teaches a universal Flood.

God dedicated four chapters, Genesis chapters 6 to 9, to the topic of the Flood. Through the Flood man recognizes that sin will be punished by a holy God. The Flood is one of the greatest motivations available to man to turn to a sovereign God in repentance. The impact of the Flood should never be underestimated by believer or unbeliever alike.

Prepare Yourself!

A few questions should be individually entertained by the enterprising reader regarding the Flood and its purposes. We shall be examining such questions in our following chapter. It is always advisable to think some of these issues through. Why is that? God requires that of all believers. That is why he granted all human beings an operational brain! The mind is to be exercised continuously. Studying God's Word is not just for preachers and teachers.

First Peter 3:15 states: "But sanctify the Lord God in your hearts, and always be ready to give a defense to everyone who asks you a reason for the hope that is in you, with meekness and fear." If a believer is not willing to consider the issues of the day, how can he then interact with those who do not believe? He must be willing and able to discuss those stumbling blocks to faith that so confuse the unbeliever. Then believers can truly be the salt of the earth and a city on a hill (Matthew 5:13–14).

Lessons Learned in This Chapter

In this chapter, we first reviewed the fact that the Flood is the only reasonable explanation for the existence of oil and coal. When studied both scientifically and biblically, the Bible satisfies all reasonable questions one might pose regarding the formation of oil and coal. Sadly, even when shown all this corroborating evidence, many simply shrug their shoulders and walk away. Their prejudiced and closed minds do not allow them to embrace the obvious empirical truths presented to them.

Second, we examined a variety of geological evidences that support the reality of the Flood. One perplexing example for the evolutionist is the existence of polystrate trees. If the earth is literally billions of years old, how could these trees penetrate through more than one coal seam? That is illogical. If, as the secular geologists claim, it takes millions of years to form a coal seam, then why did the tree not simply rot away?

Furthermore, if it really does take ten feet of vegetation to form one foot of coal, how does one explain coal seams as thick as ninety feet? That would require an astonishing pile of vegetation 900 feet high! Where does one ever find such an occurrence of such lavish vegetation in nature today? You find it nowhere. Not even the Amazon jungle, luxuriant as it is, could provide sufficient raw material to develop the massive coal deposits around the world.

Something unique and phenomenal in nature has obviously occurred in earth's history to make such massive coal seams possible. That something had to funnel these huge amounts of vegetation together and then bury them deeply and properly. Only a universal

Flood qualifies as the needed catalyst. Coal seams are massive in their breadth. While they may not be overly thick in their particular geographical situations, clearly, an astonishing amount of vegetation was buried at one time to form these huge deposits. Some of these deposits are thousands of square miles in extent.

Third, we reviewed the fact that carbon 14 allegedly has a half-life of only 5,730 years. This means that after approximately 100,000 years, there should be no measurable carbon 14 left in whatever specimen is being examined. But coal all over the world still retains carbon 14. How, then, can the coal be millions of years old? In a word, it cannot.

Carbon 14 has even been found in diamonds, which are supposedly billions of years old! Indeed, diamonds have been dated with other radioactive dating methods as being older than the earth itself. How interesting that is. Clearly, a proper understanding of the alleged dating methods has run amuck. Even relatively short-lived organisms have been dated as being alive for over 20,000 years.

For the purpose of reiteration, we once again offer the following samples. Carbon 14 has been used to date these samples:
- Living mollusks were supposedly 23,000 years old.
- Living snails were supposedly 27,000 years old.
- A freshly killed seal was supposedly 1,300 years old.
- Dinosaur bones with C-14.

If such inconsistencies characterize carbon 14, which is considered the most reliable of the dating methods, how much confidence does this engender for the other, even more fallacious dating methods? In reality, all the dating methods have been proven unworkable through systematic experimentation of many highly competent scientists and geologists.

Fourth, we explored a variety of lesser-known evidences supporting the biblical Flood. For example, aside from the Flood, what present-day activity allows for the fossilization of footprints and even raindrops? Something of an extremely unusual nature must have taken place in past history for such ephemeral markings to be fossilized. It has often been claimed by evolutionists that fossilization requires long periods of time to occur. That is almost laughable. The reality is precisely the opposite. Fossilization must take place very rapidly and under the most extreme of conditions.

Recent volcano activity has demonstrated that the fine grades of soil one finds in places like the Grand Canyon had to transpire quickly. If these layers required millions of years, there would be unconformities everywhere one looked. Such unconformities would be caused by natural events such as wind, rain, and other unforeseen forces. Only rapid rock and soil depositions, such as witnessed in the volcanic explosion of Mount St. Helens, can account for such finely graded levels. The various grades actually sorted themselves out by the size of the particles within them.

One major headache for the evolutionist is that, theoretically, older rocks are sitting on younger rocks. We provided examples of huge areas measuring hundreds of square miles where this is the case. Indeed, Mount Matterhorn in Switzerland is allegedly much older than the younger rocks upon which it rests. It must have been a truly riveting sight to behold this rather large mountain skip over to a new location. The reality is that we entirely reject the dating methods accepted by secular geologists. Their estimations of dating rocks are useless because their dating methods are entirely worthless.

We closed our chapter with a challenge to all believers to familiarize themselves with as much extra-biblical evidence supporting the Flood as is reasonably possible. This is part of the biblical injunction to prepare ourselves for worthy discussions with those who do not know Christ. Obviously, the most crucial element of sharing one's faith is to base it on holy Scripture. But to the secular mind, this is not always adequate or even desirable. Thus, it is wise to be prepared to discuss spiritual matters on a level more familiar to the unbeliever.

First Peter 3:15 serves as a constant reminder to all believers: "But sanctify the Lord God in your hearts, and always be ready to give a defense to everyone who asks you a reason for the hope that is in you, with meekness and fear." Our next chapter continues on the theme of the Flood. Much more information can be gleaned both biblically and scientifically. We pray that this information will stimulate the reader to further and deeper research on this important topic.

Cognitive Conundrum #17

Of royal heritage, I surely could claim, but this alone did not bring me fame. My husband was godly and loyal extreme; to me, his zeal sprang to excess, it did seem. Marriage for the female was coveted indeed; bearing children for growth considered a need. Resistance to God ran in my family; for resentment of worship, I paid a great fee.

Who am I?

Answer: Michal, wife of King David

Chapter 18

Seven Important Questions Concerning the Flood

(Genesis 7:6-24)

In This Chapter

Objectives for This Chapter
Seven Central Questions Regarding the Flood
Lessons Learned in This Chapter

Objectives for This Chapter

This chapter is designed to help finalize the realities of the universal Flood within the reader's mind. It is our strongest contention that the Flood was not local in extent. We shall discuss seven specific issues regarding that particular assessment. Lengthy elaboration on these points is not within the purview of this book. As we have done before, we heartily recommend that the reader avail himself of other more extended and professional books on these subjects.

We shall first begin each question with the inquiry: "If the Flood was local… ?" What would then be the ramifications if that truly were the case? In summary fashion, we shall list the seven specific questions we delve into with this chapter:

Question #1: If the Flood is local, what killed everything on earth?

Question #2: If the Flood is local, did Noah build the ark on

Mount Ararat?

Question #3: If the Flood is local, why build the ark at all?

Question #4: If the Flood is local, what difference does all of this make?

Question #5: If the Flood is local, why is there evidence for it all over the world?

Question #6: If the Flood is local, is Jesus really the God-man or not?

Question #7: If the Flood is local, can we believe in the Bible?

Second, we shall include two quotations by reputed authors. The first quotation is that of Charles C. Ryrie on the sinlessness of Christ. If Christ was not sinless, He also was not God. God cannot sin or be tempted by sin. And if Christ is not God, nor can He be the Savior of the world. If Christ is not God, His words, as recorded in the New Testament, cannot be trusted. Christ definitely believed in Noah and a worldwide Flood. To reject Christ's words means one must also reject His deity. No Christian can knowingly do this.

We also shall include an excellent quotation by Warren Wiersbe. He presents a cogent summary of New Testament teachings on the Flood. Not only does Christ adhere to the reality of the universal Flood, but so do James, Peter, and the author of the book of Hebrews. If Scripture is truly to be accepted as the eternal Word of God, it must be believed in its every teaching. To deny the universal Flood is to deny both God's Word and the worldwide evidence demonstrating the Flood. There is considerable folly in denying either one. The evidence for the universal Flood and coming judgment is overwhelming.

Seven Central Questions Regarding the Flood

As previously stated, the student of Scripture must study issues as thoroughly as possible. The first order of study, of course, is the Bible itself. Second Timothy 2:15 declares: "Be diligent to present yourself approved to God, a worker who does not need to be ashamed, rightly dividing the word of truth." If possible, every believer should endeavor to read the Bible through once every year. It takes only about fifteen minutes a day to do so. Through this important discipline, the Holy Spirit can speak and communicate truth to the listening believer. But the Holy Spirit will not read the Bible to you! You must read it for yourself or as a family.

In this chapter, we shall examine several of the more common questions asked regarding the Flood. These questions are quite instinctive and merit a worthy response. Some may not find our answers entirely exhaustive, or they may esteem them only marginally satisfactory. That is to be expected on certain issues. Furthermore, it is not within the scope of this book to address all such issues at appreciable length. Many outstanding books have been written solely on the Flood. Again, we encourage our readers to avail themselves of some of these outstanding works.

The reader must also bear in mind that God does expect us to accept some things on faith. Without faith, it is impossible to please God (Hebrews 11:6). Obstinate man tends to forget this golden and eternal principle: God is not responsible to His created beings. We are responsible to Him! God grants us answers to the level of His own choosing, not ours.

Some speculation can be healthy if not carried to excessive limits. We strive to maintain biblical parameters when addressing questions. The observant reader will note that we have already touched upon some of the following questions in earlier chapters. We include them now for review or for further enhancement.

Question #1: If the Flood Is Local, What Killed Everything on Earth?

Question #1: Why would God have had Noah build the ark if he was sending only a local flood? Noah and the animals, not to mention all of the wicked people, could simply have kept moving to higher ground. If the Flood was only local, it takes a great deal of faith to assume that people just stubbornly stood their ground and held their breath while the waters slowly went over their heads until they drowned! Obstinacy is one thing; mass suicide is quite another!

Indeed, it takes much more faith to believe in a local flood than a universal one. The Bible teaches a universal Flood, and all of the evidence cited thus far points to that fact. To deny the universal Flood is to deny the efficacy of God's judgment. One of the primary purposes of the Flood was to utterly wipe out the contamination of the earth through the Nephilim. Remarkably, only Noah and his immediate family had been spared contamination by their wickedness. Those who deny the universal Flood also deny God's purpose in it. That is an unwise course of action to take.

It's even harder to believe that cats, which generally avoid the water, would casually stand around until they drowned. You would think that at least the cats might run to higher ground. Furthermore, if the Flood was not universal, why did all the cats, not to mention all the other animals and humans around the world, drown and get buried together in huge, jumbled-up masses where it was still dry? That is indeed a perplexing mystery!

Oddly enough, according to the local flood theorists, not even the birds had the presence of mind to fly to a higher and drier place. Apparently, they simply picked at the ground and ate worms until they drowned! With such faulty reasoning, one must also assume that survival instincts did not come into play until after the Flood. If evolution were true, how could that be? How did anything survive if all creatures, including mankind, were really that stupid?

But then, again, if random and mindless evolution were true, where did the survival instinct arise from in the first place? The primordial swamp bacteria could not have devised it on their own, could they? How could these simple, one-celled creatures create that which "mother evolution" did not even inherently possess? Tis' a puzzlement, is it not? One must remember that evolution was brainless. If it had no brain, how could it have instincts?

Of course, one could offer the bland and tired old excuse that God is a liar and that the Flood is a fable. It is the skeptic's right to do so. Still, the skeptic must then reasonably explain all the world-wide evidence for a Flood. We would happily offer him the opportunity to do so. His only alternative is just to mindlessly bury his obstreperous head in the proverbial sand! That is not generally the choice of an intelligent and introspective individual.

Question #2: If the Flood Is Local, Did Noah Build the Ark on Mount Ararat?

Question #2: How could Noah have landed on the top of Mount Ararat if the Flood was only local? He would have had to drag the ark up there, which, of course, would not have been an easy task! Obviously, it would be impossible. Consider this also: Water seeks its own level. A local flood does not climb up one mountain and leave another untouched.

The water went over the top of Mount Ararat by approximately twenty-three feet. Skeptics are thus compelled to reject this statement of Scripture. Either that, or they must deny the simplest scientific observation known to man: water does not climb vertically! There is no other way to deal with it. But if one discards the straightforward statements of Scripture, then why bother studying the Bible at all? Such a person has positioned himself as a higher authority than not just the Bible but also above the God who wrote it. We refuse to bow to the whims of such self-appointed "human authorities."

Question #3: If the Flood Is Local, Why Build the Ark at All?

Question #3: Why would Noah and the animals have to stay in the ark so long if the Flood was local? Would they not become claustrophobic? One could imagine that the tigers might even get a bit edgy. One could call it "ark fever." That could result in some rather disquieting situations for the ark's inhabitants! Indeed, if the Flood was local, why build the ark at all? Why not let the tigers wander free to do what tigers do best? If God had not exercised His authority over the entire scenario, would the tigers have peacefully entered the ark in the first place? We think not! They certainly would have been highly motivated to enter the ark for a lot of free lunches, though.

Most local floods are over in a matter of days, though the water may linger longer than that. But to remain in the ark for a year after a local flood is more than just a little hard to believe. No one has ever seen a local flood last that long. If such an immense localized flood did occur, the people would simply move out of the area. That has been done on countless occasions. Generally speaking, however, they move back quite promptly.

Question #4: If the Flood Is Local, What Difference Does All This Make?

What are some of the ramifications of denying the worldwide Flood?

Ramification #1: One must be willing to call God a liar. That is not a wise decision! God cannot sin. James 1:13 states: "Let no one say when he is tempted, 'I am tempted by God'; for God cannot be tempted by evil, nor does He Himself tempt anyone" (cf. Titus 1:2). God clearly said the Flood was worldwide, not local. It is inadvisable to the extreme to question the almighty Creator on His statements. How can a person claim to genuinely worship God and then call that God a liar? What kind of God would that be? He would not be worthy of worship, only of fear.

God promised that the world would never be destroyed by a Flood again. Genesis 9:15 states: "And I will remember My covenant which is between Me and you and every living creature of all flesh; the waters shall never again become a flood to destroy all flesh." That promise has held true thus far. We trust that it always will be true. All flesh has never again been destroyed as it was in the universal Flood.

But if the Flood was only local, God would have broken His promise literally millions of times since then. Local floods of varying degrees are common around the globe every spring and summer. Indeed, probably a day doesn't go by without at least one damaging flood somewhere on the planet. In reality, there are possibly dozens. Hence, God had to be referring to a universal Flood, not a local one.

Question #5: If the Flood Is Local, Why Is There Evidence for It All Over the World?

Ramification #2: Belief in a local flood blindly denies the evidence for a worldwide Flood found all over the world. As already stated, to believe in a local flood requires far more faith than it does to believe in a biblical worldwide Flood. To what does the evidence point? We have already reviewed a sampling of the universal data.

Evolutionists make the tremendous mistake, quite intentionally, of either ignoring or misrepresenting clear scientific evidence. Christians should be careful not to follow in that same willfully ignorant pattern (2 Peter 3:5–7). God has made the evidence of a worldwide Flood so obvious that it is beyond questioning by any reasonable individual.

For the purpose of a brief summation, we shall briefly list some of the evidences for a worldwide Flood:

There are marine fossils located on the peaks of the highest mountains. This is accounted for by the mountains being elevated during and after the universal Flood. Psalm 104:6–9 offers a clear explanation as to what happened. But if one chooses to reject some plain statements of Scripture, how can he then arbitrarily accept others? To say that this is inconsistent is a remarkable understatement! One must accept all the Scripture, or he could just as well reject all of it.

(1) There are massive fossil graveyards all over the globe. Literally, trillions of fossils are embedded with each other nearly everywhere one goes. Sometimes, you can have billions of fossils jammed together in grotesque combinations of carnivores and herbivores. What could possibly account for this but a universal Flood? That is particularly true when one finds hills of fossils, such as those

in Nebraska. The state of Nebraska is not known for its breathtaking beachfront views.

Countless fossils are preserved in majestic detail. It takes unique circumstances to make a fossil. For example, fish do not simply die and then turn into fossils. They must be buried, put under tremendous pressure, be removed from decaying oxygen, and experience precise chemical reactions. Yet there is a fossil of a fish giving birth to another fish. In addition, there is a fossil of a fish in the midst of swallowing another fish. There are even ephemeral marks, such as footprints and raindrops.

Coal and oil deposits are found all over the earth. How did they form? They are composed of tremendous amounts of vegetation and animals that were buried together. What can account for this sort of a universal Flood? How does one get coal and oil in the Arctic Circle and Antarctica? There is almost no vegetation there whatsoever. How is it possible that places like northern Siberia once teemed with animals? Clearly, as the Bible teaches, there was a moderate climate all over the globe before the Flood.

Sedimentary strata were washed across entire continents and then hardened into place. Though tsunamis are destructive today, none have ever washed across an entire continent. But at one point in the earth's history, this was done repeatedly. Aside from the universal Flood, when could this have been done? These strata levels testify to rapid formation since there are rarely any gaps in between the various layers. This is only possible by extremely fast deposition and hardening, such as a global Flood would produce.

Rocks are folded in unnatural manners. Many photographs have been taken of such incredible features. This is quite common in the Grand Canyon. They can be witnessed today by anyone who ventures down into the Canyon. It is well known that rocks do not fold or bend. They break! What, then, can account for these folds in rocks all over the earth? They must have folded when still pliable and moist. This can only reasonably be explained by a universal Flood.

An additional question concerns the canyons themselves. There are many such canyons around the earth. Yet many of these canyons are in desert areas. Where did all the water come from to carve them out? A universal Flood easily explains this mystery.

The evidence for the Flood literally covers the globe. To deny it requires a volitional and curious intellectual blindness. Ignoring "rock-hard" facts does not make them go away. We trust that our readers will foster no doubts regarding the universality of the Flood. There is neither biblical nor scientific justification for doing so. To believe in a local flood envelops one in the same category as believing in evolution. There is not a shred of evidence to support evolution. Nor is there any evidence to support a local flood. Why not rather trust the Scriptures and what one can see for himself? Skeptics: Open your eyes.

Question #6: If the Flood Is Local, Is Jesus Really the God-Man or Not?

Ramification #3: Absent the universal Flood, one must decree that either Jesus was mistaken or He was lying. This is entirely inadmissible. Why? It is because both options just cited declare that Jesus truly is not the God-man. Then, who is the Christian really worshipping? Has man become superior to his Creator God? If Jesus really is the God-man and Savior of the world, He cannot be guilty of making mistakes or of lying. God does not and cannot sin.

Regarding the sinlessness of Christ, Charles Ryrie adroitly writes the following:

> The Scriptures definitely assert the sinlessness of Christ. Our Lord was announced as a holy Child (Luke 1:35). He challenged His enemies to show that He was a sinner which they could not do (John 8:46). They failed in their attempts to trap Him by using something He said (Matt. 22:15). He claimed to do always those things which pleased the Father (John 8:29). He said that He kept the Father's commandments (John 15:10).
>
> During the trials and Crucifixion He was acknowledged as innocent eleven times (by Judas, Matt. 27:4; by Plate six times, 27:24; Luke 23:14, 22; John 18:38; 19:4, 6; by Herod Antipas, Luke 23:15; by Pilate's wife, Matt. 27:19; by the repentant thief, Luke 23:41; and by the Roman centurion, Matt. 27:54). Furthermore, there is no record of our Lord offering a single sacrifice, though He frequented the temple. This silence speaks of the fact that He did not need to since He was without sin.
>
> Paul said of our Lord that "He knew no sin" (2 Cor. 5:21). Peter also declared that Christ did not commit any sin nor was deceit ever found in His mouth (1 Peter 2:22). He was a lamb without blemish and without spot (1:19). John affirmed the same truth when he said

that in Christ was no sin (1 John 3:5).

The writer of Hebrews attested to our Lord's sinlessness by several phrases: He was without sin (4:15); He was holy, innocent, undefiled, separated from sinners (7:26), and without any need of offering sacrifices for Himself (v. 27). Thus Christ's own testimony and that of the writers of the New Testament are uniform—He was sinless.[154]

No sincere believer in Christ can logically accept anything but the sinlessness of Christ. Sadly, some believers have been duped into believing that the Savior they claim to worship also had a sinful nature. Such believers are terribly deceived and need strong correction. When you call Jesus a liar or sinner, you also declare the triune God to be culpable and sinful. What type of faith is that?

In John 10:30, Jesus declared: "I and My Father are one." To this, we add Jesus' statement to Philip in John 14:9: "Jesus said to him, 'Have I been with you so long, and yet you have not known Me, Philip? He who has seen Me has seen the Father; so how can you say, Show us the Father?'" If Jesus truly is not one with the Father, who or what is He? Where, then, is holiness and eternal righteousness? If God Himself is not holy, then nothing can be. Such a theological error is not only inexcusable but also blasphemous. A child can understand that God is sinless.

Question #7: If the Flood Is Local, Can We Believe in the Bible?

To place faith in Jesus is also to place faith in the veracity of Scripture. One cannot embrace one and not the other. Hence, what

---

154 Charles C. Ryrie, Basic Theology (Wheaton, IL: Victor Books, 1986), pp. 263–264.

the Scripture teaches must be believed, even if it is not always entirely understood. Jesus emphatically stated in Matthew 24:35: "Heaven and earth will pass away, but My words will be no means pass away." For this to be true, Jesus must be God. He is declaring eternality and deity in one brief statement.

Jesus, speaking in Matthew 24:38–39, stated: "For as in the days before the flood, they were eating and drinking, marrying and giving in marriage, until the day that Noah entered the ark, and did not know until the flood came and took them all away, so also will the coming of the Son of man be."

Clearly, Jesus believed in a historical and universal Flood. He watched it happen. Indeed, He orchestrated the entire thing. This passage quite thoroughly verifies the worldwide Flood since "all" were taken away. What does "all" mean if it does not mean everything and everyone? Furthermore, it emphasizes that Jesus will likewise exact similar punishment on unbelievers at His second coming. All unbelievers will die and be cast into hell at that time (Matthew 25:31–46). Just as Christ died for all on the cross, so He will condemn all who refuse to believe on Him (John 5:24).

Wiersbe's Wise Summation

Warren Wiersbe summarizes evidences for the worldwide Flood as follows:

> The plain reading of the text convinces us that the Flood was a universal judgment because "all flesh had corrupted His [God's] way upon the earth" (6:12). We don't know how far civilization had spread over the planet, but wherever humans went, there was sin that had to be judged. The Flood bears witness to universal

sin and universal judgment. Both James and Peter used the Flood to illustrate future events that will involve the whole world: the return of Christ (Matt. 24:37-39; Luke 17:26-27) and the worldwide judgment of fire (2 Peter 3:3-7). If the Flood was only local, these analogies are false and misleading.

Peter also wrote that God did not spare "the ancient world" (NKJV) when He sent the Flood, which implies much more territory than a limited area. In spite of the devastation on the outside, Noah and his family and the animals were secure inside the Ark. No matter how they felt, or how much the Ark was tossed on the waters, they were safe in God's will.

Patiently they waited for God to complete His work and put them back on the earth. Noah and his family spent one year and seventeen days in the Ark, and even though they had daily chores to do, that's a long time to be in one place. But it is "through faith and patience" that we inherit God's promised blessings (Heb. 6:12; 10:36), and Noah was willing to wait on the Lord.[155]

Patience Is an Eternal Virtue

Like Noah and his family, may we all learn to wait on the Lord. We live in an instant "grab what we want as fast as we can" generation. The microwave has taught us that we can eat within minutes. The television gives us instant access to entertainment and news;

---
[155] Warren Wiersbe, The Bible Exposition Commentary: Genesis–Deuteronomy, p. 47.

the computer age grants us unparalleled information at our fingertips. Cell phones carried in our pockets connect us with the whole world. These conveniences, wonderful though they may be, do not promote inner qualities such as godly wisdom and patience.

But God is a patient God. He expects patience in His children as well. King David, as few others, had to learn to wait on God. He experienced the truth of Psalm 27:14: "Wait on the LORD, be of good courage, and He shall strengthen your heart; wait, I say, on the LORD!" Question: How did David learn these biblical practices and qualities so well? Answer: He endured many afflictions and dangerous trials in his life. He was abused and nearly tracked down by a jealous King Saul. He was falsely accused by others. He was hated by many who envied him. What was David's crime? He faithfully was serving God and Israel alike.

However, the most important elements in David's spiritual development were solace and seclusion. He was a keeper of the sheep. Sheep are not known for their conversation skills. That left David alone with God, his harp, and ample time for meditation. How much of God's Word he may have had in his possession is not known. But the time spent alone with God developed his spiritual life immeasurably. May all believers of today be willing to set aside their modern conveniences and contraptions at least occasionally. Time alone with God is vital to the spiritual health of every believer.

The apostle Paul, who endured so much affliction and trials for the Lord, wrote the following in 2 Timothy 3:12: "Yes, and all who desire to live godly in Christ Jesus will suffer persecution." No believer has ever experienced more suffering than Paul did for his faith. Thus has it been throughout all of mankind's long and oftentimes sordid history. May we today also patiently and cheerfully learn from David's and Paul's godly examples.

Lessons Learned in This Chapter

One of the most basic principles for the believer is to trust the Scripture. Deuteronomy 4:2 proclaims: "You shall not add to the word which I command you, nor take from it, that you may keep the commandments of the Lord your God which I command you." To this, we may add Psalm 119:89: "Forever, O Lord, your word is settled in heaven."

The Bible unequivocally teaches that the Flood was universal. God brought it upon the world to cleanse it from its thoroughly contaminated state. In grotesque fashion, demons cohabited with earthly women in an intimate fashion. Their offspring were called the Nephilim, which means "fallen ones." The world was degraded into a completely immoral state. This tragic pattern became worldwide.

No time on earth since Noah's day has ever witnessed such wickedness. The thoughts of man were evil continuously. From morning to night, men and women alike were consumed with the perpetuation of unimaginable immorality. Genesis 6:5 states: "Then the Lord saw that the wickedness of man was great in the earth, and that every intent of the thoughts of his heart was only evil continually."

In this chapter, we first examined the ramifications if the Flood was only local. We prefaced each of the seven questions we explored with the question: "If the Flood was only local…?" We repeat those questions now for the sake of the reader:

Question #1: If the Flood is local, what killed everything on earth?

Question #2: If the Flood is local, did Noah build the ark on Mount Ararat?

Question #3: If the Flood is local, why build the ark at all?

Question #4: If the Flood is local, what difference does all of this make?

Question #5: If the Flood is local, why is there evidence for it all over the world?

Question #6: If the Flood is local, is Jesus really the God-man or not?

Question #7: If the Flood is local, can we believe in the Bible?

It became quite evident in our study that the concept of a local flood is not only unbiblical, but it completely ignores all the available biblical, scientific, historical, and archaeological evidence. Some skeptics might claim that the evidence for the universal Flood is but scanty. That is an unwitting admission of profound ignorance. In reality, the evidence demonstrating that the Flood covers the entire globe is compelling. No thinking person can deny its existence. Only a lamentable ignorance of the facts allows such shortsightedness on the local flood theorists.

Second, we reviewed the most important testimony to the universal Flood. He is none other than Jesus Christ Himself. If Jesus lied or was ignorant of what He taught, He cannot be God. Thus, for a believer to deny the universal Flood is tantamount to denying that Jesus is the genuine Messiah. That is an astonishing contradiction of terms and a nearly incomprehensible lapse in faith and judgment.

Sadly, we do recognize that many believers have been so deceived. Ignorance decidedly is not bliss in theological matters. We trust that books such as this and countless others may educate them otherwise. If Jesus is not the Messiah, then He is nothing more than a clever charlatan. He shall simply disappear into the dustbins of history.

Third, we also saw that Peter gave credence to the universality of the Flood. To deny the universal Flood is to deny the Bible. To deny the Bible is to deny the God who wrote it. That is irresponsible to the extreme for any who claim to worship the Christ of the Bible. Such an inexcusable lack of awareness represents heavy chains of deceit wrapped around one's theological neck. Such besetting bonds can only be removed by exercising full faith in Christ and educating oneself both biblically and scientifically.

In our next chapter, we shall see the waters of the Flood beginning to recede. Judgment has passed, and resuscitation now begins. The world begins anew with Noah, his family, and the survivors of the ark. The Nephilim are drowned, and a new era commences. Sadly, as we shall soon see, the corruption of sin rears its ugly head once again in short order. Humanity will not completely be set free from the shackles of besmirching sin until the new heavens and earth (Revelation chapters 21 to 22).

Seven Important Questions Concerning the Flood

Cognitive Conundrum #18

At fishermen stared I in disbelief to see; in river and sea, fish thrived so abundantly. The trees monthly bore their fruits for eating; their leaves they did use for peoples' healing. Life proved hard for me. I must freely confess my diet, my calling, my message to profess. My wife, my home, and my land were taken, but through wheels in wheels, I was not shaken.

Who am I?

Answer: Ezekiel

Chapter 19

The Floodwaters Begin to Recede

(Genesis 8:1–19)

In This Chapter

Objectives for This Chapter
God Stops the Rain and the Fountains (8:1–5)
Noah Sends Out the Raven and Dove (8:6–12)
Disembarkation Time from the Ark (8:13–19)
Lessons Learned in This Chapter

Objectives for This Chapter

After the cataclysmic watery judgment on the earth, God begins to withdraw His hand. He allows the waters to retire into the newly formed ocean basins. These monumental, earth-reshaping events did not transpire overnight. They took some time. While the waters were draining into the oceans, the mountains were simultaneously ascending, thus further forcing the waters into the depths.

The earth clearly was experiencing unprecedented geological transformations. Noah and his family probably were not privileged to witness these events as they were occurring. Still, they did see the aftereffects of God's prodigious handiwork when it was already largely accomplished. Even the climate changed as a result of the Flood.

For 150 days, the floodwaters had continued to rise. In this chapter, we shall first review how God stopped the waters from rising.

There were three primary steps that God took: (1) He sent a wind to start drying off the earth's surface; (2) He sealed up the subterranean waters from flooding the earth; (3) He stopped the rain from falling.

We shall also examine some of the other topographical changes that came about from the Flood. Canyons were formed, fossils in abundance were created, and rocks were hardened. Some rocks even were deformed when they were still in the hardening stages. The Flood actually transformed almost everything on the earth. Even the Ice Age came as a direct result of the Flood. We shall examine how that unique process came to be.

Second, we shall delve into the sending out of the raven and dove from the ark. The raven is a scavenger bird. When Noah sent it out, it never returned. Being a carrion eater, it possibly found remains scattered around the earth. If not, it survived on other creatures, such as worms and bugs. The dove is more discriminating in its dietary appetites. It was a special bird and was used as a sacrifice in Israel's religious festivals. It returned to the ark two times after being sent out by Noah. The third time, the dove did not return. Then Noah knew the land was dry.

Third, we shall examine the glorious day that Noah, his family, and all the animals were released from the ark. After being confined for 378 days in the ark, this was truly a momentous occasion. We believe that God granted a high rate of fertility for both the humans and the animal kingdom. This was necessary so they could quickly increase their respective populations.

We shall also review the concept of evolution. Evolution is nothing more than a vain and empty philosophy designed to drive people away from faith in God. Tragically, in spite of no corroborating evidence, it has accomplished that in a tragic fashion. This writer offers his own personalized definition of evolution. It is by no means flattering to its proponents.

We finally take note to what the fossil record and alleged geologic column actually testify. They are a testimony of death. Henry Morris succinctly summarizes that record. The historic Flood bears witness to a future judgment upon the earth. The Tribulation is yet imminent and will, in many ways, parallel the Flood. In some ways, the Tribulation will even eclipse the Flood. For example, all the fish in the sea will die during the Tribulation. The oceans themselves will be turned to blood.

Sadly, mankind is slow to learn the lessons from its past. God has granted bountiful evidence to His existence through His Word and through nature. Romans 1:20 emphatically declares: "For since the creation of the world His invisible attributes are clearly seen, being understood by the things that are made, even His eternal power and Godhead, so that they are without excuse" (cf. Psalm 19:1–6). May our every reader heed His sacred message. One's eternal destiny will either be marvelously blessed in the presence of God or languish in agony with the diabolical devil.

God Stops the Rain and the Fountains (Genesis 8:1–5)

Genesis 8:1–5 states:

> Then God remembered Noah, and every living thing, and all the animals that were with him in the ark. And God made a wind to pass over the earth, and the waters subsided. The fountains of the deep and the windows of heaven were also stopped, and the rain from heaven was restrained. And the waters receded continually from the earth. At the end of the hundred and fifty days the waters decreased.

Then the ark rested in the seventh month, the seventeenth day of the month, on the mountains of Ararat. And the waters decreased continually until the tenth month. In the tenth month, on the first day of the month, the tops of the mountains were seen.

For 150 Days, the Waters Steadily Increased

The watery cataclysm, at long last, sees the beginning of the end! After forty days, the torrential rains finally ceased. Yet the context does indicate that intermittent rains continued. Since the waters continued to rise, it appears that the subterranean waters were still active until a total of 150 days had passed. Genesis 8:2 states: "The fountains of the deep and the windows of heaven were also stopped, and the rain from heaven was restrained."

It was not until day 150 that the phenomenal input of water finally ceased. The water level hit its peak and finally began to subside. The torrential rains ceased after forty days. The silence must have been eerie at first to the inhabitants of the ark. There was no more rain pounding on the roof. It was not until an additional 110 days passed that the ark touched the peaks of Mount Ararat.

The Flood had accomplished its divine task. All air-breathing life outside the ark, save marine creatures, insects, and the microbiological world, had been killed. However, as the fossil record amply shows, even a massive and sundry number of marine creatures were killed by the Flood waters. Untold trillions of creatures, large and small, died in the inundation.

We should add a note on Genesis 7:24, which states: "And the waters prevailed on the earth one hundred and fifty days." The Hebrew term translated for "prevailed" is related to that of the Hebrew term for warrior, "gibbor." In other words, the waters conquered the earth. The earth was totally enveloped in its watery tomb.

Leupold offers the following salient comments:

> From the idea of gabbar, "be mighty," "conquer," we derive the thought at this point that the conquering, dominating force over all the earth was the mighty mass of water. Since the verb gabbar is used (v. 18) of the time before the waters reached their maximum height and not only to mark this maximum, we feel sure that the 150 days must include the forty days of rain mentioned v. 12.[156]

The Earth Was Radically Transformed

Change #1: The entire earth had been transformed into something, which, though recognizable, was now quite different than before the Flood. The mountains had risen or were still in the process of doing so, and the ocean basins were likewise forming (Psalm 104:6–9). The continents split apart and drifted away from each other. Scripture does not tell us when some of these astounding topographical changes were completed.

Change #2: The climate changed quite drastically. This made it challenging for many different kinds of animals, such as the dinosaurs, to survive. The world was no longer the lush paradise it had been previously. Many regions of the globe became largely uninhabitable, such as the mountains, deserts, and swampy regions. Only a select few varieties of animals can live in such inhospitable regions. Evolutionists would say that these creatures slowly adapted to their environment. Creationists would say that they were designed for it.

---
156 H. C. Leupold, Genesis, p. 306.

Noah and his family disembarked from the ark and went to a world that was very different from the one before the Flood began.

Free at Last!

A total of 370 days after the Flood began would pass before the ark was emptied of its inhabitants. If the reader recalls, Noah and family were in the ark for one week before the Flood actually began, thus making 378 days. What an indescribably glorious day that would have been! To step out of the ark onto dry ground undoubtedly produced smiles of profound gratitude on the little group of saved souls. The liberation from the relatively dark confines of the ark into glorious sunshine would have few equals.

One can even envision the two tigers smiling, which probably made the herbivores nervous! Only eight human souls had been spared! Their task was before them. They were to repopulate the earth. This included both man and beast. God granted them considerable success in this endeavor. One might safely assume that God abundantly blessed the wombs of both man and beast for quite some time to come.

However, as already mentioned, some kinds of animals, such as the dinosaurs, did not ultimately fare as well. The drastic change of climate, possibly excessive hunting by man (which was now a new danger for the animals), some new or more virile forms of disease, lack of abundant food, and other factors undoubtedly contributed to their eventual demise.

One cannot determine all of the sundry causes of the dinosaur's eventual extinction with certainty. It definitely was not a mysterious asteroid strike that suddenly wiped out many species. However, in spite of these new potential difficulties, the dinosaurs did survive for a considerable length of time after the Flood. The behemoth and leviathan were undoubtedly dinosaurs of some type. They were still alive during the time of Job (Job chapters 40 to 41). Job was possibly a contemporary of Abraham's time. This would be between 350 to 450 years after the Flood.

Fiery Flying Serpents

Isaiah 30:6 presents us with one rather particular species that, to no one's regret, is now extinct:

> The burden against the beasts of the South. Through a land of troubles and anguish, from which came the lioness and lion, the viper and flying fiery serpent, they will carry their riches on the backs of young donkeys, and their treasures on the humps of camels, to a people who shall not profit.

Question: What were these fiery flying serpents? Answer: No one can identify them definitively. Whatever they were, we can rejoice that they no longer exist. They apparently could breathe out fire. Another possibility is that their bites were like fire. Commentators have spilled much ink discussing these serpents, but no real conclusions are possible in our day.

These flying fiery serpents should not be identified with the fiery serpents of Numbers chapter 21. It is not recorded that the serpents of Numbers chapter 21 that bit the children of Israel could fly. Their bites were fatal, however, if not treated in God's prescribed manner.

And what precisely was God's method of healing for the snake bites in the wilderness? It was quite unusual, to say the least. God commanded Moses to make a bronze model of the fiery serpent in Numbers chapter 21 so that if anyone would just look at the bronze serpent on the pole, he would live. This was a matter of faith on the people's part. It did not require a great deal of faith, admittedly, but the sick would still have to walk or be carried to the proper location so as to look on that strange figure on the pole. God honored that faith and healed the participants.

How counterintuitive that experience was! By looking on a symbol of death, one was granted life. Sadly, the bronze serpent was later worshiped as a god. King Hezekiah, hundreds of years later, was forced to destroy this bronze serpent. Named Nehushtan, the people of Israel had been burning incense to it (2 Kings 18:4). It is ironic how the people of Israel burned incense to this symbol of destruction, which paradoxically had brought life. They would worship and burn incense to the symbol rather than the Creator of life who empowered the symbol. Such twisted thinking, unfortunately, seems typical of human nature. The Israelites forgot that God healed them of the snake bite, not the symbol of that bite.

The Spiritual Reality Behind the Physical Symbol of the Snake

Jesus referred to a parallel incident in Matthew 23:16–22:

> Woe to you, blind guides, who say, 'Whoever swears by the temple, it is nothing; but whoever swears by the gold of the temple, he is obliged to perform it. Fools and blind! For which is greater, the gold or the temple that sanctifies the gold? And, whoever swears by the altar, it is nothing; but whoever swears by the gift that is on it, he is obliged to perform it.

> Fools and blind! For which is greater, the gift or the altar that sanctifies the gift? Therefore, he who swears

by the altar, swears by it and by all things on it. He who swears by the temple, swears by it and by Him who dwells in it. And he who swears by heaven, swears by the throne of God and by Him who sits on it.

Jesus even referred to the bronze serpent as a symbol of His future crucifixion. John 3:14–15 states: "And as Moses lifted up the serpent in the wilderness, even so must the Son of Man be lifted up, that whoever believes in Him should not perish but have eternal life." Little could anyone have realized that this symbol of death, which restored physical life in the Old Testament, would also symbolize eternal life to all who looked upon Christ and believed on Him.

Every Living Thing Left the Ark

Going back to Genesis, the animals, once off the ark, wandered off quickly to repopulate their own particular kind. An abundance of food awaited the herbivores. Vegetation would quickly take root and begin to grow. However, as already noted, the world was not as lush as in the original creation. Survival became much more of a challenge for the animal kingdom.

But it must also be remembered that at this point, only a limited number of animals consumed the available vegetation. Hence, the animal population undoubtedly increased quite rapidly. One can also rest confident that God ensured that fertility was exceptionally high during those early years among man and animal alike.

However, as time passed, many of the previously lush regions of the earth became desert. The climate modification would have contributed to these changes. The temperature was no longer uniform everywhere, and life became much harder than previously.

The world witnessed a genuinely verifiable "climate change." This transformation of the climate was, in essence, complete when they left the ark. However, slower changes would continue to descend upon the earth for some time to come. The Ice Age would be one such result.

In the beginning, carnivores probably had to survive on rapidly producing smaller creatures, such as mice and rabbits. One might speculate that the lions and other carnivores would consume everything in sight. However, there were initially only two types of carnivores. They can only consume so much. It must also be remembered that seven pairs of the clean animals entered the ark. This would give them a major advantage as far as repopulating their species around the globe.

Perhaps at first, some of the traditional carnivores also heavily subsidized their appetites on vegetation. Bears do so to this day. In recent years, at least one lion in a zoo lived on vegetation and avoided meat entirely, odd as that may seem. Fish may have also been a staple diet for the carnivores. One can assume that rivers and ponds abundantly peppered the earth's surface for many centuries to come.

A Brief Overview of the Ice Age

One unforeseen event by man that occurred after the Flood was the Ice Age. This came about as the result of warm oceans and cool continents. The volcanic eruptions would have warmed the seas considerably. Those same eruptions would have hurled vast amounts of ash and other particles into the atmosphere. That would have lessened the sunlight filtering through and reduced the temperatures over the land, particularly the land far from the seashores.

This combination of warm seas and cold continents would produce an immense amount of snow in certain regions. When heat and cold clash today, violent weather is often the result. Many of our modern storms are initiated by temperature extremes meeting in the atmosphere. Quite naturally, the increase of snow and ice in more northern climates would create a colder climate as it progressed further south. The areas most affected by the change in climate were the north and south poles and Greenland. They were buried in continent-sized ice sheets thousands of feet thick. These regions contain approximately 70 percent of the world's freshwater supply.

Eventually, the oceans would stabilize at a much cooler temperature. Some of the lower-level subterranean fountains of the deep would also have been quite warm due to the volcanic action. But over time, these magma spills diminished greatly. These initial hot-cold contrasts resulted in a volatile weather pattern, which created the Ice Age.

It is intriguing to note that uniformitarianism does not have any better explanation for an Ice Age than the global Flood. They cannot give logical or scientific reasons as to why it should ever occur. It is their privilege, of course, to listen to the creationists' logical explanation and reject it. The primary reason, however, appears to be that they "do not want to allow a divine foot in the door." The creationists' explanation, although not entirely complete, is very reasonable. Some uniformitarians actually present the viewpoint of numerous Ice Ages. Even while doing so, they cannot explain what really precipitates an ice age.

Confusion Over How an Ice Age Starts

One commendably honest individual regarding the Ice Age is Ernst Opik. He is, by occupation, an astronomer, not a geologist. He writes as follows:

More difficult is the question of the succession of several glaciations during one glacial epoch. The phenomenon seems to be of great complexity, corresponding to a perpetual variation of solar radiation according to various cycles and amplitudes, of which perhaps the sunspot cycle is one.[157]

He also adds these comments:

These fluctuations seem to be worldwide and have been most difficult to understand. My own guess is that they represent a kind of "flickering" of the disturbance in the sun—like a candle flame blown by the wind.[158]

We give credit to Opik for his acknowledged confusion. One ponders just how scientific Opik's remedy of "flickering" might be. It sounds more like the proverbial "shot in the dark" than a legitimate scientific explanation. In our opinion, however, it stands on the same level as a quantum fluctuation, the big bang, spontaneous generation, the missing links, punctuated equilibrium, and the implausibility of existing information. It is amazing that these pillars of evolutionary thought are nothing more than unsubstantiated sinking sand.

But the only other recourse atheistic evolutionists have to appeal to is a begrudging acknowledgment, submission to, and worship of a Creator God. In their incredible stubbornness, they refuse to do this. They squelch the limited biblical revelation they have received. This suppression of spiritual knowledge has dire consequences. For this flagrant disobedience, they shall suffer eternal punishment if

---

[157] Ernst J. Opik, "Ice Ages," in The Earth and Its Atmosphere, edited by D. R. Bates (New York, Basic Books, Inc., 1957), p. 172.
[158] Ernst J. Opik, "Climate and the Changing Sun," Scientific American, vol. 198, June 1958, p. 89.

they remain in their unrepentant state.

The Floodwaters Slowly Drain Away (Genesis 8:1–5)

We refer once again to Genesis 8:1–5:

> Then God remembered Noah, and every living thing, and all the animals that were with him in the ark. And God made a wind to pass over the earth, and the waters subsided. The fountains of the deep and the windows of heaven were also stopped, and the rain from heaven was restrained. And the waters receded continually from the earth. At the end of the hundred and fifty days the waters decreased.
>
> Then the ark rested in the seventh month, the seventeenth day of the month, on the mountains of Ararat. And the waters decreased continually until the tenth month. In the tenth month, on the first day of the month, the tops of the mountains were seen.

God Remembered Noah

Then God remembered Noah (Genesis 8:1a): This chapter begins with the rather odd expression that God "remembered" Noah and the animals. Did God actually forget them for a short time as they were sailing around the planet in history's worst watery cataclysm? Obviously not! If His holy eye is perpetually on the tiny sparrow, it certainly was on the ark and all its inhabitants. God never forgets anything in His creation.

Fruchtenbaum gives the following explanation of this rather curious use of the term "remember":

> The turning point begins with the remembrance of God in verse 1a: And God remembered Noah, and all the beasts, and all the cattle that were with him in the ark. The word remember does not mean remember in the sense that God temporarily forgot about the ark and its inhabitants; rather it means remembering in the sense of movement toward the object.
>
> For example, in Genesis 19:29, God remembered Abraham with a view to saving Lot; in Exodus 2:24, God remembered his covenant with the patriarchs with a view to rescuing Israel; in Jeremiah 2:2, God remembered Israel with a view toward her restoration; in Jeremiah 31:20, God remembered Ephraim with a view toward extending mercy to him, and in Luke 1:54-55, God remembered Israel with a view toward sending the Messiah to Israel.
>
> Furthermore, the sense here in Genesis is that of God remembering a covenant; though in this case the covenant itself had not yet been made. (God said earlier in Genesis 6 that He would establish His covenant with Noah.) Furthermore, in 7:4 God remembered that the rain would last only forty days. All these usages fit into the word "remember."[159]

These expressions of God's remembering His children sprin-

---
[159] Arnold Fruchtenbaum, Ariel Bible Commentary: The Book of Genesis, p. 175.

kled throughout Scripture foster great encouragement to every believer. The reality of the situation is that God will never forget nor forsake His children. Hebrews 13:5–6 declares: "Let your conduct be without covetousness; be content with such things as you have. For He Himself has said, 'I will never leave you nor forsake you.' So we may boldly say: 'The LORD is my helper; I will not fear. What can man do to me?'"

The Floodwaters Began to Subside in Three Ways (Genesis 8:1b–3)

> And God made a wind to pass over the earth, and the waters subsided. The fountains of the deep and the windows of heaven were also stopped, and the rain from heaven was restrained. And the waters receded continually from the earth. At the end of the hundred and fifty days the waters decreased.

It is intriguing to note that God used natural causes to diffuse the Flood. The Flood was caused by God's supernatural activity, of course, but He sovereignly used natural means to abate the water. First, God sent a wind. This should not be thought of as a hurricane but rather as a persistent breeze to help evaporate the water and channel it somewhat. However, it should also be noted that even with this wind, God Himself sent it. So, it was not entirely natural; it was due to God's faithful provision.

Second, God closed up the fountains of the deep. A considerable amount of mystery will always surround the opening of these subterranean fountains. These waters were one of the two primary sources to cause the flooding. Accompanying this undoubtedly were literally crust-shattering earthquakes. This changed the topography of the planet for our present age until Christ returns. Just prior to Christ's second coming, the earth will once again experience transformative geographical changes (Revelation 16:17–21).

Continents were literally broken apart, and the immense land masses drifted away from each other during the Flood. Ocean basins formed. Mountains rose! The rising of the mountains is evidenced by the marine fossils located at their summits. No reasonable person can deny that the mountains had to ascend or they could not have fossils on top of them. Hence, creationists and secularists are generally in agreement on this conclusion. The heavenly hosts witnessed the power of God in these unbelievable scenarios.

Unprecedented and climate-changing volcanic action was also initiated. The volcanos would have ejected immense beds of lava and spewed ashes all over the atmosphere. Those ashes would cool the temperatures of the earth for some time. Simultaneously, the gargantuan beds of lava would have warmed up the ocean. As already noted, this cool atmosphere would clash with the warmer oceans and usher in the Ice Age.

The release of the pent-up pressure underneath earth's crust would have blasted immense geysers of superheated water skyward with unbelievable force. Imagine what life would have been like for those outside of the ark. The terror and panic, though relatively short-lived, was horrific! One can only ponder how many people died from these two sources of horror alone.

Third, God stopped it from raining. The sound of silence (no torrential raindrops beating against the ark) must have seemed "deafening" to the inhabitants of the ark. The lack of sound must have seemed quite unnerving for a time. Even though the torrential rain stopped after forty days, the water continued to rise for an additional 110 days (Genesis 8:3). After the first 150 days were over (40 days + 110 days), the water finally started to recede.

Quoting W. D. Barrick and R. Sigler, Steven W. Boyd and Andrew A. Snelling write:

> The second mention of 150 days in 8:3 is a reference back to the same 150 days in 7:24. The turning point in the Flood is marked in 8:1. The waters began to abate at the end of the 150th day. The waters subsided just enough to allow the ark to land on high ground—in the mountains of Ararat. This occurred at some unknown hour during day 151. The tops of the mountains emerged on day 225 (8:5).[160]

Mountains, Canyons, and Rocks

Psalm 104, discussed previously, describes events pertaining to the creation week, the days of the Flood, and life after the Flood. Verses 6 to 9 are best understood as referring to the Flood. When the mountains began to rise and the ocean basins settled, it caused a tremendous runoff of the waters. This contributed to the formation of spectacular, meandering canyons. It is impossible to envision the force and impact of erosion caused by this runoff around the earth.

While the surface of the earth was still relatively moist, lakes would have burst from their natural dams. The waters quickly rushed to the lower depths, namely the ocean basins. The fact that one finds bent and twisted rocks all around the globe testifies to this. The rocks would not have bent if they had previously been formed and hardened. The rocks had to still be pliable and moist.

---

[160] Steven W. Boyd and Andrew A. Snelling (General Editors), Grappling with the Chronology of the Genesis Flood (Green Forest, AR: Master Books, 2014), p. 204.

This bending would have been further assisted by the occurrence of earthquakes.

These walls of water gushing out from bursting natural dams around the world would carve out deep river beds and meandering canyons, such as the Grand Canyon. The Grand Canyon is an astonishing maze of convoluted, smaller canyons descending into a primary one. Other less famous canyons are peppered throughout the earth. These canyons all helped drain the water away and reduce the effects of the Flood. Such flash floods would truly have been a sight to behold!

A Question of Canyon Formation

Are we really to believe that all these sensational and exceedingly complex canyons were caused by tiny rivers flowing through solid rock over millions of years? That is what the evolutionary geologist would have us to believe in spite of no evidence demonstrating this. Of course, they will always take refuge in their evolutionary closets, claiming all these things happened in the distant past. Yes, it did happen in the past, but only about 4,370 years ago at the time of this writing. A summary of the event is recorded in the book of Genesis.

It is a well-established fact that a lot of water in a short time can cause momentous topographical modification. As already noted, Mount St. Helens demonstrated that reality quite conclusively. Modern geologists watched Mount St. Helens erupt. Indeed, most of the world watched via television and the internet. The associated mudflow caused incredible damage. This one relatively small volcano triggered significant destruction in an appreciably short time. The subsequent "mudflow" flooding impacted the region markedly. One does not have to be a trained geologist to take note of what one volcano can do.

The runoff with the Flood was dramatic beyond anything ever witnessed by man. We shall never see its equal. Noah and his family were possibly privileged to witness some of the waters drain off. It certainly would have been a sight to behold! When the ocean basins dropped, and the mountains rose, the rushing water would have left immense topographical evidence.

Words are inadequate to describe the onslaught of the cascading water. One would envision that it would take an immense amount of time to drain away a globe-inundating level of water. However, considering the factors of the oceans dropping and the mountains ascending, not as much time would elapse as people might ordinarily think.

One must bear in mind that after the Flood, this was a supernaturally orchestrated runoff. God did this; it was not natural, though He used natural causes. Carving out the world's phenomenal canyons at the same time is a most reasonable conclusion. In fact, it is the only logical recourse available to the objective mind. As already noted, we can see replications of this event on a much smaller scale every day. Even a major thunderstorm can rapidly carve out new gullies on open land. Farmers must take caution to leave grass strips in highly erodible portions of their fields.

A Resting Place for the Ark

Mount Ararat was the landing place for the ark (Genesis 8:4–5): "Then the ark rested in the seventh month, the seventeenth day of the month, on the mountains of Ararat. And the waters decreased continually until the tenth month. In the tenth month, on the first day of the month, the tops of the mountains were seen."

The location of Mount Ararat and the search for Noah's ark has created much interest for centuries. To this day, the ark's location is unknown. Some claimed to have seen it, but nothing of substantive proof has been produced. Part of the problem is verifying the exact location of the "mountains" (plural) of Ararat. Naturally, the ark landed on only one spot within the mountain range. Geographically, they are alleged to be in Turkey. Geologically, they may be part of a much more extensive plateau called the Armenian Plateau. This is a range of mountains. This writer has viewed those mountains from a distance while teaching in neighboring Armenia.

Scripture correctly conveys the location, but modern man has difficulty fixing the exact area. Is the ark still there? If it still does exist, it may not be revealed until the dark days of the Tribulation. It would thus serve as a powerful testimony to God's Word in a treacherous and unbelieving world at a most opportune time. Some have speculated that the ark is entombed in snow and ice and thus hidden from view. That is entirely possible.

It is interesting to note that one of the plagues during the Tribulation is excessive heat. Revelation 16:8–9 states: "Then the fourth angel poured out his bowl on the sun, and power was given to him to scorch men with fire. And men were scorched with great heat, and they blasphemed the name of God who has power over these plagues; and they did not repent and give Him glory."

Possibly, God will utilize this period of excessive heat to melt the snow and ice around the ark if it is indeed still intact on Mount Ararat. That would be quite a phenomenal testimony to the world of God's truthfulness and eternal message through the Scriptures. Coupled with the lack of rainfall caused by the two witnesses of Revelation chapter 11, many of the rivers will dry up, and the glaciers will melt.

Although the prospect of finding the ark excites the spirit, it is not absolutely necessary to substantiate the truth of the Flood. The evidence for the Flood is already worldwide and quite conclusive to any individual with an open mind. It may well be that the wood for the ark has completely succumbed to the elements and rotted away. Or the wood may have even been used for construction or cooking fires. Though this writer's personal sentiment hopes that the ark remains intact, only time will tell.

The tops of the surrounding mountains became visible seventy-four days after the ark rested on Mount Ararat. But a longer wait before disembarkation was necessary. The floodwaters had a long way to go before dry, habitable land would appear. Still, the process passed with remarkable speed. Soon, Noah and family and all the creatures on the ark would be happily dancing on solid ground. Imagine how that must have felt after being secluded for so long in the confining ark.

Noah Sends Out the Raven and Dove (Genesis 8:6–12)

Genesis 8:6–12 states:

> So it came to pass, at the end of forty days, that Noah opened the window of the ark which he had made. Then he sent out a raven, which kept going to and fro until the waters had dried up from the earth. He also sent out from himself a dove, to see if the waters had receded from the face of the ground.

> But the dove found no resting place for the sole of her foot, and she returned into the ark to him, for the waters were on the face of the whole earth. So he put out his hand and took her, and drew her into the ark to himself.

And he waited yet another seven days, and again he sent the dove out from the ark. Then the dove came to him in the evening, and behold, a freshly plucked olive leaf was in her mouth, and Noah knew that the waters had receded from the earth. So he waited yet another seven days and sent out the dove, which did not return again to him anymore.

It is intriguing to note how God used two different types of birds to inform Noah of the earth's conditions. The ravens are considered an unclean bird. They are not fit for human consumption. God designed the raven to be a scavenger. They clean up the unclean remnants of dead animals scattered all over creation. As such, they serve a definite purpose.

The dove, on the other hand, is a gentle bird. It loathes foul scenarios and has much more delicate digestive habits. God uses both birds throughout Scripture in their own particular design. Everything God creates and everything God does serves to His ultimate glory. He cannot fail in any of His holy designs.

The Raven (Genesis 8:6–7)

"So it came to pass, at the end of forty days, that Noah opened the window of the ark which he had made. Then he sent out a raven, which kept going to and fro until the waters had dried up from the earth."

The raven, as already noted, is a scavenger bird. Hence, it could land on any remaining floating carcasses and freely dine, unappetizing as that may sound. God graciously granted certain creatures with extraordinary digestive systems. They are the "housecleaners" of the planet. It must be remembered that the mountaintops were already visible. So, even if the raven had not found anything floating on the waters to eat, it could still rest on dry ground. There certainly would have been ample bugs and worms to eat. This solitary raven had the entire world to itself. No competition existed! As Noah probably suspected, the raven did not need to return.

God created and fed the ravens, though they are unclean birds and unfit for human consumption (Leviticus 11:15). Even the noble eagle is a scavenger bird. Many other creatures also serve as carrion consumers. Where would the world be without them? Ironically, God used the unclean ravens to feed his prophet Elijah (1 Kings 17:4–6).

Warren Wiersbe comments:

> The Hebrew text says that "the ark came to rest," reminding us that Noah's name means "rest" and that his father Lamech had hoped that his son would bring rest to a weary world (Gen. 5:28-29). Though the ark had rested safely, Noah was waiting for the Lord to tell him what to do. He waited forty days and then sent out the raven; and being an unclean carrion-eating bird (Lev. 11:13-15), it felt right at home among the floating carcasses.[161]

The Dove (Genesis 8:8–12)

He also sent out from himself a dove, to see if the waters had receded from the face of the ground. But the dove found no resting place for the sole of her foot, and

---

[161] Warren Wiersbe, The Bible Exposition Commentary: Old Testament: Genesis–Deuteronomy, p. 49.

she returned into the ark to him, for the waters were on the face of the whole earth. So he put out his hand and took her, and drew her into the ark to himself.

And he waited yet another seven days, and again he sent the dove out from the ark. Then the dove came to him in the evening, and behold, a freshly plucked olive leaf was in her mouth, and Noah knew that the waters had receded from the earth. So he waited yet another seven days and sent out the dove, which did not return again to him anymore.

The dove is spoken of in positive ways throughout the Scripture. Doves are a clean bird and can even be used for sacrifice. Joseph and Mary offered two turtledoves in the temple as sacrifices for purification purposes. Luke 2:24 states: "And to offer a sacrifice according to what is said in the law of the Lord, 'A pair of turtledoves or two young pigeons.'" Doves and pigeons were the poor man's sacrifice, but they were still acceptable to God.

The Dove's Depiction and Use in the Bible

Sarfati notes: "The dove is used as a positive symbol in the Bible, depicting youth (Song of Songs 1:15; 4:1; 5:12), love (Song of Songs 2:14; 5:2; 6:9), innocence (Matthew 10:16). Indeed, at Jesus' baptism, the Holy Spirit descended on him in bodily form, like a dove" (Luke 3:22)."[162]

The first time the dove was sent out by Noah, it did not find a place to rest its foot and returned to Noah. He waited seven days and sent the dove out a second time. This time, it returned with an

---

162 Jonathan Sarfati, The Genesis Account: A theological, historical, and scientific commentary on Genesis 1–11, p. 574.

olive leaf in its mouth. This would have been greatly encouraging to Noah as he then knew that trees were already growing. The dry land was rapidly appearing, and vegetation was growing. Noah waited seven more days and sent the dove out the third time. This time, it did not return to him. Clearly, the dove, finding a clean and dry place to nest, had found solace and safety outside of the ark.

Scholars debate whether the raven and dove were both sent out on the same day or if Noah sent out only the raven and then waited one more week to send the dove. Whichever the case may be, it is not of vital importance. What was important? The time was soon approaching when every living creature could leave the ark. God's faithfulness and His preservation of every living creature and all eight humans in the ark is what one needs to remember.

Keil and Delitzsch state:

> After that, Noah let a dove fly out three times, at intervals of seven days. It is not distinctly stated that he sent it out the first time seven days after the raven, but this is implied in the statement that he stayed yet other seven days before sending it out the second time, and the same again before sending it the third time (vv. 10 and 12).[163]

There is no significant theological difference either way. The raven did not return, but the dove did, as already explained.

Disembarkation Time from the Ark (Genesis 8:13–19)

Genesis 8:13–19 states:

> And it came to pass in the six hundred and first year; in

---
163 Keil and Delitzsch, Commentary on the Old Testament: The Pentateuch, pp. 148–149.

the first month, the first day of the month, that the waters were dried up from the earth; and Noah removed the covering of the ark and looked, and indeed the surface of the ground was dry. And in the second month, on the twenty-seventh day of the month, the earth was dried.

Then God spoke to Noah, saying, "Go out of the ark, you and your wife, and your sons and your sons' wives with you. Bring out with you every living thing of all flesh that is with you, birds and cattle and every creeping thing that creeps on the earth, so that they may abound on the earth, and be fruitful and multiply on the earth."

So Noah went out, and his sons and his wife and his sons' wives with him. Every animal, every creeping thing, every bird, and whatever creeps on the earth, according to their families, went out of the ark.

Noah Removes the Roof of the Ark (Genesis 8:13–17)

The day of celebration was rapidly approaching. Noah and company certainly enjoyed a unique way to celebrate the start of a new year. Noah removed the covering of the ark and saw that the land was dry. Yet, almost two full months would pass by before they were allowed to leave the ark and step out onto dry ground.

Day 314: Noah removed the roof of the ark. What a blessed relief to all of the inhabitants to see the sun and blue sky overhead.

The fresh air blowing into the ark invigorated man and beast alike. The surface of the ground appeared dry, but apparently, it was still wet beneath the soil. It would not be safe yet to leave the security of the ark.

Indeed, it was an additional fifty-six days before they did venture out. At that point, the surface and subsurface of the ground were safe to walk on because they were totally dry. All told, Noah and his family were on the ark 371 days after the Flood actually began before they disembarked, if you count the first and last days as full days. This is fifty-three weeks. It must be recalled that they spent seven days on the ark before God initiated the Flood.

Release at Long Last (Genesis 8:18–19)!

Finally, the great day came! God commanded Noah and his family to leave the ark. One can almost imagine that even the animals were dancing and prancing upon securing their freedom. Verse 14 gloriously records: "And in the second month, on the twenty-seventh day of the month, the earth was dried."

When newborn calves are released from the confines of the barn for the very first time, they invariably kick up their heels repeatedly and sprint around the barnyard as fast as they can. Inasmuch as a tiny calf can rejoice, they definitely are rejoicing and using their energetic young legs. It must have been a sight to behold when all of these wild animals were once again released to the wild. Unnaturally penned up for a total of 378 days (counting the seven days before the Flood actually commenced), both man and beast were thrilled beyond words.

It should not be imagined that upon their freedom, the carnivores immediately attacked and killed the many herbivores. The herbivores would have been very short-lived if that were the case!

Fish would have been abundant in small pools that were drying up and in abundant streams. God would have supernaturally preserved the families of animals until a balanced population was ready for the new order.

A New but Somewhat Unwelcoming World (2 Peter 3:5–6)

Although obviously relieved to get out of the ark, the survivors of the Flood were abruptly introduced to a new and harsher climate. The old world of lush vegetation and even moderate temperatures were now gone. Second Peter 3:5–6 states: "For this they willfully forget: that by the word of God the heavens were of old, and the earth standing out of water and in the water, by which the world that then existed perished, being flooded with water."

The new climactic and topographical realities Noah's family and the animals faced definitely would make adjustments. Indeed, some of the animals, such as the dinosaurs, though part of the ark family, would not survive these new conditions for terribly long. Though the wicked Nephilim were permanently and thankfully gone, other hardships soon became evident. Deserts and extensive wilderness areas would now cover large geographical regions. Mountain ranges, beautiful though they may be, prove inhospitable save for a few select species. Weather changes required more adequate clothing and shelter. Food shortages would eventually begin to occur.

On the positive side of things, however, a new spiritual generation had emerged from a world of deplorable wickedness. Noah was the spiritual head of this family. For at least a short time, there undoubtedly was relief in the air and a spiritual rejuvenation. But as time would tell, even this fresh start would begin to "sour" within the first generation. Sin always manages to rear its ugly head in short order.

The Floodwaters Begin to Recede

This became soon evident with Ham, Noah's son. That lamentable incident, which will be discussed later, was accentuated with Noah's curse on Canaan. Specific details about Canaan and his actual character are not provided. In addition, the increased physical hardships were among the first signs of a new and less welcoming world. The telltale miseries of sin will not be eliminated until eternity commences (Revelation 21:1–4).

Changes in the World as a Result of the Flood

Henry Morris writes of these apparent physical transformations:

(1) The oceans were much more extensive, since they now contained all the waters which once were "above the firmament" and in the subterranean reservoirs of the "great deep."

(2) The land areas were much less extensive than before the Flood, with a much greater portion of its surface uninhabitable for this reason.

(3) The thermal vapor blanket had been dissipated, so that strong temperature differentials were inaugurated, leading to a gradual buildup of snow and ice in the polar latitudes, rendering much of the extreme northern and southern land surfaces also essentially uninhabitable.

(4) Mountain ranges uplifted after the Flood emphasized the more rugged topography of the postdiluvian

Corruption and Catastrophe

continents, with many of these regions also becoming unfit for human habitation.

(5) Winds and storms, rains and snows, were possible now, thus rendering the total environment less congenial to man and animals than had once been the case.

(6) The environment was also more hostile because of harmful radiation from space, no longer filtered out by the vapor canopy, resulting (along with other contributing environmental factors) in gradual reduction in human longevity after the Flood.

(7) Tremendous glaciers, rivers, and lakes existed for a time, with the world only gradually approaching its present state of semi-aridity.

(8) Because of the tremendous physiographic and isostatic movements generated by the collapse of the subterranean caverns and the post-Flood uplifts, the crust of the earth was in a state of general instability, reflected in recurrent volcanic and seismic activity all over the world for many centuries and continuing in some degree even to the present.

(9) The lands were barren of vegetation, until such time as plant life could be reestablished through the sprouting of seeds and cuttings buried beneath the surface.[164]

---

164 Henry Morris, The Genesis Record, pp. 211–212.

Lithification

Part of the geological processes that speedily proceeded during the Flood and immediately after was lithification. This means the transformation of loose grains of sediment turning into solid rock. There was an unparalleled, unimaginable amount of sediments everywhere. These assorted sediments consisted of the remnants of soil, various loose particles, vegetation, and remnants of now-deceased creatures.

While most larger creatures probably rotted, many were buried and fossilized. We cannot determine all the exact circumstances in which the fossilization took place on such a massive scale, but the evidence itself does not lie. Trillions of fossils, particularly the extremely small life forms, are scattered and fossilized all over the globe. Aside from a worldwide Flood, what else could have possibly accomplished this?

Geologists have been diligently studying the remnants of the Flood for many years and are only beginning to discover some of its secrets. There is no end of material for them to examine. The Flood quite naturally first buried marine organisms. Thus, they are found at the bottom of the alleged "geological column." In reality, there is no actual geological column. Geologists find a variety of sedimentary levels, but there is no consistent geological column anywhere on the earth. Its only real location is found in geology textbooks.

The Expected Progression of Fossil Complexity

In the successive layers above the "ground floor," so to speak, of fossilized animals, one finds larger and larger creatures. That is quite natural since the larger creatures were able to escape the Flood waters more effectively. Clams cannot run very far or fast! Man had the greatest capacity of all to escape the waters. That is one of the reasons why one does not find many fossils of man. Most of them survived until the very end possible, died, and then decomposed on the surface of the water.

Scavengers among the fish population and bacteria probably consumed the vast majority of the human remains. Human bodies tend to float, not to sink. Hence, we find very few, if any, entire human fossils. They would have been eaten and thus eliminated through natural processes.

Ardent evolutionists erroneously use the abundant fossil evidence to teach the progression of the evolutionary ladder. In reality, the fossil record proves precisely the opposite. All fossils remain in stasis, in other words, equilibrium. The variation within a species that we do witness is due to the genetic variation inherent to their DNA.

But to the scientifically anemic evolutionist, life supposedly just magically evolved from a nonliving piece of wet mineral residing placidly on a rock. For unknown and unknowable reasons, this pile of dead minerals suddenly transformed itself into a fully-functioning, living, one-celled bacteria and finally up to modern man. Perhaps a mythical bolt of tame lightning assisted in this process.

This writer is unaware of any proven incidents of lightning-producing life. How fortuitous for the atheistic evolutionist! They glibly proclaim that it must have happened once since: "Lo and behold, we are, aren't we?" Such scientific acumen boggles the imagination. It is infinitely more likely that the federal government will someday announce that the national debt has been legitimately paid off and that they have produced a balanced budget. The entire concept of evolution is laughable. It is entirely pathetic and yet firmly believed by its loyal adherents. Evolutionists turn a willfully blind eye to their complete lack of evidence for its bizarre theories.

This Writer's Characterization of Evolution

This writer summarizes evolution as follows:

The greatest evidence for biological evolution is its total lack of evidence, complete rejection of logic, strident belief in the nonconformity of all known scientific laws, and unsubstantiated faith in the unknown, unseen, and unprovable. In other words, evolution is sheer balderdash!

Though some may protest that this is an unfair characterization, it is nonetheless an accurate one. Or, as a certain politician once quipped, it is an "inconvenient truth."

For anyone who rejects the biblical record of creation and the Flood, evolution is their only logical alternative, no matter how illogical it may be. If they choose to believe life came from outer space, then how did that life originate? All that accomplishes is moving the "goalposts" further down the field, namely, to the unknown and unexplored expanse of the universe. How convenient! Their chances of finding biological life elsewhere will not improve.

Is evolution reasonable? Admittedly, it is difficult for this writer to envision intellectually empty and biologically dead field rocks sprouting legs and eventually ending up as sophisticated, white-haired professors teaching mathematics and advanced physics in Ivy League universities. This writer grew up on the farm and picked thousands of rocks out of the field. He found nary a rock capable of rudimentary conversation, let alone advanced physics. Perhaps that is due to a less-than-fertile imagination on our part. But such is the stuff that evolutionists gleefully affirm.

But imagination is one thing; proof is quite another! And so the evolutionist shrugs his wonderfully modified "bacteria-derived shoulders" and vacantly exclaims: "Whatever will be will be!" We beg to differ. A much more realistic approach to life would be to examine the available evidence in the light of legitimate science and, more importantly, Scripture.

The True Record of the Rocks

Henry Morris writes:

> The fossils in this geological column, however, speaks eloquently of death, and therefore they must have been deposited after Adam's fall and God's curse. Thus, both the Biblical and scientific data, rightly understood, show that the earth's great fossil graveyards must for the most part have been buried by the Flood and its after-effects. The record in the rocks is not a testimony to evolution, but rather to God's sovereign power and judgment of sin.[165]

Morris is absolutely correct. Fossils are a testimony to death and judgment. As such, it is a forerunner to the warnings of coming judgment on this sin-sickened world. God will once again judge the world in unimaginable ways. He has granted mankind opportunity to be spared from eternal judgment through the sacrifice of His eternal Son, Jesus Christ. All may be forgiven for their sinful ways by trusting in Him as personal Lord and Savior. But each man, woman, and child must make this decision individually. We pray that all our readers have done so.

---
[165] Morris, Henry. The Genesis Record, p. 213.

The Floodwaters Begin to Recede

Lessons Learned in This Chapter

In this chapter, we first reviewed the cessation of the worldwide Flood. After God had finished destroying the Nephilim and all air-breathing life outside of the ark, He began to clear the floodwaters away in three ways: (1) He caused a wind to begin drying the earth; (2) He stopped up the subterranean waters from rising; (3) He stopped the torrential rains. However, the floodwaters continued to rise until 150 days had passed. The highest mountains were totally inundated by that time.

Following this, as Psalm 104:6–9 informs us, the mountains began to ascend, and the ocean basins dropped. The waters drained away in rapid but controlled order. God transformed the entire world through this process of the Flood. Canyons were formed by this water cascading down to the newly formed ocean basins. Even the climate was permanently changed.

The tremendous ramifications of the Flood bear repeating. Hence, we shall include Henry Morris's brilliant summation of these radical transformations once again:

(1) The oceans were much more extensive, since they now contained all the waters which once were "above the firmament" and in the subterranean reservoirs of the "great deep."

(2) The land areas were much less extensive than before the Flood, with a much greater portion of its surface uninhabitable for this reason.

(3) The thermal vapor blanket had been dissipated, so

that strong temperature differentials were inaugurated, leading to a gradual buildup of snow and ice in the polar latitudes, rendering much of the extreme northern and southern land surfaces also essentially uninhabitable.

(4) Mountain ranges uplifted after the Flood emphasized the more rugged topography of the postdiluvian continents, with many of these regions also becoming unfit for human habitation.

(5) Winds and storms, rains and snows, were possible now, thus rendering the total environment less congenial to man and animals than had once been the case.

(6) The environment was also more hostile because of harmful radiation from space, no longer filtered out by the vapor canopy, resulting (along with other contributing environmental factors) in gradual reduction in human longevity after the Flood.

(7) Tremendous glaciers, rivers, and lakes existed for a time, with the world only gradually approaching its present state of semi-aridity.

(8) Because of the tremendous physiographic and isostatic movements generated by the collapse of the subterranean caverns and the post-Flood uplifts, the crust of the earth was in a state of general instability, reflect-

ed in recurrent volcanic and seismic activity all over the world for many centuries and continuing in some degree even to the present.

(9) The lands were barren of vegetation, until such time as plant life could be reestablished through the sprouting of seeds and cuttings buried beneath the surface.[166]

Second, we discussed the sending out of the raven and dove from the ark. The raven, being a scavenger bird, probably found many different sources of food. The dove, being a clean bird and one that is used in sacrifices, was much more discriminating in its food preferences. It returned to Noah on two occasions. On the second occasion, it brought back an olive leaf. This was confirmation to Noah that vegetation was growing more abundantly. When Noah sent out the dove the third time, it did not return.

Third, we reviewed the glorious day that Noah and all the creatures disembarked from the ark. This was a moment of unparalleled jubilation. God had proven Himself faithful to Noah, his family, and all the creatures within the ark. He would now grant them the choice responsibility of repopulating the earth after their own respective kinds.

We also explored the folly of that false philosophy dubbed evolution. The Bible explains everything necessary for man to believe in a Creator God and understand the purpose for life. Evolution, by contrast, strips away the meaning of life. The entire premise of evolution is based upon nothing. It seeks to deny the Creator God.

This writer's personalized definition of evolution is as follows:

---
166 Henry Morris, The Genesis Record, pp. 211–212.

The greatest evidence for biological evolution is its total lack of evidence, complete rejection of logic, strident belief in the non-conformity of all known scientific laws, and unsubstantiated faith in the unknown, unseen, and unproveable. In other words, evolution is sheer balderdash!

The biblical account of the Flood is to be embraced wholeheartedly. God orchestrated the entire scenario. Either God is sovereign and tells the truth, or He is not. The choice is that simple. One must choose which God he will worship. We refer once again to the eloquent testimony of Joshua as he spoke to the nation of Israel in Joshua 24:15:

> And if it seems evil to you to serve the LORD, choose for yourselves this day whom you will serve, whether the gods which your father served that were on the other side of the River, or the gods of the Amorites, in whose land you dwell. But as for me and my house, we will serve the LORD.

In our next chapter, we shall examine the Ice Age, how the world changed after the Flood, and what the ultimate future of our present earth will be. All things are within God's control. Nothing surprises Him, and nothing will ever prevent His will from being accomplished.

Cognitive Conundrum #19

Arrayed in magnificent splendor was I; for stones, pearls, and ornaments, I truly did sigh. My fame was not Godliness, that is for sure; my actions were anything but shy and demure. With kings and the wealthy, I cavorted about; of power and influence, I left not a doubt. A brand I did wear that spoke of my shame, mystery, and bloodshed came with my name.

Who am I?

Answer: the woman called Babylon (Revelation chapter 17)

Chapter 20

The Ice Age

(Genesis 8:1-19)

In This Chapter

Objectives for This Chapter
The Ice Age Explained
How About All Those Animals?
What Difference Does All This Make?
Lessons Learned in This Chapter

Objectives for This Chapter

One of the more perplexing scientific issues of our day involves the Ice Age. Those who valiantly cling to the fact-barren theory of evolution are extremely hard-pressed to explain the cause of this huge "deep freeze." The Ice Age cannot very well be denied, considering vast areas of the world are still covered with thousands of feet of ice and snow. Indeed, these regions are almost completely uninhabitable. Still, some varieties of animals manage to survive.

What complicates this matter even more is that these regions are repositories for immense amounts of coal and oil. How did that happen in these frozen wastelands? In addition, fossils of a truly bewildering assortment of animals are found in these locations. How did all of these natural resources, whether living or not, arrive there? An even bigger question is why the animals would have migrated to such inhospitable zones in the first place. Most animals seek out

709

places where the vegetation or the prey is plentiful. Is it possible that this has ever been the case in these frigid territories historically?

The wooly mammoth is perhaps the best-known of these creatures. How did they and other animals survive in such a forbidding environment? There was hardly any food to eat, particularly not sufficient for a hungry mammoth. Such a question is truly a head-scratcher for the ardent evolutionist. If the present truly is the key to the past, something simply does not compute. Where should the hapless evolutionist seek refuge in his quest for answers? His fervent and ever-playful imagination, which he uses profusely, seems his best alternative. Certainly, he cannot rely on facts!

The creationist, however, is not so fettered in his search for answers. He need not quail in fear regarding this alleged dilemma. Unlike those who unwisely adhere to uniformitarianism, the creationist is more biblical in orientation and, hence, comprehensive in these matters. He recognizes something the evolutionist refuses to acknowledge. What is that? The answer for the Ice Age resides in the biblical Flood. The Flood changed everything on earth, including the climate. Indeed, the Flood ultimately ushered in the Ice Age.

Not all questions have been resolved regarding the whys and wherefores of the Flood and the Ice Age. More than likely, some questions will remain until the Lord Himself offers the complete explanation. Nonetheless, many of the so-called mysteries can be resolved relatively simply.

In this chapter, we shall first examine why the Ice Age happened in the first place. A brief explanation can be offered even in our introductory remarks. During the Flood, tremendous volcanic action, accompanied by gargantuan geysers, took place. The crust of the earth was rocked and broken by unimaginably violent earthquakes. These combined factors spewed incalculable volumes of dust, ash, and steam into the atmosphere. In addition, the oceans heated up. The contrast in air and water temperatures produced violent storms. Precisely, the same scenario occurs in our modern world. These storms ushered in the Ice Age, as we shall soon see with more elaborate commentary by experts.

Second, we shall discuss the huge variety and numbers of animals that inhabited the northern and even southern ice-covered regions of the planet. How could they survive in those exceedingly hostile conditions? But were these territories always as they are today? Biblically speaking, they certainly were not. The world initially experienced a uniform and moderate climate. That is how God designed it. Presently, only a smattering of specified animals live in these frigid lands. Even for those relatively few animals, life is a perpetual struggle.

Third, God has promised His children a new heavens and new earth (2 Peter 3:10–14). This present heavens and earth shall be consumed by fire and then recreated. What difference should this make to the believer of today? Do believers have any reason to be intimidated or discouraged? No, we should rather rejoice in the future even if the present does contain many unwelcome challenges. God has all things under His sovereign control.

Peter, who endured many of his own personal struggles, instructs God's children to engage in holy living. Paul, who possibly experienced more opposition than any of the other original eleven apostles (2 Corinthians 11:23), believed that all of these trials and tribulations paled in comparison to what wonders lie ahead in eternity (Romans 8:18). When one meditates on God's Word, believes it, and applies it to his life, nothing should ever remain stagnant or distressing (Joshua 1:8). We can march forth as believers in triumph! God has promised always to be with His children (Hebrews

13:5–6). We can also take comfort in God's peace in our lives (Philippians 4:4–9).

As we now review this sometimes confusing issue of the Ice Age, we encourage the reader to note how it originates with the biblical Flood. The Ice Age may not be clearly specified in the Bible. Nonetheless, all these allegedly "loose ends" can be comfortably knit together for the solace of the believer and to the glory of God.

The Ice Age Explained

Why Discuss the Ice Age?

Obviously, an Ice Age took place on the earth. The evidence is found abundantly throughout the northern and southern parts of the planet. Much of Canada, the northern USA, Eurasia, Greenland, the Arctic, and Antarctica were once covered with ice and snow. Obviously, many of these regions still are smothered with a blanket of ice and snow. Little to no vegetation grows, and few animals can live in these rather extensive lands.

Evolutionists claim that there may have been many ice ages throughout earth's long and colorful history. They offer no proof for their sentiment because there is none. The primary affirmation that they extend is that the world is 4.6 billion years old. With a planet that old, there must have been many ice ages, they explain. Really? Why? Does any climactic clue necessitate such an eventuality? We think not.

But when one is given to such outrageous ages, he can easily enough envision scores of ice ages. However, as previously stated, imagination is one thing; proof is another. In reality, the earth is only about 6,000 years old.

The Ice Age

There has only been one Ice Age. But how could it have been started? Why did it end? We have already discussed some of the reasons behind the Ice Age. However, a bit of review on this particular subject may be in order. This supposed scientific mystery is related to the Flood. In actuality, the explanation is not particularly complicated. When one examines some of the catastrophic events of the Flood, the mystery is largely resolved.

An Explanation for the Ice Age

Sarfati writes as follows:

> The creationist meteorologist Michael Oard proposed that the Ice Age [possibly referred to in Job 37:10 and 38:22] was an aftermath of Noah's Flood. When "all the fountains of the great deep" broke up, much hot water and lava would have poured directly into the oceans. This would have warmed the oceans, increasing evaporation. At the same time, huge volcanic eruptions would have released massive amounts of ash and gas in the air after the Flood. This ash, and the gas forming aerosols, would have blocked out much sunlight, cooling the land.
>
> So the Flood would have produced the necessary combination of lots of evaporation from the warmed oceans and cool continental climate from the volcanic ash and aerosol "sunblock." This would have resulted in increased snowfall over the continents. With the snow falling faster than it melted, ice sheets would have built

up. This ice buildup would probably have lasted several centuries.[167]

Mount Pinatubo as a Recent Example

A recent example of the environmental damage one volcanic eruption can cause is Mount Pinatubo in Luzon, the Philippines. The eruption took place on June 15, 1991. It was approximately ten times more powerful than Mount St. Helens in America. Nearly 2.4 square miles (10 km³) of ash and other material were ejected into the atmosphere. The ash rocketed into the sky 13 miles high (21 km). At least 850 died as a direct result of this explosion, and many more as time went on due to physical complications in their lungs.

Sarfati offers the following description of Mount Pinatubo's eruption:

> Pinatubo also ejected 15-30 million tonnes of sulfur dioxide (SO_2) into the stratosphere. This reacted with water and oxygen to form sulfuric acid (H_2SO_4). The stratosphere is above normal weather patterns, so there was no rain to wash them away. So the aerosols of sulfuric acid droplets persisted for about three years after the eruption. Meanwhile, they continued to scatter and reflect sunlight, reducing the level of sunlight reaching the earth's surface by 10%. So the average global temperature over the next two years dropped by about 0.4 degrees C (0.7 degrees F).[168]

The catastrophe associated with Mount Pinatubo was apprecia-

---

167 Jonathan Sarfati, The Genesis Account: A theological, historical, and scientific commentary on Genesis 1–11, p. 587.
168 Ibid., p. 588.

ble indeed. We grieve over the loss of life and property. But even this volcanic eruption pales into insignificance when compared to the global Flood of Genesis chapters 6 to 9. That event truly changed the topography of the entire world.

What Transpired During the Global Flood?

Sarfati then elaborates on what the conditions would have been like during and after the Flood:

> Eventually, the seas gradually cooled, so evaporation would decrease, therefore, the snow supply for the continents would also decrease. And as the ash settled out of the atmosphere, it would allow sunlight through. So the ice sheets began to melt, starting about 500 years after the Flood.
>
> This would build up large lakes. Sometimes, these would have been contained by natural ice dams for a while. But when these finally cracked, the lakes would have burst through. This water can have tremendous destructive power; when ancient Lake Missoula in Montana (USA) burst an ice dam in Idaho, 2000 km^3 (500 cubic miles) of water poured westward at express train speed—the Spokane Flood. It eroded 200 km^3 (50 cubic miles) of sediment and bedrock, carving the elaborate Channeled Scablands in eastern Washington State.

This includes the Grand Coulee, an 80-km (50 mile) long trench, one to six miles wide, with steep walls up to 275 m (900 feet) high, chiseled through hard basalt and granite. The official website of the Montana Natural History Center explains how even evolutionary geologists now admit the enormous regional scale of the catastrophe.[169]

If a regional flood can cause so many topographical changes, it is impossible to imagine what a global-inundating Flood would do! This Flood was accompanied by immense natural disasters, including volcanic eruptions, crust-cracking earthquakes, gargantuan geysers of superheated water, and tsunamis. Considering these stupendous disasters, is it any surprise that few living things outside of the ark survived very long?

But people did have some time to reflect on their evil ways if they were not immediately killed by an exploding geyser underneath their feet or were instantly crushed by falling rock. Some enterprising and rugged individuals may have survived even for days. Is it possible that some of these sin-hardened people who had heard Noah's message then repented? One would like to think so. But Scripture is silent on that issue.

A Future Comparison to the Flood's Effects

A fascinating parallel to the Flood takes place in the New Testament during the seven-year Tribulation period. Throughout this unprecedented seven-year period of horror, man, the demonic world, and God Himself shall release unremitting terror and destruction on a guilty earth. The Church is removed prior to the Tribulation. What

---

[169] Ibid., p. 588.

follows are intense political, military, spiritual, and physical movements on earth. It will be a time unlike any other.

Revelation 6:12–17 states:

> I looked when He opened the sixth seal, and behold, there was a great earthquake; and the sun became black as sackcloth of hair; and the moon became like blood. And the stars of heaven fell to the earth as a fig tree drops its late figs when it is shaken by a mighty wind. Then the sky receded as a scroll when it is rolled up, and every mountain and island was moved out of its place.
>
> And the kings of the earth, the great men, the rich men, the commanders, the mighty men, every slave and every free man, hid themselves in the caves and in the rocks of the mountains, and said to the mountains and rocks, "Fall on us and hide us from the face of Him who sits on the throne and from the wrath of the Lamb! For the great day of His wrath has come, and who is able to stand?"

The sixth seal judgment will see an even fuller climax at the end of the Tribulation. But considering it is a seal judgment, it will occur in the earlier stages of the Tribulation. The order of the judgments is as follows: (1) the seal judgments, (2) the trumpet judgments, and (3) the bowl judgments.

The seventh bowl judgment (Revelation 16:17–21) will climax the impending catastrophes of which the sixth seal judgment partially forewarned. The sixth seal judgment served as an early indication of the truly disastrous events to follow later. As such, it will give people a chance to repent. According to Revelation chapters 6 to 7, great multitudes of people will come to faith in Christ when they understand the gospel.

The end time finally arrives when the Son of Man returns and judges the entire world (Revelation chapter 19). Simultaneously, the seventh bowl judgment will produce disasters all over the globe. Once Christ appears in the heavens, the time for repentance will be over for that generation. Thankfully, believers can rejoice that even during the Tribulation, countless multitudes do turn in faith to Christ. We shall have fellowship with them during the millennial kingdom of Christ. This reality is elaborated on in the fifth seal, which is found in Revelation 6:9–11 (cf. 7:9–17).

A Question of Repentance in Noah's Day

One ponders how many Nephilim-inflicted individuals repented who knew of Noah's message. It does not seem possible that these wretched souls were completely beyond God's infinite measure of grace and love. Noah preached for 120 years. If they were completely beyond redemption, why did God send Noah out to preach? People in that era did not seem overly inclined to wander over the entire earth as God had originally commanded. Hence, the majority of earth's inhabitants possibly heard Noah himself preach. If not, perhaps someone else conveyed Noah's message to them.

God is very merciful. It is entirely possible that no one repented. However, it seems more likely that at least some recognized their transgressions and repented. There is no way of knowing since the Scripture does not comment on this. But we pray that it was the latter. It also could be that Noah led the world's greatest revival after God shut the door of the ark, and it started to rain! This was not necessarily the same thing as God shutting the door of individual's hearts.

God never tires of reaching out His loving hands to the unregenerated. Jeremiah 33:2–3 states: "Thus says the Lord who made it, the Lord who formed it to establish it (the Lord is His name): 'Call to Me, and I will answer you, and show you great and mighty things, which you do not know'" (cf. 29:12–13; Psalm 91:15). Though physical deliverance was no longer available for the Nephilim, possibly spiritual deliverance still was.

Two conclusions may be offered. First, if any Nephilim-defiled individual did actually repent by Noah's preaching, they must have died before the Flood took place. If any had genuinely converted, they should have entered the ark with Noah and his family. Sadly, none did. That does not bode well for the view that there may have been any conversions to faith.

Second, if any Nephilim-defiled individual repented after the Flood began, they died by the floodwaters. The Nephilim did not survive the Flood. No land-dwelling air-breathers did. That was one of the primary purposes for God sending the Flood in the first place. Considering the overall context of Scripture, sad to say, it seems more likely that no one repented from Noah's preaching except his own family. What an incredible tragedy if that is true.

How About All Those Animals?

Did the Weather Change? Absolutely!

Question related to the Ice Age: How does one explain all the wooly mammoths and other northern creatures? Why were there so many of them if the world has always been the same?

An astonishing array of animal bones have been located in the far northern climates such as Siberia, Alaska, and the tundra regions of Canada. These areas are so inhospitable to life that few creatures are found there today. But at one time in earth's history, these northern regions teemed with abundant life and vegetation. This is further evidenced by massive oil and coal reserves. What could have caused this precipitous change in the weather? The obvious answer is the Flood.

Still, some intriguing issues remain unresolved. There have been many theories offered regarding the supposedly "quick frozen" mammoths by both secularists and creationists. A final solution has not yet been totally verified and possibly never will be. Although not completely understood in all its factors, the global Flood and what happened after the Ice Age offers the most logical explanation.

There Were a Lot of Critters Up North!

Concerning the considerable variety in animal life found in these now-frozen areas, J. K. Charlesworth writes:

> Vast herds of mammoth and other animals (the New Siberian Islands in the far north of Asia have yielded mammoth, wooly rhinoceros, musk ox, saiga antelope, reindeer, tiger, arctic fox, glutton, bear and horse among the 66 animal species) required forests, meadows and steppes for their sustenance. ... and could not have lived in a climate like the present, with its icy winds, snowy winters, frozen ground and tundra moss the year round.[170]

---

170 R. F. Flint, Glacial and Pleistocene Geology (New York, Wiley, 1957), p. 650.

The Ice Age

At one time, the northern climates were clearly characterized by abundant wildlife and vegetation. Animals thrived by the millions, including the wooly mammoth. It is well-known that mammoths require an enormous amount of food and water to survive each day. Did something sensational happen that caused all of these animals to die suddenly? The answer, as usual, lies somewhere in the middle between the more extreme positions. Something clearly did happen, and much of it was undeniably rapid. However, not everything perished instantly, as has often been reported.

Did Life End Abruptly in a Quick "Deep Freeze"?

During the Ice Age, scavengers continued to prosper for some time, feasting on larger creatures that had perished. For example, some predator(s) ate the head of an entombed horse. Portions of mammoths were also consumed. This alone demonstrates that a massive, killing cold snap could not have occurred. Nothing could have survived such a catastrophe! Rightly or wrongly, some have speculated that this cold snap would have to plummet earth's temperatures down to −97 degrees C (−175 degrees F) in order to "quick-freeze" a mammoth.

Earth's record cold temperature is 136 degrees below zero Fahrenheit, which was recorded in Antarctica. That qualifies as cold, in most people's opinion. However, such temperatures did not happen overnight in Antarctica. Nor did they probably happen in the northern climates. So what, if anything, could possibly cause such a theoretical instant freeze? Some highly speculative theories have been put forth. But are those speculations realistic? It does not appear so. Neither are they necessary.

A Cogent Explanation for Life and Death in the Ice Age

Michael Oord comments:

Carcasses and bones of woolly mammoths in Siberia, Alaska, and the Yukon have been difficult to explain. The mammoth remains are abundant over the mid and high latitudes of the Northern Hemisphere, except in formerly glaciated areas. There are probably millions of them buried in the permafrost of Siberia alone.

A wide variety of other mammals, large and small, accompanied the mammoth. Many of these animals are grazers, implying that the paleoenvironment of Beringia was a grassland with a wide diversity of plants. This diversity of plants and animals points to a longer growing season with milder winters and very little permafrost.

This paleoenvironment is contrary to what is observed in Beringia today, with its very cold winters and boggy substrate in summer. Scientists constrained by uniformitarian thinking seem to face conundrum after conundrum in regard to the life and death of the woolly mammoth in Beringia, as well as by the ice age itself.

A uniformitarian ice age climate would have been even colder still. It is difficult to conceive that the woolly mammoth and all the other animals could have lived in Siberia under these conditions. It is obvious the uniformitarian assumption does not apply. Thus, many hypotheses, both creationist and non-creationist, have been proposed. Creationists have been divided on whether the woolly mammoth perished in the Flood or afterwards. A number of creationist hypotheses involve a quick freeze, because it was thought that the state of preservation of the carcasses with only half-decayed vegetation in their stomachs demanded it.

Reasonable explanations for all these mysteries are available within the context of a unique post-Flood ice age. Astral catastrophes, pole shifts and other such exotic hypotheses are not needed. A quick freeze is also not necessary, and besides, there is much data against the hypothesis. There is strong evidence that the woolly mammoth died after the Flood during the ice age. There was enough time for the population of the mammoths to have grown to millions by the end of the ice age.

Furthermore, this unique ice age was characterized by colder summers and warmer winters, resulting in a more favorable habitat for the animals in the non-glaciated lowlands of Beringia. The animals became extinct at the end of the ice age because the climate changed to a more continental climate, with colder winters and warmer summers, and drier conditions.

There is copious data against the hypothesis of a quick

freeze. The state of preservation of the stomach contents are better explained by the post-gastric digestive system of elephants in which the stomach is mainly a holding pouch for vegetation.

The question of how the mammoths died in Beringia can be answered by analyzing the sediments surrounding the mammoths and other animals. They are mostly entombed in yedomas in Siberia and muck in Alaska. These are mostly loess and reworked loess. It is postulated that the animals were buried by dust storms, whether they met their demise directly by wind-blown silt or not.

The carcasses and other perplexing data associated with the carcasses, such as death by suffocation, entombment while in a standing position, and broken bones, can be explained by death during gigantic dust storms and post-mortem shifting of the permafrost.[171]

Not All Questions Can Presently Be Answered

The mysteries of these northern creatures and the once lush vegetation will probably always foster unanswerable questions. Oord's explanation, however, does make considerable sense. This is particularly true of dust storms suffocating the animals. This writer has personally witnessed the dire effects of a vicious winter blizzard on unprotected cattle. Their nostrils tragically become filled with ice, and the cow suffocates. They do not necessarily freeze to death,

---
171 Michael Oord, Journal of Creation 14, no. 3 (December 2000): pp. 24–34.

although that is also possible.

As time progresses, some of these questions may be resolved to greater satisfaction. One thing is certain: the universal Flood caused catastrophic and permanent changes to a once-perfect earth. Man's sin brought about this change. But at some time in the not-too-distant future, all will be made perfect once again. Only God can bring about this change. Relation chapters 21 to 22 is Scripture's most extensive description of what the new heavens, earth, and Jerusalem will be like. They shall be unparalleled in majesty.

What Difference Does All This Make?

Second Peter 3:13–14 offers all believers this wonderful promise: "Nevertheless we, according to His promise, look for new heavens and a new earth in which righteousness dwells. Therefore, beloved, looking forward to these things, be diligent to be found by Him in peace, without spot and blameless." God will always take care of His children. May we, as believers, live each day for His glory.

Two Promises and Three Commands

The above passage presents two promises and three commands. Promise #1: A new heavens and new earth is coming. Why is this necessary? It is because the original heavens and earth were corrupted by sin. God will thus create all things new again without the defilement of sin. Eternity will not be characterized by sinful behavior. Believers will be truly and permanently cleansed of all immorality. We shall never be afflicted by the presence of sin ever again. What a glorious truth that is!

Promise #2: Righteousness will characterize the new heavens and earth. Righteousness can only thrive in the absence of sin. All of creation shall be cleansed and made pure. Such a promise is beyond mankind's present imagination. We are buffeted by sin within and without. What an unimaginable time eternity shall be for the believer.

J. N. D. Kelly offers the following comments on 2 Peter 3:13:

> Christ Himself had spoken (Mt. xix. 28) of 'the new age when the Son of Man shall sit on his glorious throne', and which would be the setting of the Messianic banquet (Mk. xiv. 25), and in Paul's view (Rom. viii. 19-22) the present creation is in travail with the birth of a more glorious one. These eager eschatological expectations of early Christianity found their most colorful expression in Revelation, with its affirmation (xxi. 1 f.; 10-27) of a new heaven and earth and a new Jerusalem.
>
> All this imagery is a Christian development and adaptation of older Jewish hopes and yearnings, especially as set out in Is. lxv. 17 and lxvi. 22, which specifically forecast the creation of new heavens and a new earth; these passages presumably contain the divine promise alluded to here (cf. 1 En. lxxii. 1, which also predicts a new creation, and are in our writer's mind.[172]

---

[172] J. N. D. Kelly, Thornapple Commentaries: A Commentary on the Epistles of Peter and Jude (Grand Rapids, MI: Baker Book House, 1969), p. 368.

Believers Are to Anticipate God's Glorious Blessings

Second Peter 3:13–14 prompts the believer to obedience in several aspects. Command #1: Believers are to yearn for this day of deliverance. This is referring to the new heavens and earth and our lives within that new creation. Believers are to revel in the fact that this life on earth does not characterize eternity. In our darkest days of discouragement, we are to look up and recognize that our redemption draws nigh. Life on this earth is but a vapor which shall quickly pass away (James 4:14). Eternity has no end. Life with God will go on forever.

This great hope can sustain all who place their hope in Christ (Titus 2:13). Paul reminds us of this truth in Romans 8:18–19: "For I consider that the sufferings of this present time are not worthy to be compared with the glory which shall be revealed in us. For the earnest expectation of the creation eagerly waits for the revealing of the sons of God."

Command #2: We are to be diligent to be found by Him in peace. God grants the believer a peace that passes all understanding. But the believer must avail himself of that peace. That is where the diligent aspect is required. Spiritual complacency is forbidden. How is the believer to exercise due diligence? This is largely attained through a study of God's Word, prayer, and obedient living. Philippians 4:7 promises: "And the peace of God which surpasses all understanding, will guard your hearts and minds through Christ Jesus."

God Calls His Children to Holy Living

Command #3: We are to be found without spot and blameless. This is not to imply that we are to be sinless. That is not humanly possible. Until the Lord returns and believers are ushered into His holy presence, they will retain their evil natures. Even the apostle Paul writes of his ongoing struggle with good and evil (Romans 7:14–21). However, believers are commanded to exercise discipline in their sanctification process. Obedience to Christ demonstrates our love to Him (John 14:21).

Impetuous Peter struggled mightily with sanctification in his own life. Thus, he knew personally whereof he wrote. Nonetheless, he pens the following inspirational thoughts under the guidance of the Holy Spirit in 1 Peter 1:13–16:

> Therefore, gird up the loins of your mind, be sober, and rest your hope fully upon the grace that is to be brought to you at the revelation of Jesus Christ, as obedient children, not conforming yourselves to the former lusts, as in your ignorance; but as He who called you is holy, you also be holy in all your conduct, because it is written, "Be holy, for I am holy" (cf. Leviticus 11:44–45; 1 John 2:15–17).

With these thoughts in mind, believers can live lives of fullness and purpose. We serve a living Savior! He enables us to live our lives in ways that bring Him the glory He eternally deserves. May each believer strive for spiritual diligence in his life. Only what we accomplish for Christ will we bring with us into eternity.

Lessons Learned in This Chapter

In this chapter, we first delved into the scientific enigma of the Ice Age. It is the assessment of most creationists that the Ice Age was a natural and explainable result of the Flood. Indeed, it would have been predictable. Many unprecedented supernatural events triggered and maintained the destructiveness of the Flood. These catastrophic yet divine-induced events included earthquakes, volcanos, geysers of water under intense pressure, torrential rain, and tsunamis. Indeed, the entire climate was permanently altered by the ravages of the Flood.

We examined the examples of Mount Pinatubo in the Philippines and Mount St. Helens in America. Mount Pinatubo was considerably larger than Mount St. Helens. However, these are still relatively minor in comparison to the historic volcanic action of the Flood. The volcanic action of Noah's day was incomparably larger than anything seen today. The crust of the earth was literally shattered in many locations. The dislocation of such large areas caused magma flows of unimaginable duration and power.

Second, we explored the incredible assortment of animal fossils in what are today extremely inhospitable regions. Why did the animals move there, and how were they supported with sustenance? To the uniformitarian, this is truly a puzzle. To the creationists, a relatively simple answer is sufficient. The climate dramatically changed as a result of the Flood.

When God created the world, there was one uniform and moderate temperature. Vegetation was lush all over the planet. There was no struggle for the animal kingdom to survive anywhere on the earth. Food was everywhere! That eventually began to change. Today, large swaths of territory are incapable of sustaining much life.

Third, we discussed the future new heavens and earth. Because of the presence of sin impacting every atom of the universe today, all must be created anew. This present system shall be destroyed with fire and created afresh. Revelation chapters 21 to 22 offer a small glimpse of this future kingdom. Believers shall forever be removed from the presence of sin. Their own sinful natures shall be permanently eradicated. This is truly impossible to imagine in our sin-plagued world today.

In light of God's inspired words to man, believers have no need to fear or be overly depressed by negative events surrounding them. Ultimate victory has already been attained in Christ. The believer may rejoice in the truth proclaimed in 1 Corinthians 15:57–58: "But thanks be to God, who gives us the victory through our Lord Jesus Christ. Therefore, my beloved brethren, be steadfast, immovable, always abounding in the work of the Lord, knowing that your labor is not in vain in the Lord."

In our next chapter, we shall discuss God's covenant with Noah. The Flood, at long last, was over, and the earth dried out. The small family of eight plus all the animals disembarked from their large wooden, floating home. The world began the process of repopulation. But before anything else of importance took place, Noah worshiped the Lord. As such, he presents a powerful reminder to God's children to always exercise proper priorities. Believers of every generation and locality need to follow Noah's godly example of worship. Noah walked with God!

The Ice Age

Cognitive Conundrum #20

My husband and I, we made quite a team; the Scriptures we loved to explain, it would seem. Sewing tents for a living helped pay the bills, but the Bible we loved to others to fill. A noted preacher was our primary student; to preach and teach with alacrity was his intent. Paul was our good friend and mentor; indeed, the Scriptures and love to us he did feed.

Who are we?

Answer: Aquila and Priscilla (Acts chapter 18)

Chapter 21

God's Covenant with Noah

(Genesis 8:20-22)

In This Chapter

Objectives for This Chapter
Noah Worships God through Sacrifices
Promise #1: Astounding Agricultural Fertility (8:21–22)
Promise #2: God Will Bless Israel (Amos 9:11–15)
Promise #3: The Seasons Continue Unabated (Genesis 8:22)
Lessons Learned in This Chapter

Objectives for This Chapter

In these three short verses, a great deal of information is conveyed to the reader. The first element we shall review regards worship. Noah exercised his priorities in the appropriate order. Upon disembarking from the ark, he immediately offered up sacrifices to the all-powerful and benevolent God who had spared him. As he prepared the sacrifices, one can imagine him casting wistful glances at the immense vessel in whose holds they had resided for slightly over a year. He had invested 120 years of his life in building the ark.

Few people in the history of the world can match Noah's faithfulness. Despite all the mockery and scorn he and his family endured, they continued on with their arduous but life-saving mission. Noah shall be remembered for all time by his inspirational example all believers should follow.

Second, we shall review three promises given in this passage. All of them are germane to the present. However, some will be fulfilled to their fullest in the millennial kingdom. They are as follows: Promise #1: Astounding agricultural fertility. This fertility will be enhanced immeasurably during the millennial kingdom of Christ. But in this context, God removed the curse regarding its productivity from the earth.

Promise #2: God's blessing on Israel. As the reader will immediately note, Israel was not a nation at this time. So, why do we mention Israel? It is because the Seed Son, the Messiah, is of Israel (Genesis 3:15). This was not known, of course, in the days of Adam and Eve. Indeed, it was not until Abraham came on the scene that this promise was clarified (12:1–3). Long after Abraham died, Judah was selected as the tribe of blessing (49:10).

The fulfillment of the messianic Seed was directly tied to the Flood. The cohabitation of demons with womankind stands repugnant to the extreme. Their offspring, the Nephilim ("fallen ones"), were trying to destroy the entire human race in a spiritual sense. Hence, in the context of the Flood, some review of these prophetic principles is prudent. Under this particular promise, we shall also discuss the fact that the world would never be destroyed by a universal Flood again.

Ultimate blessing comes through the Messiah. History revolves around God's plans for His chosen people. We shall refer to Amos 9:11–15 to emphasize both the future agricultural bounty and God's plans for Israel. Coupled with this and other passages, such as Jeremiah 31:31–37, we shall see that these blessings are ultimately unconditional. However, the reception of these promised blessings has been delayed because of Israel's disobedience and the rejection of their Messiah.

God also graciously promised that this present world will never again be destroyed by a universal Flood. Those who deny the worldwide Flood are errant in at least three separate facets. Facet #1: They must deny the plain reading of Scripture. If one cannot understand simple narrative, why should any confidence be placed in their interpretive prowess for other passages? Clearly, they are lacking in fundamental hermeneutical skills. Facet #2: The local flood theory is proven wrong by the fact that literally millions of floods have taken place since Noah's day.

Facet #3: They must call God a liar. This may not be intentional on their part (we trust not), but it is precisely what they are doing. Numbers 23:19 unwaveringly states: "God is not a man, that He should lie, nor a son of man, that He should repent. Has He said, and will He not do? Or has He spoken, and will He not make it good?" God's words in Genesis 8:20–22 are not subject to allegorization or some other mystical interpretation. They are plainly evidenced for all to see in their everyday lives.

(3) The third promise is that the seasons shall continue unabated. That has also clearly held true. While some regions of the globe do not experience particularly pronounced seasons, they are there nonetheless. Such regions generally have seasons characterized by a rainy and a dry season. Many other regions are blessed with a definite change from season to season. Where this author lives, the winter season seems to linger on forever. The coming of spring and summer always causes rejoicing. God's faithfulness is not open to question. What He says He always will do.

Noah Worships God through Sacrifices (8:20–22)

Noah's first recorded act after leaving the ark was to build an altar for worshiping God. The almighty God had blessed Noah with a saga of extraordinary preservation. Needless to say, he and his family were eternally grateful. God had brought them safely through a literally earth-shaking event. Their survival and life on the ark was in itself a miracle. It is impossible to fathom the conditions transpiring all around them. The Flood was finally over, but the consequences of this remarkable, one-of-a-kind event remain with us to this day.

Noah's godly example should prove an example to all believers from every age. Worship is to be an ongoing exercise practiced daily; one might even say, continuously. Paul admonished the Thessalonians, and hence all of the Church, in 1 Thessalonians 5:16–19: "Rejoice always, pray without ceasing, in everything give thanks; for this is the will of God in Christ Jesus for you. Do not quench the Spirit." May every believer embrace these admonitions and apply them with all their strength by God's grace.

An Exercise of Proper Priorities

Genesis 8:20–22 states:

> Then Noah built an altar to the LORD, and took every clean animal and every clean bird, and offered burnt offerings on the altar.

> And the LORD smelled a soothing aroma. Then the LORD said in His heart, 'I will never again curse the ground for man's sake, although the imagination of man's heart is evil from his youth: nor will I again destroy every living thing as I have done. While the earth remains, seedtime and harvest, cold and heat, winter and summer, and day and night shall not cease."

This is the first time an altar is mentioned in Scripture. When Cain and Abel brought their sacrifices, they were not necessarily offered on an altar. Scripture offers no comment regarding that detail. Now, however, an altar is used. Noah offered one of each of the seven clean animals and one of each clean bird. The Hebrew literally says "seven seven," indicating seven pairs, and so it appears to have been a total of fourteen clean animals.

Some believe, however, there were a total of only seven birds and clean animals so that three pairs remained. If that were the case, then no creature would have lost its mate, as there was one extra in the first place. However, the stronger likelihood was that one male was sacrificed among a total of fourteen. The other males could serve as mates to the then extra female, just as is commonly true in the animal kingdom today.

God allowed the birds and animals to multiply safely. One cannot outdo the goodness of God. He did not preserve Noah and the animals simply to let them promptly go extinct. He preserved all the creatures for an extended but unknown period of time. There is no denying that due to climate changes and other unknown hardships, different species of animals have succumbed to extinction over the centuries.

An Injunction to Follow Noah's Godly Example

It is important that, as did Noah, all believers acknowledge and worship the Lord with the firstfruits of all the gifts God has granted to them. What do believers possess that God has not granted to them? In like manner, what do unbelievers retain that God has not granted to them? Everything we cherish in our lives, indeed, our very breath, comes as a gift from God.

Proverbs 3:9–10 states: "Honor the LORD with your possessions, and with the firstfruits of all your increase; So your barns will be filled with plenty, and your vats will overflow with new wine." As King David acknowledged, all that we sacrifice to the Lord is already His. We are not giving Him anything that He did not create for our benefit. Even our ability to work is a gift from God.

Deuteronomy 8:17–18 reminded the Israelites: "Then you shall say in your heart, 'My power and the might of my hand have gained me this wealth. And you shall remember the LORD your God, for it is He who gives you power to get wealth, that He may establish His covenant which He swore to your fathers, as it is this day.'"

Every Good Gift Is from God

Everything with which we are blessed emanates from the ever-benevolent hand of God. One does well to bear this in mind each moment of every day. David writes in 1 Chronicles 29:14:

> But who am I, and who are my people, that we should be able to offer so willingly as this? For all things come from You, and of Your own we have given you. For we are aliens and pilgrims before You, as were all our fathers; our days on earth are as a shadow; and without hope.

The New Testament also recognizes the blessings God bestows upon His children. James 1:16–17 states: "Do not be deceived, my beloved brethren. Every good gift and every perfect gift is from above, and comes down from the Father of lights, with whom there is no variation or shadow of turning."

Much more important than Noah's sacrifice is the fact that God accepted the sacrifice. Let the reader recall that this decidedly was not the case with Cain (Genesis chapter 4). Cain offered a sacrifice that was inadmissible. We are not informed of all the reasons why. One probable reason, however, is that it was not a blood sacrifice. Hebrews 9:22 states: "And according to the law almost all things are purified with blood, and without shedding of blood there is no remission."

Regarding Hebrews 9:22, Philip Edgcumbe Hughes writes:

> Under the law, that is, within the framework of the Mosaic system, it is, indeed, an established principle that everything is purified with blood—or almost everything, for there are a few exceptions to the rule. This principle is concisely stated in the words (perhaps a familiar saying) without the shedding of blood there is no forgiveness of sins. It is, of course, a principle which is at the very heart of the Christian gospel with its insistence that the shedding of the blood of Jesus Christ is the sole source of cleansing and reconciliation for the sinner (cf. 1 Jn. 1:7; 1 Pet. 1:18f.; Rev. 1:5; 7:14; 12:11, and v. 14 above).

> What was foreshadowed under the law is fulfilled in Christ. Once again (see page 376), the language used here is strongly reminiscent of the words with which our Lord instituted the eucharist: "This is my blood of the covenant, which is poured out for man for the forgiveness of sins" (Mt. 26:28).[173]

---

[173] Philip Edgcumbe Hughes, A Commentary on the Epistle to the Hebrews (Grand Rapids, MI: William B. Eerdmans Publishing Company, 1977), p. 378.

Although God did accept sacrifices of the fruit of the field, they could not be offered for forgiveness of sin. Innocent blood must pay for the sins of the guilty. Not only did Cain (apparently) ignore this principle, but he grew angry over his sacrifice's rejection. Surely, he had full information on how to offer a proper sacrifice, as did Abel. God counseled him to do the right thing. He refused. Instead, Cain chose the foul path of shedding the innocent blood of his righteous brother, Abel. This heinous crime was reprehensible to the extreme and entirely unwarranted.

In contrast to Cain, Scripture describes the sacrifice that Noah offered as a soothing aroma. God smelled the pleasant aroma and was pleased to honor it. The Lord, speaking to Himself, uttered three sacred promises. Again, we remind the reader that promises one and two are fulfilled more fully in the millennial kingdom.

Promise #1: Astounding Agricultural Fertility

Genesis 8:21 states: "And the LORD smelled a soothing aroma. Then the LORD said in His heart, 'I will never again curse the ground for man's sake, although the imagination of man's heart is evil from his youth: nor will I again destroy every living thing as I have done.'"

Promise #1: God would never again curse the ground for man's sake. This should not be understood as meaning that the Lord entirely removed the original curse He placed on the ground (Genesis 3:17). Clearly, land around the globe varies greatly in its productivity. Much of the world is desert or mountainous. Some of it is swampland as well. These areas are largely unproductive regions for agriculture. They do, however, oftentimes offer other benefits such as important minerals and oil or as a refuge for wildlife.

It will not be until the future millennial kingdom of Christ that

God renews and reinvigorates the land to its original productivity. Though modern agriculture has invented increasingly effective methods of growing crops, it will not even begin to compare to the millennium. It should be noted that this promise is not dependent on mankind's obedience. It is solely dependent on God's grace. Though mankind once again reverts to gross immorality, God will patiently forbear punishment. Even though man's thought life is evil from his youth, God will delay His righteous judgment. Never again will God destroy every living creature on the earth.

Agricultural Blessing

Question: How severe was God's original curse on the ground? Answer: We have no way of knowing. What we do recognize is that it meant man would have to earn his living by the sweat of his brow (Genesis 3:17–19). That is still true today. Yet, in spite of that, areas still existed that were like the Garden of Eden in fertility. Indeed, that is why Lot chose to live in Sodom and Gomorrah (Genesis 12:10). It is characteristic of God to exercise blessing in the midst of judgment. Even though He had cursed the ground, it was still sufficiently fertile to grow crops, fruit trees, and vegetables.

What will the future bring? Evidence of God's future agricultural blessing and His love for Israel is recorded in Amos 9:11–15:

> On that day I will raise up the Tabernacle of David which has fallen down, and repair its damages; I will raise up its ruins, and rebuild it as in the days of old. That they may possess the remnant of Edom, and all the Gentiles who are called by My name, says the LORD who does this thing. Behold, the days are coming, says the LORD, when the plowman shall overtake the reap-

er, and the treader of grapes him who sows seed; the mountains shall drip with sweet wine, and all the hills shall flow with it.

I will bring back the captives of My people Israel. They shall build the waste cities and inhabit them; they shall plant vineyards and drink wine from them, and eat fruit from them. I will plant them in their land, and no longer shall they be pulled up from the land I have given them, says the LORD your God.

Based on this amazing passage, God will bless both the fertility of the earth in the millennial kingdom of Christ and the nation of Israel. We shall examine both of these features momentarily.

The Importance of Petra (Amos 9:12)

However, before examining these important truths, we should ask a question. Question: Why does this passage include the "remnant of Edom?" What does that mean? Answer: It is because this is where the believing Jewish remnant will hide from the Antichrist during the Tribulation (Revelation 12:6). Revelation chapter 12 does not specifically identify this location, but it parallels what is written in Micah 2:12–13. The name Petra is not mentioned in the Bible. It came into existence later. Rather, the location is called Sela (Isaiah 16:1; 2 Kings 14:7).

The believing Jews are protected in Petra, which is a feminine Greek name for "rock," from the enemy for three and a half years. Indeed, Petra is a city carved out of rock. This writer has visited the location on two occasions. It is truly an extraordinary place! The majority of Edom shall be destroyed (Isaiah 34:6; Jeremiah 49:13;

Amos 1:12). Yet a small portion of the country shall be preserved for a season. Since this rather restricted area, known as Bozrah, or Petra, helps protect the Jewish believers, it shall be preserved during the Tribulation.

Josephus, Eusebius, and Jerome all bear witness to the fact that Kadesh-barnea was located at Petra. This location is also where Moses brought water out of the rock. Tragically, this is also where the Israelites rebelled against God and Moses. Their penalty was to wander in the wilderness for forty years until every last one of them, twenty years old and above, had perished. The only two exceptions were Joshua and Caleb (Numbers 14:30).

It is quite intriguing that the Antichrist conquers all the world except Ammon, Moab, and Edom (Daniel 12:41). Petra is within this location. These three small nations together comprise much of modern-day Jordan. When Christ returns, He first single-handedly destroys the assembled forces of the Antichrist at Bozrah, or Petra (Isaiah 63:1–6). He then will continue to advance up to Jerusalem, where He shall finish His triumph over Satan, the Antichrist, and the false prophet (Zechariah chapter 14).

Based on Amos 9:11–15, God will bless the fertility of the earth in the millennial kingdom. In our modern age, we cannot truly comprehend how fertile the earth was before God cursed the land because of man's sin in Genesis chapter 3. The entire world was at one time phenomenally productive. Vegetation grew everywhere in lavish abundance. The world was of one climate. Adam and Eve did not even require clothing to protect them from the elements (Genesis 2:25). God created a perfect environment for them.

He also blessed the soil so it could grow anything. Its fertility exceeded the best land available on earth today. The vast subterranean repositories of coal and oil attest to earth's fertility. If geologists are correct in their assessment, it takes approximately ten feet of buried vegetation to produce one foot of coal. Considering that the thickest coal seams discovered are 90 feet thick, that translates into 900 feet of buried vegetation! That is truly beyond imagination.

What sort of a cataclysmic worldwide flood could bury that much vegetation? Indeed, where in the modern world would one even find so much vegetation to bury? The Lord will someday return the earth to this level of fertility. As already stated, all the prodigious reserves of oil and coal resulted from the Flood, which was God's judgment on man and the earth.

Blessing in the Midst of Judgment

God frequently brings tremendous blessing to man through even the severest of punishments, namely, the Flood. This is characteristic of God in our everyday lives in the past, present, and future. He lovingly blesses us in spite of our all-too-often sinful behavior. His mercy and grace is everlasting. Romans 8:28 conveys the following truth: "And we know that all things work together for good to those who love God, to those who are the called according to his purpose." Believers should continuously rejoice in God's amazing benevolence.

John MacArthur comments on Romans 8:28 as follows:

> Paul is not saying that God prevents His children from experiencing things that can harm them. He is rather attesting that the Lord takes all that He allows to happen to His beloved children, even the worst things, and turns those things ultimately into blessings. No matter what our situation, our suffering, our persecution, our sinful failure, our pain, our lack of faith—in

those things, as well as in all other things, our heavenly Father will work to produce our ultimate victory and blessing.

The corollary of that truth is that nothing can ultimately work against us. Any temporary harm we suffer will be used by God for our benefit (see 2 Cor. 12:7-10). … all things includes circumstances and events that are good and beneficial in themselves as well as those that are in themselves evil and harmful.[174]

Promise #2: God Will Bless Israel (Amos 9:11–15)

This particular section is also based largely upon Amos' prophecy. Amos 9:11–15 testifies that God will bless the future of Israel. Although this is not directly related to the Flood, Amos 9:11–15 presents it as part of the restoration of the earth's fertility. One cannot exegetically separate the restoration of the soil and the future blessing of Israel. The two go together hand in hand.

The soil was cursed in Genesis; it shall be restored according to the prophet's inspired writings. Israel was shattered as a nation by the threefold threat of Assyrians, Babylonians, and Romans, but all twelve tribes shall be restored by God almighty (Ezekiel 37:15–28; Hosea 1:10–11). The Antichrist will be the final oppressor of the Israelites. The northern ten tribes do not know their identity at present, but God shall reveal this at a future time (Jeremiah 50:4).

Hosea 3:4–5 is most instructive:

> For the children of Israel shall abide many days without king or prince, without sacrifice or sacred pillar,

---
[174] John MacArthur, The MacArthur New Testament Commentary: Romans 1–8, p. 473.

without ephod or teraphim. Afterward the children of Israel shall return and seek the LORD their God and David their king. They shall fear the LORD and His goodness in the latter days.

The northern ten tribes rejected the Davidic dynasty historically. Someday in the future, however, they shall be reunited together with Judah and worship God in an appropriate fashion (Ezekiel 37:15–28).

Blessings on the Land and Israel

It is incumbent upon us to discuss the future of Israel for the moment as it is related in the context of Amos. Why is that necessary? The context of Amos relates back to the promise of the Messianic redemption (Genesis 3:15), the penalty of sin on the world (Genesis chapters 6 to 9), and the preservation of the Seed through Noah and his son Shem (11:10ff).

In the last days, God will bring the Jewish people back to the Promised Land from wherever they have been scattered throughout the globe. When we use the term "Jewish," we also include the other eleven tribes. Thus, we use the term "Jewish" generically to represent the entire nation of Israel. Technically, of course, it refers to the tribe of Judah.

All twelve tribes of Israel will become identifiable once again. Though the northern ten tribes were scattered by the Assyrians in 722–721 BC, God knows exactly where every surviving descendant resides from every tribe. Most of these individuals who are living in our modern times themselves do not recognize their Israeli heritage. That is because their genealogical records have been destroyed or lost. The Assyrians scattered the Israelites so thoroughly that almost all lost their tribal identity.

But someday, more specifically, after the Tribulation, God will dry their tears and reunite their families. They shall rebuild the cities that were destroyed by the diabolical Antichrist and his wicked forces. As Amos 9:11–15 testifies, prosperity will reign, and famine will forever be vanquished. Everyone will know of the Lord and His reign (Isaiah 2:2–4; Habakkuk 2:14).

The millennium will be a time of never-ending spiritual celebration! The unbelievers of Noah's day were granted no such reprieve after 120 years of constant preaching and testifying of God's coming judgment. But that is because they chose to remain unbelievers. All living people of today still have a choice as to whom they will serve: self or the Creator God.

The Future for Israel, According to Amos

Charles Lee Feinberg comments as follows:

Israel will in that day be restored from centuries-long captivity to rebuild her cities and inhabit them with the enjoyment of her vineyards and her gardens. (Cp. Ho 6:11 and 5:11 of this book.) Then Israel will be planted and rooted in her own land (2 Sa 7:10), never more to be plucked up and uprooted from her God-given land. The day of exile, thank God, will be past. Note carefully Isaiah 61:4; 62:8, 9; 65:21-23.

Let us summarize the remarkable prophecy of Amos to be fulfilled in the consummation of Israel's history: (1) the restoration of the Davidic dynasty, verse 11; (2) the supremacy of Israel over the nations, verse 12; (3) the conversion of the nations, verse 12; (4) the fruitfulness of the land, verse 13; (5) the rebuilding of her cities, verse 14; and (6) her permanent settlement in her own land after her return from captivity, verse 15.[175]

God's Unilateral Promise of His Faithfulness to Israel

The Jews will remain faithful to Jesus Christ throughout the millennium. They will not slip back into their former idolatrous ways. God will grant to the Jews a heart that permanently worships the Lord Jesus Christ. The millennial kingdom restores everything to the Jews that God had originally intended to give them. Their past disobedience temporarily forestalled these marvelous blessings and severed their unique relationship with God.

Jeremiah 31:31–34 eloquently testifies to this future and extraordinarily special relationship between God and His people, Israel. What is even more impressive about this promise is that it was granted to Jeremiah, the persecuted and weeping prophet. Jeremiah presented these sacred words during one of the most horrible periods Judah ever experienced... the Babylonian exile.

Though Jeremiah endeavored to bring good news in the midst of chaos, the people refused to listen to him. It mattered not how many of Jeremiah's predictions came true; the people steadfastly ignored him. Not only did they ignore Jeremiah, they desired to kill him. But God's promise of preservation of Jeremiah held fast (Jeremiah 1:17–19).

A Promise for the Ages

The incredible passage of Jeremiah 31:31–34 declares:

---
[175] Charles L. Feinberg, The Minor Prophets (Chicago, IL: Moody Press, 1948), p. 124

"Behold, the days are coming, says the Lord, when I will make a new covenant with the house of Israel and the house of Judah—not according to the covenant that I made with their fathers in the day that I took them by the hand to lead them out of the land of Egypt, My covenant which they broke, though I was a husband to them, says the Lord.

But this is the covenant that I will make with the house of Israel after those days, says the Lord: I will put My law in their minds, and write it on their hearts; and I will be their God, and they shall be My people. No more shall every man teach his neighbor, and every man his brother, saying, 'Know the Lord,' for they all shall know Me, from the least of them to the greatest of them, says the Lord. For I will forgive their iniquity, and their sin I will remember no more."

Though God had called the Jews as His chosen people, they frequently chose the path of the prodigal son (Luke 15:11–32). Unfortunately, most of them have stayed on that errant path of unbelief in their Messiah. That was true historically and sadly remains true today. They have paid a severe price for their transgressions and will, unfortunately, continue to do so until two days prior to the day of Christ's return (Hosea 5:15–6:3). On the third of the three days listed, Christ will return in triumph, slaughter the forces of the Antichrist, and establish His kingdom.

How Certain Are God's Promises to Israel?

A popular theology around the world today is that the Church has replaced Israel. This is called "replacement theology" or "amillennialism." Regrettably, that is the viewpoint of many spiritual leaders. But is that what God told Jeremiah? It decidedly is not.

Jeremiah 31:35–37 states:

> Thus says the Lord, who gives the sun for a light by day, the ordinances of the moon and the stars for a light by night, who disturbs the sea, and its waves roar (The Lord of hosts is His name):

> "If those ordinances depart from before Me says the Lord, then the seed of Israel shall also cease from being a nation before Me forever." Thus says the Lord: "If heaven above can be measured, and the foundations of the earth searched out beneath, I will also cast off all the seed of Israel for all that they have done, says the Lord."

Even the most casual of individuals can look up into the sky and see the sun, moon, and stars shining quite brilliantly. If mortal man can rid himself of these celestial objects, then God will back down on His promises to Israel. Furthermore, one must be able to measure the entire universe. Considering man has not personally traversed out of our solar system at the time of this writing, we do not believe he will ever explore the universe. Nor will he ever be able to search out the foundations of the earth. God's promises to Israel are thus completely secure.

The Jews' Misconception of Spiritual Heritage

Sadly, many Jews to this day rely on their physical heritage from Abraham for blessing. John 8:33 conveys this misunderstanding in their statement to Jesus: "They answered Him, 'We are Abraham's descendants, and have never been in bondage to anyone. How can You say, "You will be made free"?'" At the very moment, the Jews made such an outrageous claim they were under the authority of Rome. Furthermore, they had already endured the Assyrian and Babylonian captivities. Their denial of reality was truly nonsensical.

The Jews did not realize that only the spiritual sons of Abraham were legitimate heirs to God's kingdom, not merely the physical Jews. Paul also writes of that same principle (Romans 2:25–29, 9:6–9; 1 Corinthians 7:19). After the future Tribulation is finished, never again will the nation of Israel be conquered. They shall be entirely secure with their faith in the Messiah. Ironically, at the end of the millennial kingdom, there will be a rebellion against Christ. This will not include the Jews; it will only be conducted by Gentile unbelievers who are born during the millennium.

But even with this final rebellion, Israel will not be seriously threatened by their neighbors. Although Gentiles throughout the world will surround Jerusalem, they shall be destroyed by God's consuming fire (Revelation 20:7–9). The Jews will be resting securely under the everlasting wings of a sovereign and almighty God (Psalm 90:1–4). Sadly, the Gentiles who participate in this final rebellion will pay both with their lives and their souls (Psalm 2; Isaiah 65:20). Sinners beware; saints rejoice! One cannot fight against God and win.

God's Promise: No More Worldwide Floods

God promised that He would never again destroy every living thing on the earth with a Flood. There have been innumerable local floods over the millennia, but never another earth-inundating one. There never shall be such a Flood again. In this, man can rest secure. The rainbow is a sign of God's promise and testimony to His faithfulness (Genesis 9:16–17).

This does not mean that the days of God's judgments are over. That is far from the truth. God will once again bring the earth close to worldwide destruction through His holy judgments. A close parallel to the days of Noah's Flood is still coming upon the earth. However, this takes place during the future seven-year Tribulation. The Church will have been raptured out previously. God will use a huge variety of judgments to punish the earth and simultaneously draw people to faith. Many will believe on Christ. Sadly, the majority will remain obstinately in their sinful, unrepentant state.

Commenting on the Tribulation, Jesus Christ declared: "And unless those days were shortened; no flesh would be saved; but for the elect's sake those days will be shortened." By the time the Tribulation is over, the vast majority of mankind will have been killed in the various judgments. In Noah's day, only eight souls were spared from the watery cataclysm.

The Judgment of the Sheep and Goats

The unbelievers who do remain alive at Christ's second coming will promptly be put to death. The Judgment of the Sheep and Goats is recorded in Matthew 25:31–46. Hence, not a single unbeliever will survive Christ's judgment, which takes place immediately after the Tribulation. Every unbeliever will be put to death.

This non-survival rate of the ungodly exactly parallels the Flood. No evil people were spared the watery destruction of the Flood, and none will survive the judgment after the Tribulation. It does not pay to disregard the sovereign Creator of the universe. He calls, but people must personally respond to that call (Jeremiah 33:3; John 6:44; Hebrews 2:3).

In Matthew 25:31–46, the sheep represent Gentile believers; the goats represent Gentile unbelievers. The "brothers" Jesus refers to in this passage are Jewish believers. The godly sheep become believers after the Rapture of the Church. If they had been believers prior to the Tribulation, they would have gone up to heaven in the Rapture.

For the Gentile unbelievers in Matthew 25:46, Jesus pronounces a most sobering judgment: "And these will go away into everlasting punishment, but the righteous into life eternal." That was the tragic destiny of the Nephilim-plagued people of Noah's day. There is no record of anyone repenting through Noah's preaching, although possibly some did and died before the Flood took place. It is our fervent hope that was the case.

The Finality of God's Judgment

Regarding both the believer and the unbeliever, Hebrews 9:27 adds: "And as it is appointed for men to die once, but after this the judgment." The demon-men and wicked angels of Noah's time are destined for a terrible judgment. Believers do not entirely escape judgment. They will be judged on how they served Christ in this life and shall be rewarded accordingly (Romans 14:12; 1 Corinthians 3:11–15). Their salvation is not in question. Only their rewards of how they lived will be evaluated.

Second Corinthians 5:10 addresses all believers: "For we must all appear before the judgment seat of Christ, that each one may receive the things done in the body, according to what he has done, whether good or bad." Unbelievers, on the other hand, will be judged and condemned for all eternity.

The only exceptions to this pronouncement of death are Enoch, Elijah, those living believers who are raptured up to heaven (1 Thessalonians 4:13–18), and those believers who survive the Tribulation. It should be noted, however, that the two witnesses in Revelation 11:1–14, one of whom may be Elijah, will at that time be put to death. It is likely that the two witnesses are Moses and Elijah, but that cannot be ascertained with any certainty since they are never identified. However, Elijah must definitely return at some point (Malachi 4:5–6). Some scholars also feel that one of the two witnesses is Enoch because he never died.

The surviving unbelievers of the Tribulation must be put to death by Christ, and they then are cast into hell, awaiting future judgment at the Great White Throne Judgment. There, they will be pronounced guilty without exception and be thrown into the Lake of Fire for all eternity (Matthew 25:41, 46; Revelation 20:11–15).

This is a most unsettling doctrine, and to many, it seems terribly harsh, even unfair. But man is not given the right to question a sovereign God. We are given the right to submit to Him and worship Him. If a man refuses that right, he has decreed his own punishment. The Flood was a poignant example of God's holy judgment. Those who are aware of the Flood should be on their knees daily in prayer and gratitude for redemption through Christ. A future Day of Judgment yet awaits this sin-sickened earth and its unredeemed people.

Three Categories of Believers

Only believers will enter the millennial kingdom of Christ. There are three categories of believers: (1) the Old Testament saints, (2) the Church (New Testament) saints, and (3) the Tribulation saints. The Tribulation saints are not included with the Church saints because the Church will have already been raptured. All three categories are saved through faith in the Messiah. Such an expectation began with Adam and Eve (Genesis 3:15).

The Tribulation saints' belief system will precisely parallel that of the Church age. They will be justified spiritually in exactly the same way... by grace through faith in Christ. But they are not technically part of the Church. What a glorious day the first gathering of all three categories of the saints will be. That takes place when Christ returns to establish His millennial kingdom.

Noah and his family were physically secure in the ark. Believers today are spiritually secure in Christ.

During the millennial kingdom, for the saints, there shall be no more fear, no persecution, no sorrow, no tears. Following this 1,000-year glorious time on the earth, even better days follow. In reality, it is not appropriate to call them "days." That is because the eternal state technically begins for the believers. Eternity has no ending of time (Isaiah 65:17; 2 Peter 3:13; Revelation chapters 21 to 22). Eternity is the beginning of that which is "perfect," mentioned in 1 Corinthians 13:10.

Free Will Involves Making Decisions

God always grants every human being opportunity to exercise his or her own free will. That was true in the days leading up to Noah entering the ark, and it is true today as well. God does not have spiritual grandchildren in His holy kingdom. He has only children. Romans 8:16–17 declares: "The Spirit Himself bears witness with our spirit that we are children of God, and if children, then heirs—heirs of God and joint heirs with Christ, if indeed we suffer with Him, that we may also be glorified together."

It is crucial that each person come to a personal, individual faith in Christ. Faith is corporate in the sense of worship. But faith is individual in the sense of salvation. God calls each individual to Himself. It is a mystery why some are so willing to exercise their free will to follow Him and others reject Him out of hand.

As already affirmed, many will unfathomably choose to follow Satan even at the end of the millennium. The knowledge of the Lord covers the earth, and Jesus Christ is reigning in Jerusalem. Habakkuk 2:14 declares: "For the earth will be filled with the knowledge of the glory of the Lord, as the waters cover the sea." In spite of that, people will still rebel.

Christ will institute a near-perfect system, but multitudes will think they can somehow improve on Christ's benevolence and tenderness. The unrepentant people during the millennium will have no excuses whatsoever. Christ will be reigning right in front of their eyes. There will be no fallen angels cohabiting with women and creating Nephilim as in Noah's day. The contrast between the days of Noah and the days of Christ staggers the imagination. Yet, multitudes still will rebel!

The Hardness of the Heart Is Incomprehensible

We again reiterate the warning ushered in Jeremiah 17:9–10 by God's faithful prophet: "The heart is deceitful above all things, and desperately wicked; who can know it? I, the Lord, search the heart, I test the mind, even to give every man according to his ways, according to the fruit of his doing." As God judged mankind in the Old Testament in Noah's day, so will He in the New Testament.

The final rebellion should not be completely surprising, considering that Adam and Eve, who were created perfect and lived in perfect surroundings and circumstances, also chose to rebel. The primary difference is that Adam and Eve had no experiential knowledge of sin whatsoever. As such, they were truly a unique couple. They did not sin with a rebellious spirit. Rather, they did so with an ignorant one. Yet, rebel they did. All of humanity fell into the peril of sin with them.

Thus, they could neither foresee nor understand the consequences of their seemingly innocuous disobedience. How terrible can it be to eat a piece of fruit they probably reasoned to themselves? Little did they know the price that they and humanity would pay because they indulged themselves in that forbidden fruit.

The Nephilim-plagued society could not appreciate the terrible gravity of the impending Flood because their heinous thought-life and actions blinded them. Furthermore, no one had ever seen a universal Flood. It is quite likely that they had never even experienced rain. They seemed almost spiritually beyond reach, and perhaps they were after a period of time. But they could not have been born that way, or they would never have had the opportunity to exercise free will. Free will of necessity entails choice.

The doctrine of double predestination is unbiblical, though from a human perspective, logical. It means that some were born to be saved, and others were born to be condemned. No one then has any actual choice in spiritual matters, whether the saved or the unsaved. Hence, in reality, God created spiritless robots. We reject that doctrine out of hand. Free will is, in essence, put to death with the concept of double predestination. But God does not contradict Himself. From the beginning, He allowed man active choice. This theological study entails mystery, admittedly. But mortal man must leave such mysteries in the hands of a sovereign God.

In like manner, the sinful multitudes during the Tribulation will not fully understand or anticipate the horrible judgments they will have to endure. They will nonetheless have absolutely no excuse. God will reveal His eternal message in abundant ways (cf. Revelation 14:6–7). How much proof of God's sovereignty does one need? Thankfully, the end of the millennium will be the final rebellion! Those particular rebels will be the people who have the least excuse of anyone in history.

The Final Rebellion Recorded

Revelation 20:7–9 records this terrible scenario:

> Now when the thousand years have expired, Satan will be released from his prison and will go out to deceive the nations which are in the four corners of the earth, Gog and Magog, to gather them together to battle, whose number is as the sand of the sea. They went up on the breadth of the earth and surrounded the camp of the saints and the beloved city. And fire came down from God out of heaven and devoured them.

Consider and marvel at the circumstances of Christ's millennial kingdom. The knowledge of the Lord will cover the globe, a nearly perfect environment will bless the earth, and Christ will be reigning visibly in Jerusalem. Famine will have been vanquished, the weather moderated to a marvelous climate, and everyone will probably have their personal plot of ground to grow crops.

Yet, in spite of all that, the wicked nature of the ever-increasing number of unredeemed will once again come to the forefront. Though not as large a rebellion as in Noah's day, this will not be a small insurrection. Their number is as the sand of the sea. This is a use of hyperbole to emphasize a huge number. But the foolish rebellion of the nations will be instantly crushed. How tragic that the scene of the Garden of Eden is once again partially repeated, just on a massively larger scale. Such is the contagious nature of sin (Ecclesiastes 7:20; Isaiah 53:6).

These erring rebels will immediately be consumed by temporal fire, only to face eternal fire! The Great White Throne Judgment establishes their guilt once and for all. Only unbelievers will face this judgment (Revelation 20:11–15). Believers will be judged separately based on their work for Christ (Romans 14:10–12; 1 Corinthians 3:11–15; 2 Corinthians 5:10).

After this brief overview of future events related to Israel and the world, let us now return to the subject at hand, namely, Noah and his family.

Mankind Retains His Evil Nature (Genesis 8:21)

The above rather bleak commentary on man's propensity toward his evil nature is affirmed historically in Genesis 8:21: "... although the imagination of man's heart is evil from his youth ..." This phrase is sandwiched in between God's promise of (1) not cursing the ground and (2) not destroying every living thing again.

Ironically, many people reject the concept of mankind's inherent evil nature. Yet, what is one of the first words a child learns? It is the emphatic word "no!" Evil surrounds humanity on all sides. Fortunately, there are few people as wicked as Adolf Hitler of Germany, Joseph Stalin from Russia, or Mae Tse-tung from China. Incredibly, these three all lived at the same time. The havoc they brought upon the earth is incalculable.

When compared to the above three vicious monsters, most people look quite good. But sin still affects every man, woman, and child. Romans 3:10–12, 23 makes that abundantly clear:

> As it is written: "There is none righteous, no, not one; there is none who understands; there is none who seeks after God. They have all turned aside; they have together become unprofitable; there is none who does good, no, not one." ... For all have sinned and fall short of the glory of God.

That was categorically true of all but eight people in Noah's day. And even those eight were not entirely pure since all have sinned. We are all born sinners.

Regarding the evil nature, Fruchtenbaum comments as follows:

> The Hebrew word for imagine is yeitzer; and because in Hebrew the term "evil inclination" is yeitzer ba-ra, the use of this word became the source of the rabbinic doctrine of the evil inclination. Rabbi Hertz interprets 8:21b as: "The evil inclination in man, yeitzer ba-ra, which too often gains the mastery over the good inclination yeitzer ba-tov."

> Rashi writes, "From the moment the embryo bestows itself to have an independent existence, the evil inclination is given to it." While Judaism denies believing in a sin nature, it comes close to it with this concept of the evil inclination. At any rate, in spite of man's evil, there would never again be such a total destruction of

human life by water. For it will happen again, but next time by fire (Isa. 24:5-6).[176]

The Jews' History of Stubborn Denial

It is strangely ironic that the religion of Judaism rejects the concept of original sin. To do so, they must completely ignore the warning of prophets such as Isaiah. Isaiah writes in 53:6: "All we like sheep have gone astray; we have turned, every one, to his own way; and the LORD has laid on Him the iniquity of us all" (cf. Isaiah 59:2). David also offers this testimony in Psalm 51:5: "Behold, I was brought forth in iniquity, and in sin my mother conceived me."

This is not a testimony against David's mother but rather a condemnation focused on all humanity. For the Jewish people to reject the concept of original sin, they must also ignore their own colored history of rebellion against God. They clearly have no excuse for doing so. Tragically, this has fostered the concept that they do not need deliverance and forgiveness for their evil natures. They depend on their good works or Jewish identity. They were reprimanded by Christ for this very attitude. They must deliberately forget the lessons of Genesis chapter 3 and the following tragedies.

The Scriptures bear ample testimony to the Jews' errant thinking in John 8:39–41, 44:

> They answered and said to Him, "Abraham is our father." Jesus said to them, "If you were Abraham's children, you would do the works of Abraham. But now you seek to kill Me, a Man who has told you the truth which I heard from God. Abraham did not do this. You do the deeds of your father." Then they said to Him,

---
[176] Arnold Fruchtenbaum, Ariel's Bible Commentary: The Book of Genesis, p. 182.

"We were not born of fornication; we have one Father—God." ...

You are of your father the devil, and the desires of your father you want to do. He was a murderer from the beginning, and does not stand in the truth, because there is no truth in him. When he speaks a lie, he speaks from his own resources, for he is a liar and the father of it.

One can readily see, based on Jesus' words, that no man is without sin. Paul later testifies in Romans 3:23: "For all have sinned and fall short of the glory of God." Human experience testifies all too eloquently of man's inner propensity toward sin. That is why all men need a Savior. Sins must either be forgiven or eternally punished.

Promise #3: The Seasons Continue Unabated (Genesis 8:22)

Once again, in the aftermath of judgment, we see God acting in grace. That is a constant theme throughout the entire Bible. Jesus Christ even forgave those who crucified Him while He was still suffering in agony on the cross. God always seeks out reconciliation and the benefit of man. God preserved the human race through the ark. Thus, we see God uttering yet another promise to Noah in Genesis 8:22: "While the earth remains, seedtime and harvest, cold and heat, winter and summer, and day and night shall not cease."

Fruchtenbaum offers these comments:

Positively, in verse 22 the commitment is continued. As long as the earth remains, certain things will not cease and God mentions four things: first, seedtime and harvest; second, cold and heat; third, summer and winter;

and fourth, day and night. The point of this promise is that as long as the earth's cycle exists, as long as the earth exists, the cycle of life will continue. Moreover, this is what Jeremiah refers to as the covenant of seasons (Jer. 31:35-37; 33:17-26).

According to the rabbis, this oath would only be enforced "as long as the earth lasts." As long as heaven and earth endure, the oath is in effect. But in the end of days, God will destroy the earth completely and renew it; and at that time, He will not be restrained by this oath. This rabbinic view comes close to the view of Scripture since this earth will, of course, be done away with at the end of the Millennium when God will make a new earth altogether.[177]

God graciously allowed the seasons and other normal course of events to continue. The fact that the sun rises every morning bears testimony to that. Man can count fully on God's faithfulness. But rarely does he thank Him for it. Only when God destroys the present heaven and earth will things change, but it will decidedly be for the better. It is necessary to destroy the present system because sin has defiled everything. In the new heavens and earth, perfection shall reign supreme throughout eternity. Such blessedness is beyond finite human comprehension!

Lessons Learned in This Chapter

In this chapter, we first observed Noah's proper exercise of spiritual priorities. Upon disembarking from the ark, he offered burnt

---
[177] Ibid., 182.

sacrifices to God in thanksgiving. All too often, mankind just assumes that God will bless him daily with His ongoing benevolence. And that is true. God is always faithful even when man is faithless. But Noah demonstrated a spirit different from that of the typical presumptuousness of others. He actively expressed sincere and immediate thanksgiving to his holy God.

Second, within the context of these three short verses, we reflected on three promises granted by God. The first promise pertained to agricultural fertility. God had cursed the ground because of Adam's sin. How much of that curse was removed is not certain. Clearly, the world is not as fertile as it once was immediately after creation. We are encompassed by mountains, swamps, and desert regions. Most of these areas are not fit for growing crops.

Nonetheless, certain areas were extremely fertile, like the Garden of Eden. That is why Lot chose to sojourn in the plains of Sodom and Gomorrah. It was extremely fertile (Genesis 13:10). Tragically, it was also extremely wicked. Lot would pay the price for succumbing to the temptation of temporal prosperity versus righteousness.

The second promise discussed presented details on how God blessed Israel. We delved into considerable detail about how this is going to be accomplished. The reader might naturally ponder why we took this somewhat lengthy excursus. It is because Genesis chapters 1 to 11 lay the foundation of the coming nation of Israel. Genesis 3:15 is the first indication of a coming Messiah. That Messiah, Jesus Christ, is a Jew from the tribe of Judah (Genesis 49:10). Hence, we have laid out some of the biblical principles regarding Israel. Amos 9:11–15 ties the agricultural fertility with blessing on Israel. These blessings shall see full fruition in the millennial kingdom.

In the third promise, God indicated to Noah that the seasons would all remain during this present dispensation of time on the earth. Genesis 8:22 declares: "While the earth remains, seedtime and harvest, cold and heat, winter and summer, and day and night shall not cease" (cf. Jeremiah 33:20, 25). God has held true to His promises. Nothing of these three promises has fallen short or ever will. God does this in spite of mankind's ongoing sinfulness. This shall remain true even throughout the millennial reign of Christ.

Sadly, man's ongoing history is a bleak one, spiritually speaking. God provides tremendous evidence of His existence through special and general revelation. Yet the majority of mankind either ignores this revelation or outright rejects it. Thus, mankind has no excuse for his willful disobedience (Romans 1:18–22).

In our next chapter, we shall see how God blessed Noah and his sons after their departure from the ark. This blessing also extended to the animal kingdom so they could repopulate the earth. If God's eyes are on the humble sparrow, how much more is it on the sons of man (Psalm 84:3)? God created man for a relationship with Him. That relationship cannot be forced, or free will is forfeited. But when man reciprocates to God's loving mercy, a marvelous and eternal relationship is possible.

Cognitive Conundrum #21

A man of waffling spirit was I—this is true; I followed God partially in acts I did do. Not a man to be trifled with kings did find out, but the bad priests rejoiced what I was about. Deception was the name of the game I did love; though clever, I was not described like a dove. I caused the death of a most wicked woman; her burial was unique and quite quickly done.

Who am I?

Answer: Jehu

Chapter 22

God's Covenant with Noah

(Genesis 9:1–7)

In This Chapter

Objectives for This Chapter
God Blessed Noah and His Sons (Genesis 9:1–7)
Several New Developments on Earth
Lessons Learned in This Chapter

Objectives for This Chapter

God's faithfulness once again manifests itself in His interaction with His children. Not only did He accept Noah's heartfelt sacrifices, but He blessed them in new ways. We shall first observe that upon disembarkation from the ark, God reissues the mandate to repopulate the earth (Genesis 9:1). This may have seemed an impossible assignment at first. However, when God created Adam and Eve, there were only two alive to accomplish this task, namely, Adam and Eve. Now, there were eight human beings, four times as many.

Second, we shall soon see that the world dramatically changed as a result of the Flood. For one thing, the climate changed permanently. Another poignant example, different from the original creation, is that many of the animals had become carnivores. That change, however, may have occurred immediately after the fall into sin. Two lions by themselves, if they chose to do so, could have overwhelmed the eight human beings and consumed them. Although thankfully quite rare, some lions do kill and eat humans today. Hence, God placed a fear of man into the animal kingdom (9:2). This was necessary lest the small group be quickly overwhelmed.

Third, for the first time in recorded human history, man was given permission to eat meat (9:3–4). This may seem strange to modern man. Originally, in God's creation, animals and man alike were vegetarians. However, strict instructions were bestowed upon humankind with this changeover to being omnivores. They were not to consume meat without first draining out the blood. The life was in the blood (Leviticus 17:11). This was a command first given to Noah, not to Moses. We shall include Jonathan Sarfati's in-depth description of the blood system.

Fourth, we shall discuss the formation of government (Genesis 9:5–6). Strange as it may seem, previous to this time, men apparently did largely as they wanted to do. Might made right! There was no biblically designated form of government recorded in Scripture. Two tragic examples of this absence of governmentally designated authority were Cain and Lamech. Now, however, capital punishment was introduced for those who committed murder. Later on in the Mosaic covenant, the role and explanation of how capital punishment was to be incorporated was expanded.

Finally, God reiterated His command to Noah to multiply and fill the earth. Genesis 9:7 states: "And as for you, be fruitful and multiply; bring forth abundantly in the earth and multiply in it." Clearly, Noah's family and the animal kingdom performed their task proficiently. The world was soon once again repopulated with people and animals.

God Blessed Noah and His Sons (Genesis 9:1–7)

God always remembers His children. This was doubly true for

Noah and his family. Only eight human beings were left out of the multitudes that previously existed. Like Adam and Eve, they were responsible to "be fruitful and fill the earth" (Genesis 9:1). The earth, though absolutely destroyed, was now in the midst of its own restoration. Immense topographical changes had taken place, such as the mountains rising skyward and the ocean basins plummeting to fantastic depths. In our modern age, we cannot see backwards in time to understand just how much things have changed.

Fossils by the trillions had been incorporated into the steadily hardening sedimentary rock. These fossils have been explored for centuries by enterprising but often mistaken paleontologists. Though the fossils gloriously testify of the Flood, they are frequently interpreted as representing evolution. Such a counterproductive conclusion that has proven to be! The evolutionist's philosophical bent has blinded many. Creationists view the same data and reach an entirely different conclusion than the evolutionist.

Occasionally, however, a more honest but reluctant report issues from the evolutionist camp. We shall examine one such report.

A Moment of Honesty

Evolutionist Mark Czarnecki candidly admits the following:

A major problem in proving the theory has been the fossil record; the imprints of vanished species preserved in the Earth's geological formations. This record has never revealed traces of Darwin's hypothetical intermediate variants—instead species appear and disappear abruptly, and this anomaly has fueled the creationist argument that each species was created by

God as described in the Bible.[178]

Czarnecki is absolutely correct. The fossil record not only disappoints the evolutionist, but it utterly destroys any remnant of credibility the flimsy theory ever possessed. There is not even one single transition fossil demonstrating change from one species to another. If evolution were true, transition fossils are about all one should find. One must completely bury his head in the sand to deny the obvious truth derived from this complete lack of evidence: Evolution simply does not work. We do find it ironic that Czarnecki calls this an "anomaly" since it is the normal, indeed, the only pattern one finds.

Be Fruitful and Fill the Earth (Genesis 9:1)

Let us now examine the text in question. Genesis 9:1–7 states:

> So God blessed Noah and his sons, and said to them: "Be fruitful and multiply, and fill the earth. And the fear of you and the dread of you shall be on every beast of the earth, on every bird of the air, on all that moves on the earth, and on all the fish of the sea. They are given into your hand. Every moving thing that lives shall be food for you. I have given you all things, even as the green herbs.

> "But you shall not eat flesh with its life, that is, its blood. Surely for your lifeblood I demand a reckoning; from the hand of every beast I will require it, and from the hand of man. From the hand of every man's

---

[178] Henry M. Morris, *That Their Words May Be Used Against Them* (Green Forest, AR; Master Books, 1997), pp. 161–162.

brother I will require the life of man. Whoever sheds man's blood, by man his blood shall be shed: for in the image of God He made man. And as for you, be fruitful and multiply; bring forth abundantly in the earth and multiply in it."

In verse one, God repeats His original mandate given to Adam and Eve: "So God blessed Noah and his sons, and said to them: 'Be fruitful and multiply, and fill the earth.'" The basic difference is that when first commanded, Adam and Eve were sinless. Now, the entire human race and all its coming descendants would automatically possess the propensity to do evil. This, of course, had been true since the fall. Yet God showed mercy on mankind in spite of His full foreknowledge of their incurable wickedness.

The Old Man Versus the New Man

The only time the sinful nature is removed is when the believer passes away in death or is raptured directly to heaven (1 Thessalonians 4:13–18). Until that glorious time, believers must struggle with the ongoing conflict between the old and new nature.

Ephesians 4:20–24 portrays this spiritual altercation:

> But you have not so learned Christ, if indeed you have heard Him and have been taught by Him, as the truth is in Jesus: that you put off, concerning your former conduct, the old man which grows corrupt according to the deceitful lusts, and be renewed in the spirit of your mind, and that you put on the new man which was created according to God, in true righteousness and holiness.

Warren Wiersbe comments:

> When Noah came out of the ark, he was like a "second Adam" about to usher in a new beginning on earth for the human race. Faith in the Lord had saved Noah and his household from destruction, and his three sons would repopulate the whole earth (v. 18).
>
> God had told Adam and Eve to "be fruitful, and multiply, and fill the earth" (1:28), and He repeated that mandate twice to Noah and his family (9:1, 7). All of Noah's descendants were important to the plan of God, but especially the line of Shem. From that line Abraham would be born, the man God chose to found the Jewish nation. From that nation would come the Redeemer who would fulfill 3:15 and crush the serpent's head.[179]

The Fear and Dread of Man Falls upon the Animals (Genesis 9:2)

Genesis 9:2 declares: "And the fear of you and the dread of you shall be on every beast of the earth, on every bird of the air, on all that move on the earth, and on all the fish of the sea. They are given into your hand." It is hard to imagine a world where animals do not fear man. The normal exceptions to this rule are dogs, cats, cattle, horses, and donkeys. On occasion, other creatures have been tamed by man. But they definitely are a tiny minority.

The vast majority of species have an instinctive and God-given fear of man. This is appropriate as man is the chief predator on the

---

[179] Warren Wiersbe, The Bible Exposition Commentary: Genesis–Deuteronomy, p. 53.

earth. But it is also true that many larger creatures are physically much more powerful than man. If they did not naturally fear man, they might attack him as a food source. That could lead to unpleasant complications in life.

Before the advent of guns and other weaponry, man might have been overrun by the animals. Fighting a lion or tiger in hand-to-claw contact would likely have been a losing proposition for the one with the hands. The fourth seal in Revelation 6:8 seems to indicate a removal of this God-given fear by the animal kingdom. The "beasts of the earth" will be attacking man.

Behold the fourth seal judgment of Revelation 6:8: "So I looked, and behold, a pale horse. And the name of him who sat on it was Death, and Hades followed with him. And power was given to them over a fourth of the earth, to kill with sword, with hunger, with death, and by the beasts of the earth." If this passage does not grab a person's undivided attention, what will?

One-Fourth of Humanity Perishes!

One-fourth of the people of the earth will be killed in just the fourth seal judgment alone. The "beasts of the earth" will participate in this slaughter. One would assume that mankind will eventually overcome the beasts with their weapons, but what a horrible picture to envision. Lions and other ravenous beasts will be completely out of control. The human carnage they could inflict in short order will be horrific!

Those living in wilderness areas will not be safe at all. Scripture does not elaborate specifically on the beasts of the earth, but it would include most of the undomesticated animals. That is foreboding percentage of the animals on the earth. Life will become tenuous at best during the Tribulation.

Such a scenario is entirely foreign to the original creation. One must remember that from the beginning, God gave man dominion over the entire earth. This naturally included the animals. Before the fall, man was a vegetarian; he did not eat meat. Since Adam and Eve's sin, a natural animosity has existed between mankind and the undomesticated animals. Even the domesticated animals, except the dogs, cats, and horses, generally foster a cautious awareness bordering on outright fear of man.

The Fear of Today Will Be Companionship "Tomorrow"

In the millennial kingdom of Christ, this uncanny fear shall be removed (Isaiah 11:6–9, 65:25). Wild beasts and man will live in complete harmony together. That certainly is not the case in our present age. As we shall see in our passage, man was now granted permission to eat meat. Previously, he ate only vegetables. This must have been a very strange transition for Noah and his family. Obviously, God adjusted their digestive systems to go from being pure herbivores to omnivores. They could now eat both plants and animals.

The animals clearly sensed the danger to them as a result of this new system. God granted them that new instinct. This fear and dread served a double purpose: to also protect man from the animals. As is clearly evident, many wild beasts are much more powerful than man. Numerous types of animals could easily have slaughtered Noah and his entire family after disembarking from the ark. Obviously, God did not allow that to happen.

Leupold comments as follows:

> The difference between the tenor of this verse and the beautiful harmony of the original creation is immedi-

ately apparent. Now "fear" and "terror" dominate all creatures. ... There was really need of some such regulation. The beasts, by their great numbers, as well as because of their more rapid propagation, and in many instances also because of their superior strength would soon have gotten the upper hand over man and exterminated him. God, therefore, makes a natural "fear," even a "terror," to dwell in their hearts.

Even the birds, at least the stronger among them, need such restraint. "Cattle" are not mentioned, for by nature the domesticated animals stand sufficiently under the control of man. Distinct from this is the second thought that mankind shall have control of all the smaller forms of animal life as well as of the fish, to do with them as may seem good to him. For the expression "to be given in anyone's hand" signifies to be delivered into absolute control to be dealt with as the other may determine. ...

"Cattle" are not to flee from man. The truth of the fulfillment of this word lies in the fact that wild beasts consistently shun the haunts of men, except when driven by hunger. No matter how strong they may be, they dread man's presence, yes, are for the most part actually filled with "terror" at the approach of man.[180]

---

180 H. C. Leupold, Exposition of Genesis: Volume I, Chapters 1-19, pp. 328-329.

A New Diet: Meat Is Now on the Menu (Genesis 9:3–4)

In the original creation, all animals, as well as Adam and Eve, were vegetarians. It was only after the Flood that man was given permission to eat meat. Why this dramatic change in diet? The Bible doesn't give a reason, but it does provide guidelines for the new diet. Those guidelines applied to all people since the Jewish nation was not yet in existence.

Genesis 9:3–4 establishes these new changes that came upon the world after Noah and his family left the ark: "Every moving thing that lives shall be food for you. I have given you all things, even as the green herbs. But you shall not eat flesh with its life, that is, its blood." Below, we shall examine how these new developments impacted all of humanity.

Several New Developments on Earth

Animals Now Feared Mankind

Development #1: Animals now feared mankind. Prior to this, there was clearly no fear between them. This would seem to indicate that even the dinosaurs were tame, which, to modern man, is a strange thought indeed. All the animals on the ark would have been docile toward their caretakers. However, this does not necessarily mean that the animals were docile toward each other. God would have supernaturally made sure that no "fights" would have broken out on the ark.

If it is true that the fall produced a new appetite for the carnivores, God had to intervene to protect the herbivores on the ark from the carnivores. The same would be true for a time after the animals disembarked from the ark. Fish perhaps served as a meat supplement for the carnivores for a time.

Apparently, before the fall, some animals, perhaps all of them, had the gift of speech. That seems a bit odd to us today, to say the least. However, the serpent talked to Eve, and she was not alarmed (Genesis chapter 3). If animals could talk, that probably would change immediately after the fall. To this day, however, it is amazing how much dogs can understand their masters.

Meat Was Now on the Menu!

Development #2: Man could now eat meat. God apparently reorganized man's digestive system to make the eating of meat possible. Most people relish the idea of feasting on a succulent steak prepared by a master chef.

Morris offers the following salient comments:

> The reason for this change is not obvious; perhaps the more rigorous environment in the new world required the animal protein in meats for man's sustenance to a degree not normally available in other foods. Possibly the Lord also desired thus to show the great gulf between man and the animals, anticipating the dangers implicit in the evil doctrine of the evolutionary continuity of life of all flesh, which ultimately equates man with the animals and denies the Creator, in whose image man alone was made.
>
> The fact is, that doctrine had already begun to make its appearance in the early forms of paganism and polytheism. Apparently no restrictions as to which animals

man could eat were made at this point, though in the special economy of Israel only a few animals were later denominated by God as "clean" for this purpose.[181]

It should be noted that by this time, there were animals that were considered "clean," and then there were the "unclean." The clean animals were undoubtedly a tiny minority. Genesis 7:2–3 states: "You shall take with you seven each of every clean animal, a male and his female; two each of animals that are unclean; a male and his female; also seven each of birds of the air, male and female, to keep the species alive on the face of all the earth."

As previously noted, we take exception with the NKJV in their translation of "seven each." The literal translation is "seven seven," both words being singular, thus indicating seven pairs in our opinion. That means fourteen of the clean animals and of the birds. Considering that the clarifying and following phrase emphasizes a "male and his female," evidently, a mating pair is intended. Clearly, not all translators are in harmony with our conclusion of fourteen, however.

When Noah left the ark, he made a sacrifice of thanksgiving and worship with one of every clean animal and every clean bird (Genesis 8:20). The practice of offering sacrifices to God goes all the way back to Cain and Abel (4:3–5).

Eating Blood Was and Remains Forbidden

Development #3: Man must not eat the blood with the meat. God clearly communicates the principle that the life is in the blood (Leviticus 3:17, 17:10–14; Deuteronomy 12:15–16, 20–24). This may seem painfully obvious to the world today, but in more primi-

---

[181] Henry Morris, The Genesis Record: A Scientific & Devotional Commentary of the Book of Beginnings, pp. 222–223.

tive societies, this was not always understood.

Many people mistakenly believe that this command was first issued to Israel under the Mosaic Law. That viewpoint is mistaken. This prohibition was first uttered to Noah.

Victor Hamilton writes: "Eating blood and taking life are Noachian commandments, not Sinaitic ones. Here, and elsewhere in the OT, blood is equated with life, and that is why its consumption or shedding is forbidden."[182] J. Vernon McGee comments: "The blood should be drained out. The blood speaks of life; draining it indicates that the animal should be killed in a merciful way rather than prolonging its suffering and that it must be really dead."[183]

Leviticus 17:11 states: "For the life of the flesh is in the blood, and I have given it to you upon the altar to make atonement for your souls, for it is the blood that makes atonement for the soul." The blood of animals offered in sacrifice only covered sin temporarily; the blood of the Messiah took the sin away permanently. Animals were sacrificed repeatedly; the Messiah was sacrificed only once (Hebrews 9:11–26, 10:11–13). The Messiah's one sacrifice was sufficient to cover the sins of the entire world. It was perfection personified! Man must simply be willing to receive Christ's forgiveness.

The New Testament repeats the injunction against eating blood. Acts 15:28–29 makes this prohibition, along with other prohibitions, perfectly clear:

> For it seemed good to the Holy Spirit, and to us, to lay upon you no greater burden than these necessary things: that you abstain from things offered to idols, from blood, from things strangled, and from sexual im-

---
[182] Victor Hamilton, The New International Commentary on the Old Testament: The Book of Genesis Chapters 1–17 (Grand Rapids, MI: Eerdmans Publishing, 1990), p. 314.
[183] J. Vernon McGee, Thru the Bible: Genesis through Deuteronomy (Nashville, TN: Thomas Nelson Publishers, 1981), p. 47.

morality. If you keep yourselves from these, you will do well. Farewell.

Unfortunately, some Christians disobey this commandment regarding blood by indulging in food called blood sausage or by utilizing the blood in other consumptive manners. According to the New Testament, that remains a sinful behavior. The eating of blood must be strictly avoided by all believers and for all time. The Bible always overrules cultural practices!

Scientific Observations about Blood

Sarfati brings out some excellent scientific observations regarding the blood. To believe that the blood circulation system developed through hit-and-miss, purposeless, and mindless evolution requires a blind leap of faith akin to trusting in Aesop's fables. Indeed, fairy tales generally require much less faith. The blood system and everything related to it clearly required an infinite intelligence. Only a Creator God could bring such an astounding system together. Scientists can only identify, to a certain degree, how the circulatory system operates. No human technology can replicate its wonders.

Sarfati comments on this crucial subject as follows:

> The Noahic and Levitical references to the importance of blood to life mainly point to the atoning sacrifice of the Messiah. All the same, modern science has shown how vital for life blood is. Our bodies have about five litres of blood, which all circulates within a minute.
>
> Blood is red because it contains microscopic red blood cells (RBC's)—4-6 million per mm. Indeed, an adult

human has 20-30 trillion RBC's, comprising a quarter of all our cells. RBC's are red because of hemoglobin, a specially designed protein that absorbs oxygen in the lungs, but releases it at the right time where the body needs it.

The bloodstream also carries antibodies, which basically place a target on invading microbes. The immune system includes a designed mechanism for rapid variation so a wide variety of antibodies can be produced to cope with a wide range of invaders. Blood also carries white blood cells to kill them.

Our blood also has many platelets, which are vital for blood clotting, which stops blood leaking out from a hole in a blood vessel. Blood clotting requires a biochemical cascade with many steps before a clot is formed. There are also negative feedback mechanisms to prevent clotting where it should not occur—in a healthy blood vessel.[184]

The circulatory system is astounding in its complexity. Red blood cells must function with absolute precision. Every part of the body must be continuously reached, or it will die. They carry the nutrients throughout the entire organism. They interact with all of the other systems in the body, which are no less miraculous in their own right. All must work in perfect harmony.

It is hard enough to fathom how this function works once fully developed. To believe that it all eventually created itself from a dead mineral lying limp on a damp rock is truly incredible! Romans 1:22

---

[184] Jonathan Sarfati, The Genesis Account: A theological, historical, and scientific commentary on Genesis 1-11, pp. 600-601.

is absolutely correct regarding obstinate mankind: "Professing to be wise, they became fools."

Murder Now Brings a Death Penalty (Genesis 9:5–7)

Genesis 9:5–7 brings in numerous other significant changes:

> Surely for your lifeblood I will demand a reckoning; from the hand of every beast I will require it, and from the hand of man. From the hand of every man's brother I will require the life of man. "Whoever sheds man's blood, by man his blood shall be shed; for in the image of God He made man. And as for you, be fruitful and multiply; bring forth abundantly in the earth and multiply in it."

God now decrees the death penalty for those who take the life of another man. Considering how wicked the world had become, it would seem like murder had been a common crime. The Bible recounts the story of Cain's and Lamech's murders. However, in neither case was capital punishment carried out.

Regarding the institution and purpose of capital punishment, Fruchtenbaum comments as follows:

> It is God Who mandates capital punishment, and this punishment is to be applied to both man and animal. God has already exercised this prerogative of divine retribution with the Flood. However, there is also now to be human retribution, in 9:6: Who so sheds man's blood, by man shall his blood be shed. Man now has the authority to put another man to death. Capital pun-

ishment requires legal execution, and this enactment sets the stage for human government.

Under the Noahic covenant, the mandatory death penalty was only for the crime of premeditated murder. Later, the Mosaic covenant will add other crimes requiring the death penalty, but as far as the Noahic covenant goes, it is mandatory only for premeditated murder. The purpose is not to deter crime, but to punish the evildoer.

Much of the argument today about the use of capital punishment concerns whether it does or does not deter crime. Biblically speaking, that is irrelevant and not the issue. The issue for the Bible is punishing the evildoer, not reforming him or her. Genesis 9:6 concludes by giving the reason why there will be both divine and human retribution for the shedding of human blood: For in the image of God made he man. Therefore, although after the Fall it is a marred image, the image of God is still there.[185]

Government Is Established

Whatever the situation may previously have been, responsible government is clearly instituted in this passage. As later becomes evident in Moses' written law, this standard of government is not descriptive of a lynch mob mentality. Some form of organized government became necessary. When the Pentateuch was written, it was

---
185 Arnold Fruchtenbaum, Ariel's Bible Commentary: The Book of Genesis, p. 186.

not the only set of laws developed. Other nations also had written formulated laws. However, the Pentateuch was unique in the sense that God wrote it through Moses. Furthermore, the Pentateuch had logical and fair laws.

It should be observed in Genesis 9:6–7 that God reiterates that He created man in His own image. Some might speculate that man lost that image completely when he sinned, and thus, God decided to nearly obliterate mankind. That would be an erroneous conclusion. James 3:8–9 states: "But no man can tame the tongue. It is an unruly evil, full of deadly poison. With it we bless our God and Father, and with it we curse men, who have been made in the similitude of God."

D. Edmond Hiebert comments on James 3:8–9 as follows:

> The depth of the evil is clear from the fact that those cursed "are made after the likeness of God." The perfect tense "are made" indicates that the divine likeness imparted at creation has not been totally obliterated. The reference is to man as he now is. Sin has marred this likeness in fallen man; yet, as God's noblest creature, every human being retains "an indestructible nobility" that declares his divine origin and his dignity as the crown of creation.
>
> Fallen man is indeed "the scandal," but also, as God's appointed representative over creation (Gen. 1:26; Psalm 8:4-8), he is "the glory of the universe" (Pascal). "The likeness of God" consists chiefly in the fact that man is a personal, rational, moral being.

Beyond all God's creatures, he possesses the attributes of reason, will and conscience; the ability to know and serve God; and the capacity to be conformed to God's moral and spiritual likeness. Therefore, to curse a man is to insult the God whose likeness man still bears. Instead, man's innate nobility should inspire respect and goodwill, even toward those who irritate and even harm him.[186]

If the image of God had been entirely obliterated at the fall, why did He take 1,656 years, the year of the Flood, to take punitive action? Furthermore, why did He spare man at all? What eternal value would man still retain? The image of God may have been effaced, but it was not entirely erased. Noah and his sons were told to be fruitful and repopulate the earth. They did precisely that. God's eternal purpose for mankind is just beginning.

The Role of Government

Government: One of the innovations this passage develops is the role of government. This does not necessarily preclude the possibility of government prior to this, but if previously present, it was not mentioned. Considering the statement in Genesis 6:5 that the thoughts of mankind were wicked continuously, it seems there may not have been any legitimate, earthly governmental system. Judges 21:25 testifies to just such a scenario: "In those days there was no king in Israel; everyone did what was right in his own eyes" (cf. Judges 17:6).

One of the purposes of the government is to punish evildoers, particularly murderers. If someone is guilty of murder, he forfeits

---

[186] D. Edmond Hiebert, The Epistle of James (Chicago, Moody Press, 1979), p. 223.

his own life. Why is that? It is because man is created in the image of God, and thus, he must be protected. Since man is still created in God's image, the principle of the death penalty has not been entirely revoked. However, in the age of grace, the enactment of the death penalty has been somewhat lessened.

Government is theoretically designed to protect its citizens (Romans 13:1–4). Unfortunately, many governments have not only failed abysmally in their task, but they have been the primary perpetrator of many of the crimes committed against humanity. Only one government will ever truly be just and righteous. That will be the government of Jesus Christ in the millennial kingdom.

The Death Penalty

The Mosaic Law presented numerous instances in which the death penalty should be utilized. It did not always have to involve a premeditated murder. Note carefully: Two or three witnesses were always required for the death penalty to be enacted. Many precautions were taken before a governmentally supervised execution took place.

Deuteronomy 17:6–7 states:

> Whoever is deserving of death shall be put to death on the testimony of two or three witnesses; he shall not be put to death on the testimony of one witness. The hands of the witnesses shall be the first against him to put him to death, and afterward the hands of all the people. So you shall put away the evil from among you (cf. Numbers 35:30–31).

This prohibition of killing a man also extended to the animals.

If an animal kills a human, it must also be put to death. If such an event is known in advance and the owner does nothing about it, he is courting personal disaster. Even if the ox just threatened people by thrusting aggressively with its horns, it needed to be confined. The ox did not have to kill anyone to merit this confinement. But if the animal ever did kill anyone, then the owner and the ox shall both be put to death. One cannot logically reason with a wild ox. However, the owner should be open to instruction. He is thus held responsible.

Exodus 21:28–29 states:

> If an ox gores a man or a woman to death, then the ox shall surely be stoned, and its flesh shall not be eaten; but the owner of the ox shall be acquitted. But if the ox tended to thrust with its horn in times past, and it has been made known to his owner, and he has not kept it confined, so that it has killed a man or a woman, the ox shall be stoned and its owner also shall be put to death.

To the animal rights activists, the animal's life is just as important as the man or woman's life. That is, of course, if it is not their life taken by the animal! Hence, in their demented perspective, the animal should be spared. This type of mentality is a direct reflection of the view that we are all products of evolution. Such people refuse to recognize that man is created in the image of God and is thus quite distinct from the animals.

The Tragic Act of Abortion

This distorted thinking also engenders the concept of abortion. Such individuals justify abortion with the mindset that the baby is not really a baby until it is born. It is becoming increasingly popular that if the parents disapprove of the baby when it is born and fully functional, they should still have the option of putting it to death.

Even wild animals generally know better than this. God definitely begs to differ. He lovingly molded the child in the mother's womb (Psalm 139:13–16). Abortion is murder, plain and simple. Though God offers forgiveness for parents who take the lives of their own children through Christ, their crime remains repugnant. Evolution has distorted and twisted the thinking process of many. Criminal acts against the defenseless have been the tragic pattern of humanity for millennia.

We firmly believe all such aborted babies are instantly ushered into the kingdom of heaven (Matthew 18:1–7). God is a merciful God. He will take eternal care of these helpless innocents. The parents, on the other hand, will pay a huge price for their guilt. Though forgiveness can be granted, the miserable consequences of their actions remain.

The Mandate

Genesis 9:7 reiterates God's original command to multiply, be fruitful, and fill the earth: "And as for you, be fruitful and multiply; bring forth abundantly in the earth and multiply in it." In the days of Noah, that must have seemed like a daunting task. There were only eight human beings left alive. The only air-breathing animals that survived were on the ark. The earth seemed hauntingly vacant!

Obviously, both man and beast have accomplished this mandate to a commendable degree. God's grace and provision enabled both man and animals to prosper once again. Life became more difficult than previously, but it was still possible.

R. S. Candlish capably summarizes God's providence for the

earth as follows:

Such is the law of nature, or economy of life, as appointed by God for the world after the flood. It is, in part, a discipline of severity; but it is to be viewed chiefly as a provision of mercy. It does not touch any of the endearments or refinements of social intercourse, as based upon the pure and peaceful afflictions of home. Men are still to dwell in families, and in families they are to fill and occupy the earth.

But the dangers to which human society was exposed from the fearless familiarity of the subject animals and the growing anarchy of mere domestic rule, are to be remedied by the dread of man being forced upon the beasts; and by the sword of the magisterial authority being raised in terror against evil doers. And to meet the accumulating difficulty of obtaining supplies from the earth alone, the use of animal food is allowed.

Then, to guard against the abuse of these beneficent arrangements, the sword of the magistrate is ordained to be used always for the protection of the life of man, and with a reverential respect to the image of God which man bears. And even the beasts given to man for food are to be the objects of a certain scrupulous care. They are not to furnish a bloody meal. They are to be so treated as to preclude the infliction of needless pain, and to prevent any harm which the sanguinary use of them might cause.

How admirable is the wisdom of God, how great His goodness, in ordering the constitution of even a fallen world! How manifold are the provisions of His care and kindness for alleviating the ills which sin has caused![187]

Lessons Learned in This Chapter

We first reviewed the fact that God designed the earth and everything within it. Some evolutionists will candidly but begrudgingly admit that all the available scientific evidence belies a special creation. It does not support a phony fairy tale called evolution. Sadly, they nonetheless still cling to their false beliefs. We also reviewed God's repeated mandate to fill the earth (9:1). This command was first issued to Adam and Eve. Now, it is restated to man and animal alike. We also noted numerous factors that would seem to defy that divine challenge.

For example, the earth was now a much less habitable place. The climate had changed precipitously and permanently. Much of the earth was, or soon would be, characterized by vast oceans, high mountains, desert lands, and swampy territories. Although some life forms can exist in these places, they are limited. This change in climate and geography would severely restrict the amount of food available as compared to pre-Flood days.

Second, God placed a fear of man into the animal kingdom (9:2). Without this fear, man would have quickly been slaughtered by the belligerent and much stronger creatures. Almost all animals

---

[187] R. S. Candlish, Expositions of Genesis (Wilmington, DE: Sovereign Grace Publishers, 1972), p. 97.

shy away from man. Some animals, such as cattle, sheep, dogs, and cats, do not foster an inordinate fear of man. But they still possess a respect and awe of God's greatest creation, namely, man. This instinct is witnessed everywhere on the planet, with very few exceptions.

There have even been instances of brave African men walking up to a tribe of lions consuming a freshly killed carcass. These men show no fear; they chop off a portion of the fresh kill, and they walk away unharmed. The lions back away from them in fear. We would not recommend this practice for just anyone, however. It could present some rather nasty repercussions.

Third, God now allows mankind to eat meat (9:3–4). Why this is done is not explained by the Scripture. Perhaps the more arduous conditions on the earth required a higher level of protein. But restrictions were placed upon this new diet. The most important one listed at this time was that the blood must first be drained out of the creature. The physical life is in the blood (Leviticus 17:11). In like manner, the spiritual life is found in the blood of Christ shed on the cross (John 1:29, 3:16; 1 Peter 1:18–19).

Fourth, God instituted government (9:5–6). In addition, government was responsible for enacting the death penalty on those who would take another human's life. This was in reference to premeditated murder, not warfare. Later, under the Mosaic covenant, the death penalty was expanded and more thoroughly explained. Sadly, government would fail in its responsibility repeatedly throughout the history of mankind. In many cases, government itself has been the largest culprit of immorality and mayhem.

Finally, God once again repeated His mandate to repopulate the earth, both to mankind and animals, in verse 7: "And as for you, be fruitful and multiply; bring forth abundantly in the earth and multiply in it." Considering all the warfare and natural disasters that have repeatedly struck the earth, this mandate has nonetheless been abundantly fulfilled.

However, man has largely persisted in his disobedience to God. Someday, in the future Tribulation, mankind will become rarer than fine gold. Isaiah 13:11–12 warns immoral mankind: "I will punish the world for its evil, and the wicked for their iniquity; I will halt the arrogance of the proud, and I will lay low the haughtiness of the terrible. I will make a mortal more rare than fine gold, a man more than the golden wedge of Ophir."

In our next chapter, we shall explore the Noahic covenant. It is a universal covenant and is still applicable worldwide to this day. The physical emblem of this covenant is the majestic rainbow. Every time one sees the rainbow after a thunderstorm, he should rejoice in God's ongoing providence and kindness to mankind. God's ongoing benevolence toward mankind is beautifully illustrated in this natural phenomenon. More important than its physical beauty, however, is its spiritual message. Sadly, all too many people ignore this revelation of God's holiness and justice.

Cognitive Conundrum #22

A man for good deeds was I well known; my self-righteousness was indeed my throne. I desired to strive for eternal joy and life; my mentality, however, would bring me strife. Commended for my worthy life was I; deeds thought I should grant life when I die. The Savior taught me what I refused to hear: I must follow Him and give all I held dear.

Who am I?

Answer: the rich young ruler (Mark 10:17–22)

Chapter 23

God's Covenant with Noah

(Genesis 9:8-29)

In This Chapter

Objectives for This Chapter
God Establishes the Noahic Covenant
Noah's Later Years
Lessons Learned in This Chapter

Objectives for This Chapter

God perpetually demonstrates His faithfulness to His people. In this chapter, we shall first examine His marvelous and universal covenant with Noah, his descendants, and even the animal kingdom itself. In simple terms, God will never send a universal Flood that will wipe out all of humanity and every living, air-breathing creature. There will never again be need of a floating, life-preserving ark. This covenantal promise also nullifies the nonsensical claim by some that the Flood was merely a local event.

God's Three Old Testament Covenantal Signs

In the Noahic covenant, God graciously promises to spare the world of experiencing another complete obliteration by a watery cataclysm. But, in addition, He also furnishes a beautiful covenantal sign with His ongoing promise. In an absolutely splendid and creative style, He displays this covenant in the sky for all to see. (1) That covenantal sign is nothing less than the magnificent, multicolored rainbow! After every thunderstorm, anyone can look up and see God's covenantal promise in vivid display. It is a testimony to every human being of God's faithfulness.

God provides visible manifestations of His covenants on two other occasions in the Old Testament. The other two covenant manifestations are understandably not as brilliantly evident as the rainbow. They are, nonetheless, every bit as effective.

What other covenantal signs did God display? (2) He provided circumcision for the Abrahamic covenant. This, quite naturally, affects only the male population. Young baby girls are automatically registered as members of the Jewish family. The males, as future heads of the family, must experience this momentarily painful induction.

On the eighth day after a young baby boy's birth, his foreskin is surgically removed. The act of circumcision was absolutely required under the Abrahamic covenant (Genesis 17:10–14). Since this is slightly off our topic, we shall presently include only Genesis 17:10–11: "This is My covenant which you shall keep, between Me and you and your descendants after you: Every male child among you shall be circumcised; and you shall be circumcised in the flesh of your foreskins, and it shall be a sign of the covenant between Me and you."

The eighth day has been medically established as the single day in a person's life when his blood clotting capacity is at its highest. Perhaps God, who designed the human body, was privy to this information. Obviously, that is why He designated the eighth day for circumcision. However, medical science did not understand this "coincidence" for several millennia. This is yet another sign of

God's providence and omniscience. One ponders how many other medical "discoveries" that are already revealed in veiled form throughout the Scriptures await modern science.

(3) The Sabbath is the sign for the Mosaic covenant for the nation of Israel. Exodus 31:16–17 states:

> Therefore the children of Israel shall keep the Sabbath, to observe the Sabbath throughout their generations as a perpetual covenant. It is a sign between Me and the children of Israel forever; for in six days the LORD made the heavens and the earth, and on the seventh day He rested and was refreshed.

It should be noted by the reader that the Sabbath is a sign for Israel as a nation. It was never intended as a spiritual mandate for the Gentiles. Indeed, one of the Sabbath's purposes was to demonstrate a marked distinction between Jew and Gentile. The Mosaic covenant was replete with stipulations, decrees, and requirements of worship incumbent only upon the nation of Israel. The entire priestly caste system was established by God for this very purpose. It should also be recognized that the seven-day week is a demonstration of the creation week of Genesis chapters 1 and 2.

These three specific physical signs of (1) the rainbow, (2) circumcision, and (3) the Sabbath in the Old Testament represent major events in God's kingdom. In the New Testament, (4) baptism is a physical sign for new life in Christ.

Although Christianity is not specifically stated as a covenant, it may be safely thought to be subsumed under the authority of the New covenant (Jeremiah 31:31–37). Matthew 20:28 states: "For this is My blood of the new covenant, which is shed for many for the remission of sins." Christ's blood alone satisfied the stringent requirements of the Mosaic covenant (John 1:29). He alone fulfilled this covenant (Matthew 5:17–18).

God's New Testament Covenantal Sign

Water baptism is commanded for the new believer by none other than Jesus Christ Himself (Matthew 28:19–20). It is a visible, outward sign of an already existing, invisible spiritual change. One is spiritually transformed by a personal and living faith in Christ (2 Corinthians 5:17). The water baptism poignantly symbolizes that already existing spiritual rejuvenation. It is our sincere prayer that every reader has experienced a spiritual rebirth. We are born physically, but we also need to be reborn spiritually (John 3:3–8).

The second aspect of this chapter deals with a rather uncomfortable topic. Noah became drunk! He inadvertently uncovered his body within the confines of his tent. We shall enter into a discussion as to whether this lamentable drunkenness was intentional or accidental. Scholars continue to differ on this rather unfortunate discussion. A final verdict is not possible as we do not have the necessary information available.

We shall also entertain the ramifications directed toward Noah's three sons and his grandson, Canaan. Noah spoke prophetically about his three sons and his grandson, Canaan. What Canaan's culpability was in this affair is uncertain. Noah certainly qualifies as one of the most influential and godly men who ever lived. Indeed, he probably trails only Jesus Christ Himself and John the Baptist (Matthew 11:11) in biblical prominence. His steadfast obedience sets him apart from the rest of humanity. What a difference one man can make for the kingdom of God!

God's Covenant with Noah

God Establishes the Noahic Covenant (Genesis 9:8–17)

God established His covenant with Noah, guaranteeing that the world would never again perish by being inundated with water. He even included the animals in this covenant. The rainbow would serve as an ongoing testimony to God's faithfulness. Nearly every thunderstorm presents a beautiful rainbow to remind mankind of God's promise. It is one of the most sensational and ongoing evidences that God provides around the globe.

Genesis 9:8–17 states:

> Then God spoke to Noah and to his sons with him, saying: "And as for Me, behold, I establish My covenant with you and with your descendants after you, and with every living creature that is with you: the birds, the cattle, and every beast of the earth with you, of all that go out of the ark, every beast of the earth.

> "Thus I establish My covenant with you: Never again shall all flesh be cut off by the waters of the flood; never again shall there be a flood to destroy the earth." And God said: "This is the sign of the covenant which I make between Me and you, and every living creature that is with you, for perpetual generations: I set My rainbow in the cloud, and it shall be for the sign of the covenant between Me and the earth.

> "It shall be, when I bring a cloud over the earth, that the rainbow shall be seen in the cloud; and I will remember My covenant which is between Me and you

and every living creature of all flesh; the waters shall never again become a flood to destroy all flesh. The rainbow shall be in the cloud, and I will look on it to remember the everlasting covenant between God and every living creature of all flesh that is on the earth." And God said to Noah, "This is the sign of the covenant which I have established between Me and all flesh that is on the earth."

God Establishes His Covenant with Noah and the Animals (Genesis 9:8–11)

It should be noted that there are four sets of recipients named for this covenant: (1) Noah, (2) Noah's three sons (this would also include their wives), and (3) the descendants of Noah and their families. It appears that Noah fathered no additional children (Genesis 9:19). The fourth set of recipients is generally overlooked: (4) the animals. In other words, God's covenant was universal with every living thing, though not all living things are specifically mentioned.

It is quite understandable that God established His covenant with Noah and his sons. It seems initially rather strange that even the animals were included in this covenant. However, it must be remembered that the animal world was also included in the watery judgment. God remembers every creature that He designed and made during creation week. Each species is valuable and precious in His sight. Hence, it is only natural that all living things should be blessed recipients of this unique covenant.

Verses 9 and 10 make the inclusion of the animals quite clear:

Then God spoke to Noah and to his sons with him,

saying: "And as for Me, behold, I establish My covenant with you and with your descendants after you, and with every living creature that is with you: the birds, the cattle, and every beast of the earth with you, of all that go out of the ark, every beast of the earth."

All of mankind, plus the animal kingdom, were exterminated by the Flood. Animals, not having a living spirit, do not consciously contemplate the generous conditions of the Noahic covenant. God did not create animals in the image of God as He did man. Nonetheless, God graciously remembered them as an integral part of His creation. Jesus stated in Matthew 10:29–31: "Are not two sparrows sold for a copper coin? And not one of them falls to the ground apart from the Father's will. But the very hairs of your head are all numbered. Do not fear, therefore, you are of more value than many sparrows."

If God is so conscientious of sparrows and the hairs of an individual's head, it should come as no surprise that He remembered the entire living kingdom in His covenant with Noah. This in no way should be interpreted that animals are on an equal plain with humans, such as the evolutionists foolishly decree. God has not changed His original mandate. Man still has authority over the earth and the animal kingdom (Genesis 1:28).

A Cogent Summary of the Noahic Covenant

Derek Kidner offers the following comments:

This first explicit covenant (if we take 6:18 to refer to this) is remarkable for its breadth (embracing "every living creature"), its permanence ("perpetual," "everlasting," etc.) and its generosity—for it was as unconditional as it was undeserved. For good measure, its sign and seal, a feature of all covenants, was such as to emphasize God's sole initiative, far out of man's reach.[188]

Genesis 9:11 clarifies this covenant in simple terms: "Thus I establish My covenant with you: Never again shall all flesh be cut off by the waters of the flood; never again shall there be a flood to destroy the earth." That promise has been kept. Certainly, this promise nullifies the non-biblical concept of a local flood.

There have been innumerable destructive floods from time immemorial. But there has only been one universal Flood. God has promised never again to destroy the earth with water. Mankind can certainly rejoice in that. To ignore this clear promise is to entirely discount God's holy Word. Why bother reading it at all, then? Those who ignore the plain teachings of God's eternal words must someday give account to Him for their actions (Romans 14:12).

The Rainbow: God's Covenantal Sign (Genesis 9:12–17)

When a thunderstorm passes quite frequently, a beautiful rainbow graces the sky for observers below. This is a perpetual sign to all peoples that God continues to keep His promise. It is a lovely symbol and an invitation to accept the grace of Christ offered on the cross. Godly parents must instruct their children of the rainbow's meaning. It symbolizes God's grace and forgiveness. Neglect of Christ's atoning sacrifice on the cross brings eternal punishment (Hebrews 2:3). God always honors His holy Word! While the lovely rainbow does indeed testify to God's grace and mercy, it also warns

---
[188] Derek Kidner, Genesis (Downers Grove, IL: Inter-Varsity Press, 1967), p. 101.

of His judgment of sin.

Genesis 9:12–17 states:

> And God said: "This is the sign of the covenant which I make between Me and you, and every living creature that is with you, for perpetual generations: I set My rainbow in the cloud, and it shall be for the sign of the covenant between Me and the earth. It shall be, when I bring a cloud over the earth, that the rainbow shall be seen in the cloud; and I will remember My covenant which is between Me and you and every living creature of all flesh; the waters shall never again become a flood to destroy all flesh.
>
> "The rainbow shall be in the cloud, and I will look on it to remember the everlasting covenant between God and every living creature of all flesh that is on the earth." And God said to Noah, "This is the sign of the covenant which I have established between Me and all flesh that is on the earth."

Man Is Perpetually Accountable to God

God remembers that man is but "dust" (Psalm 103:14). Man would also do well to remember his humble beginnings. Although created in the image of God, we were made from the dust of the earth. Man has no reason for arrogance or excuse for ignoring his Creator. God knows that we often need a visible reminder of His covenants.

Having a pertinent illustration or sign is a marvelous teaching tool to all generations. Jesus frequently spoke in parables and used common, well-known items to assist Him in His teaching the multitudes. All teachers and preachers should follow His example of using common illustrations for communicating truth. Part of Jesus' sensational style is evident in the Sermon on the Mount (Matthew chapters 5 to 7). Jesus used common, daily objects to communicate His eternal truths. The impact on the people was marked and memorable.

Matthew 7:28–29 summarizes the people's response to Jesus' methodology of instruction: "And so it was, when Jesus had ended these sayings, that the people were astonished at His teaching, for He taught them as one having authority, and not as the scribes." Walvoord and Dyer comment as follows: "This masterful address, comprehensive and authoritative in its pronouncement, astonished the people. The teaching of Christ was in great contrast to the way the scribes taught and clearly showed that this was the truth of God."[189]

The Benefit of Visible Signs

Regarding the rainbow as a sign of the covenant, Fruchtenbaum writes:

> Then in Genesis 9:12-17, God actually focuses on the token itself. In verse 12, the token is for perpetuity: And God said, This is the token of the covenant which I make between me and you and every living creature that is with you. It is to be for perpetual generations, meaning in this context, the remainder of human history. This is the first of three signs or tokens regarding

---

[189] John F. Walvoord and Charles H. Dyer, The John Walvoord Prophecy Commentaries: Matthew (Chicago, IL: Moody Publishers, The JFW Publishing Trust and Charles H. Dyer, 2013), p. 104.

a covenant. For the Noahic covenant, the token is a rainbow; for the Abrahamic covenant, the token will be circumcision (17:11); and for the Mosaic covenant, the token will be the Sabbath (Exod. 31:16-17).

Genesis 9:13 gives the actual token: I do set my bow in the cloud. The Hebrew word for bow is keshet, the same word used of the battle bow. It is as if God hung up His battle bow on the cloud as a sign of peace in place of being a sign of war; and it shall be a token of a covenant between me and the earth. In 9:14-16, the rainbow will serve as a remembrance of God's promise.

In 9:14: And it shall come to pass, when I bring a cloud over the earth, meaning when it rains, the bow shall be seen in the cloud. The rainbow is associated with rain, and there was no rain before the Flood; therefore, no rainbows had been seen before this time.[190]

Genesis 9:15–17 emphasizes that God will never again destroy the earth with water. God perpetually reminds mankind of His grace and justice through this gorgeous symbol. The rainbow is an integral but added aspect of creation which demonstrates God's existence and promise. Its presence in the sky brilliantly testifies to God's invisible power and attributes (Romans 1:18–20).

Pity the man who disregards the benevolence of our loving God. God then reiterates His covenant in verse 17 for added emphasis. Let the reader remember: God's grace can never be exceeded; His

---
[190] Arnold Fruchtenbaum, Ariel's Bible Commentary: The Book of Genesis, pp. 188–189.

justice can never be thwarted! All the combined evidence of God's existence cannot possibly be refuted by objective man. Only obstinance of the most malevolent kind can blind man to the glories that potentially await him. Those who refuse God's offer of grace in this life will certainly witness His majesty in eternity. Tragically, it will be manifested in judgment!

Noah's Later Years (Genesis 9:18–29)

A famous movie title of yesteryear is "The Good, the Bad, and the Ugly." The Bible is a unique book in that it is similar to the title of this movie. It emphasizes the good, it reveals the bad, and it also discloses the ugly. This is not how man would have written the Bible. The bad and ugly would have been avoided, and the good alone highlighted.

A well-known and tragic example of a moral failing was King David regarding his adulterous affair with Bathsheba. In addition to his adultery, he had Bathsheba's husband, Uriah the Hittite, murdered in battle by placing him in a dangerous position (2 Samuel chapter 11). It was a sordid matter and left a permanent blotch on David's otherwise unblemished record.

Much to the Bible student's remorse, Noah also endured a momentary dark incident in his life. This regrettable scene was almost certainly a one-time failing on Noah's part. It may have been entirely accidental. That is open to debate among scholars. But the sad affair is nonetheless recorded and remembered by all. This event partially tarnishes the wonderful image of Noah, again, whether accidental or purposeful on his part. But it was true to life. All believers would do well to consider this incident and fervently pray that it may not happen to them.

Noah Got Drunk (Genesis 9:18–21)

Noah's life was one of almost unblemished spiritual victory. However, the Bible records one flaw regarding Noah's nearly unparalleled life. He got drunk! Scholars have been debating this scenario for centuries. Two opinions prevail. Opinion #1: Noah committed a sin by intentionally drinking himself into a stupor. Why he would have done so is not known. This would certainly not have been in keeping with his nature of walking with God.

Opinion #2: Noah did not realize the effects of drinking wine because of the change in climactic conditions. Fermentation had become possible for the first time in human history. The post-Flood atmospheric conditions undoubtedly had changed. If there had been a water vapor canopy, as many believe, it would have been "rained out of existence" during the Flood.

Genesis 9:18–21 relates this rather shocking incident of Noah's drunkenness:

> Now the sons of Noah who went out of the ark were Shem, Ham, and Japheth. And Ham was the father of Canaan. These three were the sons of Noah, and from these the whole earth was populated. And Noah began to be a farmer, and he planted a vineyard. Then he drank of the wine and was drunk, and became uncovered in his tent.

Our passage first relates that Noah and his family disembarked from the ark. From Noah's three sons and wives, the entire world was repopulated. It is interesting to note that one grandchild was recorded along with the three sons. This was Canaan. He would figure prominently in the immediate context as well as in the future for the nation of Israel.

Canaan symbolized wickedness in both the present and future, though none of his specific actions are recorded in Scripture at this particular point. Ironically, it is Ham's sin that is noted, but Canaan, his son, is cursed for it. It is not clear why. Perhaps Canaan participated in some unrevealed manner. However, one can see a prophetic glimpse of lamentable circumstances and rebellion ahead for the descendants of Canaan.

A Closer Examination of Noah's Drunkenness

Question: Did Noah sin in getting drunk, or was this an accident? Let us now examine more closely the two opinions previously cited. Opinion #1: The first and more popular sentiment is that Noah sinned quite intentionally. He willfully became inebriated! As mentioned earlier, King David was a fabulous king through whom the Messiah eventually descended. Yet, at one point, he became guilty of both adultery and murder. This was a major blot on his otherwise exemplary life.

In fact, the only two well-known biblical characters against whom nothing evil is recorded are Joseph and Daniel. This clearly does not mean they were flawless, but what we do know about them is nothing short of amazing. Their godly characters are to be remembered and emulated. The Bible does not hide the sins of its most precious individuals. Scripture is always honest in its appraisal. Indeed, no human being can escape the guilt of universal and individual sin (Romans 3:23).

When Did Fermentation Come into Existence?

Supporting the view that Noah sinned by excessive drinking, Sarfati writes:

Fermentation was well known from ancient times as a means of sterilizing sweet juices. The same applies to milk—yogurt is fermented milk, and is usually a healthy and safe food. So it is likely that Noah knew about fermentation and its effects. ... So far, nothing wrong—making and drinking wine is not in itself sinful. ... Indeed, what happened afterwards was: Noah "became drunk." This really is sinful. The Bible in general is unlike most ancient books—it doesn't hide the faults of even its great heroes (Jesus of course really was perfectly sinless).

For example, Moses disobeyed God once and was denied entry into the Promised Land (Numbers 20:1-12); God rebuked the righteous and blameless Job (Job 1:1) who then repented (Job 42); David, the author of most of the Psalms and a man the Bible declares to be after YHWH's own heart (1 Samuel 13:14; Acts 13:22), committed adultery with Bathsheba then had her husband Uriah placed into lethal danger (2 Samuel 12);

Jesus is rightly frustrated with the foolishness of His disciples (Luke 24:25), and rebukes even Peter (Matthew 16:22, 23). In this Genesis passage we see that even Noah, after his total obedience to God before, during, and just after the Flood stumbled as well.[191]

Opinion #2: Noah's drunkenness was accidental. This view-

---

191 Jonathan Sarfati, The Genesis Account: A theological, historical, and scientific commentary on Genesis 1–11, p. 617.

point, though decidedly in the minority, can be defended for the following reasons: Reason #1: This is the first time in Scripture that wine is even mentioned. Drunkenness is not mentioned as a sin before this. That in itself, however, does not entirely discount the possibility that it previously did exist.

However, it can certainly be argued that Matthew 24:38–39 implies drinking: "For as in the days before the flood, they were eating and drinking, marrying and giving in marriage, until the day that Noah entered into the ark, and did not know until the flood came and took them all away, so also will the coming of the Son of Man be."

Reason #2: Fermentation before the Flood is an assumption by scholars who were not there, such as Sarfati. MacArthur comments: "Fermentation, which leads to drunkenness, may have been caused by changed ecological conditions as a result of the flood."[192] Of course, MacArthur was not there either. So, there are no actual eyewitnesses as to what transpired.

What is certain, however, is that the world definitely was quite different after the Flood. It must be remembered that there had been a universally pleasant climate. Adam and Eve did not even require clothes before the fall! Sarfati claims that fermentation was a known process. Though this does seem reasonable to modern man, there is no biblical evidence affirming or denying it. Drinking, certainly, was common, but drunkenness is never mentioned!

An Issue of Character

Reason #3: Such behavior as drunkenness stands in stark contradiction to Noah's known character (Genesis 6:8–9; cf. Ezekiel 14:14, 20; Hebrews 11:7). Noah, Daniel, and Job were mentioned

---

192 John MacArthur, The MacArthur Bible Commentary (Nashville, TN: Thomas Nelson Publishers, 2005), p. 26.

by God as great intercessors in prayer. This, of course, does not eliminate the possibility that Noah intentionally got drunk. But the likelihood seems quite farfetched.

Men of his age and mature character do not normally modify their traditional behavior to such extremes. One can surmise that he got drunk while mourning over the phenomenal loss of life during the Flood. But even this does not seem realistic as this incident was at least years, if not even a full decade, after the Flood.

The Curse on Young Canaan

Canaan is mentioned as being the "youngest" of four sons of Ham if Genesis 10:4 is to be understood as chronological. This would indicate a bare minimum of five to six years after the Flood had taken place. Furthermore, some surmise that for Canaan to be cursed by Noah does not seem reasonable if he were but a small child. It is generally considered that Canaan would have been at least a teenager to have earned such a curse. That is, of course, an assumption, albeit a natural one.

Hence, it seems reasonable to many to assume Noah's drunkenness took place a minimum of ten years after the Flood and possibly more. However, such a sentiment does not take into account that this curse on Canaan could have been almost entirely prophetic. But, that would not parallel what is generally characteristic of God's working with an individual. Still, it is entirely possible.

Such a considerable passing of time would admittedly tend to support Noah's getting drunk through carelessness or even intentionally. There would have already been ample time to have witnessed the intoxicating power of fermented wine. Indeed, if this was an entirely new process, the effects of fermentation would probably have been noted quite soon after the Flood. That does not automatically mean that Noah's family had been practicing fermentation.

However, since Noah was clearly speaking prophetically, it may be that Canaan had not actually done anything particularly evil as of yet. Perhaps he was still a young boy at that point. After all, Noah spoke prophetically about his sons Shem and Japheth in the same context (9:26–27). God had granted Noah the gift of prophecy.

It is intriguing that the curse falls on Canaan, not Ham. This may be indicating a future generational sin. The future Canaanites were exceedingly immoral sexually. They even sacrificed their children to the false gods in the fire. Tragically, Israel, at certain points, imitated them. Whichever option is correct, neither represents a pleasant picture. It obviously did happen; Noah got drunk! The story grows progressively worse.

Ham Sinned Against His Father (Genesis 9:22–23)

Genesis 9:22–23 records Ham's wicked act against his beloved father:

> And Ham, the father of Canaan, saw the nakedness of his father, and told his two brothers outside. But Shem and Japheth took a garment, laid it on both their shoulders, and went backward and covered the nakedness of their father. Their faces were turned away, and they did not see their father's nakedness.

Because of his drunkenness, Noah was discovered by Ham in a state of humiliating nakedness. Noah perhaps got warm because of the excess of fermented wine and slipped his robe off, never intending to be seen. He then must have passed out or fallen into a deep sleep while in the privacy of his tent. It should be noted that he did not expose himself publicly. Hence, his nakedness was quite defensible since he was in the confines of his tent.

Regarding Noah's nakedness, Sarfati offers the following salient observations:

> Even worse, Noah's drunkenness led to further shame: becoming naked. Ever since Adam and Eve fell, nakedness in public was regarded as shameful. The phrase "and lay uncovered" is one word in Hebrew, wayyitgal. This is the Hithpael form "should be rendered as a reflexive, 'he uncovered himself.'" This may well have been an involuntary act of letting his robes slip down as he lay down to sleep off the wine. However, at least this was inside Noah's tent, not public nudity.[193]

Ham's Folly and Gross Disrespect

Ham apparently mocked Noah, his godly father. Certainly, a simple inadvertent glance at his father could not merit such a rebuttal by Noah. Ham's disrespect alone in repeating this unfortunate situation to his two brothers was bad enough. But even worse than that, his glance toward his father's nakedness apparently was not fleeting. Although his first sight of his father would have been accidental, the Hebrew text implies that his unholy gaze was lingering.

Furthermore, Ham made no effort to cover his father up. He left him in this embarrassing state. Ham seems to have been amused rather than ashamed over his father's humbling situation. That certainly is not the sign of a godly or sensitive son.

Leupold offers the following cogent comments regarding this

---
193 Jonathan Sarfati, The Genesis Account: A theological, historical, and scientific commentary on Genesis 1–11, p. 618.

regrettable scenario:

> For the right understanding of what follows we are again reminded, as in v. 18, that Ham is the father of Canaan. At the same time, the repetition of the statement in this connection seems to point more definitely to a kinship of mind between the two. The trait of inclination to the unclean is shared by father and son alike, in fact, it even appears that the trait manifested by the father has reached a higher measure of intensity in the son. But as far as Ham himself is concerned, the expression wayyar is not a mere harmless and accidental "and he saw," but "he looked at" (BDB) or "he gazed with satisfaction."
>
> What ordinary filial reverence should have restrained is given free rein. The unclean imagination feeds itself by gazing. But at the same time a measure of departure from the faith is also revealed by Ham.
>
> That the son should have treated with such levity a father eminent for true piety, the one man whom God spared in the destruction of the world, indicates that this son no longer esteemed such true godliness as he ought to have done. Similarly, wayyaggedh is not a mere "and he told," though we know of no other way of translating it. The circumstances suggest that it means; "and he told with delight." ...

In a modified sense this event may be named a second fall into sin, or the fall of the postdiluvians, yet with this proviso that, of course, since Adam's fall all men were born sinners. But the event does most assuredly show how soon the salutary warnings conveyed by the Flood were forgotten, and mankind began to incline toward a downward course.[194]

The Righteous Shem and Japheth

Shem and Japheth, in sharp contrast, carefully covered their beloved father. They walked backwards with a garment so as to conceal his nakedness. They also took great care to avert their eyes. As such, they were spared seeing the humiliation of their noble father.

No words are recorded as being exchanged between Shem and Japheth. Their silence would have served as a loud rebuke to their disrespectful and shameful brother. Clearly, as brothers, they knew previously of Ham's backsliding character. Moral perversion does not generally crop up overnight. This event possibly served as the beginning of a more permanent disruption of their partnership, brotherly fidelity, and fellowship. Sin never produces beneficial results.

Satan is always mindful of tempting those in the world. First Peter 5:8–9 states: "Be sober, be vigilant, because your adversary the devil walks about like a roaring lion, seeking whom he may devour. Resist him, steadfast in the faith, knowing that the same sufferings are experienced by your brotherhood in the world." Tragically, Ham did not heed such warnings. Rather, he willingly, perhaps even eagerly, gave into such temptations.

---

194 H. C. Leupold, Exposition of Genesis, pp. 346–347.

Noah Prophesies about Canaan, Shem, and Japheth (Genesis 9:24–29)

Rather amazingly, verses 25 to 27 are the only words recorded from Noah. Chapters 6 to 9 simply state that Noah obeyed his God. Now, he finally speaks, and part of his message is a curse. How distressing Noah's words recorded in verse 25 must have been to Ham. Ironically, and undoubtedly painfully, Noah completely failed to mention Ham in his prophecy about Shem and Japheth. The prophetic words he spoke regarding Canaan, Ham's son, were little more than a curse.

Even a father such as Ham should have lamented Noah's statement. But, considering his behavior toward his father, perhaps his heart was already hardened beyond any resuscitation of genuine spiritual concern. Although one fervently wishes that Noah's words brought Ham back to his senses, they certainly did not seem to impact his son Canaan. The Canaanites historically were legendary for their wickedness.

Genesis 9:24–27 states:

> So Noah awoke from his wine, and knew what his younger son had done to him. Then he said: "Cursed be Canaan; a servant of servants he shall be to his brethren." And he said, "Blessed be the LORD, the God of Shem, and may Canaan be his servant. May God enlarge Japheth, and may he dwell in the tents of Shem; and may Canaan be his servant."

When Noah awoke, he knew what his youngest son had done to him. The Bible does not reveal how he knew. Perhaps Shem and Japheth told Noah what had happened, although that does not seem particularly likely. They undoubtedly would have been quite uncomfortable broaching this embarrassing situation to their father. It is most likely that God Himself told Noah in preparation for his prophetic message.

It can also be that Canaan openly mocked his grandfather, Noah, thus amply earning the prophetic curse. If that is indeed how Noah found out about his humiliation of physical exposure, that would have merited even more the prophetic curse he issued on his disrespectful grandson. Several pertinent observations can be noted about this passage.

A Few Salient Observations

Observation #1: Noah cursed Canaan, not Ham. Many people have postulated that Ham is the father of the black race. This may very well have proven true historically. But Canaan was olive-brown. Indeed, it is likely that all of the brothers were of similar color. The differing pigments of skin color came gradually throughout history. Canaan's descendants moved to the land of the Canaanites, which later became the Promised Land for Israel.

There is no biblical or logical reason to believe that the black population is cursed because of Ham. One's skin color has absolutely nothing to do with his spiritual standing. Prejudice among mankind based on color is a diabolical lie of the devil. Indeed, Ham himself was not cursed. He is not even mentioned in this passage. It is highly unlikely that God would actively curse Ham since He had previously blessed him in Genesis 9:1.

The Canaanites, on the other hand, later became infamous for their evil behavior (Genesis 15:16, 18:20–21, 19:4–10; Leviticus 18:1–3; Deuteronomy 12:29–31). One biblical principle mentioned later by Moses is that the sins of the fathers are visited upon their unrepentant children (Exodus 20:5, 34:6–7). It should be understood that generational sins tend to pass from father to son. It is not inevitable, but it is sadly quite common.

Ezekiel emphasizes that a man dies for his own sins. If the son repents of his father's wickedness, he will not be punished. The father must be punished for his own sins, and vice versa (Ezekiel 18:4). Ham and Canaan both sinned. It would appear that Canaan never repented, even if his father, Ham, may have.

Shem and Japheth Are Blessed by Noah

Observation #2: Noah blessed "the LORD, the God of Shem." Through this double emphasis on the Lord, Noah seems to emphasize that Shem will be the spiritually favored brother. From Shem's descendants the Messiah would come. It is noteworthy that Shem is undoubtedly included in this blessing, but the primary focus is on the God of Shem, who is none other than Jesus Christ.

The promised Seed of the woman (Genesis 3:15) would come through Shem. He is, in essence, the father of the Hebrew race. Abraham, of course, is the actual noted father of the Hebrews, as history would play out. Shem also would dominate the Canaanites. This is truly a long-delayed fulfillment, but ultimately, it will be fulfilled completely in the second coming of Christ. It was partially fulfilled in historic times, however, with the conquest of Canaan.

Observation #3: Noah blessed Japheth, granting him the honor of dwelling in the tents of Shem. Fruchtenbaum comments: "The word dwell here has the meaning of 'having fellowship with.' So while the Japhethites would conquer the Jews physically, the Jews would conquer the Japhethites spiritually. Japhethites, more than the Hamites, adopted the God of Shem."[195]

---

[195] Arnold Fruchtenbaum, Ariel's Bible Commentary: The Book of Genesis, p. 199.

In addition, Canaan would serve Japheth and his descendants. The descendants of Japheth became the most numerous of the three brothers. This is what "may God enlarge Japheth" means. These descendants include most of Asia, Europe, the Americas, and Australia.

A Historical Anecdote regarding Immoral Semites

A historical note: The Phoenicians, who were Semites, were a seafaring people. They practiced horrendous and wicked religious practices. Carthage, a powerful city in Africa and colony of the Phoenicians, threatened and attacked the Roman Empire, afflicting them with countless casualties. Hannibal was the Carthaginian's greatest general. He was completely ruthless. They thrived militarily and also engaged ruthlessly in the slaughter of the innocents. Eventually, both the Phoenicians and their colony of Carthage were defeated.

Phoenicia ultimately became enslaved by the Persians, Greeks, and Romans, all of whom were Japhethite nations. Carthage, after numerous horrific wars, was finally overcome by the Romans.

Religiously, the Carthaginians were truly monstrous in their idolatrous practices. They had compassion on no one, particularly the vulnerable and helpless young. They shamelessly practiced child sacrifice. Such wicked people truly deserved to die.

The Greco-Roman historian Plutarch wrote the following gruesome summary of the Carthaginian people (AD c. 46–120): "But with full knowledge and understanding [the Carthaginians] offered up their own children, and those who had no children would buy little ones from poor people and cut their throats as if they were so many lambs or young birds."[196]

---
196 Jonathan Sarfati, The Genesis Account: A theological, historical, and scientific commentary on Genesis 1–11, p. 628.

How tragic that it was through Shem the Messiah would come, and yet some of Shem's descendants became absolutely heinous in their character and actions. It was for moral and political reasons that the Romans were determined to wipe out the city of Carthage from the face of the earth. Few would miss the wicked Carthaginians. They had enslaved countless people and gleefully eradicated many others.

In addition, the Romans thirsted for revenge over the merciless slaughter of their military at the Battle of Cannae on August 2, 216 BC. The victorious general Hannibal encircled a much larger Roman army and completely wiped out 50,000 soldiers! No one was allowed to surrender; no quarter was shown whatsoever. The Carthaginians were immensely cruel people. They were similar in cruelty to the Ninevites of the prophet Jonah's day.

In an additional and more practical sense, the Romans could not retain their political position in the world and allow such a humiliation as the Battle of Cannae to pass. It was under the Roman General Scipio Aemilianus in the Battle of Carthage (146 BC) that they accomplished total victory over Carthage and completely destroyed the city. The few survivors were sold into slavery.

Lest the reader be left with the impression that the Romans were a moral race, one need only recall the slaughter of Christians by gladiators and wild animals. The Romans were not much better than the Carthaginians, morally speaking. Their own moral travesties were of legendary status! They richly deserved their punishment from other invading races when it finally came.

A Summary of Noah's Godly Life

Genesis 9:28–29 finishes the summary of Noah's incredible life: "And Noah lived after the flood three hundred and fifty years. So all the days of Noah were nine hundred and fifty years; and he died." Thus ended the life of one of the most remarkable saints of all time. Noah was arguably third behind Jesus Christ and John the Baptist. Though not an entirely sinless man, he truly was a man for the ages.

It is intriguing that Noah is mentioned four times as an illustration in the New Testament.

(1) Matthew 24:37–39 and Luke 17:26–27 compare his life to the events immediately preceding Christ's second coming. (2) Noah lived by faith (Hebrews 11:7). He, in our view, had never seen rain, and he certainly had not seen a Flood. Yet by faith, he built the ark and spared humanity and the air-breathing animals from annihilation. Most people would have given up long before 120 years of faithful service and mockery had passed.

(3) First Peter 3:19–21 compares the ark to the spiritual symbol of baptism. The ark physically spared Noah and his family. Even so, baptism symbolizes spiritual deliverance for the believer. It is not actually the physical act of baptism that saves, but the faith in Christ that precedes the water baptism. Spirit baptism takes place along with salvation. It is instantaneous. Water baptism takes place shortly afterwards to symbolize openly and visibly God's forgiveness of sins and His justification of the sinner.

(4) Second Peter 2:5 states: "… and [God] did not spare the ancient world, but saved Noah, one of eight people, a preacher of righteousness, bringing in the flood on the world of the ungodly." This passage demonstrates the fact that God knows both how to spare some from judgment and to deliver others into condemnation. There is no escaping God's justice; there is no equivalent to His infinite mercy.

What a remarkable thought that Noah witnessed the Flood that destroyed the world. He then saw the dispersion of the peoples throughout the world at the Tower of Babel only a scant 106 years later. And why were the people dispersed? Once again, it was because of their rebellious spirits.

Noah: A Life Incredibly Well Invested for God

Man's obstinance and lack of faith are breathtaking! Who could possibly claim to have witnessed more significant acts of history than Noah, save Jesus Christ Himself, who orchestrates history? Noah is truly a unique man. He lived for 350 years after the Flood. His son Shem lived for 500 years after the Flood.

Even today, with all the empirical evidence covering the globe that demonstrates the Flood, people can scarcely imagine it. This event truly boggles the mind. Sadly, for many, even seeing the mountains of evidence is still not believing! But one must remember that when dealing with an infinite Creator God, nothing is impossible (Luke 1:37). May we, as believers today, recognize the power and authority of God and follow in Noah's footsteps. He was truly a man of inextinguishable faith and perseverance. Noah was a man for the ages!

Lessons Learned in This Chapter

God consistently acts in profound faithfulness and graciousness toward His people. However, God also exercises all of His eternal attributes in perfectly balanced measure. This means that He will eventually punish sin and the sinner. The Flood demonstrates beyond human equivocation the certainty of God's judgmental power.

In this chapter, we first reviewed how God acted judiciously in a unique and most impressive manner toward evil humanity. He sent the universal Flood. It wiped out all the air-breathing, land-inhab-

God's Covenant with Noah

iting humans and animals, save for what was on the ark. This act wiped out the diabolical Nephilim once and for all, save one. The future Antichrist will also be a Nephilim. Satan himself will be his demonic father. As such, there can only be one genuine Antichrist, but there are countless counterfeit ones.

After the culminating action of the Flood, God established His first genuine covenant with mankind. Called the Noahic covenant for obvious reasons, God promised never to destroy the world and its inhabitants with a Flood again. This promise was made to Noah, his immediate family, all their descendants, and even the animal kingdom.

The wording of the Noahic covenant entirely abrogates any notion of the Flood being only local. One must openly reject God's straightforward account if he insists on a local flood. What is the point, then, of even reading divine instruction if it is subservient to mortal subjectivity? The sign of the Noahic covenant is the beautiful rainbow. All around the world, the rainbow actively testifies of God's faithfulness. Sadly, many people have never been informed as to the rainbow's true biblical significance.

Second, we examined the most regrettable scenario of Noah's drunken stupor. He undressed himself and lay concealed in his tent, sleeping off his excessive wine. However, this was not a case of public exposure, which would truly have proven disconcerting. It is merely a question of excessive drinking. The question of whether this drunkenness was intentional or accidental is actively pondered. That issue may never be resolved on this side of eternity as our knowledge of what the pre-Flood world was like is too limited.

Sadly, this scenario revealed rather unsettling character flaws of Ham and his son Canaan. Ham, who discovered his father in his compromised position, apparently gazed in a most unwholesome manner at his father's nakedness. He also seemed to regale himself with the passing on of this most private observation to his brothers. In reality, he did not need to convey this sad incident to anyone. Furthermore, he apparently did not even attempt to cover his father in his lamentable exposure.

Shem and Japheth acted in accordance to more godly sons and were of more biblical character. They averted their eyes, walked backward, and graciously covered their father's nakedness. When Noah woke from his stupor, he blessed Shem and Japheth accordingly. Indeed, Shem becomes the Seed son through whom the Messiah would ultimately come.

Noah said nothing at all about Ham in his prophetic oration. He cursed Canaan. What Canaan did to merit this curse is not revealed. But we may rest assured that God does not arbitrarily foist such condemnation upon entirely innocent parties. Noah's curse was prophetic and certainly found fulfillment in Canaan's descendants. They eventually became a truly wicked tribe of people. Ironically, as important a man as Noah was, these few words are his only recorded ones in Genesis chapters 6 to 9.

We have now covered one of the most fascinating portions of Scripture with the Flood. Through this entire scenario, we have truly witnessed the good, the bad, and the ugly. These chapters are an honest though disquieting aspect of God's creation. As such, the Bible is a truly unique book. But it should be, as it is penned by a unique and singular God. He is consistent and perfectly balanced in all of His eternal attributes. That is something mankind does well to remember.

In our next book of this trilogy, we shall begin to examine the genealogy of the patriarchs and those who followed them. Admittedly, many find such sections of the Bible to be somewhat tedious. That is understandable but not commendable. God included every section of Scripture for our learning. May the reader ever be cognizant of the admonition granted us in Romans 15:4: "For whatever things were written before were written for our learning, that we through the patience and comfort of the Scriptures might have hope."

Cognitive Conundrum #23

Of foreign and suspicious blood was I; still, I climbed the ladder of great success. As chief of my king's band of servants, I possessed authority and ambition no less. As a warrior, I proved a sniveling coward; my butchery blights my life for all to see. I did not slay God's son, yes, this is for sure, but His servants I killed with evil impunity.

Who am I?

Answer: Doeg the Edomite (1 Samuel chapter 22)

Bibliography

Barbieri, Louis A. The Bible Knowledge Commentary: Matthew. John F. Walvoord and Roy B. Zuck, Roy B., eds. Wheaton, IL: Victor Books, 1983.

Barnhouse, Donald Grey. Romans III: God's Grace, God's Freedom, God's Heirs. Grand Rapids: MI: Wm. B. Eerdmans Publishing Company, 1959.

Barr, James Letter to David C. C. Watson, 1984.

Barrett, C. K. The First Epistle to the Corinthians. Peabody, MA: Hendrickson Publishers, 1968.

Blaising, Craig A. The Bible Knowledge Commentary: Malachi. Wheaton, IL: Victor Books.

Blosser, Oliver R., "Historical Reliability of Genesis 1–11." It's About Time. Spencer, Iowa: Chronology-History Research Inst. (April-July 1986); pp. 8–9.

Bock, Darrell. Baker Exegetical Commentary on the New Testament: Acts. Grand Rapids, MI: Baker Academic.

Boyd, Steven W. & Snelling, Andrew A., Editors. Grappling with the Chronology of the Genesis Flood. Green Forest, AR: Master Books, 2014.

Bozarth, G. Richard, "The Meaning of Evolution." American Atheist (February 1978). pp. 19, 30.

Candlish, R. S. An Exposition of Genesis. Wilmington, DE: Sovereign Grace Publishers, 1972.

Darwin, Charles. On the Origin of Species. New York: The Modern Library, 1856 reprint.

Deere, Jack. The Bible Knowledge Commentary: Volume 1, Deuteronomy. John F. Walvoord and Roy B. Zuck, general editors.

Wheaton, IL: Victor Books, 1985.

Feinberg, Charles L. The Minor Prophets. Chicago, IL: Moody Press, 1948.

Ferrell, Vance. Science vs. Evolution. Altamont, TN: Evolution Facts, Inc., 2001.

Flint, R. F. Glacial and Pleistocene Geology. New York, Wiley, 1957.

Fortune, A. W. The International Standard Bible Encyclopedia. General Editor Geoffrey W. Bromiley. Grand Rapids, MI: William B. Eerdmans Publishing Company, 1979.

France, R. T. The New International Commentary on the New Testament: The Gospel of Matthew. Grand Rapids, MI: William B. Eerdmans Publishing Company, 2007.

Fruchtenbaum, Arnold G. Ariel's Bible Commentary: The Book of Genesis: Exposition from a Messianic Jewish Perspective, San Antonio, TX: Ariel Ministries, 2009.

———The Footsteps of the Messiah: A Study of the Sequence of Prophetic Events. San Antonio, TX: Ariel Ministries, 2021.

Gill, John. Exposition of the Old & New Testaments: Volume 1 of 9: Genesis through Numbers. Paris, AR: The Baptist Standard Bearer, Inc., Reprinted in 2016.

Gillen, Alan. "The Genesis of Germs," Answers Magazine, July 24, 2015.

Gould, S. J. Ontogeny and Phylogeny. Cambridge, MA: Belknap-Harvard Press, 1977.

Green, Gene L. Baker Exegetical Commentary on the New Testament: Jude & 2 Peter. Grand Rapids, MI: Baker Academic, 2008.

Haeckel, Ernst. The History of Creation. Whitefish, MT: Kessinger Publishing, 2007, 1876.

Ham, Ken. The New Answers Book 1. Green Forest, AR: Master Books, 2006.

Bibliography

Ham, Ken and Hodge, Bodie. A Flood of Evidence: 40 Reasons Why Noah and the Ark Still Matter. Green Forest, AR: Master Books, 2016.

Hamilton, Victor. The New International Commentary on the Old Testament: The Book of Genesis Chapters 1–17. Grand Rapids, MI: Eerdmans Publishing, 1990.

Harrison, R. K. The Wycliffe Exegetical Commentary: Numbers. Chicago, IL: Moody Press, 1990.

Hartley, John E. The New International Commentary on the Old Testament: The Book of Job. Grand Rapids, MI: William B. Eerdmans Publishing Company, 1988.

Hiebert, D. Edmond. The Epistle of James. Chicago, Moody Press, 1979.

Hoehner, Harold W. The Bible Knowledge Commentary: Ephesians. Wheaton, IL: Victor Books, 1983.

Hughes, Philip Edgcumbe. A Commentary on the Epistle to the Hebrews. Grand Rapids, MI: William B. Eerdmans Publishing Company, 1977.

Jennings, F. C. Studies in Isaiah (Neptune, NJ: Loizeaux Brothers, 1935), pp. 184–185.

Jones, Floyd Nolan. The Chronology of the Old Testament. Green Forest, AR: Master Books, 1993–2004.

Keil, C. F. and Delitzsch, F. Commentary on the Old Testament: The Pentateuch. Grand Rapids, MI: William B. Eerdmans Publishing Company, 1986.

Kelly, J. N. D., Thornapple Commentaries: A Commentary on the Epistles of Peter and Jude. Grand Rapids, MI: Baker Book House, 1969.

Kidner, Derek. Genesis. Downers Grove, IL: Inter-Varsity Press, 1967.

Kittel, Gerhard. Editor of Theological Dictionary of the New Testament: Volume 1. Translator and Editor Geoffrey W. Bromiley. Grand Rapids, MI: Eerdmans Publishing Company, 1964.

Kroll, Woodrow. The Book of Romans: Righteousness in Christ. Chattanooga, TN: AMG Publisher, 2002.

Laetsch, Theodore. Concordia Classic Commentary Series: Jeremiah. St. Louis, MO: Concordia Publishing House, 1952.

LaHaye, Tim and Hindson, Ed. The Popular Bible Prophecy Commentary. Eugene, OR: Harvest House Publishers, 2006.

Leupold, H. C. Leupold on the Old Testament: Volume 1: Genesis 1–19. Grand Rapids, MI: Baker Book House, 1942.

Luther, Martin. Commentary on Peter & Jude. Grand Rapids, MI: Kregel Publications, 1990.

MacArthur, John. The MacArthur New Testament Commentary: Romans 1–8. Chicago: IL, Moody Bible Institute, 1991.

———The MacArthur's New Testament Commentary: Matthew 24–28. Chicago, IL: Moody Press, 1989.

———The MacArthur's New Testament Commentary: 1 Corinthians. Chicago, IL: Moody Press, 1984.

———The MacArthur New Testament Commentary: Titus. Chicago; Moody Press, 1996.

———The MacArthur New Testament Commentary: 2 Peter and Jude. Chicago, IL: Moody Publishers, 2005.

———The MacArthur New Testament Commentary: Revelation 12–22. Chicago, IL: Moody Press, 2000.

Mackintosh, C. H. Notes on the Pentateuch: Genesis to Deuteronomy. Neptune, NJ: Loizeaux Brothers, 1972.

Martin, John. The Bible Knowledge Commentary. Editors John F. Walvoord and Roy B. Zuck. Wheaton, IL: Victor Books, 1983.

Matthew, K. A. The New American Commentary: Genesis

1–11:26. Vol. 1A, Nashville, TN: Holman Reference, B&H Publishing Group, 1996.

McGee, J. Vernon. Thru the Bible: Genesis through Deuteronomy. Nashville, TN: Thomas Nelson Publishers, 1981.

McKeown, James. Genesis, Two Horizons Old Testament Commentary series. Grand Rapids: MI, Eerdmans, 2008.

Merrill, Eugene H. Everlasting Dominion: A Theology of the Old Testament, Nashville, TN: B&H Publishing Group, 2006.

Mitchell, Elizabeth. The New Answers Book 4. Green Forest, AR: Master Books, 2013.

Morris, Henry M. The Genesis Record: A Scientific and Devotional Commentary on the Book of Beginnings. Grand Rapids, MI: Baker Book House, 1976.

———The Biblical Basis for Modern Science. Grand Rapids, MI: Baker Book House, 1984,

———The New Defender's Study Bible. Nashville, TN: World Publishing, Inc., 1995, 2006.

———The Remarkable Record of Job. Green Forest, AR: Master Books, 1988, 2000.

———Treasures in the Psalms. Green Forest, AR: Master Books, 1999.

———That Their Words May Be Used Against Them. Green Forest, AR: Master Books, 1997.*

———The Revelation Record. Carol Stream, IL: Tyndale House Publishing, Inc., 1983.

Morris III, Henry M. Unlocking the Mysteries of Genesis: Explore the Science and Miracles of Creation. Eugene, OR: Harvest House Publishers, 2016.

Murphy, James G. Barnes's Notes: A Commentary on the Book of Genesis. Grand Rapids, MI: Baker Books, 1847 by Blackie & Son, London, reprinted 2005.

Newell, N. O. "Adequacy of the Fossil Record," Journal of Paleontology. Vol. 33, May 1959, p. 495.

Newman, R. C., The Ancient Exegesis of Genesis 6:2, 4. Grace Theological Journal 5(1):13-36, 1984.

Oord, Michael. Journal of Creation 14, no 3 (December 2000): 24-34.

Opik, Ernst J. "Ice Ages," in The Earth and Its Atmosphere, edited by D. R. Bates. New York, Basic Books, Inc., 1957.

———"Climate and the Changing Sun," Scientific American. Vol. 198, June 1958, p. 89.

Parker, Gary. Creation: Facts of Life. Green Forest, AR: Master Books, 1994.

Patterson, Roger. Evolution Exposed: Earth Science. Hebron, KY: Answers in Genesis, 2008.

Phillips, John. The John Phillips Commentary Series: Exploring Genesis. Grand Rapids, MI: Kregel Publications, 1980.

———The John Phillips Commentary Series: Exploring the Epistles of John. Grand Rapids, MI: Kregel Publications, 2003.

Price, Randall. Jerusalem in Prophecy: God's Stage for the Final Drama. Bellmawr, NJ: The Friends of Israel Gospel Ministry, 2020.

Rehwinkel, Alfred M. The Flood: In the Light of the Bible, Geology, and Archaeology. Saint Louis, MO; Concordia Publishing House, 1951.

Rudd, Steve. Bible Variants, November 2017.

Ryrie, Charles C. Basic Theology. Wheaton, IL: Victor Books, 1986.

———The Ryrie Study Bible. Chicago, Moody Press, 1976, 1978.

Sarfati, Jonathan D. The Genesis Account: A theological, historical, and scientific commentary on Genesis 1–11. Powder Springs, GA: Creation Book Publishers, 2015.

Bibliography

———High and Dry Sea Creatures. Answers Magazine, December 7, 2007.

Smith, Wilbur M., Egypt in Biblical Prophecy. Boston, MA: W. A. Wilde Company, 1957.

Snelling, Andrew. High and Dry Sea Creatures. Answers Magazine, December 7, 2007.

Stutzer, Otto. Geology of Coal, translated by A. C. Noe. Chicago: University of Chicago Press, 1940.

Thomas, Griffith W. H. Genesis: A Devotional Commentary. Grand Rapids, MI: William B. Eerdmans Publishing Co., 1946.

Ussher, James. The Annals of the World. Green Forest, AR: Master Books, 2003. Revised and updated by Larry and Marion Pierce.

Walvoord, John. The Revelation of Jesus Christ. Chicago, IL: Moody Press, 1966.

———Walvoord, John F. and Zuck, Roy B. (eds.). The Bible Knowledge Commentary (2 vols.: Old and New Testament), Wheaton, I: Victor Books, 1983.

Walvoord, John F. and Dyer, Charles H., The John Walvoord Prophecy Commentaries: Matthew. Chicago, Moody Publishers, The JFW Publishing Trust and Charles H. Dyer, 2013.

Walvoord, John F. and Hitchcock, Mark. The John Walvoord Prophecy Commentaries: 1 & 2 Thessalonians. Chicago: Moody Publishers, 2012.

Whitcomb, John C. and Morris, Henry M. The Genesis Flood: The Biblical Flood and Its Scientific Implications. Grand Rapids, MI: Baker Book House, 1961.

Wiersbe, Warren. The Bible Exposition Commentary: Volume 1: Matthew-Galatians. Wheaton, IL: Victor Books, 1989.

———The Bible Exposition Commentary; Old Testament: Genesis-Deuteronomy. Wheaton, IL: Victor Books, 2001.

Woodmorappe, John. Noah's Ark: A Feasibility Study. El Cajon, CA: Institute for Creation Research, 1996.

Young, Brian. Doubts About Creation? Not After This. Bend, OR: Maverick Publications, 2003.

Appendix 1

Scripture Index

Old Testament:

Amos 1:12 743
Amos 5:18–20 128
Amos 9:11–15 ...27, 168, 733, 734, 741-747, 764
1 Chronicles 29:13–14 .... 241, 738
2 Chronicles 7:14 346
Daniel 9:24–27 211
Daniel 11:41 342
Daniel 12:1–2, 4 48
Daniel 12:41 743
Deuteronomy 1:28 423
Deuteronomy 3:11 437
Deuteronomy 4:2 503
Deuteronomy 8:17–18 738
Deuteronomy 9:2 421
Deuteronomy 10:12 365
Deuteronomy 11:6 256
Deuteronomy 12:15–16, 20–24, 29–31 778
Deuteronomy 13:11 368
Deuteronomy 17:6–7 786
Deuteronomy 25:5–6 279
Deuteronomy 29:29 351
Deuteronomy 30:19–20 350
Deuteronomy 32:8 382
Deuteronomy 33:27 437
Ecclesiastes 1:2 221
Ecclesiastes 3:11 543
Ecclesiastes 5:4–5 239

Ecclesiastes 7:20 338
Ecclesiastes 8:11 367
Exodus 2:2–5, 24 .... 470, 682
Exodus 12:40–41 548
Exodus 13:11–16 238
Exodus 19:5–6 360
Exodus 20:5 818
Exodus 21:10, 28–29 787
Exodus 22:29–30 239
Exodus 25:22, 40 .... 90, 182
Exodus 31:16–17 797
Exodus 32:25–29 453
Exodus 33:12–13, 20 .... 439, 463
Exodus 34:6–7, 29–35 125
Ezekiel 3:18 69
Ezekiel 8:12 232
Ezekiel 10:1–22 182
Ezekiel 14:14, 20 .... 455, 485
Ezekiel 18:4, 23, 30–32 .. 140, 157, 272, 350, 369
Ezekiel 22:30–31 451
Ezekiel 28:11–15 379
Ezekiel 34:1–5, 11–12, 16 ...... 188, 359
Ezekiel 37:15–28 .... 207, 464
Ezekiel 38:10–12 215
Ezekiel 47:12 59
Genesis 1:26–28, 31 301
Genesis 2:5–6, 16–18, 23–25 ....
.... 66, 68, 69, 144, 161, 277, 480, 580, 743,
Genesis 3:1–6:8 39-226
Genesis 6:9–9:29 337-822
Genesis 10:1–32 36
Genesis 11:1–32 36
Genesis 12:1–3, 10 45
Genesis 15:5, 13, 16 52
Genesis 16:12 278

Appendix 1

Genesis 17:10–19 796
Genesis 18:7–8, 20–21, 23 393
Genesis 19:4–10, 29 682
Genesis 22:17 52
Genesis 25:23, 33–34 . . . . 225, 226
Genesis 32:12 226
Genesis 49:10 464
Habakkuk 2:4, 14 747
Hosea 1:10–11 745
Hosea 5:15–6:3 . . . . 210, 342, 356, 361, 749
Isaiah 2:2–4 747
Isaiah 4:1 282
Isaiah 5:1–6 114
Isaiah 6:1–3, 6, 9–10 182
Isaiah 7:14 155
Isaiah 9:6–7 202
Isaiah 11:6–9 774
Isaiah 13:11–12 792
Isaiah 14:12–15 73
Isaiah 16:1 742
Isaiah 30:6 675
Isaiah 32:6 429
Isaiah 34:6 742
Isaiah 37:16, 36 . . . . 182, 476
Isaiah 42:6–7 468
Isaiah 45:22–23 537
Isaiah 46:9–10 65
Isaiah 53:5–6 . . . . 56, 759, 761
Isaiah 54:13 56
Isaiah 55:8–9 575
Isaiah 59:2 761
Isaiah 61:1–2, 4 747
Isaiah 62:8–9, 11–12 359
Isaiah 63:1–6 743
Isaiah 64:6 549

Isaiah 65:1–2, 17, 20–23, 25
.... 42, 52, 55, 57, 751, 755
Jeremiah 1:17–19.................. 554
Jeremiah 2:2.................... 682
Jeremiah 17:9–10.................. 756
Jeremiah 18:6..................... 84
Jeremiah 22:24–30................. 229
Jeremiah 23:5..................... 84
Jeremiah 26:8..................... 69
Jeremiah 31:20, 31–37.............. 682
Jeremiah 32:17–19................. 140
Jeremiah 33:2–3, 20, 22, 25.......... 719
Jeremiah 49:13................... 742
Jeremiah 50:4.................... 745
Job 1:1, 6–12, 20–22 ....
.... 65, 365-368, 387, 456, 507, 809
Job 2:1–7, 9–10 .... 507, 542,
Job 26:10 573
Job 37:10 713
Job 38:4–7, 22 .... 78, 378, 382
Job chapter 42 809
Joel 3:20–21.................... 207
Jonah 3:4 525
Jonah 4:4, 9 246
Joshua 1:8...................... 711
Joshua 14:15.................... 421
Joshua 15:13–14.................. 421
Joshua 24:14–15............ 350, 480, 706
Judges 1:20..................... 421
Judges 17:6..................... 785
Judges 21:25.................... 785
1 Kings 2:37..................... 69
1 Kings chapter 13 101
1 Kings 17:4–6................... 691
1 Kings chapter 18 338

Appendix 1

Reference	Page
1 Kings 19:8, 10–14, 18	339, 453
2 Kings 2:11	320
2 Kings chapter 11	195
2 Kings 14:7	742
2 Kings 17:20–23	451
2 Kings 18:4	676
Leviticus 3:17	778
Leviticus 11:15, 44–45	691, 728
Leviticus 17:10–14	768, 779, 791
Leviticus 18:1–3	817
Leviticus 27:1–8	239
Malachi 1:1–3, 7–8	360
Malachi 2:1, 6	452
Malachi 4:5–6	754
Micah 2:12–13	342
Micah 6:8	365
Nehemiah 7:7	326
Numbers 12:6–8	462
Numbers 13:27, 32–33	410
Numbers 14:30–32, 36–38	411
Numbers 16:30–35	256
Numbers 18:16	239
Numbers 20:1–2	809
Numbers 23:19	436
Numbers 30:1–5	240
Numbers 32:23	146
Numbers 35:30–31	786
Proverbs 1:16	348
Proverbs 3:9–10	237
Proverbs 14:1	162
Proverbs 16:18	85
Proverbs 18:22	161
Proverbs 30:18–19	161
Proverbs 31:28	162
Psalm 2:4–9	331

Psalm 8:4–8 784
Psalm 19:1–6 503
Psalm 23:4 210
Psalm 27:14 663
Psalm 28:7 3
Psalm 29:1 382
Psalm 51:5, 17 761
Psalm 82:6 382
Psalm 84:3, 11 . . . . 439, 765
Psalm 89:6, 23, 27 382
Psalm 90:1–5, 10 399
Psalm 91:4, 15 437
Psalm 103:8–11, 14 . . . . 369, 803
Psalm 104:5–9 . . .515, 533, 552, 565-571,593,606
Psalm 116:15 350
Psalm 119:89 664
Psalm 127:3–5 54
Psalm 135:4 360
Psalm 139:7–16 788
1 Samuel 2:2 114
1 Samuel 13:14 809
1 Samuel 14:44 69
1 Samuel 15:29 437
1 Samuel 16:10 274
1 Samuel chapter 22. 826
2 Samuel 23:8–12 485
2 Samuel chapter 11. 806
Zechariah 8:2–5 . . . . 58, 70
Zechariah 9:9–10 202
Zechariah 12:10–13:1, 8–9 210
Zechariah 14:3–9 42
Zephaniah 1:18. 501

New Testament: . . . .

Acts 1:3, 5, 9–11 . . . . 139, 370, 525

Appendix 1

Acts 2:22–24 .... 45, 498
Acts 4:12, 18–20 125
Acts 5:12–16, 29 498
Acts 10:22, 34–35 45
Acts 13:22, 48 349
Acts 14:8–10 498
Acts 15:28–29 779
Acts 17:31 322
Acts chapter 18 731
Acts 20:9–12, 27–31 107
Colossians 2:6–8, 13–17 386
Colossians 3:1–12 313
1 Corinthians 3:11–15 487
1 Corinthians 6:14–15 375
1 Corinthians 7:19 751
1 Corinthians 10:12–13 111
1 Corinthians 11:7 311
1 Corinthians 13:10, 12 461
1 Corinthians 15:1–4, 51–54, 57–58 ... 320
2 Corinthians 5:6–8, 10, 17–21 .... 526, 759, 798
2 Corinthians 6:2 468
2 Corinthians 9:15 65
2 Corinthians 11:3, 23 111
Ephesians 1:13–14 138
Ephesians 2:1–9 154
Ephesians 4:8–10, 14, 20–24 .... 51, 71, 269, 770
Ephesians 5:22–33 164
Ephesians 6:16 460
Galatians 2:12 84
Galatians 3:14, 28–29 95
Galatians 4:22–26 172
Galatians 6:2, 7–8 .... 500, 501
Hebrews 2:3 753
Hebrews 4:13 .... 127, 199
Hebrews 9:1–27 .... 234, 241, 461, 527, 561

Hebrews 10:11–13, 24–31
.... 452, 501, 508, 526, 614
Hebrews 11:4–8, 10, 35–40 .... 565, 651, 810
Hebrews 12:2, 22–24 .... 92, 502
Hebrews 13:2, 5–6 .... 375, 683
James 1:13–17 468
James 2:10 323
James 3:1, 8–9 564
James 4:4, 14 727
John 1:1–19, 29 ....
.. 32, 64, 68, 82, 105, 114, 123-130, 188, 217, 291,
    296, 313, 361, 377, 383, 415, 536, 574, 791, 798
John 2:24–25 .... 498, 728
John 3:1–8, 13–21, 36 .... 541, 549, 574, 660
John 4:24 437
John 5:24, 28–29 478
John 6:27, 33, 44–45 ...... 56, 67, 139, 549, 753
John 8:12, 29, 33, 39–44, 46 .. 214, 659, 751, 761
John 9:1–3 254
John 10:9–11, 27–30 .... 188, 194, 478, 534, 545
John 11:48, 51–52 84
John 12:40 498
John 14:1–6, 9, 16, 21 520
John 15:1–6, 10 659
John 16:8–11, 21 159
John 18:35 659
John 20:12, 30–31 375
1 John 1:5, 7–10 .... 114, 187
1 John 2:15–18, 22 116
1 John 3:1–3, 5, 13–15 .... 51, 57, 71, 250
1 John 4:3, 16 532
2 John 7 411
Jude 1:6–7 .... 81, 329, 384
Jude 6 393
Jude 7 394

Appendix 1

Jude 9 182
Jude 11 271
Jude 14–15 297
Jude 20–23 194
Luke 1:26–28, 31–33, 35, 37–38, 54–55, 63
. . . . 202, 207, 217, 383, 537, 659, 682, 822
Luke 2:22–24, 34–35 . . . . 204, 205, 239, 692
Luke 3:22–38 . . . . 156, 692
Luke 4:41 376
Luke 7:5, 16 84
Luke 8:26–39 391
Luke 10:1–18 . . . . 387, 498
Luke 13:24 263
Luke 15:11–32 749
Luke 16:19–31, 48 . . . . 255, 263, 482,
Luke 17:26–27 . . . . 359, 483, 662, 821
Luke 19:10 203
Luke 20:37–38 253
Luke 21:38 428
Luke 23:2, 14–15, 22, 41–43 659
Luke 24:4, 25, 36–45, 49 . . . . . . 51, 139, 375, 809
Mark 2:7 127
Mark 5:1–13 391
Mark 8:34–38 . . . . 43, 242, 250
Mark 9:39–40 465
Mark 10:17–22, 45 793
Mark 16:5 375
Matthew 1:1–17, 20–23 . . . . 156, 301, 498
Matthew 2:9 206
Matthew 4:1–11, 24 376
Matthew 5:13–14, 17–18 500
Matthew 6:10, 14–15 133
Matthew 7:13–14, 23, 28–29 . . . . . . 260, 468, 495
Matthew 8:10–12 44
Matthew 10:16, 28–31 460

Matthew 11:11 798
Matthew 12:31 65
Matthew 16:22–23 809
Matthew 18:1–7, 12, 22 284
Matthew 20:28 797
Matthew 22:29–30 . . . . 55, 269
Matthew 23:16–22, 35, 37–39 356
Matthew 24:12, 22, 35–39 . . . .
. . . . . . 209-211, 222, 360, 436, 581, 661, 810, 821
Matthew 25:31–46 227
Matthew 28:1–7, 19–20 375
1 Peter 1:10–11, 13–16, 18–19 . . . . 560 728
1 Peter 2:22–25 . . . . 212, 497
1 Peter 3:7–9, 15, 18 497
1 Peter 5:8 . . . . 150, 153, 387, 540
2 Peter 1:19–21 502
2 Peter 2:4–8 . . . . 81, 322, 329, 384, 388
2 Peter 3:3–7, 9–14 . . . . 389, 400, 451
Philippians 1:22-25 51
Philippians 2:9–11, 15 537
Philippians 4:4–9 . . . . 712, 727
Revelation 1:7 206
Revelation 3:10, 12, 20 . . . . 209, 352, 497
Revelation 6:8–17 . . . . 57, 61
Revelation 7:9–17 57
Revelation 9:20–21 468
Revelation 11:1–13, 15, 19 . . . . 90, 203, 362, 754
Revelation 12:1–4, 6–7, 10, 12–14 . 381, 541, 742
Revelation 13:7–8, 10, 12, 14–15 . . . 64, 121, 211
Revelation 14:6–7, 9–11 . . . . 273, 341
Revelation 16:8–9, 11, 17–21 580
Revelation 19:7, 11–21 55
Revelation 20:4–15 . . . . 53, 60, 62
Revelation 21:1–4, 22–23 57
Revelation 22:2 57

Appendix 1

Romans 1:18–22, 27 359
Romans 2:25–29 751
Romans 3:10–18, 23, 29, 39 760
Romans 4:19–22 111
Romans 5:1–21 .... 119-122, 155, 170
Romans 6:5–8, 15–18, 23 .... 61, 130, 313
Romans 7:5–7, 14–25 .... 115, 313, 544, 728
Romans 8:14–17, 18–25, 28, 31–39
 .... 138, 184, 212, 329, 377, 428, 442, 454
Romans 9:6–13, 23–24, 30–33 ..... 214, 224-226
Romans 10:20–21 140
Romans 11:13, 34 351
Romans 12:1–2, 19 241
Romans 13:1–4 786
Romans 14:10–12 802
Romans 15:4, 27 825
Romans 16:4, 20 .... 153, 156
1 Thessalonians 1:2–5 .... 260, 26, 346
1 Thessalonians 4:13–18 ...... 209, 21, 227, 320
1 Thessalonians 5:16–19 485
2 Thessalonians 1:6–10 50
2 Thessalonians 2:1–12 .... 353, 411, 433
1 Timothy 2:4, 11–15............ 157, 350, 366
2 Timothy 2:15................. 212, 214, 484
2 Timothy 3:1–5, 12.................... 527
Titus 1:2............................. 655
Titus 2:13–14......................... 727
Titus 3:5............................. 32